china

TRAVELER

china

by Damian Harper
photography by Alison Wright

National Geographic
Washington, D.C.

CONTENTS

TRAVELING WITH EYES OPEN 6

CHARTING YOUR TRIP 8

History & Culture 13
China Today 14
Land & Landscape 20
Feature: Food & Drink 24
History of China 26
Feature: Religion & Philosophy 32
Arts & Culture 48
Feature: Chinese Ceramics 52

Beijing 57
Introduction & Map 58
Beijing Bike Ride 68
Feature: Beijing *Hutongs* 72
Feature: China's Gods & Goddesses 82

The North 97
Introduction & Map 98
Feature: *Gongfu* 124
Feature: Confucianism 130
A Walk Around Qingdao 137

The Yangtze Region 143
Introduction & Map 144
A Cruise Through the Three Gorges 146
Feature: Chinese Temples 156
Feature: Taiping Rebellion 164
A Bike Ride Around Suzhou 170
Feature: Grand Canal 176
A Walk Along the Bund 184
Feature: Western Architecture in Shanghai 194

The South 197
Introduction & Map 198
Gulangyu Island Walk 206
Shamian Island Walk 216

Hong Kong & Macau 221
Introduction & Map 222
Central Walk 226
Tsim Sha Tsui Walk 234
Feature: Chinese Astrology 246
Feature: Wind & Water 256

The Southwest 261
Introduction & Map 262
Li River Cruise 282

Sichuan & the Tibetan Plateau 289
Introduction & Map 290
Feature: Tibetan Buddhism 306

Inner Mongolia & the Silk Road 311
Introduction & Map 312

The Northeast 335
Introduction & Map 336
Feature: Tigers in China 342

Travelwise 349
Hotels & Restaurants 361
Shopping 386
Entertainment 387
Museums 388
Language Guide 389
Menu Reader 390

INDEX 391

CREDITS 398

Pages 2–3: Fishermen on the Li River tame cormorants to help them catch fish.
Opposite: A colorful player in Chinese opera

TRAVELING WITH EYES OPEN

Alert travelers go with a purpose and leave with a benefit. If you travel responsibly, you can help support wildlife conservation, historic preservation, and cultural enrichment in the places you visit. You can enrich your own travel experience as well.

To be a geo-savvy traveler:

- Recognize that your presence has an impact on the places you visit.
- Spend your time and money in ways that sustain local character. (Besides, it's more interesting that way.)
- Value the destination's natural and cultural heritage.
- Respect the local customs and traditions.
- Express appreciation to local people about things you find interesting and unique to the place: its nature and scenery, music and food, historic villages and buildings.
- Vote with your wallet: Support the people who support the place, patronizing businesses that make an effort to celebrate and protect what's special there. Seek out shops, local restaurants, inns, and tour operators who love their home—who love taking care of it and showing it off. Avoid businesses that detract from the character of the place.
- Enrich yourself, taking home memories and stories to tell, knowing that you have contributed to the preservation and enhancement of the destination.

That is the type of travel now called geotourism, defined as "tourism that sustains or enhances the geographical character of a place—its environment, culture, aesthetics, heritage, and the well-being of its residents." To learn more, visit National Geographic's Center for Sustainable Destinations at *www.nationalgeographic.com/travel/sustainable.*

china

ABOUT THE AUTHOR & THE PHOTOGRAPHER

Educated at Winchester College and with an art history degree and six years of bookselling under his belt, **Damian Harper** pursued an interest in Chinese martial arts to London's School of Oriental and African Studies, graduating in 1995 with a degree in modern and classical Chinese. The four-year course took him to Beijing for a year where he met his Chinese wife, Dai Min. Harper has lived and worked in Beijing, Shanghai, and Hong Kong, traveled extensively through China, and co-authored several guides on China, Beijing, and the Hong Kong region. He frequently returns to China with his wife, son, and daughter.

Alison Wright, a New York–based documentary photographer, has spent a career capturing the human spirit through her photographs, traveling to all corners of the globe photographing endangered cultures and people. Her photography is represented by the National Geographic Image collection and is published in a number of National Geographic books and publications. Wright is a recipient of the Dorothea Lange Award in Documentary Photography and a two-time winner of the Lowell Thomas Travel Journalism Award. Her memoir, *Learning to Breathe: One Woman's Journey of Spirit and Survival,* was published in 2008.

Charting Your Trip

You can visit China at any time of year, though a trip of one to two weeks in spring and autumn is recommended. The country is increasingly easy to get around, but don't expect to encounter much spoken English beyond the tourist sights. China is an unusual mix of the up-to-date and very out of date, so while you can stay in thoroughly modern five-star hotels in Beijing and Shanghai, off the beaten path you may find yourself living in very basic conditions.

Roughly equal in size (and shape) to the United States, China is impossible to experience fully on a single trip. The capital, Beijing, is located in northern China and makes for an ideal starting point. Rich in imperial history and bursting with 21st-century energy, Beijing is the heart of China, and from here, you can easily reach just about any destination on your itinerary. To the south, the ancient walled city of Xi'an and ultramodern Shanghai are also highly recommended for first-time visitors. Or create a trip that suits your interests: From centuries of architectural and religious development to stunning natural vistas and cutting-edge modern art, China has it all.

How to Get Around

Because of its size, getting around China is fun but tiring. Flying between destinations within China is simple and quick. Major domestic airlines include Air China *(www.airchina.com.cn)*, China Southern *(www.csair.com)*, and China Eastern *(www.flychinaeastern.com)*. Reliable agencies for air tickets and accommodations are Ctrip *(tel 800/820-6666, www.english.ctrip.com)* and Elong *(tel 800/810-1010, www.elong.com)*, which can help you plan ahead and get discounts.

Visitors with more time to spend may find traveling by train more enjoyable. China now boasts the most extensive high-speed rail network in the world, with trains running between major cities, like Beijing and Shanghai, and most of the country's other top tourist destinations. Buy your tickets at the local train station *(rail schedules available at http://trains.china.org.cn)*. Luxury long-distance buses also travel regularly between the big cities and towns. In more rural areas

The Chinese name for the endearing Giant Panda means "bearcat."

and for more distant sights, you must rely on fleets of overcrowded minibuses or private drivers.

How to Visit in One Week

Begin your trip in Beijing, and aim to spend three days visiting the main sights around town. On **day one,** head for the Forbidden City. Home to Ming and Qing dynasty emperors, this sprawling complex can take an entire day to navigate, so go slow and take time to enjoy all the treasures it has tucked away. In the late afternoon or early evening, visit Tiananmen Square, where you can watch soldiers lower the Chinese flag.

On **day two,** take the subway to the Ming dynasty Temple of Heaven. After you explore the temple, wander through the surrounding park. You may run across groups of people practicing tai chi or an impromptu concert in a clearing. In the afternoon, take a taxi or minibus to the splendid Summer Palace, an imperial park of temples and pavilions. Or spend the afternoon strolling through some of the city's *hutongs,* narrow avenues that will transport you back to a more traditional way of life.

NOT TO BE MISSED:

Walking Beijing's *hutongs* **72–73**

The Great Wall **89–95**

Gazing at the ineffable terra-cotta warriors **105–107**

The walls of Pingyao **109–110**

Huangshan, China's standout Yellow Mountain **154–155**

Wandering through Shanghai's French Concession **192–193**

Victoria Peak **229–230**

The transcendent landscape around Yangshuo **284–285**

Muslim Kashgar **322–323**

The Buddhist decorations of the Mogao Caves **326–327**

Beijing is within easy distance of several accessible stretches of the Great Wall, so on **day three,** head 43 miles (70 km) out of town to the Badaling section of the wall, and spend the day clambering along this colossal landmark. Check with your hotel about tours of Badaling or other sections of the Great Wall.

Take an **overnight train** (about 14 hrs.) to Xi'an, located 568 miles (914 km) southwest of Beijing. Once you arrive, catch bus No. 306 or No. 307 for the 45-minute ride to the terra-cotta warriors. Created for the emperor who first unified China some

Visitor Information

China still does not have a nationwide tourist office network that can supply foreign travelers with maps or advice. Individual large cities, such as Beijing and Shanghai, have their own tourist information offices scattered about town, but their use is limited and they may push you toward joining tours.

Branches of **China International Travel Service,** or CITS, operate in Beijing *(Beijing International Hotel, 9 Jianguomennei Dajie, tel 010 6512-0507, www.cits.net)* and across China. **China Travel Service** *(www.chinatravelservice.com),* or CTS, also has offices across the country.

Your best bet is to ask for travel advice from your hotel, a youth hostel, or expat bar. Youth hostels in particular are loaded with tourist advice, notice boards, and good English speakers; furthermore, they provide great opportunities for meeting fellow travelers and exchanging tips. Alternatively, the Internet could be your most dependable resource.

Money Matters

The currency of the People's Republic of China is the RMB (renminbi), also called the yuan (Y) or *kuai* in spoken Chinese. The renminbi is not yet internationally convertible, so it's best to wait until you arrive in China to exchange your money; spend it all before you leave unless you are departing from Hong Kong, where you can change it to Hong Kong dollars.

You cannot rely on credit cards to see you through your entire trip in China, so carry a decent amount of cash with you. ATMs accepting international cards (typically the Bank of China) have become increasingly common in China's large cities. Traveler's checks are the safest alternative to cash. They can be exchanged at banks and most large hotels, and the exchange rate is better than that for cash.

2,000 years ago, these life-size sculptures—each one of kind—are one of China's grandest artistic achievements. Spend **day five** in Xi'an, which marked the start of the Silk Road. Explore the city's Muslim quarter and perhaps rent a bike for a ride around the top of the city's walls.

From Xi'an fly or take an overnight train (about 14 hrs.) to the magnificent city of Shanghai, 757 miles (1,218 km) away on the eastern seaboard. Start **day six** with a walk along the river embankment known as the Bund, and then walk or take the subway to the Shanghai Museum in Renmin Square. Exploring the museum's unmatched collection of Chinese art and artifacts will easily take you the rest of the day. Devote your **last day** in China to Shanghai's ultra-elegant French Concession, home to charming streets, trendy shops, and a clutch of bustling restaurants.

If You Have More Time

If you have more time to spend in China, the options are legion. You could extend your stay in any or all of the cities mentioned above. Or spend the first three days in Beijing, then travel 205 miles (330 km) west by bus or train to the Shanxi city of **Datong.** An additional 10-mile (16 km) bus ride to the west of Datong brings you to the Yungang Caves. Completed primarily in the fifth century A.D., the caves will delight with a riot of Buddhist carvings and statues. From Datong, take the train 261 miles (420 km) south to **Pingyao.** Take a day or two to savor this lovely old Shanxi walled town, and then continue on to Xi'an (360 miles/580 km).

Guanxi & Mianzi

Contacts *(guanxi)* remain all important in China. The code of guanxi entails help in procuring what you want and giving what others need. As a foreigner, you may have what many Chinese want: a useful contact abroad. Before traveling to China, it is worth getting business cards printed with your name and company in both English and Chinese. Far more widespread than in the West, exchanging business cards is like a handshake and signals a desire for guanxi. Chinese proffer their business cards respectfully with both hands; do the same if you wish.

Closely related to guanxi is face *(mianzi)* or lack of it *(diu mianzi)*. The psychology of face is essentially pride in fragile form, and much maneuvering is employed to keep it intact. In this country especially, it is advisable to remain respectful, making any complaints with decorum, peppered with firmness.

After a couple days in Xi'an, fly to **Dunhuang** on the edge of the Gobi Desert in Gansu Province. Visit the Buddhist Mogao Caves, southeast of the city, and enjoy the views from the Singing Sand Dunes. From here you can venture into China's Muslim northwest, or travel southwest to **Chengdu** in Sichuan Province and then on to **Dali** and **Lijiang** in Yunnan in the far southwest; **Chongqing** and the **Three Gorges;** or the ethnic villages of Guizhou Province. Guizhou borders Guangxi, the provincial home of **Guilin** and **Yangshuo** and its stupendous karst and riverine landscapes, from where it is easy to reach the cities of **Guangzhou** (Canton) and **Hong Kong.**

Travel Restrictions

Most of China is open to travelers (including all destinations covered in this book), but some ethnic border regions and militarily sensitive zones remain closed. If you wish to visit an area that you suspect may be closed, contact the PSB (Public Security Bureau) for clarification (see Travelwise p. 355). In certain cases, travel permits will be issued. For information on travel to Tibet, see Travelwise p. 353.

Following an eastern route, take the four-hour train ride from Beijing to **Tai'an** and the holy mount of Taishan. Then pay a visit to the former German Concession of **Qingdao** (home of Tsingtao beer) on the coast, or continue south to the walled city of **Nanjing,** the canal town of **Suzhou,** and Shanghai. Picturesque home of West Lake, **Hangzhou** is about 124 miles (200 km) southwest of Shanghai, while gorgeous **Huangshan** lies about 280 miles (450 km) southwest of the city. Farther south, **Xiamen** and **Gulangyu Island** are a natural stops on the long loop to Hong Kong. ■

Once secretive, the fascinating Buddhist Lama Temple in Beijing is now open for all.

History & Culture

China Today 14–19

Land & Landscape 20–23

Feature: Food & Drink 24–25

Experience: Cooking Chinese Style 25

History of China 26–47

Feature: Religion & Philosophy 32–33

Arts & Culture 48–56

Feature: Chinese Ceramics 52–53

This huge character at the Naputuo Temple in Xiamen means "Buddha." Opposite: To Buddhists, Tibetan *thangka* painting is a manifestation of the divine.

China Today

For centuries, China seemed a remote, rarefied realm governed by inscrutable principles. These days, however, the country demands increasing attention, and Western attitudes toward this vast enigma have become more adventurous. The Chinese world is rapidly opening up, and the West has found itself in a rather unseemly rush to wedge itself in the door.

The Chinese

The Chinese are by no means homogeneous. Although Han Chinese account for 93 percent of the population, officially there are 55 other distinct ethnic minorities, from the Muslim Uighurs and Hui to the Dai and Naxi of Yunnan Province.

A night cruise along the Huangpu River affords spectacular views of Shanghai.

It is predominantly the Han Chinese, however, who are guardians of the Chinese tradition and its etiquette, language, and culture. A loyal, proud, patriotic, stubborn, quick-witted, resourceful, conservative, and family-oriented group, they are opportunistically building a new China, flaws and all.

The Chinese often note, with resigned stoicism, that one Chinese person can turn a hand to almost anything, but bring a group together and they bungle it. As individuals, the Chinese are hardworking, resourceful, and entrepreneurial. As a group, they often squabble and fight over trifles. Socially, this makes them fun and gregarious; just listen to the noise that emanates from street-side restaurants. This sociability also makes them a lovable people. There is little that is hard-edged and technocratic about the Chinese; they are emotional, haphazard, and unpredictable. Efficiency seems beyond their grasp, but flashes of insight are commonplace. Torn between the poles of compulsion (Taoism) and restraint (Confucianism/communism), the Chinese constantly charm and surprise.

The hard-and-fast barriers between the sexes that can cause discomfort in countries such as Japan hardly exist here.

Chinese men can often be soft *(wenrou)* and women strong-willed *(jianqiang)*, creating an engaging balance. The hard-and-fast barriers between the sexes that can cause discomfort in countries such as Japan hardly exist here. A deep romantic vein runs through society, finding expression in literature, film, and music (see pp. 48–56).

Despite the push and shove on the streets, the Chinese are a courteous people whose sensibilities are propped up by decorum and hospitality. This might not be clear as you unwillingly join the chaos ascending the bus in Guangzhou, but remember that this is still nominally a communist society. All people are born equal, so you need those hard-won skills of getting what you want, when you want, in the face of mass opposition. When you meet with politeness in China, however, it is often of the highest and most genuine kind.

Middle Kingdom

China calls itself Zhongguo (Middle Kingdom). In ages past, the custodians of the Middle Kingdom savored the certainty that they occupied the space at the center of the world; other cultures simply revolved in barbarian fashion around its perimeter. A sense of destiny lingers temptingly in the name the Chinese still give their land.

The Chinese are also proud of a long, magnificent history and civilization, enjoying the reassurance that their culture has survived the accumulative erosion of millennia.

In the first decade of the 21st century, China has found itself back on the road to glory after the humiliations of the 19th and 20th centuries and the errors of Communist Party ideologues. Economic reforms are being fueled by the smoldering business savvy at the heart of the national identity. China seems to have a real opportunity to regain its position in the world, and that goal—the regeneration of their country—unites the Chinese people. The goal is far less Marxist utopian than state-controlled capitalism. The country is designer-conscious, increasingly snobbish (snobbery was one of the first traits to escape the Cultural Revolution alive and kicking), materialistic, and enjoying its new guise.

An acute feeling of disorientation, however, brings a giddiness to today's China. This grand civilization has had its throne snatched by the United States and Japan. There is a feeling that the country has lost its way, for the communism that successfully exiled feudalism to the history books bred its own foibles. And the cunning about-face that allowed capitalism to reemerge made those selfless sacrifices of previous generations meaningless. The land is as if without a map; it knows what it has departed but is unsure of the destination.

China is naturally curious about the world outside, but blinkering by the Communist Party left it unprepared for the country's sudden engagement with the West. The outside *(guowai)* remains a rather distant universe piped in by television, social media, and advertising, where things—politics, business culture, philosophy—are very different.

China is in some way a bizarre pastiche of the West, with Asian ingredients. Socialist architecture the land over is based on a Western utilitarian model, and the Western suit and tie are worn without a second thought. Shanghai increasingly resembles a city from some future dimension, while the ambition of the rest of the land is to look as much like Shanghai as possible. But, as visitors discover, similarities with the West are often just skin-deep.

China Facts

Capital: Beijing
Language: Mandarin *(putonghua)*, Cantonese, and other dialects
Population: 1.3 billion
Religion: Nominally atheist, but large numbers of Buddhists, Christians, and Muslims
Telephone country code: 86
Money: Renminbi
Political system: One-party state

Politics & Economy

Today, China is undergoing a painful restructuring, with reform *(gaige)* the engine of growth. The result is spectacular economic expansion and a dramatic increase in prestige abroad.

The country is effectively trying to drag itself from the 1940s into the new millennium in half the time; the nation has been revitalized and the burden of Marxist dogma jettisoned into history's trash can.

In economic terms, China's dramatic rise under the leadership of Deng Xiaoping, Jiang Zemin, and Hu Jintao has dazzled the world. A palpable sense that China has advanced in great leaps and bounds is obvious on the streets of Shanghai, Beijing, and other large cities, which are awash with smart cars and fizz with commercial energy. The feel-good factor may not infect the whole nation, but it is extending its reach, and many

Chinese know they have never had it so good. China has sent a man into space (twice), the Three Gorges Dam was finished ahead of schedule, and the nation is assuming its position on the world stage with an increasingly bold voice.

The Communist Party is under siege from its reformist agenda, but the student idealism of the Tiananmen Square era (see p. 47) has seemingly evaporated in the face of undergraduate enthusiasm for work opportunities at home and abroad. Economic advancement has become a personal as well as national goal. China now has a "Me" generation with only a dim notion of the relentless frugality of the Mao era (see pp. 42–45).

A boy enjoys sipping from a coconut at Sanya beach on Hainan Island.

Behind the impressive economic statistics and hype, however, lurks a confusing picture: The banking sector is in dire need of reform, yawning regional disparities remain, the gap between rich and poor is best described as a chasm, the political system has resisted evolution, restrictions on free speech and access to information are if anything intensifying, the Internet is zealously censored by cyber-police, a healthy forum for political discussion does not exist, dissent is ruthlessly quashed, rural unrest is on the increase, and the environment is in a state of crisis (the last two being directly linked). The government pays lip service to Marxism-Leninism while knowing that its grip on power may depend purely on economic growth. The consequent gulf between ideology and the reality is an ever present fact, the result a stagnant political drama whose occasional change of cast is hobbled by an unchanging, drab script.

The baton of discontent has been handed to those who are not aboard the gravy train. The country's losers include the unemployed, peasants robbed of their land by government projects like the Three Gorges Dam, and those—writer and human rights activist Liu Xiaobo, for example—persecuted for taking on the government.

The behemoth of the Chinese government finds that it must evolve further or perish. The oft-quoted argument that China is too large to be a democracy is debatable. India (population 1.1 billion) has achieved democracy, and it could well be argued that China is equally too large to be a one-party state.

Religion & Politics

The Chinese Communist Party has tried to replace religion with Marxism-Leninism *(makesilieningzhuyi)*, with varying success. Chairman Mao attempted to purge China of superstition with the Cultural Revolution (see pp. 44–45) but instead turned himself into a demigod who is still idolized and worshipped in shrines around

China. The current bankruptcy of communist theory has left a spiritual vacuum in China that has been filled with a medley of religious beliefs. Recent riots involving Chinese Christians point to the growing toehold Christianity has in China and the problems the authorities have in dealing with it. It should not be forgotten that the Christian Taiping came close to overthrowing the Qing dynasty (see pp. 164–165).

The Communist Party reacts with concern to any creed that offers an alternative vision to that bequeathed by Karl Marx. Falun Gong ("art of the wheel of the law"), a quasi-Buddhist "cult," was banned because of fears that it challenged the primacy of the Communist Party. Despite being marshaled by middle-aged women and the elderly, Falun Gong has managed to worry the Communist Party, whose grip on power is fretful and insecure. Its adherents periodically demonstrated in Tiananmen Square, only to be bundled off to prison. Banning Falun Gong has not solved the problem of spiritual emptiness in China and may simply have exacerbated it.

Travel in China

Early Western inroads into China explored the peripheries of several of the country's more familiar aspects: *fengshui* (see p. 156), tai chi, medicine, and an enviable cuisine. These days, however, China's numerous dialects are no longer the exclusive domain of eccentric Western scholars in smoking jackets and missionaries on Christianity's front line, while the formerly distant and mysterious ways of the Chinese government are suddenly staring Western speculators in the face.

Those on the imperial China trail will explore the Forbidden City, the stately imperial tombs, and the Great Wall in and around Beijing.

In voyaging to China, visitors coming from the West are making up for lost time. An appreciation of the range of sights that the country offers will help in your choice of route through this huge land.

Those on the imperial China trail will explore the Forbidden City, the stately imperial tombs, and the Great Wall in and around Beijing. Further imperial remnants can be found in the cities of Nanjing and Xi'an and add a splash of grandeur to Shenyang.

China inherited marvelous architectural gems from its unfortunate historical liaison with the West (see pp. 38–41). Guangzhou's Shamian Island is an outdoor museum, but the Bund in Shanghai has the last word. Gulangyu Island in Xiamen is a delight, but don't overlook the mountain retreats of Lushan and Moganshan.

The embankment known as the Bund follows the course of the Huangpu River in Shanghai.

Harbin boasts some extravagant Russian architecture, as does Dalian. Part of Germany has been delightfully re-created in Qingdao in Shandong Province, and Tianjin enjoys a cosmopolitan nobility. Hong Kong, the former British colony, is an alluring jumble of modern architecture, Cantonese cooking, and pastoral, verdant islands. A small slice of Catholic Portuguese culture washes up on the south China shoreline with Macau.

China's sacred Taoist and Buddhist mountains lie strewn with traditional temples. Taishan is the country's holiest Taoist mountain, although most visitors agree that secular Huangshan is more beautiful. Putuoshan is China's Buddhist mountain island, suffused with the spirit of the Goddess of Mercy, Guanyin (see pp. 180–181). Shine a light on Buddhist cave art at Dunhuang, Longmen, and Yungang, or gasp at the immensity of the Buddha at Leshan.

Adventurous travelers will be tempted by China's peripheral regions. Lhasa, the capital of Tibet, is an enticing mix of Buddhism, magic, and mystery. Xinjiang fosters an Islamic culture that immigrated via the old Silk Road. Yunnan Province borders Tibet, Myanmar (Burma), Laos, and Vietnam and is home to a quirky patchwork of ethnic communities. The sublime volcanic lake of Tianchi straddles the border with North Korea.

Those who have long been on the China travel circuit rest their feet in Dali and Yangshuo, the two most famous backpacker retreats in the land, with some of China's most magical scenery on all sides. ■

Land & Landscape

In the shrinking global village, traveling through China recalls the excitement of being a true adventurer. Any journey through this vast nation throws open to visitors a geographical encyclopedia and a breathtaking exploration of diverse worlds.

Geography

China is the world's third largest country, after Russia and Canada. Its most mountainous terrain rises in the west with Tibet and the mighty Himalaya, and in the northwest with the Kunlun, Tianshan, and Pamir mountain ranges. At 29,028 feet

Man and yak cross the waterfalls at Jade Dragon Snow Mountain near Lijiang, in the foothills of Tibet.

(8,848 m), Mount Everest is the highest peak in the world. China's lowest point, the Turpan Depression (505 feet/154 m below sea level), is scooped out from the vast northwest region. The land increasingly flattens out the farther east you travel.

As the great mountainous highland of west China acted as a huge barrier, Chinese expansion was also resisted by the forbidding deserts, including the Gobi and the parched Taklimakan (see sidebar p. 323), that punctuate the great plains of the north.

Many of China's most colorful and engaging regions lie on its periphery, a cocktail of different cultures and ethnic minorities.

The vast majority (90 percent) of the population lives along China's coast or in the fertile lands that line the Yangtze River (Chang Jiang), the Yellow River (Huang He), the Pearl River (Zhu Jiang), and the Mekong River (Langcang Jiang). Most of the cultivable land is irrigated by these river systems, which course through China and bring fertility to a place that perennially suffers from cycles of water abundance and shortage. The Three Gorges Dam (see pp. 146–149) on the Yangtze River aims to help reverse this tradition. China's coastline is an affluent bundle of Special Economic Zones (SEZs) and thriving ports. Two-thirds of the land is too mountainous, arid, or otherwise unsuitable for agriculture.

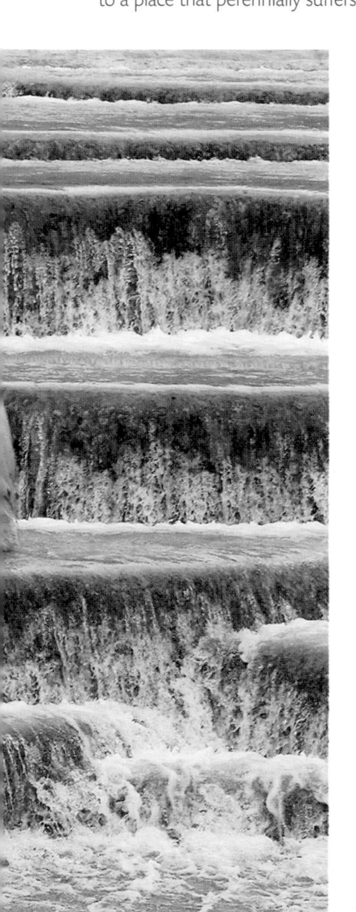

China's Provinces & Borderlands

China is composed of 22 provinces, four municipalities (Beijing, Tianjin, Chongqing, and Shanghai), five Autonomous Regions, and two Special Administrative Regions, or SARs (Hong Kong and Macau). The "renegade province" of Taiwan is being heavily wooed into a reunion.

China's borderlands make for a fascinating cultural tapestry. North Korea, Russia, Mongolia, Tajikistan, Kirgizstan, Kazakhstan, Afghanistan, Pakistan, Bhutan, India, Nepal, Myanmar (Burma), Laos, and Vietnam border the country. Many of China's most colorful and engaging regions lie on its periphery, a cocktail of different cultures and ethnic minorities.

Chinese-drawn maps show an unlikely national boundary line lassoing the far-flung Spratly Islands (Nansha) to the south, a large group of islands also claimed by Vietnam, Malaysia, the Philippines, and other countries.

Climate

From the arid, desert expanses of the northwest to the humid south and ice-clamped winter seizure of the northeast, China has wide disparities of climate.

Winter in China north of the Yangtze River is typically cold, becoming increasingly frigid the farther north you go. The vast northwest alternates between summer's scorching aridity and the blistering chill of the winter months. Come December, glacial temperatures stupefy Heilongjiang ("black dragon river") Province in the northeast, although it enjoys hot summers. Winter in southern Yunnan Province and along China's southern coastline is comfortable, but regions of high elevation (most notably Tibet) can be dangerously cold.

Virtually the land over is hot in summer, with heavy monsoon rainfall (originating over the Pacific) in the south, southeast, and parts of the southwest. The gray skies over Shanghai continuously open, while the warm and heavy August rains in Beijing flush away the desert dust that clogs the roads. Warm, late summer rains in Xishuangbanna fall relentlessly. Summer in Xingjiang's Turpan, China's hottest and lowest spot, is punishing. The season also turns on the "three ovens" of China–Chongqing, Wuhan, and Nanjing–which sweat under the steam of the Yangtze River.

South Yunnan Province, Guangxi, Guangdong, Hong Kong, Macau, and Hainan Island enjoy a tropical climate. Hong Kong's August humidity relentlessly clings like a warm, wet sheet until a typhoon blows into town. Typhoons can be constant hazards to the southern coastal regions in the summer. Much of Yunnan Province is unexpectedly fresh year-round.

Flora & Fauna

China supports a wide diversity of plants and animals reflecting the huge geographical disparities characteristic of the country. A vast array of species crowds into the tropical, forested regions of Yunnan Province in the southwest, among them the snub-nosed monkey, the elephant, and the elusive Indochina tiger *(Panthera tigris corbetti).* Hainan Island sustains shrinking pockets of tropical rain forest.

China supports a wide diversity of plants and animals reflecting the huge geographical disparities characteristic of the country.

At the other extreme, the rugged northeast is a sanctuary of the Manchurian tiger *(Panthera tigris altaica),* reindeer, bear, and other species suited to Siberian forest conditions. The northwest (former Chinese Turkistan) is a desiccated expanse of desert and hardy, drought-resistant plants, punctuated by green oases and pine-covered mountains. The region supports wild cats, leopards, camels, and hares, among others.

Environmental Threats

The plants and wildlife of China are suffering serious degradation, however, principally due to the country's rapid economic growth. Acid rain, industrial pollution, and urban toxic palls threaten China with ecological catastrophe. The outlook is bleak, and even officials have warned that China's pollution problems could quadruple by 2020. Hong Kong's harassed pink dolphins *(Sousa chinensis)* battle pollution, overfishing, and collisions with surface vessels. In mainland China, strict new regulations on logging are battling to preserve the country's shrinking forests. There is concern that a shift to a more green consciousness in China will prove to be too little, too late.

A gorge in Xinjiang, the mighty northwestern province formerly known as Chinese Turkistan

Many rivers and lakes steam with pollution, choking life. Industry has scarred the land, and the encroachment of agriculture into habitats has further reduced plant and animal numbers. China needs to feed itself and lacks the arable land to do so; wildlife is consequently driven into the forested, mountainous, and desert regions.

The other threat comes from superstition and Chinese medicine. Exotic animals are trapped for their tendons, organs, and skin. Tigers, bears, pangolins, and deer are among the prized specimens.

Endangered animals include the giant salamander *(wawayu),* the colossal Manchurian tiger, and the giant panda *(xiongmao),* whose last refuge is located in western Sichuan Province. China's cheerless zoos are generally not worth visiting except for a rare view of the giant panda.

There are a number of sanctuaries that are ideal for bird-watchers and for those in search of wilder destinations, including Hong Kong's Mai Po Marsh, the Zhalong Nature Reserve in Heilongjiang Province, and Qinghai Lake in Qinghai Province (but check on bird flu outbreaks). ■

Food & Drink

Chinese cooking can be enjoyed in Chinatowns the world over; but if it's the real thing you want, it's mandatory you come to China. A history of famine coupled with a delight in food preparation has produced an obsession with mealtimes. An indispensable part of the China experience, eating is not just a necessity here but an event.

Steamed dumplings are a staple of Shanghai cooking.

Historically, pork *(zhurou)* was the most popular meat in China, followed by chicken *(jirou)*; beef *(niurou)* and lamb *(yangrou)* are eaten less due to their strong flavor, but Muslim Chinese and Mongolians (from Inner Mongolia) retain a strong affection for them. Fish *(yu)* is also popular.

A host of culinary exotica also makes its way onto tables in China, including tortoises, sea snails, snakes, bear paws, cicadas, scorpions, and rats. If you are presented with a menu exclusively in Chinese, one way to avoid these is to look at the prices; exotic food tends to be more expensive. Chinese also eat dog meat *(gourou)*, especially in the colder winter months.

Popular vegetables include Chinese cabbage *(baicai/qingcai)*, spinach *(bocai)*, and potatoes *(tudou)*. Apples *(pingguo)*, oranges and tangerines *(juzi)*, bananas *(xiangjiao)*, pears *(lizi)*, watermelons *(xigua)*, and grapes *(putao)* are seasonal.

Tofu *(doufu)* is eaten for its versatility and as a meat substitute. Rice *(baifan)* accompanies most meals, usually in small bowls. Often served at the start of a meal, peanuts *(huasheng)* feature in a range of dishes. Watermelon seeds *(guazi)* are also widely eaten, and pistachios *(kaixinguo)* and cashew nuts *(yaoguo)* can be found in most shops and supermarkets.

Regional Cuisine

Beijing *(jingcai)* and Shandong *(lucai)* typify northern cooking, embracing salty flavors and wheat-based staples. Pork-filled dumplings *(jiaozi)* dipped in soy sauce and rice vinegar are enormously popular, as are noodles and steamed bread *(mantou)*. The most famous Beijing dish is Peking duck, a rich preparation of oily duck flesh, plum sauce, and onion, which you eat rolled into a water-thin pancake.

Stir-frying is the hallmark of southern Cantonese *(yuecai)* cooking, along with boiling and steaming. Lightly fried dim sum snacks and pastries are wheeled around restaurants, served on plates and steamers, and dipped in an array of sauces. Chaozhou cuisine, another southern style, is sweet and seafood-based.

Eastern cooking is typified by Shanghai cuisine, reveling in soups and seafood. Quite oily dishes include "drunken chicken" and *xiaolong bao* (small parcels of meat wrapped in pastry).

Sichuan, the heartland of western Chinese cooking, introduces a galaxy of searing dishes. In Sichuan cooking *(chuancai)*, an idiosyncratic herb called *huajiao* numbs the mouth, while the remaining herbs and spices blister the taste buds. Famous Sichuan dishes include *suancai yu*, a pickled vegetable and fish soup, and *shuizhu roupian*, in which slices of pork cook slowly in a sea of chili oil and cabbage leaves. Hunan food *(xiangcai)* and Hubei cuisine are also renowned for their fiery dishes.

Drink

With meals, the Chinese drink beer *(pijiu)*, wine *(putaojiu)*, or a strong, clear spirit called *baijiu* (literally "white wine"). Baijiu is a sharp shock of a drink, the most famous of which comes from Maotai in Guizhou Province. *Erguotou* (literally "two pot head") is one of the strongest at 65 percent proof.

Chinese everywhere drink tea *(cha)*, especially at mealtimes. It comes in various guises, including chrysanthemum *(juhua cha)*, Western *(hong cha)*, green *(lü cha)*, and lovely eight treasures *(babao cha)*, a potpourri of flower petals and buds, sweetened with rock sugar.

Not popular outside of cafés, coffee *(kafei)* is on the menu at most restaurants, though it is likely to be instant. The Chinese also enjoy drinking boiled, hot water *(baikai shui)*.

Fruit juice *(guozhi)* and mineral water *(kuangquan shui)* are widely available.

EXPERIENCE: Cooking Chinese Style

If you want to learn to cook Chinese style, you can't go wrong in Beijing, the heart of northern Chinese cooking. Tucked away off Nanluogu Xiang along the lovely Heizhima ("black sesame") Hutong is the Black Sesame Kitchen *(3 Heizhima Hutong, Dongcheng, tel 1369 147-4408, www.blacksesamekitchen.com)*, a restaurant and cooking school founded by Jen Lin-Liu, the author of *Serve the People: A Stir-Fried Journey through China.*

You can take one class or attend an entire series. The staff will teach you how to *bao jiaozi* (wrap dumplings) the local way. You might bring tears to your eyes frying up Chongqing spicy chicken or learn the secret of a perfect plate of *mapo doufu*, literally "grandma's tofu." Hands-on classes *($$$$)*, with English instruction, cook up on Thursdays *(11 a.m.–1:30 p.m.)* and on Saturday afternoons *(1 p.m.–4 p.m.)*. Attend one of the Friday evening *(7 p.m.–10 p.m.)* Wine 'n' Dine events *($$$$)*, and watch the preparation of a ten-course gourmet dinner.

Far less well known outside China than either Cantonese or Sichuan cuisine, Shanghai cooking uses an abundance of fish and seafood. Stir-frying is used as well as steaming, the latter employed in signature dishes like *xiaolong bao* (see above). To try your hand at Shanghai cooking, contact The Kitchen at... *(383 South Xiang Yang Rd., Bldg. 20, 3rd Floor, tel 021 6433-2700, www.thekitchen at.com)*, which runs cooking courses *($$$$–$$$$$)* in Shanghai and other cuisines on Tuesdays and Saturdays.

History of China

China's history is a captivating chronicle that reaches deep into the past to dim and obscure origins. As you explore the strata of this profound history, an epic tale emerges, peopled by a cast of savage tyrants and shrewd opportunists who steered this huge country to the present.

Myths & Legends

Some historians earmark 6000 B.C. as the dawn of Chinese civilization. Ancient legends speak of Pangu who created the world, dividing heaven and Earth. Three divinities successively created humans and brought them animal husbandry,

A spectacular failure, the Great Wall was built to protect China from northern invaders.

agriculture, and the medicinal properties of plants. The first of them, Fuxi, formulated the eight trigrams of the *I-Ching*, known in English as the *Book of Changes* (an ancient book for predicting the future). They were succeeded by other mythological beings. The Yellow Emperor is accorded the greatest respect as the primeval ancestor. Also regarded as the founder of Taoism (see p. 32), among his many contributions to Chinese civilization, the mythical emperor invented the boat, improved cattle breeding, and introduced bamboo to China. Chinese myth also recalls how the Great Yu harnessed the floods and tamed the Yangtze River, leaving Chang Jie the task of inventing words.

Peking Man Site

The Peking Man Site *(Sinanthropus pekinensis zhoukoudian)* ($), located 30 miles (48 km) southwest of the city of Beijing, features caves where primitive humans lived some 300,000 to 600,000 years ago. Exhibits at the museum include remains unearthed at the site: flint tools, bone needles, and animal parts, all labeled with English explanations.

Xia & Shang Dynasties

Archaeological evidence adds credence to the existence of the primordial Xia dynasty (ca 2205–1766 B.C.), although a much larger body of historical evidence relating to the ensuing Shang dynasty (ca 1766–1122 B.C.) survives. Finds reveal an agricultural society whose domain reached along the Yellow River basin from Xi'an to Shandong, buffered by the Yangtze River to the south. This area is the heartland of Chinese civilization.

Shang dynasty society acknowledged a single leader, who was also a religious figure. Rulers were both military commanders and leaders of community activities, with succession either from brother to brother or from father to son. As this society became increasingly sophisticated, the king delegated more and more tasks to a cadre of officials. Much of the king's authority derived from his ancestors, who were worshipped and consulted in matters relating to affairs of state. The practice of divination (to gauge the seasons, aid farming, engage in warfare, etc.) using inscriptions on oracle bones shows that writing had evolved.

Tamed elephants were reportedly used in large building works, indicating advanced techniques in construction. The city of Anyang, in Henan Province, was built on the site of Yin, the last city of the Shang. The dynasty is also synonymous with its fabulous bronze art, notably the ferocious and mysterious animal-like designs embellishing vessels. Under the Shang, commerce and trade must have evolved as the term "Shang" is still found

China's Dynasties

Xia: ca 2205–1766 B.C.
Shang: ca 1766–1122 B.C.
Zhou: Western ca 1122–771 B.C., Eastern ca 771–221 B.C.
Qin: 221–206 B.C.
Han: Western 206 B.C.–A.D. 9, Xin (Wang Mang) A.D. 9–25, Eastern A.D. 25–220
Three Kingdoms period: 220–265
Jin: Western Jin 265–316, Eastern Jin 317–420
Northern: Northern Wei 386–534, Eastern Wei 534–550, Western Wei 535–557, Northern Qi 550–577, Northern Zhou 557–581
Southern: Song 420–479, Qi 479–502, Liang 502–557, Chen 557–589
Sui: 581–618
Tang: 618–907
Five Dynasties: Later Liang 907–923, Later Tang 923–936, Later Jin 936–947, Later Han 947–950, Later Zhou 951–960
Song: Northern 960–1127, Southern 1127–1279
Yuan: 1279–1368
Ming: 1368–1644
Qing: 1644–1911
Republic of China: 1911–1949 (maintained in Taiwan)
People's Republic of China: 1949–present

today in the words for business *(shangren)* and commerce *(shangye)*.

Zhou Dynasty

The house of Zhou, whose name frequently appears in Shang oracle bone inscriptions, eventually overthrew the Shang. They differed little from their Shang predecessors and inherited much of their culture, which coalesced under a feudal state structure.

There are sparse data on the history of the Western Zhou (ca 1122–771 B.C.), but by the ninth century B.C., the monarchy was significantly weakened, finally perishing during the reign of Yu Wang. Yu Wang's successor moved the capital from Hao (southwest of present-day Xi'an) to Luoyang. During this period, known as the Eastern Zhou (ca 771–221 B.C.), turbulent feuds swept the states.

Pre-Qin Philosophical Foundations

Historians generally divide the Eastern Zhou into the Spring and Autumn (ca 771–476 B.C.) and the Warring States (476–221 B.C.) periods, a time also termed Pre-Qin. More than any other epoch, this violent period forged the philosophical culture of China that survives today. Confucius (551–479 B.C.) was a product of his times (see pp. 130–131), with constant war and bloodshed urging him to develop a system of social behavior that would edify and instruct. His model was the *junzi,* or gentleman, who was upright, loyal, and civilized. Confucius's intellectual successor, Mencius (372–289 B.C.), further championed his philosophy, emphasizing the concept of the Mandate of Heaven. This held that heaven could confiscate the mandate to rule from a corrupt or bad ruler, through rebellion or withdrawal of support by the people.

Incipient Taoism found a mouthpiece with the sage Laozi (ca 580–500 B.C.), whose mystical reflections on the cosmos he distilled into the seminal *Daode Jing (The Classic of the Way and Its Power)*. His musings were more fancifully presented by the insightful allegories of storyteller cum philosopher Zhuangzi (ca 369–286 B.C.). Other philosophical ideas arose, chief among these being those of the Mohists under Mozi (ca 468–376 B.C.), who promulgated a doctrine of universal love–*jian'ai*–despite being keen military strategists. The Legalist school under Han Feizi (ca 280–233 B.C.) also engineered an influential realpolitik philosophy of law fused with statecraft.

Qin Dynasty

The constant warring between states was halted by the inexorable rise of the state of Qin, which unified China's fragments. Qin ultimately lent its name to the foreign word for the Middle Kingdom: China. Qinshi Huangdi was its first, terrible emperor, engineer of mass death and oppression against his countrymen. His reign lasted from 221 B.C. to his death in 210 B.C. During these years, he instigated a purge of Confucian scholars *(kengru)* and a great burning of books *(fenshu)*, reducing most of China's literature to carbon.

The emperor also led China on a course of territorial expansion, which necessitated the linking up of previously built earthen ramparts into the Great Wall to prevent barbarian incursions. Another lavish building project was the extravagant underground mausoleum of the terra-cotta warriors outside Xi'an. Under Qinshi Huangdi, the Chinese script and weights and measures were standardized.

Provincial rebellion against oppressive Qin power (principally in the hands of Chao Kao) led to a massacre of the Qin army by Xiang Yu, who was in turn defeated by Liu Bang, founder of the Han dynasty.

Han Dynasty

The Han preserved much of the state structure instituted by the Qin dynasty before it. The 400-year dynasty did so much to define Chinese culture that the character "Han" is still used to refer to China (for example, Hanzu: the Chinese race; Hanyu: the Chinese language).

The dynasty is divided into the Western Han (206 B.C.–A.D. 9) and the Eastern Han (A.D. 25–220). Separating the two was the short rule of the Xin, who seized power with the usurpation of the throne by minister Wang Mang at a time of growing incompetence in the Han court.

The Western Han had the massive task of rescuing the country from decline and consolidating the state; in its structure, the Han state was closely modeled on that of the Qin. Confucianism effectively infiltrated the bureaucracy after recovering from the Qin edict outlawing it, adding a veneer of morality to otherwise coercive government.

The Eastern Han was brought to its knees by social discontent, which spawned the Yellow Turban Sect (a secret Taoist group) uprising. In the ensuing chaos, the Han dynasty collapsed under the pressure of feuding warlords. The *Shi Ji*, or *Records of the Historian,* by Si Maqian (ca 145–85 B.C.) is the most

Unearthed near Chengdu in Sichuan Province, this bronze sculpture may be more than 4,000 years old.

The ruthless first emperor of the Qin dynasty left China the legacy of the terra-cotta warriors.

notable literary legacy of the period, an epic record of the rise and fall of the great ruling families of China.

Period of Division

The disintegration of the Eastern Han marked the end of the centralized state. For almost 400 years the country was mired in incessant war and division. Three states arose from the rubble of the Han—Wei, Shu, and Wu—known as the Three Kingdoms (A.D. 220–265). They are romantically recalled in the Ming dynasty novel *The Romance of the Three Kingdoms,* while in reality their shared history was stained with blood. Each state considered itself the true successor of the Han dynasty. Wei conquered Shu in 263, which was soon followed by the birth of the Jin dynasty and the conquest of Wu. The country was temporarily reunited, but it soon unraveled again under attack from the "barbarian" Xiongnu and other nomad invaders. The Jin lost control of North China and moved the capital to Nanking, prompting a huge migration south.

Three states arose from the rubble of the Han—Wei, Shu, and Wu—known as the Three Kingdoms (A.D. 220–265).

In the fifth century, the Tuoba (a Turkic tribe) took control of North China, establishing the Northern Wei (A.D. 386–534) while rapidly adopting the customs and ways of the Chinese (as the Mongols and Manchus did after them). The country was effectively divided into what is known as the Northern and Southern dynasties, with the Northern Wei and its successors in the north, and the Eastern Jin and the states that succeeded it in the south.

Social disorder split the Northern Wei into Eastern Wei (534–550) and Western Wei (535–557), whose Tuoba rulers soon lost power, hatching the Northern Zhou (557–581) and the Northern Qi (550–577). The two new states indulged in a period of immorality and bad government.

In the south, a succession of generals forged a series of dynasties on the backs of incessant war and death.

Buddhist Beginnings: The period of division was chaotic, but, amazingly, a rich culture flowered from the mess. Taoism responded to a heightened spirituality of the times, while the famous Seven Sages of the Bamboo Grove, a group of intellectuals, got together to discuss Taoist philosophy, write poetry, and drink wine. A more metaphysical mood reigned, bringing a deep and intense searching for meaning in a violent world. Buddhism flourished, as did Buddhist art, including the entrancing Wei Buddhist sculpture. Captured on the faces of bodhisattvas and Buddhas (see p. 82) of this period is a mesmerizing transcendence and divinity; the most famous extant caves with art from this era are at Yungang, Longmen, and Dunhuang. The Taoist poet and hermit Tao Yuanming fashioned beautiful verse.

Sui Dynasty

The fleeting Sui dynasty (581–618) again unified China when Yang Qian overthrew the ruler of the Northern Zhou in 581 and began reincorporating the states in the

(continued on p. 34)

Religion & Philosophy

China is a deeply religious country, with the main faiths being Buddhism, Taoism, and, to a lesser extent, Confucianism (after atheism). Confucianism is not strictly a religion but a philosophy, and Buddhism was imported from India, leaving Taoism as China's only true indigenous faith.

A young Buddhist monk spins a prayer wheel decorated with flags.

Taoism

Taoism *(daojiao)* is essentially more mystical than religious, although certain strains are presided over by deities (see p. 83). Supposedly founded by Laozi (ca 580–500 B.C.), who wrote the *Daode Jing (The Classic of the Way and Its Power),* Taoism aims to cultivate a philosophical awareness of life. Lacking an anthropomorphic god, it seeks revelation of "the Way"—the term used to describe the dynamism of nature and the operating force behind the universe.

Taoists believe in achievement through inaction *(wu wei),* allowing things to develop and occur of their own accord. Readers who wish to experience a sensation of the Way should peruse Laozi's classic, a book that has, as closely as is humanly possible, captured the feeling of the Tao. The Way is also experientially revealed through the practice of tai chi *(taiji quan)* (see p. 125), a martial art that draws on the Taoist precepts of softness, heightened awareness, and avoidance of conflict.

Buddhism

Most temples in China are Buddhist, pointing to the importance of Buddhism *(fojiao)* among the Chinese. Founded in India by the Indian prince Siddhartha Gautama (563–483 B.C.), Buddhism migrated to China from the third to the sixth centuries A.D., where it slotted in alongside Taoism. The faith seeks to cure suffering through the neutralization of desire; following the "eightfold path" leads to nirvana, a transcendent state of freedom.

The type of Buddhism generally found in China is Mahayana Buddhism (greater vehicle), which differs from Theravada Buddhism (doctrine of the elders) in its belief that bodhisattvas (see p. 82) should delay Buddhahood in order to help others. The distinctive Tibetan Buddhism (see pp. 306–307) is found in Tibet and Inner Mongolia.

Buddhist Art: Buddha is an object of veneration in China, and Buddhist sculpture is principally devotional rather than artistic in nature. Nevertheless, Chinese Buddhist sculptures and frescoes, especially those at the famous grottoes at Dunhuang (see pp. 326–327), Longmen (see pp. 122–123), and Yungang (see pp. 114–115), are also fabulous works of art in their own right.

Buddhist sculpture evolved with the reinterpretation of Buddhism over the dynasties. Examples from the Northern Wei (A.D. 386–534) are notable for their slightly smug smiles and divine beauty. They seem remote, metaphysical, and abstruse. Those from the Tang and Song dynasties are more human and of this world.

Confucianism

Confucianism *(rujia sixiang)* (see pp. 130–131), named after the sage Confucius, is a paternalistic philosophy of social behavior that teaches the Chinese people their codes, rules, and norms of conduct. Many Chinese consider genuflecting to one's elders as ordained by strict Confucianism a thankless task, yet the philosophy permeated the soul of the nation and was successfully transplanted to Japan, Korea, and Vietnam. Through time, Confucianism has became decorated with religious trappings and institutionalized, despite being a very human philosophy that offers an answer to suffering and bad governance.

Islam

Arab merchants brought Islam *(yisilan jiao)* to China along the Silk Road and across the sea to the southern coast, where they established their mosques. Xinjiang Province in the northwest has a prominent Muslim population in the Uighurs, descendants of these Arab traders. The other large Muslim group, the Hui, live in Gansu, Ningxia, Qinghai, and Xinjiang (see p. 315).

Christianity

The Nestorians (a Syrian Christian sect) arrived in China in the seventh century A.D., followed later by the Jesuits, who helped in the building of the Old Summer Palace in Beijing and gave assistance in the sciences (see p. 76). The 19th-century Taiping Rebellion was led by Hong Xiuquan (see pp. 164–165), who believed he was the Son of God. Today, Christianity *(jidu jiao)* is China's fastest growing faith, partly due to associations made between the spirit of capitalism and Protestantism, the spiritual bankruptcy at the heart of society, and the flourishing number of (illegal) house churches, unregistered places of assembly and worship for the swelling number of Christians (who by some estimates now number 100 million).

Most temples in China are Buddhist, pointing to the importance of Buddhism *(fojiao)* among the Chinese.

Judaism

Judaism *(youtai jiao)* in Kaifeng (see p. 126) can be traced back to the Tang dynasty, having arrived along the Silk Road. The first synagogue was built in the 12th century, but it was destroyed twice during floods. After the second flood in the mid-19th century, it was not rebuilt. A large population of non-Chinese Jews settled in Shanghai during its heyday and heavily contributed to the city's prosperity and development.

south. The dynasty prospered under its ambitious first emperor, Wendi. The second emperor, Yangdi, however, indulged in mammoth building projects that drained the treasury coffers and incensed the peasants. The Grand Canal (see pp. 176–177) was extended with the help of forced labor. Luoyang was extravagantly rebuilt, as were sections of the Great Wall, all at enormous cost. A disastrous war against Korea and a subsequent humiliation by the Eastern Turks further infuriated the luckless peasants, and Yangdi was strangled by a member of his entourage in 618.

Tang Dynasty

The Chinese consider the Tang (618–907) the most glorious of dynasties. Hatched by an official of the Sui dynasty, Li Yuan, the Tang quickly reasserted Chinese influence over Korea and Central Asia. The civil service developed under the aegis of neo-Confucianism, a philosophy that had been eclipsed by Taoism and Buddhism in preceding dynasties. The Confucian classics-based, conservative examination system for recruiting civil servants (see p. 64) was set in amber.

To avoid the mistakes of earlier dynasties, appeasement of the peasants became policy through a system of land equalization. The early Tang saw impressive economic growth, which encouraged manufacturing and foreign trade. The dynasty also wielded considerable influence over Central Asia and saw growing relations with Tibet. Ample cultural commerce with Japan led to the adoption of the Chinese writing system there.

Fruitful contact with other cultures along the Silk Road (see pp. 312–313) was fostered by a tolerant policy toward foreigners, resulting in a sense of cosmopolitanism. A number of religions, including Nestorianism, Manichaeism, Islam, and Judaism made their way to China, but none of them flourished as successfully as Buddhism.

Tang culture was a high point in China's history, especially during the reign of Xuanzong, and its poetry reached an unsurpassed zenith.

China's sole female emperor, the notorious Wu Zetian (or Wu Hou) reigned during the Tang. She rose from imperial concubine to empress and reigned from 698 to 705, when she was forced to abdicate. Buddhism flourished under her tutelage, largely because of her penchant for Buddhist monks. Her story is fascinating: A soothsayer at the court warned the emperor not to admit any woman with the surname Wu to the palace, for such a woman would destroy the Tang dynasty. Wu Zetian was infuriated by attempts to sideline her and set her sights on the royal throne, which she eventually seized.

The reign that followed, under Xuanzong (712–756), is often referred to as the Tang's golden age. However, the dynasty was weakened severely by defeat in battle against the Arabs in 751 (which resulted in a spate of successful incursions by the Tibetans) and the revolt of An Lushan, a Turkish general. The rebellion was eventually crushed, but the state's control was greatly diminished in the process.

The Tang monarchy then came under the sway of the eunuchs, and several emperors were poisoned. The Buddhists encountered a period of repression, the economy nosedived, and the peasants, exploited to the hilt, rose once more in revolt. The Tang dynasty was leveled by rebellion, and China fell into the hands of warlords.

Tang culture was a high point in China's history, especially during the reign of Xuanzong, and its poetry reached an unsurpassed zenith. The poets Li Bai and Du Fu were poised at the very summit; Han Yu is renowned principally for his marvelous prose writing. Printing in China dates from the Tang dynasty, and the world's first known printed book, the *Diamond Sutra,* was found stored away at Dunhuang. Buddhist art also reached its peak in this era, but anti-Buddhist repression destroyed many examples. A selection of the statues at Longmen and Dunhuang survive as a record of this fabulous period. Painting also matured to a form that paved the way for the success of the ensuing Song dynasty.

Five Dynasties & the Song Dynasty

Following the Tang dynasty came a period of division, with decentralized power in the hands of a number of states. The ephemeral dynasties in the north charted an oppressive rule alongside ten kingdoms from 907 to 960, a period often called the Five Dynasties.

China was reunited by Zhao Kuangyin, commander of the Imperial Guard of the Later Zhou (the last of the Five Dynasties), under a new dynasty: the Song (960–1279). This dynasty is generally divided into the Northern Song (960–1127) and the Southern Song (1127–1279).

Beijing or Peking?

The name of China's capital has changed over the centuries. At one time or another it has been known as Yanjing, Dadu, and Beiping. Indeed, you could be forgiven for thinking Peking and Beijing were two different places. Peking is simply the old transliteration of the Chinese pronunciation for "Northern Capital"; Beijing is the officially sanctioned Pinyin spelling, based on the Mandarin dialect.

The administration was rebuilt and the official examination system resurrected; the economy flourished. Paper money was invented, and a period of reform *(bianfa)* was instigated by Wang Anshi (1021–1086). The greatest cultural legacy of the Song lies in its landscape painting, its poetry, and a thriving neo-Confucian philosophy.

The Song, however, were under constant threat from attacks from the outside. The Jurchen, marauding invaders from the north, forced the northern court south after the capture of the capital, Kaifeng, in 1126. The capital was moved to Linan (present-day Hangzhou), while the Jurchen established the Jin dynasty (1125–1234) in the north. The Jin managed to extract a vast amount of tribute from the Song in return for peace, and the Huai River was deemed the dividing line between the two. The Southern Song still managed to progress, despite the Jurchen presence to the north, and a newfound prosperity emerged in agriculture, foreign commerce, and manufacturing.

This glittering period, however, was soon eclipsed by the Mongol menace. Under Ghenghis Khan, the Mongols devised a fanatical form of scorched-earth warfare that obliterated all in their path. The Mongols conquered the Jin, and the wealth of the Song lay before them. The naive Song had allied with the Mongols against the Jurchen, only to see their new allies turn about and muster on their borders. The Mongols devastated the Song and, in 1279, imposed foreign rule on the whole of China for the first time.

Yuan Dynasty—Mongols

The victorious Mongols held sway over a vast domain from Asia to Eastern Europe; their control over China is known historically as the Yuan dynasty (1279–1368). When in China, they made Beijing (Dadu) their capital (see sidebar this page), while still reserving a capital of their own in Inner Mongolia.

The Mongols imposed their own culture on the Chinese in the form of an uncompromising and oppressive regime. China was divided into four groups, with the Mongols at the top, their foreign allies below them, the Chinese and other inhabitants of North China further down, with the last rung of the ladder reserved for southern Chinese.

The Mongols used China as a springboard to launch costly attacks on the surrounding regions, including Vietnam and Japan. Again, a rebellious peasantry fired up

Statue from a fourth-century temple built during the Eastern Jin dynasty

by agrarian crises overturned the dynasty. Directed by Buddhist secret sects, such as the White Lotus and the Red Turbans, rebellious foment cohered under the leadership of Zhu Yuanzhang (*r.* 1363–67). He overthrew the overlords who were by then squabbling among themselves, and established the Ming ("bright") dynasty.

Ming Dynasty

Zhu Yuanzhang, ruling under the name of Hongwu, established the capital of the Ming dynasty (1368–1644) at Nanjing ("southern capital"), constructing his palace there and surrounding the city with huge walls.

Hongwu (*r.* 1368–1398) ruled China effectively but quickly slid into despotism, displaying a savagery matched only by his severe paranoia. The problem of succession on his death led to civil war, and the throne ultimately went not to his grandson (his chosen successor) but to the Prince of Yen, who seized power and ruled as the emperor Yongle (*r.* 1403–1424). Yongle moved the Ming capital to Beijing and built the Forbidden City (see pp. 60–66).

It was during this period that Europeans, who were later to have a huge effect on the history of the Qing dynasty, began to arrive. The Portuguese captured Macau in Guangdong Province, the English arrived in Canton (Guangzhou), and the Jesuits, led by Matteo Ricci (1557–1610) in the 1580s, tried to graft Catholicism to China's register of religions.

The Mongols continued to harass China on the country's northern borders, and sections of the Great Wall were rebuilt. The Japanese invasion of Korea (a vassal state of China) during the reign of Wanli (*r.* 1573–1620) prompted a tardy and costly Ming military response.

By the 15th century, the eunuchs were again manipulating the emperors like puppets at the palace. Eunuch domination of state policy often brought the empire close to ruin. Ming authority had degraded in the face of peasant rebellion, and the last Ming emperor hanged himself from a tree on Jingshan Hill in Beijing as rebels swarmed through the capital.

The Ming dynasty's chief cultural advancement was the novel, which was welcomed by a growing audience. *Shuihu Zhuan (The Water Margin)* and the *Sanguo Yanyi (Romance of the Three Kingdoms)* narrated historical stories in an accessible vernacular language, while eroticism found a voice in *Jin Pingmei.* Much admired blue-and-white Ming dynasty porcelains built upon a style fashioned in the Yuan dynasty under Middle East influence.

Mongol Achievements

Despite ruling with a determination to exert control over every corner of China, the Mongols administered the empire with a modicum of skill and foresight. The Grand Canal was rebuilt, roads were renovated, and foreign trade began to mushroom. After contact with Europe increased, Venetian traveler Marco Polo visited China and later penned his famous travelogue. The destruction wrought by the Mongol invasion of China brought huge losses of Chinese art, but despite the upheaval, painting continued to refine in technique, especially in landscapes (see pp. 48–50). The dynasty also nurtured the development of Chinese drama and the novel.

Qing Dynasty—Manchus

A massive famine in Shaanxi Province in 1626 ignited a vast peasant rebellion that coincided with a growing threat to China from its northern neighbors, the

Manchus, descendants of the Jin dynasty Jurchen. With the rebels failing to unite against the Manchus, the northern invaders slipped in to establish a new dynasty. From their triumphant entry into Beijing in 1644, the Manchus took four decades to completely wrest power from the disparate Ming elements.

The fragmented Manchus had been united by Nurhachi under a banner system and forged into a formidable fighting force. They first established the Qing ("clear") dynasty in 1636 in northeast China's Manchuria. The banner system *(baqi),* a military and governmental organization that regimented the upper echelons of society, was maintained; it formed the basis of the state, but many Ming officials were allowed to keep their positions to appease the Chinese. The overlords sought to impose their own stamp on China, however, and top posts were reserved for those of Manchu stock.

Male adult Chinese were forced to wear the *bianzi,* or long braided ponytail, to mark their subservience to the Manchus, while Manchu men were forbidden to marry Chinese women. Manchu women, moreover, never emulated the Chinese custom of binding their feet. With time, however, the Manchus thoroughly absorbed Chinese culture.

The early Qing dynasty was an auspicious period and an era with some of the most competent rulers China has ever seen. The Kangxi, Yongzheng, and Qianlong emperors represent a golden age in Chinese history. Under the Kangxi emperor (1661–1722), treaties were made with Russia and the empire was expanded to include Outer Mongolia, Tibet, Nepal, and chunks of Central Asia. Mongol and Tibetan leaders were courted by way of imperial patronage of Tibetan Buddhist temples, such as the Lama Temple in Beijing. The Kangxi emperor oversaw the construction of the Tibetan-style imperial summer retreat at Chengde and encouraged Jesuit tutelage in the sciences, principally mathematics and astronomy (see p. 76).

The early Qing dynasty was an auspicious period and an era with some of the most competent rulers China has ever seen.

The reigns of Yongzheng (*r.* 1723–1735) and Qianlong (*r.* 1736–1795) saw growth in industry and commerce throughout China and healthy patronage of the arts and sciences. Most important, tax reforms and flood control projects pacified the insurgent peasant population. China had become weakened, however, by a series of campaigns in Central Asia and the southwest.

Western Encroachment: The greatest challenge to imperial authority arrived in the 19th century, once more from outside the empire. The technologically advanced foreign powers, including Britain, France, and Germany, had become increasingly bewitched by China's great riches and weakness. A rapid encroachment on China became the objective of the West, which sought to establish trade links.

The Qianlong emperor had rebuffed the overtures of the British Lord Macartney and his embassy at Chengde (see p. 119) in the closing years of the 18th century, a precedent that cast them into opposition. The belligerent mood of 19th-century relations with the foreign powers resulted in wars ending in defeat for China, along with equally humiliating treaties.

The result of the first Opium War (1840–1842) led to Hong Kong being parceled off to the British with the Treaty of Nanking. The second Opium War (1856–1860) and further treaties saw packets of land slide into the clutches of Britain, Japan, France, and Russia. China was in danger of being carved up like a turkey.

China's woes were manifold during this period. The Middle Kingdom was not equipped to deal with the sophistication of the Western model of warfare. The situation could have been saved by modernization of its military and government institutions, but conservative elements in the Qing court blocked the way. The West was treated by the Chinese court with a mixture of awe and contempt, a neurotic formula that led to insoluble paralysis.

In the aftermath of the mid-19th century Opium Wars, parts of China drifted into foreign hands.

Nineteenth-century China was also split by internecine strife. Popular anti-Qing unrest flared up afresh with the hugely damaging proto-Christian Taiping Rebellion of 1850–1864 (see pp. 164–165) that leveled numerous cities and left millions dead. China's plentiful smoking ruins were further turned over by the Nien Rebellion (1853–1868) and a massive Muslim rebellion in the northwest (1862–1873). The Taiping, in particular, almost brought the Manchu dynasty to its knees.

Fall of the Qing: China's stagnation continued further under Empress Dowager Cixi (1835–1908), a former concubine who appropriated power through luck and deceit. Famed for her lengthy, clawlike fingernails, Cixi liked to pose as Guanyin, goddess of mercy, lending her the epithet "Old Buddha." Behind the divine facade, however, lay the reality of an inept tyrant.

Her nephew, Emperor Guangxu, was nominally sovereign, but in reality Cixi held the reins of power. The catastrophic Sino-Japanese War (1894–1895) fueled China's shame.

The Reform Movement (1895–1898), which tried to shoehorn in modern ideas, failed and led to Cixi imprisoning Emperor Guangxu (who sympathized with the movement) in the Summer Palace.

By the end of the century, the tectonic collisions between Chinese and Western culture erupted in the ill-fated Boxer Rebellion (1899–1901), signaling the last gasp of the old order. Emperor Guangxu and Empress Dowager Cixi died within a day of each

Chinese soldiers escort Europeans during the Boxer Rebellion of 1899–1901.

other in 1908, leaving the juvenile Emperor Puyi in charge of China at the tender age of two.

The dynasty collapsed around him in the successful uprising of 1911, which installed the republic.

Modern China

The fruitless Reform Movement of 1898 and the failure of the Boxer Rebellion to expel the "foreign devils" from China signaled a paradigm shift in the Chinese consciousness. It had become increasingly evident to all Chinese that the country must modernize. This grudging awareness, however, came too late.

Among the torch-bearing Chinese intellectuals who were committed to reform was Sun Yat-sen (1866–1925), also called Sun Zhongshan, the pioneering father of Chinese republicanism. Sun Yat-sen melded together principles of nationalism, democracy, and the people's livelihood into his vision of a modern China.

When the Qing dynasty finally crumbled, Sun returned from America, where he was raising funds in Denver, to be elected provisional president of the Republic of China in 1911. His position was opportunistically wrested from his grasp by the general Yuan Shikai, who had helped light the bonfire under the failed Reform Movement of 1898.

Yuan set himself up as emperor in 1915 but died in 1916, effectively leaving most of China in the hands of feuding warlords, while Sun Yat-sen retained power in Guangzhou. The subsequent dislocation would survive until the Communist Party seized power in 1949.

Experimentation with foreign political concepts in China had encouraged the formation of the Chinese Communist Party in the city of Shanghai in 1921.

Arrival of Communism

With China in disarray, the Nationalist Party (Kuomintang or KMT) maintained its republican ethos under the leadership of Sun Yat-sen. On Sun's death in 1925, the mantle of the KMT passed to Chiang Kai-shek (1888–1975), also called Jiang Jieshi. The KMT's goal was to vanquish the warlords in the north of China and unite the land under a Nationalist government.

Republicanism, however, was not the only credo fomenting new ideas. Experimentation with foreign political concepts in China had encouraged the formation of the Chinese Communist Party in the city of Shanghai in 1921 (see p. 188).

With Soviet encouragement, the Communists decided to unite with the KMT in 1923. But when Chiang Kai-shek replaced Sun Yat-sen, he dissolved the union and blackballed the Communists, seduced by the hope of establishing a capitalist state on his own terms. His northern expedition against the warlords in 1926, aided by Shanghai moneymakers, led to a massacre of Shanghai workers and Communists. Harried, expelled, and radicalized, the Communists undertook to survive and take control by other means.

The northern expedition persisted in its course and installed a government in Beijing, but large swathes of China remained under the control of despotic warlords. Many Communists, led by the young Mao Zedong and Zhu De, retreated to the countryside and mountains in Jiangxi and Hunan Provinces. Mao chose a rural-based revolutionary formula directed at China's peasantry, as opposed to urban-based centers of communism.

The Long March

Chiang Kai-shek, whose hatred of the Communists eclipsed his hatred of the warlords, launched a series of punitive campaigns that finally evicted Mao and his combatants from their mountain stronghold.

During the Long March (see sidebar) to a safer base of operations, Mao Zedong had won a war of wills over the direction of Communist resistance and risen to the unchallenged position of Communist leader, asserting his authority at the famous Party Conference of Zunyi in Guizhou Province. The experience also allowed other veterans who would have great influence on the shape of the party—Zhu De, Zhou Enlai, Lin Biao, Liu Shaoqi, and Deng Xiaoping—to assert themselves.

The Long March

In October 1934, Communist leader Mao Zedong and his force of 100,000 men and women—determined to escape destruction at the command of Nationalist Chiang Kai-shek—left their mountain stronghold and embarked on the arduous 6,000-mile (9,659 km) Long March. Mao intended to find a more secure base in Shaanxi Province from which to wage his "people's war." A year later, and after massive detours, fewer than 10,000 people struggled into Yan'an and the mountains of Shaanxi Province; the rest had fallen victim to a mixed bag of Nationalist attacks, illness, and desertion. The marchers who had set out from Jiangxi had traversed 11 provinces.

War With Japan

A divided China failed to escape the attention of Japan, which swiftly occupied Manchuria in 1931. The last Qing emperor, Puyi, was ignobly installed as puppet sovereign of Manchukuo, the renamed kingdom of Manchuria, with Changchun as his capital.

The Japanese, however, were only clearing their throats. They invaded China in 1937, in the face of a shaky alliance between the Communists and the KMT. Their advance was swift and successful, swallowing up much of northern and eastern China. Shanghai fell, and the citizens of Nanjing were subjected to the infamous Rape of Nanjing.

The KMT fled west, halting temporarily at Wuhan and then going on to Sichuan to establish a new capital at Chongqing. Obsessive hatred of the Communists blunted KMT resistance against the invaders, and an ambivalent, spineless mood reigned. The Communists, however, grew in strength, organization, and mobility. The great tragedy was China's lack of a firm common front against the forces of the "island kingdom."

A second alliance between Communists and Nationalists failed, and the entry of the United States into World War II after the Japanese attack on Pearl Harbor coalesced American and KMT interests. The United States supported the KMT effort with weapons and money, but the Nationalists, riddled with corruption, still lacked the patriotic resolve to wholeheartedly resist the Japanese. Japan's unqualified surrender in 1945, after the destruction of Hiroshima and Nagasaki, again left China victim to civil war. The Communists made startling gains, using captured KMT equipment (largely supplied by the United States) and defecting troops.

The People's Republic

Mao Zedong inaugurated the People's Republic of China from Tiananmen Gate in Beijing on October 1, 1949. The KMT troops were forced to withdraw to Taiwan,

Mao Zedong exercised a powerful spell over the hearts of the Chinese people.

where the Nationalists remain to this day (before they left, the Nationalists took China's gold reserves and palace treasures with them).

For the Communists, the jubilation of victory was accompanied by the daunting task of national construction, as the country lay in tatters. But land reform, new laws, nationalization, mass projects, and the mobilization of the people led to a rise in optimism during the 1950s. The Korean War (1950–1953), however, was a period of uncertainty and nationalism. In industry, the Soviet model of five-year plans *(wunian jihua)* was copied, while a collectivist agenda governed rural production.

Hundred Flowers Movement to the Cultural Revolution

China was a one-party state, but moves to restrict intellectual freedom were ambivalent. The confident Mao sanctioned the Hundred Flowers Movement (1957), which encouraged criticism of policy from intellectuals. His dictum "Let a hundred flowers bloom, let a hundred schools contend" opened the floodgates to an outpouring of criticism for which the party was unprepared. Mao instigated an anti-rightist campaign that branded intellectuals as enemies of socialism. Vast numbers had to recant and saw their careers destroyed, while others were deported to labor camps. Chinese communism was slipping into the tyranny it had tried desperately to eradicate.

Toward the end of the 1950s, the search for ideological purity led to society becoming more radicalized. The Mao-dictated Great Leap Forward *(dayuejin)* in 1958 was a victory of economic idealism over common sense, creating divisions in the party and leading China to ruin. An obsession with quotas led to artificial production figures, gross economic imbalance, and mass starvation.

The 1960s saw a damaging Sino-Soviet split (with a freezing of Soviet aid) following Mao's concerns at the apparently revisionist nature of President Nikita Khrushchev's Soviet Union. The possibility of war hung over both countries, and air-raid shelters were built.

China sought to reinforce its ideological credentials through the Great Proletarian Cultural Revolution (1966–1976). The Mao-instigated revolution forced itself into every nook and cranny of the nation's consciousness, hunting out the Four Olds: old culture, old customs, old habits, and old ideas. The objective was nothing less than the erasure of traditional, nonsocialist China.

Young Red Guards launched a wave of terror as radical China tore at itself with the sharp tools of self-denunciation and criticism. Confucian standards were inverted as the young criticized their elders, and teachers and intellectuals were herded off to work on farms.

Buddhist, Taoist, and Confucian temples were destroyed or desecrated and their resident monks educated in Maoist doctrine. The monasteries of Tibet suffered in particular. Mao became the object of a personality cult, and his collected quotations or "little red book" became a bible for the young. Liu Shaoqi and Deng Xiaoping were both branded "capitalist roaders" for offering commonsense corrective solutions to the excesses. Liu Shaoqi, banished to Hunan Province, reportedly died in detention, while Deng Xiaoping eventually went on to

Chinese Architecture

Sadly, history has given traditional Chinese architecture a beating. The fires of war that constantly swept the land reduced many wooden buildings to ash, while dynastic succession was regularly marked by the wholesale destruction of important buildings. The Cultural Revolution attempted to annihilate China's historical fabric, and today's wrecking ball continues in the same way. The traditional buildings that survive are exercises in harmony, decorum, and balance. *Fengshui* (see p. 156) was a deciding factor in design and location.

China's great buildings of the past were not temples but structures erected for imperial use, such as those in the Forbidden City (see pp. 60–66). Restrained in outline, they occupy the horizontal rather than the vertical plane and tend to be large, interconnected complexes. A sign that China is losing touch with its cultural roots is the contemporary obsession with skyscrapers.

Tibetan monks at Shershul Monastery engage in debate.

become China's leader (see p. 46). The legacy of the Cultural Revolution has still not been properly addressed by either the Communist Party or the Chinese people. A new generation has grown up with little understanding of the era and its consequences.

From the mid-1970s, China picked up the pieces. Premier Zhou Enlai (who groomed Deng Xiaoping as his successor) did much to restore balance, and China found a seat in the United Nations in 1971. President Richard Nixon came in 1972, visiting the Great Wall and repairing Sino-U.S. relations.

Within the party, however, a wide rift had developed between reformers and conservatives, with Mao and his chosen successor, Lin Biao, deeply at odds. Lin Biao died in a plane crash while fleeing the consequences of a failed plot to kill Mao (or so the official version went). Zhou Enlai was opposed by Jiang Qing (Mao's wife) and her clique, the Gang of Four (she ended up in prison, where she killed herself).

The death of the hugely popular Zhou Enlai from cancer in January 1976 sparked an outpouring of grief in Tiananmen Square that escalated into a riot. Branded the Tiananmen Incident, it fed from the huge reservoir of desperation and anger at the culmination of the Cultural Revolution. Deng Xiaoping was blamed and removed from his party posts.

Mao died in the same year, a year that was also marked by the massive Tangshan earthquake. A huge mausoleum was built on Tiananmen Square for his body, which still lies there in state.

After Mao

Mao's death saw the blame for the Cultural Revolution being apportioned to the Gang of Four. Deng Xiaoping and his acolytes returned. After a transitional period with Hua Guofeng as leader, Deng found himself in command of China's belated modernization drive.

Ideological concepts were replaced by more pragmatic solutions. In the 1980s, Special Economic Zones (SEZs) emerged. Inaugurated by Deng Xiaoping, SEZs enjoyed special economic regimes outside the socialist economy, thus attracting foreign investment. The first ones were Shenzhen, Zhuhai, Shantou, Hainan Island, and Xiamen. China's economy began to flourish in a way undreamed of under Mao, albeit at the price of diluting communist policy; "socialism with Chinese characteristics" was the official parlance.

The Monument to the People's Heroes marks the center of Tiananmen Square.

The future of Hong Kong was decided in the Sino-British agreement of 1984. It guaranteed that Hong Kong's Western economic and legal model would remain for at least 50 years after the return to Chinese sovereignty. Portugal prepared a similar agreement for the 1999 return of Macau.

Tiananmen

The 1980s ended tellingly with the expression of deep-lying stresses in society. Economic liberalization had not been matched by political reform, and there was endemic corruption in the party. Galloping inflation further tightened the screw on social harmony.

The sovereignty of Hong Kong was transferred from Britain to China in a somewhat muted ceremony on June 30, 1997.

The death of the reformer and moderate Hu Yaobang in 1989 prompted a display of mass mourning in Tiananmen Square that escalated into a movement for democracy. Led by student leaders Wang Dan, Chai Ling, and Wu'er Kaixi, the sit-in was brutally crushed by the People's Liberation Army (PLA) on June 3 and 4, with hundreds of innocent deaths. Party Secretary Zhao Ziyang lost his job for sympathizing with the students, and China suffered worldwide condemnation, not least from the citizens of Hong Kong.

1990 to the Present

In 1990, Deng Xiaoping's economic reforms were extended, and Shanghai was chosen to become the nation's new economic powerhouse, retaining, for the first time in 40 years, the bulk of its fiscal revenues to reinvest in the city's faded infrastructure. In addition, Pudong, the area to the east of the Huangpu River, was declared an SEZ, which Deng hoped would rival and overtake Hong Kong, at the time still a British colonial enclave.

The sovereignty of Hong Kong was transferred from Britain to China in a somewhat muted ceremony on June 30, 1997. These days, Taiwan is front-page news in Chinese papers almost daily, revealing Beijing's obsession with pressuring the island into unification. The threat of force remains in the growing number of missile batteries along the south coast, while the U.S. pledge of support to Taiwan in the event of a conflict remains a constant thorn in the side of Sino-American relations.

Deng's successors, Jiang Zemin (1992–2004) and Hu Jintao (2004–), have made substantial contributions to China's economic development. ■

Arts & Culture

Within the dramatic pages of Chinese history is an unbroken and highly idiosyncratic aesthetic that expresses the nation's characteristic nobility and sense of propriety. To understand its language is to fathom the soul of China.

"When I was in China I was struck by the fact that cultivated Chinese were perhaps more highly civilized than any other human beings that it has been my good fortune to meet," wrote Bertrand Russell in the 1920s.

The Chinese might demur but would privately agree with this accolade from the great British philosopher, for they are proud of their country's cultural and artistic achievements.

The languorous introspection so characteristic of Chinese landscapes is passive and inviting.

Much traditional Chinese art appeals to Western sensibilities because its aesthetics tend to avoid tension and insist instead on a softness and elegance of touch. The Western preoccupation with forthrightness and realism traditionally never found a home in Chinese art, which instead was more economical, metaphorical, and restrained. This in turn can help explain the popularity of, for example, Chinese landscape painting in the West. Contemplation of landscape art can be liberating and philosophically rewarding, for it reveals a vision of life that is very different from that in the West.

These opposing views resulted in two different philosophies. The West saw itself as more apart from nature and sought to dominate it, while the instinctive involvement of the Chinese in nature denied it the empirical, objective tools with which to dissect it. A more passive acceptance of nature meant that the existential conundrums infusing much of Western art found no place in traditional Chinese aesthetics. In Western culture, God is represented in human form. In Chinese philosophy, the Tao (Dao), or "the Way," is the closest the Chinese come to expressing an overall deity, yet it is formless. Whether concerning landscape painting or the landscape itself, the Tao permeates without revealing itself.

Chinese Painting

A number of styles make up Chinese painting, but none is more evocative of the Asian sensibility than landscapes. A meditation upon the mists, spaces, and mountains brings the Chinese aesthetic, with its grace and composure, into relief. Landscape painting originated in China as early as the fourth century A.D. but did not reach technical maturity until the Tang dynasty. Its apotheosis came in the Song and the Yuan dynasties, where an unsurpassed legacy has been handed down to this day.

The landscape is of actual and symbolic importance to the Chinese for its physical presence in such a huge land and because it reflects the divine. The languorous introspection so characteristic of Chinese landscapes is passive and inviting. Commotion is absent, and a spirit of acceptance governs the waterfalls, pines, and peaks. Technically, the correct depiction of atmosphere and light is paramount. Air is a significant material because it stores *qi*, the energy that inhabits all living things (see pp. 124–125). Blank spaces, washes, contrast, and a temperate use of color create light, while often adding a hazy mood. The use of ink on silk was the preferred medium for artists, which meant that changes could not be made once the ink had been applied.

The traditional Chinese folk art of weaving has a long history.

Painted dragons enliven many of China's spectacular national festivals.

The landscape must be vital, not just a vapid portrait. This effect is achieved through a suffusion of mood and feeling permeating the scene, rather than through realistic portrayal.

Specific feelings are generally shunned in this style of painting; there is a pervasive mood but no particular message. This lack of focus reflects the Chinese desire to avoid the obvious and the clear-cut. The vaporous mood invites the viewer to enter and encourages him or her to be quiet, creating an unobtrusive and welcoming atmosphere.

Yuan dynasty landscapes are more personal than their Song dynasty cousins. Attention to brushwork and inking became more important in the Yuan dynasty, with greater emphasis given to experimentation. The union of calligraphy and art was made in the Yuan dynasty and continued from there. In the Ming and Qing dynasties, the search for the subjective led to the romanticism of such artists as Shi Tao (1641–1720) and Zhu Da (1625–1705).

Techniques of traditional landscape painting are still copied today, although the 20th century heralded a revolution in both method and materials. The socialist realist artists of the Mao era emulated European techniques, forcing a political message onto a protesting landscape. In some ways this signified a change in Chinese consciousness, as the country became more westernized (via Marxism-Leninism, a Western political philosophy). Art became highly subjective and idealistic and, later, more experimental.

Oil on canvas is now a common medium for the artist in China. The successful Ningbo-born artist Chen Yifei painted in oil in a realist vein, largely taken from European schools. Copies of his works, often portraits of musicians, can be found in hotels and street markets all over China.

Literature

The written word in Chinese bears no relation to its equivalent in English. English recreates sounds alone, which makes listening to English poetry so absorbing. Reading Chinese literature differs because painted on the page is an accompanying portrait of the piece. This is important in the appreciation of classical Chinese poetry, for example, where visual impressions are conveyed by the characters.

Classical poetry: The earliest collection of poems in China is the *Shi Jing (Book of Songs)*, a bundle of verse allegedly compiled by Confucius. Many of the poems are lively songs bursting with bucolic lyrics and infused with agrarian melody.

An animist China comes to life in the poetry of Qu Yuan (340–278 B.C.), whose most famous poem, "Li Sao" ("The Lament"), is a fragrant and luminous work, full of passion, primitive belief, and mythical beings. During the Han dynasty, a longer type of prose poem *(fu)* evolved at the royal court.

One of China's most revered poets, Tao Yuanming (365–427), is enjoyed chiefly for the simplicity of his verse and his delightful Taoist pursuit of wine and nature. His most famous work (actually a piece of prose)—"Taohua Yuanji"—magically narrates the discovery of an ancient, forgotten community.

Classical Chinese poetry reached its zenith during the Tang dynasty. The sensitivities of the age are beautifully communicated in poems characterized by a charming economy and balance. The Tang era produced China's two most famous poets, Li Bai (701–762) and Du Fu (712–770). Li Bai was a Taoist eccentric who explored a mystical communion of poetry and wine. Du Fu was a Confucian man of letters whose stoic verses speak of a deep grief juxtaposed with an equally deep sense of grace and charity. Their poems respectively reveal a glimpse of the soul of the nation, a country torn between romanticism and restraint. Other famous poets of the Tang dynasty are Meng Haoran, the poet-painter Wang Wei (see sidebar this page), Zhang Jiuling, and Li Shangying.

Poetic Painting

Poetry and painting were enthusiastic bedfellows in China, and the Tang dynasty poet-painter Wang Wei (699–759) probably best personifies this. His frequently snow-filled landscapes embody poetic concepts while his poetry is alive with vivid images of nature. The Song dynasty further nurtured the marriage of the two arts. Ma Yuan (1165–1225) was a master of the technique of leaving large areas of the picture blank, giving the impression of vast space and depth and light.

The Tang dynasty ushered in a more regulated poetic form known as *lü shi.* These poems are typically eight lines long, with each line of five or seven characters. This established strict rules for tonal patterns and symmetry that imposed constraints on poetic form but resulted in closer attention to balance and harmony. Language is chosen for its tone so that harmonies of pitch echo throughout the poem.

The end of the Tang dynasty saw the development of the *ci* poem. Sung to music and composed of lines of irregular length, the ci form fully blossomed in the Song dynasty. Famous masters include Su Dongpo (1037–1101) and Ou Yangxiu (1007–1072).

Modern verse is much freer in style and content, influenced by Western innovations in form and theme.

(continued on p. 54)

Chinese Ceramics

Famed for centuries the world over, China's porcelain enjoys a long and splendid heritage. Designed as works of art, ceramics from the Middle Kingdom were also objects of utilitarian value.

Ceramic ship on display in the Guangdong Museum of Folk Arts and Crafts

Pottery fragments in China date back to Neolithic times and to a primitive society known as Yangshao in North China. Surviving specimens from the Shang dynasty show a slow evolution to the important development of glaze, possibly during the Zhou dynasty. A relatively large number of pieces survive from the Han dynasty, which reveal a growing mastery of glazing techniques and stylistic energy, especially in statues and effigies.

Porcelain made its important appearance during the Tang dynasty as did colored glazes, most notably in the world-renowned *sancai* (three color) pieces that are typically green, yellow, brown, orange, and blue against an earthenware body. Song dynasty ceramics, which survive in fair number, are noted for their undecorated, monochrome simplicity.

The Yuan dynasty saw the arrival from the Middle East of underglaze cobalt blue (*qinghua,* or blue-and-white), a technique that flourished under the Ming and Qing dynasties. Blue-and-white often characterized the Ming period, but the style reached its peak during the Qing dynasty, which left us numerous pieces of perfection. The Qing dynasty is notable for colored porcelain and complex decoration. The luxuriously painted, often spectacular pieces are balanced by restrained monochromic ones.

Much Qing porcelain was destined for export to the European market, and consequently Western decorations were incorporated into Qing ceramics. Porcelain is still produced at numerous kilns today, but the golden days of porcelain production are over.

Symbols

At first glance, many ceramics are hidden behind a jungle of decorative motifs. An understanding of the prominent decorative symbols used on Chinese ceramics will help appreciation. The dragon often denotes the emperor and could indicate that the piece is imperial porcelain. The phoenix represents the empress. Peaches symbolize longevity, as do pine trees, tortoises, bamboo, and the bald-headed god of longevity. The Chinese character for long life *(shou)* is also a popular pattern.

Homophones are liberally used. Bats are common motifs. They are pronounced *fu,* the same sound as good fortune. Fish *(yu)* also appear, denoting abundance *(yu).* Other designs include landscapes, flowers, and historical scenes. Literature often embellishes later pieces with a poem or a piece of prose in appropriate calligraphy. Religious imagery includes the eight immortals (see p. 83), the eight *I-Ching* trigrams, and the eight Buddhist symbols.

Color, Glaze, & Mark

Chinese ceramics can be categorized by their color and glaze. Pale green celadon is a typically thick and creamy green glaze that the Chinese adore for its similarity with jade, symbol of both long life and purity. Produced mostly in Jiangxi Province, Qingbai, a transparent pale blue glazed ware, was very popular in the Song dynasty (960-1279). Crisp blanc de Chine *(dehua)* ware originated at the Quanzhou kilns in Dehua, Fujian Province. This pure white glazed ware is typically used for small Buddhist figures, such as Guanyin, the goddess of mercy (see pp. 82–83), and mythological characters. Dehua's first appearance in the west is associated with Marco Polo's visit to China. Ding plates and bowls are usually a creamy white, although black specimens exist, fired between the Tang (618–907) and Yuan (1279–1368) dynasties.

The most famous colored porcelain is cobalt underglaze (a technique of painting the ware before it is glazed and fired) blue-and-white. Qing polychrome *doucai* (joined colors) pieces are characterized by green, blue, and red overglazed colored enamels on white porcelain backgrounds. Although often playful and simple, they can appear in a fantastic tangle of detail. *Wucai* (five colors) is a polychrome enameled decoration like doucai.

Famille rose, called *falangcai* (enamel colors) or *yangcai* (foreign colors), is a lush type of *ruancai* (soft colors). These are low-fired overglaze pieces finished in various shades of rose. Imperial monochromes are gorgeous pieces of uniform coloring; imperial yellow *(minghuangse)* is a typical example, the bright yellow signifying the emperor. The rough texture of *zisha* (purple sand), produced in Yixing (see p. 172), is usually found in the form of teapots.

The mark, used to help identify the date of manufacture, is found on the foot of the ceramic. It is typically square or circular, with the name of the dynasty preceding the emperor, read vertically from right to left. It is, however, very risky to date a piece by the mark alone. Marks were often copied by later ages, and forgeries are manifold. Fake ceramics from China are improving technically all the time, often fooling inexperienced buyers and occasionally confounding the experts. The 1980s and 1990s saw an upsurge in the quantity of forgeries, and the majority of what you see in China's markets is fake. Most decent pieces are historical items that belong to private collections around the world.

This cobalt blue-and-white ceramic (ca 825) is the oldest of its kind discovered in China.

Prose & Literature: The abstruse *Yi Jing (I-Ching)* is a very early work, but it is more a book of prediction than a work of literature. Apart from the *Shi Jing (Book of Songs)*, the origins of Chinese literature are marked primarily by philosophical works. These include the *Daode Jing (The Classic of the Way and Its Power)* by Laozi (ca 580–500 B.C.), the charming writings of the Taoist sage Zhuangzi (ca 369–286 B.C.), the sayings of Confucius (551–479 B.C.), and the works of Mencius (373–289 B.C.). The *Shi Ji (Records of the Historian)* by the Western Han historian Si Maqian (ca 145–85 B.C.) is a monumental and engaging chronicle of Chinese history. The Tang dynasty writer Hanyu (768–824) is notable for his lucid prose and an innovative approach that made classical literature more accommodating to spontaneity. The

Naxi musician from Lijiang, in northwest Yunnan Province

Song dynasty writers Su Dongpo and Ou Yangxiu excelled in classical writing; drama developed in the Yuan dynasty.

Classical Chinese, with its arcane grammar and characters, was elitist and an impediment to literacy and creativity. The famous Ming and Qing dynasty epic stories, *Shuihu Zhuan (The Water Margin)*, *Xiyou Ji (The Journey to the West)*, and *Honglou Meng (The Dream of the Red Chamber)*, were penned in a semiclassical vernacular that helped pave the way for the novel.

It wasn't until the appearance in 1918 of *A Madman's Diary* by Lu Xun, however, that colloquial *baihua* (literally "white speech") was adopted for novel writing. Western fiction techniques had considerable influence on 20th-century Chinese writers. The Chinese novel evolved under the patronage of such eminent writers as Lao She (1899–1966), author of *Rickshaw Boy* and *Teahouse*, and Shen Congwen (1903–1988), author of *The Long River*. Both suffered from political coercion at the hands of the Communists, as did a whole generation of writers.

As with poetry, calligraphy reached its peak in the Tang dynasty. The Shanghai Museum is an excellent place to admire some of China's best examples.

Calligraphy: Accompanying poetry, calligraphy is the oldest of China's arts. Despite being closely governed by structure and form, it ranges from an exacting and pure form (*lishu*, or regular script, and *kaishu*, or clerical script) to the more spontaneous and complex (*xingshu*, or cursive, and *caoshu*, or grasshand script). The latter is extremely challenging, even for Chinese. Regular and clerical script draw characters of equal size and style, while running script encourages a more cursive rendition. Grasshand script approaches the abstract in the fluid scrawl of its form, where characters may just appear as a line or as a smudge of meaning.

Before tackling the more expressionist cursive and grasshand script, the student of calligraphy has to spend years perfecting regular script. The apparent ease and spontaneity of grasshand script conceal a lengthy apprenticeship. The form of grasshand script emerges from an intuitive understanding of regular technique in much the same way that students of Chinese martial arts deliver inspired performances from a deep knowledge of the basic moves (see pp. 124–125). Intention *(yi)* and technique *(jishu)* must correspond perfectly.

As with poetry, calligraphy reached its peak in the Tang dynasty. The Shanghai Museum is an excellent place to admire some of China's best examples.

Music

You will most likely encounter traditional Chinese music through the Beijing Opera (see sidebar p. 56). Traditional instruments include the *erhu*, a stringed instrument that makes a mournful wailing sound, the lutelike *pipa*, and the *dizi* (flute). Much traditional music has been lost, having fallen prey to the rapacity of the Cultural Revolution and the banality of socialist art theory. Valiant orchestras such as the Naxi Orchestra in Lijiang (see sidebar p. 273) have managed to preserve their art.

Chinese popular music tends to seek inspiration from Hong Kong, Taiwan, and Singapore, the distillation of which is Canto-pop. Predominantly sugary, romantic ballads, Canto-pop can be initially repellent, but perseverance pays off. Western music is enjoyed, but real devotion is reserved for homegrown singers. Andy Lau and Wang Fei enjoy demigod status in China, and even though big names such as Bob Dylan play in Beijing, a limited number of foreign bands include China on their tours.

Film

Modern Chinese film tends to be a sumptuous exploration of texture, color, lighting, and mood, often heavily streaked with tragedy. Despite the straitjacketing of Chinese cinema by a government fondness for safe subject matter, the results are sometimes impressive. Often lavish, classical period pieces, Chinese film is an accessible introduction to the Chinese aesthetic. Directors such as Zhang Yimou and Chen Kaige have created such fables as *Raise the Red Lantern* (1991), *Farewell My Concubine* (1993), *Hero* (2002), and *House of Flying Daggers* (2004). Gong Li and Zhang Ziyi are the most famous Chinese actresses of the past two generations.

Contemporary Chinese cinema is caught in a bind. Uncontrollable DVD piracy makes filmmaking in China far less lucrative than it could be, while directors continuously choose safe subject matter to avoid run-ins with the authorities. Historical epics will always entertain fascinated Chinese audiences but may—sooner or later—alienate foreign viewers. The result is an industry hobbled by a lack of imagination and freedom, both essential ingredients in filmmaking. In a controversial protectionist move, China also caps the number of Western films that can be shown in cinemas to around twenty a year.

Hong Kong cinema is often violent, crass, and given to slapstick, but it enjoys a cult following. There's more to Hong Kong cinema than vampires, ghost stories, martial arts, and romantic comedies, however. The city's confused cultural identity, covert romanticism, and violent substrata find expression in excellent art cinema. Wong Kar Wai wonderfully celebrates a sense of longing tinged with brutality in *Chungking Express* (1994) and *Fallen Angels* (1995). *As Tears Go By* (1988) traces the tragic slide into Triad society by two young brothers. ■

Chinese Opera

Opera emerged from popular theater, an art form that flourished in the Mongol Yuan dynasty. There are many regional forms of Chinese opera, with their own stories, costumes, makeup, and music. The most famous of the regional operas, the Beijing Opera (Jingju), reached its apex during the Qing dynasty.

Chinese opera has little relation to Western opera. The popular stories are shrilly sung to a clashing of cymbals by heavily made-up performers (usually male). The roles can be very demanding, with leaping, jumping, and other energetic routines that require both flexibility and endurance. In this sense, Beijing Opera is closer to Western ballet, although the choreography is very different. Characters are identified by their makeup and clothing. The roles are generally divided into male *(sheng)*, female *(dan)*, warriors and heroes *(jing)*, and clowns *(chou)*. For Westerners, the language is sadly a major hurdle to comprehension. Shanghai, Beijing, and Hong Kong have the best venues for Chinese opera.

Training for the Beijing Opera is severe, and it was usually reserved for orphans. The 1993 movie *Farewell My Concubine* delivers a vivid account of the hardships endured by young opera students. Martial arts supremos Jackie Chan, Samo Hung, and Yuan Biao learned their moves through training in Beijing Opera.

China's intriguing capital city, filled with hallmark sights as well as unexpected surprises and hidden worlds

Beijing

Introduction & Map 58–59
Forbidden City 60–66
Beihai Park & Jingshan Park 67
Beijing Bike Ride 68–69
Tiananmen Square 70–71
Feature: Beijing *Hutongs* 72–73
Experience: Overnight in a Courtyard Hotel 73
Temple of Heaven 74–75
Ancient Observatory 76
Experience: Blind Massage 76
Experience: A Chinese Education 77
Lama Temple 78
Confucius Temple 79
Other Religious Sites 80–81
Feature: China's Gods & Goddesses 82–83
Summer Palace 84–86
Old Summer Palace 87
Around Beijing 88–95
Experience: Local Chinese Village Life 89
Experience: Take a Trip to Jiankou Great Wall 90

Door knocker in a Beijing *hutong*

Experience: Sleep Near the Great Wall 92
More Places to Visit in & Around Beijing 96
Experience: Hike into the Hills With Beijing Hikers 96
Hotels & Restaurants in Beijing 362–365

Beijing

At the center is the capital, Beijing, the seat of power in China and a good starting point for your journey in the Middle Kingdom. The Chinese universe orbits Beijing, and political power radiates from here, as do flight connections to just about anywhere in the land.

Imperious seat of political power, proud capital of the Middle Kingdom, and China's showcase to the world, Beijing ("northern capital") has a powerful allure. The rest of China has at least one eye on this repository of the nation's soul. Wherever you go in China, the city either follows or is waiting for you, in its dialect (Mandarin), its cuisine, and its political (un-)certainties.

Beijing was not always the dynastic capital, but you get the impression it has presided over China's fate since time immemorial. The Forbidden City, Beijing's walled heart, is an arcane yet majestic labyrinth of imperial custom and lore. The plan of this sovereign core extends outward, framing Beijing in a broad grid pattern of wide boulevards and delightful *hutongs.*

In its entirety and beyond its showcase commercial areas, the city is a splendid microcosm of today's China. In its breathless race into the 21st century, the city remains a lovely tangle of the old and the new in its hodgepodge of daily life. Skyscrapers rocket into the sky above low-lying districts of crumbling alleyways and shuffling old folk, while immaculately dressed white-collar types disappear into a deluge of bicycles, as the streets jostle with the flotsam of itinerant workers, long-haired students, entrepreneurs, and hordes of out-of-towners.

Despite its wholesale modernization, Beijing has no deficit of history. The Forbidden City and the Temple of Heaven are two of the best examples of imperial-era architecture in the land. Both monolithic fence and symbol of a defensive mentality, the Great Wall snakes its way north of the capital, while the extravagance of the Summer Palace makes for an excellent day out.

The mouthy Beijing dialect, eternal bane of students of Mandarin, is China's best known tongue, carrying considerable cachet across the land. Chinese cuisine converges from all corners, but Peking duck is an almost mandatory local dish, and don't forget: Once bitten, forever smitten. ■

NOT TO BE MISSED:

The Forbidden City **60–66**

Taking to the streets of Beijing—on a rented bike **68–69**

Getting lost in Beijing's fascinating old *hutongs* **72–73**

Waking up after a night spent in a Beijing courtyard hotel **73**

Fathoming the cosmic harmonies of the Temple of Heaven **74–75**

An afternoon exploring the splendid Summer Palace **84–86**

Local village life in Chuandixia **89**

Trekking along the Great Wall from Jinshanling to Simatai **92–93**

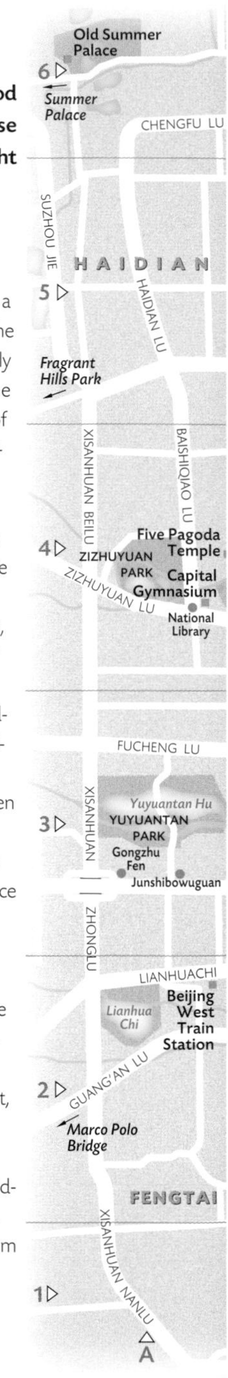

Area of map detail
Beijing
Wudaokou
OLYMPIC PARK
National Olympic Sports Center
Qinghuayuan Railway Station
Great Bell Temple
Beijing Normal University
Xihuang Temple
Hepingli Railway Station
Lufthansa Center Youyi Shopping City
Beijing North Railway Station
Beijing Zoo
Planetarium
XICHENG
DONGCHENG
CHAOYANG
Song Qingling Museum
Bell Tower
Drum Tower
Confucius Temple
Lama Temple
Temple of Earth
Sanlitun YaShou Clothing Market
Worker's Stadium
White Dagoba Temple
Lu Xun Museum
North Cathedral
Nine Dragon Screen
China Art Gallery
St. Joseph's Church
Dongyue Temple
Yong'an Temple
Forbidden City Palace Museum
Zhihua Temple
Temple of the Moon
Worker's Cultural Palace
DONGDAN
Temple of The Sun
Silk Street
Monument to the People's Heroes
Great Hall of the People
China National Museum
Ancient Observatory
Beijing Railway Station
Capital Museum
South Cathedral
White Clouds Temple
Mao Zedong Mausoleum
Qianmen Gate
National Centre for the Performing Arts
Dongbianmen Watchtower
CHONGWEN
Cow Street Mosque
Fayuan Temple
Museum of Natural History
Pearl Market
Temple of Heaven
Guang'anmen Railway Station
XUANWU
TIANTAN PARK
LONGTAN PARK
TAORANTING PARK
GRAND VIEW GARDEN
Yongdingmen Gate
Panjiayuan Market
Beijing South Railway Station
0 2 kilometers
0 1 mile
B
C
D
E

Forbidden City

The Forbidden City (Zijin Cheng), a 78-acre (32 ha) pied-à-terre to the emperors of the Ming and Qing dynasties, is Beijing's most alluring and magnificent Chinese treasure.

The ornate rooftops of the Forbidden City reflect the Chinese tradition of myriad buildings composing palace design. Access was denied to all except those with imperial permission until 1911.

When the Yongle emperor (see p. 37) moved the capital to Beijing from Nanjing in 1421, he built the walled Forbidden City near the site of the palace used by the Yuan dynasty emperors. In today's China, the lackluster name of **Gugong,** or **Palace Museum,** describes what was a territory out of bounds to the hoi polloi. The Chinese name translates as Purple Forbidden City, which is not an allusion to the color of the walls but to the Polar Star, at the center of the celestial world and symbolic of the emperor. Purple is also a color associated with royalty.

Considerably restored and embellished since the Ming dynasty (most of the buildings you see today were built during and after the 18th century), the Forbidden City signified the distant and unapproachable emperor. It is also the finest example of Chinese imperial architecture.

INSIDER TIP:

If you enter the Forbidden City from the Northern Gate early in the morning, you will escape the throngs coming from the south.

—PAUL MOONEY
National Geographic author

The Forbidden City reflects the Ming practice of dividing Beijing into walled sections. This is the heart of China, the nucleus of the Middle Kingdom—a receptacle for the mandate of Heaven and the source from which imperial dictates were issued to even the most far-flung of the country's provinces. The complex is not one stately building as was the Western practice (for example, Versailles or Buckingham Palace), but rather a series of halls and buildings separated by passages, like a small city. It is said that the complex consists of 9,000 rooms in 800 buildings.

The palace was built primarily of wood, so fire was a constant hazard. The Manchus (who swept down from Manchuria to install the Qing dynasty) torched the palace in the 17th century. The Japanese ransacked it, as did the Kuomintang (the Chinese nationalists who fled to Taiwan in 1949). The whole, labyrinthine complex was almost torn apart during the intoxication of the Cultural Revolution, but it was saved from destruction by the intervention of Premier Zhou Enlai. He interceded more than once to spare national treasures from demolition.

China's great buildings were constructed for the use of the emperors. Chinese architecture has preferred to explore the horizontal human plane rather than occupy space vertically. As a result, the palace's buildings are not tall, but the space around them can be breathtaking. China has no equivalent of the West's huge cathedral, a towering structure used to emphasize human smallness (this does not apply to modern Chinese architecture). The interconnected system of the Forbidden City represents a harmonious network of form and allegiance of shape.

Getting Around Town

Beijing is a huge entity whose roads are governed by chaos and precision in equal measure. Walking around town is possible but very tiring because the city is so big. Taxis are plentiful or you can try your luck with the buses, but prepare for gridlock on anything but short journeys: Beijing's roads are close to vehicle saturation point. By far your best bet is Beijing's massively expanded subway system, which now covers the city in a tangle of subterranean lines; trains are frequent and tickets are cheap. For the intrepid, renting a bicycle will thrust you into a fascinating and exciting world (see pp. 68–69).

Forbidden City

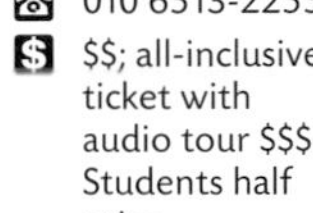

59 C3

010 6513-2255

$$; all-inclusive ticket with audio tour $$$. Students half price

Subway: Tiananmenxi, Tiananmendong

www.dpm.org.cn

Approaching the Palace

Ideally, approach the Forbidden City from the south, which gives you the chance to admire the huge port-red walls that thrust out from either side of the Meridian Gate (Wumen). You can enter from the northern gate, but the audio tour guides you from the south. The major halls and palaces are set out along a line bisecting the complex, running south to north. All Chinese temples lie along this same axis (see pp. 156–158).

INSIDER TIP:

The outer buildings are interesting, but plan to spend most of your time on the treasures housed in the inner courtyards.

—KIRSTEN CONRAD
Conservationist

Leaving Tiananmen Square and crossing under Chang'an Dajie by subway brings you to the entrance to the palace. As you traverse the

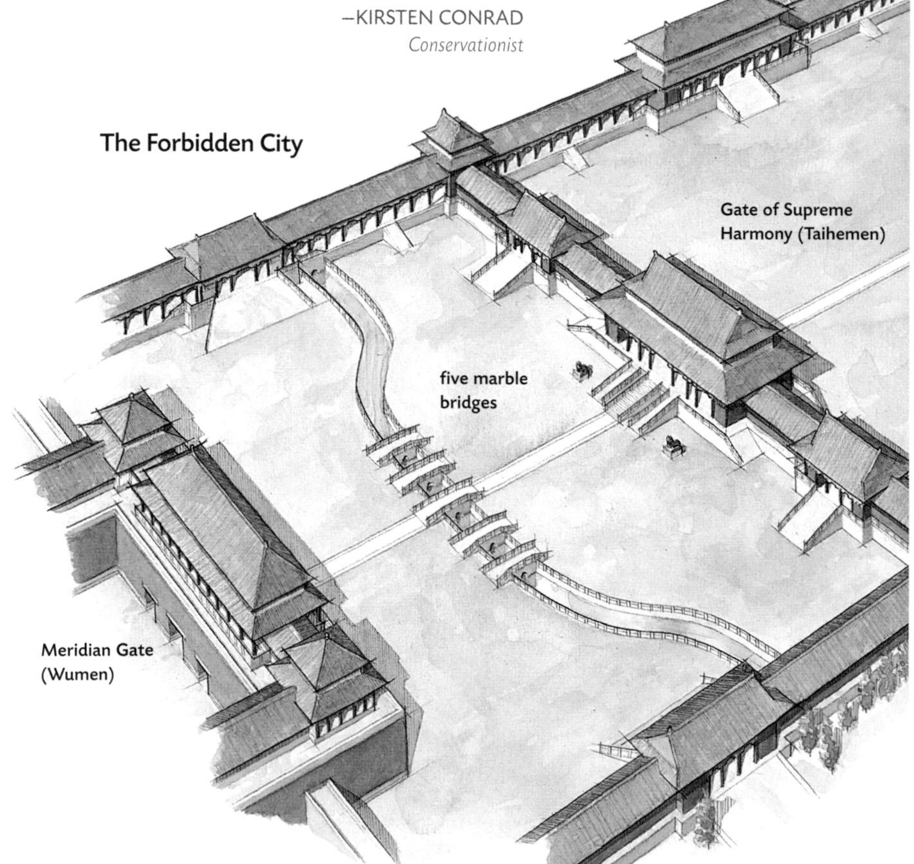

arched marble bridges, you come face-to-face with the **Gate of Heavenly Peace (Tiananmen)** and its monumental portrait of Mao. The painting was defaced during the democracy protests in 1989, when three workers from Hunan (Mao's home province) flung eggs filled with paint at it. The white characters on the red background to the left of the portrait urge the government mantra "Long Live the People's Republic of China." From this gate Mao proclaimed the founding of the republic in 1949, and it is used today as a spot for watching military parades. For a fee, and a frisking, you can climb up onto the gate for views over the square.

Walking through the gate brings you into a large courtyard lined by souvenir stalls and restaurants. West of the courtyard is the attractive **Zhongshan Park,** where the emperor used to make sacrifices in spring and autumn to ensure a fruitful harvest. East are the magnificent triple halls of the **Supreme Temple (Taimiao),** more prosaically called the Worker's Cultural Palace. The most sacred imperial temple after the Temple of Heaven, the complex is often devoid of visitors, and entrance is a pittance.

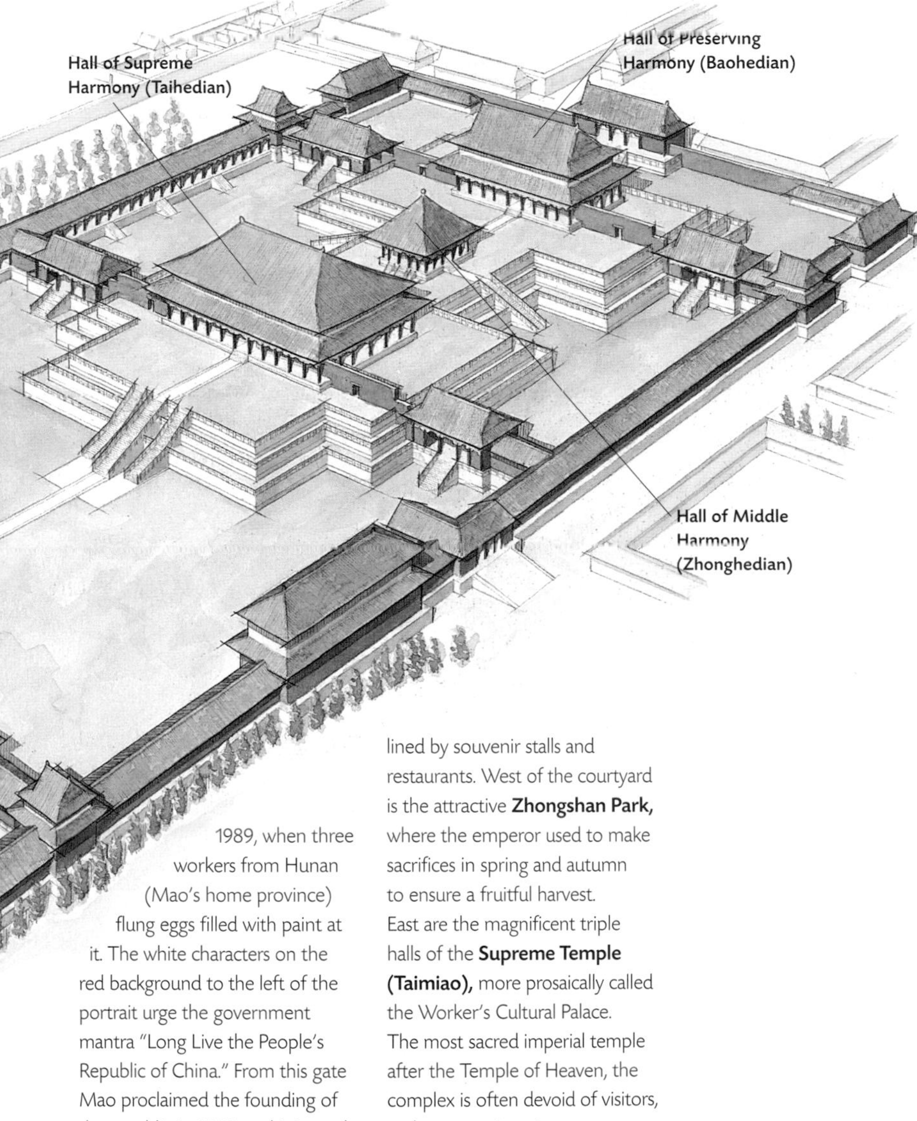

Entrance

Passing through the next gate leads you to the fortresslike **Meridian Gate (Wumen).** This marks the entrance proper to the Forbidden City. The gate was reserved for the sole use of the emperor, with drums and bells sounding his approach to the Hall of Supreme Harmony. The 170-foot-wide (52 m) moat begins its circuit around the walls here. The dwarfing walls, a massive 28 feet (8.5 m) wide at the base, create colossal silhouettes at twilight. Obtain your ticket (and audio tour guide) from the booths on the left or right.

Through the Meridian Gate you come to a huge paved courtyard with five bridges straddling a central strip of water. The **Gate of Supreme Harmony (Taihemen)** lies beyond. This gate was built in 1420, destroyed by fire in 1888, and rebuilt the following year. The ceiling is a blaze of emerald green and gold. As you walk through the gate, you will see to the east the **Hall of Literary Glory,** which contained the Imperial Library; to the west is the **Hall of Martial Valor** (academic and military functions are often counterposed in Chinese culture).

Three Big Halls

Ahead of you stands the imposing **Hall of Supreme Harmony (Taihedian),** the first of what are known as the Three Big Halls, where the emperor performed state functions. In fact, the emperor used the hall conservatively, reserving it for such mundane events as his birthday and the announcement of the list of successful imperial examination candidates. Passing the imperial examinations was an essential step up the ladder of the official elite. Spread over three days and two nights, the exams tested candidates' knowledge of huge tracts of Confucian classics

Raised on a three-tiered platform, the Hall of Supreme Harmony was for many years the tallest building in Beijing, and a law forbade commoners to construct anything higher. No one could look down upon this

A splendidly colored decoration juts from one of the city's walls.

Symbols

You will see the dragon motif carved and painted throughout the Forbidden City. The dragon denotes the emperor *(huangdi)*, and the phoenix represents the empress *(huanghou)*. The two are often depicted together. The image of the dragon chasing the flaming pearl portrays the quest for purity, while the lavish yellow tiling of the roofs denotes the emperor, a color often seen in imperial porcelain.

The dragon seems to have had a claw-hold on the Chinese imagination since the earliest times: Fuxi (see p. 27) had a dragon tail. The Chinese believe in several of these serpents: The *long* is the dragon that surges through clouds chasing pearls; the *li* is the dragon of the sea; and the *jiao* is the dragon of marshy land.

The Chinese lion, a playful-looking creature with a curly mane, is often seen sitting in pairs outside buildings of note. The female holds her baby under one paw (the Chinese believed that lions could secrete milk through their paws), while the male plays with a ball. Lions are de rigueur in Hong Kong, where you may even see a few Western-style ones (for example, outside the Hong Kong & Shanghai Bank building).

most sacred of imperial buildings (there was also the *fengshui* belief that benign spirits flew at a certain altitude, a height that should not be exceeded by buildings). Twin sets of stairs ascend to the hall, divided by a decorated stone slab over which the emperor's sedan chair would be conveyed (see sidebar p. 66). Inside sits the imperial throne. The large water drums outside supplied water for fighting fires. Altogether 308 such drums were in the palace.

Tucked away behind is the smaller **Hall of Middle Harmony (Zhonghedian),** where ministers from the Ministry of Rites were received. The rectangular **Hall of Preserving Harmony (Baohedian),** where the emperor oversaw the final stages of the imperial examinations, occupies a space just before you reach the **Gate of Heavenly Purity (Qianqingmen).** The carving on the marble slab by the stairs shows a flying dragon.

INSIDER TIP:

It's worth paying an extra fee to see the Forbidden City's Eastern Axis, which includes the Hall of Jewelry and the Clock Exhibition Hall.

—BARBARA NOE
National Geographic Books editor

The Inner City

The courtyard behind the gate of Heavenly Purity marks the entrance to the nucleus of the Forbidden City, access to which was restricted to eunuchs, maids, and imperial relatives. As the republic surrounded this last bastion of the Manchu empire in the early 20th century, it was theatrically presided over by the last Qing emperor, Puyi.

The Gate of Heavenly Purity leads to what were essentially

A turret of the Forbidden City in winter

the residential quarters of the Forbidden City. The first building, the **Palace of Heavenly Purity (Qianqinggong),** served as the emperor's bedchambers. Behind this is the smaller **Hall of Heavenly and Terrestrial Union (Jiaotaidian),** where the empress slept. Other buildings housed eunuch and imperial advisers.

North of this lies the **Palace of Terrestrial Tranquillity (Kunninggong).** Manchu shaman ritualistic ceremonies took place here, with shaman priests and priestesses overseeing the sacred rites. In the southeast of the Forbidden City a temple known as the Tang Temple, or the Shaman Temple, once stood; its services were later transferred to the Palace of Terrestrial Tranquillity. The Qing Manchu court never gave up the shaman belief in nature spirits and incorporated this primitive faith into its sinicization. Immediately behind is the **Gate of Terrestrial Tranquillity,** which leads on to the **Imperial Garden.**

You can leave the Forbidden City at this point, through the **Gate of Divine Prowess (Shenwumen),** which opens to a bridge over the moat that rings the walled city. Empress Dowager Cixi and Emperor Guangxu fled for Xi'an in August 1900 from a gate in the northern wall, as foreign powers descended on Beijing.

Several halls in the palace have been converted into exhibition halls, including the magnificent **Clock Exhibition Hall,** where a glittering array of antique timepieces—many of which were gifts to the emperors from abroad—garner rave reviews from appreciative travelers. ■

Sedan Chairs

This genteel means of transport gradually disappeared as road surfaces improved. Until then, sedan chairs were identified by a color code system. The reigning sovereign was carried in a yellow sedan and imperial concubines were given orange chairs. Green sedans identified high-level mandarins, while lesser mandarins were conveyed in blue.

Beihai Park & Jingshan Park

These two parks, to the north and west of the Forbidden City, offer a natural balance to the imperial thoroughfares of the palace.

Beihai Park

Beihai Park (Beihai Gongyuan) is a romantic sojourn for young couples who meander from pavilion to pavilion at dusk and look out over the city below from the hill on Qiong Island.

The larger part of Beihai Park is a lake, a frozen mass in winter, crisscrossed by children's paddle-boats in summer. The Yong'an Bridge straddles the water to **Qiong Island (Qiongdao).** Folklore attributes the scooping out of the lake and its subsequent pile of earth to the great Kublai Khan. He used Beihai as his stomping ground before the Ming dynasty upstaged him with the Forbidden City. The Buddhist **Yong'an Temple** climbs the island's hill in layers.

The dumpy **White Dagoba** crowning the hill is a Lamaist stupa inaugurated for a visit by the Dalai Lama in the 17th century. Rattled by earthquakes, the dagoba virtually collapsed in the big Tangshan tremor of 1976. You can ascend a platform behind the dagoba for a sweeping view over Beijing, with the Forbidden City to the east.

The paths snaking down from the summit thread through fanciful pavilions, halls, and rock gardens bordered by pines. North of the island is the **Nine Dragon Screen (Jiulongbi).** This spirit wall, 88 feet (27 m) long and 16 feet (5 m) high, was designed to deflect bad spirits. Located at the entrance to a temple since destroyed, the screen is a serpentine assortment of more than 400 glazed tiles.

Jingshan Park

Jingshan Park (Jingshan Gongyuan), or Scenic Mountain Park, was known as Coal Hill by Western residents in Beijing at the end of the 19th century. The hill was called Meishan ("beautiful mountain"), and Westerners confused it with the word *mei* meaning "coal" (same pronunciation, but with a different tone). This artificial hill was piled up from the earth scooped out to make the moat ringing the Forbidden City. The park is directly opposite the north exit of the Forbidden City, and the view from the summit over the imperial palace is peerless. ■

Beihai Park
- 59 C3
- Wenjin Jie
- $
- Subway: Zhangzizhonglu

Jingshan Park
- 59 C3
- Jingshan Qianjie
- $
- Subway: Tiananmen East

Prayers written on small tags hang from trees in Beihai Park.

Beijing Bike Ride

Flat as a Peking duck pancake, the capital's wide avenues and vast distances are awash with a sea of cyclists. Bicycles get their own (broad) lanes, where they jockey for position through sheer number and lobby successfully for control at intersections. It looks terrifying, but this is one of the best ways to bring this huge city to heel. Go with the flow.

North Around Beihai Park

Set out from Chang'an Jie, north of Tiananmen Square (see pp. 70–71), and head up Nanchang Jie, the road running just to the west of the Forbidden City (see pp. 60–66). To the west is Zhongnanhai, the political nerve center of Beijing, named for the two lakes of Zhong Hai ("middle sea") and Nan Hai ("south sea"). Beijing's leaders control the destiny of the land from here, hidden away behind the wall on your left.

Ahead is **Beihai Park** ❶ (see p. 67), the stomping ground of the Yuan dynasty emperors. Strike out west along Wenjin Jie. If you are feeling energetic, continue west to Fuchengmennei Dajie and the **White Dagoba Temple** (see p. 96). If not, turn north onto Xishiku Dajie, where you will see the twin spires of the Gothic **North Cathedral (Bei Tang)** ❷. This Christian monument is one of several in Beijing, serving a growing population of worshippers. It served as a school during the Cultural Revolution and later as a warehouse. Now it is once more an active place of worship. The church's Jesuit sisters—the baroque South Cathedral (see p. 81) and the marvelous St. Joseph's Church on Wangfujing Dajie—both endured repeated destruction.

Keep going north up to Di'anmen Xidajie and turn right. After about half a mile, turn left up Longtoujing Jie opposite the north end of Beihai Park, and continue up Liuyin Jie after the intersection with Qianhai Xijie.

At No. 14 is the marvelous **Mansion of Prince Gong (Gongwangfu)** ❸ *(Liuyin Jie 14, $)*, originally the home of a high-ranking Manchu official. This abode is considered to be the inspiration behind the great house in *Dream of the Red Mansions* (also called *Story of the Stone*), written by Cao Xueqin circa 1715–1763. The book is considered one of the greatest Chinese novels, written in a semiclassical vernacular. The mansion consists of a series of elegant courtyards enclosed by rocky arrangements and walls and gardens threaded with restful walking paths.

Backtrack to the crossroads. Turn east along Qianhai Xijie to the fringes of the Shicha Qian Hai Lake and cross the bridge.

Hou Hai Lake & Around

Turn left and run along the bar-littered edge of Hou Hai Lake, which freezes over in winter, attracting ice skaters. The small **Guanghua**

NOT TO BE MISSED:

Beihai Park • Drum Tower & Bell Tower • Nanluogu Xiang

Cycling Around & Beyond Beijing

Perhaps the ultimate way to see Beijing is on a pair of wheels—preferably off the main roads and along the small *hutongs* that crisscross old Beijing. By far the best plan is to rent a bike from your hotel or youth hostel; alternatively, there are numerous small rental shops in tourist areas such as Dazhalan Xijie, where you can rent a bike. If you're fit, renting a mountain bike can be an excellent way to experience the hilly and frequently dramatic landscape around Beijing—away from the crowds and into the municipality's great rural vastness.

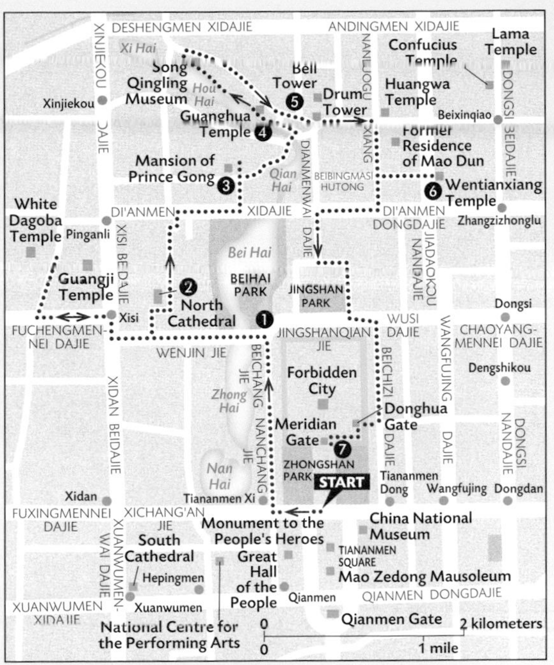

- See city map pp. 58–59
- Chang'an Jie
- Half day; whole day (including side trips)
- 9 miles (14.5 km)
- Meridian Gate

Temple ❹ is tucked away down Ya'er Hutong to your right; cycling at will around this area will turn up a pleasant mix of lake views and old traditional *hutongs*. Alternatively, loop back and head east along Yandai Xiejie, a fun café-lined street that takes you to Dianmenwai Dajie. From here, cycle directly north to the **Drum Tower** *(Gulou Dongdajie, $)*, which stands on the remains of the original 13th-century structure. A drum used to beat out the hours of the day and night from here, with the night divided into five two-hour periods.

To the north of the Drum Tower, the **Bell Tower (Zhonglou)** ❺ *($)* was first erected during the Mongol era in the 13th century but rebuilt by both the Ming and the Qing. The huge bell rang as the city gates closed at night. You can climb up the steep steps for views of the nearby Drum Tower and beyond. There is a small fee for both.

From the Drum Tower, cycle east along busy Gulou Dongdajie all the way to the intersection with Nanluogu Xiang, and head south down the alley. On the north side of the intersection, you will spot the **Huangwa Temple,** on the corner of Gulou Dongdajie and Beiluogu Xiang.

South Along Nanluogu Xiang

Cycling south down Nanluogu Xiang is a fun and fascinating journey. Only ten years ago, the alley was just beginning to reinvent itself as a trendy strip of bars, cafés, and restaurants. Today Nanluogu Xiang and the lanes off the main alley teem with courtyard hotels, boutiques, micro-bars, ceramics shops, and legions of tourists. Some of the hutong names here are lovely, including Rain Hutong (Yu'er Hutong) and Black Sesame Hutong (Heizhima Hutong).

The small **Wentianxiang Temple (Wentianxiangci)** ❻ can be found just to the east of Nanluogu Xiang on Fuxue Hutong, east of Dongmianhua Hutong. The truly energetic should continue along through the hutongs and head north along Dongsi Beidajie to the Buddhist Lama Temple (see p. 78) and the Confucius Temple (see p. 79).

From the foot of Nanluogu Xiang, turn west along Di'anmen Dongdajie, before heading south along Dianmenwai Dajie to Jingshan Park (see p. 67). Cycling down Beichizi Dajie will bring you to a bridge over the moat of the Forbidden City and Donghua Gate. Follow the road south along the wall to the **Meridian Gate** ❼ (the palace entrance).

Tiananmen Square

The sweeping Square of the Gate of Heavenly Peace—Tiananmen Square—is the soul of China. This vast expanse of paving stones, scene of the 1989 student demonstrations and their gory climax, is an ordered microcosm of the Communist universe and a colossal statement of power. Chairman Mao is interred here, and the monolithic Chinese parliament overlooks the square.

Fireworks light up Tiananmen Square on National Day (October 1).

Tiananmen Square
59 C3
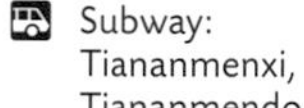
Subway: Tiananmenxi, Tiananmendong

Chairman Mao Memorial Hall
Tiananmen Square
Open a.m. Tues.–Sun.
Compulsory bag storage, $
Subway: Tiananmenxi, Tiananmendong

In & Around the Square

A motley assortment of historical buildings, garish, Soviet-style monuments, and huge museums flank the square. To the north is the **Gate of Heavenly Peace,** viewing stand for military parades, with its huge portrait of Mao. On the north–south axis in the center of the square stands the **Monument to the People's Heroes,** last bastion of the students before their denouement with the People's Liberation Army. The monolith remembers martyrs to the cause of the Communist revolution.

South of this is the **Chairman Mao Memorial Hall (Mao Zhuxi Jiniantang),** where the waxen-faced Great Helmsman lies in state. The hall was constructed the year after Mao's death in 1976. A long line of people still files through to pay respect to the ex-chairman, who lies on a slab of black granite from Taishan, one of the five sacred Taoist mountains. The hall is periodically shut for maintenance.

North and south of Mao's mausoleum, socialist realist **statues** depict a group of idealized workers rallying behind the party line. Such anachronisms pitch a last-ditch struggle against the free-market mutiny sweeping China.

The **Qianmen Gate** in the very south is one of the few remaining gates of the old wall of Peking. It was originally constructed during the reign of Yongle (r. 1403–1423). The wall formerly ringed the old city, and no one was allowed to climb it (the first people allowed to stroll along it were foreigners in 1860). The towers bordering Qianmen were burned down in 1900 by the Boxers as a punishment for selling foreign goods (there used to be a small bazaar running between the gates).

The west side of the square is dominated by the **Great Hall of the People (Renmin Dahuitang),** where China's parliament meets. You can enter the building when the National People's Congress (NPC) is not in session.

Opposite is the hulking **China National Museum,** shut in 2007 and reopened in 2011 after a massive and costly renovation. Captions are largely in Chinese, and not all halls are open at the same time, although there are regular temporary exhibitions. Those who take delight in the museum's Marxist thrust will most appreciate the exhibits.

West of Tiananmen Square you will find the egglike, supermodern titanium and glass **National Center for the Performing Arts,** the design of which sparked considerable controversy.

Center of Protests & Celebrations

Tiananmen Square (Tiananmen Guangchang) was the riotous scene of exultation at the launch of the Cultural Revolution in 1966 (see pp. 45–46). Today it is the backdrop to vast military parades that grind down the northern perimeter of Chang'an Jie ("avenue of eternal peace").

Despite the authoritarian design, the square has become a battleground in the lopsided tussle between government and disaffected groups. Democracy protests in the spring of 1989 were molded from public grief over the death of reformer Hu Yaobang. Sadness smoldered to anger when the authorities rebuffed the people. Bizarrely, the government sent tanks against unarmed workers and students, rather than riot police and tear gas.

The square is a tempting destination for numerous disaffected groups, but plainclothes police ensure it remains "harmonized." South of the arrow tower just south of Qianmen Gate ranges Qianmen Dajie, in recent years remodeled and restored to resemble a street from the early 20th century. October 1 is China's National Day, and half of Beijing descends on the square to commemorate the event. ■

INSIDER TIP:

Try to catch the National Flag Ceremony, which occurs exactly at sunrise, when soldiers march through the gate of Tiananmen Tower and raise the flag.

—BARBARA NOE
National Geographic Books editor

China National Museum

- ✉ Tiananmen Square
- $ $
- Subway: Tiananmenxi, Tiananmendong

National Center for the Performing Arts

- ✉ Tiananmen Square
- Open for visits 1:30 p.m.–5:30 p.m. Tues.–Fri.; 9:30 a.m.–5 p.m. Sat. & Sun.
- $ $
- Subway: Tiananmenxi

Beijing *Hutongs*

Beijing's wide avenues, vast squares, huge palaces, and great distances can leave you feeling rather small. A vanishing labyrinth of charming decay, however, awaits you on a more human scale. It's the unique world of Beijing's *hutongs*–a mesh of narrow lanes that thread across the city. Hutongs (from a Mongolian word for a passageway) often harbor another picturesque world, that of the *siheyuan* (four-walled courtyard).

A pedicab tour through Beijing's narrow back streets, or *hutongs,* is an unbeatable experience.

It is said that there are more hutongs in Beijing than there are hairs on a cow. Today, though, this particular cow has had quite a shearing, and sadly, many hutongs have been swept aside to make room for tower blocks and new hotels.

Hutongs are primarily lanes where people live, but they also bustle with markets and commerce of all kinds. They are often charmingly complicated: a tangle of minute passages compressed into a tight area, with sub-hutongs adding to the confusion. Locals navigate their small, private world with ease, while taxi drivers enter a twilight zone, driving in circles and leaning out of the window to ask directions. This is the place to come to really get a sense of community in Beijing.

The thoroughfares are loved by Beijing residents. Bicycles scythe down the narrow passages, bells jingling. Bundles of swaddled schoolchildren race back home from school in the winter air, past glowing brickwork outhouses, chimneys pumping smoke, and the occasional carved doorway laden with snow. Some hutongs are so narrow they pinch; others are broad, breezy thoroughfares, shaded by trees.

Their often fanciful names give an idea of their original function or the people who once lived there. Some names are seemingly plucked from a child's imagination: Rain Lane, Earth Lane, Bright Lane, Luck Lane, Happiness Lane. Others echo the old markets that set up shop there, such as Stir-Fried Bean Lane, Chrysanthemum Lane, Cap Lane, Rice Granary Lane,

Aromatic Bait Lane, and Black Sesame Lane. Others have more obscure origins deep in Beijing's history, such as Clean Earth Lane (Buddhist), Three Never Get Old Lane, and Horsetail Cap Lane.

Most of the lanes run east to west in accordance with the dictates of *fengshui* (see pp. 256–257), and the doors and portals face south as they do in Chinese temples (see pp. 156–158). Only occasionally do some hutongs run north to south, linking the major ones.

Hutong Courtyards

Hutongs are honeycombed with four-walled courtyards, which for centuries were the standard housing units in the capital. These picturesque nests consist of a communal courtyard, hugged on four sides by a house. Often they are clustered together, or in strings, where whole communities live. Some courtyards are fronted by doorways wonderfully adorned with Chinese characters or religious motifs. In places, the sooty buildings are still decorated by deliciously ornamental tiling; others are more modest. Occasionally, the door to a hutong may be left open so you can peer into the courtyard lying behind. The courtyards are roofless, admitting light and the elements, however fair or foul.

Sidelined by the socialist building programs of the 1960s and 1970s, the courtyards have been further left out in the cold by the slick developments of the past decades. Despite their obvious charm, they lack efficient insulation and central heating and are inconvenient for car-owning families. Despite this, they remain home to a huge number of Beijing's residents.

Finding Hutongs

You can stumble upon hutongs all over Beijing, but they tend to survive within the second ring road. Rather than leap from one district to another in your quest, navigate the historic grid southeast of the Bell and Drum Towers (see p. 69). This block of hutongs, surrounded by Gulou Dongdajie, Dongsi Beidajie, and Di'anmen Waidajie and divided by Jiaodaokou Nandajie, is a small township of these charming lanes. Another historical reach is around the nearby Hou Hai Lake.

Riding a rented bike is the best way to survey this cozy little world, but you can also do it on foot. Tour companies that offer rides through the hutongs are everywhere, and you only have to wander to the area around Qian Hai Lake to be pounced upon by pedicab riders looking for customers. It's always best just to take the hutongs at your own speed, by yourself.

EXPERIENCE: Overnight in a Courtyard Hotel

For a taste of the traditional way of life in Beijing, you can spend the night in one of the many courtyard hotels that have opened for business in the city over the past decade. Some of these can be found in the alleyways off Nanluogu Xiang, an attractive and lively north–south alleyway lined with bars, shops, and restaurants to the east of Qian Hai Lake.

Rooms in courtyard hotels are small, and you won't find a swimming pool. Nevertheless, peace and quiet, age-old charms, traditional Chinese rooftops, grey brickwork, carved lintels, trees, birds, greenery, and the engaging flurry of hutong life will all be on your doorstep.

All of Beijing's courtyard hotels lie within the second ring road (mainly in Dongcheng) and range from budget to luxury. Recommended hotels include Courtyard 7 ***(7 Qiangulouyuan Hutong, tel 010 6406-0777, $$$, www.courtyard7.com),*** **just off Nanluogu Xiang, and Haoyuan Hotel** ***(53 Shijia Hutong, tel 010 6512-5557, $$$, www.haoyuanhotel.com),*** **west of Wangfujing Dajie.**

Temple of Heaven

This supreme example of Ming dynasty architecture is one of Beijing's truly prized landmarks. The temple, a diagram of Chinese cosmology, is both a transmitter to heaven and a splendid icon of Beijing. Designed according to Confucian principles, the temple—more accurately an altar—is a tranquil and harmonious retreat from Beijing's congested streets.

The Hall of Prayer for Good Harvests represents the meeting point between heaven and Earth.

Temple of Heaven
- Map: 59 C2
- Address: Yongdingmennei Dajie/Tiantan Beilu
- Admission: $
- Subway: Tiantandongmen

Set in a vast 660-acre (267 ha) park a mile south of Qianmen Gate, this sacred plot of land was where the emperor conducted the most significant ceremonies and rites of the year. The rituals established the divine link between heaven (*tian*) and the son of heaven (*huangdi*), channeling eternal law to the Earth.

The Temple of Heaven (Tiantan) was a regal domain and out of bounds to the common people (*laobaixing*). In 1918, the temple's former functionaries stepped aside to admit the public, and extensive renovation work has since been carried out. Its sacred geometry retains the cardinal east–west, north–south axis and its celestial metaphors. Buildings are spread through the park, but the principal structures lie along the south–north axis, as with all temples in China.

Hall of Prayer for Good Harvests

The most striking edifice in the park is the tall, circular Hall of Prayer for Good Harvests (Qiniandian), built in 1420 during the reign of Yongle, when Beijing was designated capital. The emperor's geomancers (*fengshui* masters) determined this as the point where heaven and Earth meet. The hall was the focus of sacrificial rituals and prayers for fruitful harvests (*qigu*).

It was rebuilt during the reign of Jiajing in 1545 into a triple-eaved structure that glistened with blue, yellow, and green glazed tiles. This chromatic scheme symbolized, in turn, heaven, Earth, and the mortal world. The Qing Emperor Qianlong replaced the tiles with the present azure roofing. During the reign of the feeble Guangxu (*r.* 1875–1908), lightning struck the hall, which burned for a day and a night, and the entire hall was again rebuilt.

The conical roof is a beautiful sight, its roundness symbolizing the extent of heaven. The 120-foot-high (36.5 m) vault was skillfully slotted together without using a single nail. The four inner pillars represent the seasons, and two further sets of 12 columns denote the months and the division of the 24-hour day into two-hour units (their concentric configuration supports the three tiers of the roof).

South of the Hall of Prayer for Good Harvests is a raised platform called the **Red Platform Bridge (Danbiqiao),** along which the emperor approached the hall.

Other Sites in the Park

The **Imperial Vault of Heaven (Huangqiongyu)** lies south, a round hall tiled in blue and standing on a white platform. The **Echo Wall (Huiyinbi)** ingeniously conveys sound around its circumference, but any personal interface with this technology is usually blotted out by the commotion of tour groups.

The **Circular Altar (Yuanqiu)** to the south resonates with astronomical significance, a cosmic hub that was also the site of the annual winter solstice ceremony. The solemnities involved sacrificial offerings of animals to the accompaniment of music. The altar was also requisitioned during times of natural disasters to entreat heaven.

Built in 1530 of blue stone (later replaced with the present white stone), the mound consists of three tiers that represent Earth, the mortal world, and heaven.

INSIDER TIP:

Step into the past and approach the altar along the traditional ceremonial route, through the south gate (Zhaohengmen).

—DAMIAN HARPER
National Geographic author

Nine steps separate each tier, nine slabs are laid on each tier, and the upper tier is adorned with nine stone rings. The number nine has special significance in Chinese cosmology, for there are nine layers to heaven.

The central feature of the **Fasting Palace (Zhaigong)** near the west gate (Xitianmen) is its large port-red "beamless hall." The neighboring **Living Hall,** surrounded by wilting bamboo, is where the emperor observed abstinence before the sacrificial rites. ■

VISITING THE TEMPLE OF HEAVEN: The temple park is generally accessed via its west gate from Yongdingmennei Dajie, but gates puncture the wall of the park at all the cardinal points.

Ancient Observatory

Surrounded today by a roar of traffic, the Ancient Observatory (Guguanxiangtai), built near remains of the old city walls, allowed the Middle Kingdom access to the stars.

Ancient Observatory
- 59 D3
- Jianguomenwai Dajie
- Closed Mon. & 11:30 a.m.–1 p.m.
- $
- Subway: Jianguomen

Beijing's first observatory was Kublai Khan's, a wooden tower designed to aid astrological predictions; the Mongols were keen sky-watchers. Construction of the present building began in 1437, and its role included astronomy, astrology, and seafaring navigation. At one time run by Muslims, it was later under the control of the Jesuits.

The Chinese originally thought that the Earth was the center of the universe, orbited by the celestial spheres. In the 17th century, the Jesuits arrived with astrolabes, heavenly mathematics, and other devices to set the record straight.

Chinese astronomers were generally (but not always) successful, as Juliet Bredon notes in her book *Peking* (1922). Under the tutelage of Father Verbiest, the Belgian Jesuit priest who came to China in 1659 and was made president of the Board of Works, they learned to predict eclipses accurately; on eclipse day, members of the official board would appear, beating drums to scare away the dragon about to swallow the moon or sun (the Chinese word for eclipse is still *shi*, to eat).

The observatory houses a museum dedicated to Chinese astronomy. Displayed on the roof are pieces designed by the Jesuits in 1674 on the orders of Emperor Kangxi. These include an ecliptic armillary sphere, a theodolite, a sextant, and a dragon quadrant. The large azimuth was a present from Louis XIV to the emperor. Fantastic Chinese designs adorn the instruments. The Jesuits encouraged the Chinese to construct these instruments to replace the old Mongol versions that had been used for centuries. Most survive, despite being stolen by Germans during the Boxer Rebellion; they were returned after World War I.

Near the observatory were the Imperial Granaries and the Examination Halls (Gongyuan), both of which have long disappeared. The Examination Halls housed the candidates for the imperial examinations (see p. 64), a highly conservative selection method that was reformed out of existence by Empress Cixi. ■

EXPERIENCE: Blind Massage

A massage from a blind masseur is perhaps just the ticket after pounding the pavement in Beijing. Blind masseurs are famed for their heightened sense of touch and tactile sensitivity; furthermore, the occupation provides employment for the blind. You may see groups of blind masseurs on the street; otherwise try Aixin Ziqiang Blind Massage Center ***(2a Baijiazhuang Lu, tel 010 6595-0997, $$)*** **or Comfortable Blind Massage** ***(18 Zhongfangli, Sanlitun Nanlu, Chaoyang, tel 010 6507-0036, $$).*** **Both offer a range of massage techniques to restore vitality to your aching muscles.**

EXPERIENCE: A Chinese Education

Beijing offers a fascinating range of lectures, classes, workshops, and tours to suit the needs and tastes of every visitor who comes to town.

Run by the enthusiastic Feng Cheng, the resourceful **Chinese Culture Center** *(Kent Centre, A 101, Anjialou, 29 Liangmaqiao Lu, Chaoyang, tel 010 6432-9341, www.chinaculturecenter.org)* has a busy schedule of events, from calligraphy classes for beginners to workshops on Chinese medicine, meditation, kite-making, *fengshui,* Peking Opera, tai chi, and Chinese landscape painting. You can also sign up for back street walks around Beijing, as well as trips to the Great Wall, the Shanxi town of Pingyao (see pp. 109–110), and as far away as Xinjiang.

Practicing *qigong,* traditional Chinese breathing exercises

Qigong

Similar in some ways to yoga, the technique of *qigong* (meaning literally "breath work") combines breathing with the circulation of *qi* (energy) around the body, while allowing the mind to enter a state of meditation.

Some martial arts—such as tai chi—are moving qigong forms, but many other styles of qigong are stationary. The most common qigong posture is to bend the knees while keeping a straight back and lift your arms—palms facing you—to roughly shoulder height, holding your arms there in a rounded form. Then you maintain this posture for around ten minutes, breathing regularly and circulating the qi around your body. Relaxation is key to this style, especially as your legs and shoulders will get tired.

The best place for practicing qigong is in the open air (although you may have your reservations considering Beijing's reputation for atmospheric pollution!). The **Beijing Milun School of Traditional Kung Fu** *(tel 138 1170-6568, www.kungfuinchina.com)* offers one-to-one lessons in Ritan Park.

Mandarin

Students of Chinese quickly discover that the Beijing dialect is the cream of Chinese accents. It's also a particularly tricky brogue to master, however. But if you really want to learn some Chinese, attending a class in Beijing is the best place as you will pick up a respectable accent rather than some provincial inflection that will raise eyebrows across China.

The **Hutong School** *(8 Shuangsi Hutong, off Jiugulou Dajie, Xicheng district, tel 010 6403 8670, www.hutong-school.com)* offers either courses or private classes for beginners—its Gulou branch in Shuangsi Hutong (Double Temple Alley) is located in the historic Xicheng district not far from Gulou Dajie subway station. The school also provides a range of cultural activities—including cultural immersion, where you can turn your hand to learning a classical Chinese musical instrument or how to play the game of mahjong. It also provides accommodation.

Lama Temple

Beijing's premier Buddhist temple attraction, the Lama Temple was converted from a palace to a temple in 1744 and stood by the old northern wall of the Mongol City. The complex is one of the largest in China.

Lama Temple
- 59 D4
- 28 Yonghegong Dajie
- 010 6404-4499
- $; audio guide $
- Subway: Yonghegong

Fronted by huge *pailou* (decorative arches) to the east of Yonghegong Dajie, the massive Lama Temple is a colorful and exotic Buddhist temple complex that once rose up just within the massive Tartar City Wall that ringed the Manchu sector of Beijing. The wall has disappeared, leveled in the 1950s to ease traffic circulation, but its gates survive in the name of the ring road just to the north—Andingmen Dongdajie.

Today, the ebullient Future Buddha greets all, accompanied by the Four Heavenly Kings on either side. Above him is written: "If the heart is bright, the wonderful will appear." Behind him is trusty Weituo, the defender of the faith, holding his staff.

In the next courtyard, the **Yonghe Palace** houses two statues of the 18 Luohan (see p. 83) and three golden, robed Buddhas. The decorated ceiling is startlingly beautiful. The **Yongyou Hall** has a statue of the Longevity Buddha. On the altar of the Qing dynasty **Hall of the Wheel of the Law** stands a statue of Tsongkhapa, the founder of the Yellow Hat Sect of Lamaism (see p. 304). The **Wanfu Pavilion (Wanfuge)** is built around a colossal effigy of the Maitreya Buddha, a vertigo-inducing 55-foot-tall (17 m) statue, with an additional 20 feet (6 m) below ground, carved from a single block of sandalwood.

At the rear lies a display of Qing dynasty Tibetan articles and an exhibition on Tibetan Buddhism and the Lama Temple. The collection of Tibetan items includes dharma wheels (wheels of the law), scepterlike *dorjes* (see p. 307), bells, effigies of Buddha, and a multiarmed statue of the goddess Guanyin (see pp. 82–83). This collection is possibly the most fascinating aspect of the temple. There's also an explanation of the gold lots used for the nomination of the next lama. You can chart the succession of the Panchen and Dalai Lamas (see p. 308) along the walls. English-language guides can be hired at the temple entrance. ■

Mysteries of the Lama Temple

As a reliquary for the frightening spirits and forces of primitive Tibetan Buddhism, the Lama Temple was often associated with strange goings-on. For many years, the temple was out of bounds to Beijing residents. Juliet Bredon's book *Peking* (1922) relates how a Russian bribed his way into the temple with a packet of Huntley & Palmer's biscuits (which he knew the head Lama enjoyed). When he tried to leave, the monks shut door after door in his face and asked for payment before opening each in turn. A number of foreigners went missing after visits to the temple, and the rumors of human sacrifices heightened the fear and suspicion.

Confucius Temple

Along the *hutongs* opposite the entrance to the Lama Temple is the Confucius Temple (Kongmiao). Like many temples to Confucius, it is dusty, neglected, and redolent of a disappearing age or a forgotten book. Second in size only to the Confucius Temple in Qufu, this is a tranquil reserve of ancient cypresses, stelae (inscribed stone tablets), crumbling buildings, and a forlorn air.

Around the Confucius Temple *(13 Guozijian Jie, $, Yonghegong subway)* the cypresses claw at the sky. Several of the halls sheltering stelae on the backs of *bixi* (mythological tortoiselike dragons) have been renovated.

INSIDER TIP:

Each year, the Confucius Temple attracts high school students before the very competitive university entrance exam takes place.

—PAUL MOONEY
National Geographic author

Standing in front of the **Dacheng Hall (Hall of Great Achievement)** is the largest cypress in the compound, planted in the Yuan dynasty by an imperial official. The hall's mammoth interior swallows up the feeble lighting, but you can pick out a collection of dusty musical instruments and devotional objects. Immediately west is the impressive **Imperial College,** with its staggering decorative archway, and **Biyong Hall,** both well worth a look. ■

A statue of Confucius stands in the temple's first courtyard.

Other Religious Sites

Beyond the more well known temples, Beijing is studded with an eclectic assortment of other houses of worship—Muslim, Buddhist, Taoist, and Christian.

Cow Street Mosque
- 59 B2
- 88 Niu Jie
- 010 6353-2564
- $

Fayuan Temple
- 59 B2
- 7 Xuanwai Fayuansi Qianjie
- 010 6353-3772
- $

Cow Street Mosque

Cow Street Mosque (Niu Jie Libaisi) in southwest Beijing is a fascinating little world, inhabiting a small preserve on the east side of Cow Street (Niu Jie). This perfectly preserved, active mosque is in the Chinese style and was originally built during the Song dynasty.

Ancient Muslim worshippers with white beards sit in the shadows reading Islamic texts. Lush vegetation covers the grounds, and pines soar gloriously aloft. Astronomical observations were made from the **Wangyuelou (Moon Observation Tower)** for calculations of the Islamic calendar. The minaret stands in the middle of the courtyard.

Inside the mosque are a **prayer hall** (you can't enter unless you are a Muslim), side halls, a reserve for female Muslims, and vases inscribed with Arabic. Stelae on the grounds commemorate the history of the temple, including two inscribed with Arabic at the rear. Dress respectfully.

The area around Cow Street (so named because of the local Muslim predilection for beef) is also notable for its selection of Muslim restaurants.

Tranquil Fayuan Temple offers a welcome retreat from the hustle and bustle of modern Beijing.

Fayuan Temple

Not far from Cow Street Mosque is the large Fayuan Temple (Fayuansi). The complex is extremely quiet but active, so be respectful. More than a hundred monks live here, and the most venerable monk has not left this holy domain for nearly 20 years. The Buddhist brothers inhabit a tranquil world apart, a frugal and restrained alternative to the world of today's China. The highlight of the temple is its distinctive and ancient copper Buddha and Qianshou Guanyin statue.

White Clouds Temple

Mainstay of the Quanzhen School of Taoism, the White Clouds Temple (Baiyunguan) off Baiyun Lu is a fascinating multiplex of courtyards and different shrines. Originally founded in the Tang dynasty, it is presided over by Taoist monks, chattering on cell phones. On the walls of the small **Hall for the Tutelary God (Lingguandian)** are portraits of four famous marshals, including the famous Song dynasty general, Yue Fei. Note the *bagua* prayer mats decorated with trigrams (see p. 292).

There's another temple dedicated to three famous Taoist officials, containing some vivid murals, and the **Hall for the Jade Emperor (Yuhuangdian),** the celestial Taoist god (see p. 83). The walls used to be lined with a set of Taoist statues, which have disappeared. The hall in the fourth courtyard is dedicated to Chang Chun, a famous Taoist monk from Shandong Province, who lived and died at the temple.

Citizens come to worship Karl Marx's nemesis (greed) in the **Hall to the God of Wealth.** They congregate to have their ailments healed at the **Hall of the King of Medicine,** otherwise known as Sun Si Miao (dedicated to a deified doctor of the fifth–sixth century). At the rear of the complex is a temple dedicated to the four celestial emperors.

The **Shrine Hall for the Savior Worthy** has depictions of the Taoist realm of hell (with its apparent shortage of women).

Dongyue Temple

Dedicated to the god of Taishan, the vibrantly colorful Dongyue Temple (Dongyue Miao) is well worth visiting for its numerous spooky "departments," small side halls peopled by fiendish deities and creatures from Taoist myth.

Zhihua Temple

Here is one of those rare temples in today's Beijing, largely unrestored and kept in its original state. See the enticing **Ten Thousand Buddhas Hall,** arranged over two floors.

INSIDER TIP:

The Ming dynasty Zhihua Temple features regular performances of traditional Chinese music, with scores dating back more than 500 years.

—MARY STEPHANOS
National Geographic contributor

Churches

The baroque **South Cathedral (Nantang),** or the Church of the Immaculate Conception, is a 20th-century replacement for an earlier church that was leveled during the 1900 Boxer uprising. This is the focus of Catholic activity in Beijing, with an English mass on Sundays at 10 a.m. Its cousins, **St. Joseph's Church** (on Wangfujing Dajie) and **North Cathedral** (see p. 68), survive. ■

White Clouds Temple
- 59 B3
- Baiyun Lu
- 010 6346-3531
- $
- Subway: Nanlishi Lu

Dongyue Temple
- 59 D3
- 141 Chaoyangmenwai Dajie
- Closed Mon.
- 010 6551-4148
- $
- Subway: Chaoyangmen

Zhihua Temple
- 59 D3
- 5 Lumicang Hutong
- $
- Subway: Chaoyangmen

South Cathedral
- 59 C3
- 141 Qianmen Xidajie
- Subway: Xuanwumen

China's Gods & Goddesses

A host of deities preside over the sacred domain in China. Your visit will be that much more enjoyable if you can lift the lid on the local pantheon and learn to recognize a few of the more popular celestial beings.

Two of the Four Heavenly Kings guard the Tang dynasty Jietai Temple just outside Beijing.

Buddhas & Bodhisattvas

Future Buddha (Milefo or Maitreya): This jovial, golden fellow greets you at the entrance to temples. Buddhists believe there are Buddhas whose time is already in the past and others who are yet to come. Milefo is a bodhisattva (see below) who will eventually manifest himself on Earth. He is sometimes portrayed with a small group of children. In China, Milefo is a chubby incarnation, based on a real monk called Chang Dingzi.

Historical Buddha (Sakyamuni): The main hall of a temple contains a trinity of golden Buddhas, and the central statue is the Historical Buddha, his hand touching the ground. This represents Gautama Siddhartha, founder of Buddhism, in his pre-Nirvana incarnation. He is also represented reclining on a couch, preparing for death.

Bodhisattva: The term refers to the Historical Buddha and to those who are capable of becoming Buddhas; in other words, they have attained a pre-Buddha stage of enlightenment. The most prominent bodhisattvas in China are the goddess Guanyin (see below) and the Future Buddha (see above), both of whom typify the essentially compassionate mission of the bodhisattva.

Goddess of Mercy (Guanyin or Avalokiteshvara): Guanyin, the Goddess of Mercy, is the Chinese incarnation of the Buddhist Bodhisattva Avalokiteshvara.

Legend holds that Guanyin was once Prince Bu Xun, who lived on the southern coast of India. The prince renounced the material world and became the disciple of Buddha, vowing to deliver people from all their suffering.

Bodhisattvas are traditionally asexual, but during the Yuan dynasty, images of Guanyin as a female were erected in temples as it was believed many of the bodhisattva's tasks, such as bestowing and delivering children, were more appropriate for a female deity.

This ruling deity of the island of Putuoshan (see pp. 180–181) is manifest in the Dalai Lama (see p. 308). In temples, her statues often face north at the rear of the main temple; she may also have a separate hall dedicated to her. See also sidebar p. 181.

Wenshu (Manjushri): This bodhisattva carries a sword and sometimes a book, rides a lion, and represents wisdom. He rules over the Buddhist mountain of Wutaishan (see p. 111) and often appears as a trinity with Puxian and the Historical Buddha.

Bodhidharma (Damo): This Indian monk is usually shown with a heavy brow and thick beard. Patron of the Chan (Zen) Buddhist sect, his spiritual home is the Shaolin Monastery (see pp. 128–129), where he left his legacy in the form of *gongfu* (see pp. 124–125).

Luohan (Arhat): The Luohan are perfect humans who have been freed from the cycle of rebirth. There are usually 18 of them, often depicted worshipping Guanyin or ranked in two lines of nine alongside temple walls. Occasionally they appear as a gilded group of 500. They remain in this world until the coming of the next Buddha.

Weituo: The defender of Buddhism can be found standing with a staff behind the Future Buddha at the entrance to a temple.

Four Heavenly Kings: The kings are usually present in pairs on either side of the Future Buddha and Weituo. Large and ferocious, they are dressed in armor and carry musical instruments.

Taoist Gods & Goddesses

Laozi: Born in the seventh century B.C., this founder of philosophical Taoism is often displayed riding an ox and holding a book, his *Daode Jing (The Classic of the Way and Its Power)*.

Eight Immortals: This famous group from Taoist legend is often portrayed crossing the sea in a boat.

Jade Emperor (Yuhuang Dadi): This is the supreme god of Taoism, and he is often shown with a black beard, seated on a dragon throne.

Three Pure Ones (Sanqing): These are the three large statues grouped together in Taoist temples: Laozi, the Yellow Emperor, and the Jade Emperor.

Queen of Heaven (Tianhou): Reigning principally in the southern coastal regions of China, Tianhou, also known as Niangniang and Mazu, is the protector of seafarers. A large number of temples in Hong Kong are dedicated to her.

God of War (Guandi): This god, typically depicted red-faced, adorned with a black beard, and clad in armor, is also the god of literature and represents both civil and military aspects.

Taoist door gods: Taoist temples—and some private houses, too—employ similar defenses against evil spirits as Buddhist temples. The Green Dragon and the White Tiger (see p. 256) are Taoist door gods, who guard temple entrances.

Summer Palace

The Summer Palace is a sprawling imperial encampment of temples, pavilions, and halls set in a park around the vast Kunming Lake. The imperial family once used this wonderland of noble follies as a summer residence. If the weather is fine, a visit here can make for a memorable day. Expect to stay at least half the day, and pack your camera, especially for sunset over the lake.

Once an imperial retreat, the Summer Palace is a huge domain of halls and temples.

The Summer Palace (Yiheyuan) was conceived in the 12th century, although the buildings here today date from the Qing dynasty. Long before that, the site was a royal garden and retreat, but it was not until the reign of the Qianlong emperor (*r.* 1736–1795) that the transformation was made.

From the main entrance east of Kunming Lake you come first to the **Hall of Benevolence and Longevity (Renshoudian).** Here Empress Dowager Cixi (see sidebar opposite) sat on her throne during her time of power. The throne is still there, but unfortunately, the hall interior is fenced off and inaccessible to visitors.

The fascinating bronze statues in front of the hall include a *qilin,* a mythical chimera that appeared on Earth only during times of harmony. The creature is often seen in Confucian and imperial buildings, a hybrid of dragon, lion, deer, and other animals. To the left of the hall are statues of a dragon and a phoenix, symbols of the emperor and the empress.

North of the Hall of Benevolence and Longevity lies the **Court of Virtue and Harmony (Deheyuan),** with its impressive theater in which Empress Cixi is said to have dressed up as Guanyin, the goddess of mercy.

On the northern shore of the lake sits the **Hall of Happiness and Longevity (Leshoutang),** where Cixi used to spend the summer months. South of the hall is a pier where she would disembark after crossing the lake.

To the south is the **Hall of Jade Billows (Yulantang),** where Emperor Guangxu was kept under lock and key after his involvement in the 1898 Hundred Days of Reform movement (see p. 41).

Follow the shoreline south for sweeping views over the lake. Jutting out from the shore is an island, upon which stands the **Zhichun Pavilion.** Farther along, rows of benches look out over the water. The temple-encrusted hill north of the lake is called **Longevity Hill (Wanshoushan).**

At the southern end of the loop, you will pass a large bronze ox, next to the fabulous **Seventeen Arch Bridge (Shiqikongqiao),** a 492-foot (150 m) span of graceful curves over the water to South Lake Island (Nanhudao). Here resides the **Dragon King Temple (Longwangmiao),** where the empress dowager would pray for rain. Alongside the temple is the pier where she would alight from her boat. Inside you can catch a glimpse of the rather ferocious Dragon King. Above the door are characters that translate as "always moist like spring."

From here, jump aboard a tourist boat at the island's northern fringe, and chug to the other side of the lake. The trip offers engaging views of the lake: To the north you can see the stepped arrangement of temples climbing Longevity Hill. The boat ferries you to the decadent **Marble Boat,** a superbly decorated folly, symbolic of the wasteful decline of the Manchu court. The empress dowager paid for its construction with funds earmarked for the Qing naval fleet. To the east extends the Long Corridor

Cixi—The Old Buddha

The Qing Empress Cixi (1835–1908), also known in the West as empress dowager, or Old Buddha, began her rise to power when, as a concubine, she had a son by the Xianfeng emperor. The boy became the Tongzhi emperor at the age of five. On his death, Cixi installed her nephew as the Guangxu emperor in contravention of the laws of succession. Throughout her life she dealt in political intrigue and eventually ruled the imperial court with an iron fist.

Summer Palace

- Map: 58 A6
- Address: Yiheyuan Lu
- Phone: 010 6288-1144
- Price: $$ (some sights have separate tickets); $ (audio guides)
- Subway: Xiyuan

GETTING TO THE SUMMER PALACE: The Summer Palace is 7 miles (11 km) northwest of central Beijing and is best reached by taking the subway to Xiyuan or Beigongmen. In the summer months, boats run along the canal to the Summer Palace from a jetty north of the Exhibition Center east of Beijing Zoo; boats also depart from the zoo.

(Changlang) with its Pavilion for Listening to Orioles (Tingliguan).

Follow the path to the west to some excellently preserved Qing dynasty roofed docks, where Empress Cixi moored her boats. If you want to see inside, rent a paddleboat from the dockside and take a flashlight.

Longevity Hill

From here, take the path through the trees up Longevity Hill and work your way east to the **Sea of Wisdom Temple (Zhihuihai)** on the crest. This temple is covered with small glazed-tile Buddhas, many of which had their heads smashed off (especially on the lower tiers) by French and British troops who swarmed through the Summer Palace in 1860, during the second Opium War. The foreign troops returned in 1900 after the Boxer Rebellion for a repeat performance.

Work your way downhill to the octagonal **Pagoda of Buddhist Fragrance (Foxiangge).** The descent takes you through a network of steep steps and corridors. **Cloud Dispelling Hall (Paiyundian)** was used by Cixi for holding grand ceremonies. In front are bronze phoenixes marked with the reign of Guangxu.

INSIDER TIP:

The Summer Palace stays open late, so visit it in the evening after the crowds have left. You may just have the place to yourself.

—ALISON WRIGHT
National Geographic photographer

Long Corridor

At the base of Longevity Hill is the **Cloud Dispelling Gate (Paiyunmen),** in front of which sit a pair of lions. From here, you can enter the Long Corridor, which runs along the northern shore of Kunming Lake and links the Marble Boat with the Hall of Happiness and Longevity (Leshoutang). Originally built in 1750, the corridor is decorated with thousands of paintings from Chinese myth and legend, including views of Hangzhou's **West Lake** (see pp. 173–174). It was torched by Anglo-French troops in 1860 and reconstructed in 1888. The corridor swarms perennially with visitors.

Around Kunming Lake

Over the hill to the north, a string of lakes leads from west to east, culminating in the **Garden of Harmonious Interest (Xiequyuan),** a copy of a Wuxi garden (see p. 172). The area called Suzhou Creek, near the North Palace Gate, has been restored and comes replete with "Olde China" teashops.

A popular walk runs west of Kunming Lake along West Causeway, passing willows and charming Chinese bridges. The summer weather is refreshingly cooler than in central Beijing, but in winter Kunming Lake is transformed to a sheet of ice. ■

Old Summer Palace

The magnificent ruins of the Old Summer Palace, torched and plundered by Anglo-French troops in 1860, are scattered through a park in northwest Beijing. The vast grounds of the park are a sprawl of lakes and ponds surrounded, in summer, by the somnolent figures of fishermen.

The walks here are enchanting—past ponds thick with lilies, along shaded paths, and away from the grinding snarl of Beijing's traffic. The perfect antidote to the mayhem of the metropolis, the Old Summer Palace (Yuanmingyuan) attracts couples seeking a romantic retreat, especially at twilight.

The main attraction is the sublime tangle of marble pillars, column bases, and stone slabs that once formed the European-style palace. The remains are scattered in the **Eternal Spring Garden (Changchunyuan).** If they are not crawling with visitors posing for photos, something of their silent beauty can be enjoyed. The original palace was a colossal estate, with more than 200 buildings and a circumference of 4.5 miles (7 km). A few remaining photographs capture its magnificence. A giant reproduction ancient bronze vessel has been added, presumably to give some local flavor. Looting troops filled their knapsacks with treasures, which still pass through auction houses and private collections in Europe and the United States.

Apart from the palace structures, a huge number of ruins dot the park. Some appear to have been moved to create the proper mood, and a stone pavilion set in a maze has been built for the benefit of visitors.

The ruins of the Old Summer Palace symbolize the humiliation of China at the hands of foreign powers.

The wooden palace buildings were all burned to the ground by the British and French in 1860, but the marble structures largely survived in tumbledown fashion, although the site was repeatedly ransacked after 1949. ■

Old Summer Palace

- 58 A6
- Yuanmingyuan Donglu
- $
- Subway: Yuanmingyuan Park

Around Beijing

The region around Beijing is where you will find that eternal symbol of China, the Great Wall, the solemn grandeur of the imperial tombs, and a crop of temples in the surrounding hills.

The ancient ancestors of the Chinese cut more than a hundred cave homes outside Beijing.

Western Hills

The Western Hills (Xishan) stretch out 12 miles (19 km) west of Beijing, not far from the Summer Palace (see pp. 84–85). Excellent hiking options lie in the hills, most easily accessed through **Fragrant Hills Park** in the eastern section. Temples once dotted the park, but many were damaged by the French and British in 1860 and later during the Boxer Rebellion.

You can reach **Incense Burner Peak (Xianghufeng),** the summit of Fragrant Mountain, either by cable car or by clambering up its slopes, beyond which sprawl the remainder of the Western Hills.

Not far from the park's North Gate is the **Azure Clouds Temple (Biyunsi),** distinguished by its unusual Indian-style, 110-foot-high (33.5 m) **Diamond Throne Pagoda.** Before finally being laid to rest in Nanjing, Dr. Sun

Yat-sen's body remained in the pagoda for four years. Five hundred carved, lacquered Luohan figures (see p. 83) congregate in the Luohan Hall.

To the south of the Western Hills is the area known as **Badachu (Eight Great Sites),** celebrated for its eight nunneries and temples. Temples here include the Ming dynasty **Changan Temple,** the **Lingyuan Temple,** which houses a tooth belonging to Buddha, and the **Xiangjie Temple.** To reach Badachu, take the subway to the last stop west at Pingguoyuan, then a taxi.

INSIDER TIP:

The northern hiking route in Fragrant Hills Park leads to gorgeous Yanjing Lake and an 18th-century Tibetan-style lamasery.

—MARY STEPHANOS
National Geographic contributor

EXPERIENCE: Local Chinese Village Life

For a taste of the life that many ordinary Chinese experience, take a day trip to the ancient village of Chuandixia in the far west of Beijing municipality. The journey plunges you into the hilly countryside around Beijing and leads you into China's most charming and often overlooked dimension: its bucolic and rural aspect.

Dating from the Ming and Qing dynasties, Chuandixia's lovely houses rise up the side of a hill. Some of them now operate as guesthouses (ask around), and spending the night here promises a tranquil escape.

The fastest way to reach Chuandixia is to take a taxi from Pingguoyuan subway station in west Beijing. Alternatively, two 929 buses make the two-hour trip directly to Chuandixia from Pingguoyuan subway station, leaving at 7:30 a.m. and 12:40 p.m.

Tanzhe & Jietai Temples

About 28 miles (45 km) west from Beijing is the **Tanzhe Temple,** on the slopes of Tanzheshan (Pool and Mulberry Mountain). The temple's history goes back to the third century A.D. (predating Beijing).

Jietai Temple, or Ordination Terrace Temple, 5 miles (8 km) southeast of Tanzhe Temple, is a Tang dynasty house of worship, although most of the surviving buildings are of later construction. The chief features of the temple are a 10-foot-high (3 m) terrace, which was built in the Liao dynasty (907–1125), and its community of pine trees in the courtyard.

The Great Wall

Colossal endeavor, brave folly, futile contrivance, or splendid achievement, the Great Wall of China inspires awe. Sections have been restored outside Beijing, but for the larger part, it staggers fitfully over North China.

Not so much one wall as an articulation of ramparts, the punctuated Great Wall (Wanli Changcheng) straddles China from remnants in Liaoning in the northeast to its crumbling finale in the Gobi desert of Gansu. In its entirety, the wall is almost

(continued on p. 91)

EXPERIENCE: Take a Trip to Jiankou Great Wall

If you prefer your Great Wall unspoiled, uncommercialized, and authentically ragged-looking (as it should be), then make a visit to Jiankou in Huairou County. The mountainous scenery is jaw-dropping, with a long, ragged section of wall running dramatically along a high ridge. It's about an hour-long trek from the village of Xizhazi uphill through the woods to the north side of Jiankou wall, and the approach is pretty strenuous. Once you reach the wall, however, you have the freedom to explore in either direction.

Be warned that the wall here is in its natural state: shedding bricks, with saplings sprouting from the brickwork and entire sections having collapsed into piles of rubble. You will have to tread carefully, otherwise you could sprain an ankle.

This is how the Ming dynasty brick-clad wall is supposed to look, before the kind of tourist reconstruction that rebuilt the masonry at **Badaling** and **Mutianyu.** It is far more sublime here than elsewhere, and there is a magnificent sense of seclusion, away from tour buses and crowds.

It is possible to hike east 6.8 miles (11 km) all the way from **Jiankou** to Mutianyu, but you should do this with a sense of caution. Take food and water with you, and always remember to check the weather before you set out. The full hike takes around four hours, involving some rather steep sections as well as tracts of overgrown wall bristling with saplings. Never climb on crumbling sections of the Great Wall alone in case you have an accident. Take good shoes and a sense of adventure, but note that the expedition may not suit children or the elderly.

The best way to reach the north side of Jiankou is by taxi either from Beijing or Huairou, which can be reached by bus from the Dongzhimen long-distance bus station. Be sure also to ask at your hotel as it may conduct tours. You can also reach Jiankou from the south side, which is easier to approach from Beijing, but the climb to the wall is more difficult and you have fewer options for exploring.

You will have no problem completing a return trip to Jiankou in one day. However, if you would rather spend a few days or longer exploring the area, it is possible to stay in simple hostels in the village of Xizhazi.

The sun descends behind a watchtower at Jiankou.

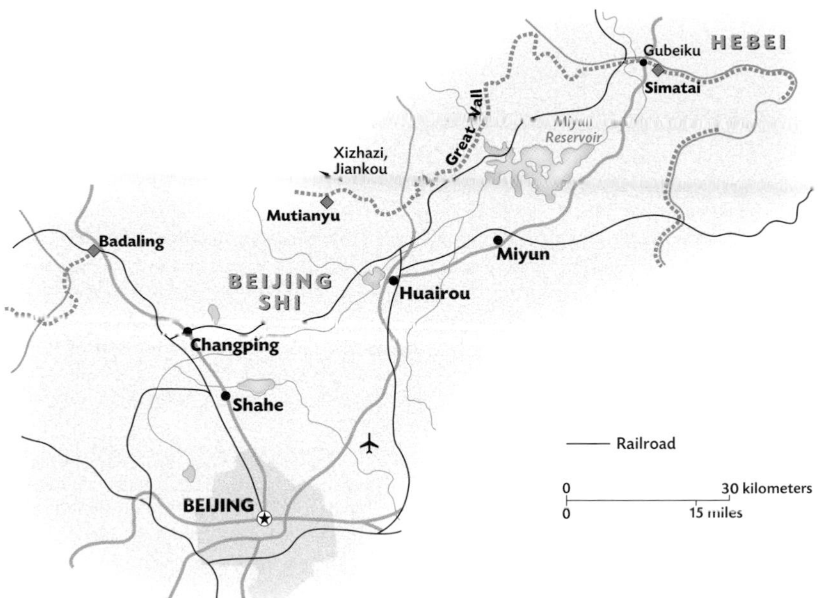

4,000 miles (6,430 km) long. Schoolboys love to quip that it is the only man-made structure observable on Earth from space, but this is totally untrue.

History of the Wall: The wall is not the work of one dynasty. Begun as early as the seventh century B.C., it took on its gargantuan character under the first emperor of the Qin dynasty that unified China, Qinshi Huangdi (*r.* 221–210 B.C.). Qinshi Huangdi, whose other lasting legacy was the terra-cotta warriors (see pp. 105–107), threaded together the existing ramparts, erected watchtowers, and constructed beacons to alert the capital (near present-day Xi'an) of attack.

The wall advanced with the Han dynasty, which further extended Qinshi Huangdi's fine efforts into the Gobi desert, but was chiefly dormant during the flourishing Tang and Song dynasties. The Jin and Ming dynasties heralded a spate of enthusiastic construction. The Ming, in particular, encased sections of the wall (constructed principally of rammed earth) in brick. Slaving at the wall was a motley assortment of disaffected farmers, soldiers, and prisoners, many of whom died of exhaustion or malnutrition.

The purpose of the defense was to keep the hostile tribesmen of the north out of China. The wall failed spectacularly, most notably with the incursions that established the dynasties of the Jin (Jurchen), Yuan (Mongols), and Qing (Manchu). Perhaps that's why the Qing spent so little time on the wall. Ultimately, the wall was superseded by technology and circumvented by forces that emptied into China from other directions: the Western powers

EXPERIENCE: Sleep Near the Great Wall

After some intense sightseeing in town, taking a few days out from Beijing is highly recommended, to flee the smog and ceaseless traffic noise and to immerse yourself in the raw scenery around town.

Several hotels have established themselves near or next to the Great Wall. Not far from Badaling, **Commune by the Great Wall** *(tel 010 8118-1888, www.communebythegreatwall.com)* is a stunning piece of modern architecture with a Great Wall section to boot and magnificent views. A hunting lodge backing on to parts of the Great Wall in Huairou County, **Red Capital Ranch** *(28 Xiguandi Village, Yanxi tel 010 8401-8886, www.redcapitalclub.com)* is magnificently located, while the popular **Schoolhouse at Mutianyu** *(tel 010 6162 6506, www.theschoolhouseatmutianyu.com)*, near the wall at Mutianyu, has an excellent selection of houses.

Badaling Great Wall

Map 91
Badaling
$

that mustered along the coastline and the Japanese.

Like other symbols of division (the Berlin Wall, the Iron Curtain), walls are out of fashion these days, and the Great Wall serves only to attract visitors (in huge numbers).

INSIDER TIP:

Take a tent and sleeping bag when visiting Simitai Great Wall. There are fewer tourists, and you can enjoy sunrise at the wall with tea.

—JINZHONG FU
National Geographic grantee

Visiting the Wall: The wall is impressive for its magnitude. The sections you can realistically visit have been rebuilt and touched up for the benefit of visitors; this gives a false impression of the condition of the wall (in large measure derelict). The fortresslike segments around Beijing quickly peter out.

You don't have to go to Beijing to visit the Great Wall; trips can be made at Shanhaiguan (see p. 142), where the wall meets the sea, and Jiayuguan (see p. 328), in the far west of Gansu, among other points.

Most people, however, visit the wall on day trips from the capital. **Badaling,** 43 miles (70 km) northwest of Beijing, heads the thrust of the local tourist industry.

The wall here snakes dramatically over undulations in the land, punctuated occasionally by watchtowers and gates. The Ming sections, clad in stone, surround a core of rubble and earth. Parts of the wall at Badaling can be steep to the point of being mountainous, so take shoes with good grip. To the west, this stretch of wall eventually dissolves into ruins.

Badaling is generally besieged by tour buses and full-on commercialization (the authorities still need to fine-tune profit with preservation), so don't expect a romantic sojourn with just you and the wall. Unless, of course, you go in midwinter. This is actually a good idea, for you will be rewarded with peace and quiet and a wonderfully frosted landscape. In addition, you won't be besieged by hawkers. If you do go in the glacial Beijing winter, however, be warned. It's colder than central Beijing and more exposed to the biting winds.

Many hotels and hostels can arrange trips to Badaling. You can also catch bus No. 919 from Deshengmen Watchtower all the way, or jump on a morning tourist bus from the Beijing Sightseeing Bus Center *(tel 010 8353-1111)* west of Tiananmen Square.

Another fragment of wall was rescued from oblivion at **Mutianyu,** 56 miles (90 km) northeast of the capital. This part was restored in an attempt to divert the crowds from Badaling. The section of wall here is just a mile long, however, and has also succumbed to the commercial onslaught, especially on the lower levels. Tours to Mutianyu are easily arranged through your hotel. Also, tour bus No. 6 runs on weekend mornings from the South Cathedral in summer.

Among the official tourist sections, the most secluded and genuine part of the Great Wall can be found at **Simatai.** At 68 miles (110 km) northeast of Beijing, it is farther away than either Badaling or Mutianyu. This distance has protected it from overexposure to tour groups but, equally, has made it harder to reach.

Only partially restored, the wall here offers a more authentic stretch of ruins. The powerful landscape backdrop makes for marvelous hiking along the crumbling remains, but the wall can be dangerous in parts and at the time of writing was shut for restoration. Ask at your hotel for the latest.

Mutianyu Great Wall

91

Mutianyu

$$ (including cable car)

Simatai Great Wall

91

Simatai

$

Sometimes climbing, sometimes plunging, the Great Wall follows the contours of the hills.

Ming Tombs
$ (charge per tomb)

The wall here begins at **Simatai Village.** Hire a private car or taxi, or sign up for one of the early morning tours run by hotels and youth hostels in Beijing. Less conveniently, buses from Dongzhimen bus station run to Miyun, from where minibuses run to Simatai.

Imperial Tombs

The tombs of Ming and Qing emperors lie to the north, south, and east of Beijing. Grandiose and solemn, the tombs display some of the finest of Beijing's carved stone and the majesty of centuries of imperial lineage.

Ming Tombs: The Ming Tombs (Shisanling) or 13 Tombs, located 30 miles (48 km) northwest of Beijing, constitute one of the city's major historical sites. They can be disappointing, however, unless you have a knowledge or appreciation of imperial history.

The founder of the Ming dynasty, Hongwu (*r.* 1368–1398), is buried in Nanjing, but there are 13 Ming emperors interred here, including Xuande (*r.* 1426–1435), Jiajing (*r.* 1522–1566), and Wanli (*r.* 1573–1620). In all, three tombs have been opened to the public—Changling, Dingling, and Zhaoling.

The tombs are reached under a five-arched gateway *(pailou),* behind which stands a further three-arched brick gateway *(da gongmen).* Through the gates stands the **Stela Pavilion (Beilou),** which holds a large engraved stela eulogizing the Ming emperors.

Beyond lies the long **Spirit Way (Shendao),** lined with statues of animals (some mythological) and officials. The emperor's coffin would have been conveyed

The Ming Tombs are laid out on a strict geomantic scheme according to the laws of *fengshui*.

Tomb Architecture

When the imperial tombs were originally sealed, they contained a hoard of gold, silver, lacquer, porcelain, and other riches to accompany the departed emperor; these were later plundered by thieves. Often designed during the emperor's lifetime, tombs would consist of either one chamber or an interconnected cluster. Geomancers would faithfully determine the superlative site for the tomb, paying strict attention to the surrounding *fengshui* of hills and rivers. The south-facing complex typically consisted of a crypt covered in a mound of earth, fronted by altars and halls, and a strip of water (to deflect bad spirits). It should be noted that the governing aesthetic is imperial and Confucian, rather than Buddhist or Taoist.

along this route and through the **Dragon and Phoenix Gate (Longfengmen)** to his tomb.

To reach the tombs, the avenue crosses a seven-arched bridge before fanning out to the individual crypts.

Changling, the first tomb ahead, is the resting place of Emperor Yongle (*r.* 1403–1423). The tomb complex contains an impressively large hall whose roof is supported by 32 cedar pillars.

Dingling, the tomb of the rather hopeless Wanli, was opened in the late 1950s. You can visit the underground passageways and chambers (Dixia Gongdian).

The last tomb open to visitors is **Zhaoling,** where Emperor Longqing (*r.* 1567–1572) was buried. The rest of the tombs at this site await excavation.

Travelers generally tie in visits to the Ming Tombs with the Great Wall. Line A buses from the Beijing Sightseeing Bus Center, west of Qianmen Gate (Tiananmen Square), take in the Great Wall at Badaling and the Ming Tombs, with buses leaving between 6 and 10:30 a.m. Also ask at your hotel for details of other buses.

Eastern Qing Tombs: Entombed 78 miles (125 km) east of Beijing are five Qing emperors, including the Kangxi emperor, the Qianlong emperor, the Xianfeng emperor, and a multitude of empresses. The layout echoes that of the Ming Tombs, with a series of stone gates funneling a Spirit Way to the tombs. **Empress Cixi's tomb (Dingdongling)** is an extravagant feat of self-congratulation. The carved ramp leading to her sacrificial hall depicts the phoenix (representing the empress) above the dragon (the emperor).

The tomb of the Qianlong emperor was a costly money pit from which the Qing dynasty had to extricate itself. The chamber is notable for its Buddhist images, usually absent in imperial tombs.

Western Qing Tombs: If you want to pay further homage to the Qing dynasty, you can do so at the Western Tombs of the Qing emperors. Seventy miles (112 km) southwest of Beijing are the final resting places of the Yongzheng, Jiaqing, Daoguang, and Guangxu emperors. ■

Eastern Qing Tombs
$ $

Western Qing Tombs
$ $

More Places to Visit in & Around Beijing

798 Art District

In the Dashanzi district of northeastern Beijing, the fascinating **798 Art District** (798 Yishu Xinqu) is a vast collection of art galleries and studios in a former electronics factory built by the East Germans. Admission is free (some galleries close on Mondays), and several cafés and restaurants are at hand.
✉ Jiuxianqiao Lu

Capital Museum

This stunning museum contains a fabulous collection of porcelain, statues, jade, bronzes, paintings, and other treasures.
www.capitalmuseum.org.cn ✉ 16 Fuxingmenwai Dajie ☎ 010 6337-0491 🚇 Subway: Muxidi

EXPERIENCE: Hike into the Hills With Beijing Hikers

The city of Beijing is remorselessly flat, but the environs of the municipality are hilly and even mountainous, with hiking trails winding around gullies, ravines, lakes, and remnants of the Great Wall that beckon outdoor lovers.

For fun and energetic treks in the countryside, contact Beijing Hikers ***(tel 010 6432-2786, www.beijinghikers.com, $$$$),*** **which offers regular weekend, and some midweek, hikes, as well as some overnight trips. Reservations are a must, and prices include transportation, guides, and snacks. Hikers meet at the Starbucks in the Metropark Lido Hotel** ***(6 Jiangtai Lu, Chaoyang)*** **in the far east of town.**

Beijing Hikers can arrange tours for small groups, as long as you give five days' notice, and also conducts tours to other parts of China. Kids are welcome.

Great Bell Temple

The Great Bell Temple (Dazhongsi) is a Qing dynasty complex housing a stout Ming dynasty bell. The bell, cast in 1406, is more than 22 feet (6.5 m) high, 8 inches (20 cm) thick at its widest point, and weighs 46.5 tons (42 metric tons). Furthermore, it is adorned with Buddhist sutras. It was one of six cast, designed to be hung at the six corners of the old city walls.
Map 59 B5 ✉ Beisanhuan Xilu $ $

Liulichang

This is the place to come for souvenirs, ersatz imperial porcelain, and mementos. Littered along Liulichang, southwest of Qianmen Gate, are "Olde Beijing"–style teahouses, antiques stores, and art galleries, which join forces to preserve something of the flavor of China's pre-Communist era.
Map 59 C3

Marco Polo Bridge

Students of the Japanese invasion of China in the 1930s may like to pilgrimage to the Marco Polo Bridge (Lugouqiao) *($),* 10 miles (16 km) southwest of Beijing. The bridge was the scene of the July 7, 1937, skirmish that finally ignited the war between Japan and China. The marvelous bridge, dating from 1189 and decorated with carved lions capping its balustrades, was described by the great Venetian writer in his travel memoir, a book some scholars declare to be fiction.
Map 59 A2 $ $

White Dagoba Temple

The White Dagoba Temple (Baitasi) is topped with a 13th-century bottle-shaped dagoba that originally housed Buddhist relics. The temple's highlight, however, is its riveting display of Tibetan Buddhist statues.
Map 59 B3 ✉ Fuchengmennei Dajie $ $

Dynastic capitals, the Shaolin Temple, Taishan, and a coastline harboring a medley of Western treaty port architecture

The North

Introduction & Map 98–99

Xi'an & Around 100–104

Experience: Snacking Around the Muslim Quarter 102

Army of the Terra-cotta Warriors 105–107

Huashan 108

Pingyao 109–110

Experience: Walk an Ancient Town Wall 109

Wutaishan & Taihuai 111

Datong 112–113

Yungang Caves 114–115

Tianjin 116–117

Chengde 118–120

Luoyang 121

Experience: The Peony Festival 121

Longmen Caves 122–123

Feature: *Gongfu* 124–125

Kaifeng 126

Songshan 127–129

Feature: Confucianism 130–131

Terra-cotta statues made for the tourist market

Qufu 132

A Climb up Taishan 133–135

Qingdao 136–141

A Walk Around Qingdao 137–139

Experience: Qingdao Brewery 141

More Places to Visit in the North 142

Hotels & Restaurants in the North 365–368

The North

The North is the historic heartland of China. Chinese civilization first blossomed along the lower reaches of the muddy Yellow River (Huanghe), charting its colossal course through this historic domain.

The provinces of Shaanxi and Shanxi are stained with the yellow earth *(huangtudi)* that dyes the Yellow River ocher and with which the Chinese mythically associate themselves. As China's cradle *(fayuandi),* the North is unequivocally Han in custom and folklore, possessing a cultural continuity missing in the minority-rich border regions.

Southern Chinese see their northern counterparts as unsophisticated, simple, and honest *(pushi)* folk. In today's competitive China, this may seem demeaning, but there is brotherly respect for the region's historical legitimacy. Northern Chinese may only be taking up the rear of China's economic drive, but all Chinese traditions flow from this northern fountainhead.

Chinese from the south furthermore vaunt their "many mountains, rivers, and saints" *(duo shan, duo shui, duo shengren).* Those from the solitary northern province of Shandong curtly reply they have the cream of the crop, "one mountain (Taishan), one river (the Yellow River), and one saint (Confucius)" *(yi shan, yi shui, yi shengren).* Unassuming Shandong, where the Yellow River leaves China for the Bo Hai Sea, also sports Qingdao, one of China's most attractive port cities and one-time German concession.

China was first united by the northern state of Qin, whose capital was at Xianyang, outside of Xi'an, itself capital to 11 dynasties. The vast ranks of the terra-cotta warriors assemble outside of Xi'an, guardians of an imperial birthright that belongs to North China.

Other past and present dynastic capitals—Anyang, Luoyang, and Kaifeng (all in Henan Province) and Beijing itself—endow the North with a pageantry and heritage envied by the rest of the land.

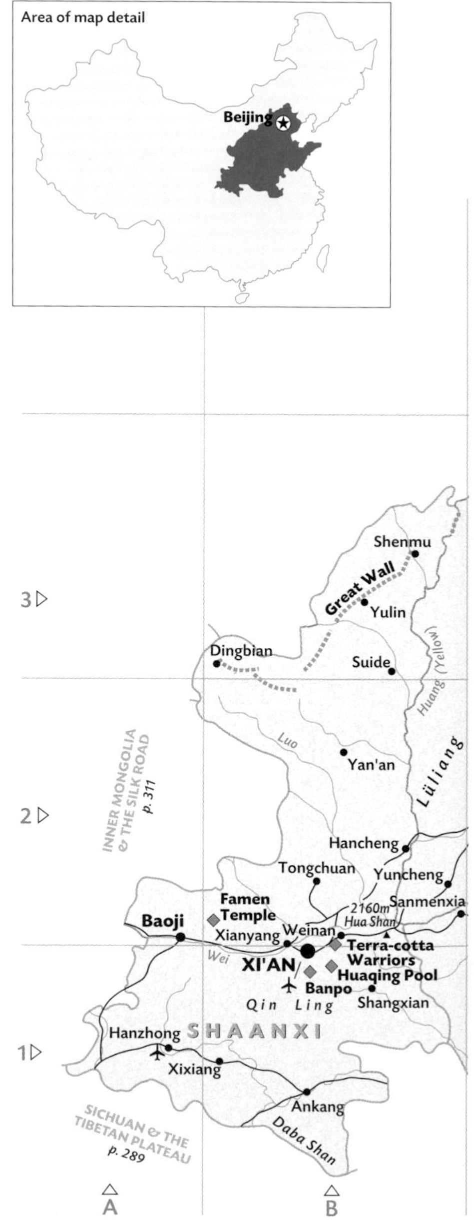

The West's 19th-century colonial imprint barely reaches inland, but foreign architecture of the period has left an indelible mark on the eastern coastal outposts of Tianjin, Yantai, and Qingdao.

Sacred monuments dot the North. Temples cluster at the imperial resort of Chengde and cling to the slopes of Huashan, Taishan, Wutaishan, Songshan, and Laoshan. Buddhist carvings at Longmen and Yungang pay homage to this religion, further evidenced by the legendary monastic order of Shaolin. ■

NOT TO BE MISSED:

Snacking around Xi'an **102**

The stunning army of the terra-cotta warriors near Xi'an **105–107**

A trip back in time to the walled town of Pingyao **109–110**

Exploring the Buddhist temples on the slopes of Wutaishan **111**

Admiring the Buddhist caves of Yungang **114–115**

Coming to grips with martial arts at the Shaolin Temple **128–129**

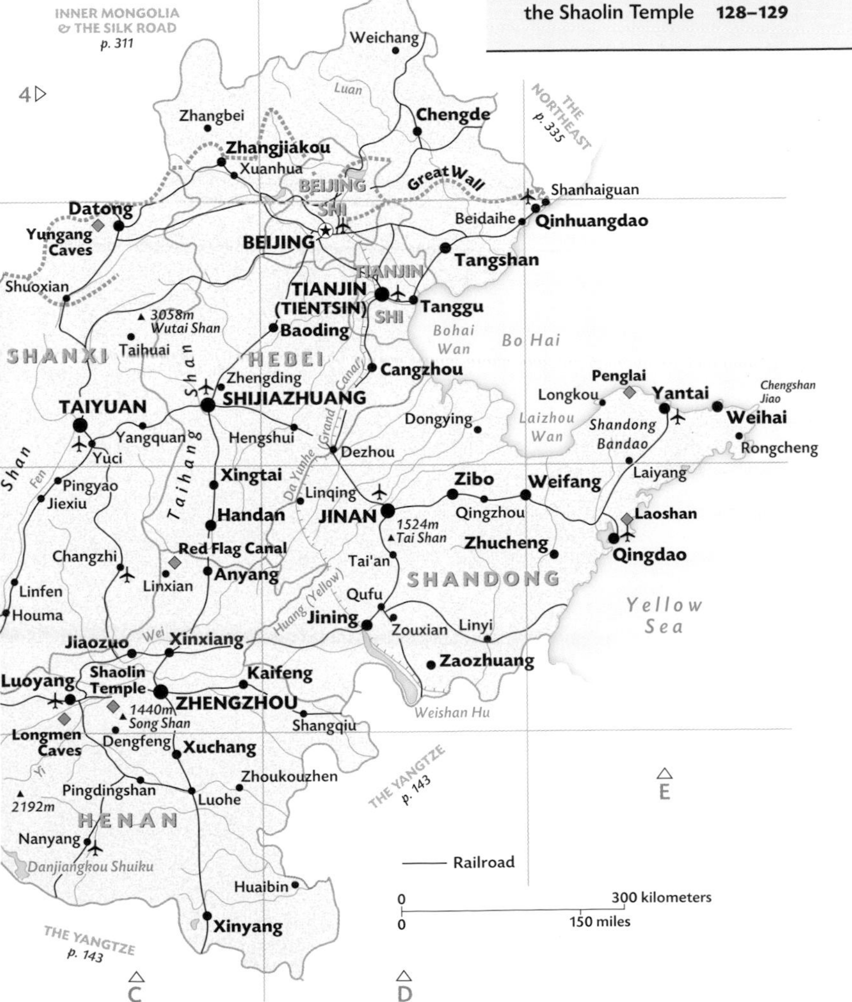

Xi'an & Around

Venerable and eternal Xi'an, one of China's most important cities, sprang from almost mythological beginnings. Some Chinese scholars attest to a flourishing town coexisting with the dawn of Chinese civilization. The affluent Silk Road began here, and incoming foreign traders and emissaries brought with them an Islamic flavor that lingers today.

Today as during the Tang dynasty, Xi'an is a prosperous city.

Xi'an
98 B1 & 101
CITS Visitor Information
101
48 Chang'an Lu
029 6288-9999

The city was apocryphally the Yellow Emperor's capital, and some Chinese believed that Xi'an was thriving when the god Fuxi was born, although he appears in the earliest pages of Chinese myth (see p. 27). What is certain is that the capital of the Zhou dynasty existed near here. Xi'an grew considerably under the first emperor of the Qin, Qinshi, who instigated his infamous mass book burning in 213 B.C. not far from the city. Often sacked and rebuilt (even being taken by invading Tibetans in A.D. 763), the city has been the national capital of 11 dynasties; its apogee was reached in Tang dynasty China, when it was called Chang'an.

Numerous religions entered Xi'an along the Silk Road (see pp. 312–313). Islam found a toe-hold here, and Christianity arrived when the Nestorians established an outpost in Xi'an, while Buddhism crept in from India.

The City Today

Xi'an is the capital of Shaanxi Province. The Tang grid pattern of old Chang'an survives in Xi'an today (making navigation straightforward), as does a considerable quantity of historic architecture. The Ming city walls encompass downtown Xi'an, itself divided into sections by major avenues and streets. Running north–south from the Bell Tower are Bei Dajie and Nan Dajie; east–west of it are Dong Dajie and Xi Dajie. Try to pick up a copy of the easy-to-use Xi'an Traffic & Tourist Map, which can be found across the city.

A host of historic attractions lie beyond the city walls, including the Big Wild Goose Pagoda, the Small Wild Goose Pagoda, the Shaanxi Museum of History, the Eight Immortals Temple, and, farther afield, the Army of the Terra-cotta Warriors, Banpo Neolithic Village, the imperial tombs that ring Xi'an, and Famen Temple.

Within the Walls

The imposing defensive walls, 8.5 miles (14 km) long, 40 feet (12 m) high, and 50 to 60 feet (15–18 m) thick at the base, were built by the founder of the Ming dynasty, Hongwu. Each flank has a gate and a chain of watchtowers. Add to that almost 6,000 battlements and a wide moat. From the ramparts, the walls give an enduring sense of impregnability. Like most city walls in China, these have been restored.

You can access the battlements from a number of points, mainly the southern reaches. The walls are not high enough to offer a bird's-eye view over the city, and the ramparts have attracted a swarm of substandard amusement attractions, but you get a good idea of the grand scale of the undertaking. Rubber-wheeled buses are on hand to ferry around those who prefer not to walk.

Xi'an's sizable Islamic population converges on the **Great**

Ming City Walls
Map 101
$ $

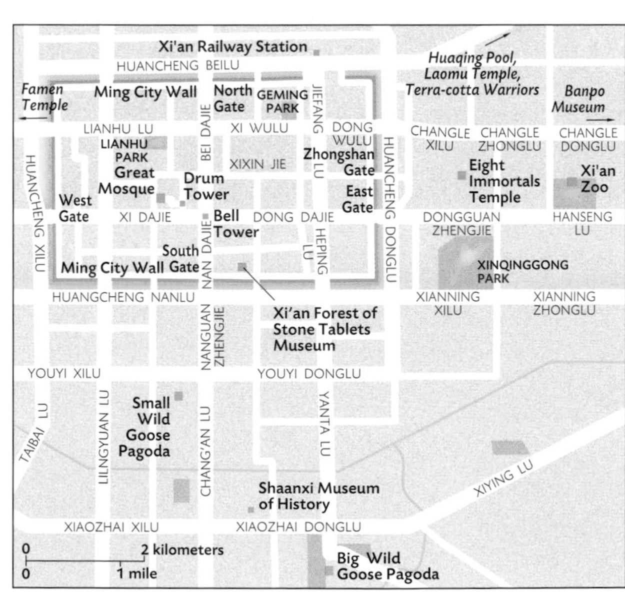

EXPERIENCE: Snacking Around the Muslim Quarter

One of the culinary highlights of Western China, Xi'an's Muslim Quarter is full of the aroma of Silk Road cuisine. You'll find *roujiamo* (shredded lamb or beef in a bun) in abundance; often described as "China's hamburger," it's a delicious mouthful and excellent for eating on the go. Look out also for *yangrou paomo* (lamb soup with noodles and bread), one of Xi'an's best known dishes, *fenzheng yangrou* (chopped and fried lamb), and, of course, *yangrou chuan* (lamb kebabs) and *yangrou shuijiao* (lamb dumplings).

Great Mosque
- 101
- $

Bell Tower
- 101
- Nan Dajie
- $

Xi'an Forest of Stone Tablets Museum
- 101
- 15 Sanxue Jie
- $$

Eight Immortals Temple
- 101
- Off Wudaoshizi Dongjie
- $

Mosque (Da Qingzhensi) in the Muslim quarter, the area to the northwest of the Bell Tower (see below). The mosque has been styled with a Chinese temple handbook and built with several courtyards. The prayer hall is barred to non-Muslims. Elsewhere this engaging corner of the city has a fascinating Islamic complexion.

The **Drum Tower** is similarly rooted in the Muslim quarter, set in a seemingly distant land of Islamic aromas and motifs. This is an excellent area to find a good Muslim restaurant. The **Bell Tower** sits on Xi'an's north–south axis, at a point upon which the main thoroughfares converge.

The **Xi'an Forest of Stone Tablets Museum (Beilin Bowuguan)** near the city wall in the south was originally a Confucian temple, as can be discerned from the two characters on the main wall outside *(kong miao)* and above the secondary entrance *(wen miao);* both mean "Confucian temple." Many of the stelae celebrate such Confucian virtues as filial piety, and they are inscribed with the complete text of ancient classics, documents, and historical records.

Among the texts carved on stone here are the *Book of Songs* (the first collection of Chinese poems), the *Book of Rites,* and the *I-Ching* (*Book of Changes*). To prevent copying errors, the classics were inscribed on stone and kept in Chang'an (the former name of Xi'an) during the Tang dynasty. Students of classical Chinese will find the collection fascinating, but it may prove inaccessible to most foreign visitors.

An intriguing item kept here is the **Nestorian Tablet.** The Nestorians were Christians from Syria who argued that Christ's human and divine natures were separate. Another tablet is an imperial announcement made during the Boxer Rebellion (see p. 40), and it concerns an uprising against Christian missionaries in Luohe Town, Shaanxi Province.

Beyond the Walls

The **Eight Immortals Temple (Baxianan)** lies east beyond Zhongshan Gate. The eight immortals are central characters in Chinese Taoist mythology. You can find images of them in the **Hall of the Eight Immortals** inside the temple complex. At the rear is a temple dedicated to Doumu, the Taoist goddess of the 12 stars and goddess of all the stars in heaven.

The **Hall of Master Qiu** at the rear on the left is where Empress Dowager Cixi and Emperor Guangxu lived after fleeing to

Xi'an following the Boxer uprising in 1900. The plaque in front of the hall is signed in red by the empress and dated the 30th year, the 8th month, and the 21st day of the reign of Emperor Guangxu.

On the corridor to the left of the main courtyard are a number of fascinating black plaques. One rare item relates to the *Neijing* (a book treasured by Taoists for its lessons on correct breathing and the cultivation of *qi*, essential for the quest for immortality). Another plaque celebrates the five Taoist mountains. Other plaques describe the principles of Taoist spiritual alchemy.

There is little to see at the **Small Wild Goose Pagoda (Xiaoyanta),** on Youyi Xilu, just south of the city walls. Founded in the eighth century, the pagoda was originally 15 stories high, but earthquake damage reduced it to 13 and left a jagged top to the elegant building. Although sometimes inaccessible, you can occasionally climb to the top for good views, but be warned: The pagoda is more than 130 feet (40 m) high.

Big Wild Goose Pagoda (Dayanta) was originally built by Emperor Gao Zong in A.D. 648 in honor of his mother Empress Wende. The pagoda was the most famous temple in Chang'an during the Tang dynasty. In the main temple, three statues of Buddha are flanked by the 18 Arhats, or Luohan (see p. 83).

Xuan Zang (602–664), the famous Buddhist emissary who collected scriptures from India, managed the temple. The Big Goose Pagoda was built to store the hundreds of volumes that he brought back. It was rebuilt as a square, brick pagoda in Tang dynasty fashion during the reign of Empress Wu Zetian (see p. 34).

The **Shaanxi Museum of History (Shaanxi Lishi Bowuguan),** northwest of the Big Wild Goose Pagoda, displays a couple of the life-size terra-cotta warriors from the army of Qinshi Huangdi (see p. 105). Their facial expressions are worth studying in detail; of the thousands of warriors found, no two faces are alike. A pottery horse from the same tomb shows exceptional skill and artistry. The warriors and horse indicate a technical expertise that was rarely repeated in later dynasties.

The collection includes a range of pottery figures from other

Small Wild Goose Pagoda
- 101
- Youyi Xilu
- $

Big Wild Goose Pagoda
- 101
- Yanta Nanlu
- $

Shaanxi Museum of History
- 101
- 91 Xiaozhai Donglu

Temple of the Eight Immortals Market

The road leading up to the Temple of the Eight Immortals has a flourishing market of relics and fakes, operating on Wednesdays and Sundays. Take a close look at what's on offer. Antique Chinese round eyeglasses in their pouches and ceramic busts of Chairman Mao nestle up against heads of Buddha. The latter are clearly forgeries, but they look as if they have been hacked from the Longmen cliff face. Scattered piles of old Chinese coins with a heavy (and fake) patina heap up against fossils (they look carved), suspicious-looking ceramics (but you never know), jade jewelry, faded photos of Empress Cixi, Taoist volumes on alchemy, old pipes, and magic funeral paper.

Banpo Museum
98 B1 & 101
Banpo Lu
$

Huaqing Pool
98 B1 & 101

Famen Temple
98 B2 & 101
Fufeng County
$

dynasties. The Han dynasty pieces exhibit the brute vitality typical of this forceful people; however, ceramics from the less interesting earlier dynasties far outnumber those made during the more skillful Yuan, Ming, and Qing dynasties.

A stunning collection of Shang dynasty bronzes reveals how advanced early metalwork was in China. Admission to the museum is free with a valid passport.

INSIDER TIP:

Don't leave Xi'an without sampling some of the street food in the Muslim Quarter. The fried persimmons are especially delicious.

—SUSAN STRAIGHT
National Geographic Books editor

Around Xi'an

Fragments of imperial history as well as primitive remains dot the environs of Xi'an. The most arresting of all is the awe-inspiring army of the terra-cotta warriors (see pp. 105–107).

Banpo Museum: This site just east of town celebrates the Banpo period (4800–3600 B.C.) of the neolithic and matriarchal Yangshao culture that lasted from around 5000–2800 B.C. and saw the dawn of China's painted pottery tradition (see pp. 202–203). **Banpo Neolithic Village (Banpo Bowuguan),** as the museum is otherwise known, was excavated in 1953. The remains of the village and its cemetery are open to the public, accompanied by the more interesting pottery pieces. Viewing the ancient remains is a rather dry experience, but renovations aim to inject more attraction for the average traveler.

Huaqing Pool: The hot springs at Huaqing first became popular in the Tang dynasty, when emperors visited a complex of bathing houses and pools. You can still bathe in the 123°F (43°C) mineral water.

Tombs: Emperor Qinshi Huangdi's burial mound is yet to be excavated and is not worth a visit unless you wish to pay homage to the despotic monarch. You can glean much more from the nearby terra-cotta warriors. It is likely that grave robbers have ransacked the interior, but if they never broke into its vaults, a veritable treasure trove awaits. Other imperial tombs near Xi'an are testament to the city's importance as a dynastic capital. They are difficult to reach except on a tour that covers Xi'an's environs.

Famen Temple: Situated 73 miles (117 km) northwest of Xi'an, Famen Temple has a history that dates back to the Eastern Han (A.D. 25–220). The temple's **pagoda (Zhenshen Baota)** is one of a legendary total of 84,000 built to accommodate relics of the body of Sakyamuni (Buddha), making Famen a place of pilgrimage. ■

Army of the Terra-cotta Warriors

Stumbled upon by peasants digging a well in 1974, the 2,000-year-old army of the terra-cotta warriors (Bingmayong) is a fascinating record of artistic achievement and a grandiose expression of imperial power.

Emperor Qinshi Huangdi united China for the first time under the Qin (see p. 29) and embarked on a series of huge construction projects including the Great Wall. The best preserved of these undertakings is probably the army of terra-cotta warriors, interred within the outer wall of the emperor's mausoleum (which was built during his lifetime) as his eternal imperial guard.

The thousands of pottery warriors stand inside three vaults. These were originally covered with wooden roofs, under a layer of earth. Remarkably, no historical records acknowledged the existence of this army, so they were lost to time.

The tallest warrior stands more than 6 feet (1.8 m), and all were equipped with still-sharp bronze weapons–swords, spears, crossbows, and longbows (the weapons have been removed and are not on view). Soldiers and horses were modeled from yellow clay and painted after firing, but the paintwork, which must originally have been vivid and colorful, has faded almost completely.

Pit No. 1

The main army stands in Pit No. 1; 6,000 of the 8,000 soldiers and horses are here. As you enter, the silent ranks of the terra-cotta warriors stare fixedly back through the millennia. The rows of figures are separated by walls roughly 8 feet (2.5 m) wide; high-level walkways lead between the rows so that you look down

Army of the Terra-cotta Warriors

101
Ticket: $$$. Audio guide: $

www.bmy.com.cn

Each terra-cotta warrior represents an individual man.

VISITOR TIPS:
Recorded tours and guides are available on site. Running the gauntlet of hawkers outside the museum can be trying.

Most hotels can arrange trips to see the terra-cotta warriors, 18 miles (29 km) east of Xi'an, taking in other sights en route. Getting there yourself by bus is simple; just take bus No. 306 or 307 from Xi'an train station, both of which terminate at the museum. The trip takes one hour.

Qin Warrior Museum
$

on the warriors. (Photography is not permitted). The ranks of soldiers face east, away from the emperor's tomb. A group of terra-cotta horses wore harnesses with brass fittings and perhaps drew chariots, which must have been wooden and are long since gone. Toward the rear of the vault you can see a pile of collapsed warriors with smashed heads; in fact, a number of the statues at the front are headless. Archaeologists are trying to reassemble whole figures from this jigsaw puzzle of shattered fragments.

The scale of the endeavor is awe-inspiring, and the image of warriors (many toppled by earthquakes) solemn and moving. Close examination reveals the superlative skill that has given each figure a unique expression. The figures are hollow from the legs up; hands and heads must have been modeled separately and then connected to the bodies.

The find propelled Xi'an into the tourist age when the first vault was opened to a clamoring public in 1980. Rivaling China's other premier attractions—the Great Wall and the Forbidden City in Beijing—the terra-cotta warriors were just one part of the enormous imperial necropolis planned by Emperor Qinshi Huangdi.

Terra-cotta horses and a rider

Pit No. 2

More recently excavated, this pit was discovered in 1976 and opened in 1994. Buried here were chariots, cavalry, and statues of infantrymen, terra-cotta effigies that numbered 1,300 in all. On view are several figures, including archers, an officer, a horseback soldier, and further soldiers, all modeled with an exacting eye to detail and craftsmanship.

Pit No. 3

Of the three chambers in this small vault, one is still unexcavated. The two others have been opened, and their contents look to be reasonably intact. They contain 72 soldiers and a war chariot; the figures appear to be high-ranking officers because they are dressed in more elaborate costumes than the infantrymen in vault No. 1; was this the command center for the ghostly army? Photographs taken during the original excavations carried out in the 1970s line the walls.

Qin Warrior Museum

This small museum (Tongchema Chenlieshi), located near the warriors' site, contains a pair of highly detailed bronze chariots unearthed 65 feet (20 m) west of Emperor Qinshi Huangdi's tomb (see p. 104). ■

Army of the Terra-cotta Warriors

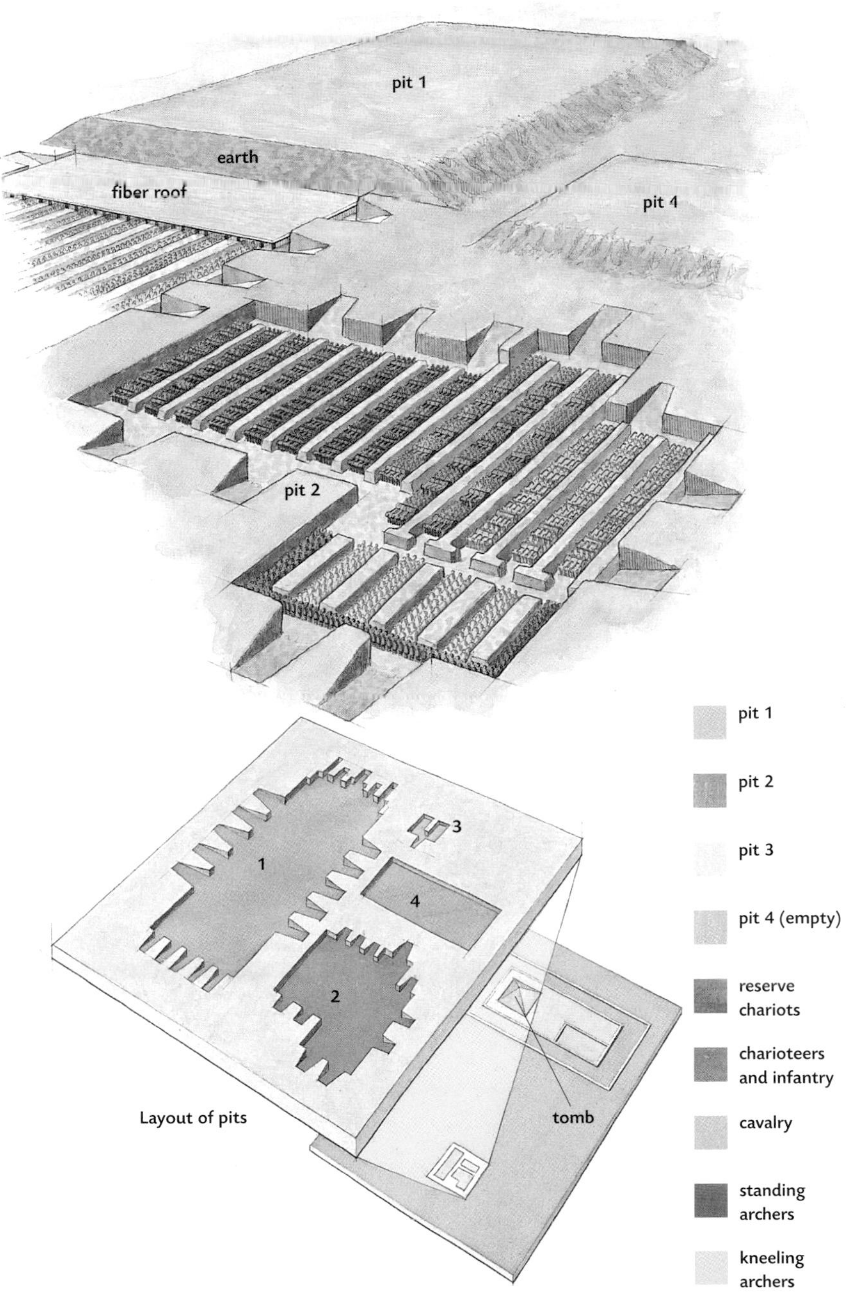

Huashan

Huashan is the western peak of the five holy Taoist mountains. In ages past, the mountain, which overlooks the lower Shaanxi plain 75 miles (120 km) east of Xi'an, swarmed with cave-dwelling Taoist hermits reputedly endowed with magical powers.

Though popular, the climb up Huashan is precipitous.

Huashan
98 B2
Visitor Information
$$$ (Cable car: $$)

Huashan has five peaks: East, South, West, North, and Central. Among them lies a valley with cascading waterfalls. The sight of the mountain in the mist is a most beguiling spectacle. As with Taishan (see pp. 133–135) and Emeishan (see pp. 296–297), sun watchers make the ascent to see the dawn sun, and there are accommodations on the summits, such as North Peak Hotel *(tel 029 430-0062)*. Spring and autumn are the best seasons for climbing Huashan.

North Peak

The climb to the first peak—North Peak—from Huashan Village, at the foot of the mountain, is comfortable to begin with, but after a few miles it becomes increasingly strenuous. The path clings to the mountainside, rising through the **Huashan Gate** near the **Jade Spring Monastery (Yuquanyuan).**

Huashan has a reputation for being a dangerous climb, as some terrifying sections consist of little more than incisions in the perpendicular rock (a few fatalities occur every year). The ascent is about 9 miles (14 km), so you will need a day for the round-trip. Another option is a cable car that ferries you from the eastern base to the North Peak, from where you can access the other summits.

Cratering the mountain rock surface are caves bedecked with carved statues, silent companions to the hermits who sought sanctuary here. Many of the caves suffered violence at the hands of Red Guards during the Cultural Revolution. Some hermits still live on the mountain, but the groundswell of tourism has made such an ascetic life difficult. The hermits are served by a sprinkling of Taoist temples. Although Huashan is a Taoist mountain, there's also a temple dedicated to Guanyin, the Buddhist goddess of mercy.

South Peak

A footpath winds up to the summit of South Peak, the highest point (7,085 feet/2,160 m). Here lies the **Laozi Cave,** dedicated to Taoism's enigmatic founder, also called Laojun. ■

Pingyao

One of China's premier sights, Pingyao is the most authentically preserved walled town in the land. Its age-old charms, gorgeous red-lantern-hung streets, and splendidly hoary Ming and Qing dynasty architecture give it the look of the China we all go to find but rarely discover. Here you'll also find fine courtyard hotels, and some excellent side trips lie just outside town.

Ringed by magnificent Ming dynasty walls dating to the 14th century, the merchant town of Pingyao rose to prominence as a banking center in the 17th century. The town's wealth left a supreme collection of Ming and Qing dynasty courtyard houses and some impressive temples as well as a charming lattice-work of ancient alleyways and lanes.

Admission to the town is free, but if you want to see the town wall or the Rishengchang Financial House Museum, you should purchase a ticket at one of these or another sight in town *($$$$; valid for all sights for two days).*

Exploring Pingyao

By far the best way to enjoy the town is to amble around the streets and back alleys. With more than 100 rooms, the impressive **Rishengchang Financial House Museum** was established as a bank in 1824, before covering the nation with branches. For worthwhile views over town, climb the intact Ming **city wall** (see sidebar

Pingyao
99 C2

NOTE: Take enough cash with you when visiting Pingyao as there is nowhere to change money, although you can withdraw cash from bank ATMs such as the Industrial and Commercial Bank of China.

EXPERIENCE: Walk an Ancient Town Wall

As ancient Chinese towns go, Pingyao is very unusual. Unlike other walled towns in China, Pingyao retains not only its wall but also many of its old buildings, their symmetry and architectural logic having survived the calamitous 20th century (and so far the 21st century). In contrast, Xi'an's city wall, although lovely, embraces a city that has preserved precious little of its ancient heritage.

Pingyao's 39-foot-high (12 m) wall has 72 watchtowers (representing the 72 sages) and six gates, one each in the northern and southern walls and two each in the eastern and western ramparts. Some say the wall resembles a tortoise: The south gate is the tortoise's head and the north gate its tail. Originally two wells outside the city walls represented the tortoise's eyes. The four eastern and western gates represented the reptile's four limbs. A section of the southern city wall collapsed in 2004 but has been restored, and a moat still survives on the far side of the ramparts.

A walk along the wall *(access included in the main ticket that grants admission to all the town's sights)* is one of the highlights of a trip to Pingyao, affording excellent views over town and beyond. For the best light and vistas over town, try to arrive at the wall either early in the morning or at sunset. Once upon the wall, you can walk the entire length of the ramparts and its 3,000 crenellations—around 3.7 miles (6 km)—in about two hours. Also try to walk around the outside of the wall for a different perspective.

p. 109). In the southeast of town stands the **Confucius Temple,** the main hall of which dates to the 12th century. The attractive and elegant **City Tower** *(Shilou, $)* rises up over Nan Dajie, the busy north–south street lined with shops and restaurants.

Pingyao is particularly attractive at night, when the red lanterns come on and the town settles beneath a nocturnal hush. You will find several bars in the old town, or just pop into one of the courtyard hotels for a beer.

INSIDER TIP:

In September, Pingyao's ancient buildings become galleries during the city's annual photography festival, the largest of its kind in the world.

—CRISTINA MITTERMEIER
National Geographic grantee

Ancient Pingyao is also a UNESCO World Heritage site.

Outside Town

A cycle or taxi trip south of town, the **Shuanglin Temple** (Double Forest Temple; $$) contains a collection of exquisite and rare statues from the Song and Yuan dynasties. The very grand **Wang Family Courtyard** *($$$$$)* is typical of Qing dynasty Shanxi courtyard homes. To get there, take a bus from Pingyao to the town of Lingshi and then a bus or taxi to the sight.

The lovely **Qiao Family Courtyard** *($$$$)*, about 17 miles (30 km) north of Pingyao, was the setting for Zhang Yimou's glorious movie *Raise the Red Lantern.*

Getting to Pingyao

Travelers to Pingyao normally reach town from Taiyuan, two hours away by bus or train. (Many guesthouses and hotels pick up visitors at the train station.) Book your room in advance: The town can become very busy, especially during major holidays. ■

Wutaishan & Taihuai

The slopes of Wutaishan, the northernmost of China's four sacred Buddhist mountains, are scattered with a profusion of temples set against a marvelous alpine backdrop. Wutaishan's peaks group around the charming hamlet of Taihuai.

Wutaishan

Not long ago, 200 temples congregated around Wutaishan (10,000 feet/3,058 m), but the ravages of war and revolution have reduced the figure to about 40 (Chinese guides say there are 58). The peaks are presided over by Wenshu (Manjushri) (see p. 83), the Buddhist god of wisdom.

Wutaishan (Five Terraces) is around four to five hours by bus from either Taiyuan (see p. 142) or Datong (see pp. 112–113). The highest part of the mountain is the **Northern Peak (Beitaiding),** at more than 10,000 feet (3,050 m). Purchase a map in Taihuai.

Taihuai

Swamped by visitors in summer but relaxed in winter, Taihuai village is a cornucopia of temple architecture, much of which displays Tibetan and Mongolian Lamaist features. The most distinctive example of this is the white Tibetan-style dagoba of the **Tayuan Temple** in the south of the village. The dagoba stands more than 150 feet (45 m) tall and is hung with 250 bells.

Behind lies the vast **Xiantong Temple,** whose origins stretch back to the Eastern Han (A.D. 58–75). The enticing **Bronze Pavilion** is made entirely of glistening metal. Just to the east, the **Luohou Temple** contains a wooden lotus flower with eight movable petals, a Buddha figure sitting on each. Next to it stands the small **Guangren Temple,** run by Tibetan and Mongolian monks.

The yellow-roofed temple of **Bodhisattva Peak (Pusading)** is 108 steps up Central Terrace, 108 being a significant number in Buddhist numerology. On either side of Taihuai village, you can trek to several other temples overlooking the valley.

The large complex of the Yuan dynasty **Nanchan Temple** (see sidebar) is 1.5 miles (2.5 km) south of Taihuai, on the Southern Terrace. Other temples around the terraces of Wutaishan include the **Shuxiang Temple,** the **Longquan Temple,** and the **Cifu Temple.** Accommodation is available in the village and in some temples. ■

Nanchan Temple

The peaks of Wutaishan are home to one of the oldest temple halls in China. One of the halls of Nanchan Temple dates to A.D. 782, and the temple itself perhaps dates back even further. Due to its remote location, the hall and its Tang dynasty frescoes eluded the great anti-Buddhist destruction heaped on Wutaishan by Tang emperor Wuzong. Also protected by its isolation, the main hall of Foguang Temple, more than 25 miles (40 km) northeast of Nanchan Temple, dates to A.D. 857.

Wutaishan & Taihuai

- Map: 99 C3
- $: Wutaishan: $$$$$

CITS Visitor Information

- Taihuai
- ☎ 139 9410-4419

NOTE: Due to its altitude, Wutaishan can be snowed in from late September through May, making access and departure tricky. Be sure to check the weather before heading out, and take warm, waterproof clothing.

Datong

The walled city of Datong was the imperial capital under the Northern Wei (A.D. 386–494) before Luoyang took its place, but today it wears an industrial face. Travelers make a pilgrimage west of the city to the splendid Buddhist caves at Yungang. Digging deeper beneath the city's dirty countenance exposes a rich vein of temples. Across the desolate wastelands to the south, the vertiginous Hanging Monastery miraculously suspends itself over a dizzying void.

The Hanging Monastery clings to its perpendicular perch on the Taoist mount of Hengshan.

Datong
99 C3
CITS Visitor Information
Datong Train Station
0352 502-1601
Yungang Hotel, 21 Yingbin Donglu
0352 712-4882

Datong sits in Shanxi Province, with Inner Mongolia's wide sweeping plains sprawling just to the north, a contrast to this grimy city surrounded by China's leading coalfield. But Datong has several points of interest in its ancient center.

In the western part of the old walled city off Da Xijie is the **Huayan Monastery** *(Huayansi Jie, $)*, whose roots reach back to the northern dynasty of the Liao (907–1125), though it was largely built by the nomadic Jin (1125–1234). The monastery houses the marvelous **Mahavira Hall,** at 16,785 square feet (1,560 sq m) one of China's largest temple buildings. Its scale is a pronouncement of the city's former importance. Inside are

31 lifelike, colored clay figures from the Liao period representing the Buddha and bodhisattvas.

About half a mile to the east along Da Dongjie (the eastern extension of Da Xijie) you will come across the **Nine Dragon Screen (Jiulongbi).** This 150-foot-long (45 m) tiled "spirit wall" *(Da Dongjie, $)*, built in 1392, protected a former palace. Spirit walls are *fengshui* defenses for deflecting demon spirits (see p. 156), although the palace itself burned down!

Shanhua Temple *(Nansi Jie, $)*, abutting the old Ming city walls in the south, also contains a small dragon screen. Datong's city walls are being slowly restored (see sidebar below).

From a distance, the **Hanging Monastery (Xuankongsi),** 47 miles (75 km) to the southeast, is seemingly wallpapered to the cliff face. This eccentric achievement dates back more than 1,400 years and is a spectacular sight. The temple buildings *($$)* are linked together by boardwalks and bridges laid over piles rammed into the rock. Caves along the temple length are decorated with sculptures, one of which depicts the three faiths of Taoism, Buddhism, and Confucianism.

INSIDER TIP:

Reminiscent of Tiger's Nest in Bhutan, Datong's Hanging Monastery is well worth a visit.

—ALISON WRIGHT
National Geographic photographer

The **Wooden Pagoda (Muta),** in Yingxian 43 miles (70 km) south of town, is one of the oldest wooden structures in China. Built in A.D. 1056 in the Liao dynasty, the pagoda *($$)* has miraculously survived earthquakes and war to struggle through to the present. ■

The New Look of Datong's Old Town

In recent years, Datong's old town, which lies at the heart of the city within the old city walls, has been undergoing a massive and costly face-lift. In a bid to resurrect its past, the city's authorities—like many others in old towns across China—have quite literally rebuilt the old town.

This rebuilding, or more accurately "re-imagining," of the past, is intended to boost the city as a tourist destination in a highly competitive market. In Datong's case, this has been fueled by rampantly growing real estate values, as well as the city's heritage as the capital of the Northern Wei dynasty in the fifth century.

The old town walls in Datong are being frantically reconstructed, and many of the city's temples now sport rebuilt, old-style Chinese halls. Because much of what you see at the site has been built in recent years, you will need to bring a critical eye for history and its repackaging.

Some of the revenue for this project has come from rapidly escalating admission fees, including the Yungang Caves (see pp. 114–115), now lashed to the city by a brand-new highway, where ticket prices have increased by almost 300 percent in the past three to four years.

Yungang Caves

The caves at Yungang are both a major landmark of Buddhist art and a place of veneration and worship. An army of some 40,000 workmen, under the direction of devout Buddhist artists, carved the caves and statues from the sandstone rock. Protected from inquisitive eyes for centuries, the remaining artifacts have survived plunder, weathering, and industrial pollution.

Stunning Buddhist statues and carvings like the ones pictured here fill the Yungang Caves.

These entrancing Buddhist cave-temples in the Wuzhou Mountains of Shanxi, 10 miles (16 km) west of Datong, were largely completed during the Northern Wei dynasty. One of the earliest chronicles of Buddhist art in China (and the earliest grottoes containing stone carvings), the major caves were hollowed out between 460 and 494, when Datong was the dynastic capital.

The caves were carved from a sandstone cliff by a massed workforce of 40,000, and they have survived better than many of the wooden temples of the early dynasties. For centuries, they were appreciated only by devout Buddhists. In the early part of the 20th century, however, statues stolen from Yungang found their way into collections in Japan and the West, where they remain.

Conservation efforts today extend to protecting the Yungang statuary from the combined effects of rock fractures, groundwater, weathering, and pollution from nearby Datong. Despite successes, many unsheltered statues have been irretrievably scoured away by wind and rain.

Foreign Influence

These carvings show the effect of many artistic influences. Hellenistic themes had made their way to Gandhara in north India, gathering Persian elements on the way, and a fused aesthetic had emerged. From here, Buddhism was exported along the Silk Road to China, passing through the lands of Central Asia and acquiring their flavor.

Buddhist Themes

The 45 caves house a gathering of 51,000 statues. Stylistically, some of the caves are simply capsules containing colossal statues of Buddha (the tallest is 55 feet/17 m high). Others are designed as temples, enclosed behind wooden galleries and decorated with numerous carved murals and effigies.

Recurring themes focus on Buddha himself or recount Buddhist stories and legends from India. Buddhism found a comfortable niche in China during the Northern and Southern dynasties (386–586), possibly as an antidote to the incessant wars and relentless human suffering of the period.

Buddhist parables, or *jataka,* adorn the walls, including the tales of the man who gave his own flesh to save a dove and the 500 bandits who had their eyes gouged out. Sakyamuni (the historical Buddha) is pictured having strips of flesh cut from his legs to feed a hungry eagle preparing to feast on a dove, a test of faith designed by the gods. The lively facial expressions of the statues animate the scenes.

The Caves

The south-facing caves stretch for about half a mile and are more accessible than those at Dunhuang (see pp. 326–327). They are grouped in three clusters. Of the four caves in the eastern section (1–4), the largest, **Cave 3,** once contained a temple and now houses a seated Buddha and two bodhisattvas.

The caves in the central section, including caves 5 to 8, are magnificent, protected by wooden temple exteriors. They are shielded by a much later, Qing dynasty temple. **Cave 5** shelters a colossal 55-foot (17 m) Buddha. The walls of **Cave 6** revel in stunning detail (relating Buddhist stories) and revolve around an intricately carved central pillar. **Cave 8** is peopled by Indian gods and goddesses, including Vishnu and Shiva, while the remaining caves in this central section teem with Buddhas.

INSIDER TIP:

When visiting any of the Buddhist caves in China, be sure to bring a flashlight in order to fully appreciate their stunning beauty.

—MU SU
National Geographic writer

Many of the western section caves (14–53), the largest group, are badly eroded, though there are a few surprises. **Cave 19** reveals another 55-foot (17 m) Buddha, and **Cave 21** wraps around a central pagoda. The statue of Buddha in **Cave 20** shows Central Asian influence in its wide features, cloth folds, and broad chest. ■

Yungang Caves
- Map: 99 C3
- $: $$$$$

CITS Visitor Information
- North of Datong Train Station, on Zhanbei Jie
- ☎ 0352 712-4882

Tianjin

Recently swept by a gale of investment that has left this former concession city bristling with newfangled architecture and tidying up its concession districts, Tianjin can be reached in half an hour by train from Beijing.

The Tianjin skyline sparkles at twilight.

Tianjin
99 D3
CITS Visitor Information
22 Youyi Lu
022 2810-9988
www.tianjinexpats.net

Great Compassion Monastery
40 Tianwei Lu
$

Wanghailou Cathedral
Shizilin Dajie
Closed Mon.–Sat.

Its proximity to the sea and to Beijing, and its location at the northern reaches of the Grand Canal (see pp. 176–177), made Tianjin (Tientsin) the economic hub of North China by the time of the early Qing dynasty. The Treaty of Tientsin (1858) opened the city to British and French concessions, followed in due course by others. Foreign troops shelled and occupied the city during the Boxer Rebellion and destroyed its old walls. It was badly rocked by the notorious Tangshan earthquake of 1976.

Religious Landmarks

Tianjin has a variety of places of worship that survived the great earthquake and symbolize the city's cosmopolitan history. The **Great Mosque (Qingzhensi)** in the northwest of the city near Xibeijiao subway station has a Chinese look, but it remains an active place of worship (non-Muslims may not enter).

Great Compassion Monastery (Dabeiyuansi), also in the northwest of the city, is Tianjin's most impressive Buddhist temple. The earthquake gave the temple a bad shake, but it has been restored.

Bordering the river not far to the south of the Dabeiyuan Monastery is the **Wanghailou Cathedral (Wanghailou Jiaotang).** Outside this solemn, dust-choked Gothic church, a plaque (in Chinese) commemorates an incident in 1870, when an irate mob burned the cathedral and the French Consulate. The notice relates that some 20 missionaries were killed after rumors circulated accusing the European Christian community of kidnapping children for nefarious purposes (in fact, the children were orphans), including human sacrifice. The cathedral was later rebuilt, torched again during the Boxer uprising, and rebuilt again. It suffered further during the Tangshan earthquake and also at the hands of the Red Guards who gave the church a battering during the Cultural Revolution.

Poking out from the bric-a-brac of Ancient Culture Street (see opposite) is the fabulous **Tianhou Temple (Tianhougong),** dedicated to Tianhou, the goddess of seafarers. The restored frescoes in the main temple show exploits from the life of Tianhou (also known as Niangniang or Mazu). Here, too, are models of Ming and Qing dynasty sailing ships from the provinces of Fujian and Zhejiang (where Tianhou is most actively worshipped). Fierce-looking weapons displayed on either side in the temple are there to protect her. At the rear is a small temple to Guanyin, goddess of mercy.

A block west stands the **Confucius Temple (Wenmiao),** a rather dry and mothballed monument to the sage. Confucius sits on his altar, surrounded in perpetuity by dust and ancient musical instruments. The temple sits toward the eastern edge of the old–formerly walled–town of Tianjin, marked at its center by the Drum Tower.

The massive **Xikai Cathedral (Xikai Jiaotang)** was originally dedicated to St. Vincent de Paul and was managed by missionary priests from the order he founded. Its towers sport green domes, the whole edifice a copy of Notre Dame de la Garde in Marseilles.

Markets

You can hunt for souvenirs and relics at the massively revamped **Ancient Culture Street,** near the Confucius Temple. Meant to re-create an ancient Chinese street, the buildings here have carved balconies, red- and green-painted shops, and curling tiled roofs. It's worth exploring for the occasional rarity, such as documents from the Cultural Revolution era (including 1960s pamphlets screaming, "Down with Deng Xiaoping!").

Tianjin's bustling **Antique Market** can be found on Shenyang Dao, south of Heping Lu. It operates every day but is at its busiest and most fascinating on Sundays.

Concession Architecture

As soon as you exit Tianjin train station you will see Liberation Bridge, leading to the much spruced up **British Concession** along Jiefang Nanlu, on the far side of the Hai River. The entire area is a treasure trove of stately European architecture. West of Liberation Bridge, the newly restored **Italian Concession** on the north side of the river has been converted to house restaurants and bars. In the south of Tianjin, the area known as **Wudadao** ("five big roads"), a district of European villa architecture from the early 20th century, makes for a pleasant walk or ride in one of the horse carriages that clop about the streets. ■

Tianjin by Bus

A very handy bus route that lassoes in most of Tianjin's sights is bus No. 600 (*$*), which leaves from the street behind Tianjin train station. Traveling in a huge loop, the bus passes within reach of Wanghailou Cathedral, Ancient Culture Street and Tianhou Temple, the Old Town, Xikai Cathedral, and Jiefang Nanlu (for the British Concession).

Confucius Temple

✉ 1 Dongmennei Dajie

Xikai Cathedral

✉ Binjiang Dao

🕒 Closed Mon.–Sat.

🚇 Subway: Yingkou Dao

Chengde

Called Jehol ("warm river") by the Manchus, the imperial resort of Chengde was established during the reign of the Kangxi emperor (*r.* 1662–1722) in the early 18th century. The spectacular complex, set on a sheltered river plain, was known as Bishu Shanzhuang, or "mountain hamlet for escaping the heat." Today it is called Chengde after the adjacent town.

The Putuozongcheng Temple was built to impress the Buddhist lamas of Tibet and Mongolia.

Chengde
99 D4
Imperial Resort: $$$$

CITS Visitor Information
3 Wulie Lu
0314 202-4816

The mountain-fringed resort, 159 miles (255 km) northeast of Beijing, was much expanded during the reign of the Kangxi emperor's grandson, the Qianlong emperor (*r.* 1736–1795). Work continued during the reign of Jiaqing (*r.* 1796–1820), but his death from a fire at the resort (ignited by a bolt of lightning, rumors said) tarnished Chengde's standing. The kiss of death came with the demise of the Xianfeng emperor here in suspicious circumstances in 1861. Chengde never recovered from its reputation for misfortune, and even the feeble last emperor, Puyi (see p. 40), refused to visit the resort, although he had nowhere to go as he fled from Beijing.

Chengde today is a sprawl of palaces, pavilions, temples, and monasteries. Though a number of buildings are in ruins, much survives and forms an impressive architectural museum.

A 6-mile (10 km) wall encloses the imperial resort. The main entrance is called Lizheng Men; another entrance (Dehui Men) pierces the wall to the east. Through the Lizheng Men you come to the **Main Palace (Zhenggong),** with its nine courtyards (nine being the number of heaven) set amid pines and rocks. It houses a museum of imperial memorabilia: furniture, costumes, and weapons of the period.

Leaving the palace by the north gate brings you to the main park, threaded by lakes. From here, you can see the wooded area to the west. The plain stretching to the north was the site of imperial hunting parties and archery competitions, and the lake to the east (divided into Ideal Lake and Clear Lake) is studded with temples and pavilions. The **Hall of Mist and Rain (Yanyulou)** sits on a small island hill in the north of the lake; it was once an imperial study.

On the eastern shore of the lake stands **Gold Mountain (Jinshan),** a small hill topped by the elegant hexagonal pagoda and temple, the **Building of God (Shangdilou),** built for the Kangxi emperor in imitation of the Jinshan Temple in Zhenjiang (see p. 167). Also on the lake, and erected as one of the Qianlong emperor's 36 beauty spots of the resort, are the **Water's Heart Pavilions (Shuixinxie).**

North of the lakes and visible from afar is the tall **Yongyousi Pagoda,** rising from the grounds of its vanished, namesake temple (destroyed by the Japanese).

Eight Outer Temples

The Eight Outer Temples (Waibamiao) lie north and east of the imperial resort (catch a bus from the road outside the resort's main gate). Of the original 12 temples, eight remain today, built mainly during the reign of the Qianlong emperor. Most were designed in non-Han style to impress visiting Tibetan and Mongol envoys.

The temples have suffered the ravages of time: Some were damaged during the civil war of the 1930s and 1940s, and some were marred by the war with

Culture Clash

In 1793, Lord Macartney and his embassy from Britain arrived at Chengde for an audience with the Qianlong emperor. Macartney's brief was to make diplomatic overtures and secure trade links with the Middle Kingdom.

The audience went awkwardly. Lord Macartney would only kowtow to the Chinese emperor if courtiers would likewise bow in front of a portrait of the English sovereign, George III. This request was refused. Despite the extravagant gifts presented to the emperor, his final message was, "We possess all things. I set no value on objects strange or ingenious, and have no use for your country's manufactures." This marked the beginning of a war of wills that saw Britain try to force trade on China. Ultimately, China would buckle and accept things foreign.

Japan, while others fell victim to the iconoclastic Cultural Revolution. This neglect is being slowly reversed, but you may find that some temples are closed or parts are off-limits. Sadly, many have been ransacked of their former treasures.

Largest is **Putuozongcheng Temple** *($$)* in the hills to the north of the imperial complex, built in 1771—a small-scale copy of the Dalai Lama's Potala Palace

Putuozongcheng Temple rises powerfully from the hills.

in Lhasa. It was built by the very religious Qianlong emperor in the hope that the Dalai Lama would visit Chengde (he didn't). The dagoba-topped temple is the largest in Chengde, containing 60 halls. Inscriptions in Tibetan, Mongolian, Manchurian, and Chinese illustrate the link with Potala Palace.

To the east of the Putuozongcheng Temple, the **Temple of Sumeru Happiness and Longevity (Xumifushouzhimiao)** *($$)* was built in honor of a visit from the sixth Panchen Lama in 1779. It imitated his Tibetan monastery in Shigatse. High outer walls with many windows surround the magnificent temple, adorned with a huge, dragon-encrusted roof.

INSIDER TIP:

While in Chengde, consider a side trip to the gorgeous Bashang Grassland, about 170 miles (274 km) northwest of the city.

—ZHONGHE ZHOU
National Geographic grantee

Tibetan motifs also dominate the **Temple of Universal Tranquillity (Puning Si)** *($$)* to the northeast, likewise styled after a Tibetan monastery. This is Chengde's most famous temple, celebrated for its hallmark attraction, the behemoth of a gilded statue of Guanyin in the huge Mahavira Hall up the steps at the rear. A staggering 72 feet (22 m) high, the mind-boggling statue is carved from five different woods and sports 42 arms. It is an awe-inspiring sight.

A few miles south is the circular, two-tiered roof of the **Temple of Universal Happiness (Pulesi)** *($$)*, which resembles Beijing's Hall of Prayer for Good Harvests at the Temple of Heaven (see pp. 74–75). Other temples include the **Anyuan Temple, Puren Temple, Shuxiang Temple,** and in Chengde itself, the Taoist **Guandi Temple,** west of Lizheng Men, the main gate to the imperial resort. ■

Luoyang

The ancient city of Luoyang, south of the Yellow River on its sweep through Henan Province, was capital to ten dynasties. China's first Buddhist temple opened its doors here, and the awesome endeavor of the Longmen Caves lies outside town.

Luoyang's eminence ended with its sacking by Jurchen invaders during the Northern Song dynasty and the fleeing of the court to Kaifeng (see p. 126). Communist-era industrial development has transformed the little town to a city of more than a million people. Artifacts and artwork, including some stunning jade pieces, in the **Luoyang Museum (Luoyang Bowuguan)** guide you through local history.

White Horse Temple

The enchanting White Horse Temple (Baimasi) *($$$)*, located 6 miles (10 km) east of Luoyang, is considered China's first Buddhist temple.

A colorful legend lies behind the temple's inception. When Luoyang was capital of the later Han dynasty, in A.D. 64, Emperor Ming had a dream. In his vision, a golden deity flew in front of his palace. Asking his advisers for an interpretation of this symbol, one replied that it was Buddha. The king promptly dispatched men to India to bring back scriptures.

After several years, they returned on two white horses with sutras (scriptures of Buddhism). These were ostensibly the first Buddhist writings to come to China. A temple, named for the two horses, was built to house the manuscripts. The story is probably apocryphal. Buddhism was already finding a tentative toehold in China along trade routes during this period, although the faith did not flourish in the Middle Kingdom for several centuries.

The present buildings date from a later time, but the timeline of the temple dates to the first century A.D. Within the temple are two **tombs,** the final resting place of two Buddhist missionaries from India, and the adorable **Qiyun Pagoda.** ■

Luoyang
Map 99 C2

CITS Visitor Information
Changjiang Lu
0379 432-3212

Luoyang Museum
298 Zhongzhou Zhonglu

EXPERIENCE: The Peony Festival

Luoyang's best known celebration is its annual Peony Festival, held in **Luoyang National Peony Garden** just outside town along the road that leads to Luoyang Airport. Splashes of color saturate the garden as soon as the flowers start to bloom, which can be any time from late March through April.

During the festival, which takes place April 15–25, hawkers at the park's entrance sell huge clumps of colorful peonies, but be careful: The flowers may be artificial, so check carefully if you consider buying them. Within the park, girls and even men walk around with floral bouquets and flowers in their hair.

The Peony Festival is popular with Chinese and tourists, and crowds can get intense, with long lines forming just to enter. A light show is held in the evening.

Longmen Caves

The Longmen statuary outside Luoyang in Henan Province is an exhilarating legacy from master Buddhist sculptors. Like the Yungang Caves and the Mogao Caves at Dunhuang, Longmen constitutes one of the most treasured reliquaries of Buddhist cave art in China.

Legend tells how the cliffs of Longmen suddenly appeared, adorned with Buddhist statues.

The majority of the statues took shape between 473 and 755. The colossal endeavor began when the capital of the Northern Wei moved from Datong to Luoyang (see p. 121). The hard rock of the cliffs along the Yi River, 9 miles (14.5 km) from Luoyang, provided an ideal site for further carving.

Among the Buddhas and bodhisattvas recorded in stone are Guanyin, Amitabha, Sakyamuni, Maitreya, and other celestial beings (see pp. 82–83). Buddhas from the Northern Wei are ethereal and subtle, divine and idealistic, while those from the Tang appear more mundane. Also reflected in the carvings is a maturing of technique that accompanied successive dynasties. The Tang dynasty empress Wu Zetian (*r.* 698–705), a famous patron of Buddhism (see p. 34), commissioned a number of pieces.

Scars of History

A sense of loss and defilement may accompany your admiration of the carvings. The large number of headless Buddhas and bodhisattvas is a depressing statistic. Many were plundered for sale to antiques collectors, but many appear to have had their faces smashed off, possibly during anti-Buddhist episodes. Years of neglect have also taken their toll. This damage creates a powerful sense of sacrilege, but there is an equally strong sense of immortality in their remains, partly due to the toughness of the rock they are chiseled from and partly from the sheer magnitude of the undertaking.

Altogether, there are nearly 1,400 caves, 2,800 inscriptions, and 100,000 statues (the smallest about an inch/2 cm high). Among the scars of repeated vandalism and the onslaught of the elements, flakes of paint still gleam from ceilings and walls, and the larger Buddhas are largely still whole.

Many of the grottoes are high up and accessed by steps and walkways. It is difficult to get a good view of the statues, though, as fences keep you at a distance and the English translations of the informative signs are hard to read. A journey to Dongshan on the other side of the Yi River (cross the bridge to the east side) puts the undertaking into colossal relief. Dongshan contains a further net work of caves worth exploration

The Caves

The Longmen caves are clustered together, generally reflecting the period in which they appeared. From the entrance at the north end of the site, you walk along the west bank of the river just below the caves. The three **Bingyang Caves,** near the entrance, are some of the earliest carvings here, dating mainly from the Northern Wei.

Farther along is the spectacular **Cave of the Ten Thousand Buddhas (Wanfodong),** from the late seventh century. It is crammed with small Buddha figures and a large central statue.

In the **Lotus Flower Cave (Lianhuadong),** whose ceiling is decorated with a lotus flower, stands a headless Buddha that was carved in 527.

The Tang dynasty **Ancestor Worshipping Cave** is the most impressive sight at Longmen. The central statue is 55 feet (16.5 m) tall and flanked by bodhisattvas and a ferocious guardian figure. The face of the central figure supposedly captured the visage of Empress Wu Zetian.

INSIDER TIP:

Try to visit the Longmen caves in the morning rather than in the afternoon to avoid the shadows that blanket the caves later in the day.

—MU SU
National Geographic writer

The size of the larger Buddha statues reveals the diligent efforts of the Longmen sculptors. A fascinating set of large, unfinished Buddhas reveals the deities emerging unformed from the rock, suggesting the Buddhist themes of metamorphosis, transcendence, and eternal change.

The **Medical Prescription Cave (Yaofangdong)** is carved with small medical prescriptions; the ancient Guyang Cave was first carved in 495. The **Shiku Cave (Shikudong),** decorated with ceremonial figures, was carved during the Northern Wei. ■

Longmen Caves
99 C2
$$$$

CITS Visitor Information
Changjiang Lu
0379 432-3212

GETTING TO THE CAVES: The Longmen caves lie 9 miles (14.5 km) south of Luoyang. They are easily reached by bus No. 53 or No. 81.

Gongfu

Whether it is esoteric or athletic, *quanfa* (Chinese boxing) is a mysterious and captivating art. The enticing path to *gongfu* (which you may know as kung fu) is a strenuous one for its disciples, fraught with hardship and littered with failure. For the spectator, it is a colorful and dazzling performance that offers a glimpse of transcendent skill.

A monk demonstrates *gongfu* at the Shaolin Temple.

Skill

Gongfu simply means "skill." This can mean perfection in calligraphy, painting, martial arts, or any other endeavor. It has, however, become irretrievably embedded in the notion of the fearless and exceedingly skilled fighter.

The concept has been warped by its cinematic variant: the high-kicking, wrathful, and fearless hero. This perception swamps *gwoon* (Chinese kung fu schools, *guan* in Mandarin) the world over with suspect personalities.

The high-kicking and elastic fighter of the movies could not be further from real gongfu. True gongfu stresses not awesome flexibility but more the ability to change quickly from ethereal to solid. It is an internal ability, rather than an external piece of equipment. Flashy displays often belong to those who have lost their way on the road to mastery. The Chinese call those who make a lot of noise "half a bottle of vinegar," for the insubstantial sloshing sound it makes. True skill in gongfu can be elusive and difficult to retain, once discovered.

Patience

Gongfu stresses depth, rather than what is "up in the air." "Pretty flowers, but no roots" is another Chinese saying, describing what is visually impressive but lacks solidity. This is perhaps best demonstrated by the emphasis paid to standing, for long periods, in fixed postures. It develops the "root" of the student and the circulation of *qi* or "energy" within the body, and it also instills an essential ingredient into the student; only through patience and endurance can gongfu be attained.

The rewards of gongfu appear in equal measure to the amount of work put in. Even students of the "soft" or "internal" arts of *taiji quan* (supreme ultimate boxing, also known as tai chi) and *bagua zhang* ("eight trigram palm"), an esoteric Taoist martial art that employs the palm as a striking weapon, rather than the fist, have to invest pain in pursuit of their art.

Students who attain true gongfu are physically and mentally different from the disciples who first set foot on the path to skill. Not only are the students more aware of their body and its capabilities, but they have also endured a long and punishing voyage where the virtues of perseverance and reward are understood. Furthermore, they are no longer necessarily aware that they have skill for it feels inherent. Humility results from this.

Hard & Soft Schools

Fighting tactics tend to fall into two groups, the "soft" or "internal" school and the "hard" or "external" school. Taiji quan, with its slow moves and ethereal lightness, typifies the former group, while *baimei quan* (white eyebrow boxing), characterized by ferocious and rapid strikes and grabs, belongs to the latter.

In its purest form, softness in boxing equals nothingness and is a Taoist pursuit (see p. 48). The soft arts of taiji quan, bagua zhang, and *xingyi quan* (body-mind boxing) all take Taoism as their guiding creed. The hard arts such as *laohu quan* (tiger boxing) and white eyebrow boxing are Buddhist in inspiration.

Softness may seem like a recipe for defeat, but the aim is to approximate a vacuum at one moment and solidify the next, so an attacker is led into nothingness and then repelled by an attack. In the soft armory, taiji is the most weightless, while bagua zhang is weightier and xingyi quan is the most aggressive.

In practice, many schools mix hard and soft moves, and *wing chun* is an example. Invented in the 18th century by a nun called Ngmui from the Shaolin Temple (see pp. 128–129), the art combines evasiveness and yielding with hard and fast, snappy punches. Wing chun is what Bruce Lee studied, and it is one of the more successful arts for the beginner who seeks a speedy acquisition of skills.

In *zui quan* (drunken boxing) the student moves as if drunk, a state of mind that relaxes the body and deceives the aggressor, who is lured into a trap. A high degree of flexibility is necessary for this style. Other styles include praying mantis boxing, five ancestors boxing, red sand palm, wuji, white crane boxing, monkey boxing, and long boxing.

If you want to find a teacher, a multitude of martial arts schools can be found at the Shaolin Temple and in Shanghai, Beijing, Hong Kong, and other large cities.

Every style of *gongfu* enhances spiritual awareness and demands physical strength.

Kaifeng

The walled city of Kaifeng served as capital to seven dynasties, including a glorious period during the Northern Song (960–1127). Once prosperous and cosmopolitan, Kaifeng is an attractive city still decorated with a smattering of traditional architecture, and a concerted effort has been made to restore the buildings that reveal its imperial heritage.

Kaifeng
99 C2
CITS Visitor Information
98 Yingbin Lu
0378 393-4702

Da Xiangguo Temple
Ziyou Lu
$$

Yanqing Temple
Guanqian Jie
$

Most of its historic sites lie within the city walls. **Da Xiangguo Temple** was originally founded in A.D. 555. During Kaifeng's heyday as capital of the Northern Song, it was China's foremost temple. Da Xiangguo was washed away in 1642 when the Yellow River was deliberately allowed to flood the city in a botched attempt to halt the invading Manchu army. Rebuilt by the Manchu victors, the temple resumed its position as the focal point of the city. Dine at the temple vegetarian restaurant for a taste of China's Buddhist cuisine.

The temple's bell tower contains a vast bronze bell and an umbrella that belonged to Cixi, empress dowager. The many-armed figure of Guanyin, goddess of mercy, in the octagonal pavilion at the rear was carved from a single piece of ginkgo wood.

About half a mile (0.8 km) to the west on Dazhifang Jie is the tiny Taoist **Yanqing Temple,** badly damaged by the floodwaters of the Yellow River. The **Pavilion of the Jade Emperor** (supreme god of Taoism) remains.

Rising up in its namesake park just within the city walls in the northeast of Kaifeng, the slender **Iron Pagoda (Tieta)** *($)* is wrapped in rust-colored tiles. The tiles on the lower flanks of this octagonal pagoda display damaged Buddhist images. The temple that was attached has vanished. You can climb to the top of the pagoda for unobstructed views over the city.

The Qing dynasty **Dragon Pavilion** stands within Longting Park in the northwest. The park can be reached by walking along the reconstructed **Imperial Way (Songdu Zhengjie),** the Song capital's main thoroughfare. ■

Tracking Down Kaifeng's Jewish Heritage

Until the late 19th century, the city of Kaifeng had a thriving Jewish community, which may have originally come along the Silk Road from central Asia. Matteo Ricci, the Jesuit missionary, was the first Westerner to stumble upon the city's Jews in the early 17th century.

Sadly, little remains today of Kaifeng's unique Jewish heritage, although a handful of Chinese Jews survive in town.

All that remains of the city's synagogue *(youtai jiaotang)* is a sorry-looking well beneath a modern iron lid. The building once stood near or under the No. 4 People's Hospital on Beixing Tujie.

Three stelae from the synagogue recording the history of the Jews in Kaifeng are on display upstairs in the Kaifeng Museum *(26 Yingbin Lu, closed Mon., $$ to see stelae).*

Songshan

Songshan, the mountainous home of the legendary fighting monks of the Chan (Zen) Buddhist Shaolin Temple, is also the central mountain of the five sacred Taoist peaks and site of possibly China's oldest Taoist shrine–Zhongyue Temple.

Chinese throughout the country worship the compassionate goddess Guanyin.

A mile (1.6 km) to the northeast of Dengfeng–the usual point of departure for tours of Songshan–is the **Songyang Academy (Songyang Shuyuan),** founded in the Song dynasty (960–1279) and one of the four great Confucian academies (it was previously both a Buddhist and a Taoist monastery). The other academies are in the provinces of Hunan and Jiangxi. Despite being a major Confucian monument, Songyang offers little to see, apart from two (originally three) old twisted cypresses. These trees were promoted to the rank of general by the Han emperor Wudi, when he ascended the mountain in 110 B.C.

Three miles (5 km) farther to the northwest is the pagoda of the **Songyue Temple.** The pagoda and the temple, which date from the sixth century A.D., are sadly crumbling away. Empress Wu Zetian (see p. 34) was a guest during the Tang dynasty, when she came to Songshan to offer ritual sacrifices.

Heading northeast from the Songyang Academy, you will reach **Central Peak,** the highest of Songshan's mountains at 4,893 feet (1,490 m). To the east of Dengfeng is the start of another route to the summit. Here you will find

Songshan
Map 99 C2

CITS Visitor Information
Address: Beihuan Lu (Dengfeng)
Tel: 0371 6288-3442

the Taoist **Zhongyue Temple (Zhongyuemiao)** *($$)*. It claims a venerable ancestry, reaching back to 215 B.C., although all the present buildings are of a later date. The two carved pillars south of the main temple were erected in the second century A.D.

Shaolin Temple

The warrior monks of the Shaolin Temple are synonymous with Chinese *gongfu* (see pp. 124–125). Buddhism and martial arts are their dawn-to-dusk staples. Theme of countless films and schoolboy make-believe, Shaolin's mystery emanates from the very real religious fraternity that worships here.

The Shaolin Temple dates from the fifth century A.D.

The Shaolin Temple, on the slopes of Songshan between Luoyang and Zhengzhou, was founded in the fifth century A.D. by a monk named Ba Tuo, a martial arts exponent.

Bodhidharma, the Indian sage who founded the Chan (Zen) sect of Buddhism, a tolerant strain of the religion, visited in 527. He developed a series of physical exercises for the monks to perform after their long periods of seated meditation. The seeds for the great flourishing of *wushu* (martial arts) at the temple had been sown. Unlike karate, tae kwon do, or kick boxing, the Shaolin martial arts foster a religious sense and a way of life.

The temple welcomed artistic and idiosyncratic monks who were refused by other monasteries. It also became a refuge for hundreds of soldiers, militiamen, and bandits, who were often skilled in the fighting arts. These regular arrivals helped protect the temple against the threat of outside attack, while growing imperial patronage added to its fortunes.

The monks of Shaolin were sometimes called upon to fight for the court, and a standing army of monk-soldiers was formed. By the time of the Ming dynasty, the monks were at their zenith, only to face a decline during the Qing dynasty. The temple suffered numerous sackings and torchings in its history, including a visit from Red Guards in the 1960s.

Today, thousands of would-be Shaolin monks come to the temple, often for what amounts to a crash course in self-defense. The temple's accountants long ago noted there was a yuan or two to be made out of opening up to the masses. Martial arts schools have sprung up around the temple, and you may see their students practicing in the precincts. Many foreigners also enroll in the hope of becoming tomorrow's David Carradine, star of the TV series *Kung Fu,* but some sadly get fleeced and return disconsolate.

INSIDER TIP:

In addition to the temple, Songshan has plenty of other ancient sites that are worth spending an afternoon exploring.

–ZHU JUN
Architect & historian

Shaolin Temple

99 C2

Songshan, Henan Province

$$$$$

The Temple: The main courtyard bristles with a series of commemorative stelae, some from as far away as fighting clubs in England. This testifies to Shaolin's powerful sway over the global imagination. Three golden Buddhas and an effigy of Bodhidharma are displayed in the main temple. Bodhidharma stands, slightly obscured by a velvet curtain to the right-hand side, and can be identified by his beard and Indian countenance.

Toward the rear of the temple is **Standing Snow Pavilion,** where a monk named Huihe cut off his arm while standing in the snow to commune closely with the substance of Chan (Zen) Buddhism. Adjacent **Wenshu Hall** houses a stone whose surface has captured the likeness of a bodhisattva.

The deep impressions on the floor of the **Pilu Pavilion** behind, whose walls are covered with murals, were made by the feet of legions of fighting monks. The **Guanyin Temple** to the right displays the famous frescoes of Shaolin monks fighting.

Chuipu Hall displays large ceramic figures depicting gongfu and meditational postures. A number of different forms of Shaolin boxing are represented, including Luohan fist, a vigorous style named after the famous Luohan of Buddhist mythology (see p. 83).

A number of the "monks" have taken up begging, although the rest continue their ascetic, disciplined fighting existence, despite the flurry of commerce around them.

The famous **Forest of Dagobas** lies 650 feet (200 m) up from the main temple, but it is not difficult to locate (follow the map on your ticket). Each of the hundreds of small dagobas commemorates a notable monk.

A cable car from the temple takes you into the Songshan range to the west for walks among cliffs and woods.

Visiting the Temple: Thousands of gongfu enthusiasts visit Shaolin every year. Behind the flashing cameras and souvenir stalls they find a great monument, still the home of all the Eastern fighting arts. The weekends see the temple at its commercial worst, so plan to visit on a weekday if possible. ■

Confucianism

The influences of China's greatest social philosopher, Confucius, upon Chinese values and political doctrine have been colossal. Furthermore, his teachings found fertile ground in other Far Eastern countries. The Chinese characteristics of frugality, diligence, and veneration of the family structure owe much to the Confucian vision.

The once reviled philosopher Confucius is now basking in newfound popularity.

Confucius (551–479 B.C.), whose name comes from the Chinese pronunciation of his name, Kong Fuzi, or Master Kung, was born into poverty in the state of Lu (in present-day Shandong). He lived during the pre-Qin era, a period of great division when China was assailed by immoral government, internecine strife, and oppression (see p. 28). Despair prompted Confucius to seek a code of ethics that would encourage rulers to govern fairly and win the hearts of the people.

There was little of the metaphysical about his philosophy, which hoped to offer rational solutions to the problems of the age. Central to his beliefs was respect for the past and for authority, whether the elders of the family or leaders of the social hierarchy. Confucius stressed the importance of education and the study of classical texts and rite; his teachings formed the basis of the grueling civil service examinations all the way up to the 20th century.

Permeating his teachings was a strong sense of humanity and sympathy that heralded an escape from superstition. The emphasis on respect for your elders and the political hierarchy, however, encouraged the static nature of Chinese society. Confucius never lived to see the practical application of his theories and achieved fame only in the centuries after his death. Even so, he attracted around him a group of disciples to whom he conveyed his body of thought. Confucius encouraged his disciples to better themselves through the study of poetry, music, history, and the rites *(li)* or ceremonies that formulated the etiquette of the period. He hoped his converts would fashion a society governed by principles of uprightness and honesty.

After his death, his teachings were brought together by his disciples into a volume called *Lunyu (The Analects)*. Later Confucianism was championed by the philosophers Mencius (372–289 B.C.) and Xunzi (ca 313–238 B.C.).

Confucianism is often contrasted with Taoism (see p. 48): The former system embraces the human world, while the latter seeks to escape it. Taoism is nature-bound and spontaneous, while Confucius's goal was a utilitarian philosophy; they represent the two sides of the human mind, one cognitive, the other emotional. The balance between both systems creates a satisfying order.

Confucianism Through History

Confucius has ridden a roller coaster of praise and condemnation through successive dynasties. The Qin, who unified China, condemned his works to the bonfire, but the Han dragged them out of the embers. The Wei Jin era (A.D. 220–420) was a period of metaphysical flights of fancy, and Confucius was outclassed. The 19th-century Taiping (see p. 39) were zealously anti-Confucian, as were the Red Guards in the next century, but today the sage is championed. The cycle of condemnation and worship points to the ambivalence in Chinese society regarding Confucius. Although a rationalist philosophy, Confucianism failed to evolve. Its patriarchal nature, coupled with the respect accorded to long-deceased ancestors, led to its gradual but steady ossification.

Confucianism Today

Confucius today is enjoying another upswing in popularity. Though Confucianism represents an anachronistic impediment to China's drive to fully implement science and technology and would seem to be in opposition to the Chinese Communist Party's autocratic governance, it is also lauded as a corrective to the spiraling greed and selfishness that are overwhelming Chinese society. A fundamental reading of Confucius sits awkwardly with modern China, but the Chinese Communist Party has redirected the sage's emphasis on harmony toward its own obsession with removing evidence of social discontent. Confucius has also become an ambassador of sorts for Chinese culture abroad, with Confucius institutes opening across the world. The Chinese Communist Party has in fact become so recently enamored with Confucius that a huge statue of the philosopher is earmarked for Tiananmen Square, only four decades or so after statues of Kongzi (Confucius) were put to the torch.

A multitude of Confucian temples (often called *wenmiao*) lie scattered across China, but it is at Qufu (see p. 132), Confucius's birthplace, that the finest example can be found. This is a place of sacred pilgrimage not just for millions of Chinese but for devoted bands of Japanese and Koreans who also flock here.

The Confucius Mansions in Qufu

Qufu

Qufu, the hometown of Confucius and his family and capital of the state of Lu during the Zhou and Han dynasties, is a pilgrimage site for Chinese, Japanese, and Korean visitors, with some of China's finest examples of Confucian temple architecture.

Direct descendants of Confucius can still be buried in the Confucian Forest.

Qufu
99 D2

The importance of Confucius (see pp. 130–131) to the cultures of the Far East is inestimable, but the philosophical resonances require a Confucian upbringing to appreciate fully. What can be enjoyed, however, are the architecture and the sense of history permeating the place. The Chinese rank the town alongside the Forbidden City and Chengde in the importance of its buildings.

The **Confucius Temple (Kongmiao)** *($$$$)* has grown considerably since its humble inception as a memorial hall, with the complex now covering a large part of central Qufu. Inside you will find twisted cypress trees and more than a thousand stelae, both hallmarks of Confucian temples (see pp. 156–157). Also rooted in the grounds is a juniper tree planted by Confucius himself; the pavilion from which he taught his students is here, too. The impressive **Dacheng Hall (Dachengdian)** is the hub of the complex and the site of Confucian rites and festivals celebrating the philosopher.

The **Confucius Mansions (Kongfu)** *($$$)*, just to the east of the temple, was the abode of the aristocratic Kong class, who apparently lived in great luxury, protected by their own laws and imperial favor. Just over a mile (1.6 km) to the north of Qufu lies the **Confucian Forest (Konglin)** *($$$)*, the burial place of Confucius and his family and heirs. You can either walk there or take bus No. 1. ■

A Climb up Taishan

Mount Tai in Shandong Province is the holiest of China's revered Taoist mountains. The twisting climb to its summit is the *dao* or "the Way," a voyage and a metaphor for life, making the ascent a spiritual journey.

The mountain is a place of creation. It was commonly believed that the sun began its daily trek from Taishan, and many pilgrims stay overnight at one of the guesthouses on the summit to catch the famed dawn. The souls of the dead also flee to Taishan. Much of the allegory and legend associated with Mount Tai predates Taoism, rooted in a deeper, more primordial ancestry.

The Chinese take climbing Taishan (5,000 feet/1,524 m) seriously. Streaming up its slopes are the old and decrepit, businessmen from Taiwan, Hong Kong accountants, peasants, soldiers, and tourists. Pilgrims flow past sinewy porters making more routine assaults with bottled drinks, food, and building materials. In ages past, devout climbers would knock their heads (kowtow) on the stone steps during their ascent.

At least one climb is a mandatory pilgrimage for Taoists. Shandong ("east of the mountains") Chinese are justifiably proud of Taishan, and they look down on China's other sacred peaks.

The mount, being in the eastern realm, is further governed by the Green Dragon of *fengshui* lore (see p. 256), lord of springs and streams. The emperor would come to Taishan to offer sacrifices to the god of Taishan and seek his blessing in times of crisis or lack of rain.

The ravines, gullies, twisted outcrops, trees, and temples of Taishan are also infused with the spirit of the Princess of the Azure Clouds, a Taoist deity (and daughter of the god of Taishan) worshipped in this region.

Taishan

Map: 99 D2

Admission: $$$$

Visitor Information

Address: 22 Hongmen Lu

Phone: 0538 218-7989

A seemingly endless path of steps greets pilgrims at the foot of Taishan.

The Route

It's not Everest and you won't need ropes, but the 6,660 steps will knock the stuffing out of the unfit. If you feel weak-kneed, glance at the bright-eyed, aged wayfarers and the one-legged hopping up alongside you. The Pan Lu, or "pilgrim's road," is marked with inscriptions and calligraphy.

You have a choice of two paths up Mount Tai: the central or the western route. The **central route** is the most popular with visitors, littered as it is with places of historical interest; along this path the emperor sauntered on horseback. The **western route** is longer, more circuitous, and with fewer historical sites, but it is scenically pleasant.

Regardless of the route you take, you should start your journey from the **Dai Temple** in Tai'an, at the foot of the mount.

Sunrise from the Summit of Taishan

The Chinese say you'll live to 100 if you climb holy Taishan, China's most sacred Taoist peak. The most easterly of the four Taoist peaks, the mountain is the ideal place to see the sun rise. You will need to spend the night on or near the summit (or climb up the mountain at night); the Shenqi Hotel (a very short walk from Riguan Feng—the viewing point for the sunrise) can put you up for the night and wrap you up in a thick jacket to fight off the bone-numbing cold. Be warned that crowds can be dense and there can be quite a hubbub, so definitely avoid weekends and big holiday periods.

INSIDER TIP:

Stone steps cut into the side of Taishan lead to spectacular, ancient temples, where you can also spend the night.

—SIMON WORRALL
National Geographic writer

The temple, a huge, walled complex of halls, cypresses, and stelae, has a history reaching back 2,000 years. The main temple is the **Palace of Heavenly Blessing,** dedicated to the god of Taishan. It contains a retouched Song dynasty fresco depicting the journeying god in the form of an emperor.

Leave the temple to start your ascent of the central route and pass Daizong archway along Hongmen Lu. The **Pool to the Cloud Mother (The Queen Mother of the West)** is marked by a small nunnery. Ahead, you will see the archway of **Yitianmen** ("first gate of heaven") precedes this inscription: "the place where Kongzi (Confucius) began to climb."

The temple of **Red Gate Palace (Hongmen)** pays homage to the Princess of the Azure Clouds. Past the tower of the **Building of 10,000 Immortals (Wanxianlou)** rises a revolutionary monument, a jarring effigy of socialist China (Mao climbed Taishan). Beyond that lies **Doumu Hall (Doumugong),** the Nunnery of the Bushel Mother, the Taoist equivalent of Guanyin (goddess of mercy). A path twists down to your east, leading to a carving of the Buddhist Diamond Sutra on the mountainside, unusual considering this is principally a Taoist mountain.

Horse Turn Ridge marks the point where the horse of Emperor Zhen Zong (*r.* 998–1023) died. Pilgrims drag themselves up to **Zhongtianmen** ("middle gate of heaven"), where a cable car awaits those gasping for breath. This is a major resting post and the climb's midpoint. Zhongtianmen is a bit of a circus, like much of Taishan, but try to look beyond the cola vendors and hawkers.

Continuing up, cross over **Cloud Step Bridge** and ahead is the **Five Pines Pavilion (Wusongting),** marking the spot where Emperor Qinshi Huangdi, invoking the blessings of the mountain, instead ran into a tremendous thunderstorm. He sheltered under pines and promptly promoted them to the rank of ministers of the fifth degree. You may need divine intervention to scale the steep **Path of Eighteen Bends,** which ends with the temptingly close but ever distant **Nantianmen** ("south gate of heaven").

You still have a short way to go to get to the summit, where the small **Azure Clouds Temple (Bixiaci)** finally awaits the triumphant pilgrims. The **Jade Emperor Temple (Yuhuangding)** stands at the highest point of Taishan. Below is the **Wordless Stela,** whose writing has long been worn away by inquisitive hands.

If you are planning to see the sun rise, the assembly point is the **Gongbei Rock.** In times past, devout pilgrims would throw themselves off the edge of the peak in a religious trance. ■

Taoist shrines pepper the slopes of sacred Taishan.

Qingdao

The refreshing town of Qingdao ("green island"), on the Shandong Peninsula, is dotted with parks, caressed by ocean breezes, and heavy with the aroma of the sea and kebabs (the local delicacy). This port is also home to world-famous Qingdao (Tsingtao) beer. Branded "China's Switzerland" because of its European heritage, Qingdao boasts a jumbled fabric of styles that architectural enthusiasts will admire.

Qingdao's picturesque pier entices many people out for a nighttime stroll along the water.

Qingdao
99 E2

CITS Visitor Information

73 Xianggang Xilu

0532 8389-2065

Sleepy Qingdao had a rude awakening at the end of the 19th century, when it became the focus of foreign ambitions. As China was sliced apart by the Western powers, the Germans joined the land-grabbing game in 1897 and occupied the port after the murder of two German missionaries. Qingdao woke to find its streets cobbled, the town electrified, a university in place, and the famous brewery installed. A railroad snaked to the provincial capital, Jinan, and heavyset Bavarian architecture followed wholesale.

The Japanese took delight at the prospect of a modernized port on the Shandong Peninsula, and they successfully wrested Qingdao from German clutches at the end of World War I. Qingdao

(continued on p. 140)

A Walk Around Qingdao

Qingdao is not a large town, and the most interesting sights can be enjoyed while ambling through its pleasant streets rather than by racing between points. The walk will take you through the picturesque reaches of Qingdao and its historic German area.

Zhanqiao Pier to St. Michael's

Start your walking tour of Qingdao by strolling up Zhanqiao—the pier reaching out into Qingdao Bay—to the **Huilan Pavilion** ❶ at its tip. Look out over the bay to the southeast and you can see the **Little Green Isle (Xiao Qingdao),** which lends its name to the town. The pavilion is the symbol of Qingdao and graces the label of Tsingtao beer brewed in town. In summer you will see vendors advertising speedboat trips around the bay and beyond.

Just west of Zhanqiao is **No. 6 Bathing Beach,** a stretch of beach that is active in the early hours with locals exercising and children playing.

Heading north up Zhongshan Lu (opposite the pier), you will pass a number of kebab sellers serving up their irresistible snacks. Go for the ones with the crowds out front: Try the lamb *(yangrouchuan)*, pork *(zhurouchuan)*,

Also see area map p. 99
➤ Zhanqiao
4 hours
3.5 miles (5.5 km)
➤ Huashilou

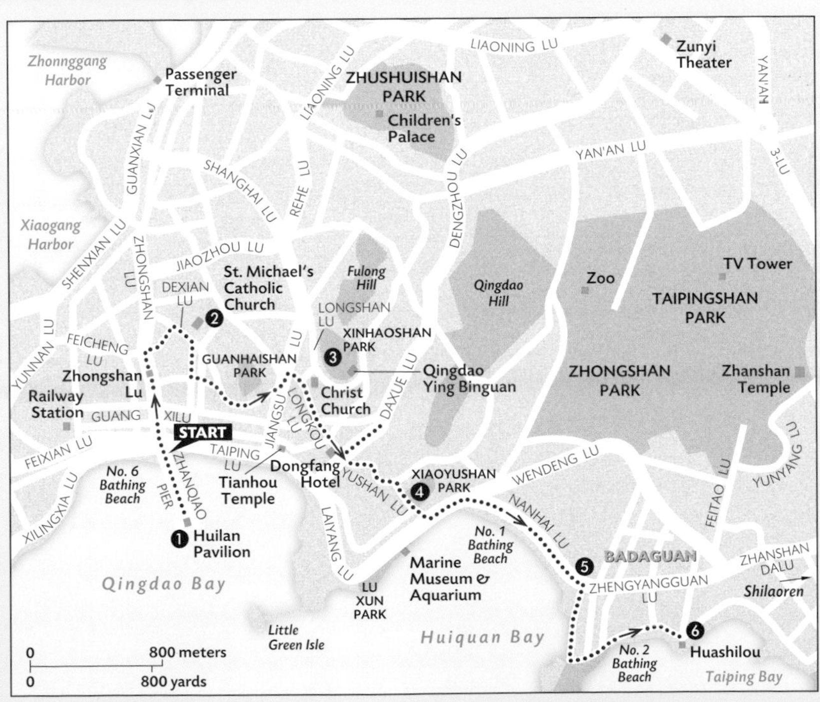

or squid *(diankao youyu)*; grab a stool, a drink, and enjoy. This is an inexpensive and appetizing way to dine.

Continue up **Zhongshan Lu**—once a premier shopping street until all the money went east to the new commercial area of Qingdao—and take Feicheng Lu to your right, which leads uphill to **St. Michael's Catholic Church (Tianzhu Jiaotang)** ❷ *($)*. This twin-spired church dominates the town, and it still holds regular Sunday services. A couple of Red Guards fell to their deaths while trying to knock the crosses off the steeples during the Cultural Revolution; the crosses were later hidden by locals in the hills around Qingdao. Next to the church stands a convent. A daily fish market sets up nearby in the former German Concession.

INSIDER TIP:

Zhongshan Park is home to a Buddhist temple and several gardens. Visit in late April or early May for the annual Cherry Blossom Festival.

—MARY STEPHANOS
National Geographic contributor

"Red Tiles, Green Trees"

From St. Michael's, walk south down Zhejiang Lu, over Qufu Lu (named after Confucius's birthplace), and turn left (east) onto Hubei Lu. The road twists south and becomes Yishui Lu. There is a charming diversion not far from here up to the top of the minute **Guanhaishan Park (Guanhaishan Gongyuan),** where you are rewarded with an expansive view over the red-tiled rooftops of Qingdao and out to sea. A plaque (in Chinese) states that the park was originally used as a golf course by the Germans. The park is not easy to find. From Hubei Lu, roads corkscrew up to the small summit; turn left into Guanhai Lu, which twists around the hilly park (you will find steps leading up to the park).

NOT TO BE MISSED:

St. Michael's Catholic Church • Qingdao Ying Binguan • Christ Church • Xiaoyushan • Huashilou

Keep going along Yishui Lu to Jiangsu Lu; then take Longkou Lu (Dragon's Mouth Road) south, which runs south of **Xinhaoshan Park (Xinhaoshan Gongyuan)** ❸. In the eastern section of the park is the former hotel known as the **Qingdao Ying Binguan** *($)*, Qingdao's most prized chunk of German architecture that is now a museum. Originally built for the German governor, the ex-hotel once hosted Mao Zedong as a guest. The interior is a snapshot of the early 20th century, replete with dark wood paneling and a German grand piano made in 1876. The building's exterior is constructed from block-like stone, similar to many other Teutonic vestiges visible around the west of town.

Opposite the park you will see the patina-green-towered Protestant **Christ Church (Jidu Jiaotang)** with its fine, white clockface. Sledgehammer-wielding Red Guards smashed the stained glass of this evangelical church, built in 1910, during the Cultural Revolution. The interior is typically austere and Lutheran, but the outside is impressively well kept. The church is generally accessible, and you can climb the clock tower for views out over the sea.

Continuing south down Longkou Lu, you will pass the **Dongfang Hotel** on your right. It is worth taking a short diversion up Daxue Lu (University Road), similarly notable for its historic architecture, including the German buildings of the Haiyang Daxue ("ocean university").

Qingdao's *hongwa lüshu* (red tiles, green trees) make a splendid panorama.

Backtrack to the continuation of Longkou Lu on the south side of Daxue Lu. This is the rather steep Yushan Lu, which takes you to the picturesque small park of **Xiaoyushan** ("little fish mountain") ❹ *($)*. The peak is graced by a three-tiered pagoda (Lanchaoge), which once served as an observation tower. From the peak you can see all around the *hongwa lüshu* (literally "red tiles, green trees") that give Qingdao its charming picture-postcard appeal.

The Waterfront

Yushan Lu leads to Laiyang Lu, running east along the waterfront. **Lu Xun Park (Lu Xun Gongyuan),** named after China's most famous modern writer (see p. 179), is to your right. Speedboats also muster here for trips across the bay (worth considering if the sun is out). Carrying on east brings you shortly to **No. 1 Bathing Beach** and, just beyond that, the smart **Badaguan** ❺ area, a shady, tree-lined haven of sanatoriums and quiet guesthouses. This sheltered area of villa-lined streets is worth strolling around.

Overlooking Taiping Bay is **No. 2 Bathing Beach,** a quieter and more secluded beach. At its easternmost end stands the magnificent castle-like **Huashilou ❻,** otherwise known by locals as the **Chiang Kai-shek Building** (the Kuomintang leader stayed here in 1947). This was the former German governor's residence, modeled on a German palace. You can visit the grounds and rooms of this marvelously Teutonic and brave folly. The bird's-eye view out to sea from the roof is excellent.

The building stands on the rise up to **Zhongshan Park (Zhongshan Gongyuan),** previously called Mount Diederich by Qingdao's German colonials. To the northeast of Zhongshan Park is **Taipingshan Park (Taipingshan Gongyuan),** where you will find the **zoo (Dongwuyuan),** the **Zhanshan Temple,** and the **TV Tower (Dianshita),** capped by a revolving restaurant.

slipped back into Chinese hands in 1922, returning to the Japanese between 1938 and 1945 during the war with Japan. Since 1950, Qingdao has developed rapidly, and today this wealthy enclave makes Shandong one of China's most dynamic provinces. The walk on pp. 137–139 offers the best way to enjoy the sights.

through walls on Laoshan. Rumor has it that the first emperor of the Qin dynasty visited Laoshan in search of the pill of immortality. The magic no doubt still permeates the local water, for Laoshan is famed far and wide for the springs that put the crispness into Qingdao beer.

The famous Chinese beer Tsingtao is brewed in Qingdao.

Laoshan
99 E2
$$

Around Qingdao

Twenty-five miles (40 km) to the east of Qingdao is **Laoshan,** a mountain infused with Taoist mystery and legend. It is associated with the Eight Taoist Immortals. It also features in the popular Taoist fairy tale about the Laoshan Daoshi (a monk), who perfected his transcendental technique of walking

Most travelers visit only a few temples (there were once 72 Taoist temples on Laoshan) and merely scratch the surface of this dramatic area; the farther you penetrate Laoshan, the more you will unearth wild hiking opportunities.

The principal shrine is the Song dynasty **Taiqing Palace,** a Taoist monastery. The main temple is the **Hall of the Three Pure Ones,** where three large statues represent Laozi, the Yellow Emperor, and the Jade Emperor (see p. 83). To the left is the **Three Emperors Hall** and to the right the **Three Officials Hall.** The temple also contains a proclamation from Genghis Khan calling for the protection of Taoism.

From the temple, a cable car climbs up the side of the neighboring peak. Clinging precariously to the mountainside is the **Songqing Palace,** while below plunges the **Dragon Pool Waterfall (Longtanpu).** The highest peak is Jufeng, at 3,700 feet (1,127 m). Beyond lies a huge swath of undulating territory, drilled with caves and washed by waterfalls.

To the north, steep rock formations punctuate **Beijiushui,** a wild area laced by rivers, streams, and cascading waterfalls.

One of Qingdao's best beaches is around 40 minutes by bus to the east of town at **Shilaoren,** reachable on bus 304 from Taiping Lu in the east of Qingdao. The beach is not as serene as it once was, but it is still less mobbed during the summer months. Alternatively, the beaches on the island of Huangdao, lashed to Qingdao by the longest bridge in the world (see sidebar below), are also superior to those in town. ■

EXPERIENCE: Qingdao Brewery

China's first and most famous brewery, the Qingdao brewery *(56 Dengzhou Lu, tel 0532 8383-3437, $$)* contains a museum dedicated to the history of the now world-famous Tsingtao beer, the beer on which many other beers were modeled. Find out how the beer was first brewed here in 1903, look out over the bottling line, and sample some of the product at the end. To get to the brewery, take bus 221 or 205. The Qingdao International Beer Festival is held in August every year—the ideal opportunity for beer lovers to visit the town.

World's Longest Sea Bridge

In 2001, China continued to break engineering records with the completion of the world's longest sea bridge—the Jiaozhou Bay Bridge, which connects Qingdao with the island of Huangdao. The bridge is strung out upon 5,200 pillars, consumed more than 80 million cubic feet (2.25 million cu m) of concrete in its construction, and stretches 26 miles (42 km)—3 miles (4.8 km) longer than the previous record-holder, the Lake Pontchartrain Causeway in Louisiana. Built at an official cost of US$1.55 billion (other reports suggest it went well over budget), the bridge can accommodate 30,000 cars per day and withstand a magnitude 8.0 earthquake.

Mighty as it is, the six-lane Jiaozhou Bay Bridge is due to be overtaken in length by another Chinese bridge, scheduled for completion in 2016 and set to link southern Guangdong with Hong Kong and Macau. Both sea bridges, however, have already been eclipsed by the Danyang–Kunshan Grand Bridge. Opened in 2011, this rail viaduct ranges over an astonishing 102 miles (164 km), making it the longest bridge in the world.

More Places to Visit in the North

Anyang

The city of Anyang, in Henan Province, is built on the ruins of Yin, the last capital of the Shang dynasty (ca 1766–1122 B.C.). Fragments from the old city can be found in the **Yin Ruins Museum (Yinxu Bowuguan)** *(Yinxu Lu, $)* in the west of town. Anyang's other historical landmark is the **Tomb of Yuan Shikai (Yuan Shikai Mu),** who tried to restore imperial authority in 1915 (see p. 41).

Trips can be made to the **Red Flag Canal,** west of Anyang. A utopian vision during the days of the Cultural Revolution (1966–1976), this 900-mile (1,450 km) irrigation canal was cut through a mountain by hand.

99 C2

INSIDER TIP:

If you are a fan of ancient bronze and jade artifacts or oracle bones, don't miss the fabulous Yin Ruins Museum in Anyang.

—GEORGE RAPP
Regents Professor of Geoarchaeology Emeritus, University of Minnesota

Penglai

Legend has it that the Eight Immortals of Chinese Taoism (see p. 83) set out for their sea crossing from the ancient castle of Penglai, 40 miles (64 km) west of Yantai. A cable car connects this fascinating place to the cliffs opposite.

99 E3 $ $$$$

Shanhaiguan

Shanhaiguan is where the Great Wall meets the sea. Ascend the towering **First Pass Under Heaven** *(Dongda Jie, tel 0335 505-2894, $$, and visit the nearby Great Wall Museum on the same ticket),* or visit the more dramatic backbone of wall at **Jiaoshan,** just north of town. Restored **Laolongtou** ("old dragon head") south of town marks the wall's conclusion at the sea. Just across the border in Liaoning Province, **Jiumenkou** affords a unique spectacle of the arched wall crossing a river.

99 D3 & E3

Taiyuan

Taiyuan, capital of Shanxi Province, was lauded by Marco Polo, and despite today's industrial scars, it is still blessed with a few temples. The **Chongshan Temple,** off Shangma Jie, was once the largest Buddhist monastery in China. The **Jinci Temple,** 15 miles (24 km) southwest of Taiyuan, is noted for its Song dynasty clay figures.

99 C3 **Visitor Information**
88 Yingze Dajie 0351 567-9966

Zhengding

The **Longxing Temple (Dafo Si)** in the Hebei temple town of Zhengding is notable for its bronze, multiarmed, 70-foot (21 m) statue of Guanyin, dating from the Song dynasty. The town is also decorated with several attractive Tang dynasty pagodas, including the pagoda at the **Kaiyuan Temple (Kaiyuansi)** and **Lingxiao Pagoda.**

99 C3

Zoucheng

Zoucheng is the ancestral home town of the great Confucian philosopher Mencius (372–289 B.C.). The **Mencius Temple** *($)* is a marvelous piece of Confucian heritage, and the adjacent **Mencius Mansions** is a similarly harmonious arrangement of ancient buildings. Buses run to Zoucheng regularly from Qufu for the 30-minute journey.

99 D2

A watery world of canal towns and the gushing Yangtze River, which exhausts itself in the sea by glittering Shanghai

The Yangtze Region

Introduction & Map 144–145
A Cruise Through the Three Gorges 146–149
Chongqing 150
Wuhan 151–152
Yixian & Shexian 153
Huangshan 154–155
Feature: Chinese Temples 156–158
Jiuhuashan 159
Nanjing 160–163
Feature: Taiping Rebellion 164–165
Yangzhou 166
Zhenjiang 167
Experience: Moganshan Trek 167
Suzhou's Gardens 168–169
A Bike Ride Around Suzhou 170–171
Lake Taihu & Around 172
Hangzhou 173–175
Feature: Grand Canal 176–177
Shaoxing 178–179
Putuoshan 180–181
Shanghai 182–193
A Walk Along the Bund 184–187
Experience: Art in the M50 190
Experience: Zhujiajiao 192
Feature: Western Architecture in Shanghai 194–195
More Places to Visit in the Yangtze Region 196
Hotels & Restaurants in the Yangtze Region 368–373

Delicate art of painted snuff bottles

The Yangtze Region

Tumbling from the Tibetan Plateau, the Yangtze River nourishes the fertile valleys below but also causes catastrophic flooding. Some of China's great cities cluster around this major artery of communication and irrigation. The river pumps through Chongqing, cuts Wuhan in two, and is later straddled by Nanjing's great bridge. It leaves the waterlogged province of Jiangsu, emptying into the East China Sea just north of mighty Shanghai.

Cherry trees and traditional Chinese buildings line the banks of the Yangtze River.

Enthusiasts can navigate the Yangtze all the way from Chongqing to Shanghai, but most settle for the splendor of the Three Gorges. Temples, historic walled towns, and eccentric rock formations stud the dramatic route. The massive Three Gorges Dam has altered the topography of the region, however, submerging towns and monuments and transforming the Three Gorges.

The river slices through poor Anhui Province to the east, anonymous perhaps but for China's most famous peak, Huangshan. Farther east, the river flushes through its last province, Jiangsu. Here, the Grand Canal feeds in from the north, leaving the province awash with lakes and charming canal towns. Historic Nanjing, the provincial capital, deserves exploration.

Glittering Shanghai sits south of the river's final plunge into the sea. Fiercely independent and inherently rebellious, Shanghai is

simultaneously a museum of European antiquities and a showcase of newfangled architecture.

The famous city of Suzhou is a graceful vignette of bridges and gardens. Lake Taihu, Yixing, and picturesque Yangzhou further stock the province of Jiangsu with sights.

The Grand Canal feeds farther south to northern Zhejiang Province and Hangzhou, one of China's premier tourist destinations. South again, more reserved Shaoxing is cut by pleasant canals. Off the coast lies a string of islands, including the sacred Putuoshan, home of China's goddess of mercy, Guanyin. ■

Area of map detail

Beijing

NOT TO BE MISSED:

Escaping the city for a day into the hills of Moganshan **167**

Wandering around Hangzhou's West Lake in the evening **173–175**

The outstanding collection at the Shanghai Museum **189–191**

Ambling through Shanghai's ultra-chic French Concession **192–193**

Dinner and a cocktail on the bustling Bund in Shanghai **194–197**

Exploring the canal towns of Zhouzhuang and Changzhou **196**

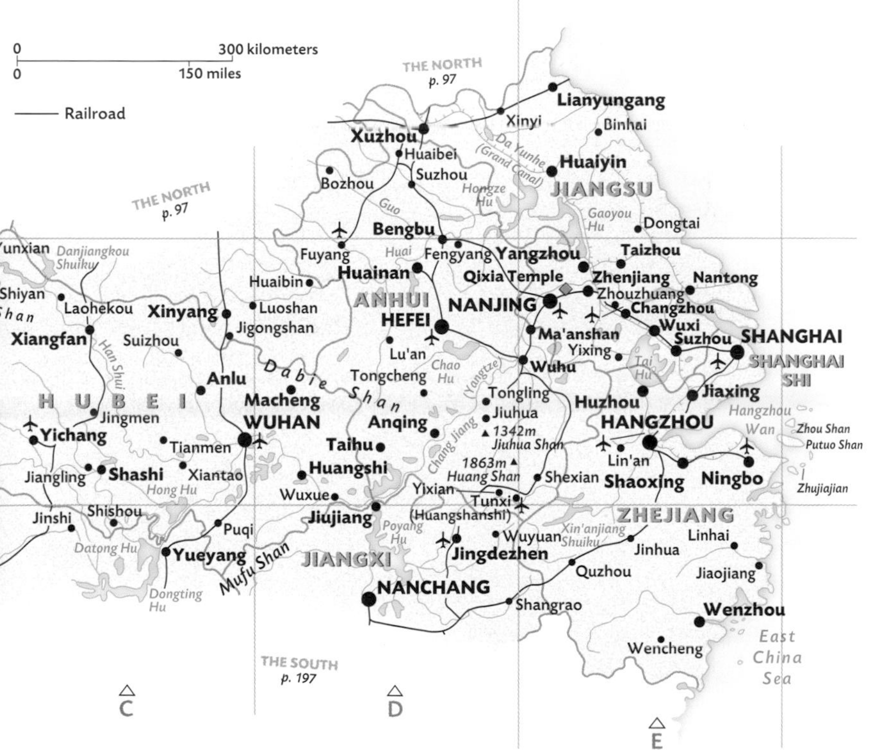

A Cruise Through the Three Gorges

Called the Yangtze Kiang or the Chang Jiang (literally "long river"), the Yangtze River is China's longest, starting out as a trickle in the Tanggulashan Mountains in Qinghai, swelling through the Tibetan highlands, then plummeting into Yunnan Province and surging through the Sichuan Basin. It courses 3,500 miles (5,630 km) through a string of provinces and finally disgorges its waters into the East China Sea above Shanghai.

The Yangtze basin is a highly fertile valley, but a dangerous one: Floods occur during the seasonal summer rains and are made worse by the deep silting up of the riverbed. Every 50 years or so the Yangtze basin sees a disastrous flood, although the Three Gorges Dam was designed to lessen the chance of serious flooding. The vast Three Gorges Dam was completed in 2006, and the waters behind the dam have not risen to their full height. The gorges have consequently been visibly reduced in stature, but for first-time visitors, the gorges remain spectacular and one of China's top sights.

The Route

This cruise, starting at Chongqing, funnels you past dramatic rock formations, vast, hanging curtains of stone, mist-shrouded peaks, the fragments of ancient settlements, and swirling eddies. Rocks, eroded by the elements or split by water, adopt fanciful forms that resemble a legion of abstract shapes long ago given whimsical names by the Chinese who traveled the river.

It is still possible to journey all the way from Chongqing to Shanghai, although most tours just cover the stretch between Chongqing and Yichang just beyond the Three Gorges Dam, which is where this tour terminates. The most celebrated and interesting section lies between Fengjie and Yichang—the famous and dramatic Three Gorges. Boats stop at towns and historical sights along the route, allowing you time to ponder the dramatic story as it unfolds. The cruise can be done in the other direction (for instance, Wuhan or Yichang to Chongqing). It is also possible to jump on a hydrofoil from Wanxian for the six-hour high-speed journey

Also see area map p. 145
➤ Chongqing
4 days
840 miles (1,350 km)
➤ Wuhan

NOT TO BE MISSED:

Fengdu • Qutang Gorge • Little Three Gorges • Wu Gorge • Peaks of Wushan

through the gorges; you get to see the gorges, but vessels do not stop at the tourist sights.

A passenger boat makes its way through the Lesser Three Gorges.

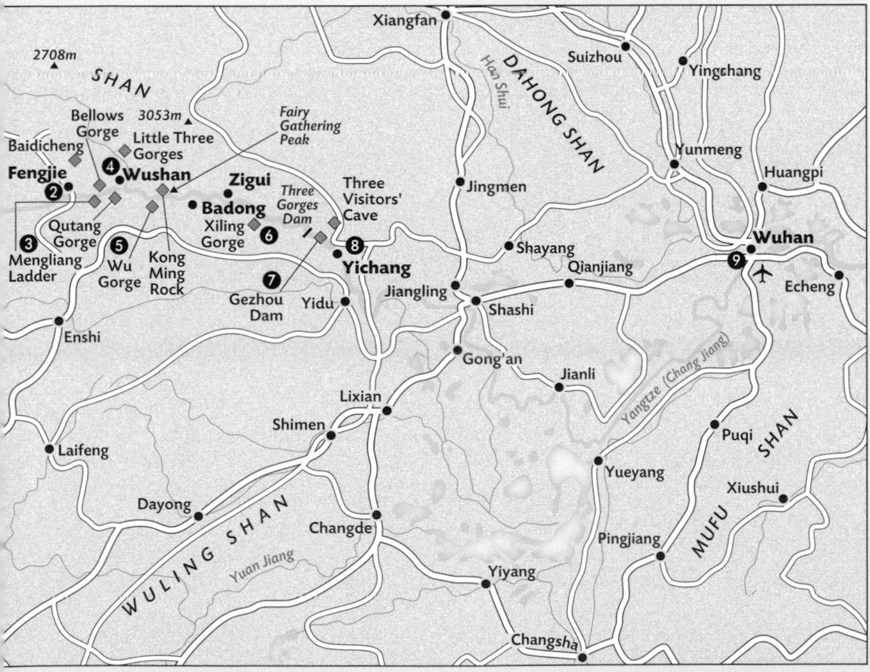

Chongqing to Fengjie

From mighty **Chongqing** (see p. 150), the boat initially travels past a long belt of uninspiring scenery. The haunted "Ghost City" of **Fengdu** ❶ has literally become a ghost town, as most of its residents have been relocated due to the rising river level. A spooky crop of temples and statues of Yinwang, god of the netherworld, survive on the mount of Mingshan overlooking Fengdu. Boats used to moor midstream in case of attack by phantoms!

The boat drifts past **Shibaozhai** ("stone treasure storehouse"), a 100-foot (30 m) rock resembling a seal-chop (a type of small, cylindrical marble seal). A towering, crimson **temple**, dating from the Qing dynasty and shaped like a pagoda, crowns the peak.

Perched above the river, the functional town of **Wanxian (Wanzhou)**—its lower slopes deserted to the rising waters—provides an overnight berth for many boats. If time is tight, you can take a three-hour bus ride from Chongqing to Wanxian and then board the hydrofoil here for rapid seven-hour trips to Yichang through the Three Gorges. Farther downstream beyond Wanxian, the 2,000-year old town of **Fengjie** ❷ marks the western entrance to Qutang Gorge (Qutangxia), first of the Three Gorges. The two great poets of the Tang dynasty, Li Bai and Du Fu, lived here and captured the great river in song. Li Bai wrote the following verse entitled "Departing Early from Baidicheng":

A cruise liner waits in the lock at the Three Gorges Dam.

> *In the morning, I leave Baidi between colorful clouds,*
> *A thousand miles of river and land, to return the next day.*
> *On each bank the gibbons scream without pause*
> *My boat has already drifted past endless hills.*

The partially submerged **Baidicheng (White King Town)** in the poem, at the entrance to Qutang Gorge, was christened by a king of the Western Han who saw a well emitting a white vapor "like a white dragon." He promptly called himself White King and named White King Town his fief. The town is rife with folklore from the time of the Three Kingdoms period (A.D. 220–265, see p. 31), most notably in the White King Temple.

The Three Gorges

The splendid Three Gorges (Sanxia) start at this point with **Qutang Gorge,** the shortest of them at 5 miles (8 km) long. The water flows rapidly through the gorge, pinched between the cliffs that narrow at points to 328 feet (100 m). The effect is thrilling, and many say that this is the most amazing of the gorges. The geological oddity of the Monk Hung Upside Down certainly resembles a suspended figure.

At the eastern entrance to the gorge, the **Mengliang Ladder** ❸ is a series of holes made in the rock; these originally supported piles driven into the rock face, upon which a pathway was laid for travelers. The other type of pathway that lined the gorges was cut out of the rock, and this can be seen from the boat on the northern face of Qutang Gorge. The furrows for the ropes that hauled boats up against the current of the river also remain.

On the opposite bank to the Mengliang Ladder is a set of crevices high in the rock face called the **Bellows Gorge.** These were the final repository for coffins of an ancient tribe called the Ba. For centuries, the boxes positioned there were believed by wayfarers on boats to contain the bellows of a blacksmith or carpenter called Lu Ban, who helped the mythical Yu the Great cleave the Yangtze gorges and dredge the river.

Travelers can explore the **Daning River (Daninghe),** and boats wait for them to transfer from the larger tour vessels. This stretch is called **Little Three Gorges,** a narrower and fiercer section than the larger gorges, and a thrilling ride. A coffin can be seen high on the rockface in Iron Coffin Gorge, the second gorge. The round-trip takes around five hours.

The ancient walled town of **Wushan** ❹ may make for an overnight berth, at the point where the Yangtze and the Daning Rivers meet. The town has 12 streets named after the mountain peaks in the next gorge.

Bewitching **Wu Gorge (Wuxia)** ❺—the Gorge of the Witches—towers ahead with its supernatural peaks and frequently misty cliffs. It starts in **Golden Helmet and Silver Armor Gorge,** pleated and fractured shafts of rock resembling a warrior's battle dress.

The 12 cloudy peaks of Wushan ("witch mountain") lie ahead: Fairy Peak, Immortals Gathering Peak, Clean Altar Peak, Climbing Dragon Peak, Holy Spring Peak, Emerald Green Screen Peak, Flying Phoenix Peak, and others rise up on both sides.

The spirit of Yaoji—the daughter of the Queen of Western Heaven, who came to Earth to assist Yu the Great in his labors—is believed to occupy Fairy Peak. Yaoji chased away wild animals and helped farmers grow crops, while tending magical herbs to cure the sick.

Kong Ming Rock, on the side of **Immortals Gathering Peak,** is supposedly carved with an inscription by Zhuge Liang, the master military strategist from the Three Kingdoms period.

At the port of **Badong,** you can take a rowboat along the tributary of Shennongxi, past caverns to an attractive beach by the river

Farther ahead the Fragrant Stream (Xiangxi) empties into the Yangtze River, and **Xiling Gorge (Xilingxia)** ❻—the longest and perhaps least spectacular—begins. At 50 miles (80 km), it's a marathon stretch, but it's still impressive. The **Sword and Military Strategy Book Gorge** is associated with Zhuge Liang, and the eccentrically named **Ox's Liver and Horse's Lung Gorge** may impress you if you actually know what a horse's lung looks like. There's also **Shadowplay Gorge.**

Three Gorges Dam

The controversial construction of the Three Gorges Dam, which aims to control flooding on the Yangtze River while generating vast amounts of hydroelectric power, was completed ahead of schedule in 2006. When fully functioning, the reservoir built up behind the dam at Sandouping will have submerged entire towns and villages. The Three Gorges will have been reduced in stature, and in the end, more than a million people will have been relocated.

Xiling Gorge was historically the most hazardous of the gorges for vessels plying the river, but it was long ago tamed by dredging and the rising waters. A particularly nasty stone, wonderfully called Here It Comes, sent many a boat to a watery grave until it was blown up by soldiers.

Beyond, the river widens, announcing the locks of the **Gezhou Dam** ❼. Farther ahead and shortly before boats pull in at **Yichang** ❽, the gargantuan Three Gorges Dam rears into view. Some boats stop here for trips to the dam, and hydrofoils also berth at the terminal; otherwise you can visit by bus from Yichang *(CITS visitor information, Yunji Lu, tel 0717 625-3088)*, the next town downstream. The voyage through the Three Gorges can also be done in reverse from Yichang to Chongqing. Tour boats stop at Yichang, although passenger boats continue to **Wuhan** ❾ (see pp. 151–152). From here on, towns begin to blur into a gray stream of industrial buildings.

What largely remains on the river from this point are cargo vessels shipping coal and cement to Shanghai. Some passenger boats still struggle on despite the competition from far faster routes to the east of China, but if you continue, you will pass through **Nanjing** and terminate at the mouth of the Yangtze River just north of **Shanghai.**

Chongqing

A vast municipality, rapidly developing Chongqing is also the starting point of the popular cruises through the Three Gorges. The hilly city is also home to blazing Sichuan cuisine and its namesake hotpot, which will fire up even the most seasoned chili aficionados.

Traditional structures meld easily with modern architecture in Chongqing.

Chongqing
Map 144 A1

CITS Visitor Information
Address: 151 Zourong Lu
Phone: 023 6387-6537

Luohan Temple
Address: Luohansi Jie
Admission: $

The largest city in the world (by some estimates), rapidly developing Chongqing is also one of the three hottest cities in China come summer.

Glinting from the smog of central Chongqing is the **Luohan Temple.** The Luohan (see p. 83) are usually fashioned in numbers of 18, but 500 lifelike Luohan effigies reside here. On the wall behind the huge Buddha effigy, look for the likeness of Siddhartha Gautama cutting his hair to renounce the world.

Pipashan Park (Pipashan Gongyuan) presides over Chongqing on a hill that rises some 1,100 feet (335 m); at the summit, **Hongxing Pavilion** offers long views over the city.

The **Huguang Guildhall** *(Dongshuimen Zhengjie, $$),* a lovely collection of restored traditional buildings, stages performances of Chinese opera. ■

Wuhan

Wuhan, capital of Hubei Province, is an amalgam of three cities clustered around the Yangtze River. Wuchang was a former capital of the state of Wu during the Three Kingdoms period (A.D. 220–265) and served as an anti-Qing center during the Taiping Rebellion. Hankou became a treaty port in 1861, with a complement of European concessions. Hanyang, the smallest of the three, became heavily industrialized during the 20th century.

Guiyuan Temple

Inside the courtyard of this temple in Hanyang is a sizable pool with two large, carved lotus flowers in the water. The Maitreya Buddha (see p. 82) welcomes all in the initial temple, and behind him is Weituo, standing with natural poise and grace on a splendidly carved altar.

The **main temple (Daxiong Baodian)** contains a magnificent altar with a central golden effigy of the goddess of mercy, Guanyin (see sidebar p. 181), surrounded by a host of other colorfully painted deities.

The hall at the rear on the right is where the Buddhist scriptures were stored. There is also a fascinating hall containing 500 almost life-size Luohan and seated monks. Each one displays its own individual temperament. In front is a black statue of Guanyin dressed in a robe, surrounded by a constellation of pottery figures. Signs in Chinese warn worshippers away from the hordes of fortune-tellers outside.

Hubei Provincial Museum

Over the Yangtze River in Wuchang, Hubei Provincial Museum (Hubeisheng Bowuguan) has an absorbing collection of relics from the state of Zeng, a small Zhou dynasty kingdom (1100–221 B.C.) in the middle of the Yangtze region. Of particular note are grave relics from the tomb of the Marquis of Zeng, who was buried in Zeng in 433 B.C. Ritual vessels, chariot fittings, musical instruments, weapons, gold, jade, and lacquerware make for a fascinating display. The bronzes are particularly interesting. The crane piece with deer antlers is

Wuhan
Map 145 C2

CITS Visitor Information
Zhongshan Dadao
027 5151-5955

Guiyuan Temple
Cuiweiheng Lu, Hanyang
$

Hubei Provincial Museum
156 Donghu Lu
Last admission at 3:30 p.m.

China by High-speed Rail

High-speed rail has become a crucial plank in China's burgeoning economy, shifting people and goods across the nation at great velocity. Today, it has become increasingly possible to cover huge distances quickly without having to take a flight.

For travelers, the D-, C-, and G-class high-speed trains are the most useful, shuttling passengers in comfort along major routes between large cities. Popular routes include Beijing to Shanghai, Beijing to Xi'an, and Wuhan to Guangzhou, but the list of high-speed routes is continually expanding.

With the opening of the G-class route between Beijing and Shanghai in 2011, the journey takes just four hours. The Beijing-Tianjin high-speed train takes a mere 30 minutes.

Villa of Mao Zedong
✉ Donghu Lu
$ $

Yellow Crane Pavilion
✉ Snake Hill (She Shan) Wulou Lu, Wuchang
$ $$$

arresting, but the main attraction is the marquis's magnificent coffin. Consisting of an inner and outer coffin, it is covered with early Zhou designs and motifs. You will see a reproduction of the coffin chamber as you enter.

Twenty-two sacrificial coffins were also found at the site—mainly containing women. Other bronzes that accompanied the coffins in the tomb show an evolved stage of craftsmanship. Pieces include bronze picks, ladles, a wine cooler, *ding* and *zun* (types of vessels), filters, and an exquisitely detailed bronze weight. There is also a vast bronze for serving wine at important ceremonies, inscribed with these words: "For the permanent use of the Marquis of Zeng."

Also unearthed was a huge set of bronze bells; the amount of bronze alloy controls the note of each bell. Along with the bells was a large set of chimes, both commonly seen in Confucius temples across China (see pp. 156–157).

Historic Architecture

For a taste of Wuhan's foreign concession past, wander around Hankou, which contains several buildings from concession days, when the city was a major center of trade (and missionary activity).

Wander along the premier shopping street of **Jianghan Lu** and note its sporadic historic architecture. Pop into the **Xuangong Hotel** *(57 Jianghan Yilu)* just west of Jianghan Lu; built in 1931, the building is typical of the Old World charms of the area. Also note the imposing historic building that houses the **Bank of China,** where Jianghan Lu meets Zhongshan Dadao.

Yanjiang Dadao runs along the Yangtze River in Hankou, punctuated with pompous old architecture, including the **National City Bank of New York** building, at No. 142. Also worth a look is the former **Hankou Railway Station** building, built by the French and still sitting at the northern end of Chezhan Lu.

INSIDER TIP:

Trains are a fast and great way to travel in China. When planning a train trip, it's worth it to book first-class passage; the price may be higher but the comfort is unbeatable.

—ALISON WRIGHT
National Geographic photographer

The impressive **Former Headquarters of the Wuchang Uprising** in Wuchang is now a museum, while the **Villa of Mao Zedong** is a weary remnant from Mao's itinerant past. The villa itself is more like a dreary two-star budget hotel, but you see his swimming pool, bathrobe, and other scattered objects from his life.

Yellow Crane Pavilion

Yellow Crane Pavilion, located by the Yangtze River on Snake Hill, is a much restored tower lauded by the Tang dynasty poet Cui Hao. ■

Yixian & Shexian

Yixian county is characterized by its Huizhou culture and architecture. Little authentic traditional village character of this kind survives in modern China, and visits here are highly recommended, especially if you are en route to nearby Huangshan (see pp. 154–155).

Yixian

Yixian's two most famous villages are the gorgeous **Xidi** *($$$)* and **Hongcun** *($$$)*, both easily reached by bus from Yixian town itself, 30 miles (47 km) west of Tunxi (Huangshan Shi). Both UNESCO World Heritage sites, each village is typified by picturesque and distinctive Huizou buildings, painted creamy-white, topped by black tiles, and bookended by the lovely horse-head gables you see throughout this region. The building's interiors reveal further hallmarks of the Huizhou style, including the use of oblong light wells (openings in the roof), courtyards, and upper galleries.

Introduced by way of a splendid *paifang* (decorative arch), Xidi's charming streets are flanked by delightful Huizhou architecture. Numerous halls and former residences are open to the public, so you can wander in and absorb the pleasures of their interior arrangements. Once you have finished exploring the village, opportunities exist for short treks into the surrounding countryside.

Nearby Hongcun has a different and altogether unique aspect. Reputedly designed to resemble an ox from above, the village is centered on the pond of Yuezhao, linked to the lake bordering the south of Hongcun by small water channels. Follow the signs around the village for a tour of its halls and residences. Other villages in the Yixian area can also be explored, although reaching them can be inconvenient.

The distinctive ancient houses of Hongcun village

Yixian
145 E2

Shexian
145 E2

Shexian

The town of Shexian, less than an hour by bus from Tunxi, was the former capital of the Huizhou region. In exploring the old town, seek out the magnificent and richly decorated **Xuguo Archway** *($)*–one of China's most elaborate paifang. Nearby, the Huizhou residential architecture of **Doushan Jie** *($)* can be explored with a guide; otherwise just meander the charming streets with your camera. A few miles west of Shexian, a sequence of seven paifang called the **Tangyue Decorative Arches** *($$)* stand alone in a field. ■

Huangshan

Adorning piles of coffee-table books on China is stunning, pine-tree-clad Huangshan in south Anhui Province, China's most famous, probably most beautiful mountain.

A sea of clouds settles on the fairy-tale archipelago of Huangshan's lofty peaks.

The 160-mile-long (257 km) Huangshan range is a dramatic panorama of 72 peaks, capped by Lotus Flower Peak (Lianhuafeng). During the Qin dynasty, the mountain was called Qianshan, but it was renamed Huangshan in A.D. 747, in honor of the Yellow Emperor (Huangdi). The mount was later the hideaway of Chan Buddhist recluses, who foraged for inspiration among the pines, waterfalls, and hot springs.

On the summit, Xihai ("west sea") and Beihai ("north sea") are famed for their jaw-dropping misty panoramas. The main loci of interest on Beihai are **Lion Peak (Shizifeng), Monkey Which Looks Out Over the Sea (Houzi Guanhai),** and an old, twisted pine tree charmingly labeled **Flowers Springing from a Dreaming Writing Brush (Mengbi Shenghua).** Come sunrise, bleary-eyed wayfarers muster in padded coats on **Refreshing Terrace (Qingliangtai)** along the slopes of Lion Peak. If you have the time, spend the night at one of the hotels on the summit, where the view can be astonishing. From **Cloud-Dispelling Pavilion (Paiyunting)** on Xihai, the view reaches out over layers of small peaks emerging through the clouds and mist.

Climbing Huangshan

The first hurdle is the very steep entrance charge. Ahead lie various routes, the easiest being the eastern one. Ride up on the cable car to pursue the eastern route from the **Yungu Temple,** which marks the start of the trail. This is an option if you just can't face the walk, but your patience can wear thin after hours of waiting in line. Sedan chairs await the truly decadent.

The eastern ascent is a 5-mile (8 km) stretch, and this should take you about three hours to finish. There's less to see than on the western route, but the climb is far easier and it's pleasantly shaded.

Huangshan's Spectral Mists

The famous mists that swathe Huangshan's slender pine trees and pour into the gullies and ravines of the mountain form a bewitching spectacle. At the peak, the summits and pinnacles may poke out of a "sea of clouds" *(yunhai)*, separated into the east sea *(donghai)*, west sea *(xihai)*, north sea *(beihai)*, and south sea *(nanhai)*. Even though Huangshan sees more than 250 misty days a year, there's no guarantee you will catch the mountain smothered in fog. In fact, there may not be a cloud in sight during your visit, but rest assured: The views remain fabulous.

INSIDER TIP:

Scenes from the movie *Crouching Tiger, Hidden Dragon* (2000) were filmed in Huangshan's spectacular bamboo-covered valley.

—MARY STEPHANOS
National Geographic contributor

The western ascent is a gut-wrenching 10 miles (16 km); around every corner waits a further flight of steps, mocking your stamina and testing your endurance. Along the western trail are the **Merciful Light Pavilion (Ciguangge)** and, farther up, the **Halfway Mountain Temple (Banshansi),** now a hotel and restaurant. The dwarfing granite pinnacle of **Tiandu Peak** rises south of **Jade Screen Tower Hotel (Yupinglou Binguan),** with its spectacular vista. The path then winds around **Lotus Flower Peak** before grinding on to **Bright Summit Peak (Guangmingding)** and the summit proper.

Many visitors ascend by the eastern route and descend by the western trail. Guides are available, but they are unnecessary as exploration is straightforward and English signs numerous. The best weather occurs when the peaks are shrouded in mist (which is much of the time), and the Chinese insist on climbing to the very top for the breathtaking views over the "sea of clouds" (see sidebar above).

The thermometer can dip, so take warm, waterproof clothes and extra layers. Summer sees Huangshan infested with climbers and is best avoided, if possible.

The nearest town is **Tunxi (Huangshan Shi)** served by an airport from where buses reach Huangshan. Alternatively, stay in the pleasant village of Tangkou at the foot of Huangshan and climb early the next day. ■

Huangshan

Map: 145 D2

$: $$$$$ (Cable car: $$$)

CITS Visitor Information

6 Xizhen Jie, Tunxi

Tel: 0559 252-6184

Chinese Temples

If you can interpret the sacred symbols of the temples you visit, you will be well rewarded. The divine architecture of Chinese temples is a world governed by the sacred science of *fengshui* (see pp. 256–257) and other mysterious forces. This short guide aims to ease open the door to that rich domain and help you to understand it more fully.

The customs and lore of traditional China can be found in temples—and on the street.

Fengshui

Regardless of faith, Chinese temples are principally laid out on the advice of a fengshui (geomancy) expert. The axis runs north–south, with temple gates and doors facing south. Temples are often perched on mountainsides, not only because mountains are sometimes infused with Taoist or Buddhist myth but also because the Green Dragon and White Tiger (see p. 256) follow mountain ranges and imbue hilly land with *qi* or "cosmic energy."

Water acts as a repellent, guarding against attack from evil spirits, which cannot travel over water; hence the common positioning of pools and canals in temples. Most temples are also protected by menacing door gods, including the Four Heavenly Kings (see p. 83), who act as a further line of defense.

The five elements of fengshui (metal, water, wood, fire, and earth) are important aspects of temple design, interwoven into the structural fabric of the buildings and statuary. The Wong Tai Sin Temple in Kowloon, Hong Kong, is an example of this (see p. 238).

Confucian Temples

The primary courtyard of Confucian temples is typically a small grove of stelae inscribed with the names of dignified local scholars. The stelae are frequently supported on the backs of vast *bixi* (mythical tortoise-like dragons), themselves occasionally housed in individual pavilions. A statue of Confucius with clasped hands often welcomes visitors, although the statue is generally a recent carving.

The main hall surrounds an effigy of the sage flanked by two rows of disciples, including a statue of the Confucian philosopher Mencius. Also on show is an assortment of musical instruments, a set of bells, and stone chimes. The chimes are an important part of the Confucian canon, for they were apparently tuned in accordance with the Dao, or Way; a fluctuation in pitch indicated earthly imbalance and consequent implications for the imperial sphere. Statues or effigies of the *qilin*, a mythical chimera, are often found at these temples. The animal sometimes appears in Confucian literature, signifying earthly harmony.

The significance of religious Confucianism dwindled with the emergence of Communism, and many temples suffered from neglect. They are often quite lifeless and deserted, despite Confucius' recent renaissance. Other Confucian temples have been converted to museums or, as is often the case, schools (because of Confucius' association with learning).

Confucian temples are called *wenmiao* (cultural temple) or *kongmiao* (Confucius temple). Famous examples can be found in Qufu (the

The Flower Pagoda at the Buddhist Temple of Six Banyan Trees in Guangzhou

largest of them all), Beijing (the eponymous Confucius Temple), Yixing, Harbin, and Jilin.

Buddhist Temples

As loci of spiritual power, Chinese Buddhist temples hum with sacred energy. Balls of incense smoke rise from braziers, cross-legged monks sit reading sutras, and worshippers divine their futures with bamboo slips *(qian)* and prayers. Often you will find temples hidden among the cool pines of a forest or clinging to a mountainside.

Entering, you are traditionally greeted by a golden Milefo, the plump and jovial Buddha of the future. Standing back to back with him is Weituo (see p. 83), carrying his staff. On either side are the colossal Four Heavenly Kings, who protect the temple from evil spirits.

The jovial bodhisattva reminds Buddhists that the future awaits those who believe. Two strips of calligraphy on either side of him generally tell of his toleration of what is unendurable and his hilarity at life's comedy. Milefo often sits within a hall called the Hall of Heavenly Kings.

Behind Milefo lies the first of several courtyards. Large bronze incense burners, often fantastically decorated, send up smoke in vast plumes. On either flank stand the bell and drum tower, which sound to alert the faithful to prayer. Ahead is a succession of temples.

The main hall, the Daxiong Baodian, or "great heroic treasure hall," is first. Here you will encounter a trinity of bodhisattvas. Guanyin, the goddess of mercy, is often present, generally facing north at the rear.

INSIDER TIP:

If you're lucky enough to be in Shanghai during the Tomb Sweeping Festival in early April, join the throngs making offerings at the Chenghuang Temple *(247 Middle Fangbang Rd., $).*

—SUSAN STRAIGHT
National Geographic Books editor

The second hall is not usually notable, but the third generally contains the salvationary Amitabha Buddha or Wenshu. The 18 Luohan line the sides in rows of nine (see p. 83). There may be a fourth hall, which will contain a group of male and female bodhisattvas.

Some temples retain pagodas, but many pagodas survive without companion temples. The pagoda was used for storing sacred sutras and translations from India. Surviving spirit walls, often decorated with dragons, deflected bad spirits. Buddhist temples also feature a number of small side halls and temples.

Buddhist temples are called *simiao* (temple) or *chansi* (Zen temple). They are found all over China in greater numbers than their Confucian and Taoist peers. Famous examples include Nan Putuo Temple in Xiamen, the Lama Temple in Beijing, the Jade Buddha Temple in Shanghai, and the Jokhang Temple in Lhasa. The four sacred Buddhist mountains of China are dotted with them.

Taoist Temples

Taoist monks *(daoshi)* differ in appearance from their yellow-robed, shaven-headed Buddhist brethren *(hesheng)*. Their hair is long and twisted up in a knot, and they wear small, squarish jackets and straight trousers.

The sequence of temples also diverges from the Buddhist pattern. The main hall holds the Three Pure Ones (see p. 83), representations of the Dao, or Way. This hall is often surrounded on either side by clusters of lesser halls.

Other deities who have their own halls include the Eight Immortals, the Jade emperor, Laozi (author of the classic *Daode Jing*), the goddess of seafarers Tianhou (otherwise called Mazu, or Niangniang), and the Queen of the West. The temple guardians are represented by the fearsome combination of the Green Dragon and the White Tiger.

Laozi can often be found seated in an octagonal pavilion whose design echoes the arrangement of the *bagua,* or the eight trigrams of the *I-Ching* or *Yi Jing* (see p. 54).

There is a relaxed atmosphere in Taoist temples, which reflects the passive doctrine of *wuwei,* or inaction. Taoism is less concerned with salvation and more preoccupied with the manifestation of the Way and living in accordance with its rhythm. The internal martial art of tai chi is a Taoist practice that attempts to move with the Way.

Taoist monasteries are called *guan,* or *gong* (palace), although the latter are occasionally Buddhist. Famous temples include the Qingyang Palace in Chengdu; the temples that dot Qingchengshan, also near Chengdu; Taiqing Palace on Laoshan; the Eight Immortals Temple in Xi'an; and the White Cloud Temple in Beijing.

Jiuhuashan

Located in southern Anhui Province, Jiuhuashan ("nine flower mountain") is easily climbed in a day, making it a practical alternative to the more rigorous ascent of nearby Huangshan **(see pp. 154–155).**

The divinity ruling Jiuhuashan is Dizang, a salvationary god of the dead and the underworld, called Ksitigarbha in Sanskrit, to whom pilgrims flock to pray for the souls of the departed. Dizang has apparently manifested himself on the mountain more than once in human form. A Korean monk named Kim Kiao Kak came to Jiuhuashan in the eighth century to dedicate a temple to the god.

As with other Buddhist mountains in China, Jiuhuashan was occupied by Taoist recluses before being converted wholesale to Buddhism. The enigmatic Tang poet Li Bai wrote a devotional poem to Jiuhuashan after living on its slopes, lending the mountain its name.

The lofty peak of **Tiantaishan** lies a staggering 5 miles (8 km) of steps up in the clouds from Jiuhua village, itself about halfway up the mountain from Wuxi Town below. Many temples, shrines, and nunneries still decorate the slopes, despite a spate of desecration and torching during the Taiping Rebellion (see p. 164–165) as troops surged through Anhui Province.

The Dongya Temple is just one of many on Jiuhuashan.

Jiuhua to the Summit

In the village of Jiuhua you will find the Ming dynasty **Zhiyuan Temple,** the largest of the local monasteries. On the ridge behind stands the **Baisui Temple,** which contains the remains of a wandering monk who came to the temple in the 1600s. When he died at the age of 126, his body refused to decay, and it remains, seated and embalmed by his faith (and a coating of gold).

A cable car also runs to the peak. Near the summit are two nunneries, before the path trails up to the **Ten Thousand Buddhas Temple** on the peak.

How to Visit

Spring and autumn are the most refreshing seasons for the climb up Jiuhuashan; summer is hot and humid. Daily buses arrive at the mountain from Huangshan, and services also run from Nanjing and Hangzhou. ■

Jiuhuashan

Map 115 D2

$ $$$$

CTS Visitor Information

✉ 135 Baima Xinchen

☎ 0566 283-1890

Nanjing

Nanjing is an attractive city with wide boulevards and an enduring sense of history; it was frequently the capital of regional empires and twice the capital of China.

A statue of a merchant selling his wares brightens a Nanjing street.

Nanjing

145 E2 & 161

CITS Visitor Information

202 Zhongshan Beilu

025 8342-1125

City Wall

161

Zhonghua Gate, Zhonghua Lu. Alternative access via Jiming Temple or Zhongshan Gate

$

The provincial capital of Jiangsu, Nanjing lies on the Yangtze River's southern bank. It is probably best remembered in the West for the devastation brought on it by the invading Japanese army in 1937.

The treaty ending the first Opium War was penned in this former Ming capital in 1842. Eleven years later, the city was capital of the terrestrial heaven of the remarkable Taiping (see pp. 164–165). They demolished the city's famous Ming imperial palace, only to have their replacement structures leveled by the Qing. The city later served as the Kuomintang capital (see p. 41).

There's a palpable sense of confidence among Nanjing citizens, despite their traumatic past. Getting around is easy; taxis are cheap and plentiful, and a new subway system shuttles passengers through the center of the city.

Ming Legacy

Nanjing retains much of its Ming heritage. The most stunning example is the Ming **city wall (Chengqiang)** that encircles Nanjing; at more than 20 miles (32 km), it is the longest city wall in the world. It was too long to defend adequately against the Taiping, but although some of the fortifications were demolished during their occupation, a good portion stands.

The wall avoids the standard square layout and instead follows the contours of the land, creating a fluid shape. Some of its gates survive, most notably **Zhonghua Gate** to the south and **Zhongshan Gate** to the east. Zhonghua Gate, an elaborate barrier of tiered portals and vaults, was used to house troops. Follow the steps to the overgrown ramparts and fine views over the city.

If visiting **Zijinshan** (see pp. 162–163), take bus No. 20W back to the city, which gives dramatic views of the city wall, terminating at **Jiming Temple.** Here you can ascend the ramparts and a section of wall that runs south of Xuanwu Lake Park. The north exit of the temple crosses a bridge to the wall. You can also walk along a 0.75-mile (1.2 km) length of wall to the east, with views over the lake and hillside pagodas. It's overgrown in parts, but easily passable.

Wuchaomen Park sits on the ruins of the former **Ming Imperial Palace (Ming Gugong),** built by the first Ming emperor, Hongwu (*r.* 1368–1398). The buildings, which were the model for the Forbidden City in Beijing (see pp. 60–66), were destroyed during the anti-Manchu Taiping Rebellion in the mid-19th century. All that remains are some strewn, though enchanting, fragments, and the park is sublimely attractive. The ruins of the Gate of Heavenly Worship consist of stone pedestals overlooked by cypresses.

Five old Ming bridges cross a moat, behind which stands a stela carved in the 40th year of the reign of the Wanli emperor (*r.* 1573–1620). Also still standing is the ancient wall of **Wumen,** overgrown with creepers and topped with the symbol of the current dynasty, the PRC (People's Republic of China) flag. The **Drum Tower** and the **Bell Tower** standing on either side of Zhongshan Lu were both originally constructed during the Ming dynasty.

Museums

The **Taiping Museum (Taiping Tianguo Lishi Bowuguan)** is essential viewing for anyone interested in the troubled history of Christianity in China. The Taiping was one of the bloodiest rebellions in Chinese history, led by the obsessed Hong Xiuquan. Much to the chagrin of historians (and the Taiping faithful), Hong's palace in Nanjing was razed, and only a few documents and tablets remain to record their whirlwind social experiments.

As you enter the museum gate, you pass a bronze bust of Hong Xiuquan and a row of cannon used during the rebellion. Some of them

Jiming Temple
161
¢

Wuchaomen Park
161
Zhongshan Donglu

Taiping Museum
161
128 Zhonghua Lu
$

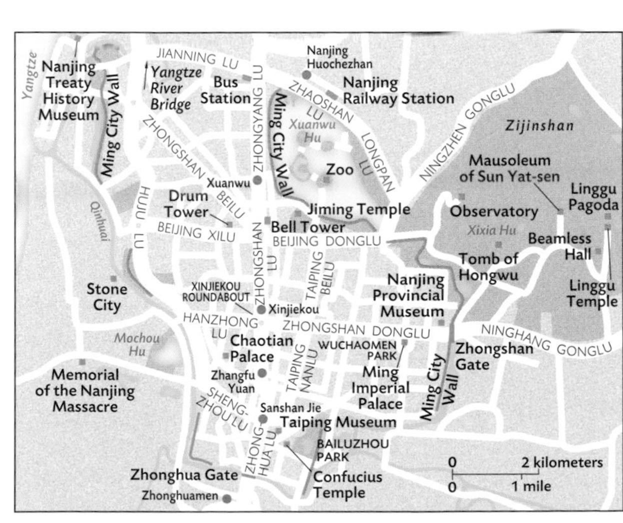

Memorial of the Nanjing Massacre
- 161
- 418 Shui Ximen Dajie
- Closed Mon.

Confucius Temple
- 161
- Gongyuan Jie
- $

Chaotian Palace
- 161
- Mochou Lu
- Closed 10:30 a.m.–2 p.m.

Mausoleum of Sun Yat-sen
- 161
- Zijinshan
- $$$

are stamped with the characters Tianguo, or Heavenly Kingdom. You will also find a diagram of Hong Xiuquan's palace and intriguing documents, including a treatise called *The New Guide to Government.* The treatise, written by Hong Rengan, reveals considerable borrowing from Western political models. The jade seal of the Heavenly King, called the great seal of the Taiping, is a square seal (chop) composed of Chinese characters.

INSIDER TIP:

Touching, informative, and beautifully crafted, the Memorial of the Nanjing Massacre should not be missed by anyone.

—ALISON WRIGHT
National Geographic photographer

The daring exploits of the Taiping are recorded in murals in chronological order, and some weapons are displayed.

The **Memorial of the Nanjing Massacre (Datusha Jinianguan),** outside the city walls to the west, remembers the appalling barbarity of the invading Japanese army in December 1937. A hideous but necessary memorial to those who suffered, it makes for fascinating (though nauseating) viewing. The museum resembles a colossal tomb, emblazoned on the facade with the number 300,000 (the upper estimate of those killed). A visit is essential viewing for those wanting to comprehend why Sino-Japanese relations remain fraught and why China insists on a full apology from Japan.

Temples

A stone's throw from the Taiping Museum is the **Confucius Temple (Fuzimiao).** This Song dynasty temple has been continuously added to after repeated damage; most of the structures you see today are from the late Qing dynasty. The cells where students prepared for the official civil service examinations are displayed.

Inside an expansive hall is a vast portrait of Confucius overseeing a set of bells, chimes, and musical instruments, and along the wall are some rather gaudy bas-reliefs in colored glass, which relate stories from Confucius's life. One parable tells of a *qilin* (a mythical chimera that only appeared during times of morality) slaughtered in a world without ethics. The hall at the very rear offers classical Chinese music and performances by singers and dancers in period costumes. The area around the temple is a lively shopping/restaurant district.

The focal point of the **Chaotian Palace** on Mochou Lu is a Confucius Temple. In front of the palace is a statue of Confucius, clasping his hands. Inside the Dacheng Hall is a fascinating exhibition of pottery and model ships illustrating life during the period of the Southern dynasties.

Zijinshan

East of Nanjing lies Zijinshan, a wooded hill hosting a collection of historical sights. The overblown **Mausoleum of Sun Yat-sen**

(Zhongshanling), founder of the Republic of China, is approached along a long avenue bordered with pines. The roof is grandly tiled in blue. Through the main gate stands a large stela emblazoned with gold characters declaring that the Kuomintang (Nationalists) buried Sun Zhongshan (Sun Yat-sen) here. Sun swore to make Nanjing the Nationalist capital, and Chiang Kai-shek made it so in 1928. In the mausoleum itself, a seated statue of Sun sits beneath a huge mosaic on the ceiling of a white sun on a blue background—the Kuomintang (Taiwan) flag. Signs in Chinese remind visitors to salute.

Nearby are the remains of the **Tomb of Hongwu (Mingxiaoling),** the first Ming emperor. The tomb was devastated by the Taiping, but the Spirit Way (Shendao) survives, set at an angle and lined with statues of animals, including elephants and camels.

The main approach takes you to the Military and Civil Gate, a large construction with bright red doors. Behind that is a stela inscribed by the Kangxi emperor and a Ming bridge that takes you to the Soul Tower. The original yellow-glazed tiles and double-eaved roof of the tower, behind which is the mound of the emperor's tomb, were all damaged during the Taiping Rebellion. Also leveled during the rebellion was the Xiaoling Palace, but you can make out the original foundations.

On the slopes of Zijinshan is the small **Zixia Lake (Zixiahu)** and **Linggu Temple.** Near the temple stands the simple but impressive **Beamless Hall,** now a museum celebrating the life of Sun Zhongshan and highlighting the foreign menace of the Opium Wars. There are no English captions. Tall pines grow in the courtyard of the quiet, gracious **Linggu Temple.** The nine-story Linggu Pagoda, designed in 1929 by American architect Henry Killam Murphy, rises behind.

Yangtze River Bridge

An engineering feat of considerable importance straddles the Yangtze to the north of Nanjing. The Yangtze River Bridge opened at the height of the Cultural Revolution in 1968, at the same time as the Confucius Temple was being daubed with Maoist graffiti. Until it opened, trains crossed the river by ferry, a two-hour trip. The hefty Bolshevik lines and monumental scale will appeal to students of socialist iconography. You can get a good view if you are taking a day train to or from Beijing. ■

Tomb of Hongwu

Map p. 161
Mingling Lu, Zijinshan
$$$

Linggu Temple

Map p. 161
Linggusi Lu, Zijinshan
$

The Mausoleum of Sun Yat-sen

Taiping Rebellion

The bloody Taiping Rebellion (1850–1864) caused the deaths of an estimated 20 million Chinese during the middle of the 19th century. While the violence was indescribable, the Taiping doctrine was transfixing. The movement's founder, the Hakka Hong Xiuquan (1814–1864), believed he was the Son of God and brother of Jesus.

Engraving of the Franco-Chinese Treaty of 1858

Christian Communism

Fired by feverish Christian visions (inspired by his dealings with missionaries in the city of Guangzhou), and harboring a grudge after failing the civil service examinations, Hong Xiuquan embarked on his religious quest to conquer China. In 1851, he proclaimed the founding of the Taiping Tianguo (Heavenly Kingdom of Great Peace), encouraged by a multitude of disaffected peasants. His ambition was to rid the world of the Qing dynasty and to establish a radically new society. The Manchus were biblically seen as devils fit for destruction.

The Taiping devised an innovative form of Christian communism where property was shared, a common treasury was established, and the sexes were separated. Women were led by their own battle-hardened veterans, and homosexuality was forbidden on pain of death. Prostitution, opium smoking, and foot binding were similarly outlawed.

Spreading Violence

The egalitarian promise of the rebellion cemented together a devout assortment of anti-Qing faithful, and a disciplined fighting force a million strong was built. After an unsuccessful 33-day siege of Guilin, the Taiping erupted out of south China and swept along the fertile Yangtze Valley via Wuchang to storm the great walled city of Nanjing on March 9, 1853; the city's entire Manchu population was put to the sword.

En route, the Taiping besieged the capital of Hunan Province, Changsha, but failed to take the city; in their wake, the provinces of Hunan and Hubei lay devastated. Nanjing became their capital and was renamed Tianjing—the Heavenly Capital. Hong Xiuquan conferred upon himself the absolutist title of Heavenly King.

From Nanjing the Taiping struck out at the rest of China, with the city of Hangzhou suffering great devastation and falling to the rebels in 1861. The hard-won advantage began to slip from the rebels' grasp, however. Although the capture of Nanjing was a dramatic success, it signaled the start of a decline for the Taiping.

Decline of the Taiping

Conquered domains fell back into Qing control, and the 1853 northern expedition to take Beijing failed, as did the later western expedition to occupy Shanghai. Hong Xiuquan sought a powerful alliance with the Christian Western powers, but they shunned his heretical brew. If the West had accepted Hong's style of Christianity, the Qing dynasty would almost certainly have been overthrown.

Fearing usurpation, Hong eliminated a number of influential high-ranking rebels, encouraging desertions from the Taiping ranks. Power was shared by Hong's hopeless relatives, and a creeping malaise set in. By the end of 1863, many of the gains in eastern China had been lost and the disastrous expedition to seize Shanghai was repelled by a Western-trained Manchu army known as the Ever Victorious Army, which eventually besieged the Heavenly Capital of Nanjing. Hong Xiuquan

The ill-treatment of Europeans in the Taiping Rebellion depicted by W. Dickes, ca 1860

died during the city's encirclement. The city capitulated on July 19, 1864, after a mammoth siege, with the Taiping fighting to the last man or taking their own lives. The rest of the rebels, scattered through south China, were rooted out and ruthlessly eliminated.

Lasting Influence

The Taiping system is unique in Chinese history and is seen by many as a progenitor of Chinese communism. Defying Chinese traditional beliefs, fiercely anti-Confucian and radically experimental, the Taiping creed stressed brotherhood, equality, and common ownership. Some of the Taiping furthermore promoted democratic principles and incubated inventive plans for economic transformation. The whole edifice of Taiping social planning was glued together by the dictates of the Christian gospels. The Communist Party remembers them as champions of the people and dresses them up suitably for public consumption. The Taiping Museum in Nanjing (see p. 161) is a fascinating chronicle of the period.

If the Taiping had succeeded in their ambitions to conquer the nation, China would have become the most populous Christian domain in the world. The apostasy of its Christianity, however, would have ultimately led to a clash with the rest of Christendom.

Yangzhou

Enriched by the burgeoning trade of the Grand Canal (see pp. 176–177) yet devastated in the 19th century by Taiping rebels, Yangzhou in Jiangsu Province is a pleasant city noted for its picturesque grid of waterways, bridges, parks, and gardens.

Yangzhou's Tang-style city wall museum

Yangzhou
145 E2

Daming Temple
Pingshantang Lu
$

He Garden
Xuningmen Jie
$$$

Ge Garden
Yanfu Donglu
$$

Tomb of Puhaddin
Jiefang Nanlu
$ (temple & gardens)

Many of Yangzhou's sights are settled on the periphery of town, and taking a taxi is the best way to reach them. The **Daming Temple,** to the northwest, was originally established in the Southern dynasty of the Liu Song (A.D. 420–479). It was rebuilt in the late Qing dynasty after being torched by the Taiping (see pp. 164–165). It is celebrated for its **Jianzhen Hall,** dedicated to a pioneering Tang dynasty monk who, after many failed attempts, succeeded in reaching Japan to further the cause of Buddhism there. The temple is not far from the remains of the Tang **city wall.** The nearby **Pingshan Hall** belonged to the Song dynasty writer Ou Yangxiu (see p. 51).

Shouxi Lake Park (Shouxihu Gongyuan) *(Dahongqiao Lu, $$$$)* is a Tang dynasty lake historically exalted by visiting wordsmiths and forever seething with tour groups, so weekends are best avoided. The elaborate **Five-Pavilion Bridge (Wutingqiao)** spans the lake, and nearby stands a white **dagoba** *(baita),* based on the example in Beijing's Beihai Park (see p. 67).

Yangzhou is famous for its gardens, bequeathed by merchants who made their fortune in salt. **He Garden (Heyuan),** not far from the hook of the moat in the southeast, between Nantong Donglu and Guangling Lu, is surrounded by pavilions, while the **Ge Garden (Geyuan)** is a Chinese classical contrivance of bamboo and rockeries.

To the east of the Ge Garden, across the Grand Canal, is a Muslim monument called the **Tomb of Puhaddin (Puhading Muyuan).** Puhaddin was a wayfaring Yuan dynasty Islamic missionary. The tomb shelters the remains of other Muslims and is devoted to the history of Muslim contacts with China.

The city also preserves a small Catholic church and a Baptist church in the center of town. A reminder of the once sizable Protestant population in Yangzhou, the Baptist church still functions and contains a baptismal pool. ■

Zhenjiang

Zhenjiang is another Jiangsu city whose riches came with the building of the Grand Canal (see pp. 176–177). Although it is now busy and industrialized, its hilly parks are attractively dotted with temples, and there are enduring shades of treaty port architecture.

Jinshan Temple lies on the slopes of **Jinshan ("golden mountain") Park** in the northwest of town. This active temple is a layered sequence of halls and steps that mount the hill (formerly an island in the Yangtze River). Don't miss the three golden, seated Buddhas in the main hall.

The **Cishou ("benevolence and longevity") Pagoda** above was supposedly built to celebrate the 65th birthday of Empress Dowager Cixi in 1900. Caves punctuate the hills, and the "First Spring Under Heaven" is celebrated for the quality of its water.

To the east, also abutting the Yangtze River, lies **Beigushan Park,** with the intoxicatingly named **Sweet Dew Temple (Ganlusi),** most of which dates from the Qing dynasty. Nearby is a rather peculiar and weather-beaten **iron pagoda,** sitting on the site of the original Tang dynasty version that was destroyed.

On a street north of the railway station stands a monument to American Pearl S. Buck, author of *The Good Earth.* The **Pearl S. Buck House** *(6 Runzhoushan Lu)* is a well-preserved testament to Buck, who wrote so vividly about China and its people.

The attractive hilltop **museum (Bowuguan)** *(85 Boxian Lu, $),* housed in the former British consulate and set in the grounds of Boxian Park, is a reminder that Zhenjiang was a foreign treaty port. The surrounding area is the historic core of the city, with cobbled streets and river-port views.

Jiaoshan ("burnt hill"), a delightful park, lies beside the river in the northeast of town. The views over the river are excellent. There are pavilions galore, venerable pine trees, and the **Dinghui Temple,** whose current buildings replace previous incarnations that failed to weather the tempest of Chinese history. ■

Zhenjiang

115 E2

CITS Visitor Information

92 Zhongshan Xilu

0511 523-7538

Jinshan Temple

Xinhe Lu

$

Sweet Dew Temple

Zhenjiao Lu

$

EXPERIENCE: Moganshan Trek

For a wilder trek through the hills, head south to Moganshan in the hills of north Zhejiang Province. Similar to Lushan (see pp. 203–204) and a delightfully cool escape in the humid Yangtze summer, the hills attracted Europeans in the early 20th century, who built stone villas, churches, and post offices on Moganshan's wooded slopes. The villas survive today, and many of them have been converted to hotels and guesthouses (see Travelwise p. 369). Aim to spend at least a few days here, climbing the stone steps and breaking off into treks through the woods.

To get to Moganshan, take a bus from the north bus station in Hangzhou (see pp. 173–175) to the town of Wukang, and then take a taxi the rest of the way.

Suzhou's Gardens

Suzhou is one of China's premier attractions, fabled for its picturesque canals and traditional gardens. Chinese gardens aim to inspire a meditative mood, so there's no need to rush from one to another in a bid to see them all in one day.

The flowers of the Humble Administrator's Garden bloom proudly.

Suzhou
145 E2 & 171
Visitor Information
345 Shiquan Jie
0512 6530-5887
www.classicsuzhou.com

Master of the Nets Garden
Off Shiquan Jie
$

Suzhou's gardens are not beautiful in the idyllic sense, and they depend heavily on the weather for mood. They are microcosms of nature and bring elements of *shanshui,* or mountains and rivers, to the city. As such, the weather is as much a part of the garden as its physical features. Depending on the season and the weather, Suzhou's gardens can be golden with autumn colors and frosty, clear, and bright, or grey and downcast. This interplay of the elements (wind, rain, snow, frost, sunlight) with the garden is critical. On a colorless day, the gardens can look limp and washed out; in the right light conditions, however, an inspirational mood reigns. Some of the gardens contain teahouses, where you can rest and enjoy the view over a steaming cup.

Master of the Nets Garden (Wangshiyuan)

The arrangement of pavilions, halls, music rooms, winsome bamboo groves, and waterside perches is an exercise in natural harmony. The garden's hub, surreptitiously tucked down an alleyway, is a large pool surrounded by ribbons of walkways and pavilions reflected in the water. Visit the gardens early in the morning to escape foraging tour groups blotting out the view. When approaching a garden such as this, aim to sit down and find peace within its natural setting.

Blue Wave Pavilion (Canglangting)

The best feature of this garden is its charming canalside setting. The rustling of wind in the bamboo leaves creates a tranquil mood, and stone recesses offer shelter from sudden showers. The rising and dipping contours distinguish the pavilion from the flatland of other Suzhou gardens.

INSIDER TIP:

In summer you can hear an outdoor concert or watch artists paint in the Master of the Nets Garden, a favorite of the locals.

—SUSAN STRAIGHT
National Geographic Books editor

Garden of Happiness (Yiyuan)

The Garden of Happiness is one of Suzhou's more relaxing gardens—not too large and a real pleasure to explore. The rock garden within is an intricate network of narrow stairways.

Humble Administrator's Garden (Zhuozhengyuan)

Considered one of Suzhou's finest, this is a harmony of water, stone, pavilions, bamboo groves, islets, and bridges in the north of town. Designed in the 16th century, it is the largest garden in Suzhou and is divided into two balanced sections.

Couples Garden (Ouyuan)

A pleasantly designed space near the moat in the eastern part of Suzhou, the Couples Garden offers an unruffled escape, a quiet retreat of birdsong and slowly sauntering couples rather than hordes of vacationing Chinese. The attractively named **Moon-viewing Pavilion** overlooks the water. The small figures on the plaque outside the **Zaijiu Tang** have had their heads smashed off—possibly the work of Taiping rebels.

East Garden (Dongyuan), north of Couples Garden, is more of a modern sprawl, offering noisy animal shows and lions riding on horseback when the fair's in town.

Lion Grove (Shizilin)

The origin of this garden's name is rather a mystery, though some say the shapes of lions can be discerned in its stones. It is easy to get completely lost in the cave-filled rock garden here, so take note. Once attached to a monastery, the garden was tended by architect and designer I. M. Pei. Most popular with Chinese tour groups and constantly overrun, the garden is rarely peaceful.

Garden for Lingering In (Liuyuan)

This is probably the least successful of Suzhou's gardens, with a contrived mystique and a rather tired feel to the gardens. ■

Blue Wave Pavilion
✉ Off Renmin Lu
$ $

Garden of Happiness
✉ Off Renmin Lu
$ $

Humble Administrator's Garden
✉ Dongbei Jie
$ $$ (free audio guide)

Couples Garden
✉ Off Cang Jie
$ $

Lion Grove
✉ Yuanlin Lu
$ $

Garden for Lingering In
✉ Liuyuan Lu
$ $

A Bike Ride Around Suzhou

From the Panmen Scenic Area near the city moat, this bike ride takes you along Suzhou's pretty streets past gardens, canals, and noteworthy temples. Bicycles can be rented from many places around town, including a number of hotels and opposite the train station.

Tourists consult a map before setting out on a tour of Suzhou.

NOT TO BE MISSED:

Master of the Nets Garden • Suzhou Museum • West Garden Temple

Before you set out at the start of the tour from the Panmen Scenic Area—an attractive, historic place in Suzhou's southwestern corner—leave your bike and clamber up this section of the old city wall. Below is the **Wuxiang Temple (Wuxiangci),** included in the price of your ticket to Panmen.

Cycle north to Xinshi Lu, passing the restored **Ruiguang Pagoda (Ruiguangta).** Follow Xinshi Lu, and then go left along Renmin Lu to the double-eaved, 11th-century **Confucius Temple (Kongmiao) ❶,** presiding over a collection of ancient stelae. Take your bike up the path along the canal opposite the **Blue Wave Pavilion** (see p. 169). Around the corner along Shiquan Jie, the **Master of the Nets Garden ❷** (see p. 168) is tucked down an alleyway.

Return to Shiquan Lu. Take the first right north up Fenghuang Jie (Phoenix Street) past the tenth-century **Twin Pagodas (Shuangta) ❸** on your right. The temple that accompanied them was torched by the Taiping in 1860.

Cross the canal and continue heading north along Lindun Lu. At the next major intersection is Guanqian Jie, a pedestrian-only street (you may have to leave your bike behind) marked by the **Xuan Miao Temple (Xuanmiaoguan) ❹,** a Taoist temple originally built in A.D. 276. In the **Sanqing Hall** are the Three Pure Ones (see p. 83), accompanied by images of the 12 Heavenly Generals. At the rear of the temple stands golden Taoist figures; a separate temple holds an effigy of eight-armed Doulao, the goddess who governs the Big Dipper constellation.

Continue north along Lindun Lu, turn right on Baita Donglu and then left on Yuanlin Lu, where you will find the **Lion Grove** (see p. 169). North again is the **Humble Administrator's Garden ❺** (see p. 169) on Dongbei Jie.

Just west is the new and magnificently designed **Suzhou Museum ❻,** designed by I. M. Pei. You'll want to spend quite a bit of time here examining the architecture and the museum's standout pieces. Farther along, as the road becomes Xibei Jie, rises the **North Pagoda (Beita),** which can be climbed.

Cycle south on Renmin Lu, then west along Dongzhongshi, which follows the canal, and turn right and then left into Liuyuan Lu. You will pass the **Garden for Lingering In** (see p. 169), but far more interesting is the **West Garden Temple (Xiyuansi) ❼** ahead.

The main temple houses imposing statues of Buddha and, behind, a colossal statue of Guanyin, draped in a robe and standing on the head of a fish. Clustering around her are the supplicant Luohan (see p. 83) in acts of benediction. The miniature palace to her on the far left is called the Crystal Palace.

A truly mesmerizing sight here is the **Arhat (Luohan) Hall,** first built in the Ming dynasty (and later burned down and rebuilt). The Guanyin facing you as you enter has 1,000 arms. There are 500 gilt clay Luohan in small corridors, surrounding the four sacred Buddhist mountains sculpted in the center.

Each breathtaking figure has a different facial expression, from laughter to sadness and everything in between, and stands encapsulated in a glass box, though some break out of their cages. The arms of one Luohan shoot out through holes in the glass, and others have staffs that pierce the ceilings. Models of children clamber over other Luohan. The Luohan with the completely mad expression is the Jigong monk.

Farther east on Fengqiao Lu stands the **Hanshan ("cold mountain") Temple.** It's not worth making an expedition to the temple unless you want to explore what inspired the Tang dynasty poet Zhang Ji to write his famous poem "Night Mooring by Maple Bridge":

The moon lowers, crows call and the whole world is frost
Facing the riverside maples and the fisherman's torch light I feel troubled in my sleep
In the middle of the night, the sound of the bell reaches my boat
From the Hanshan Temple outside the city of Gusu.

> Also see area map p. 145
> Panmen Scenic Area
> Whole day, including time spent in gardens
> 6.5 miles (10.5 km) to West Garden Temple
> West Garden Temple or Hanshan Temple

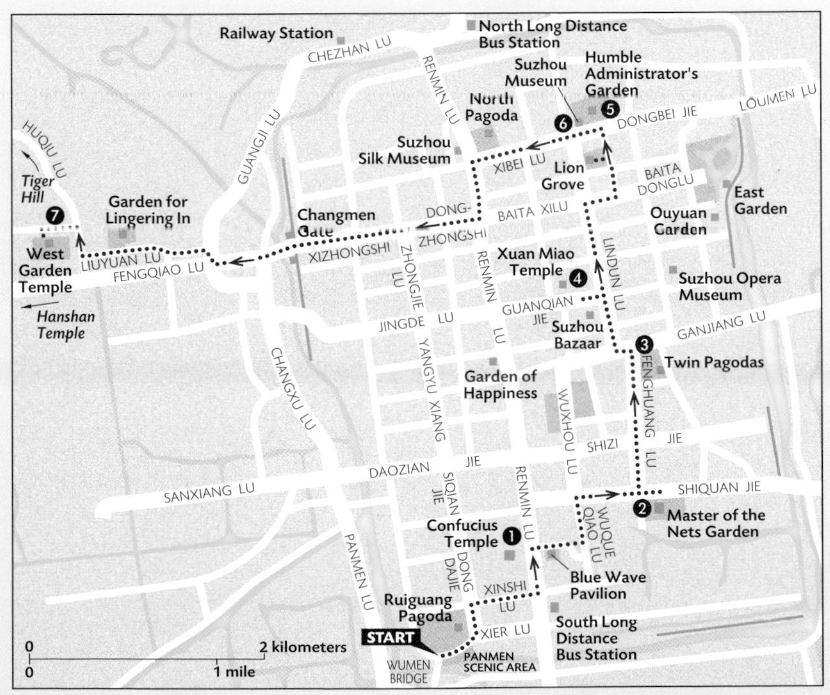

Lake Taihu & Around

Not far from Suzhou in Jiangsu Province is China's third largest freshwater lake, Taihu. Studded with islands, it lies next to the port city of Wuxi on the Grand Canal, and Yixing town, home of its famous namesake pottery.

The silhouette of a pagoda at Lake Taihu

Wuxi
145 E2

Xihui Park
Huihe Lu, Wuxi
$

Li Garden
Hubin Lu, Wuxi
$

Lake Taihu
145 E2

Wuxi

The city of Wuxi has buried its long history under a modern face. **Xihui Park (Xihui Gongyuan),** in the west of town, has some items of note. From the **Longguang Pagoda** adorning the hill you can cast long looks over Taihu. **Jichang Garden (Jichangyuan)** is an echo of Suzhou's famous gardens. An artificial lake, a zoo, and the **Huishan Temple** complete the park. In the south of town, **Li Garden (Liyuan)** adjoins the lake, which remains more popular with the Chinese, for around Taihu lie vestiges of two ancient kingdoms, Wu and Yue.

Lake Taihu

The most famous sights cluster on the lake's northern edge. The peninsula southwest of Wuxi, **Turtle Head Island (Yuantouzhu),** offers a vantage point over the water. At the south end of the island is a collection of amusement parks.

Ferries travel routes from the peninsula to islands in the lake. The short trip to the 5-acre (2 ha) **Three Hills Isles** (also called the Fairy Islands) is a popular excursion. The island supports a population of wild monkeys, and the views are excellent; overblown classical Chinese structures, however, seem rather contrived. Speedboats also cross the lake for two-hour trips.

Dingshan

Dingshan, in Yixing County on the western shore of the lake, is home of the purple sand *(zisha)* Yixing teapots. Found all over China, these teapots appear in a range of dark colors and have a porosity that best augments the color and fragrance of tea. The **Ceramics Exhibition Hall (Taoci Zhanlanguan)** features pots from Yixing over the ages.

Caves

Yixing County is also riddled with limestone caves. Navigate the recesses of **Shanjuan Cave (Shanjuandong)** along an underground river, or explore **Zhanggong Cave (Zhanggongdong),** honeycombed with a network of smaller caves. ■

Hangzhou

Famed throughout China for its silk and the idealized West Lake, Hangzhou has had a checkered history. It prospered as capital of the southern Song but was destroyed by the Taiping between 1860 and 1862. The Zhejiang city may be only a shadow of its former self, but the area around huge West Lake is delightfully picturesque.

Hangzhou's origins lie in the Qin dynasty (221–206 B.C.), though it was not until its connection to the Grand Canal (see pp. 176–177) in the seventh century that it flourished. The southern Song fled here from Kaifeng to establish their capital (then called Linan). Marco Polo and other Western travelers eulogized Hangzhou, as did many Chinese emperors. In the 19th century, however, the Taiping destroyed many of Hangzhou's temples and notable buildings, prompting a reversal of fortunes.

West Lake

The Chinese consider West Lake to be a heavenly, archetypal lake, the model for others. As such, it is stormed by tour groups, stampeding from one sight to another and crowding out the view. A visit to Hangzhou is obligatory for all Chinese, so it's often preferable to slip away to less visited sights.

West Lake may be commercialized, but the area has enjoyed considerable beautification over recent years. The lake is vast, so consider renting a bicycle from one of the numerous outlets as cycling

Hangzhou

145 E2 & 173

Visitor Information

Leifeng Pagoda, Hangzhou Train Stations, and other locations

0571 8796-8560

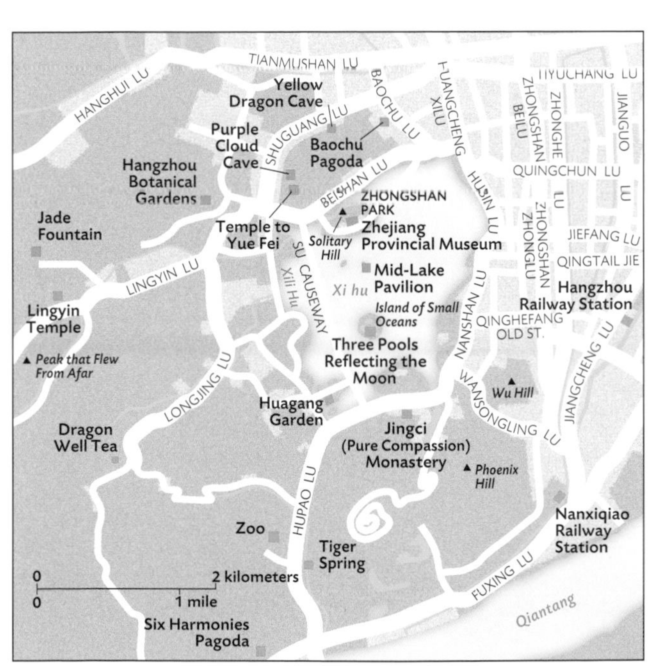

Temple to Yue Fei
Beishan Lu
$

Lingyin Temple
173
Lingyin Lu
$$

is possibly the best way to get around the lake and its sights.

The **Temple to Yue Fei (Yuefeimu)** on the northwestern shore tells the story of the heroic Song dynasty general who is buried here. Master strategist, loyal patriot, and inventor of a popular Chinese martial art (see pp. 124–125) linked with tai chi, Yue Fei was imprisoned and executed despite his successful incursions against the northern Jurchen invaders. He was posthumously exonerated and later elevated to the status of hero and demigod. He is also feted by the Communists, who admire his patriotic example. On the temple grounds are kneeling statues of the perfidious Qin Hui (the man who betrayed Yue Fei), his wife, and two treacherous generals.

To the west are the **Hangzhou Botanical Gardens (Hangzhou Zhiwuyuan),** and spanning south over West Lake is the Su Causeway, named after the Song dynasty poet Su Dongpo, who was also governor of Hangzhou for a period. The causeway stretches past **Huagang Garden** near the southern shore, famed for its goldfish.

Across the causeway, to the east, lies the **Island of Small Oceans,** with its four lotus-choked ponds. South of the island a cluster of small pagodas rises from **Three Pools Reflecting the Moon.** Candles are placed in each pagoda on nights of the full moon.

The largest island in the lake, **Solitary Hill (Gushan)** is attached to the north shore by the Baidi Causeway and Xiling Bridge. Dotted with small pavilions and pagodas, the island is home to **Zhejiang Provincial Museum,** where you can find **Zhongshan Park** and exhibits relating to Hangzhou and Zhejiang Province.

The slender **Baochu Pagoda** overlooks the lake from the hills to

This bamboo forest and other areas around Hangzhou evoke classic Chinese beauty.

Qinghefang Old Street

East of West Lake, Qinghefang Old Street is a lively, bustling, and fun collection of stalls selling snacks and knickknacks, shops selling silk and gifts, and the diverting Huqingyu Tang Chinese Medicine Museum, a traditional medicine shop.

the north. Originally built in 968 and repeatedly restored, it stands 125 feet (38 m) high.

Hangzhou was also a center of Christian missionary activity, an impressive remnant of which survives in the **Catholic Church** and the Chinese-style **Sicheng Church,** both of which you can enter.

Lingyin Temple

To the west is Hangzhou's most celebrated sacred site, Lingyin Temple. In the fourth century A.D., an Indian Buddhist noted that nearby rocks resembled a holy peak in India and suggested they had flown to China from there. The rocks were named Feilai Feng or the Peak That Flew From Afar.

Lingyin Temple was promptly built on the spot. Destroyed and rebuilt at least 16 times in its history, it miraculously survived the menace of the Cultural Revolution.

The chubby Qing dynasty Future Buddha (supposedly based on a real Chinese man who loved children) greets all with his welcoming laugh, while Weituo (see p. 83) stands behind him. The Four Heavenly Kings stand on either flank.

The Great Hall behind presents its magnificent 65-foot-tall (20 m) statue of Sakyamuni (see p. 82), carved from camphor wood. The hall was constructed in the 20th century to accommodate the statue, which was completed in 1956. On either side of the Great Hall stands a stone pagoda.

Opposite the Lingyin Temple, a network of caves and Buddhist statues in the Peak That Flew From Afar, one of few Buddhist art grottoes in southern China, makes for an interesting tour. The statues date from as early as the Five Dynasties (A.D. 906–960), and many are from the Song and Yuan dynasties. The most popular is a statue of the corpulent Laughing Buddha.

Dragon Well Tea

The town of **Dragon Well (Longjing),** southwest of West Lake, is celebrated throughout for its distinctively flavored tea. Nearby you can explore the **China Tea Museum** and the tea-making industry in Hangzhou.

Six Harmonies Pagoda

Farther to the southwest, nudging up against the Qiantang River, is the Six Harmonies Pagoda (Liuhe Ta). Situated on a hill, the octagonal structure served as a lighthouse and was thought to exert an esoteric influence over the annual tidal bore that swamped Hangzhou. It is named after the Six Codes of Buddhism. The hillside above the pagoda offers pleasing walks among statues and shrines. ■

Catholic Church

415 Zhongshan Beilu

Sicheng Church

132 Jiefang Lu

China Tea Museum

Longjing Lu

Closed Mon.

Six Harmonies Pagoda

173

Zhijiang Lu

$

Grand Canal

The Grand Canal, like that other mammoth engineering endeavor—the Great Wall—has sadly decayed through old age, neglect, and the dawn of new technologies. The remnants of this network of watercourses, however, constitute the longest man-made waterway in the world, cutting a 1,000-mile (1,610 km) route from Hangzhou to Beijing.

Boatmen ferry wood along the Grand Canal through Hangzhou.

History of the Canal

Segments of the canal system date back almost 2,500 years, but the first concerted effort to enmesh north China and the basin of the Yangtze River in a web of waterways came during the reign of a single megalomaniacal emperor.

The second emperor of the Sui dynasty, Yangdi (*r.* 604–618), was a man of extreme vision. His designs included the rebuilding of the capital Luoyang and the Great Wall. There was method to his imperial madness, however, and the logic behind the titanic canal scheme was to afford a transport link between the fertile Yangtze region and Luoyang. This would allow the smooth and efficient transport of both grain and soldiers in times of unrest.

In keeping with the tradition of great construction projects in China, forced labor made up most of the muscle (any surplus manpower was dispatched to the Great Wall). Up to 5.5 million workers slaved on the project, which was overseen by a large and quite brutal police force.

The new waterways were, in many places, carved out from the shells of existing canals cut during the Han dynasty. Upon its completion, Yangdi made a number of ostentatious outings along the canal until he was hanged in Yangzhou by justifiably mutinous members of his entourage.

Later dynasties made full use of the waterways. The Tang dynasty availed itself of the Grand Canal, while the Song dynasty grafted its capital Hangzhou onto the system. It was further extended during the Yuan dynasty to transport food to the new capital in Beijing; thus appeared the canal in its present route.

The emperors in Beijing relied upon the canal to bring north the produce of the fecund southern regions, which included rice, silk, and tea. Much of the brick and other material that made up the Ming dynasty Forbidden City and the Temple of Heaven in Peking was ferried up the Grand Canal.

The canal maintained its structure (which was not one canal but a linked chain of waterways) until the 19th century, when catastrophic flooding of the Yellow River caused major damage to both the waterways and vessels. The Taiping, who established their capital in Nanjing, further jeopardized the canal industry with their constant assaults on north China, and the canal's northern reaches gradually fell into disuse and disrepair.

The 20th century saw a host of rival transport options emerging to challenge the redundant technology of the Grand Canal. Railways and, more recently, air travel have led to further stagnation along the reaches of Yangdi's great enterprise.

The Canal Today

Save for a few sections, the canal today has largely fallen into disuse. The ambitious and overwhelmingly expansive South-North Water Diversion Project—which aims to divert river water from the Yangtze River to the dehydrated north of China—is employing sections of the canal in its eastern operation; however, severe pollution has created problems.

Stretching across China, the Grand Canal is a primary transport route.

The section between Suzhou (with its wonderful gardens and temples) and Hangzhou remains open, and flat-bottomed boats regularly float between the two, making for an interesting overnight journey.

Don't expect the Grand Canal of Venice, though. For centuries the waterway served as a conveyor belt of produce and was a functional, rather than an aesthetic, masterpiece. This has resulted in grubby boats plying the route and sooty factories scarring some of the shoreline. Nevertheless, if you are planning to travel between Suzhou and Hangzhou, this is an alternative to taking the bus or train.

Making the Journey

Boats *($$$)* depart from Suzhou for Hangzhou daily at 5:30 p.m. for the 11-hour journey to Hangzhou, arriving the next morning. Tickets can be bought in Suzhou at the Lianhe Ticket Center *(1606 Renmin Lu)*, or ask at your hotel.

Shaoxing

The Chinese celebrate the pretty town of Shaoxing for its charming canal scenes and the picturesque decay of its waterside houses. It is also the birthplace of the iconoclastic writer Lu Xun, one of China's greatest modern novelists. Shaoxing wine, a strongly flavored culinary wine, has been fermented here since the sixth century; it has since found its way into kitchens throughout the land.

Shaoxing's canals add charm to Zhejiang Province's waterlogged north.

Shaoxing
145 E2

Former Home of Lu Xun
208 Lu Xun Zhonglu

The old city of Shaoxing, capital of the state of Yue in the seventh century, lies in the middle of a heavily irrigated region of Zhejiang Province. One of the best ways to enjoy this town is to amble along its waterways and narrow, quaint streets.

The **Former Home of Lu Xun (Lu Xun Guju)** is where the author of "Diary of a Madman" (see sidebar opposite) lived before moving to Shanghai. Admission is free with a valid passport. Nearby is the **Lu Xun Memorial Hall (Lu Xun Jinianguan)** and the school where he studied.

The area around the memorial hall is an attractive part of Shaoxing and is well worth exploring for its canal textures and enchanting arched bridges. At the western tip of Lu Xun Zhonglu is **Lu Xun Cultural Square,** which marks an intersection of waterways.

Shaoxing's other darling son was the much loved Zhou Enlai, China's premier who died in 1976. He was an effective counterbalance to Mao Zedong's bad judgment and a sane voice in a time of madness. He never actually lived in Shaoxing, but his family came from here. Zhou's

Ancestral Home (Zhou Enlai Zuju) houses a museum dedicated to the man.

Head east along Changqiao Zhijie ("long bridge straight street"), and turn south on Guangningqiao Zhijie ("extensive peace bridge straight street"). This will take you across the canal and down to the Jin dynasty **Eight Character Bridge (Baziqiao),** one of Shaoxing's oldest.

The hexagonal and much restored **Dashan Pagoda (Dashanta)** rises on Guangming Lu southwest of the intersection of Jiefang Lu and Shengli Lu. Shaoxing's other pagoda, **Yingtian Pagoda (Yingtianta),** is in the south of town. It was rebuilt after a visit by the Taiping in the mid-19th century.

The Great Yu, China's famous water worker and mythical founder of the Xia dynasty (see p. 27), has an unlikely grave outside town. The **Tomb of the Great Yu (Yuling),** 2.5 miles (4 km) southeast of Shaoxing, is marked with a statue of the man, pavilions, cypresses, stelae, and memorial halls (take bus No. 2, which runs along Jiefang Lu).

Orchid Pavilion (Lanting) appeals most to Chinese visitors. The pavilions are especially noted for their association with the fourth-century calligrapher Wang Xizhi. His most famous piece, the *Lanting Xu* or *Preface to the Orchid Pavilion*, marks a literary feast held there in A.D. 353. ■

INSIDER TIP:

Use *ctrip.com* to book internal flights and hotels in China. The website and phone service are in English.

—ALISON WRIGHT
National Geographic photographer

Ancestral Home of Zhou Enlai
✉ 369 Laodong Lu
$ $

Tomb of the Great Yu
$ $$

Lu Xun

China's first great modern novelist, Lu Xun (Lu Hsun, 1881–1936) was born in Shaoxing and originally studied medicine in Japan before turning his attention to fiction. He became involved with the nascent Chinese May 4th literary movement, which aimed to replace the use of classical Chinese in literature with the spoken form of Chinese; in 1918 his best work, "Diary of a Madman," was published. This was the first short story to eschew classical Chinese, the establishment language that had exercised a stranglehold on literary creativity. The sinister and discomforting tale depicts a lunatic who feels enveloped by a man-eating society. The story is a thinly veiled critique of the self-consuming nature of Confucian society.

Lu Xun's anti-conservatism found free reign in *The Story of Ah Q* (1921), probably his most famous work, and "Medicine," a short story that dealt with the messy world of superstition in Chinese society.

The writer also excelled at prose writing, penning *A Brief History of Chinese Fiction* and translating a large body of literature from other languages. He lived his last years in Shanghai, increasingly sympathizing with the Communist cause, which he saw as offering salvation to China. His tomb is in Shanghai.

Putuoshan

Putuoshan, one of the four sacred Buddhist mountains, lies off the coast of Zhejiang Province in the East China Sea. Its sympathetic goddess, Guanyin, presides over her maritime dominion of caves, pavilions, and monasteries.

Incense is an important part of Chinese worship.

Putuoshan
145 F2
$$$

CITS Visitor Information
117 Meicen Lu
0580 609-1414

GETTING TO & FROM PUTUOSHAN: The nearest airport is on the island of Zhujiajian, but most visitors arrive by ferry from either Shanghai or Ningbo. Regular ferries leave daily for the island from Ningbo (2 hrs) and Shanghai (4 hrs). A 12-hour overnight ferry to Shanghai, leaves Putuoshan at around 4:40 p.m.

"Putuo" is the Chinese approximation of the Sanskrit Potala, or Potalaka—the mountain home of Guanyin. The same bodhisattva inhabits the Potala Palace in Lhasa (see pp. 304–305).

Putuoshan was originally a Taoist preserve (a few Taoist shrines still remain). Its appropriation by Buddhist folklore was assured, however, when a vision of Guanyin appeared on the island, quickly succeeded by further sightings. A spate of temple building generously sprinkled the island with shrines, though most were destroyed by pirates and Red Guard fanaticism.

Putuoshan is only 3.5 miles (5.5 km) long and 2 miles (3 km) wide. If you have the time, it is better to walk around, but minibuses also travel the routes between the major sights. Despite modernization, the island retains an insular Buddhist charm, but avoid weekends and holidays.

Pleasant beaches border Putuoshan's eastern shore. **One Hundred Step Beach (Baibusha)** and **One Thousand Step Beach (Qianbusha)** are attractive and clean but can be crowded in summer. Lonely **Houao Beach** looks out to sea on the island's northern fringe. Small **Roaring Tiger Beach (Xiaohusha)** lies on the northeast shore next to Lotus Sea.

Puji Monastery

Upon arrival at the ferry terminal, take the road leading left through the trees north to the Puji Monastery *($)*, also known as the Front Temple (Qiansi). This area is also the island's hub—a knot of small hotels, shops, and restaurants. The temple, which was begun in the northern Song dynasty, is fronted by a lotus pond, its main hall filled with manifestations of Guanyin. To the southeast of the temple lies the Yuan dynasty **Many Treasures Pagoda (Duobaota),** a adorned with Buddhist images.

Buddha's Summit Peak

At the far end of One Thousand Step Beach, on the east flank of

Putuoshan, is **Law Rain Monastery (Fayu Chansi)** *($)*. Also known as Rear Temple (Hou Si) It clings to the slope of Buddha's Summit Peak (Foding Shan) and safeguards a huge statue of the merciful bodhisattva.

A path leads up the northern hill—Buddha's Summit Peak—to **Huiji Monastery (Huiji Chansi).** Over the centuries this monastery has mushroomed from its humble beginnings as a solitary structure to a cluster of halls and pavilions.

Other Temples & Caves

The Taoist **Meifu Nunnery (Meifuan),** west of Puji Monastery, was built where a Taoist recluse, Wei Meifu, came during the Han dynasty to smelt cinnabar (a major ingredient in the Taoist elixir of life) and achieve immortality. Farther along the road to the south is the nunnery of **Guanyin Cave,** overshadowed by a large camphor tree.

South of One Hundred Step Beach, on a promontory of land, is the **Hall of the Unwilling to Depart Guanyin (Bukenqu Guanyinyuan).** Legend records that a Japanese monk was returning home from Wutaishan in 916 with a statue of Guanyin. As he passed Putuoshan, his boat was unable to continue; the monk believed that Guanyin wished to remain on the island. The hall celebrates the beginning of the worship of Guanyin on Putuoshan.

Farther south along the shoreline is **Sound of the Tides Cave (Chaoyindong),** where the foaming waves are funneled with a crash into hollows in the cliff.

A number of other caves pockmark Putuoshan. Carved from the promontory of land reaching out east, **Buddhist Tidings Cave (Fanyindong),** with its small Guanyin temple, offers a thrilling view down to the roaring waves. **Morning Sun Cave (Zhaoyangdong)** lies sandwiched between One Hundred Step Beach and One Thousand Step Beach.

Zhujiajian

South of Putuoshan is the larger and less visited island of Zhujiajian, with its crop of temples. ■

THE SOUTHSEA GUANYIN: Visible from many parts of the island, the Southsea Guanyin (Nanhai Guanyin) is a giant golden effigy of the goddess of mercy. A moving sight at sunrise and sunset, the huge goddess at the southern tip of the island stands above exhibition space dedicated to effigies of Guanyin and her relationship with the island.

Guanyin

The ruling deity on Putuoshan, Guanyin is a salvationary goddess who emanates a powerful sense of compassion, not unlike the Virgin Mary. She is a bodhisattva or Future Buddha, who is worshipped over the length and breadth of China. Women in particular show keen devotion to her, especially if they are praying for a child. A Songzi (literally "offering son") Guanyin is shown holding a child, but she appears in many other manifestations. The thousand-armed Guanyin (Qianshou Guanyin) is also common, as is the Dripping Water Guanyin (Dishui Guanyin); she is also portrayed holding a lotus flower or a cup of nectar.

There is a question as to the true sex of Guanyin. Some argue that the deity is without gender, and some statues attest to this ambiguity. It appears that Guanyin was originally male and then endowed with female characteristics. Certainly, early representations of Guanyin exhibit a distinctly masculine appearance.

Shanghai

Stylish Shanghai, metaphor for decadence, class division, spectacular riches, corruption, nepotism, sophistication, and snobbery, is also a stylish byword for today's China and the glittering offspring of an enticing engagement between the East and the West.

Shanghai is a sparkling appendix to the revolutionary chronicle of 20th-century China.

Shanghai
145 E2

Challenging orthodoxy and leading the country on its dramatic journey to modernity and wealth, Shanghai has often shunned decency and temperance in favor of a wilder agenda. It is here to make history and not to follow it.

The great Yangtze River empties into the Yellow Sea just north of Shanghai, as if sapping the country's ingenuity and depositing it on the shores of this great city. Many locals admit the wherewithal comes from its peculiar hybrid culture of Occident and Orient—a potent formula that leaves the rest of the country fumbling for the switch to success.

Unlike Shenzhen or Zhuhai, which beneath the veneer were recently mere specks on the map, Shanghai (literally "on the sea") gives the impression of having been great once and is arguably great once more.

In earlier centuries, the town of Shanghai earned its living through cotton and silk production. By the mid-18th century a huge task force of 20,000 was engaged in the cotton industry.

INSIDER TIP:

During World War II, European Jews found sanctuary in the Jewish quarter that still surrounds the Ohel Moishe Synagogue and Shanghai Jewish Refugees Museum *(62 Changyang Lu).*

—JAY PASACHOFF
National Geographic field researcher

The British established their first concession here after the treaty of Nanking, which ended the first Opium War in 1842 (see p. 39). They were followed quickly by other powers. With the foreign powers in charge of an unrestricted trading base, Shanghai quickly emerged as China's greatest port. Along with the inflow of money came the big Western names of commerce and banking, and some dashing architecture.

Built on the back of the opium trade, Shanghai was from the very start a lawless endeavor. It was administered by greed and exploitation, becoming a very rich but insurgent domain of brothels, gambling, and opium dens.

(continued on p. 188)

SHANGHAI TRANSPORT CARD: Travelers who intend to spend a lot of time in Shanghai should invest in a transport card. You generally won't net discounts for your journeys, but the card will save you the inconvenience of waiting in long lines for subway tickets. The card can also be used on buses and taxis, and it can be purchased at subway stations, some banks, and convenience stores with a refundable deposit.

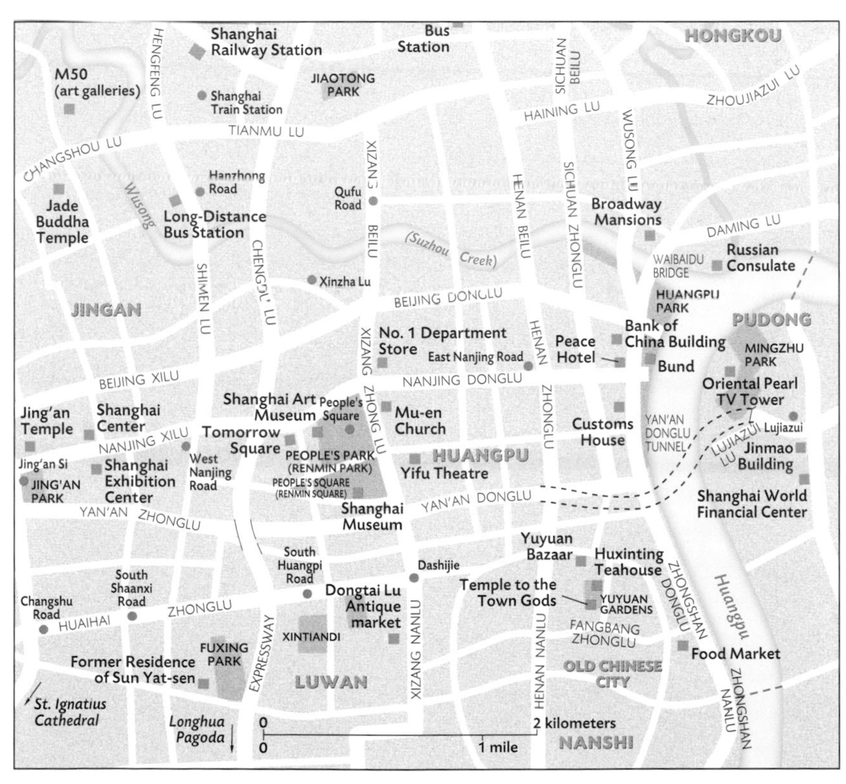

A Walk Along the Bund

The embankment known as the Bund, with its elegant sweep of European architecture and landmark hotels lining the low bow of the Huangpu River, is perfectly evocative of old Shanghai. Stoically facing the glittering panorama of Lujiazui in Pudong across the water, the Bund is a proud and gentrified chapter of Shanghai history, housing, as it did, the many movers and shakers of this rich city.

Head out along the Bund in the early morning, and you may run across people doing tai chi.

The Bund (an Anglo-Indian term for a muddy embankment) was the financial motor behind Shanghai's success and Europe's corporate perch in China. It was renamed Revolution Boulevard during the Cultural Revolution, but as Shanghai reemerged as a city of huge financial importance, its original significance was reestablished.

The waves of visitors that surge up and down the Bund (Waitan in Chinese) do so in amazement. Other cities (such as Qingdao) have their colonial stamp, but nowhere, apart from Hong Kong, is this statement so loud and so bold.

The most romantic way to take in the Bund is from the decks of the Huangpu River cruise (see p. 196). Alternatively, walk along the Bund promenade at nightfall and watch the dazzling display of evening neon in Lujiazui across the Huangpu River as the lights come on.

A slow walk along the Bund itself will, however, equally immerse you in the location's history and unique character. Shanghai's first hotel, the **Astor House Hotel** (see Travelwise p. 370), north of Suzhou Creek, is a good place to start. Pop into the reception area to gauge the scale of the place, and clamber up to the galleries for a sense of its history. This is a museum of old, varnished floorboards, high ceilings, faded photos, and wooden rafters. Everywhere is the pervasive aroma of the 1920s. Albert Einstein and Charlie Chaplin both stayed here.

Opposite the Pujiang Hotel, on the bank of the Huangpu River, stands the **Russian Consulate** *(20 Huangpu Lu)*, built in 1917.

South Toward Yan'an Donglu

The brick 1935 **Broadway Mansions**—a hotel with good views of the Bund—looms up to your right as you head south to **Waibaidu Bridge** ❶, looking out over Suzhou Creek. Cross Waibaidu Bridge (originally known as Garden Bridge), with its excellent view east to the glittering buildings of **Pudong** (see p. 188). Setting foot on the Bund itself, note the ornate building hidden away behind the garden and foliage at No. 33 Zhongshan Donglu; it was formerly the British Consulate. Unfortunately, you are not allowed to enter.

Flush with the banks of the Huangpu River is Huangpu Park (formerly called the British

NOT TO BE MISSED:

Astor House Hotel • Peace Hotel • Hong Kong and Shanghai Bank

Public Gardens), site of the Bund History Museum (currently closed for restoration).

A long stretch of neoclassical grandeur starts at No. 29, the old address of the French Bank de Indochine. The edifice at No. 28 was originally the Glen Line building, and the heavyweight, chunky, and grandiose affair at No. 27 was owned by the venerable Jardine & Matheson trading company that built its fortune from opium. The Corinthian pillars say it all. Now it's the **Foreign Trade Building.**

No. 24 was originally the Yokohama Bank, built in 1924. No. 23—the **Bank of China Building** ❷—interrupts the Occidental theme with its accent on traditional architecture, with a strong art deco twist. It was jointly designed by Palmer & Turner and a Chinese architect (hence the traditional Chinese roof). The building was the highest in Shanghai when completed in 1937.

Sitting on the eastern extremity of Nanjing Donglu, the art deco **Peace Hotel** ❸ *(20 Nanjing Donglu, tel 6321-6888)*, formerly the Cathay, was built in 1926 and opened in 1929. The Chinese outpost of businessman Victor Sassoon, it was the place to stay on a visit to Shanghai, attracting such types as English playwright Noel Coward, who penned *Private Lives* here. Stiff competition from the ever burgeoning Shanghai five-star hotel market led

Also see area maps on pp. 144 & 183
➤ Astor House Hotel
0.5 to 1 hours
1.2 miles (2 km)
➤ Nanjing Donglu

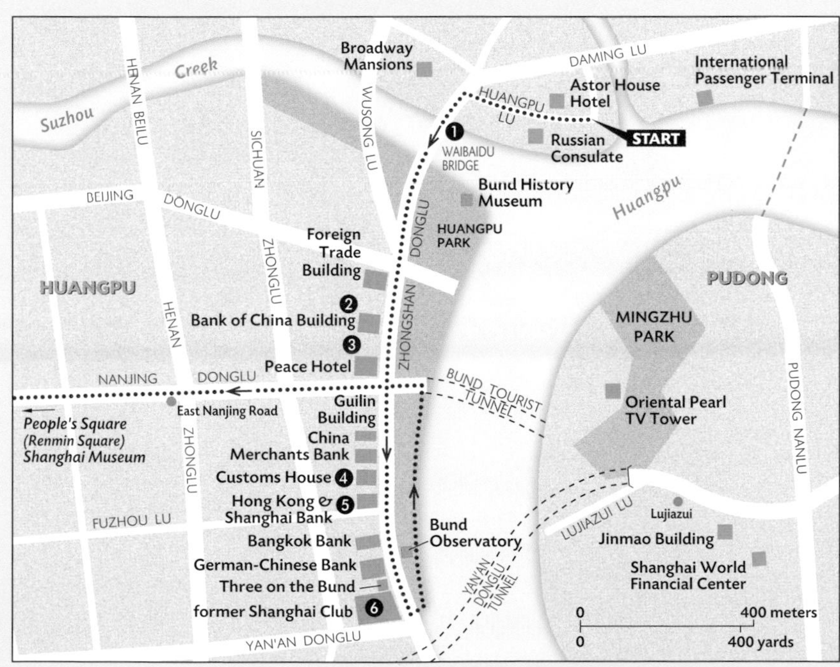

to the hotel's shutting in 2007 for a three-year restoration before a high-profile reopening in 2010. The hotel remains a grand slice of Shanghai art deco heritage: Peek at the interior, especially the marvelous lobby and stained glass. The legendary Peace Hotel Jazz Band put down its instruments for the refit but is serenading guests once more.

The Peace Hotel extends to No. 19 on the next block—the red-and-white brick building called the Peace Palace Hotel. No. 18 is a boastful affair—previously the Chartered Bank of India, Australia, and China building—and now the very smart Bund 18, a constellation of chic bars, restaurants, and shops. Once known as the Guilin Building, the building at No. 17 housed the offices of the *North China Daily News.* Slip in through the side entrance and take in the gold mosaics on the ceiling.

On the next block down, No. 16—the **China Merchants Bank,** again overdone in classical style with huge pillars—was the old address of the Bank of Taiwan.

No. 14 is an arresting 1940s construction, sharp-edged with vertical lines and a then futurist agenda. Note the brass doorway, and inside, '40s handrails and balustrades.

Tracing Shanghai's Jewish History

Shanghai's famous and wealthy Jewish families—from the Sassoons to the Kadoories and Hardoons—are forever associated with the city's age of splendor and excess. Shabby Hongkou in north Shanghai received a vast influx of stateless Jewish refugees during World War II, when it grew to be known as "Little Vienna." Several synagogues have survived to the modern day, including the Ohel Moishe Synagogue *(62 Changyang Lu, $$)* in Hongkou and the Ohel Rachel Synagogue *(500 Shanxi Beilu)*, north of Nanjing Xilu.

No. 13, the **Customs House ❹**, was built in 1927. It was home to the "People's Peace Preservation Corps," who operated from room 410. A huge plaque on the wall outside commemorates this and shows the citizens of Shanghai waving banners that read: "Welcome, People's Liberation Army" and "10,000 years for the Chinese Communist Party." Inside are some period art deco features and mosaics. The Customs House is crowned by **Big Ching,** a clock that chimed every quarter hour. The bell was silenced during the Cultural Revolution and substituted with propaganda broadcasts and the Mao anthem "The East Is Red."

At No. 12 you'll find the extravagant former headquarters of the **Hong Kong and Shanghai Bank ❺**. Along with the Peace Hotel, this domed structure is probably the most famous building on the Bund. A plaque reveals that it was opened by Sir Ronald Macleay, minister to China, on June 23, 1923. It was designed by the architectural firm Palmer & Turner. The original mosaic floor remains intact, and a stunning octagonal ceiling with panels depicts Tokyo, New York, London, Paris, Calcutta, Bangkok, Hong Kong, and Shanghai. Classical figures (Probitas, Historia, Fides, Sapientia, Veritas, and so on) ring the walls. This is one of the most alluring interiors in the whole of the city. The pair of bronze lions that guarded the door were removed during the Cultural Revolution; one of them can be seen in the Shanghai History Museum (see p. 189). The red star on a pole hoisted above the building finishes the picture, and the building is currently occupied by the Pudong Development Bank.

In the next block, on the corner with Fuzhou Lu, No. 9 is an interesting building partially overgrown with ivy and surrounded with hedges. It was constructed in 1912. The **Bangkok Bank** at No. 7 was the China Mercantile Bank in a previous incarnation.

The Gothic windows and arches of No. 6 belong to the former German-Chinese Bank. On the other side of Guangdong Lu, **Three on the Bund** is one of Shanghai's most celebrated

Expat Magazines

One of the first things you should do when you arrive in Beijing, Shanghai, or other major Chinese city is to grab a copy of the local entertainment and events magazines, available at expat bars and restaurants. The monthly *Beijinger (www.thebeijinger.com)* lets you hit the ground running with complete bar, restaurant, and club listings, as well as much more other useful miscellany. A similar publication, *That's Shanghai,* is the equivalent in the eastern seaboard metropolis. In Hong Kong, get hold of *HK Magazine* or *bc magazine,* both of which have complete listings. *Time Out* is available in all three cities.

addresses, converted to house an assortment of luxurious restaurants, bars, shops, and the **Shanghai Gallery of Art.**

Farther down, No. 2 was the former address of the **Shanghai Club** ❻. Built in 1910, the club was the site of the world's longest bar and the venue of the most exclusive colonial coterie in town. In more recent years it served as the Tung Feng Hotel, but it is now closed and inaccessible to the public.

River Promenade & Nanjing Donglu

From the former Shanghai Club, cross over Zhongshan Donglu to the promenade overlooking the Huangpu River and walk back up the Bund, savoring the views. The **Bund Observatory** tower contains exhibits related to the Bund. Turn left at the Peace Hotel into the shopping strip of **Nanjing Donglu** to taste Shanghai's commercial fever. You can either walk along Nanjing Donglu or take the subway from Middle Henan Road station to Renmin Square and the magnificent **Shanghai Museum** (see pp. 189–191).

While sauntering down the Bund, steal a glance at Pudong opposite. The Pudong New Area is larger than Shanghai itself and fronted by some daring architecture, including the spectacular **Jinmao Building,** the skyscraping **Shanghai World Financial Center,** and the bizarre **Oriental Pearl TV Tower,** resembling a 1950s monument to the atomic age.

The clock tower of the Customs House overlooks the Bund.

Pudong
183

Shanghai World Financial Center
183
100 Shiji Dadao
Observation deck: $$$$
Subway: Lujiazui
www.swfc-observatory.com

By the early 20th century, Shanghai had added an industrial base to complement its trading success. With half of the city dandified and the other half in rags, however, the stifling inequality rapidly incubated protesting sentiments. The Chinese Communist Party, with its creed of justifiable outrage and accurate sense of destiny, was born here in 1921.

The Communists liberated the city in 1949, filled the gaps of inequality, eradicated child labor and prostitution, and restored respect to the poor. The city's drive stalled as a by-products followed by a creeping passivity.

Since the 1980s, however, Shanghai has been exploring the outer fringes of capitalist permissibility. China's highest salaries and property prices are to be found here, as well as the nation's tallest buildings.

Shanghai's dubious history has equipped it with all the tools of success: confidence, panache, money, and a brain up top. Here you will find not just socialism with Chinese characteristics but capitalism with textbook characteristics.

The Oriental Pearl TV Tower highlights modern Pudong.

Pudong

Newfangled Pudong challenges the antiquated arrogance of the Bund (see pp. 184–187). To understand what the Chinese want China to look like, come to Pudong, a shrine to international finance, a concrete expression of vanity, and a symbol of the Chinese reform drive.

Paving its way through its heart is 2.8-mile (4.5 km) **Century Avenue (Shiji Dadao).** Splitting the Pudong New Area, it is a grand gesture of the new zeitgeist.

China's tallest buildings have been earmarked for Pudong since 1990, when the wrapping came off the blueprints. The crystalline **Jinmao Building,** a searing 1,379 feet (420 m) high, is a bold testament to China's newfound confidence. The nearby **Shanghai World Financial Center** is quite awesome and home to the world's highest observation deck above ground level (three decks in all) and the standout Park Hyatt, briefly the world's highest hotel above ground level (now in Hong Kong).

Pudong's other eye-catching edifice is the concrete tripod **Oriental Pearl TV Tower,** with excellent views over town and home to the highly informative **Shanghai History Museum** in the basement. Pudong was also the site of the 2010 World Expo and some of its edifices remain, including the China Pavilion.

Most Western visitors come to see old China, not an American derivative. As it is so modern and concrete-saturated, most visitors quickly discover that Pudong lacks soul, substance, and history. Pudong is growing, however, with a flourishing retail and restaurant scene and a sightseeing tunnel linking it to the Bund.

Maglev

If you're traveling with kids or just like speed, consider a trip on the Maglev—the world's fastest high-speed train in commercial service—which runs to and from Pudong International Airport. Floating on a magnetic cushion, the train reaches a top speed of 268 miles an hour (431 kph). With departures every 20 minutes during operating hours (6:45 a.m.–9:40 p.m.), the rocketing Maglev journey is a mere eight minutes. If you have an air ticket for the same day, tickets are cheaper.

Shanghai Museum

Occupying a prime piece of real estate in Renmin Square in the heart of Shanghai, the unique and inspiring **Shanghai Museum (Shanghai Bowuguan)** hoards a magnificent collection of Chinese art and antiquities. If you only have time for one museum in China, make sure it is this one. It's easy to spend the whole day here, and many visitors come back for more.

Styled to resemble a *ding* (an ancient Chinese bronze vessel), the Shanghai Museum is a splendid transformation of its original incarnation on South Henan Nanlu. The entrance fee is a bargain, but you may wish to avoid the expensive coffees in the Yen Yu Yun Pavilion teahouse upstairs. The bright interior, lit by an impressive atrium, is exciting, as is the ascending floor plan, accessed by a sweeping staircase. And the galleries are intelligently laid out, with utmost consideration to the visitor. Gone is the stuffy, monotonous, and somnolent atmosphere of socialist museums of old.

The millennia of Chinese history are beautifully illustrated via the stories of each individual gallery. Whether you are interested in Chinese bronzes, sculptures, calligraphy, paintings, seals, jade, Ming and Qing dynasty furniture, or the flawless perfection of the ceramic pieces on view in the Zande Lou Gallery, the museum is an education. These are some of the best pieces left in China.

First floor: The **Gallery of Ancient Chinese Bronzes** takes you on a dazzling journey through the millennia of early bronze design from its earliest days to its subsequent apogee. Observe the ferocious *taotie* designs on the Shang dynasty bronzes, which point to an animist creed. The exhibition then continues to chart the development of this art form through the successive dynasties of the Zhou (1122–256 B.C.) and the Spring and Autumn period (770–476 B.C.).

Oriental Pearl TV Tower (Shanghai History Museum)
- Map 183
- Museum: $$ (audio tour: $$)
- Subway: Lujiazui

Shanghai Museum
- Map 183
- 201 Renmin Ave.
- 021 0372 3500
- Subway: People's Square

GETTING TO PUDONG: Pudong is easily reached by taking subway line No. 2 to Lujiazui station. Alternatively, take the Bund Sightseeing Tunnel from the Bund to the far side of the river; or take a ferry or taxi. To ride the astonishing Maglev train to Pudong International Airport, take the subway to Longyang Road station.

Exploring the **Ancient Chinese Sculpture Gallery,** also on the first floor, is like nosing through the cave sculptures of Dunhuang, Longmen, or Yungang, without the rattling bus ride. The stone and wooden Buddhas, bodhisattvas, and other figures have been gathered from the four corners of China, and range from the Warring States period (475–221 B.C.) to the Ming dynasty (1368–1644). Coming together under one roof, they give you the excellent opportunity to compare how the countenance of Buddhist images has changed over the dynasties.

The shop on this floor stocks an impressive range of books on the arts of China and general literature on Chinese culture.

Second floor: For many, the highlight of a visit to the museum is the **Ancient Chinese Ceramics Gallery,** which feeds chronologically into the **Zande Lou Ceramics Gallery.** This wonderful collection of Chinese ceramics ranges from the Neolithic era to the late Qing dynasty. There's a medley of colors from brightly glazed Tang horses to the cool jade of celadon bowls, from playful *doucai* stem cups to the fragile crackle of Song Ge ware and overblown Qing famille-rose. Crowning them all are the exquisite underglaze cobalt blue-and-white pieces known as *qinghua* (see p. 52). The earliest blue-and-white pieces appeared in the Yuan dynasty, but they reached their apogee in the Ming and Qing dynasties.

Third floor: The superb layout of the **Chinese Painting Gallery** is intelligently illuminated and inviting. Paintings are lit as you approach them, in an effort to preserve their ancient colors. Primarily landscapes, they range from the Tang through the Song, Yuan, Ming, and Qing dynasties.

The **Chinese Calligraphy Gallery** displays all the major calligraphic styles, from the formal and exacting *kaishu* (regular) to the dynamic and exciting *caoshu* (grasshand). Though difficult to appreciate fully unless you read the language, Chinese calligraphy is mesmerizing nonetheless.

The **Chinese Seal Gallery** displays more than 500 pieces from the Zhou to the Qing dynasty.

EXPERIENCE: Art in the M50

The industrial complex known as the M50 *(50 Moganshan Lu, www.m50.com.cn)* is the best place in Shanghai to satisfy a craving for contemporary art. The M50's industrial architecture is redolent of Beijing's 798 Art District (see p. 96), a kind of lucrative fusion between proletarian heritage and the art-buying middle classes that troop here. There's a lot to see around here, so you'll need plenty of energy and the better part of half a day. Cafés and shops round out the picture. The galleries—the best known is the high-profile ShangART *(www.shangartgallery.com)* in buildings 16 & 17—are shut on Mondays.

Fourth floor: Jade occupies a prime position in Chinese culture, and the **Ancient Chinese Jade Gallery** presents excellent specimens. The exhibition musters together prize examples of jade carvings from the Shang dynasty and earlier cultures through to later dynasties.

The **Ming and Qing Furniture Gallery** guides you through the functional beauty of classical Chinese furniture. The pieces range from restrained yet voluptuous Ming pieces to their elaborate and overblown Manchu equivalents.

The vivid cultural traditions of China's ethnic minorities are represented in the **Minority Nationalities' Art Gallery,** while the **Chinese Coin Gallery** paints the story of China's currency.

Located in the center of the old city, the classical Yuyuan Gardens are Shanghai's most famous.

Old Chinese City

Southwest of the Bund lies the old Chinese quarter, an echo of the original town of Shanghai. Many of the city's old buildings remain, along with labyrinthine gardens and the Yuyuan Bazaar, a busy, commercial tangle of souvenir and antique shops.

Designed by a rich Ming dynasty family of officials, the **Yuyuan Gardens** are a pleasant side step off the city's busy streets. Altogether, the gardens were destroyed three times, once being carpet-shelled during the first Opium War (a museum in the gardens chronicles the disasters). The French also destroyed the place during the Taiping Rebellion in the mid-19th century. Later restored, the gardens are now made up of inner and outer sections and are comparable to Suzhou's (see pp. 168–169). Paths wind under rocky outcrops, past pools thick with goldfish, and through caves and rockeries. Avoid the gardens on weekends, when crowds of visitors annihilate the last remaining shred of tranquillity, and try to get here in the morning.

At the Yuyuan Bazaar and the shops along **Fangbang Zhonglu,** you can hunt through a mound of bric-a-brac and fake antiques to find the occasional gem. The whole setting is ersatz-period China with a theme-land feel, but it is an ideal hunting ground for souvenirs and gifts. After shopping, pop upstairs to the **Old Shanghai Teahouse** *(385 Fangbang Zhonglu)* to sip tea and snack among its fascinating jumble of collectibles.

In the middle of the lake, China's famous **Huxinting Teahouse** (see p. 371) serves pots of tea. It is connected to the shore

Old Chinese City
Map 183
Visitor Information
✉ 149 Jiujiaochang Lu, located a short walk southwest of Yuyuan Gardens
☎ 021 6355-5032

Yuyuan Gardens
$ $

Jade Buddha Temple
183
170 Anyuan Lu
$

Jing'an Temple
183
1686 Nanjing Xilu
$
Subway: Jing'an Si

Longhua Pagoda
183
$
Longcao Lu Light Rail Station

by a zigzag bridge (Jiuqu Qiao), a picturesque structure that also serves as a *fengshui* device to deflect bad spirits, which can travel only in straight lines.

Jade Buddha Temple & Other Temples

Shanghai is largely a modern city with few temples. In the northwest of town, however, you'll find the city's holiest spot, the saffron-colored **Jade Buddha Temple (Yufosi).**

About 70 monks live in the temple, whose centerpiece is its jewel-encrusted white jade Buddha. Standing more than 6 feet (1.8 m), the statue was brought back from Burma (Myanmar) in 1882 by a devout monk from the Buddhist island of Putuoshan.

Adorning the walls are 7,000 Buddhist sutras. At the rear stands a resplendent figure of Guanyin, surrounded by a host of little figures. Behind the main hall is a small courtyard attractively arrayed with plants; here you will see the tower where the Buddhist scriptures from India were stored.

The **Jade Buddha (Yufo)** can be found upstairs inside a small wooden hall. The gorgeous statue is clearly Southeast Asian in origin, with its luminous sheen and delightfully calm features. Unfortunately, a barrier prevents you from approaching the sacred effigy. It miraculously eluded the sledgehammers of the Cultural Revolution (1966–1976).

Downstairs in the **Reclining Buddha Hall** is a supine Buddha on a couch. It represents Buddha giving his last homily to his disciples before entering nirvana.

The **Jing'an Temple,** which sits above its namesake stop on the underground subway, is being slowly restored and boasts well-designed exterior walls and partially renovated interior walls.

The Buddhist **Longhua Temple (Longhuasi)** in the south of town is Shanghai's largest temple complex; you can see the city's seven-story **Longhua Pagoda (Longhuata)** rising across the way.

EXPERIENCE: Zhujiajiao

Shanghai is not a city that you would normally associate with canals, yet within Shanghai municipality lies the lovely Ming dynasty water town of Zhujiajiao. Easily reached from the city, Zhujiajiao is a charming panorama of narrow lanes, ancient arched bridges, and temples. A crop of hostels and guesthouses has also recently opened up, so spending the night away from the bright lights of the big city is a definite attraction. There is no admission price to the town, but some sights require tickets. The five-arched Fangsheng Bridge is a real picture, and you can hop onto river boats for waterborne tours of town. Buses depart in the morning for Zhujiajiao from the Shanghai Sightseeing Bus Centre in Shanghai Stadium *(tel 021 5351 4830).*

French Concession

Shanghai's most charming streetscapes, trendiest shopping zones, and most ultrachic restaurants and bars belong to the former French Concession, an elegant swath of Paris-meets-Puxi that extends through the districts of Luwan to Changning and hinges north–south roughly

Shikumen & Lilong

Shanghai's French Concession is filled with *shikumen* housing and *lilong* lanes waiting to be explored. A kind of synthesis of Western terrace housing and Chinese courtyard architecture, shikumen houses in many ways typify the hybrid architecture of the city.

While Xintiandi is more accessible and more high-profile as a dolled-up and chic quadrant of shikumen housing, the more hidden-away domain of Tianzifang (also called the Taikang Road Art Centre) is perhaps more genuine and appealing. It is also home to some lilong lanes. The lanes off the eastern end of Yuyuan Road near Jing'an Temple subway station are typical of Shanghai's famous and well-kept alleyways.

on the bustling shopping street of Huaihai Zhonglu.

One of the best ways to appreciate the charms of this area is to walk around its leafy backstreets. **Xintiandi,** an ambitious and ultra-trendy upscale retail, restaurant, and bar enclave south of Huaihai Zhonglu, is an excellent place to start exploring the eastern edge of the French Concession. Consisting of recently restored *shikumen* (literally "stone gate house") architecture, a kind of hybrid Chinese- and European-style brick residential building divided up by *longtang* (alleyways), Xintiandi is ideal for sauntering. If you want to know more about shikumen buildings, pop into the **Shikumen Open House Museum,** a restored shikumen building.

Also located in Xintiandi is a crop of celebrated restaurants, including T8 (see Travelwise p. 371), and the **Site of the 1st National Congress of the Chinese Communist Party** *(76 Xingye Lu),* also housed in an attractive former shikumen house.

Wandering around **Tianzifang (Taikang Road Art Centre)** on Taikang Lu to the south is great for art galleries, chic boutiques, arts and crafts shops, and cafés, all in a manageably charming area.

A fascinating diversion to the west of the French Concession, the **Propaganda Poster Art Centre** is in the basement of a residential block. Hanging from the walls are excellent original examples of Mao-era propaganda art, lambasting the United States and celebrating the irrepressible onward march of Chinese communism. Many of the posters can be purchased.

At the time of writing, Shanghai's leading knockoff clothing bazaar Xiangyang Market had shut, but Huaihai Zhonglu remains an excellent street for window shopping. The French Concession is also one of the hubs of the expat drinking scene, with well-known drinking holes along Taojiang Lu and Dongping Lu (both off Hengshan Lu) and the south end of Maoming Nanlu. Hordes of popular restaurants similarly congregate along the streets of the French Concession, cashing in on the district's indelible panache and easy sense of style. Huaihai Lu is excellent for upscale window shopping, while trendy boutiques cluster along Xinle Lu and Changle Lu, but don't forget Xintiandi and Tianzifang. ■

Xintiandi

Map 183

Subway: South Huangpi Rd.

Tianzifang (Taikang Road Art Centre)

Lane 210, Taikang Lu

Shikumen Open House Museum

Lane 181, Taikang Lu

$

Subway: South Huangpi Rd.

Propaganda Poster Art Centre

Room B-OC, President Mansion, 868 Huashan Lu

021 6211-1845

$

Subway: Jiangsu Rd.

www.shanghaipropagandaart.com

Western Architecture in Shanghai

The Western businessmen and financiers who effectively colonized Shanghai built a metropolis in their own image. Wall Street and the City of London came to sit on the Bund, Paris helped fashion the French Concession, and elsewhere Spanish, German, Japanese, Russian, Byzantine, and even Swedish flavors drifted in from abroad. An eclectic medley of building styles resulted that could have converged in only one city–Shanghai.

The buildings in Shanghai's French Concession offer an intriguing glimpse of the city's past.

A stroll around Shanghai brings with it a fascinating taste of yesteryear. The concoction–a melee of venerable clubs, apartment blocks, churches, showy banks, hospitals, cinemas, and hotels–is an engaging brew. With styles ranging from the modest (villas) through the decorative and trendy (art deco) to the monumental (bank architecture), Shanghai is a yellowing photograph of late 19th-century and early 20th-century architecture.

The Japanese unfortunately destroyed many buildings, but today surviving heritage buildings are well preserved, due to their enormous real estate value and historical significance. Wherever you are in the former concession areas of Shanghai, keep your eyes open. Even a casual glance above the street level (often the best place to look) reveals a riot of Corinthian columns, European lintels, art deco plasterwork, brick houses, red-tile roofs, and carved facades. Throughout Shanghai, small ripples of Western styling gradually amass to result in the crashing wave of the Bund.

The Taipans (foreign owners of the *hongs*, or trading companies) constructed the most ostentatious buildings. The wealthy Jews (such as the Sassoons, Ezras, and Kadoories) also lived in regal style.

Much of the hotel architecture in Shanghai was fastidiously trendy. The 1934 **Park Hotel** (designed by Ladislaus Hudec) at 170 Nanjing Xilu has been robbed of a lot of its art deco finesse, but the **Peace Hotel** (see p. 185) still exudes sophistication. The **Pacific Hotel**

(104 Nanjing Xilu), opposite what was the old Racetrack (now Renmin Square), displays considerable historic charm.

The eminent 1928 **Cathay Mansions** (Shanghai's first high-rise) on Maoming Nanlu and the neighboring **Grosvenor House** are now owned by the nearby, glittering Jinjiang Hotel. The **Crystal Palace,** the **Astor,** the **Ritz,** and the **Metropole** were all cinemas. The art deco outline of the **Cathay Theater** still stands, south of the Jinjiang Hotel at 870 Huaihai Lu (formerly known as Avenue Joffre).

Other extant art deco edifices include the plaster-worked exterior of the **Savoy** apartments *(131 Changshu Lu),* near the junction with Huaihai Lu, and the brick **Astrid** apartments *(301–309 Maoming Nanlu).*

Suzhou Creek was lined with massive apartment blocks, such as the Sassoon-built **Embankment House** (equipped with its own artesian well). The huge **Post Office,** built in 1924 and adorned with Corinthian columns, is still on the corner of Sichuan Zhonglu (opposite stood the British American Tobacco Company). Check out its interesting museum.

Robust consular architecture, such as the **Russian Consulate,** also fringed the International Settlement north of Suzhou Creek. The **Chinese People's Association for Friendship With Foreign Countries,** a huge white affair at 1418 Nanjing Xilu, stands next to the **Shanghai Exhibition Center.** From the streets you can get a good view of the balconies and balustrades.

Wandering the backstreets of the French Concession—such as Julu Lu—is an excellent way to get a feel for the Shanghai of the early decades of the past century. The 1930s villas of the well-to-do are still preserved on leafy Xinhua Lu on the western borders of the French Concession. Other buildings to look out for are the former addresses of eminent people, such as Song Qingling's residence at 1843 Huaihai Zhonglu and the residence of Sun Zhongshan (Yat-sen) at 7 Xiangshan Lu, both serving as museums.

The fairy-tale towers of the **Moller Mansion** (now a hotel) rise surreally over the rooftops at 30 Shaanxi Nanlu. Both Lin Biao and Jiang Qing stayed at the European-style, red tile residence at 145 Yueyang Lu (south of the western end of Fuxing Zhonglu).

Much old architecture survives as department stores. The Sun Company long ago was renamed the **No. 1 Department Store,** at the junction of Nanjing Donglu and Xizanglu.

The Jesuit-built **St. Ignatius Cathedral** *(158 Puxi Lu)* near the Xujiahui subway station is just along the road from the **Bibliotecha Zi-Ka-Wei** *(tel 021 6487-4095, ext. 208),* the former Jesuit library, which can be toured between 2 p.m. and 4 p.m. on Saturday afternoons. The huge **Catholic church** on Sheshan south of Shanghai was built between 1925 and 1935.

INSIDER TIP:

Beautifully preserved, the early 20th-century Jin Jiang Hotel *(59 Maoming Lu)* lies in the heart of the French Concession.

—DAMIAN HARPER
National Geographic author

East of the Shanghai Museum on the corner of Hankou Lu *(No. 766)* is the charmingly simple **Muen Church (Mu En Tang),** formerly the Moore Memorial Church. Completed in red brick, this Protestant church was attacked in 1966 by Red Guards and its Bibles damaged (a plaque outside in Chinese testifies to the event).

A Russian Orthodox church can be found on Xinle Lu in the French Concession. Sadly, most ecclesiastical stained glass in Shanghai was destroyed during the Cultural Revolution, but some remains in private houses (the Peace Hotel has wonderful examples).

Western architecture has entered a new age with the buildings on Pudong opposite the Bund. Many may have Chinese architects, but the inspiration is largely Occidental.

More Places to Visit in the Yangtze Region

Huangpu River Cruise

Pumping through Shanghai, the Huangpu River is the city's vital lifeline to the sea and the Yangtze. Boats leave from the wharf on the Bund for cruises to the mouth of the Yangtze River and shorter one-hour cruises.
145 E2 501 Zhongshan Dongerlu (40-minute trips also leave from the Pearl Dock in Lujiazui) 021 6374-4461 $$–$$$ 3.5-hour trip with dinner, $ one-hour trip

Mudu

Much less commercialized than Zhouzhuang (see below), Mudu is another canal town that has become popular for its canal scenes and gardens. The best approach is to wander around the old town or ride one of the tour boats along the canal. Prime sights within the old town include the **Hongyin Mountain Villa** and the **Bangyan Mansion.**
145 E2 Canal tour: $$

INSIDER TIP:

The ancient town of Mudu and its remarkable natural scenery are accessible as a day trip from Suzhou or Shanghai.

—DAMIAN HARPER
National Geographic author

Ningbo

Chiefly a port for the island of Putuoshan (see pp. 180–181), the town of Ningbo lies huddled on the jagged Zhejiang coastline. It has a few notable buildings, including the **Tianyige,** an ancient private library. On Zhongma Lu, north of Xinjiang Bridge, the **Portuguese Catholic Church** is a mummified slice of old Europe in China.
145 E2

Tongli

A day trip from either Shanghai or Suzhou, the town of Tongli on the Grand Canal (see pp. 176–177) is typical of the picturesque canal towns that dot Jiangsu Province. Less touristy than other canal towns that have been deluged in recent years, Tongli remains a charming portrait of old bridges, whitewashed houses, and traditional residences; weekends are busy so try to come during the week.

One of Tongli's most famous assets is the **Chinese Sex Museum** *($)*, famed for its honest look at the fascinating world of Chinese erotica. Not far from the museum, the **Tuisi Garden** *($)* is an attractive and retiring arrangement of rockeries and pavilions.
145 E2 Town admission: $$$

Wudangshan

The temple-strewn Wudangshan mountains stretch across the northwestern portion of Hubei Province and are wrapped in Taoist lore. Also associated with the martial arts, they are a pilgrimage destination for students of *gongfu* (see pp. 124–125).
145 B2 & C2

Zhouzhuang & Changzhou

West of Shanghai awaits the ancient canal town of Zhouzhuang. It is crisscrossed by very picturesque bridges and waterways and studded with traditional houses. Trains pass through Kunshan City, close to Zhouzhuang on the Shanghai-Suzhou railway.

Beyond Suzhou lies Changzhou, a town similarly threaded by canals and home to the refined **Tianning Temple.** The temple once had a contingent of more than 800 monks but suffered during the Cultural Revolution, and its numbers are much reduced now. The temple boasts a collection of 500 gilded Luohan (see p. 83).
145 E2

From the sandy beaches of Hainan Island to the sheer energy of Guangzhou and the enchanting legacy of Gulangyu Island

The South

Introduction & Map 198–199

Fenghuang 200–201

Wulingyuan 202

Lushan 203–204

Xiamen 205

Gulangyu Island Walk 206–208

Yongding County 209

Experience: Spend the Night in a Hakka Earth Building 210

Guangzhou 211–215

Shamian Island Walk 216–217

Hainan Island 218–219

More Places to Visit in the South 220

Hotels & Restaurants in the South 373–375

Rambutans from the local market

The South

Down south, Beijing's political hegemony meets resistance, especially in the more experimental economies of Guangdong Province and Hainan Island. The city is checked by a tangle of tongues that confounds Mandarin *(putonghua)* speakers. Shrewd business sense, savoir faire, diligence, and greater exposure to the West further shape a resourceful regional character.

South China's frontier town, Shenzhen is far removed from Beijing's conservatism.

Droopy and lush, China's rice-growing south sees abundant summer rains, typhoons that blast the ragged coastline ports, and green vegetation choking the land. This is a fecund and wealthy region.

The late Deng Xiaoping's maxim "To get rich is glorious" allowed the free market to enter through the backdoor of Guangdong Province. Guangdong is South China's heartland, a region forced open to trade by the foreign powers in the 19th century and an exit point for legions of overseas Chinese. The return of Hong Kong in 1997 may have boosted China's gross domestic product by 25 percent, but the province had long prospered from its wealthy neighbor.

Guangdong's capital, Guangzhou, evinces a maelstrom of free enterprise, noise, and traffic. Shenzhen and Zhuhai continue to probe the waters of the free market and international finance. Together they typify the end of the altruistic economy built up by the older generation.

China's southernmost province, the island of Hainan, seems even more estranged from Beijing than Guangdong. A free-market haven, it is a place of greenery, beaches, sun, and skyrocketing house prices.

East along the coastline lies the ancestral homeland of many Taiwanese: Fujian Province. Fujian's port of Xiamen squarely faces the Taiwan-controlled island of Jinmen, within artillery range off the coast. Xiamen is a peaceful place, however, further tranquilized by its picturesque island of Gulangyu, awash with colonial remains and fading history.

Hunan, to the north, is home to some of China's hottest food and a liberal sprinkling of Chairman Mao iconography (he was born and educated in the province). ■

NOT TO BE MISSED:

Spending a day ambling around the historic walled town of Fenghuang on the Tuo River **200–201**

Exploring the magnificent karst scenery of Wulingyuan **202**

Rambling around the charming island of Gulangyu **206–208**

The astonishing size and simplicity of Hakka earth buildings **210**

A relaxing walk on Guangzhou's old-world Shamian Island **216–217**

Sunbathing on the beaches around Sanya, Hainan Island **219**

THE YANGTZE p. 143
SICHUAN & THE TIBETAN PLATEAU p. 289
THE SOUTHWEST p. 261
THE YANGTZE p. 143
WULINGYUAN
Cili
Jinshi
Datong Hu
Yueyang
Changde
Dayong
Wuling Shan
Dongting Hu
Yuan Jiang
Dehang
Yiyang
CHANGSHA
Jishou
Shaoshan
Fenghuang
Loudi
Xiangtan
Yichun
Zhuzhou
Huaihua
Liling
Pingxiang
Shaoyang
1290m Heng Shan
Hongjiang
HUNAN
Hengyang
Jingxian
Dong'an
Xiang Jiang
Leiyang
Yongzhou
Chenzhou
Daoxian
Nan Ling
Lechang
Jianghua
Shaoguan
Lianxian
Bei Jiang
GUANGDONG
Huaiji
Qingyuan
GUANGZHOU (CANTON)
Zhaoqing
Xi Jiang
Foshan
Xiqiao Hills
Luoding
Jiangmen
Yunwu Shan
Zhongshan
Zhuhai
Macau
Shenzhen
Hong Kong
Yangjiang
Maoming
Leizhou Bandao
Zhanjiang
Xuwen
Qiongzhou Haixia
HAIKOU
HAINAN
Wenchang
Hainan Island
Dongfang
1867m Wuzhi Shan
Xinglong
Tongshi
Xincun
Monkey Island
Sanya
South China Sea
Jiujiang
Hukou
Guling
Poyang Hu
Mufu Shan
1474m Lu Shan
Jiuling Shan
Boyang
Wuyuan
Jingdezhen
NANCHANG
Shangrao
Gan Jiang
Yingtan
Linchuan
2158m
Pucheng
Fuding
Shaowu
Nancheng
Zhenghe
Wuyi Shan
Ji'an
Guangchang
Nanping
JIANGXI
FUZHOU
Min Jiang
Suichuan
Yong'an
Sanming
FUJIAN
Putian
Ganzhou
Zhangping
Qingyuan Shan
Meizhou
Longyan
Quanzhou
Longnan
Zhangzhou
Jinmen
Xiamen
Gulangyu Island
Lianping
Meizhou
Zhangpu
Chaozhou
Raoping
Shantou
Lufeng
Taiwan Strait
TAIWAN
0 300 kilometers
0 150 miles
Railroad
4 3 2 1
A B C D

Fenghuang

Fenghuang—"phoenix town"—is one of China's most photogenic cities, a picturesque assortment of covered bridges, ancient temples, waterwheels, crumbling town walls, narrow alleyways, and charming riverside hotels, their rooms propped up on stilts.

Fenghuang's old town gives a delicious taste of life in ancient China.

Fenghuang

199 A3

Visitor Information

Daomen Kou, north of Fucheng Gate in the south of the old town

0743 322-9364

South of the Tuo River

The best way to tackle the town is simply to wander around on either side of the Tuo River. Fenghuang's **City Wall (Chengqiang)** runs alongside the river, sandwiching a long seam of hotels and guesthouses against the water. As you walk down Biaoying Jie, which runs next to the wall south of the river, look out for ethnic Tujia and Miao hawkers selling jewelry and keepsakes. The impressive **North Gate City Tower (Beimen Chenglou)** overlooks the river, with the **Yang Family Ancestral Hall (Yangjia Citang)** standing nearby.

Perhaps the most iconic sight in Fenghuang is the magnificent wooden **Hong Bridge.** Several nearby hotels have rooms with views overlooking the bridge.

Also in the old town south of the river are the **Confucian Temple,** the **Tianhou Temple,** and the **Former Home of Shen**

Congwen, the famous 20th-century author of *Border Town.*

The North Bank

Cross Hong Bridge, or feel your way across the fun stepping-stones that stud the river a few hundred feet (about 100 m) west of the bridge. The elegant **Wanming Pagoda (Wanming Ta)** rises up above town not far from the **Wanshou Temple (Wanshou Gong).** West of here is **Laoying Shao,** a long alley lined with cafés and bars that are lively in the evening.

The most photogenic images of Fenghuang are from the north bank, looking over the river at the rickety houses and rooms on stilts on the far shore.

How to Visit

You'll probably need two or three days to fully savor the sights. You can purchase a through ticket *($$$$)* to town that will give you access to many of the sights and a boat ride along the river. Alternatively, you can pay for the boat ride separately and still enjoy Fenghuang without visiting any of the specific sights.

Hotels are everywhere in the old town but are generally of the guesthouse variety, with small rooms. Book early, especially during the busy period, as rooms go rapidly.

There's no shortage of restaurants in Fenghuang, but food is not one of the town's highlights. The **night market** along Hongqiao Lu north of Hong Bridge that kicks off in the late afternoon is a good place for snacks. Makers of brittle ginger candy are everywhere in town, pulling the gooey golden-colored mixture into long ropes before it sets.

The town is sadly mobbed by domestic tourists throughout the year, but as long as you avoid weekends and major holiday periods, you may catch tourist numbers at low ebb.

To reach Fenghuang, hop on a bus from the nearby town of Jishou, about an hour away. Buses also run to Fenghuang from Zhangjiajie and Changsha. Jishou is accessible by train from a number of towns, including Huaihua, Changsha, and Zhangjiajie.

INSIDER TIP:

There is nowhere to change money in Fenghuang, so make sure you arrive in town with enough Chinese cash or an ATM card.

—DAMIAN HARPER
National Geographic author

Other Sights

Nearby sights accessible from Fenghuang include the **Southern Great Wall (Nanfang Changcheng),** west of town, originally dating from the Ming dynasty and built to guard against uprisings by the Miao minority. **Huangsiqiao Old Town** is a picturesque old town farther to the west of the Southern Great Wall, almost on the border with Guizhou. ■

Wulingyuan

The mountainous reserve of Wulingyuan is often touted as one of China's most magnificent karst landscapes. Officially named the Wulingyuan Scenic and Historic Interest Area, this park in northwestern Hunan is a magnet for hikers, rafters, and escapees from city life. The Chinese tout Wulingyuan as a geological museum, and it is also a UNESCO World Heritage site.

Wulingyuan

 199 A4

Zhangjiajie, Northwestern Hunan

$$$$$

www.zhangjiajie.com.cn

CITS Visitor Information

CITS Building, 631 Ziwu Lu, Zhangjiajie

0744 820-0885

Dehang

199 A4

Wulingyuan is known for its small communities of Miao, Bai, Tujia, and Hui (Muslim) minorities, as well as its spectacular forest of splintered, rocky columns. The huge grove of stone columns numbers in excess of 3,000. The park is cut by the Suoxi River, while waterfalls, limestone caves, and surface and subterranean pools add to the adventure. During the summer months, white-water rafting trips can be taken on the river.

Most travelers plunge into Wulingyuan from neighboring **Zhangjiajie Village** or nearby **Zhangjiajie Town.** You can spend the night in either, but the village is more attractive and right next to the main entrance to Wulingyuan.

Just beyond the entrance, a path trails to the top of **Dragon Woman Peak.** To the north lies **Huangshizhai** (3,400 ft/1,035 m), a real climb. Cable cars *($)* run up the sides of both, and from the summits you are treated to excellent views.

Surrounding Tianzi Peak in the north of the park are some of the loftiest pinnacles, alongside natural stone arches and bridges. The spectacle, generally draped in cloud and mist, is very steamy in summer.

A tangle of caves and underground streams perforates Wulingyuan. **Yellow Dragon Cave,** 12 miles (19 km) to the east of Suoxiyu Village, is a labyrinthine 7 miles (11 km) long, with a subterranean waterfall and rivers. **Jiutiandong,** 10 miles (16 km) north of the park, is a massive cave.

Wulingyuan has a rich and varied collection of plants and wildlife. It is home to serows, clouded leopards, giant salamanders, Asiatic black bears, red magnolias *(honghua yulan)*, and other rare species. ■

A Side Trip to Dehang

On a far smaller scale, and in many ways a more charming alternative to Wulingyuan, is a trip to the Miao village of Dehang in west Hunan Province. The area is actually a huge geological park with a tantalizing variety of walks awaiting exploration, including the one-hour trek up to the attractive and elegant Liusha Waterfall along the Nine Dragon River Scenic Area. The landscape of karst peaks and terraced fields is particularly breathtaking, and several charming hotels have opened up near the river in the village, so spending the night is no problem. Dehang can be reached by bus (one hour) from outside the train station in the town of Jishou, also the town of access for Fenghuang (see pp. 200–201).

Lushan

The mountains of Lushan to the south of Jiujiang rise to 4,827 feet (1,474 m). Poets and artists have immortalized their wooded slopes and distant views, and the pleasant summer climate has drawn vacationing visitors in growing numbers.

Chinese poets have extolled Lushan's cool, mountainous landscape for centuries.

At the end of the 19th century, when it was known as Kuling, Europeans and Americans came in droves to clement Lushan in Jiangxi Province to escape the oppressive summer heat of nearby Jiujiang and the Yangtze River. As with other foreign centers in China, Lushan was almost a complete society, with post offices, hospitals, schools, and its own police force.

The resort was divided into valleys—Russian Valley, Long Valley, Lotus Valley—and crisscrossed with streets bearing Western names such as Princeton Road and Cambridge Road. A charming and picturesque community of red-roofed bungalows, villas, and cottages was built in a mishmash of European and American styles, much of it still standing.

Guling

The focal point of Lushan is the village of Guling, a cluster of wood-front buildings, old

Lushan
- 199 C4
- $$$$$

Meilu Villa
✉ Hexi Lu
$ $

cottages, and villas at the northeast end. Six-sided towers spring up all around on the hillsides. Guling was originally a retreat for missionaries, and this is reflected in the church architecture that survives on the pretty streets (maps are plentiful in the village). The Red Guards swarmed through Guling adding their bit of desecration to the story of Lushan, but most of the churches were let off lightly.

Gaily painted woodwork (most of it a soft blue) decorates many of the porches, windows, and shutters. The stonework is worthy of close attention; the heavy blocks used in the construction have been fitted together with superb craftsmanship.

A creek runs through Guling and feeds a number of serene lakes. Here, too, past visitors built the occasional colonial house or now deserted boathouse.

Lushan is also much admired by the Chinese for its association with Chairman Mao, Chiang Kai-shek, and Chiang's wife, Song Meiling, all of whom had villas in Guling. One of the most famous buildings here is the **Meilu Villa (Meilu Bieshu),** Chiang Kai-shek's summer retreat. You can poke around his living quarters, but it's a bit forbidding inside. There are relics of Chiang Kai-shek found here; photographs of him and his wife still hang on the villa's walls.

The times are, however, catching up with Guling. Many of the villas have been sold, and quite a large number have been converted to guesthouses to supply the hordes of vacationing Chinese who swarm about the Lushan slopes in summer. The nobility of Guling is further under attack from relentless tour buses.

When to Visit

Thanks to its mountain position, Lushan has a pleasant climate in summer—the best time to visit weatherwise—but it also coincides with the tourist crush. The mountain tends to be wet, cold, and misty during the rest of the year, and in winter a mantle of snow settles upon its inclines and ridges. ■

Wuyuan

The villages around Wuyuan in northeastern Jiangxi Province—located about 62 miles (100 km) east of Lushan and best reached from Jingdezhen or Tunxi—are beautiful snapshots of traditional Huizhou culture, similar to that seen in Yixian and Shexian (see p. 153). Hunt out the old villages of Likeng, Xiaoqi, Qinghua, and Jiangwan, set in lovely countryside, where scenic river views are vaulted by old stone bridges and simple accommodation is available for those who want to spend several days traveling from village to village. The settlements, barely even heard of by outsiders ten years ago, are now much visited by travelers, but the communities continue as before and their traditional livelihoods have not been lost. They remain very attractive and photogenic, and finding a place to spend the night is not hard. Beyond the villages, excellent opportunities also exist for trekking around the nearby countryside.

Xiamen

Called Amoy by Westerners, the island-city of Xiamen has picturesque pockets of historical interest. The port, fortified in the Ming dynasty, is entwined with the Taiwanese, whose forces still occupy the nearby island of Jinmen. The neighboring island of Gulangyu (see pp. 206–208) is a delightful museum piece of meandering lanes and colonial history.

An important stronghold of resistance against the invading Manchus in the 17th century, Xiamen was later wooed by the European powers, and the British prized it open with gunboats as a treaty port in the mid-19th century. Xiamen later became one of China's first Special Economic Zones (see p. 46).

The most attractive part of Xiamen is found in the port area that faces the island of Gulangyu. The colorful bustle of Zhongshan Lu runs east from the harbor front. Peek down its small side streets for a taste of a bygone age.

A worshipper at the Nanputuo Temple lights incense.

The famous **Nanputuo Temple** in the south of town is a wonderful complex, set against **Drum Hill (Gushan)** opposite Xiamen University. The Laughing or Future Buddha offers a welcome from **Tian Wang Hall;** backing onto him is Weituo, protector of the Buddhist faith. Flanking them are the Four Heavenly Kings, defenders of the temple.

The courtyard behind contains incense braziers, the **Drum Tower (Gulou)** to the west, and the **Bell Tower (Zhonglou)** to the east. The **Great Treasure Hall (Daxiongbaodian)** (north) houses three statues (Guanyin, the present Buddha, and Wenshu), while in adjacent halls sit the 18 Luohan (see p. 83) in ranks of nine. Behind stands the **Hall of Great Mercy (Dabeidian)** with four effigies of Guanyin, where most of the worshippers are women. At the rear stands the **Hall of Sacred Scriptures,** where the original sutras were stored.

Across from the temple, **Xiamen University** has a pleasant campus that you can wander around. To the southeast of the university, along Daxue Lu (University Road), is the **Huli Cannon (Hulishan Paotai)** on **Huli Mountain (Hulishan).** The battery was installed by the Germans at the close of the 19th century. On a clear day, look east at **Jinmen** and **Xiao Jinmen,** the two islands still occupied by the "rebellious province" of Taiwan. ■

Xiamen
199 C3

www.amoymagic.com

Gulangyu Island Walk

The enchanting island of Gulangyu ("drum wave island") became a foreign concession in 1903, quickly acquiring a medley of building styles and textures. The island was blueprinted for churches, hospitals, schools, villas, and post offices—a home away from home for the foreigners who lived here. Crisscrossed with narrow, intriguing lanes, Gulangyu obliges with languorous walks amid palms, and a relaxed temperament holds sway.

Quiet, car-free lanes add to Gulangyu's allure.

Jump on a ferry from Xiamen's terminal (Lundu Matou) across the way from the waterfront Chinese-style Lujiang Hotel for the five-minute excursion to the island. The old ferry cuts diagonally across to the pier toward the south of the island.

No cars are allowed on Gulangyu, and the only traffic noise is the whine of electric buggies straining to climb up the inclines—the island undulates with small hills, threaded through by little cobbled roads. There are wonderful European-style villas here, a grand collection of columns, verandas, and red roofs surrounded by palms, banyans, and creeper-choked trees.

This walk is a rough guide only; it's easy to lose your way on Gulangyu, but because the island is so small, wandering around without a map or itinerary is just as much fun. If you do get lost, head for a high point and set your bearings in relation to Xiamen across the water.

Disembarking the ferry, you will see Xiamen Underwater World (a fun place for the kids). The hills in front of you sport a cluster of imposing buildings, including the former British

---

NOT TO BE MISSED:

Statue of Koxinga • View from Sunlight Rock • Gulangyu Guesthouse

---

Consulate, which you can climb up to. The Amoy Telephone Company, the German Consulate, and the King George Hotel were all situated here.

Ferry Pier to Yanping Park

Following Lujiao Lu south around the island you will pass the old Bo'ai Hospital, built by the Japanese. Farther south, the road becomes Zhangzhou Lu and follows the waterfront. On your right is **Flag Raising Hill (Shengqishan).** At the southeastern tip of Gulangyu is a **statue of Koxinga ❶**, otherwise called Zheng Chenggong. This hero pirate commanded a huge armada of junks, and, with a massive army of fellow pirates, drove the Dutch from Formosa (Taiwan) in 1661. Koxinga championed the Ming cause and to his death defied the Qing government. His anti-Manchu motto, "Resist the Qing and restore the Ming," was often accompanied by the Shaolin salute (flat left palm pressed tightly over the right fist and held at chest level).

Zhangzhou Lu winds around to the right and climbs to a sports field. Turn left on Huangyan Lu ("bright rock road"), passing by the former **Gulyangyu Guesthouse** at No. 25, a magnificent old colonial building. The road then wraps around **Sunlight Rock (Riguang-yan) ❷**, the island's highest point. Buy a ticket (*$*) and climb to its peak—where you look over the town's pretty tiles and redbrick buildings. To the north, the large, red-domed, and colonnaded building is the Xiamen Museum.

Also see area map p. 199
- Gulangyu pier
- 1.5–2 hours
- 3 miles (5 km)
- Gulangyu pier

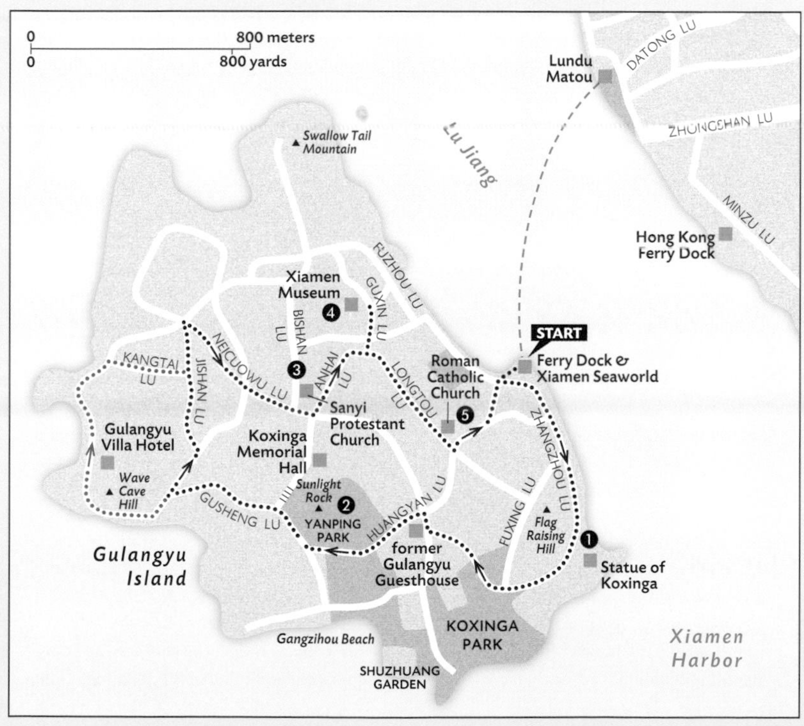

The locals call it the Bagua Lou or "eight-trigram building," a Taoist description of its octagonal form. You will visit the museum later on this walk. Way off to the east lie the two Nationalist-held islands of Xiao Jinmen and Jinmen.

Small **Yanping Park** sits at the base of Sunlight Rock, where you will also find the **Koxinga Memorial Hall (Zheng Chenggong Jinianguan).** Keep an eye out for colonial architecture in the area.

South & West of Sunlight Rock

South of Sunlight Rock lies **Gangzihou Beach,** just to the east of which is **Shuzhuang Garden (Shuzhuang Huayuan),** laid out in 1913 by a Taiwanese resident who fled to Gulangyu after the Japanese invasion of Taiwan. The garden is the site of the fascinating **Piano Museum.** With the largest number of pianos per capita in the nation, the music-loving island is well known throughout China as "Piano Island."

From Sunlight Rock, follow Gusheng Lu, which hugs the island's western shoreline. It wraps around **Wave Cave Hill (Langdongshan),** upon which sits the **Gulangyu Villa Hotel,** and continues on to Kangtai Lu. Otherwise, from Sunlight Rock, head along enchanting Jishan Lu ("chicken mountain road") and turn right onto Neicuowu Lu. Both roads are lined with a wonderful potpourri of architectural styles. Standing ahead on the corner of Anhai Lu and Yongchun Lu is the large, plain **Sanyi Protestant Church ❸,** originally built in 1904 as the London Missionary Society hall.

North Gulangyu

Turn left along Anhai Lu, bear left, and join up with Guxin Lu, which leads to the impressive **Xiamen Museum ❹,** which contains an organ museum. The path returning south along Guxin Lu reveals a fascinating collection of buildings that continues along Longtou Lu ("dragon's head road").

Along Lujiao Lu—heading back toward the ferry pier—is the whitewashed **Roman Catholic Church ❺** (No. 34), dating to the early 20th century. Follow Lujiao Lu back toward the pier area, or head back up Longtou Lu for its collection of cafés and restaurants.

Taiwan's Golden Gateway

The Taiwan-controlled island of Jinmen (Kinmen in Taiwan, Quemoy to Westerners) lies 173 miles (278 km) from Taiwan, but it is just a few miles off the coast of Fujian Province. When the Nationalists withdrew to Taiwan (Formosa) in 1949 after fierce fighting, they managed to keep the island as an outpost. The name Jinmen means "gold gate," appropriate considering that the Nationalist forces retreated to Taiwan with all of China's gold reserves.

Formed from granite, Jinmen belongs to an archipelago of 15 small islands that includes neighboring Xiao Jinmen (Little Kinmen). Today, a number of these islands are in the hands of the People's Republic of China.

Jinmen has often sheltered refugees, most notably those fleeing the Mongol invasion of China. It also harbored Ming partisans fighting the Manchus; the pirate Zheng Chenggong (Koxinga, see p. 207), was among them.

Along with the island of Matsu, Jinmen was heavily shelled for 44 days in 1958 by Communist forces, generating an international crisis. China's periodic saber rattling is a fact of life on Jinmen, and the large military population of this fortress island is prepared for an overwhelming Communist onslaught should Taiwan (the Republic of China) officially declare independence from the mainland.

The island is open to tourism, but only if you approach it from the Taiwan side.

Yongding County

The borderlands between Jiangxi, Fujian, and Guangdong provinces meet in splendid rural seclusion, characterized by some of China's most magnificent architectural spectacles: the earth buildings *(tulou)* of the Hakka.

Built of stout walls made of tamped earth and wooden beams, the fortresses are several stories tall and designed to accommodate hundreds of Hakka, persecuted Han Chinese who historically migrated south from north China. The buildings are typically accessed by a single large door, which is still locked every evening.

Most earth buildings are circular, but others are oval, square, or rectangular. Some of those destroyed in war have been restored, and a number of them have recently been listed as UNESCO World Heritage sites, raising their profile and perhaps guaranteeing increased protection.

The interior of a traditional Hakka *tulou* earth building

Although you can visit Hakka earth buildings in Jiangxi and Guangdong Provinces, the most accessible and best known area is Yongding County in southwestern Fujian Province, about 130 miles (209 km) from Xiamen. Base yourself in Yongding town, in the town of Hukeng, or even in an earth building itself (see p. 210), because the region warrants weeks of exploration.

Many earth buildings cluster together. The most famous earth is the four-story **Zhencheng Lou** *($$$$)*, an impressive circular edifice built in Hongkeng in 1912. Enveloping an ancestral temple in the middle of the central courtyard and a sequence of internal rings, the galleried four floors rise up around the interior. The square **Kuiji Lou,** built in 1834, is a short walk away. Other nearby earth buildings include **Fuyou Lou** (see p. 210) and **Rusheng Lou.**

The cluster of earth buildings at **Tianluokeng** *($$$$)* is particularly impressive, especially when seen from above.

The earth buildings are spread out around a large area, and getting from one earth building cluster to the next by public transportation is not easy. It's best to ask at your hotel for a driver to hire for a day or more to transport you around. Alternatively, you can book an all-inclusive tour from Xiamen. ■

EXPERIENCE: Spend the Night in a Hakka Earth Building

One of the highlights of a trip to southern China is the opportunity to visit and even spend the night in a Hakka earth building *(tulou)*. Erected by the Hakka—originally a community of migrants who fled south from persecution in North China—in the border regions between the provinces of Fujian, Guangdong, and Jianxi, these multistory walled forts can each house hundreds of families.

Although similar in concept if not in design to the Hakka walled villages of Hong Kong, the stout tulou of southern China were designed for defence, with thick walls and robust architecture.

Many earth buildings today are only partially populated, as young people have left to find work in the city. This means that an increasing number of earth buildings have empty rooms that can be rented out for the evening or overnight, providing a livelihood for some of the families that still remain.

Overnighting in a Hakka earth building can provide a unique experience of life in one of these magnificent structures. Furthermore, the exclusively rural setting totally withdraws you from the city and immerses you deep within the countryside.

Tulou walls are made of earth, stone, and other materials.

It is not hard to find a room in an earth building: If you like the look of any particular tulou, just ask the family members inside if they have rooms to rent.

What to Expect

The rooms that you will find in a Hakka earth building are very simple and often just contain a simple bed and a fan. Lavatories will be very basic indeed and are generally outside the earth building. It's a good idea to bring mosquito repellent and also a flashlight. Check when the huge wooden door to the tulou is shut so you are not locked outside at night.

Fuyou Lou

Near the huge (and most famous) earth building, Zhencheng Lou in Yongding County (see p. 209), simple rooms are available in the impressive, square Fuyou Lou *(tel 0597 553-5900)*.

The earth building dates from 1880 and contains some magnificent carpentry and woodwork. Rooms are very cheap and come with television, and the owners can cook up local dishes for their guests.

Guangzhou

Astride the Pearl River, Guangdong Province's capital has long enjoyed proximity to Hong Kong. This helps explain its sky-high economic figures, Special Economic Zones (SEZs), excessive property prices, mercantile nature, and infamous sweatshops. China's gravy train set out from Guangzhou in this corner of the south, but in its wake, thankfully, it left charming pockets of history and a distinctive cuisine.

A riot of neon highlights a bridge across the Pearl River.

There has been a settlement here since the time of the Qin (221–207 B.C.); by the Tang dynasty (618–907) it had evolved into a flourishing market town. Foreign trade, first with the Middle East and Central Asia, focused the attention of the West. By the late 17th century, Guangzhou (also called Canton by Westerners) was partially opening its doors to the West. In time, the Cantonese through trade and emigration established Chinatowns the world over. Their culture harbored revolutionary forces in the Taiping leader, Hong Xiuquan (see pp. 164–165) and republican Sun Zhongshan (Yat-sen; see p. 41). Both were influenced by contact with the West. Guangdong Province was later earmarked by Deng Xiaoping as the vanguard of China's modernization.

The dry run of capitalist experimentation nosed Guangdong Province into a commanding lead

Guangzhou

Map 199 B2 & 213

CITS Visitor Information

✉ 8 Qiaoguang Lu

☎ 020 8333-6888

Temple of the Six Banyan Trees

- Map 212
- Address: Liurong Lu
- $ $
- Subway: Ximen Kou

over the rest of China. Guangzhou epitomizes the successes and stresses of modern Chinese society. Vast new hotels sparkle, and building projects shape the skyline. Simultaneously, China's jobless migrants race to the city to swell unemployment figures and the crime rate, stretching the creaking infrastructure in the process.

Getting about Guangzhou can be difficult. The city is a gridlocked sprawl of honking cars, although the subway is changing this. Sights are scattered around haphazardly, and negotiating a route to encompass them all can fray tempers. The best advice is to make a choice, and stick to it. For Western visitors, Shamian Island (see pp. 216–217) in the south part of Guangzhou is a blessed sanctuary of quiet streets.

INSIDER TIP:

Unless you're interested in shopping, skip Shenzhen in favor of Guangzhou, which is just an hour away from Hong Kong.

—RORY BOLAND

National Geographic contributor

Temples, Mosques, & Churches

Although history takes a backseat to Guangzhou's modernization drive, nuggets glint from the fog of construction dust. The **Temple of the Six Banyan Trees (Liurongsi Huata)** is Guangzhou's most celebrated temple. Devoid of its fabled eponymous trees, the temple

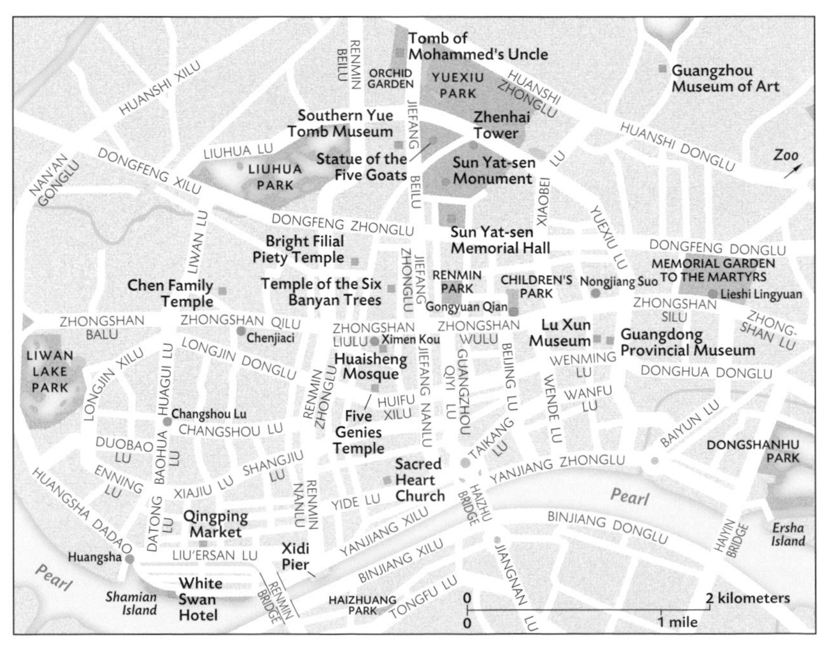

receives shade from the 17-story Flower Pagoda. Dating from the mid-sixth century, the temple was built to provide a reliquary for some of Buddha's ashes.

Upon entering, you are greeted by a statue of chubby Milefo, the Laughing Buddha. To his right are the Chinese words "The big belly can endure all that is unendurable"; on his left the words read: "He opens his mouth and laughs at all the laughable people in the world." Behind him stands Weituo (see p. 83), with his staff to the ground.

The three golden Buddhas in the back of the temple represent the Buddhas of the past, present, and future. Within the main temple are two other temples: The small **Sixth Ancestor's Temple** has the words "One Flower, Five Leaves" embroidered above it. Inside it stands an effigy of the sixth patriarch of the Chan Buddhist sect, Huineng (637–731). The **Guanyin Temple** houses a huge statue of the Buddhist goddess of mercy.

The octagonal **Flower Pagoda (Huata)** is the tallest pagoda in Guangzhou; previously it held the aforementioned sacred ashes of Buddha. It has 17 floors, despite the external illusion that it contains only nine. You can climb the pagoda for excellent views over the city. The road leading to the temple bustles with stalls selling souvenirs, religious accessories, and jade objects.

Not far away is **Bright Filial Piety Temple (Guangxiaosi),** parts of which date from the fourth century. The Laughing Buddha again greets you with the jovial message "Spirited eyes, full chest." To your left as you enter is the **Drum Tower,** and to your right is the **Bell Tower.** A reclining Buddha lies in the **Fahua Altar (Fahuatan).** The characters on the entrance read: "As if asleep, but not asleep; sex is empty, empty is sex," and on the left the words read: "Truly awake, pretending to be awake, the heavens connect with water, water connects with heaven."

The main temple contains three golden Buddha statues that sit under a vast, beamed roof. To the rear, the ancestor temple is pleasantly shaded by trees. Women file into the Guanyin Temple to burn incense and pray to Guanyin, the goddess of mercy, while monks wander around in saffron robes.

Nearby, **Huaisheng Mosque (Huaishengsi Guangta)** testifies to the penetration of Islam into Guangdong. The mosque traces

Shops selling medicinal herbs and plants are easy to find.

Bright Filial Piety Temple
- Map: 212
- Address: Guangxiao Lu
- Price: $
- Subway: Ximen Kou

Huaisheng Mosque
- Map: 212
- Address: Guangta Lu
- Price: $
- Subway: Ximen Kou

Five Genies Temple
212
Off Huifu Xilu
$
Subway: Ximen Kou

Sacred Heart Church
212
Yide Lu
Closed Mon.–Sat.
$
Subway: Haizhu Square

its lineage back to the Tang dynasty (618–907) and is notable for a smooth minaret, which lends its name to the neighboring street, Guangta ("smooth minaret") Lu.

To the south, the **Five Genies Temple (Wuxianguan)** is a Taoist complex and site of the mythical creation of the city. The Five Genies correspond to the five elements (fire, water, earth, wood, and metal), the five planets (Venus, Mercury, Jupiter, Saturn, and Mars), and the five seasons (spring, summer, autumn, winter, and middle). If the clapperless, 5-ton, Ming dynasty bell rings, it means affliction will hit the city. The bell was apparently struck by a shot from an English gun during one of the Opium Wars.

Down by the Pearl River, the Gothic-style **Sacred Heart Church (Shishi Jiaotang)** was designed in the 19th century by the French architect Guillemin and built in granite. Unfortunately, as with most churches in China, much of its stained glass is missing. The Cantonese call it the Church of the House of Stone.

The **Chen Family Temple** (Chenjiaci; *west off Zhongshan Lu, Subway: Chenjiaci*) was built at the end of the 19th century with funds donated by the families of that name (it is a common name in Guangdong Province). This traditional complex contains a main hall, lesser halls, courtyards, and sculptures. The temple survived the Cultural Revolution, when many others dedicated to ancestor worship were destroyed. Today, handicraft exhibitions are held here.

With its cages of live animals, Qingping Market is not for the squeamish.

Other Sights

Qingping Market (Qingping Shichang), opposite Shamian Island, is an institution. This legendary market, a menagerie of Cantonese cooking and medicinal ingredients, is a Noah's ark of the exotic and bizarre, both alive and dead: Vegetarians should avoid it. The market sprawls through a labyrinthine checkerboard of streets; you could spend an afternoon with your eyes popping out.

Starting innocently enough with the pungent aroma of fungi and dried herbs, an A–Z of Chinese medicine, things soon move into squeamish territory. Owls are crammed into cages, skinny cats sit stuffed into tight boxes, and turtles rasp in the heat. Animal products galore are scattered hither and thither, including deer horns, bear paws, unidentifiable tendons, piles of dried animal parts; sea horses, geckos, and

Kilns

Ceramics were often named for the kiln where they were fired, including Dehua, Ding, and Longquan.

The Jiangxi town of **Jingdezhen** is home to high-quality porcelain. Records trace kiln activity here back to the Eastern Han (A.D. 25–225). The community of potters expanded during the Tang dynasty and flourished under the subsequent Song, with many fine porcelain pieces specifically designed for imperial use. Production here continues today.

The **Jingdezhen Pottery Culture Exhibition Area (Jingdezhen Taoci Wenhua Bolanqu)** is in the west of Jingdezhen. Tours of potteries in the area can be arranged through the local branch of **CITS** *(tel 0798 851-5888)*.

The **Shiwan** kilns in Foshan (see p. 220), near Guangzhou, first fired up in the Song dynasty. Demand increased in the Ming and Qing dynasties, and the kilns continue to operate today.

Yixing (see p. 172) teapots were made in vast quantities during the Ming and Qing dynasties. The range of colors (from purple to green) results from the high concentration of metallic oxides in the clay.

For those who appreciate fine ceramics, a visit to the Shanghai Museum (see pp. 189–191) is essential.

bluebottles all play their part. The moving, heaving, and slithering end of the market may turn some stomachs; then again, as they say in China, the Cantonese will eat anything on four legs, unless it's a table.

Yuexiu Park (Yuexiu Gongyuan) is a vast diversion where you will find the rather ghastly Statue of the Five Rams, symbolic founders of the city, and the **Zhenhai Tower,** a pagoda built in 1380 and once part of the old city wall. Today it houses the city museum, devoted to the history of Guangzhou. In the south section of the park lies the **Sun Yat-sen Monument,** dedicated to China's famous revolutionary.

To the west of the park, the **Southern Yue Tomb Museum (Nanyuewangmu)** stands on the site of the tomb of the second king of Yue, a breakaway kingdom that lasted until 111 B.C. with Guangzhou as its capital. Yue is the name given to the whole province of Guangdong to this day. On display is an array of jade funeral objects found in the tomb.

If you want to voyage south of the river, visit restored **Haizhuang Park (Haizhuang Gongyuan),** which is home to the Ocean Banner Monastery.

You will find the **Guangzhou Museum of Art (Guangzhou Yishu Bowuguan)** south of Luhu Park in the north of town. Displayed here is a collection of modern and traditional works by Chinese artists and sculptors.

The **Pearl River cruise (Zhu Jiang Youlanchuan)** takes you along Guangzhou's main artery, the Pearl River. The neon lights along the southern shore illuminate the evening trip *(Apr.–Oct.)*. Boats depart in the evenings from Tianzi Pier, or you can book a tour through your hotel; the White Swan Hotel (see p. 373), on Shamian Island, has its own tour. ■

Southern Yue Tomb Museum

Map 212

867 Jiefang Beilu

$

Guangzhou Museum of Art

13 Luhu Lu

$

Guangzhou Star Cruises (Pearl River cruise)

Tianzi Pier

020 8333-2222

$$

Shamian Island Walk

Shamian Island, a captivating museum of colonial architecture, sits on a half-mile-long (0.8 km) lozenge of sand in the Pearl River just south of Qingping Market. This is Guangzhou's equivalent to London's Kensington and Chelsea, a preserved snapshot of 19th-century Europe in the Far East.

Time's bell jar has been dropped over Shamian's delightful European colonial architecture.

Spearheaded by the British, the West carved this little slice of Europe for itself after forcing open the doors of China to trade in 1843. The island quickly assumed a foreign guise, with banks, churches, administrative offices, and all the trappings of Western culture.

The island was joined to Canton by the "English Bridge," which was closed nightly to keep the locals out. Symbolic of the power and organization of the "foreign barbarians," Shamian remained in Western hands until salvaged by the founding of the People's Republic in 1949.

Shamian Island (Sameen Do in Cantonese; the name means "sand surface") is another world when compared with the traffic-locked snarl elsewhere in Guangzhou. Set against the ceaseless roar of construction, Shamian languishes in a delightful reverie that dwells upon a faded era. As towering hotels erupt from the ground across the river, Shamian crumbles slowly away in the melancholic Canton damp.

NOT TO BE MISSED:

Christ Church • Shamian Dajie • Our Lady of Lourdes Chapel

Many buildings have been restored, and several now bear plaques detailing their history. The real estate value of the island can only be guessed at, and cafés and restaurants add to the European feel, while several hotels can be found on the island if you want to overnight.

Only a mile (1.6 km) in circumference, the island makes for a leisurely stroll. Start at the **White Swan Hotel** (one of the few distinctly modern structures on the island; see Travelwise p. 373) and head west along Shamian Nanjie.

Ahead on your right is **Christ Church ❶**, managed by the Guangdong Christian Council. It is disappointing that you can't just walk in, but visitors are welcome to the service each Sunday from 9:30 to 10:45 a.m. Continue west around the western tip of the island in the direction of Shamian Beijie on the north of Shamian. Small residential streets lead into very tranquil backwaters, offering a glimpse into courtyards and the occasional open doorway leading to old wooden stairs that climb into cavernous interiors.

Continuing in a loop around the island's tip and onto Shamian Beijie (Shamian "north street"), you will pass the **Shamian Traditional Chinese Medical Center** at No. 85, where you can get a restorative and reinvigorating traditional massage; perhaps leave this until the end of the walk, when you need a complete recharge, or pop it in your diary for a later date. When you reach the Guangdong Victory Hotel, turn right to head south along Shamian 4-Jie, a lively street with restaurants, antiques galleries, souvenir stores, and bars (the island sports a flourishing crop of Western watering holes).

Turn left onto **Shamian Dajie,** the island's main boulevard. Along its length are a motley collection of prestigious buildings with a pleasant green strip of grass, trees, and park benches down the middle.

Once full of dilapidated and roofless houses rotting away through neglect, Shamian Dajie, is a very pleasant and genteel stretch of restored buildings and tranquil street scenes. The overgrown trees and palms recall a time when Shamian was shrouded in greenery. Farther down Shamian Dajie, the central parks become tidier and better groomed. There is even a small running track.

Walk on east along Shamian Dajie, and after crossing Shamian 1-Jie you will find **Our Lady of Lourdes Chapel ❷** *(14 Shamian Dajie)*, a late 19th-century French church, which remains open for services. Check the blackboard outside for details of the next sermon, if you would like to attend.

Turn right onto Shamian Nanjie and follow the road south, where you will pass **Cuizhou Park ❸.** Take the road alongside the park to the riverside, and stroll past the tennis courts. Here you will encounter **two cannons.** Inscriptions on them reveal that they were forged on nearby Foshan, or Buddha Mountain, and used against the "imperial invaders." You are also told that they are 6,000 *jin* (6,600 pounds/2,994 kg) each in weight and were moved to Shamian Island in 1963. Continue walking west back to the White Swan Hotel, your starting point.

Also see area map p. 199
White Swan Hotel
30–40 minutes
1 mile (1.6 km)
White Swan Hotel

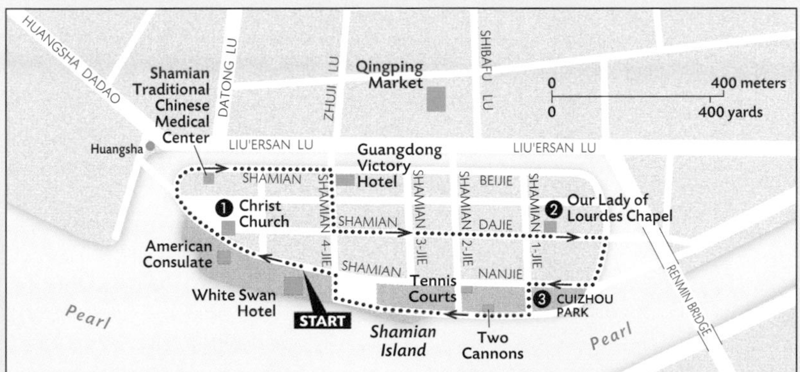

Hainan Island

Hainan ("south of the seas") is a large tropical island and erstwhile place of exile. Disgraced officials were (permanently) dispatched here, and it was only in the late 1980s that the island was reinvented as a Special Economic Zone. A new free-market prescription galvanized Hainan's economy, and the blend of a sultry climate, the proximity to increasingly lawless Guangdong Province, and the political and geographical removal from Beijing encourages a lax atmosphere.

Fishermen reenact a traditional ritual on the beach at Sun and Moon Bay.

Hainan Island

Map: 197 A1–B1

CTS Visitor Information

Address: Haifu Dadao

Phone: 0898 6530-6003

Sweltering in greenhouse temperatures from March onward and typhoon-lashed in summer, Hainan attracts a massive influx of winter visitors from the mainland. At a time when Hong Kong Chinese venture to glacial Harbin (see pp. 344–347) in northernmost Heilongjiang Province to see snow, half of Manchuria comes to Hainan to catch some rays.

The mountainous and forested central belt that forms the island's spine supports minority Li and Miao tribes, whose communities can be visited by the more adventurous (see sidebar opposite).

Haikou

The capital, Haikou ("sea mouth"), is the island's access point. Elements of colonial architecture have survived the damp climate, and there are a few historical sites of note, but a day here at most will suffice. Strolling around Haikou quenching your thirst with coconut milk, readily available from streetside sellers, is fun.

The attractive **Five Officials Memorial Temple** lies in the southeast of town and is dedicated to five unfortunate officials who were exiled to Hainan. The temple was built in the Ming dynasty, though it was later restored. The memorial temple is surrounded by pleasant walkways, ponds, and greenery. The **Tomb of Hairui** *(off Haixiu Dadao)* is dedicated to an honest and well-respected 16th-century official. Recent restoration has given it a thoroughly modern and bright new look.

Sanya

The beaches of Sanya, on the south coast of Hainan, are the principal reason for coming to the island. By far the best is the long curve of **Yalong Bay (Yalongwan)**—a white ribbon of sand more than 4 miles (6.5 km) long, on the hook of land east of Sanya. This is the southernmost reach of China, and it feels like it. If you come here any time other than winter, bring plenty of sunscreen, as the sun can be ferocious.

The bay is reached via Yalong Bay Square in Sanya, where an 88-foot (29 m) **totem pole** has been erected. The primitive totemic engravings on the pole are of auspicious animals and gods, including the dragon, Pangu (see p. 26), and the Great Yu (see p. 27), who harnessed the floodwaters.

Closer to Sanya lies the smaller and more crowded beach at **Dadonghai,** just south of town. Running along the edge of the Luhuitou Peninsula are other beaches, while a half-hour bus ride away is the beach of **Tianya Haijiao,** west of Sanya. A stone etched with the characters *tianya* (edge of sky) and *haijiao* (rim of sea) stands on the beach. The stone is famed, as it is pictured on the back of the old Y2 note.

Around the Island

Wenchang, on the east coast of Hainan, is famed for its coconut plantations, beaches, and seafood.

Hotels have sprung up around the famous hot spring baths at **Xinglong,** farther down the east coast toward Sanya. The nearby **Indonesian Village** celebrates Indonesian culture with music and dance. Xinglong is also renowned for its coffee, a major crop here.

Monkey Island, a narrow peninsula on the coast, is home to more than a thousand Guangxi monkeys *(Macaca mulatta),* but they are elusive and numbers are beginning to shrink. A wildlife research center has been established to study them. ■

Minority Villages

Perched up in the Limuling Mountains is the town of Tongshi (also called Wuzhishan), putting you within reach of Li and Miao minority villages. Some communities have been requisitioned by the tourist industry, which parades them for the benefit of visitors. Other communities farther in the interior are more genuine. Not far from Tongshi is Five Fingers Mountain (Wuzhishan), at 6,122 feet (1,867 m) the island's highest peak.

TOURS: The best way to see the outlying parts of the island is to join one of the tours that depart from Haikou. They race to Wenchang, Xinglong, Monkey Island (sporadically), and Sanya, and then do a whistlestop return via Tongshi. Tours can be arranged with English guides through the tourist office, and they are expensive; a Chinese tour is much cheaper—but viable only if you speak the language.

More Places to Visit in the South

Foshan

Buddha Mountain, or Foshan (Fatsan in Cantonese), 17 miles (27 km) southwest of Guangzhou, is home to the intriguing **Ancestor's Temple (Zumiao).** The temple oversees a huge bronze statue of Beidi, the Emperor of the North, and a wonderful panoply of colorful ceramic figures. Shiwan, famed for its porcelain, lies southwest.
199 B2

Hengshan

The southernmost of the five sacred Taoist Mountains, Hengshan is famed for its greenery and temple architecture, especially **Nanyue Temple (Nanyue Damiao).**
199 B3 $ $$$$

INSIDER TIP:

The trading city of Chaozhou in Guangdong Province *(map p. 199 C2)* is famous for its cuisine, a tasty rival to Cantonese food. The Tang dynasty Kaiyuan Temple is not far from the remains of the old city walls.

—DAMIAN HARPER
National Geographic author

Meizhou

The small island of Meizhou, one of the myriad islands along the shore of Fujian Province, is celebrated as the birthplace of Tianhou, the goddess of seafarers.
199 C3 **CTS Visitor Information**
0753 225-9650

Qingyuanshan (Qingyuan Mountains)

Sites in this mountain cluster just north of Quanzhou include a Song dynasty **statue of Laozi, Buddhist caves (Qingyuandong),** and a **Muslim tomb (Lingshan Shengmu)** dedicated to two Islamic missionaries.
199 C3

Quanzhou

Quanzhou in Fujian Province was formerly a port city on the maritime silk route. *Dehua,* or "blanc de chine," porcelain originated here. Tang dynasty **Kaiyuan Temple** *(Xi Jie, $)* leads to a museum with the remains of a Song dynasty junk. Quanzhou has a number of temples, and **Qingjing Mosque** testifies to its once flourishing Muslim community.
199 C3 Kaiyuan Temple

Shantou

Shantou in Guangdong Province is a Special Economic Zone, though the Midas touch has somehow eluded it. Pockets of disintegrating colonial architecture near the quayside make for engaging walks; a boat trip to **Mayu Island** brings pilgrims to its **Tianhou Temple.**
199 C2

Xiqiao Hills

The Xiqiao Hills (Xiqiao Shan), 42 miles (67 km) southwest of Guangzhou, are a scenic area of caves, waterfalls, and peaks. Trails start from Xiqiao town, reached by bus from Foshan.
199 B2

Zhuhai

Zhuhai ("pearl sea") is a Special Economic Zone on the border with Macau. Most people who visit are either en route to somewhere else or on business. Haibin Park has pleasant walks, and the **Zuhai City Museum** *(191 Jingshan Lu, closed Mon.)* explores the history of the town. The old house of **Dr. Sun Yat-sen (Sun Zhongshan Guju)** can be visited in Cuiheng, north of Zhuhai.
199 B2

A dynamic outpost fringed with sleepy islands and a romantic port city with Portuguese charms and a mushrooming casino circuit

Hong Kong & Macau

Introduction & Map 222–223

Hong Kong 224–250

Central Walk 226–228

Hong Kong Island 229–237

Experience: *Wing Chun Gongfu* 231

Tsim Sha Tsui Walk 234–236

Experience: Free Tai Chi 237

Wong Tai Sin Temple 238

New Territories 239–245

Experience: MacLehose Trail 240

Feature: Chinese Astrology 246

Outlying Islands 247–250

Macau 251–259

Macau Peninsula 252–255

Feature: Wind & Water 256–257

Macau's Islands 258–259

Experience: Biking & Hiking 259

Statue of Sakyamuni

More Places to Visit in Hong Kong & Macau 260

Hotels & Restaurants in Hong Kong & Macau 375–379

Hong Kong & Macau

Hong Kong and Macau share unique histories but are very different. Hong Kong, the robust ex-colony perched on an uncertain political faultline, is a success story of magnificent proportions. Macau, the former Portuguese enclave, is blessed with a Latin mood and a charm that eludes Britain's former territory.

"One Country, Two Systems"

The return of Hong Kong and Macau to the "motherland," in 1997 and 1999 respectively, ended a humiliating chapter for China, and it couldn't have come at a more opportune moment. Coinciding with a period of unprecedented Chinese economic development, the restoration of colonial spoils at the end of the 20th century was an apt finale. Of course, there were other reasons to celebrate; Hong Kong's return to China automatically increased China's gross domestic product by 25 percent.

Hong Kong and Macau are Special Administrative Regions (SARs) within China, retaining their own laws, tax systems, budget, and freedom in all areas except defense and foreign policy. The promise of the "one country, two systems" policy—which China wants to get right in a bid to lure Taiwan back into the fold—will protect the Hong Kong way of life for 50 years from 1997, and Macau has a similar proviso.

What was remarkable was that a society in the Western vein had been successfully grafted onto Communist China, an achievement made possible because China found itself more open to Western ideas than ever before.

Hong Kong & Macau Today

Is Hong Kong the ultimate Trojan horse of Western values? Or is the Hong Kong and Macau way of life hostage to an unpredictable power? To date, Hong Kong's free press, freedom of speech, and its evolved and fair legal system have had negligible impact on

China. Apart from capitalist know-how, China has shunned Hong Kong's more progressive formula; how the fickle winds of Chinese politics will blow in the future is anyone's guess. ■

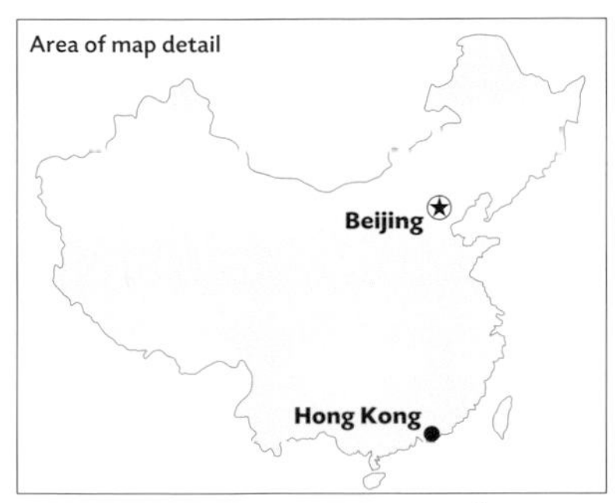

NOT TO BE MISSED:

A ride up Victoria Peak on Hong Kong Island's Peak Tram **230**

Delving into history at the Hong Kong Museum of History **236**

Enjoying a daylong adventure to the Outlying Islands **247–250**

Admiring the illuminated ruin of St. Paul's in nocturnal Macau **252**

Macau's pastoral islands **258–259**

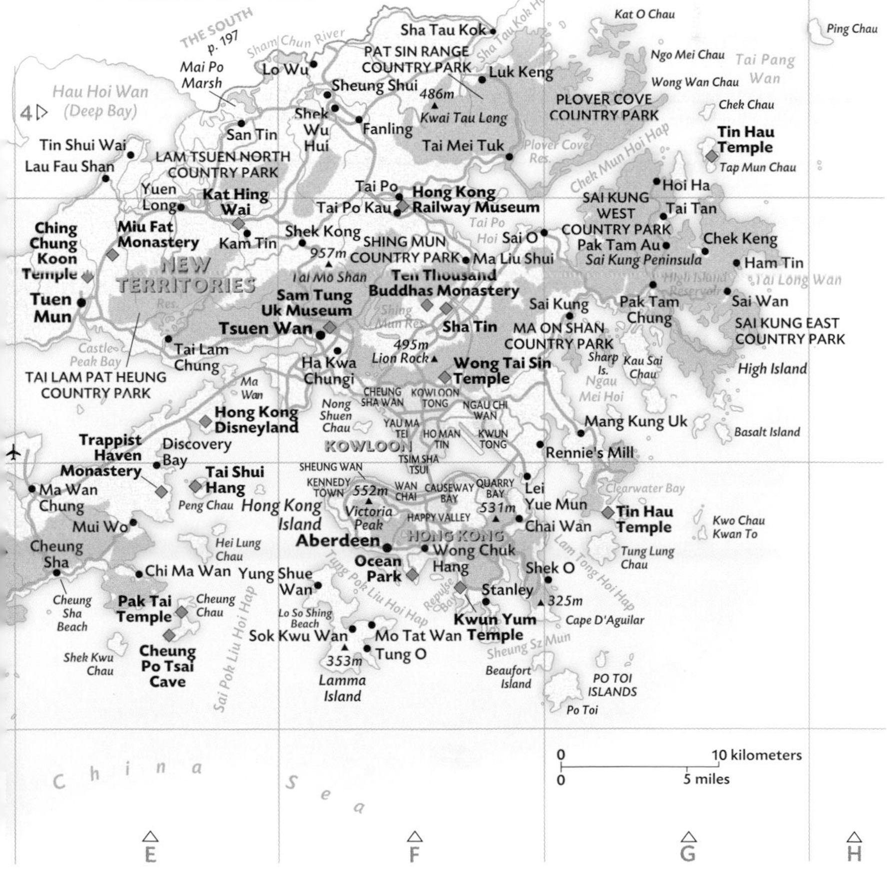

Hong Kong

Hong Kong panders to its cosmopolitan image with international restaurants at every turn, five-star hotels, shopping malls, plush bars, horse racing, and more. But it is the unexpected side to Hong Kong—a territory of overgrown islands, temples, hills, beaches, and wild walks—that makes this destination so rewarding.

The Hong Kong Convention & Exhibition Centre overlooks the harbor.

Hong Kong Island was originally ceded to the British "in perpetuity" with the Treaty of Nanking in 1842, which concluded the first Opium War (see p. 39). This was expanded to include Kowloon in 1860, mushrooming later to embrace the New Territories in 1898, on a 99-year lease. China understandably nursed feelings of grievance for many years. During the Cultural Revolution (1966–1976), Hong Kong braced for the Chinese invasion that never quite came: Mao Zedong was keenly aware that Hong Kong was a useful portal to the outside world and a fundamental source of foreign exchange.

The year 1997 signaled the expiration of the 99-year lease for the New Territories, and the idea was that the whole colony should be handed back. The only demand was that Hong Kong's way of life be guaranteed for the next 50 years. The Sino-British Joint Declaration was signed between then British Prime Minister Margaret Thatcher and Deng Xiaoping in 1984, and a basic law was drawn up for Hong Kong.

The decade preceding the handover was fraught with tension. The Tiananmen Massacre (see p. 46) sent a chill through the territory, and the last British governor, Chris Patten, regularly locked horns with Beijing as both sides maneuvered to shape Hong Kong's postcolonial future.

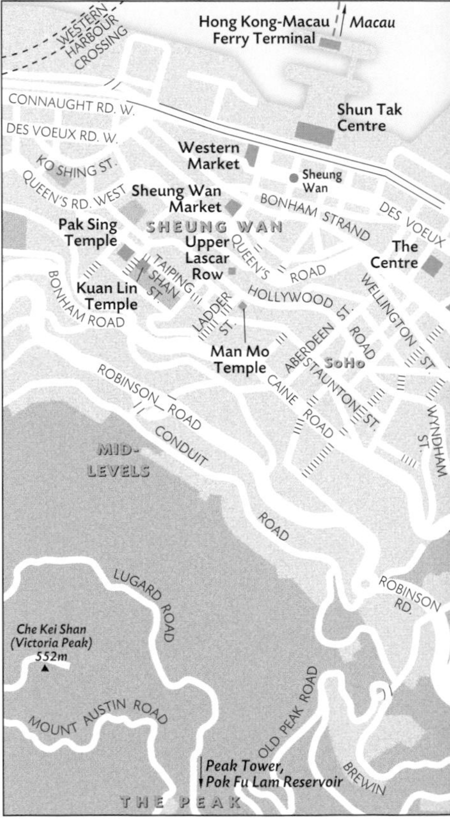

The handover on July 1, 1997, was a rainy, melancholic affair. The immediate aftermath of return to Chinese sovereignty and the ensuing years saw Hong Kong going all wrong, albeit in unpredicted fashion. A long-term economic downturn, bird flu, and SARS all conspired to knock the stuffing out of the territory, but in recent years Hong Kong has recovered its confidence and economic drive, while Chief Executive Donald Tsang has proved popular.

Hong Kong, more fully called the Hong Kong Special Administrative Region (SAR), is an ambivalent city. While the outward guise of British culture—the wigged judges, historic buildings, and afternoon tea in postcolonial hotels—remains intact, the people, language, food, and culture are predominantly Cantonese.

INSIDER TIP:

Make sure you pick up an Octopus Card *(www.octopuscards.com.hk)*, which can be used on most public transportation and in some shops.

—RORY BOLAND
National Geographic contributor

It is best to visit Hong Kong after you have seen the rest of mainland China. If this is your first port of call, however, it may be too redolent of the West to surprise you. Nevertheless, the city's forthright blend of Occident and Orient will make perfect sense. ■

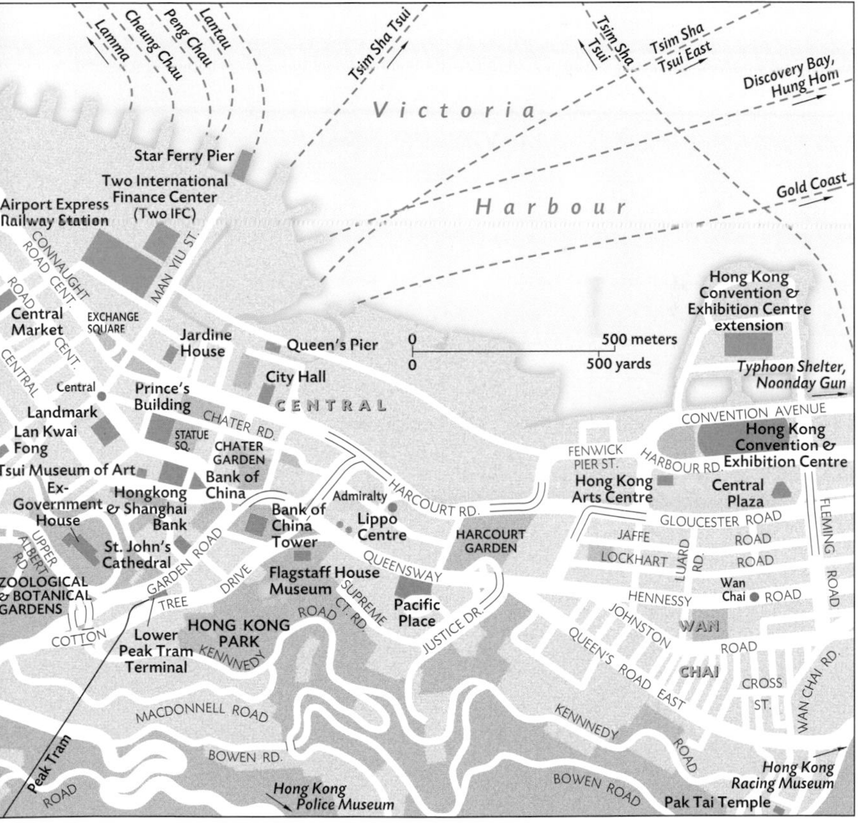

Central Walk

This walk through Hong Kong's Central District explores the territory's extrovert face. It's a splendid crush of refined shopping malls, cosmopolitan restaurants, and triumphant skyscrapers with relaxing diversions of parks and historic buildings.

For a bargain sightseeing tour, hop on one of the city's double-decker trams.

Begin this walk by disembarking the ferry at the Star Ferry Pier and walking south along the Man Yiu Street walkway past **Two International Finance Centre** (Two IFC), currently the tallest building on Hong Kong Island at 1,378 feet (420 m). Next door is the luxury **IFC Mall,** an exclusive zone of brand-name outlets, attracting Hong Kong's indefatigable shoppers.

To the west is **Exchange Square,** three towers encircling a public area of statues and fountains. Ahead is the impressive, 52-story, 1973 **Jardine House (formerly the Connaught Centre),** which rises above Connaught Road Central. Built on reclaimed land, this sophisticated and towering aluminum-clad building features circular windows; square windows were avoided to maximize the strength of the structure.

NOT TO BE MISSED:

Statue Square • St. John's Cathedral • Zoological & Botanical Gardens • Lan Kwai Fong

---

Statue Square & East

Walk east along Connaught Road Central to **Statue Square** ❶, whose statues are long gone (Queen Victoria's statue now stands in Victoria Park). The only survivor from the Japanese occupation during World War II is a figure of Sir Thomas Jackson, a former manager of the Hong Kong and Shanghai Bank. The colonial-era building to the east is the **Legislative Council Building (LegCo),** with the premier shopping experience of **Prince's Building** *(Chater Rd., Subway: Central)* to the west. The **Landmark,** southwest of Prince's Building, plays host to a further spread of elegant outlets, supported by the Gallerie and Alexandra House. Many of these buildings are linked by a web of overhead walkways, rising above the traffic.

Cross Des Voeux Road Central to visit the elaborate genius of Sir Norman Foster's **Hong Kong & Shanghai Bank** ❷ *(1 Queen's Rd., Subway: Central).* The space under the edifice is a public area, and two escalators feed into the belly of the structure. When it was completed in 1985, it was the world's most expensive building at almost a billion dollars. Note the two huge bronze lions that guard the entrance. Foster's robotic building looks down upon the old **Bank of China.** The top three floors play host to the ostentatious China Club (note the two sets of lions outside—one traditional, the other 1940s).

Not to be outdone, the Bank of China enlisted architect I. M. Pei to resurrect itself in more dramatic fashion in 1990 (beyond the mighty, gleaming Cheung Kong Centre) in the geometric guise of the 70-story **Bank of China Tower** *(1 Garden Rd., Subway: Central).* The tower thrusts up like a gleaming crystal, challenging with its sharp lines and ingenuity. It's designed to withstand typhoon stresses four times the equivalent for earthquake requirements in Los Angeles. The landscaping on either side of the shaft and the lobby are muted Chinese gestures that remain smothered in the building's overall modernity. Take the express elevator to the 47th floor for sweeping

Also see area map p. 223
- Star Ferry Pier
- Half a day
- 2 miles (3 km)
- Lan Kwai Fong

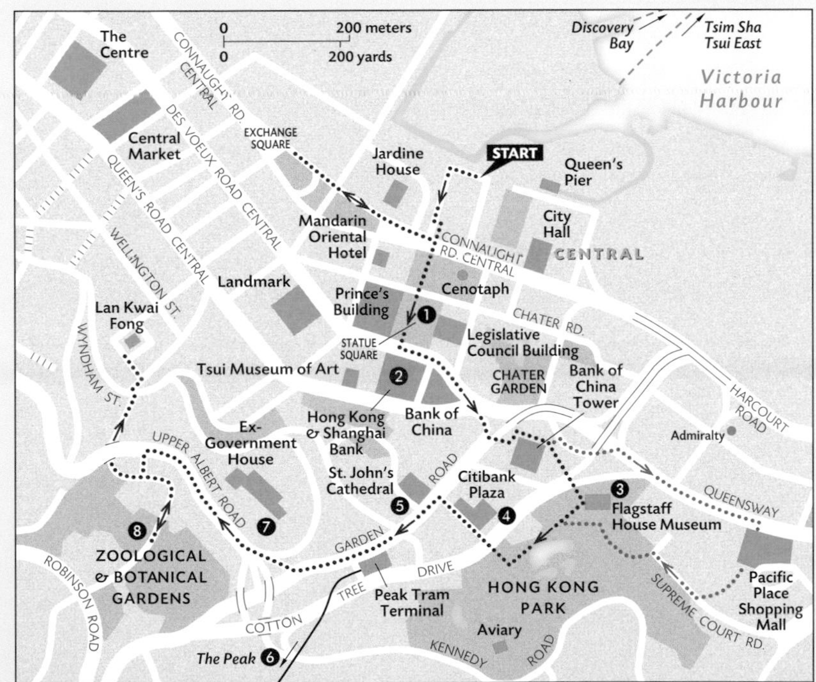

views over Victoria Harbour. Admiralty, to the east, feeds into famous Wan Chai, but not before making its pronouncement with the huge **Pacific Place Shopping Mall.**

Hong Kong Park

Walk south of the Bank of China Tower to reach Hong Kong Park, a welcome escape from the overwhelming presence of the city's tall buildings and busy streets. The park contains an aviary with a fascinating collection of brilliantly plumed tropical birds, a visual arts center, and a tai chi garden. The **Flagstaff House Museum** ❸ *(Hong Kong Park, 10 Cotton Tree Dr., tel 2869-0690, closed Tues. & some public holidays, Subway: Admiralty),* with its display of Chinese tea ware, dates from 1846. It's a great place to spend an hour or so.

INSIDER TIP:

If you want to eat at the Peak, don't miss out on the amazing views at family-friendly Cafe Deco *(www.cafedecogroup.com)*. The restaurant can get crowded, especially on weekends, so make reservations.

—JULIA MULROY
National Geographic contributor

You can access Hong Kong Park via Cotton Tree Drive, or alternatively you can enter via the park's main entrance on Supreme Court Road, accessible by the Pacific Place Shopping Mall in Queensway (follow the tram lines or take a tram).

Overlooking the park south of the Bank of China Tower is another wonderful example of architecture—**Citibank Plaza** ❹ *(3 Garden Rd., Subway: Central).* The interplay of curved and straight lines lends a powerful grace to this 1992 building.

Colonial Hong Kong & the Peak

Take the park exit to Cotton Tree Drive and cross over to Garden Road and **St. John's Cathedral** ❺. Built in 1847, this is one of the last colonial pieces of architecture left in Hong Kong. It was badly damaged during the Japanese occupation in World War II. Services are still held here regularly, and an information booklet is available inside the church. Farther up Garden Road, you can hop aboard the Peak Tram, which drags itself up an impossible angle to the summit of **the Peak** ❻ (see pp. 229–230).

Alternatively, walk south up Garden Road, turn right on Upper Albert Road, and pass **Ex-Government House** ❼. Dating from the mid-19th century, this was the residence of colonial governors during British rule. Hong Kong's present chief executive refused to live here, complaining that the *fengshui* was not up to scratch. The house is not open to the public, except for one Sunday in March; contact the Hong Kong Tourism Board *(Ground floor, The Centre, 99 Queen's Rd., tel 0852 2508-1234)* for details.

Albany Road runs south from Upper Albert Road to the splendid **Zoological & Botanical Gardens** ❽ *(Albany Rd., Central, tel 0852 2530-0154),* home to a surprising number of exotic creatures, including a family of orangutans and a black jaguar.

Lan Kwai Fong

Backtrack along Albany Road and then continue onto Glenealy. At D'Aguilar Street. Turn left to reach Lan Kwai Fong. This is a tight jam of pubs, clubs, discos, restaurants, sandwich places, and cafés. Hong Kong's bright young things converge here to parade themselves and escape the stresses of office life. Farther west are the bars, cafés, and restaurants of SoHo, abbreviated from "South of Hollywood Road," and NoHo, or "North of Hollywood Road"—two of Hong Kong's most popular drinking and eating spots.

Hong Kong Island

Take the Star Ferry from Tsim Sha Tsui on the southern reaches of the Kowloon Peninsula to Hong Kong's Central District for a classic approach to one of the world's most photographed vistas. The Bank of China Tower and other landmarks of modern architecture that thrust skyward define the sophistication of Hong Kong.

The only way to build is up in high-density Hong Kong.

Hong Kong Island is the place where you can find the stock exchange, the financial district, the legislature, government offices, the most exclusive hotels (apart from the Peninsula) and restaurants, and the most expensive real estate, plus the best stores and nightlife in town.

Nevertheless, it's not all business and commerce. Above the futuristic landscape of Central rises the most expensive piece of real estate in the world: the Peak. Victoria Peak, at 1,810 feet (552 m), is home to Hong Kong's elite, and the closer to the summit you get, the more stunning the cost. Property prices here, like the mist-wreathed paths that circle the Peak, are well and truly in the clouds.

To the south of the island lies a scattered retreat of small communities, seaside restaurants, and beaches. Tempting walks snake across the island, and several bus rides pass very dramatic and inspiring scenery.

Hong Kong Island is also the springboard to the picturesque outlying islands (see pp. 247–250).

Victoria Peak

The Peak is the most exclusive residential area in Hong Kong, a confluence of huge bank

Hong Kong Island

223 F2

Hong Kong Tourism Board (HKTB)

✉ Ground floor, The Centre, 99 Queen's Road, Central

☎ 0852 2508-1234

www.discoverhongkong.com

Cantonese & Mandarin

While Mandarin is by far the most useful dialect to learn in China, Cantonese opens up the door to understanding the culture of Hong Kong, Macau, Guangdong Province, and of course, myriad overseas Chinese communities dotted around the globe. The name Hong Kong itself derives from Cantonese for "fragrant harbor"—*heung gong*. The Mandarin equivalent, *xiang gang*, is a far more distant sound, hailing from north China.

For students of Mandarin, learning Cantonese offers fascinating insight into how Chinese sounds and tones change across the dialect boundaries, while also demonstrating how all Chinese languages are related.

In some respects, Cantonese is an easier dialect to learn than Mandarin. Although there are a larger number of tones, the tones are more widely spaced apart in pitch and are more regular in usage. Sounds in Cantonese are also easier for foreign students to reproduce; some sounds in Mandarin take students years to mimic correctly.

Victoria Peak
Map 223 F2 & 224

Peak Tower
Tel 0852 2849-0668
$ Peak Tram: $$$$
www.thepeak.com.hk

STAR FERRY: The Star Ferry *(tel 0852 2367-7065, $, www.starferry.com.hk)* runs between Central and Tsim Sha Tsui every 6 to 10 minutes, 6:30 a.m.–11:30 p.m., and between Wan Chai and Tsim Sha Tsui every 10 to 20 minutes, 7:30 a.m.–11 p.m.

accounts, massive real estate value, and panache. It was rapidly colonized by a British establishment eager to escape the suffocating summer heat below.

The best way to get up here is by the **Peak Tram,** a unique ride. The angle of the railway slope approaches 45 degrees; just try not to think what might happen if the cable snaps! In fact, the tram has never had an accident since opening in 1888. It operates from 7 a.m. to midnight, running every 15 minutes. A one-way trip takes about 8 minutes.

The Peak Tram terminus is located on Garden Road, Central, and is connected to the Star Ferry Pier by a free shuttle bus that runs every 20 minutes between 9 a.m. and 7 p.m. (8 p.m. on Sundays and public holidays).

A great place to bring the kids, the impressively dissonant **Peak Tower** (designed by British architect Terry Farrell) doubles as the upper tram terminus. Climb up to the **Sky Terrace** *($; joint ticket with Peak Tram also available)* on the roof for some truly outstanding views. The upper terminus is not the peak per se; that's farther uphill, and you'll have to walk. Apart from the views, however, there is little to do on the summit.

The nearby **Peak Galleria** has another collection of shops and the excellent **Peak Lookout** (see p. 377). If you can get a table for dinner here, do so; the nocturnal view down to the neon foothills of the Peak is unforgettable.

Harlech Road and Lugard Road run around the Peak and make for an attractive, undemanding walk. More strenuous walks lead away from the Peak downhill, one of which takes you along Pok Fu Lam Reservoir Road past the reservoir. The brisk **Hong Kong Trail** (see p. 237) also commences here.

On a misty day, the trails around the Peak make for a very refreshing and atmospheric day out. On a clear night, the twinkling view down to Central is simply bewitching. You can understand why residents are willing to pay so much to live here.

Sheung Wan

Though Sheung Wan is more down-at-the-heels than Central, it is also more authentically Cantonese in flavor. Located to the west of Central, this ramshackle area comprises temples, shops, and pungent pockets of dried-seafood stores.

Hollywood Road, a fascinating jumble of antique stores, burrows into Sheung Wan from Central. Sift through a sea of ceramics, Ming furniture, Tibetan artifacts, and relics from the Cultural Revolution. Half a day can be spent here, trawling for those elusive treasures.

The **Central-Midlevels Escalator** (the world's longest outdoor escalator) ferries shoppers and commuters up to the Mid-Levels from Central—it's more than 2,600 feet (790 m) long. It descends from 6 a.m. to 10 a.m. and ascends from 10:30 a.m. to midnight. Jump on if you want (the journey takes 20 minutes).

The **Man Mo Temple**, one of the oldest temples in Hong Kong, also lies on Hollywood Road. It predates the British arrival and is dedicated to the civil and the martial (in Cantonese *man* means "literature" and *mo* means "military"). Huge, picturesque incense coils hang from the roof. Farther into Sheung Wan, on Tai Ping Shan Street, are two smaller temples, the **Pak Sing Temple** and the **Kuan Yin Temple.** Nearby Possession Street marks the spot where the Union Jack was first raised over Hong Kong.

The Edwardian **Western Market,** on New Market Street at the corner of Des Voeux Road (Central), is built on what was one of Hong Kong's busiest food markets. The brick building is a nostalgic nod to the past, equipped with an old London phone booth, cafés, and trinket stalls.

High-speed catamarans travel the route to Macau (see

Sheung Wan
223 F2 & 224

Man Mo Temple
224
124–126 Hollywood Rd.

Western Market
224
323 Des Voeux Rd. Central
Subway: Sheung Wan

EXPERIENCE: *Wing Chun Gongfu*

The *wing chun* school of *gongfu* can be traced back to the Shaolin Temple (see pp. 128–129) and a nun called Ng Mui, who taught her skills to a young girl named Wing Chun. In fact, despite its predominantly male student body, wing chun has many techniques that suit women or those of a slighter build. The wing chun style of gongfu does not emphasize strength so much as evasion, deflection, and a combination of very fast punches and low kicks.

A training routine called *chi sau* (sticky hands) teaches the wing chun student to relax when under attack and promotes softness and "listening" in his or her arms. This listening—or awareness of the movements of others through touch—can be used to put an attacker off balance or to neutralize a punch.

The wing chun style of gongfu is forever associated with Bruce Lee, whose snappy punches and simple economy of movement are its trademarks. Although he eventually parted ways with wing chun to devise his own martial arts style (Jeet Kune Do), Lee remains a figurehead of the wing chun lineage.

To learn this style for yourself, contact the Wan Kei Ho International Martial Arts Association *(tel 0852 2544-1368, www.kungfuwan.com)* in Sheung Wan.

Wan Chai, Happy Valley, & Causeway Bay
223 F2 & 225

pp. 251–259) from the Ferry Terminal behind the **Shun Tak Centre** *(200 Connaught Rd.).*

Toward Kennedy Town along Des Voeux Road West, stores spill over with dried seafood Jump on an eastbound tram back to Central,

INSIDER TIP:

Hong Kong offers tons of great hiking opportunities. The easy but stunning Dragon's Back Trail runs through Shek O. The hike takes about two hours.

–JULIA MULROY
National Geographic contributor

and go on to Admiralty, Wan Chai, Causeway Bay, or Happy Valley (check the front of the tram). Grab a seat at the top and sail back through a forest of store signs.

Wan Chai, Happy Valley, & Causeway Bay

Head east on the double-deck tram from Central to Wan Chai, a knot of Western bars, sandwich parlors, and brisk side streets. Causeway Bay beyond caters to eager shoppers and diners, while Hong Kong's gamblers converge on Happy Valley's racecourse.

The buildings get progressively more frayed to the east, while Wan Chai south has interesting pockets of historic architecture.

The rest of Wan Chai itself is a rather tacky strip of bars, clubs, and pubs, its reputation still feeding remorselessly off its red-light association with the 1950s novel *The World of Suzie Wong,* by Richard Mason. Wan Chai is a *gwailo* (foreign devil) stomping ground, jammed with snack bars and cafés.

One of the best sights here is the **promenade** around the **Hong Kong Convention & Exhibition Centre extension.** The promenade allows fabulous views over Victoria Harbour to both Kowloon and Central. The new wing itself is a gorgeous extension of the waterfront; pop inside and stroll around its spacious interior.

Not far away is the **Hong Kong Arts Centre** *(2 Harbour Rd., tel 2582-0200),* where contemporary art exhibitions are held. The **Police Museum** *(27 Coombe Rd., tel 2849-7019, closed Mon., & Tues. before 2 p.m.)* is devoted to the history of Hong Kong's police force.

For a diversion, jump on a tram headed to Happy Valley and visit the horse-racing track. The racing season here lasts from September to May. You can glean some of the history of horse racing in Hong Kong at the **Hong Kong Racing Museum** *(2nd floor, Happy Valley Stand, Happy Valley Racecourse, tel 2966-8065, closed Mon.).* West of the track lies a collection of well-tended Catholic, Muslim, Parsi, and Hindu cemeteries.

Continue by tram to Causeway Bay. Much of this former warehouse district was under water until a land reclamation program transformed it into a vast restaurant and retail zone. A lasting symbol of the departed colonial presence is the **Noonday**

Gun. Fired daily at noon, it can be found in a garden by the **Typhoon Shelter** on Gloucester Road.

Farther to the east are **Quarry Bay** and **Chai Wan.** Not far from the Chai Wan subway station is the **Law Uk Folk Museum** *(14 Kut Shing St., tel 2896-7006, closed Sun. a.m., Tues. & Thurs.)*, a restored dwelling of the Hakka, a traditional Chinese group living mainly in the New Territories and recognizable by their broad-rimmed hats.

Around Hong Kong Island

The southern coastline of Hong Kong Island harbors an enticing world of seaside retreats and beach life that is far removed from the strip of urban congestion on its northern shore. The thrills and spills of Ocean Park and Water World make for a fun family destination.

Beaches line most of the small communities sheltered along the coast, but a casual glance at Hong Kong's pollution figures should deter you from flinging a towel into your luggage. The beaches make for attractive strolls, with swimming only for the thick-skinned.

On the southeast coast is tiny **Shek O.** A tip: Go during the week; it's not easy to get to, but it's worth it, and you will have a lot of space to yourself (including the excellent beach). The No. 9 bus from Shau Kei Wan subway station takes an attractive route there.

Another popular hamlet on the south coast of the island is **Stanley,** a *gwailo* (foreign) refuge famous for its market. Again, the weekends see the place crammed with visitors, so try a weekday. The nearby **St. Stephen's Beach** is an attractive stretch of sand, and the village is packed with a choice of popular restaurants and bars. To the west of Stanley is a small

(continued on p. 237)

Horse racing is a favored pastime in Hong Kong.

Tsim Sha Tsui Walk

Tsim Sha Tsui in Kowloon (Kowloon or Gaulong means "nine dragons" in Cantonese) is altogether a land of rougher textures than Central. This walk takes you past hallmark locations of sophistication (the Peninsula) and culture (the Hong Kong Cultural Centre), with a dazzling view over to Hong Kong Island. Kowloon Park patiently waits for those exhausted by the shopping frenzy of Nathan Road.

The Signal Tower provided time signals to ships in Victoria Harbour.

Start at the **Star Ferry Pier** in Tsim Sha Tsui; visit the Hong Kong Tourism Board *(Star Ferry Concourse, tel 2508-1234)* if you need extra information. Follow the promenade to the east. The splendid waterfront walk along the edge of Victoria Harbour offers an ideal view of the sparkling districts of Central and Wan Chai on Hong Kong Island, and the nighttime vista is one of the most breathtaking urban sights imaginable. The 20-minute **Symphony of Lights laser show** takes place at 8 p.m. every night from the Avenue of the Stars to the east. The vast tower in West Kowloon is the recently completed International Commerce Centre, the tallest in the territory.

You will pass the **Hong Kong Cultural Centre** *(10 Salisbury Rd., tel 2734-2009)*, one of Hong Kong's landmarks, and the **Clock Tower ❶**. The clock is a remnant of the old Kowloon-Canton (Guangzhou) Railway station, built in 1915 and demolished in 1978. The Cultural Centre houses an impressive range of cultural amenities, including a concert hall, a theater, and an arts library. The bookstore has a varied selection of books on art and is worth a browse.

Part of the Cultural Centre is the **Hong Kong Museum of Art** *(10 Salisbury Rd.,*

NOT TO BE MISSED:

Waterfront Walk • Hong Kong Cultural Centre • The Peninsula Hong Kong • Nathan Road • Hong Kong Museum of History

---

tel 2721-0116, closed Thurs. & some holidays, $), which holds regular exhibitions of home-grown and international art. The adjacent **Hong Kong Space Museum & Theatre** *(10 Salisbury Rd., tel 2721-0226, closed Tues., & a.m. Mon. & Wed.–Fri.)* has a constellation of facilities, including a planetarium (where films are regularly screened).

Cross over Salisbury Road to the fabled **Peninsula** ❷ *(Salisbury Rd., tel 2920-2888),* an oasis of luxury in a rather run-down neighborhood. This is the grandest building in Tsim Sha Tsui, boasting an equally luxurious view over Victoria Harbour. If you have the good fortune to be a guest here, it will put an ornate frame around your memories of Hong Kong. If not, catch a glimpse of this sterling establishment through its ritual of afternoon tea in the foyer. Peruse the lobby and the excellent shopping arcades.

Nathan Road

Turn left onto Nathan Road (called the Golden Mile for its sky-high real-estate value), cutting a mercantile swath through Tsim Sha Tsui to Mong Kok. This is the place to come if buying a copy Rolex is on your list; you're bound to be approached by street sellers.

The notorious **Chungking Mansions,** a low end backpacker hotel, is at 36–44 Nathan Road, with its poor stairwells and minute rooms. Be careful if shopping for cameras or electrical goods at one of the many outlets here: They prey off the tourist market (note the absence of price tags on items in the windows). But Nathan Road has to be experienced because it is pure, unadulterated Hong Kong.

Kowloon Park ❸ provides a nearby retreat from exhaust fumes and the general chaos of Tsim Sha Tsui. The swimming pools are open between April and October, but go during the week when they are less crowded. The park sits at the edge of some of the priciest real estate in the world. Like other parks in Hong Kong, it is a sculptured, rather contrived garden, but it is still attractive and an essential refuge for local residents. On the southeast corner of the park rises **Kowloon Mosque,** which you can enter only if you are Muslim.

If you want to return to the Star Ferry Pier to go to Central (see pp. 226–228), turn left onto Haiphong Road, which skirts south of the high wall of Kowloon Park. The network of streets south of Haiphong Road is another sanctuary of *gwailo* (foreigners') watering holes and international restaurants that come alive at dusk. Beyond lies Canton Road, hemmed in on either side by cinemas, top-end hotels, and shopping arcades, taking you south back to the Star Ferry

Also see area map p. 223
- ➤ Star Ferry Pier
- Half day, with museum visits
- 2.5 miles (4 km)
- ➤ Star Ferry Pier

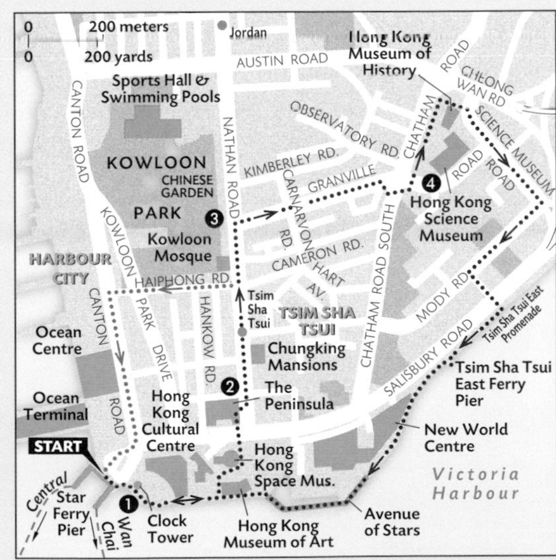

Pier. Otherwise, from the southeast corner of Kowloon Park you can take the MTR (Mass Transit Railway) north to Yau Ma Tei and Mong Kok (see p. 260).

Hong Kong Museum Pass

Although admission to all museums in Hong Kong is free on Wednesdays, visitors who plan to spend more than a few days in the city should consider investing in the Hong Kong Museum Pass (*$*), which permits repeat entry to a large number of museums over the course of a week. Museums on the pass include the Hong Kong Museum of History, Museum of Art, Space Museum, Science Museum, and Heritage Museum.

Tsim Sha Tsui East

Back on the main walk, the roads running off to the east of Nathan Road (Carnarvon Road, Mody Road, Hanoi Road, and so on) journey through an energetic domain of Western pubs, clubs, discos, and restaurants.

Follow Granville Road, opposite the Parklane Shopper's Boulevard, and take the walkway from the Ramada Hotel Kowloon over Chatham Road South, which accesses Energy Plaza before traversing north to the **Hong Kong Science Museum** ❹ *(2 Science Museum Rd., tel 2732-3232, closed Thurs. & some holidays, $)*. Imaginative and up-to-date displays and exhibits make for a lively experience that will keep kids amused. North of the Science Museum, the **Hong Kong Museum of History** *(100 Chatham Rd. South, tel 2724-9042, closed Tues., $)* offers a thorough and resourceful chronicle of the ex-British colony.

This area is Tsim Sha Tsui East, a domain of nightclubs, hotels, restaurants, and shopping emporiums built on reclaimed land salvaged from Victoria Harbour. Walk south from the Museum of History down Science Museum Road, and turn right onto Mody Road. At the Urban Council Centenary Garden about 150 yards (140 m) down Mody Road, take the walkway to the Tsim Sha Tsui East Promenade and walk past the **Avenue of the Stars** (a tribute to the Hong Kong film industry) back to the Star Ferry Pier. Alternatively, catch a ferry to Central from the Tsim Sha Tsui East Ferry Pier.

Calm Kowloon Park is a welcome respite from the go-go pace of modern Hong Kong.

Tinhau temple, and a temple to **Kuan Yin (Guanyin)** perches on a hill overlooking the sea.

West along the coast is **Repulse Bay,** Hong Kong's most popular beach, though it suffers from sludgy water. An enticing feature of the bay is the **Kwun Yum Temple** at the eastern end, where you will find a fascinating collection of Buddhist effigies wreathed in pearls and jewelry. **Deep Water Bay** is a quieter beach farther around the coast to the west.

Ocean Park, a huge marine/amusement park, sits west of Deep Water Bay and makes an ideal outing for children. The shark aquarium is particularly instructive and exciting. Water World is a fun complex of swimming pools and water slides.

Aberdeen, opposite the island of **Ap Lei Chau ("duck's tongue island"),** was where boatpeople lived on junks and sampans, but many have now moved ashore. It is worth noting that you can get to **Mo Tat Wan** and **Sok Kwu Wan** on the south of lovely **Lamma Island** (see pp. 247–248) from Aberdeen. You can take tours of the harbor from one of the private sampans, which will take you on a meandering chug past the houseboats. Walk along the waterfront and sea dogs offering rides will quickly encircle you. Otherwise, find the pier for the harbor's floating restaurants and get a free ride (boats leave every five minutes).

Hong Kong Trail

If you want to get the blood pumping and see a rawer side to the island, this 31-mile (50 km) trail will guide you through the nature spots. It winds from Lugard Road on Victoria Peak, down to **Pok Fu Lam Reservoir** (you can join this section from Aberdeen), before snaking through parks in the east of the island and stopping in Shek O.

Wilson Trail

The 48-mile (78 km) Wilson Trail cuts across Hong Kong Island, submerges under Victoria Harbour, and re-emerges in the New Territories. The trail commences just above **Stanley** on the south of Hong Kong Island, cuts roughly north, straddles Violet Hill, traverses **Mount Butler,** and drills through the Eastern Harbour Tunnel (take the subway from Quarry Bay to Lam Tin) to the other side. Once in the New Territories (see pp. 239–245), the trail charts a breathtaking course through **Lion Rock Country Park** (bisecting the MacLehose Trail, see sidebar p. 240), over hills, and on to the **Pat Sin Range Country Park.** ■

Ocean Park

- 223 F2
- Ocean Park Rd.
- 2552 0291
- Water World closed Nov.–May
- $$$

www.oceanpark.com.hk

EXPERIENCE: Free Tai Chi

Free one-hour tai chi classes are held four mornings a week (Mon., Wed., Thurs., and Fri.) at 8 a.m. in Tsim Sha Tsui in Kowloon. The classes are organized by the Hong Kong Tourism Board *(www.discoverhongkong.com)*, and they are an excellent opportunity to see if tai chi is the right kind of martial art for you. Instructors can also help advise on your next steps if you find the art appealing.

TRAIL MAPS: A very useful Hong Kong Trail map, published by the Country Parks Authority, is available from the Government Publications Centre *(Rm. 402, Murray Bldg., 22 Garden Rd., Central, tel 2537-1910)*. A map of Hong Kong Island, published by Universal Publications, is available at most bookstores. Universal Publications also has a map of the Wilson Trail.

Wong Tai Sin Temple

Bringing a splash of vibrant color to New Kowloon, Wong Tai Sin Temple swarms with worshippers casting *chim*—bamboo sticks used to interpret the future—amid pungent clouds of incense.

Wong Tai Sin Temple

223 F3

Exit B, Wong Tai Sin MTR

Wong Tai Sin (Huang Daxian in Mandarin), a Taoist deity much lauded in Hong Kong and the surrounding region, reigns from this fabulous temple. Once a shepherd in Zhejiang Province, he learned the art of healing from an immortal. Consequently, those who are ill seek his guidance and restorative powers.

The temple is a splendid mish-mash of faiths. The main temple contains an image of Wong Tai Sin and the Monkey God, a mythical being who appears in the classic tale *Journey to the West*. The **Three Saints Hall** behind has a statue of the Buddhist Guanyin (pronounced Kwan Yam in Cantonese), Guandi (Kwan Ti), and one of the Eight Taoist Immortals (see p. 83). The Confucian hall is called the **Qilin Pavilion (Linge)** after a mythical animal often associated with Confucius and royalty.

Chinese Divination

***Chim* are an assortment of numbered bamboo sticks placed in a container. After lighting incense and kneeling in front of an altar, the worshipper shakes the container in both hands until one of the sticks escapes and falls to the ground. The number is then interpreted for its message.**

Visit on the weekend, when the temple is most active, to catch the faithful praying (but be unobtrusive). A carnival atmosphere also reigns during Chinese New Year and on Wong Tai Sin's birthday, the 23rd day of the eighth lunar month.

The Five Elements

The fabric of the temple taps directly into the *fengshui* lore. The **Bronze Pavilion** to the east represents metal (which produces water and is itself produced by earth in the phase of creation and destruction of the five elements). The other elements (wood, fire, earth, and water) manifest themselves in other halls.

The **Yue Heung Shrine (Yue Heung Ting)** contains a portrait of the Buddha of the lighting lamp; the portrait embraces fire, and the brick wall in front of the hall represents earth. The **Scriptures Hall (Ging Tong)** preserves the teachings of Wong Tai Sin; its wooden structure represents wood in the elemental cycle, and the fountain in front of the hall represents water.

Fortune-tellers

If you want your fortune told at the temple, there are booths of commercial fortune-tellers (some speak English) who will read your palm or consult the *I-Ching* (see p. 54). ■

New Territories

There's much more to Hong Kong than the bright lights of the big city. The rural New Territories introduce a more pastoral side, a pressure valve for the grinding stresses of high-density living. Along with the outlying islands, this is Hong Kong's garden.

The Ten Thousand Buddhas Monastery actually houses nearly 13,000 effigies of Sakyamuni.

Technically speaking, all that lies between Boundary Street in Kowloon and the border with China proper is the New Territories, which were leased to Great Britain in 1898 for 99 years. The area embraces a wide range of sights and activities, and a potentially vast region in which to explore. To see it all would take several days of rigorous trekking, so it pays to make a judicious selection.

Sai Kung Peninsula

The ragged expanse of the Sai Kung Peninsula out to the east offers a number of opportunities for exploration. The old fishing town of **Sai Kung** acts as a launchpad to the surrounding region, and boats venture out to an assortment of small islands.

Pak Tam Chung, on the borders of the **Sai Kung East Country Park,** ushers you onto the start of the **MacLehose Trail** (see sidebar p. 240). The 62-mile (100 km) route winds its length through the New Territories. South of Sai Kung town, the road penetrates to the rough tip of land around **Clearwater Bay (Tsing Sui Wan),** where you can find pleasant beaches and an aged **Tin Hau Temple** overlooking Joss House Bay. The island to that lies to the south is **Tung Lung Chau** (see p. 260).

New Territories
223 E3

MAPS: Universal Publications prints the *Hong Kong Guidebook,* with a highly detailed map of the entire territory of Hong Kong; look for it in Hong Kong bookshops. Arm yourself with this guide if prospecting for far-flung sights in the New Territories and islands. Taking plenty of food and drink, sunscreen, a sun hat, and a basic medical kit is advisable.

Sha Tin

The **Ten Thousand Buddhas Monastery** lies west of Sha Tin, a town easily accessed by taking the KCR (Kowloon Canton Railway). A steep 15-minute climb brings you to the temple, so named because hoarded there are roughly 13,000 statues of Buddha. The **Heritage Museum** *(1 Man Lam Rd., tel 2180 8188, closed Tues., $)* is one of Hong Kong's best museums, with displays on traditional Hong Kong culture.

You will also find Hong Kong's second racecourse here. There's an entrance charge on days when there are races.

Tai Po

Farther north on the KCR is Tai Po, a new town that has little value for the traveler apart from the **Hong Kong Railway Museum** *(13 Shung Tak St., tel 2653-3455, closed Tues.),* which should be of interest to railway enthusiasts and children.

Tsuen Wan

Tsuen Wan is easy to reach from either Kowloon or Hong Kong Island since it is located at the end of the MTR (Mass Transit Railway) line. The main draws here are the **Yuen Yuen Institute** *(tel 0852 2492-2220)* and the Buddhist **Western**

EXPERIENCE: MacLehose Trail

The 62-mile (100 km) MacLehose Trail is a daunting prospect if you have only a few days in Hong Kong. Don't be put off though; it can be chopped up into manageable sections. The MacLehose Trail (named after one of Hong Kong's former British governors) starts in Pak Tam Chung in the Sai Kung Peninsula and finishes in the western New Territories town of Tuen Mun. The trail can also be done in reverse.

The first section takes you from **Pak Tam Chung** and initially skirts south around High Island Reservoir, before winding through the tiny villages of **Ham Tin** ("salty field") and **Tai Long** ("big wave") along the shoreline. The trail curls on up through the village of **Chek Keng** ("red path") and on to **Pak Tam Au.**

The path then enters the **Ma On Shan Country Park** and leads up the mountain of **Ma On Shan.** From this point, the climb can become an exerting affair. If you don't wish to continue, you can jump on bus No. 99 at Pak Tam Au to **Sai Kung** (see p. 239).

Persevering on the trail through Ma On Shan Country Park, you will come to the next peak of **Tai Lo Shan** (1,892 feet/576 m). The trek (stage 5 of the MacLehose Trail) then passes **Lion Rock** (a path north leads to Amah Rock), the ancient lookout post of **Beacon Hill,** and **Eagle's Nest. Kowloon Reservoir** lies ahead (where you can catch a bus back on Tai Po Road) and beyond that, to the north, **Shing Mun Reservoir.**

You are now wandering around **Tai Mo Shan Country Park.** Pause for breath before clambering up **Tai Mo Shan** (see p. 241). This is stage 8 of the trail, and you still have almost 14 miles (22 km) to get to **Tuen Mun.** Alternatively, catch bus No. 51 to Tsuen Wan MTR station from Tai Mo Shan Road.

To the west, the trail wraps itself around the north of **Tai Lam Chung Reservoir,** before ending in Tuen Mun.

Monastery *(tel 0852 2411-5111);* both are worth a look. The Yuen Yuen Institute is a Taoist temple with a vegetarian restaurant and panoramic views.

A taste of simple, traditional Hakka (the "guest people," and one of Hong Kong's minority groups) life can be gleaned by visiting the **Sam Tung Uk Museum** *(2 Kwu Uk Ln., tel 2411-2001, closed Tues.).* The name means "three beam house," and it was originally peopled by a migrant Hakka community from Fujian Province (adjoining Guangdong to the east). The museum is actually a small, walled village, of which there are other examples in the New Territories. The setting wins acclaim due to its authenticity.

The **Airport Core Programme Exhibition Centre** *(410 Castle Peak Rd., closed Mon.),* west of Tsuen Wan, guides you through the civil engineering feat of Chek Lap Kok airport and the stupendously long Tsing Ma, a railroad suspension bridge.

Tai Mo Shan

Big Misty Mountain, or Tai Mo Shan, is Hong Kong's tallest peak at 3,139 feet (957 m). It lies on the MacLehose Trail (see sidebar opposite), but you can also reach the peak from Tsuen Wan to the south (take bus 51 from Tsuen Wan MTR station).

Tuen Mun

Tuen Mun is a new town to the west of the **Tai Lam Pat Heung Country Park.** In the north of town is the **Ching Chung Koon Temple,** a Taoist house of worship dedicated to a Taoist Immortal, replete with ancestral hall and drum towers. The most active time to visit is during the Ching Ming Festival, a period of remembrance for the dead, which occurs at about the same time as Easter (Easter is known as the Foreigner's Ching Ming in Hong Kong).

Tuen Mun is best reached by hover ferry from Central, but you can get there by bus from Tsuen Wan. It can also be accessed along the MacLehose Trail as Tuen Mun marks the trail's culmination.

Miu Fat Monastery

Take the Light Rail Transit (LRT), whose terminus is Yuen Long, from Tuen Mun to Lam Tei, where you can find the Miu Fat Monastery. Three golden Buddhas preside over the monastery's top floor. The vegetarian restaurant here makes for a healthy diversion.

Courtyard of the Ten Thousand Buddhas Monastery, west of Sha Tin

Sha Tin
223 F3

Tai Po
223 F3 & F4

Tsuen Wan
223 F3

Tai Mo Shan
223 F3

Tuen Mun
223 E3

Miu Fat Monastery
223 E3

Kat Hing Wai
223 E3

Mai Po Marsh
223 E4

Kat Hing Wai

The walled village of Kat Hing Wai, with its traditional architecture, will bring you face to face with old Hakka women in traditional garb, bunching together for photo ops. A donation box is set up at the gate where you are encouraged to submit a small fee. Outside Kam Tim is **Shui Tau,** another walled village.

Mai Po Marsh

Bird-watchers and nature enthusiasts will hardly expect Hong Kong to host a thriving wetland in the northwest of the New Territories. However, Mai Po is a hidden natural gem full of birdlife—at least for now. It's under threat from Shenzhen's chronic pollution. Trips to the marsh, north of Yuen Long, can be arranged through the World Wildlife Fund *(1 Tramway Path, Central, tel 2526-4473).*

Located in the unlikeliest of spots in the northwestern New Territories, the Mai Po Marshes lie sandwiched between the high-rises of Yuen Long to the south and those of the Shenzhen Special Economic Zone across the border to the north. The marshes and the mudflats of adjacent Inner Deep Bay make up one of the world's most important wetlands. The area's significance is underscored by **Hong Kong Wetland Park** (see p. 244), a nature reserve that lets visitors explore its biodiversity.

The area provides a unique habitat for huge numbers of resident species and a crucial stopping-off point for vast flocks of migrating birds. About 60,000 birds gather in the ponds,

Countless thousands of migratory and resident birds seek haven in Mai Po's wetlands each year.

marshes, mangroves, and mudflats during the winter. More than 340 different species have been recorded here, many of them endangered, including a quarter of the world's remaining 600 black-faced spoonbills.

What brings these birds to the 3,700 acres (1,500 ha) of Mai Po and Inner Deep Bay is the opportunity to rest and refuel on their long migratory journeys between north Asia and Australia.

One of Mai Po's biggest attractions for the birds is the man-made, **earth-walled ponds** known as *gei wai.* The ponds attract other wildlife such as fish, crabs, and oysters, which flourish in the environment.

Bird Flu

Hong Kong put avian flu on the map, so it's a good idea to have at least a working knowledge while visiting, and what better place to start than a bird sanctuary? Avian flu is, simply put, a strand of influenza caused by viruses adapted to birds. Entire populations of domesticated birds, such as chickens and turkeys, have been slaughtered to stop the spread, which can rapidly infect other populations. In 1997, the virus first jumped the species barrier, killing six people in Hong Kong. Mai Po is temporarily closed by the government when birds are found to have contracted avian flu.
The last outbreak was in February 2008.

Mai Po Nature Reserve: The Mai Po Nature Reserve, which is managed by the World Wide Fund for Nature Hong Kong, is active in promoting the importance of the region. The **Education Center** has displays highlighting the area's geology, ecology, and settlement, and the exhibition gallery's interactive exhibits feature the art of gei wai–building, farming techniques, wetland ecology, the area's abundant land-based wildlife species, and, of course, birdlife and migration.

Mai Po's network of paths, bridges, and boardwalks, with access for the disabled as well as ten **observation hides,** brings you within feet of thousands of birds. A **floating boardwalk** runs out into the mangroves of Deep Bay. Request a boardwalk permit when you reserve a visit.

Although it's unlikely you will encounter any of them on your visit, Mai Po also attracts a wide variety of mammals, including mongooses, pangolins, and leopard cats.

Despite the determined efforts at conservation and protection, the reserve remains under threat from development in the surrounding areas. Pollution in Deep Bay, flowing down from the manufacturing centers in southern China, and agricultural waste from Hong Kong have had an impact, as has air pollution.

Mai Po Nature Reserve

- ✉ Mai Po Wildlife Education Center, Tam Kon Chau, Yuen Long
- ☎ 2526-4473
- $ $$ (guide fee)
- 🚌 MTR to Sheng Shui Station, then bus 76K

www.wwf.org.hk

Hong Kong Wetland Park

✉ Wetland Park Road, Tin Shui Wai

☎ 2708-8885

$ $

🕒 Closed Tues.

🚌 MTR: Tin Shui Wai Station, then LTR to Wetland Park Station; Bus: 967 from Admiralty

www.wetlandpark.com

Access to the reserve is limited, and you need a permit, so make a reservation well in advance. You can rent binoculars at the site. Children under five years of age are not admitted.

Hong Kong Wetland Park: Set up to replace a section of the ever shrinking wetlands, and as a center for education and tourism, these man-made wetlands attached to the Mai Po marshes are slightly less wild but just as rewarding.

The 151-acre (61 ha) park attracts much of the wildlife that also calls the marshes home and is designed to provide a more interactive learning experience than the Mai Po Nature Reserve. It has a huge **visitor center,** with a number of exhibitions on biodiversity around the world, including frozen tundras and a tropical swamp, and displays on how humans interact with and affect wetlands.

However, it is outside, in the actual wetlands, that the park really impresses. Themed walks allow visitors to see local wildlife in its natural habitat, with fixed binoculars, telescopes, and even closed-circuit television set up along the paths. The park can get very busy, particularly on weekends. Bringing your own pair of binoculars is advisable.

The park's star is Pui Pui the crocodile, who was moved to an enclosure here after being found in the Yuen Long area. ■

Designated a Wetland of International Importance in 1995, the Mai Po marshes are some of the most important wetlands in the world. They make a major stop-off and feeding area for birds migrating between Asia and Australia.

Chinese Astrology

Behind the image of Hong Kong as a 21st-century city, with its gleaming skyscrapers and booming economy, a more ancient force can sometimes be seen at work. The moon, with its phases and movements, continues to hold sway over the lives of many people.

Fortune-tellers pore over charts of the movements of the moon to calculate whether days will be good, bad, or average. The right day could mean the difference between a good or bad marriage, a great or poor business. The moon has been used to divine important occasions, such as marriages, harvests, and festivals, for thousands of years in China. Since the lunar month differs in length from those used in the Gregorian calendar, the date for the start of the Lunar New Year changes every year, at least according to calendars in the West.

Each lunar year is governed by one of a dozen animals—rat, ox, tiger, rabbit, dragon (the only mythical beast in the list), snake, horse, goat, monkey, rooster, dog, and pig—creating a 12-year cycle. People are said to take on the characteristics of the animal in whose year they are born.

Both smart and charming, **rats** like to get their own way. They also love a challenge.

The dependable, sometimes stubborn **ox** is able to achieve great things by adopting a careful, methodical approach.

A **tiger** is sensitive and likes to be in control, but can also have a bad temper.

Rabbits can be pushovers and will handle problems at their own, slow pace.

Clever and powerful **dragons** are said to be lucky in love but lacking in compassion.

Snakes have the ability to charm, are hardworking, and also lucky with money.

Horses are natural-born wanderers and love to travel, but have an impatient streak.

Creative and artistic, **goats** need lots of support and understanding from those around them.

Monkeys love fun and are full of energy. Their devil-may-care attitude, however, can cause them problems.

The truth is all-important to the **rooster,** who likes to be in charge. Strutting is important, with appearance a priority.

The faithful **dog** can make a loyal friend, but can also be stubborn.

And **pigs?** Those born in the last year in the cycle are considered to be polite perfectionists, always willing to see the best in people.

Chinese Birth Signs

Rat: 1900, 1912, 1924, 1936, 1948, 1960, 1972, 1984, 1996, 2008

Ox: 1901, 1913, 1925, 1937, 1949, 1961, 1973, 1985, 1997, 2009

Tiger: 1902, 1914, 1926, 1938, 1950, 1962, 1974, 1986, 1998, 2010

Rabbit: 1903, 1915, 1927, 1939, 1951, 1963, 1975, 1987, 1999

Dragon: 1904, 1916, 1928, 1940, 1952, 1964, 1976, 1988, 2000

Snake: 1905, 1917, 1929, 1941, 1953, 1965, 1977, 1989, 2001

Horse: 1906, 1918, 1930, 1942, 1954, 1966, 1978, 1990, 2002

Goat: 1907, 1919, 1931, 1943, 1955, 1967, 1979, 1991, 2003

Monkey: 1908, 1920, 1932, 1944, 1956, 1968, 1980, 1992, 2004

Rooster: 1909, 1921, 1933, 1945, 1957, 1969, 1981, 1993, 2005

Dog: 1910, 1922, 1934, 1946, 1958, 1970, 1982, 1994, 2006

Pig: 1911, 1923, 1935, 1947, 1959, 1971, 1983, 1995, 2007

Outlying Islands

Along with the New Territories, the outlying islands show the rural side of Hong Kong, a rich and diverse aspect to the ex-colony often overlooked by travelers. They are a treasure chest of charm and essential for anyone who wants fresh air, lush vegetation, and superb views.

A gondola ride up to Lantau Peak offers panoramic views of Lantau Island.

Before embarking for the islands, it pays to get hold of the Hong Kong and Yaumati Ferry Co.'s timetable from the outlying islands' ferry piers, in Central. If you plan to do some hiking, drop in on the Government Publications Centre (see p. 237) in Central, which publishes a useful series of detailed regional maps.

Lamma Island

Lamma Island, a hilly patch of land crisscrossed with atmospheric pathways, bordered with beaches, and supporting two vibrant villages, makes for a superb half-day trip.

Yung Shue Wan, in the north of the island, is the hub of the *gwailo* (foreign) community—a lively strip of bars, seafood restaurants, and cafés. Surrounding it is a host of smaller villages (such as Tai Peng to the north), slotted in among the hillocks and fields.

The hourlong walk from Yung Shue Wan to the southern community of **Sok Kwu Wan** will take you across the backbone of the island, passing the small but unspoiled beach of **Hung Shing Ye** on the west of the island. The beach is protected by a shark net, which is (supposedly) checked daily during the swimming season. Note the conspicuous industrial

Lamma Island
223 F2

Typhoons

During the May to November typhoon season, Hong Kong is usually skirted by a couple of typhoons or tropical cyclones. Typhoons bring severe rainstorms and strong winds, which can affect business and public transportation. Although these storms' danger shouldn't be underestimated, Hong Kong is well prepared and quickly returns to normalcy.

A warning system alerts the public of impending typhoons. Warning Number 1 (the letter T) means a typhoon is within 500 miles (800 km) of Hong Kong. This is followed by Number 3 (an upside-down T), which means strong winds between 25 to 38 mph (41–62 kph) are blowing or expected. Next is Number 8 (a triangle), which means gale force winds between 39 to 73 mph (63–117 kph) are blowing or expected—businesses close and ferry service and public transportation are suspended. Number 9 (double triangles) means winds are increasing and a direct hit is imminent. Number 10 (a cross) is a direct hit, and winds are now above 73 mph (117 kph). All interior doors should be closed; you should shelter away from windows. Warnings are posted on Hong Kong radio and TV (in the right-hand corner) and in many buildings' lobbies.

Cheung Chau
223 E2

addition to the skyline, the Lamma Island Power Station (the cables of which burrow through the island and provide electricity to the whole of Hong Kong Island). Farther on is the small but attractive **Lo So Shing beach.**

If you plan your walk right, you can enjoy lunch or dinner in **Sok Kwu Wan,** which has a row of popular seafood restaurants. The **Lamma Hilton Shum Kee Seafood Restaurant** *(tel 2982-8241)* enjoys a loyal following. Once you have finished, you can take the ferry from Sok Kwu Wan to either Aberdeen or Central.

The more adventurous can clamber over the hills to the lovely driftwood-littered bay of **Tung O** on the southeast coast (no shark net), and from there cut your way west through to unspoiled **Sham Wan** ("deep bay"). From Tung O Bay, there is a superb walk through bamboo groves and banana trees to **Mo Tat Wan,** where you can catch the ferry out to Aberdeen.

Ferries for Yung Shue Wan and Sok Kwu Wan generally leave hourly from the Outlying Islands ferry piers in Central on Hong Kong Island. The last boats to Central leave from Sok Kwu Wan and Yung Shue Wan at 11:40 p.m. and 12:30 a.m. respectively.

Cheung Chau

Cheung Chau ("long island") has lovely walks, temples, and a bay filled with sampans and junks. Pirates once used the island as a base, and some historical remnants can be found. The main event of the year is the Cheung Chau Bun Festival, which takes place in May, climaxing in a procession of costumed children, some of whom ingeniously appear to float down the streets (suspended by invisible wires). The famous bun towers were banned after one of them collapsed, injuring participants.

Praya Street, running north and south from the ferry pier, overlooks the bay. A nice assortment of cafés and restaurants has grown up around the view. Walk north along Praya Street, and pay homage to the brightly painted **Pak Tai Temple.** Built in 1788, it is dedicated to a thoughtful god who rescued the inhabitants of Cheung Chau from a plague. Inside the temple are relics associated with Pak Tai: a Song dynasty sword and a sedan chair that was used to ferry aloft an effigy of the god on festival days. A marvelously dilapidated altar, depicting a coiling dragon, sits in a roofless chamber under the sun.

Cheung Chau Village is worth exploring for its mix of herbal stores, shrines, mah-jongg parlors, traditional Chinese houses, sacred trees, and shops selling brightly colored decorative paper for funerals. Tung Wan Beach, on the village's east coast, is a popular venue for windsurfing. The smaller beach farther south is **Kwun Yam Wan Beach** ("afternoon beach"), named after Guanyin, the Buddhist goddess of mercy; a temple dedicated to her is nearby.

Worth exploring for magnificent vistas out to sea, **Peak Road** winds in a long loop around the south of the island. Lined with trees and shaded from the sun, the road passes cemeteries on its way to **Sai Wan** ("west bay"). Here you can see a **Tin Hau Temple** and the **cave of Cheung Po Tsai,** a notorious pirate who frequented Cheung Chau and stashed his booty here. From Sai Wan, hop aboard a sampan back to the pier at Cheung Chau Village in time for lunch or dinner.

Ferries for Cheung Chau leave hourly from the Outlying Island ferry piers in Central on Hong Kong Island. The last boat returns to Central at 12:30 a.m.

Lantau

Not as easy to navigate as Lamma and Cheung Chau, the huge island of Lantau greets you as you fly into Hong Kong. **Chek Lap Kok airport** was built on a mass of reclaimed land north of the island, and the airport express shuttles over the vast Tsing Ma bridge that straddles the waters across to Kowloon.

Lantau Island
222 D2 & 223 E2 & E3

Popular with visitors, this enormous statue of Buddha overlooks the Po Lin Monastery on Lantau Island.

Harboring a number of important temples and monasteries, the island boasts the world's largest outdoor, seated bronze Buddha and a sprinkling of seaside communities.

INSIDER TIP:

The New Territories and the outlying islands have more than 30 designated campgrounds. Check *www.afcd.gov.hk* for a full list.

—RORY BOLAND
National Geographic contributor

The ferry from Central drops you at **Mui Wo** ("plum nest") on Silvermine Bay (named for the abandoned silver mines there), which has an attractive stretch of beach and a waterfall north of the village. Buses to the rest of the island radiate from Mui Wo.

Tricky to reach but worth the hike is the **Trappist Haven Monastery,** a 90-minute clamber north of Mui Wo. Alternatively, you can grab a ferry to the island of **Ping Chau** (see p. 260) from Mui Wo and then take a *kaido* (small ferry) to the monastery (destination Tai Shui Hang).

Most people who visit Lantau make a beeline for the **Po Lin Monastery** *(www.plm.com.hk),* a large Buddhist complex on the Ngong Ping Plateau. A thrilling cable-car ride called **Ngong Ping 360** *(www.np360.com.hk, $$)* can convey you from either Ngong Ping or Tung Chung to the monastery. The colossal **statue of Buddha,** on the hill overlooking the monastery, is a staggering 111 feet (34 m).

Lantau Peak, the highest mount on the island, rises southeast of the monastery. Dawn-watchers race energetically to the 3,063-foot (934 m) summit for panoramic views as far as Macau.

The seaside village of **Tai O,** on the western shore, is a mildly charming diversion, while most of the local and mainland Chinese crowds surge to **Hong Kong Disneyland** *(tel 1-830-830, www.hongkongdisneyland.com, $$$$$).*

Cheung Sha Beach on the southern fringe of Lantau is a popular magnet for the weekend crowd, so be warned. More secluded are the beaches at **Fan Lau,** on the Lantau Trail. Fan Lau is also host to an ancient fort, near which rest the timeless remains of a primitive stone circle.

Ferries to Mui Wo leave roughly every hour from the Outlying Islands ferry piers in Central. The last return boat departs at 12:20 a.m. During the week, faster hover ferries also make the trip.

Lantau Trail: You can do short sections of this dramatic trail or the whole knee-wobbling 43 miles (69 km). Starting from Mui Wo, it loops over Lantau Peak, passing south of Tai O, hooking around Fan Lau, threading through Shek Pik, and running alongside Cheung Sha beach before returning to Mui Wo. Remember to take enough water and sunscreen. ■

Macau

The romantic enclave of Macau may be back in the hands of the People's Republic of China, but its atmosphere is still heady with the flavors of Portugal. Moreover, despite its customary pairing with Hong Kong across the water, Macau comfortably stands alone as a unique travel destination in China. A leisurely mood here helps you unwind after the breathlessness of the former British colony.

Macau, the successful result of Portugal's foraging for trade routes in the 16th century, was leased from China in 1557 The territory was called Macau after the local name: Amagao, or island of A-Ma. The local name for Tianhou (Tinhau or Mazu), the goddess of seafarers, is A-Ma (see p. 83).

Macau thrived on its trade of sandalwood, tea, and other commodities, but by the 19th century Canton (Guangzhou) had become an important rival. Macau further lost its shine to Hong Kong, whose star was on the rise, and the gradual fading of the Portuguese empire. By the early 20th century, its significance had dwindled to the mere picturesque.

Macau—never a colony like Hong Kong—was only under the temporary administration of Portugal, which twice tried to hand it back, with no success. With an agreement on Hong Kong's return on the table, the question of its future arose again, and a settlement was made with China in 1987.

On December 20, 1999, Macau returned to China and was ushered in as a Special Administrative Region (SAR) enjoying a high degree of autonomy (in official parlance). As with Hong Kong, Macau has a level of self-determination denied other areas of China.

Macau consists of a peninsula and two islands, capped by the city of Zhuhai to the north. Beyond its many casinos, the peninsula is a charming checkerboard of Portuguese ruins, decaying churches, and colonial buildings. The islands of Taipa and Coloane each shelter small communities, where life continues in an unhurried and traditional way. In recent years, Macau has emerged as one of the world's leading casino center, luring ever growing crowds of gamblers for a throw of the dice and the chance to strike gold. ■

Travel to Macau

The journey between Hong Kong and Macau via high-speed ferry takes about 60 to 70 minutes. From Hong Kong Island, ferries depart from the Shun Tak Centre with Turbojet *(tel 2859-3333, www.turbojet.com.hk)*. Ferries run every 15 minutes between 7 a.m. and midnight, and less frequently overnight. One-way tickets cost HK$142 (about $18US) for economy class, more for weekend and night sailings. Similarly priced ferries also leave Tsim Sha Tsui's China Ferry Terminal with New World First Ferry *(www.nwff.com.hk)*, every 30 minutes from 7 a.m. to 7 p.m., with reduced service overnight. Both ferries dock at the Macau Ferry Terminal.

Tickets for both services can be bought at the ferry terminals. Booking ahead for weekends and night sailings is recommended.

Passengers arriving at Hong Kong International Airport can take ferries directly to Macau without going through Hong Kong immigration and customs. Macau Express Link *(tel 853-2886-1111)* runs the same service between Macau Airport and Hong Kong (HK$215/$27US).

Macau Peninsula

The Macau Peninsula is a wonderful canvas of grand colonial monuments, interesting church architecture, and charming side streets.

Central Macau

Cutting an impressive slice across the peninsula, the **Avenida de Almeida Ribeiro** runs east to west and south of the grand **Largo do Senado,** the main tiled square of fountains, colonnades, and Portuguese architecture. Here you will find the Macau tourist office. Opposite is the **Leal Senado,** the august seat of the municipal government. North of the main square on Rua de São Domingo sits **St. Dominic's Church,** a 17th-century Dominican building that is open to the public.

A UNESCO World Heritage site, St. Dominic's Church stands in Leal Senado plaza.

Probably the most awe-inspiring sight is the glorious ruin of **St. Paul's (São Paulo),** just to the west of Monte Fort. The crumbling facade is all that remains of St. Paul's, an apt metaphor for the decline of European ecclesiastical power in Asia. The wooden church was destroyed by fire during a typhoon. The structure becomes even more inspirational at night, when it is illuminated.

The annals of Macau's past unfold at the **Macau Museum.** Hollowed from the slopes of the hill capped by **Monte Fort,** the museum offers a comprehensive chronicle of the enclave.

The cannons at the Jesuit-built **Monte Fort (Fortaleza do Monte),** above the museum, only roared once, in 1622, repelling the Dutch who had designs on Macau. Today, the muted weapons stand guard over the fort, while bells still hang here and there, their peals now muffled. The fort offers sweeping views, and the best time to come here is when the city darkens into twilight.

The **Camoes Gardens,** located toward the Inner Harbour, are dedicated to Luis de Camoes, the 16th-century Portuguese poet. There is no substantial proof that the writer ever came to Macau, but the gardens offer a pleasant departure from the streets. Come in the morning to see old men walking their caged birds; stroll to the top where old practitioners perform tai chi and *qigong* in the cool air to traditional Chinese music. Middle-aged folk walk over the pathways of rounded pebbles, massaging acupressure points in the feet. Botanists will love the wealth of flowers and vegetation; there's a splendid collection of trees, many festooned with long, hanging creepers.

Nearby is the **Old Protestant Cemetery,** the final resting place of artist George Chinnery (1774–1852), renowned for his depictions of the China coast. Also buried here is British missionary Robert Morrison (1782–1834), who had the unenviable task of translating the Bible into Chinese.

Wine enthusiasts will enjoy the **Wine Museum,** near the outer

Macau Peninsula
222 B2 & 253
Visitor Information
Edificio Ritz, 9, Largo do Senado
0853 2831-5566 or 0853 8397-1120
www.macautourism.gov.mo

Macau Museum
253
Monte Fort
0853 2835 7911
Closed Mon.
$$

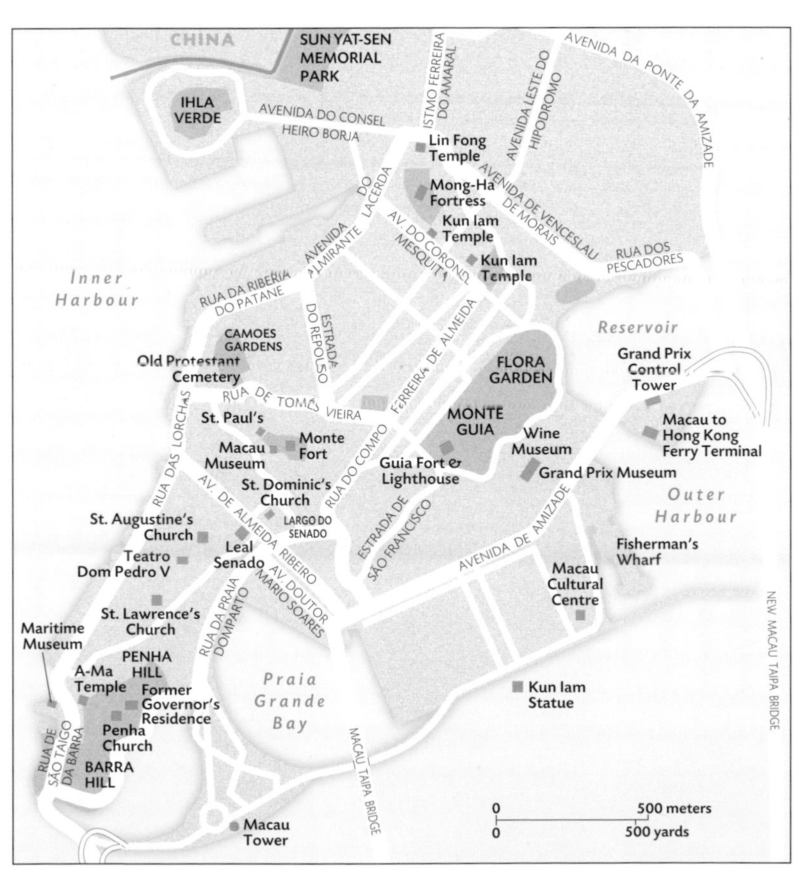

Wine Museum & Grand Prix Museum

- 253
- Macau Forum
- 0853 8798 4188
- Closed Tues.
- $

Kun Iam Temple

- 253
- Avenida do Coronel Mesquita

Macau Grand Prix

This race *(http://gp.macau.grandprix.gov.mo)*, held annually in November, first screamed around the sleepy streets of Macau in 1954. The main race is the FIA International Cup for Formula Three; others events include customized touring cars (the Guia Race), saloon cars (the Macau Cup), and the Super Car Race.

harbor; the ticket price includes a tasting. The **Grand Prix Museum,** housed in the same building, lets you try out some simulation rides (without the acrid smell of burnt rubber and gas fumes).

Part of the **Macau Cultural Centre,** a noteworthy architectural experiment that contains three museums and two auditoriums, is the rewarding **Macau Museum of Art,** well worth exploring for its temporary exhibits as well as its permanent collection.

Nearby, a walkway stretches across the water to a gargantuan golden effigy of **Kun Iam (Guanyin),** built in 1999. It is immediately obvious that the statue has Western elements; this was the intention of the Portuguese sculptress Christina Maria de F. R. Leiria. The effigy is wonderfully illuminated at night. Beneath it, the interior walls of the **Kun Iam Ecumenical Centre** are painted with excerpts from the great Chinese classical philosophers: Confucius, Mencius, and Laozi. The center seeks to embrace all faiths under one roof, with a common expression of spirituality permeating its design.

North Macau

You can join worshippers at the fascinating **Kun Iam Temple,** dedicated to the goddess of mercy. The complex opens onto a small courtyard with the main temple behind. In front stands a large copper incense burner. Trees pleasantly shade the courtyard, and stone lions lie among creeping vegetation.

Signs exhort those who are dirty (of conscience) not to enter. The effigy of Guanyin is in the temple at the rear, and above her is the customary inscription *daci dabei,* or great charity, great compassion. The 18 Luohan worship her from glass cages on either side. Incense hangs in spirals from the ceiling.

To the right of this building lies a gorgeous little garden temple, and around it stands a fascinating assortment of smaller temples. Fortune-tellers offer their magical wares in the temple. Farther west on Avenida do Coronel Mesquita is another, smaller **Kun Iam Temple** that is equally appealing.

South Macau

Just south of Leal Senado is **St. Augustine's Church (São Agostinho),** near the cool green of the **Teatro Dom Pedro V,** built in 1873. The ravaged paintwork of **St. Lawrence's Church (São Lourenço)** farther south shows the effects of Macau's humid climate.

Running along the eastern seaboard is the picturesque **Rua de**

Gambling is Macau's major drawing card, especially for big spenders from Hong Kong.

Praia Grande, the location of the **Former Governor's Residence.** Painted bright rose, the building can be admired only from outside. Nearby is the stately building that was once Macau's finest hotel—the **Bela Vista.** This eight-room former *pensione* is characteristically colonial and sophisticated.

A steep climb up the hill behind takes you to the granite **Penha Church,** which affords extensive views of the southern reaches of the peninsula.

Around the tip of the peninsula is the **A-Ma Temple (A-Ma Miu),** elements of which have a 600-year-old history. A-Ma is the goddess of the sea and the queen of heaven (also called Tinhau or Tianhou), and it is she who lends her name to Macau. Visit during the spring festival for an explosive display of bangers, crackers, and cymbals. In addition, A-Ma has her own festival in April or May.

Nautical enthusiasts will find what they are looking for at the **Maritime Museum,** opposite the A-Ma Temple. Macau's rich and glorious maritime history is on display in the form of vessels, equipment, clothing, techniques of boatbuilding, and more. ■

Maritime Museum

- Map: 253
- Address: Opposite A-Ma Temple
- Phone: 0852 2859 5481
- Hours: Closed Tues
- Cost: $

Bigger Than Vegas

Macau has become the capital of world gambling, putting even Las Vegas firmly in the shade. Gambling revenues in Macau are four times those of Vegas, with some predictions that they could total almost $44 billion by 2014. Gamblers from China flock to Macau to bet with some of their hard-earned cash, and casinos are multiplying to feed the insatiable appetite. With the world's largest casino here (the Macau Venetian), casinos in the territory being the world's most profitable, and around 25 million visitors a year (around half from China), the only way is up for gambling in Macau.

Wind & Water

The sacred science of *fengshui* (literally "wind water" in Mandarin) is a conservative tradition that reaches back to the earliest origins of Chinese civilization. You may consider it rather surprising, therefore, that fengshui should cast such a spell in modish, technocratic Hong Kong.

Despite its innovative modernism, Hong Kong is rife with superstition. The number four *(sei)*, for example, is obsessively avoided for its similarity with the word for death *(sei)*, despite having a different tone. The number eight *(baat)*, on the other hand, is fortuitous–associated with good luck and health. Few Hong Kong Chinese will live in a place overlooking a graveyard.

The Cantonese culture's penchant for the occult spawns a massive film industry revolving around ghosts and vampires. Fengshui, or *fungsui* in Cantonese, accommodates itself easily to this spontaneous persuasion for things mystical.

INSIDER TIP:

The view at night across Victoria Harbour to sparkling Hong Kong Island is truly one of the finest in the world.

–LAWRENCE M. PORGES
National Geographic Books editor

What Is Fengshui?

Put simply, fengshui is an understanding that one's life and destiny are shaped by one's physical surroundings. Man and environment react with each other via *qi*, or energy (Cantonese *hei)*, a relationship that fengshui seeks to harmonize. This relationship is also called the *Dao* (Cantonese *Do*) or Way; any action that helps cultivate the Way is beneficial.

Fengshui is most importantly used for the siting of buildings, for interior design, and for the positioning of graves (you will see graves in Hong Kong pointing out to sea). With buildings, the *fengshuishi* (fengshui expert or geomancer) looks for places with *ling*, or spirit. Ling is also a kind of elemental form of qi. Temples are generally well sited and charged with ling. Qi is channeled by certain landscape features, which become veins of energy, and these can be tapped. Some places are intrinsically luckier and more positive than other places, for they positively channel qi, improving our physical and spiritual existence. Such places tend to be open, airy, elevated, and hilly; green with vegetation; and near a water source (waterfalls, rivers, lakes, or ponds). Despite the specific vocabulary, fengshui is often just common sense.

Hills accommodate two mythical animals–the Green Dragon (in the east) and the White Tiger (in the west)–from which large amounts of qi can be harvested. Houses should ideally be positioned in the lap between the two and never at the crest of the hill.

Places that are dark, dank, dull, and stagnant, where qi is largely absent, should be avoided. Rocky soil is shunned, loamy, airy soil preferred.

Harmony is of paramount importance. *Yin* (the female, dark, cold, quiet, shadowy, and lunar realm) should be balanced with *yang* (male, light, warm, noisy, solar, and bright) for the optimum amount of qi. A glut of either is best avoided.

Five Elements

A further system of relationships that must be observed is the *wu xing* (five elements). Wood, fire, earth, metal, and water exist in a cycle of mutual creation and destruction, and their importance in fengshui can best be seen by the colors associated with them. Wood is green, fire is red, earth is yellow, metal is gold, and water is black. If an element needs to be emphasized, its color can

Even modern Hong Kong architecture pays homage to the old laws of fengshui.

be accentuated. A skilled fengshui master can quickly ascertain the elemental condition of a place and identify imbalances. In temples like the Wong Tai Sin Temple in New Kowloon (see p. 238), the five elements are represented by the fabric of the buildings.

Fengshui is taken very seriously in Hong Kong. As it endows a business location with good luck, it is a weapon in Hong Kong's highly competitive armory. If your business is ailing, a fengshui master can maximize the arrangement of your office to attract good fortune.

Macau's Islands

The two islands of Taipa and Coloane are refuges of tranquil charm, just like the outlying islands of Hong Kong (albeit easier to reach). Their Mediterranean-like pace invites you to saunter through pastoral villages and enter a long-lunch frame of mind.

Shoppers on Cunha Street in Taipa Village, Taipa

Taipa
222 B2
Macau Government Tourist Office
Edificio Ritz, 9, Largo do Senado
315566 or 333000 (hotline)
www.macautourism.gov.mo

Taipa House Museum
Avenida da Praia
Closed Mon.
$

Taipa

Originally two islands but now fused by silt, Taipa still musters considerable rural appeal despite the threat posed by the new airport and the metropolitan aspirations of Taipa City. Make a beeline for **Taipa Village** in the south, and skirt around all the construction.

In permanent siesta, Taipa Village seems oblivious to the construction roar besieging it. The leisurely mood inspires a desire to take root and buy a chicken farm on the edges of the village.

Near the waterfront, the **Avenida da Praia** used to border the sea, but a tide of silt has pushed it back. Regardless, this promenade of trees, benches, and colonial buildings is a restful and picturesque synopsis of Macau. Take your time languishing here, and enjoy the postcard view.

The **Taipa House Museum** on the promenade has preserved the life enjoyed by a middle-class family in the last years of the 1900s. Period furniture and authentic decorations take you on a historic tour. West of the museum and elevated on a rise of land, the ubiquitous presence of Portuguese Catholicism appears in **Our Lady of Carmel Church (Igreja Nossa Senhora do Carmo),** which overlooks gardens leading down to the silted seafront. In the west of the village you will find the small **Tin Hau** and **Pak Tai temples.**

The village has a famous assortment of Portuguese restaurants that can serve as an indulgent end to your visit. **Rua de Fernao Mendes Pinto** is a picturesque walk of restaurants, and **Rua do Cunha**, at right angles to it, is a pleasing stretch of eateries.

You can rent a bike cheaply from a few places in Taipa Village. This is an excellent way to see the

INSIDER TIP:

Macanese cuisine marries Cantonese and Portuguese cooking. First on your plate should be *minchee,* a meat and potato hash.

—RORY BOLAND
National Geographic contributor

rest of the island, and you can even cycle over to Coloane.

If the thought of being separated from Macau's casinos (see sidebar p. 255) leaves you cold, a gambling rush can be had at the **Macau Jockey Club** *(tel 0853 2883-7788),* west of Taipa Village. Races are held twice a week, so call beforehand to check dates.

Coloane

Coloane
222 B1

Coloane is joined to Taipa by a causeway swollen through land reclamation that is fusing the two islands together. **Coloane Village** has some colonial treasures worth exploring.

The **Chapel of St. Francis Xavier (Capela S. Francisco Xavier)** is subtropical Christianity's bastion in the village. The white church rises magisterially from the dusty streets and can be carefully contemplated over a coffee from one of the cafés opposite. The chapel dates from 1928 and is dedicated to St. Xavier, a missionary who trawled the Far East for converts to Christ. Among relics previously sheltered here was the saint's elbow bone, which had been held at St. Paul's (see p. 252) until the big fire; it was returned to the museum there in the mid-1990s.

Other temples in the village are the **Kun Iam Temple,** the **Sam Seng Temple,** and the interesting **Taoist Tam Kong Temple,** housing a detailed whalebone carving of a boat with oarsmen.

At **Cheoc Van Beach (Bamboo Bay),** about a mile (1.6 km) around the coast to the south, you can take a dip in the silted waters. There are a swimming pool and a few restaurants/cafés, but it's a bit dormant.

There's more of a sense of activity and beach life at the **Hac Sa Beach,** on Coloane's eastern fringe. Not only can you find one of Macau's best restaurants, **Restaurante Fernando** *(tel 0853 2888-2264),* but the whole area is attractive, the views are excellent, and a recreation park is bursting with activities. Here you will find tennis courts, Ping-Pong tables, football, and badminton courts; you can also rent sailboards and Jet-skis. ■

EXPERIENCE:
Biking & Hiking

Two cycling trails wind around Taipa island's two highest hills: the 1.4-mile (2.2 km) **Taipa Grande trail** and the 1.2-mile (2 km) **Taipa Pequeña trail.** Note that if you are cycling on Taipa, you are not allowed to cross over from the Macau peninsula on bike; however, you can rent a bike at one of several outlets in Taipa Village.

For hikers, there are several trails on Coloane, but the longest is the 5-mile (8 km) **Coloane Trail** that wraps its way around the island.

More Places to Visit in Hong Kong & Macau

Hong Kong

Peng Chau: The small island of Peng Chau has a handful of small seafood restaurants and a **Tin Hau temple**; its highest point is the diminutive **Finger Hill** (310 ft/95 m). You can look out over to the glitter of **Discovery Bay** to the west.
223 E2

Ping Chau: Just within the orbit of Hong Kong, Ping Chau has a dash of Chinese temple architecture, small sandy beaches, and shells of deserted buildings. There's also a radiation shelter in case an accident occurs at China's Daya Bay nuclear power station, 7 miles (11 km) away.
223 H4

Guia Fort & Lighthouse

The Guia Fort, sitting on Guia Hill in the east of the Macau Peninsula, was built between 1637 and 1638 on Macau's highest point. It also has a 17th-century chapel and excellent views spanning out over the territory. Hiking trails encircle the hill, while a small cable car *($)* ascends to the top.

Plover Cove Reservoir: This is excellent hiking territory, up in the wilder reaches of the northeast New Territories. You can follow the **Pat Sin Leng Nature Trail,** which starts at Tai Mei Tuk and ends at Bride's Pool, or join the **Wilson Trail** (see p. 237) and head south. Weekends are crowded.
223 F4 & G4

Tap Mun Chau: This secluded grassy knoll in the northwest of the New Territories has a Qing dynasty **Tin Hau temple.**
223 G4

Tung Lung Chau: South of Joss House Bay on the Clearwater Bay peninsula is the uninhabited island of Tung Lung Chau. A **fort** was built in the 18th century on the northeast fringe to protect the island from pirates. Rock carvings show traces of early inhabitation.
223 G2

Yau Ma Tei & Mong Kok: The overhyped **Jade Market** sells its wares from Kansu Street, Yau Ma Tei, a dilapidated area north of Tsim Sha Tsui (see pp. 234–237). Unless you know your subject, it is very easy to buy inferior jade, so do some research before you haggle. North of the market is a **Tin Hau temple.** A wander around the **Temple Street Night Market** reveals a profusion of stalls. Some real bargains surface from the bustle, but be prepared for a tide of pirated goods.

The Chinese fascination with birds can be explored in the **Yuen Po Street Bird Garden,** Mong Kok. It has hundreds of birds, many of which sing from the confines of exquisitely carved, wooden cages. The garden is a short walk from Prince Edward Subway.
223 F3 **Hong Kong Tourism Board (HKTB)** Star Ferry Concourse, Tsim Sha Tsui; or Ground Floor, The Centre, 99 Queen's Rd., Central; or Hong Kong International Airport 0852 2508-1234

Macau

Gambling: With 33 casinos, Macau makes more revenue from gambling than Las Vegas. Casinos are the principal reason behind the weekend exodus to Macau from Hong Kong.

Lou Lim Ieoc Gardens: The 19th-century gardens in this quiet enclave to the west of Guia Hill are a profusion of plants, interspersed with ponds, paths, and pavilions. It is named after a famous merchant of Macau.
222 B2 Avenida do Conselheiro Ferreira de Almeida $

One of China's must-see regions, teeming with minorities and rewarding travelers with some breathtaking landscapes

The Southwest

Introduction & Map 262–263
Kunming & Around 264–266
Stone Forest 267
Dali 268–271
Lijiang 272–275
Experience: Naxi Music 273
Xishuangbanna 276–279
Guilin 280–281
Li River Cruise 282–283
Yangshuo & Around 284–285
Experience: Cycle Around the Southwest 285
Experience: Getting Physical in Yangshuo 286
Beihai 287
More Places to Visit in the Southwest 288
Hotels & Restaurants in the Southwest 379–382

Delightfully decorated children's shoes make a colorful display.

The Southwest

If you thought China was in danger of becoming a washed-out blur of socialist housing, the Southwest throws color back into the mix. Historically under vacillating Chinese control, it's a magnificent patchwork of minority cultures stitched into a dreamy landscape. This is an enthralling region if you want to explore rather than tour. Guilin, Yangshuo, Dali, Lijiang, and Xishuangbanna are a roll call of China's must-sees.

The Southwest's secret lies with its unique combination of geography and ethnic culture. Yunnan, situated high up on the Yunnan–Guizhou plateau, is overlooked to the north by the roof of the world—Tibet. The jungles of Myanmar (Burma) encroach from the west, while the flavors of Laos and Vietnam spill over from the south. The province's sheltered relief endows it with clement weather in both winter and summer; the provincial capital, Kunming, is called Spring City.

Half of China's 55 ethnic minorities call this area home, from the industrious, blue-clothed Naxi of Lijiang to the often elusive tribes of the southern border regions. Together they cling to a colorful way of life that 50 years of Communist supervision have failed to bleach.

Not long ago, primitive transportation and terrible roads put many important destinations in the Southwest tantalizingly beyond reach of those with little time. Dali and Lijiang should be savored slowly, but airports have opened them up to whistle-stop approaches.

Xishuangbanna, in the lush south, lures visitors with the chance to explore tropical jungles. The regional pivot, Jinghong, is surrounded by a domain of ethnic villages, deep in the green tangle of foliage.

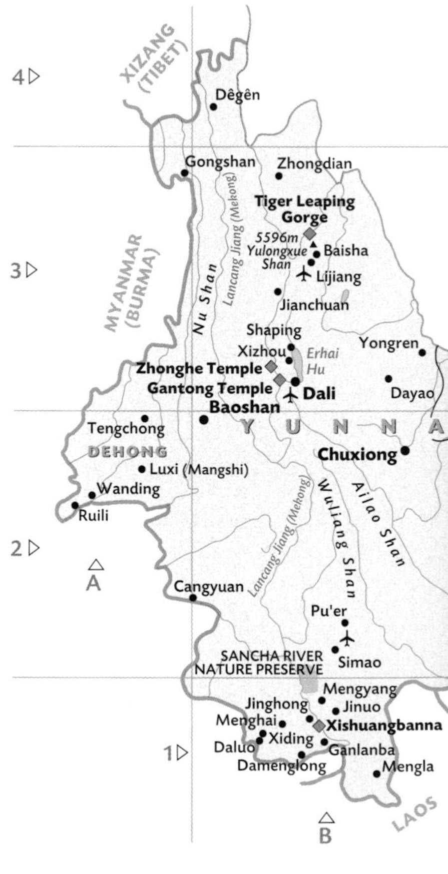

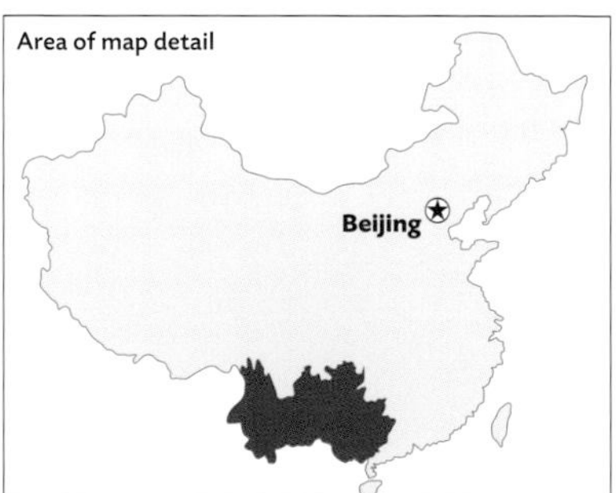

Guilin, in adjacent Guangxi Province, has suffered from overpopularity and the resultant plague of trinket sellers and insistent guides, but nearby Yangshuo has much more to offer in its enticing dreamland karst scenery, which is simply spellbinding.

Opportunities exist in all these regions to jump on a bicycle and work out a route as you go along. And you will find an energetic service sector dedicated to entertaining and feeding Westerners. In most of China, visitors tend to be left to fend for themselves; in the Southwest, a lively tourist industry has equipped itself with the trappings of banana pancakes, cappuccino, and not half-bad English. ■

NOT TO BE MISSED:

Exploring the beautiful landscape around Dali **268–271**

The sublime town of Lijiang, home to the Naxi people **272–273**

Trekking along the outstanding Tiger Leaping Gorge **274–275**

Villages in Xishuangbanna **276–279**

Drifting into a verdant landscape on the Li River Cruise **282–283**

The transcendent scenery around the city of Yangshuo **284–285**

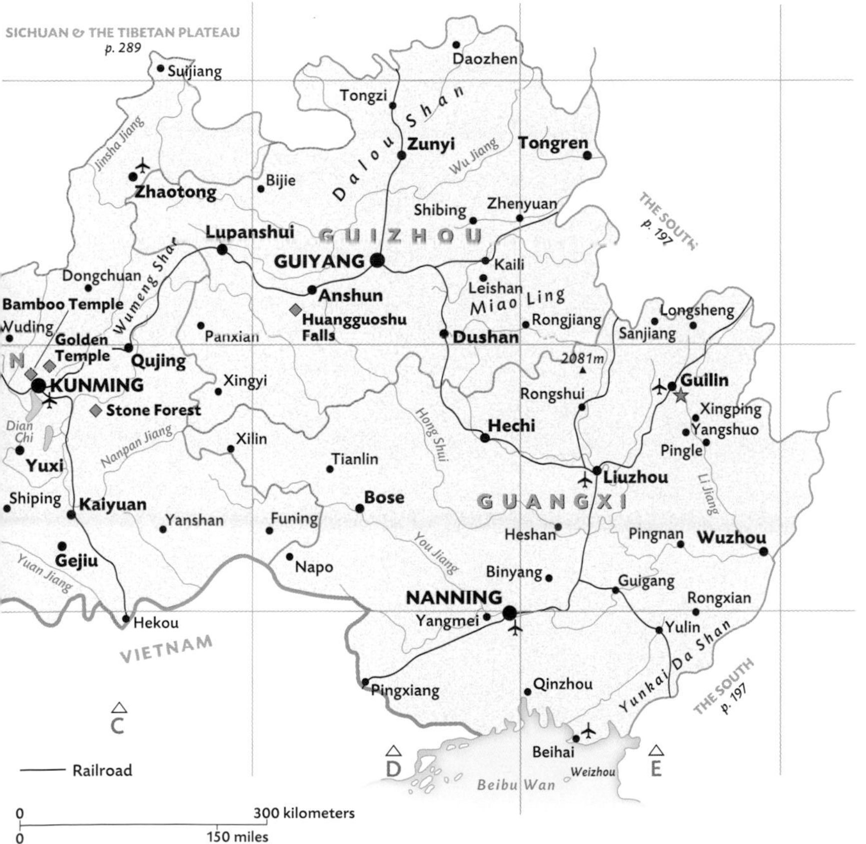

Kunming & Around

The name Kunming comes from a vanished minority group called the Kunmi. Capital of Yunnan ("south of the clouds") Province, Kunming has historic temples and pagodas and is an ideal springboard to the rest of this area.

Meat for sale in a local Kunming market

Today, the city has prospered from being drawn into the whirlwind of economic change sweeping China. Unfortunately, this may be the kiss of death for Kunming's historic architecture, which is being moved aside for modern building projects.

Foreign involvement came with British and French influence in Burma and Indochina respectively. In the 1930s, the daring Burma Road cut 625 miles (1,000 km) through the mountains here, enabling the British and Americans to funnel supplies through Kunming to aid the resistance against the Japanese.

Temples & Mosques

The **Yuantong Temple,** in the north of the city near the zoo, is a huge and fascinating Buddhist complex worthy of an hour or two. Through the secondary gate and past a refreshing stretch of gardens you come to the main "courtyard." From the center of the large, square pool rises an octagonal temple to Guanyin. Inside are two statues of the goddess of mercy standing back to back; one is a thousand-armed Guanyin (Qianshou Guanyin), the other an offering-child Guanyin (Songzi Guanyin). In the main temple lies a white marble statue of Buddha, presented by the king of Thailand in 1985.

Hui (Muslim) Chinese worship at the rebuilt **Nancheng Ancient Mosque (Nancheng Gusi),** on Zhengyi Lu. The area around the mosque has sadly been largely demolished in recent years, so much of the old Hui atmosphere has gone.

The **West Pagoda (Xisita),** tucked away in the south on Dongsi Jie, was built during the Tang dynasty and can be found in an original part of town. Not far away, on Shulin Jie, are the remains of its brother, the **East Pagoda (Dongsita),** which was toppled by an earthquake in 1833 (tremors are common in Yunnan Province). Both pagodas were once accompanied by now vanished temples.

Around Kunming

The region surrounding Kunming is more tempting than the city itself. The **Golden Temple (Jindian)** *($$),* also known as the Copper Temple, is a Taoist place of worship 7 miles (11 km) northeast of Kunming on a pine-forested hill.

This double-roofed, Ming dynasty structure (completed in 1604) replaces the original that was transported to Dali prefecture. It is amazingly made of copper, built upon a base of marble. The panels are intricately created and decorated: A stylized motif of the character *shou,* or long life, is plentifully employed. There isn't an abundance of metal temples in China, but another exists in Wutaishan (see p. 111). You can climb the steps and examine the Golden Temple close up, if you can wedge yourself between the visitors; it's a good idea to get here early to avoid the crowds. The surrounding forest offers inviting walks, threading along paths among the trees.

The Tang dynasty **Bamboo Temple (Qiongzhusi)** *($),* located 8 miles (13 km) northwest of Kunming, contains 500 eccentric clay Luohan modeled at the end of the 19th century by the Chinese sculptor Li Guangxiu and his students. The Luohan usually appear in a dignified assembly of 18; when portrayed in a group of 500, they tend to be a wilder bunch. Other Chinese temples host such plentiful Luohan, but none have the mannerisms and energy of these. The full range of human emotion is fashioned in clay by Li's creative fingers. Some are grotesque, others mad, sad, or joyful.

INSIDER TIP:

Shopping comes to you in Kunming, not the other way around. A vast population of hawkers sells pipes, trinkets, costumes, hats, ceramics, tea, and "angel hair" (Yunnan tobacco) right on the city's streets.

—DAMIAN HARPER
National Geographic author

Lake Dian (Dian Chi) is heavily promoted in tourist literature

Kunming
263 C2

Yuantong Temple
Yuantong Jie
$

South of the Clouds Cuisine

Kunming is a virtual delicatessen. Famous nationwide, ***guoqiao mixian*** (across-the-bridge noodles) is a hot chicken, chili, and vegetable noodle broth that seethes beneath a layer of insulating oil. Served throughout the province is black, gritty, and strong **Yunnan coffee** *(yunnan kafei)*. Toasted goat's cheese (which you dip into herbs and spices), Yunnan mushrooms, and Yunnan ham could well rob you of the motivation to do anything else but eat during your stay. Interestingly, ***nailao*** (cheese) is eaten here; it is generally shunned by Chinese, who opt instead for Chinese cheese *(furu)*, a kind of fetid tofu preserved in oil. If you buy a chicken drumstick from a street vendor, check first that it's well cooked.

as a worthwhile destination, but it's best to avoid its industrial southern edges.

A trip to **Daguan Tower (Daguanlou)** in **Daguan Park (Daguan Gongyuan),** located 2 miles (3 km) to the southwest of the city on Daguan Jie, offers excellent views over the water. An inscription by the Qing dynasty poet Sun Rangwen lauds the view, but that was before industry began polluting the lake. The tower was torched by Muslim rebels in the mid-19th century and later rebuilt.

Parks in Kunming offer the ideal spot for relaxing and people-watching.

Also on the shores of the lake is the **Yunnan Nationalities Village (Yunnan Minzu Cun)** *($$$)*, a concentration of ethnic minority exhibits from around the province. There are a number of places like this in China, but if you are interested in China's minorities and want to learn about their customs, the best strategy is to visit the areas where the people live (such as Xishuangbanna and northern Yunnan). You can drift over to the summit of the Western Hills, on the western flank of Lake Dian, by cable car from near the Village.

It's more fun to explore the **Western Hills (Xishan)** on foot. From the bus station at Gaoyao, you can make your way up the paths and steps to the **Dragon Gate (Longmen)** at the summit. Expect the ascent to take three or more hours. The cliffs on the way up bristle with temples, including **Huating Temple** at the base, **Taihua Temple** farther up, and, as you approach the summit, the Taoist **Sanqing Temple (Sanqingge).** Farther on still, a cluster of Taoist grottoes, statues, and pavilions clings to the sheer cliff face. Plunging views sweep over Lake Dian below. ■

Stone Forest

The limestone outcrops known as the Stone Forest (Shilin) bristle 75 miles (120 km) southeast of Kunming. The ashen stone pillars, abandoned by the sea as it receded hundreds of millions of years ago, bunch together into a geological thicket. Their twisted and shattered form is the result of excessive weathering, similar to that found at Wulingyuan (see p. 202).

Stone Forest
263 C2
$$$$$

The journey to the Stone Forest is as beautiful as the landscape that surrounds it. Scattered around the forest are villages populated by the local ethnic minority, the Sani. They also congregate at the entrance to the Stone Forest and will gladly accompany you as tour guides; you may prefer to go at your own pace. Paths bore between the limestone pillars, past pools, pavilions, and peaks.

INSIDER TIP:

Visit the Stone Forest early in the morning or late in the afternoon, when the throngs of tourists have gone home. The place turns quiet, and the sun makes the rock pillars glow.

—BARBARA NOE
National Geographic Books editor

Visiting Chinese are enchanted by the game of identifying shapes among the columns, an activity that has given names to many of the formations (for example, **Buddha Stone** and **Rhinoceros Gazing at the Moon**). The shapes act as points of reference around which you can explore.

For many Chinese, the Stone Forest is Yunnan Province's main attraction. Visitors give it mixed reports; some say it's a waste of time, while others sing the praises of penetrating into the inner regions. Late in the day is the best time to visit, when the tourists drift away and twilight creates a shifting mood.

Spending the Night

You can spend the night at one of the on-site hotels or in the nearby **Five-Tree Village.** The **Stone Forest International Youth Hostel** *(tel 0871 771-0768)* has clean single and double rooms. In the evenings, Sani singing and dancing troupes often perform.

Getting There

A highway enables visitors to get rapidly to and from Kunming. Many hotels in the city can arrange trips to the Stone Forest.

If you want to travel independently to the forest or stay the night there, catch a bus leaving from the bus station or the long-distance bus station on Beijing Lu in Kunming. Buses *($$)* run regularly to the Stone Forest from Kunming's east bus station, taking two hours. ■

Dali

Despite being a busy tourist mecca for overseas and Chinese travelers, Dali—one of Yunnan's top sights—has the old-town charms, scenic beauty, ethnic Bai minority heritage, and bustling markets that still make it a great place to explore.

Erhai Lake, east of Dali, is popular for cormorant fishing.

Dali
262 B3

Dali Museum
111 Fuxing Lu

Dali was once the capital of the Nanzhao Kingdom, a powerful entity separate from China. In the 13th century, the Mongols invaded and subjugated the region. The largest ethnic minority is the Bai, who speak a Tibetan-Burmese language and whose traditional architecture can be seen at Xizhou, north of town. Dali is famous for its marble, lending its name to the Chinese word for the stone *(dalishi)*. You can buy marble pictures along the main shopping street or view them at the Dali Museum.

Dali Museum

Most of the bronzes and ceramics featured in the Dali Museum (Dali Bowuguan) are from the Nanzhao and Dali state period (eighth to tenth century A.D.), and some of the Ming period blue-and-white porcelain is interesting. But the layout is yesteryear Soviet style, and the museum is hampered by a lack of English captions. Escape to the courtyard outside, where decapitated statues (probably victims of Red Guard sledgehammers) preside over rows of stelae (inscribed stone slates).

At the rear is an enticing (although, again, Englishless) gallery of polished marble slabs whose grain resembles clouds and rivers in the mountains. Try to find the one called "Mountain Devil," an image of a demon caught in stone.

Foreigner's Street

Foreigner's Street (Yangren Jie) is where visiting Chinese come to watch foreigners eating Western food and buying souvenirs. The real name of the street is Huguo Lu. If you want a change from rice and noodles, you will love the homemade apple pie, cheeseburgers, pizzas, and more offered here. Many restaurants and cafés also serve foreign beers and wines and an increasing range of international cuisine, often staying open until the early hours. You will also find travel agents here, as well as information about local tours and tickets.

Erhai Lake

Dali sits near the shore of Erhai Lake (Erhai Hu), a ten-minute bike ride away. The best views are from the Zhonghe Temple (see below). Arrange for cormorant fishing (see sidebar this page) through your hotel.

The lake also acts as a waterway to **Wase,** a traditionally built village on the eastern shore that throws together a lively market on the 5th, 10th, 15th, 20th, 25th, and 30th of each month. **Putuo Island** supports a small community with a temple dedicated to Guanyin. Check with one of the cafés on Foreigner's Street first, because a group could well be going. Three-hour boat rides *($$$$$)* around the lake are popular; some of them run to the town of Xiaguan at the south tip of the lake.

Cormorant Fishing

The cormorant *(Phalacrocorax carbo)* has long been trained for fishing in China. The sleek swimming birds have rings or tight cords fitted around their throats before fishing. The ring constricts the throat so the bird does not swallow the fish, and the fisherman can retrieve his catch. Cormorant fishing continues today, albeit largely for the tourist market.

Zhonghe Temple & Beyond

The countryside around Dali has dazzling scenery, fascinating temples, and the occasional village showcasing exquisite traditional Bai architecture. A good start is to visit the Zhonghe Temple, right outside Dali, up the hillside. You can climb the paths that snake their way up, but it's far better to take a 20-minute cable-car ride *($$$)* and see the

Zhonghe Temple
262 B3

Three Pagodas
1.2 miles (2 km) NW of Dali
$$$$$

marvelous view of Erhai Lake. The cable car trims the pine trees on the way up, passing numerous Chinese tombs, the occasional tumbledown house, and streams.

At the top, you'll be at the gate to the temple, which embraces both Taoist and Buddhist features. The people guarding the temple are welcoming, and guides (armed with bad English and ponies) will offer to lead you into the woods and on to distant springs, creeks, and waterfalls.

Third Moon Fair

Try to time your arrival in Dali with the weeklong Third Moon Fair (Sanyue Jie), which kicks off on the 15th day of the third lunar month (usually April or May). Commemorating the appearance in Dali of Guanyin, the Buddhist goddess of mercy, this once religious Bai festival is an opportunity for much singing, horse racing, dancing, and merrymaking, with local people dressing up in their finest ethnic clothes.

These are in the marvelous **Cangshan Mountains,** which form the backdrop to Dali. You can hike out by yourself, but be prepared for changeable weather. A good walk begins from the cable car: Head left on the path through the pine forest, and after about 6 miles (10 km), you will reach seven pools and waterfalls. From here, you can either walk back the way you came or down to the road and get a bus back to Dali.

Three Pagodas

The famous Three Pagodas (Santasi) stand just a short distance northwest of Dali. They are attractive from a distance, especially early in the morning or at dusk, although hardly worth visiting. The tallest of the three pagodas has 16 tiers, reaching 234 feet (72 m) high, and was originally constructed in the ninth century. The cable-car trip up to the Zhonghe Temple affords an excellent view of all three pagodas.

Guanyin Temple

Three miles (5 km) south of Dali is the fascinating little Guanyin Temple (Guanyintang), dedicated to the Buddhist goddess of mercy. In the small shrine in front of the **main temple (Daxiong Baodian)** is an effigy of the goddess worshipped by the 18 Luohan (Arhat). The Luohan stand on little niches carved into a cliff face, all exhibiting vivid and lively facial expressions. One has a huge, extended arm that grabs at what appears to be the moon in the clouds. Another holds his trousers up and has telescopic legs. On his left swoons a drunken Arhat; another rides a tiger, while yet another pulls open his stomach to reveal a Buddha inside. Spot the one with the extra-long eyebrows.

The complex is an active nunnery. The large hall at the rear houses a collection of *pusa* (bodhisattvas), while the inner courtyard has a small, square temple built over a boulder and encircled by a pond crossed by a bridge. The boulder was apparently rolled into position by the goddess to stall an advancing army. The two golden characters on the right-hand door as you enter mean "wheel of the law," or *falun* in Chinese.

Gantong Temple & Jizhao Nunnery

Tucked away in the pine-clad mountains above the Guanyin Temple is the tiny Buddhist **Gantong Temple.** It's quite a hike up the hill (about an hour; come out of the Guanyin Temple, turn into the first right, and keep going). Horse carts often plod by, however, and will take you up for a small fee.

Just above the temple in the trees is a small **dagoba,** where you may find monks practicing *gongfu.* Another five minutes into the woods is the **Jizhao ("quiet illumination") Nunnery,** with a peaceful courtyard laid out with beautiful gardens.

Xizhou

Fifteen miles (24 km) north of Dali is this gem of a village, a must-see for architecture enthusiasts. Much of the original Bai architecture is well preserved, and that which is not stands in picturesque decay. A few interesting Bai courtyards have been sectioned off, and here there is an entry fee. A slow amble through the streets is by far the best approach.

Doors with colorfully painted eaves yield to active courtyards where children play, chickens squawk, dogs fight, and all the rhythms of family life play out. Here and there, amazingly, you will see a 19th-century Western door, complete with marble pillars and classical pomposity, relic of an early European presence.

The village is exceptionally photogenic and the maze of little streets a charming place to get lost in. Cultural Revolution buffs will revel in hunting down the former local party headquarters and graffiti of the Cultural Revolution era. One such, on a gaunt and lifeless building, proudly declares "Serve the People," in Mao's calligraphy with his signature next to it. Flanking it are the scrubbed-out characters "Study Mao Zedong Thought." They remain ghostly, indelible shadows.

Shaping Market & Butterfly Spring

The town of Shaping, about 20 miles (32 km) north of Dali, buzzes with a popular market on Mondays. The **Butterfly Spring (Hudie Quan)** *(3 miles/5 km south, west of road)* swarms with butterflies in spring. ■

Gantong Temple
262 B3

Shaping
262 B3

Much of Dali's traditional way of life has been preserved.

Lijiang

In the foothills of the Himalaya lies the splendid little town of Lijiang, in northwest Yunnan Province. The town has transformed considerably—including a pounding from a 7.0-magnitude earthquake in 1996—since drifting onto the tourist radar in the 1980s, but valiant efforts have been made to preserve its ancient culture. The stunning Jade Dragon Snow Mountain hints at the Land of Snows to the north, and Tiger Leaping Gorge awaits the adventurous.

Lijiang's old town was named a UNESCO World Heritage site in 1997.

Old Town

The old town of Lijiang is a wonderful maze of traditional Naxi architecture, pitted against the new section, an encroachment of breeze blocks and ceramic tiling. It's a marvel at night, when the Chinese roofs, festooned with lights, sparkle against the evening sky; the old quarter is a dreamscape of dark cobbled streets, gushing canals, and paths trailing away from the main street. Wooden doors open to reveal the cozy interiors of Naxi and Western restaurants.

Study the architecture. Unlike other buildings in town, many of the traditional structures survived the 1996 earthquake. The buildings charm you with their engaging and satisfying harmonies. Substantial half-timbered and earthen houses have solid wooden gates, central courtyards, and eaves carved with fish and symbols for good luck. Wander around to your heart's content, and even get lost if you wish.

The morning sees a bustling local market animating the streets of the old town, providing a lively montage of blue-clothed Naxi women. As well as local produce, you can buy tourist staples such as embroidery, hand-beaten copper pots, or carved wooden birds.

Black Dragon Pool (Heilongtan) *($$$)* in the north of town is a large park with fantastic photo ops of Jade Dragon Snow Mountain and a museum dedicated to the shamanistic Dongba religion that the Naxi people brought with them from Tibet.

If you are out for a twilight stroll, walk along the narrow street south along the canal that borders the main street to the west, and try one of the restaurants here. Several of these serve traditional Naxi food such as *baba,* a local flatbread; others celebrate food from around the world. Western cafés are common in the old town, providing Internet access and knowledgeable advice on jaunts into the surrounding region. Round off the evening by taking in one of the shows featuring Naxi music (see sidebar this page).

For a panoramic view of Lijiang, take one of the roads west away from the canal, climb up the hill past the radio station, and go on to **Wangulou** *($),* a pavilion that overlooks the town.

Jade Dragon Snow Mountain

If the weather is clear, a visit to the breathtaking Jade Dragon Snow Mountain (Yulongxue Shan), 21 miles (34 km) north of Lijiang, is a recommended, albeit very expensive, diversion. The mighty mountain rises raggedly above Lijiang, encrusted with snow and (if you're lucky) set against a sharp, blue sky. It's an alluring sight that can make for dramatic photography. Be warned that the elevation can make some people feel queasy: Lijiang sits at 7,924 feet (2,415 m), high enough to affect some, and the mountain's summit soars to 18,354 feet (5,596 m).

EXPERIENCE: Naxi Music

For good evening entertainment, attend a performance by a Naxi orchestra in Lijiang. The more authentic presentation is at the Naxi Music Academy *(Dong Dajie, tel 0888 512-7971, $$$$),* introduced by Naxi musician Xuan, with performances at 8 p.m. The other is at the Dongba Palace *(Dong Dajie, $$$$),* with performances at 7 p.m. Many of the songs you'll hear were rescued from oblivion by elder members of the band (some in their 70s and 80s). Colorful dancing and solo singing spice up the show, and a venerable Naxi sage does a sword dance. You can take photographs.

If it's cloudy or misty, don't bother. Avoid the rainy season at the end of summer; late autumn and winter are the ideal seasons. Cable cars (one from the Snow Flower Mountain Village, itself reachable by local bus from Lijiang), take you to idyllic spots for the best views.

Baisha

Baisha village, about 5 miles (8 km) north of Lijiang, is noted for its collection of faded religious **frescoes** *(bihua)* that took a hammering during the Cultural Revolution. As with many Buddhist treasures around China, the collected scars tell a vivid story. In Baisha, some of

Lijiang

262 B3

Visitor Information

Any of the hotels or cafés in the old town

Jade Dragon Snow Mountain

262 B3

21 miles (34 km) north of Lijiang

$$$$$

Baisha

262 B3

Tiger Leaping Gorge
262 B3
37 miles (60 km) north of Lijiang
$$

the figures have had their faces scratched away, while here and there vandals have etched their names into the paintwork.

You can't photograph the frescoes; expect a big fine if you do. The lighting is very gloomy and it is difficult to make any coherent sense of the pictures without a guide. Naxi dancers perform for a fee as you exit.

The other gem of Baisha is the legendary Dr. Ho, an enthusiastic Taoist physician who operates from his Clinic of Chinese Herbs in Jade Dragon Mountains of Lijiang. Patients come away with sachets of a powdery tea. Some people swear by his potions.

INSIDER TIP:

Ride a bike through the gorgeous region around Lijiang. Head toward Baisha at the foot of Jade Dragon Snow Mountain.

—BARBARA NOE
National Geographic Books editor

Generally, visitors rent bikes and pedal out on unpaved roads to visit the sites around Lijiang. To reach the nearby unspoiled village of **Longquan,** turn left off the road about 2 miles (3 km) north of Lijiang. In the village, the Ming dynasty **Dajue Temple** still retains its frescoed walls. Across a narrow bridge over roaring water lies the **Nine Vessel Dragon Pool (Jiuding Longtan),** a clear blue pool otherwise simply called Dragon Spring; behind it is an attractive hall.

Tibetan Monasteries

Also in the foothills of Jade Dragon Snow Mountain is the **Yufeng Monastery,** a Tibetan lamasery about 3 miles (5 km) north of Baisha. The monastery is famous for a 500-year-old camellia tree that flowers profusely in spring.

A number of other Tibetan temples survive in the region. You will find frescoes at the **Fuguo Monastery** not far from Baisha, and the **Puji Monastery** just northwest of Lijiang contains some original Tibetan features.

Tiger Leaping Gorge

Many travelers come to Lijiang for the adventure of visiting Tiger Leaping Gorge. If the weather is fine, it is one of the most striking treks in China.

With Jade Dragon Snow Mountain as a breathtaking backdrop, the Jinsha River flows through the gorge, later swelling into the mighty Yangtze River. The gorge is a dramatic and thrilling journey, but changeable weather (especially during the rainy season at the end of summer) can catch hikers without warning. Periodic landslides and falling rocks can be lethal. Several travelers have been killed while navigating the gorge.

That said, the majority of ramblers experience no mishap. Time is a factor, and you will need two days for the trip, but if you have a generous schedule, this can be extended to three or four days, or as long as you like. You can spend

The gorgeous countryside around Lijiang is perfect for riding bikes—or horses.

the night at a string of hostels and guesthouses along the way, such as the comfortable Naxi Family Guesthouse *(tel 0887 880-6928),* not far from the start of the trek from **Qiaotou,** or Sean's Spring Guesthouse *(tel 0887 820-2223, www.tigerleapinggorge.com)* in Walnut Garden. Both come with single and double rooms as well as dorms. Spending the night is an excellent way to recharge, plan the next day, and talk to others.

To tackle the gorge, most travelers set out from Qiaotou village, reachable from Lijiang by bus. The hike takes you toward Daju village, a trek that is completed in several stages. It will take you around eight to ten hours to reach **Walnut Garden**—where there's a cluster of guesthouses and where many trekkers overnight before continuing to **Daju** the next day—but there are several villages and guesthouse options along the way if you want to stop off and add a day or two to your hike. Most hikers take the more scenic upper trail rather than the lower trail with its vehicular traffic. Be warned, however, that some of the high trail can be heavy going and strenuous. Take water and good shoes, of course.

It's advisable to check at one of the foreign cafés in Lijiang for news about conditions along the trek, or phone one of the guesthouses in the gorge for an update. Cafés in Lijiang can also supply you with maps of the gorge, as well as addresses and phone numbers of guesthouses in Walnut Garden, Qiaotou, Daju, and at all points in between. They can also supply you with essential information such as temporary stoppages of the ferry services across the river and other crucial advice. ■

Xishuangbanna

Yunnan merges with Southeast Asia in the region of Xishuangbanna. Bordering Laos and Myanmar (Burma), it is an abundant, though dwindling Eden of plant and animal life. Hiding off trails that snake into the forest are scattered temples, stupas, and a host of minority communities, some of which have marginal contact with the outside world. The farther you delve, the more you will discover.

The name Xishuangbanna is derived from Sip Sawng Panna—"twelve rice-growing districts."

Xishuangbanna
262 B1

Jinghong
262 B1

Tropical Flowers & Plants Garden
28 Jinghong Xilu, Jinghong

$$

Jinghong

At the hub of the Xishuangbanna (or just "Banna") region, Jinghong is best used as a base from which to explore the surrounding territory. The Lancang River, otherwise known as the Mekong River, flows through the city before coursing into Myanmar. Jinghong has a varied ethnic mix (the Dai are the largest minority), which finds expression in the food, skin color, and bone structure of its residents. But much of the more traditional, regional architecture is missing. It's best to treat the city as a communications center.

At the **Tropical Flowers & Plants Garden (Redai Huahuiyuan),** you can leaf through an encyclopedia of tropical plant life.

There are more than a thousand species of plants here, many under threat in their natural habitat. The institute, lying off Jinghong Xilu in the west of Jinghong, vividly captures the range of Xishuangbanna's diverse plant life.

Manting Park (Manting Gongyuan), on the city's southern edge, can make for a reasonable distraction. The local tourist authorities dress up visiting Chinese in ethnic costumes to pose in front of a statue of ex-premier Zhou Enlai (also garbed in local costume). There's an aviary here with hundreds of peacocks strolling around: Spring is the best time to catch them in boisterous plumage. A couple of Buddhist temples on the grounds are worth a visit, including the **Manting Temple** just next to the path. As with most temples in the region, you have to remove your shoes before entering.

The **National Minorities Park (Minzu Fengguangyuan),** off Minhang Lu in the south of the city, is rather tired and should be avoided.

Around Jinghong & Surrounding Villages

The secret to getting the most out of Xishuangbanna is to put on your explorer's hat and get off the beaten path. Around Jinghong is a plethora of small villages and towns on forest fringes, many of which are reachable by bus or bike. You have to rein in your wanderlust, as some destinations (such as Demenglong) are virtually on China's borders and trespassing without a visa may not go down too well with the Myanmar (Burma) or Lao authorities. Arm yourself with decent mosquito repellent, food, and water.

Before you bolt into the undergrowth, do yourself a favor and work out a plan of attack on the region. A good idea is to call in at the **Mei Mei Café** *(tel 0691 216-1221),* on Menglong Lu in Jinghong, or the **Forest Café** *(tel 0691 898-5122, www.forest-cafe.org)* on Mengla Lu. The Mei Mei Café has books of collected wisdom from travelers and excellent advice from those who have explored the region. This is also a great place to meet others and negotiate a strategy for tackling Xishuangbanna.

Water-splashing Festival

The traditional Dai minority Water-splashing Festival is held every year in mid-April. The Buddhist Dai celebrate the occasion by drenching everything that moves in a bid to cleanse away the dirt and ills of the old year. This is the most popular time of the year, and Jinghong is generally packed with visitors. The event is a three-day gala that culminates with the great soaking. The ritual has been hijacked by the local tourism industry, which performs daily Water-splashing events at select sites, including Manting Park.

Traveling by bike is feasible and puts you within reach of a number of adventures. It's important to check the tires and brakes carefully before you set out. You can head for Ganlanba by bike (which should take you about three hours) and cross the Mekong River by barge at Ganlanba, where

Ganlaba
262 B1

you will find a cluster of little villages on the other side.

If you do head into the wilds for a few nights, it's imperative to take sunblock, a flashlight, insect repellent, toilet paper, food, water, and water sterilization tablets. Despite the low incidence of malaria, antimalarial tablets should also be taken if heading into village areas, and be on your guard against snakes.

Jinghong's Manting Park is the oldest imperial garden in Xishuangbanna.

Ganlanba

Ganlanba (Menghan), south along the Mekong River, is an exciting minibus drive away, following the great river. The **Ganlanba Temple (Menghan Chunman Dafosi),** originally built in A.D. 583, was badly damaged during the Cultural Revolution and last restored in 1997. The building features traditional Dai architecture, with cross beams, ocher-and-gold paint, and expertly laid roof slating. The huge statue of Buddha inside is surrounded by a group of smaller effigies.

Part of the main temple is put aside as a classroom for the children of the Buddhist school in the compound. Outside the temple, hedged in by plants and shrubs, stands a bright golden stupa. The monks seem very relaxed about visitors passing through; they offer souvenirs for sale in the main temple.

The temple is set on the grounds of a **Dai minority garden (Daizuyuan)** *($$$$)*. If you head away from the temple, you can explore the countryside and visit traditional Dai communities (the road follows the river, and you might find a boat that will ferry you to small, inhabited islands).

Heading farther out of town will take you into agricultural

INSIDER TIP:

Check at the Dai minority garden about local performances of the Peacock Dance, the most popular Dai folk dance.

—MARY STEPHANOS
National Geographic contributor

countryside. Travelers report joining tours such as a three-day expedition from Ganlanba back to Jinghong, via Jinuo and Mengyang. Mengyang has a banyan tree *(rongshu)* shaped like an elephant that attracts tour groups. You may well get the opportunity to stay with Dai families in the area.

Mengla

The countryside around Mengla, 125 miles (200 km) southeast of Jinghong (six hours by bus), has exciting treks and traditional Yao villages. People are sometimes welcomed into minority homes to spend the night, although invitations should be accepted cautiously; there are a few negative tales.

Damenglong

In and around Damenglong, 43 miles (69 km) south of Jinghong, are the rather gaudy **Black Pagoda** and **Manfeilong Pagoda.** The Black Pagoda sits on the hill above town, and the Manfeilong Pagoda is a short motorbike taxi ride out of town. The sight of saffron-robed monks wearing sunglasses and riding motorbikes is a treat.

Striking out in almost any direction from the main road of Damenglong will take you into a countryside of forests and farmland, with occasional temples twinkling from the foliage (but remember the border is only a few miles to the south). Other temples crumble and return to nature.

Alternative expeditions from Damenglong can be made by the more intrepid to **Manguanghan village** and **Guangmin,** where the Hani minority lives, or to **Manpo** and its Bulang people.

Other Villages

Other villages reachable by public transport from Jinghong include **Menghai, Menghun,** and **Xiding.** All have Sunday markets full of ethnic flavor. The Thursday market in Xiding starts in the morning, with Dai and Hani villagers coming in from the surrounding area. Take the bus from Jinghong to Menghai and Xiding. ■

Wild Elephant Valley

A symbol of good luck to the Dai minority, hundreds of elephants live in Wild Elephant Valley (Yexiang Gu), part of Sanchahe Nature Reserve *($$$$)*, located about 28 miles (45 km) north of Jinghong. You can view the great animals from a specially built observation tower. The best times to visit are at dawn and dusk. Ask at your hotel about transportation *($$)*.

Mengla
262 B1

Damenglong
262 B1

Guilin

For centuries, Chinese poets, painters, and aesthetes have used Guilin and its environs in Guangxi Province as a yardstick for natural beauty. Celebrated for its karst limestone pinnacles, the city was unsuccessfully besieged by Taiping rebels in 1852; some complain that tour groups have put the city under similar duress. Nonetheless, Guilin has considerable appeal, and Yangshuo, a boat trip away along the scenic Li River, is a delight.

Light from Guilin's modern airport casts beautiful reflections in the waters of the Li River.

Guilin

263 E2 & 281

Visitor Information

South Gate, Ronghu Beilu

0773 280-0318

Along the River

The Li River flows right through Guilin, and Rong Lake and Shan Lake rest next to each other in the center of town. Two elegant pagodas—the **Sun and Moon Pagodas** *($$)*—rise up from Shan Lake, splendidly illuminated at night. The Sun Pagoda is constructed from copper and contains an elevator.

The geological oddity of **Elephant Trunk Hill (Xiangbishan)** *($$)*, with its "trunk" in the Li River, is worth a peek and perhaps a paddle in the river's clear water (unless it's winter). You can then dry your feet on the banks and eat a toasted fish bought with small change. Clamber up to a cave, take a trip on a bamboo raft into the river for more comprehensive views, or spend some time watching cormorants fishing.

Seven Star Park

The well-tended **Seven Star Park (Qixing Gongyuan)** *($$)*, east across the Li River by way of Liberation Bridge, is studded with seven peaks thought to resemble the Great Bear constellation. Picturesque scenery, bridges, woods, and lily-choked ponds can also be found. The grass is especially lush in front of **Camel Hill.** Enter over Flower Bridge, and look out for the large Maoist slogan carved indelibly into the cliff face.

About half a mile (0.8 km) north of Seven Star Park is the **Minorities Cultural Park,** an artificial tour through the minority realms of the Guangxi Zhuang Autonomous Region (the full name of this province).

Mountain Hikes

Rising from the center of Guilin, **Solitary Beauty Peak (Duxiufeng)** commands stunning views over town. To the east, caves punctuate the slopes of **Wave-subduing Hill (Fuboshan).**

Folded Brocade Hill (Diecaishan) is an attractive hike north of Solitary Beauty Peak. Hot, summer climbs are cooled by the refreshing **Wind Cave** to your right soon into your ascent, one of two caves here. For good luck, put your arms around the small, supine laughing Buddha (Milefo). A larger Milefo sits joyously in the other cave.

At the summit of **Four Views Hill,** climbers enjoy excellent views of other peaks. A museum at the base of the mount houses a fine collection of colorful butterflies.

Reed Flute Cave

A pleasant bike ride takes you to Reed Flute Cave (Ludiyan), northwest of town. The cave has some of the most arresting scenery in Guilin. The whistle-stop tour gushes through a cavernous labyrinth of gaudily illuminated stalactites and stalagmites. Water drips, covering the rocks in a cold sheen and making the way slippery, so hold on to the rails. The tour leader casts a flashlight here and there, illuminating a snowman, a lion, or a giant sunflower leaping out from the gnarled formations. It's a magnificent product of nature, especially the vast crystal palace of the Dragon King, a huge cave partially suspended over a very cold lake. Unfortunately, the production-line tour commercializes the mystery out of the place: Ignore the sales pitch and enter without a guide, if you can.

Word of Warning

Crime flourishes in Guilin, primarily because of the large number of foreign tourists in town. Try to establish prices (such as taxi fares) before committing yourself. ■

Wave-subduing Hill
Map: 281
Address: Binjiang Beilu
Price: $

Folded Brocade Hill
Address: Diecai Lu
Price: $

Reed Flute Cave
Map: 281
Address: Ludi Lu
Price: $$$$

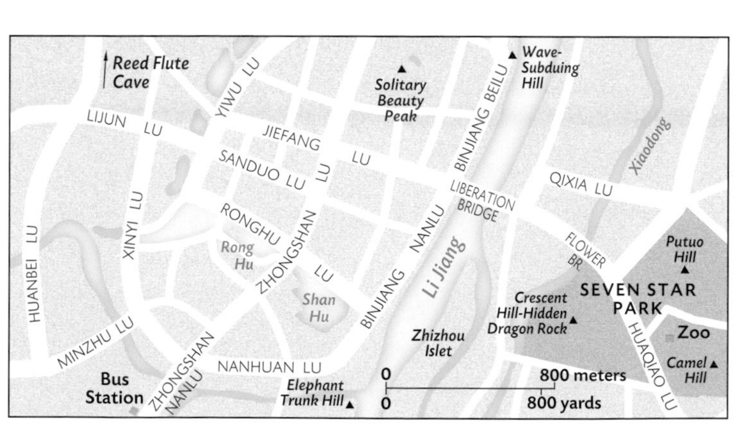

Li River Cruise

One of the most popular trips in China, the Li River (Lijiang) cruise takes you past a panorama of bamboo groves, sleepy villages, and karst peaks. This is also the most picturesque way to reach fabled Yangshuo to the south of Guilin. The scenery en route is a splash of coffee-table book colors and, as you approach Yangshuo, some of the most idyllic in China.

A fisherman on the Li River near Yangshuo prepares for an evening's work.

A cruise to Yangshuo takes between five and six hours. The river is not navigable along its complete length through the year, and the best seasons are spring and autumn. Winter waters are too low to allow boat tours, and the summer heat is oppressively sticky.

The boat trip down the Li River from Guilin to Yangshuo is considered by many travelers to be extortionately priced (*$$$$$*), and there is a markup for the foreign tourist boats. As a result, some travelers instead take the bus to Yangshuo, where even better scenery awaits. Once you get there, Yangshuo has the advantage of being far more easygoing than Guilin.

Some boats depart from **Zhujiang Pier** south of Millstone Hill, a 30-minute bus ride from Guilin, in which case the first section of the cruise will be skipped. Vessels will take you past rock formations fancifully named by painters and poets. The names of the mountains compose a dictionary of the fantastic, religious, and decorative: Look for Dragonhead Hill, Boy Worshipping Guanyin, Bat Peak, and Nine Horses Painting Hill. Nestling between the peaks are sleepy villages, while fishermen move along the riverbanks.

Departing from **Elephant Trunk Hill (Xiangbishan),** an ungainly formation that appears to drink from the river, **Pagoda Hill (Tashan)** drifts by to the east, a peak topped by the tapering form of a Ming dynasty pagoda.

NOT TO BE MISSED:

Looking Out for Husband Rock
• Boy Worshipping Guanyin
• Nine Horses Painting Hill

Cock-Fighting Hill (Douji) ❶ gives the impression of battling roosters, while Moon Cave drills through the side of **Tunnel Hill (Chuanshan).**

Rising south of Millstone Hill (beyond the riverside town of Daxu) is **Bat Peak (Bianfushan)** ❷, its sheer cliffs resembling the airborne mammals. Bats are lucky symbols in China; the words for bat and good fortune are homonyms.

Farther down the river are **Dragons Play in the Water (Qunlong Xishui),** rocky outlines of the magical dragons dispatched by the Jade Emperor (see p. 73) to gather sweet-scented osmanthus flowers.

Looking Out for Husband Rock (Wangfushi) ❸ resembles a maiden with a young child on her back. She gazes into the distance, awaiting the return of her spouse.

The boat nudges past **Caoping** village and the dark depths of **Crown Cave (Guanyan)** on the eastern bank. Beyond lies the thatched village of **Yangdi** ❹, among the dense bamboo fronds that stretch out over the river. **Wave Stone Misty Rain (Langshi Yanyu)** is a hazy phenomenon conjured up by the mists that cloak the river in autumn, absent in clear weather.

The **Boy Worshipping Guanyin** ❺ is supposed to resemble a respectful toddler communing with the goddess of mercy. Before you reach Xingping you will see **Nine Horses Painting Hill (Jiuma Huashan)** ❻, a jagged monument to the forces that molded this landscape. Among the sharp lines and dramatic fissures dance the images of nine horses. The full herd of steeds is elusive, but those with a good imagination can usually count seven.

Surrounding picturesque **Xingping** ❼ (see p. 285) is some of the most breathtaking scenery on the voyage. You can easily return to it from Yangshuo for a closer inspection.

Wave good-bye to **Five Fingers Hill (Wuzhishan),** creep by **Snail Hill (Luoshishan),** and float on to **Dragonhead Hill (Longtoushan).** This marks the arrival of the boat in Yangshuo, where it moors under **Green Lotus Peak (Bilianfeng).**

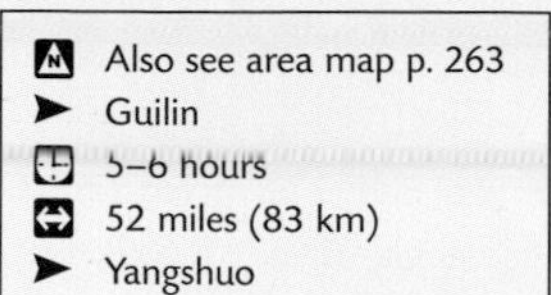

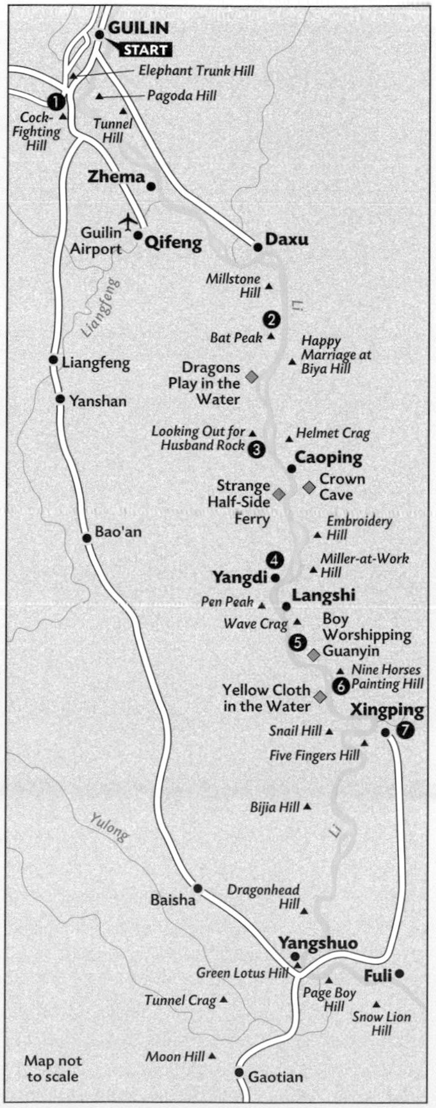

Yangshuo & Around

Yangshuo is an idyllic corner of China, a pastoral patchwork of fields, rivers, and limestone peaks. Its uniqueness has attracted a mixture of Western cafés, dazed travelers, musicians, poets, and itinerant idealists. It is the China that some travelers make the journey specifically to find. Green Lotus Peak (Bilianfeng), Yangshuo's most famous peak, overlooks the Li River, with long views up- and downstream.

Tradition and modernity mix on the streets of Yangshuo.

Yangshuo
263 E2

Yangshuo

Pantao Lu and **Xi Jie** are the crossroads of the local Western food and entertainment industry, with bags of tourist advice to boot. Basing yourself here and taking a stroll around the district is essential to get laid-back Yangshuo in perspective. Plentiful Chinese restaurants serve the legions of domestic travelers.

Xi Jie shows genuine Western-focused resourcefulness absent elsewhere in China, but be constantly alert to rip-offs. Xi Jie also swarms with souvenir stores, silk bargains, calligraphy, and leechlike trinket sellers who will doggedly pursue you. Eating alfresco at any of the cafés will invite them to stand next to you during your meal, bleating occasionally.

An evening attraction is the riverside Impressions Liu Sanjie *(www.yxlsj.com, performances begin at 8 p.m., $$$$$)*, a spectacle involving hundreds of performers to a backdrop of floodlit karst peaks, directed by Zhang Yimou.

Moon Hill

Yangshuo has a few peaks, but the true gems lie outside town. By renting a bike, you will throw open the entire surrounding countryside to exploration.

The otherworldliness of **Moon Hill** *($)* is about a 30-minute bike ride to the south *(take Pantao Lu out of town)*. This journey alongside the Li River from Yangshuo is a dream. Towering karst peaks surround, rivers glitter, and herds of water buffalo munch lazily at the wayside. After you arrive at the base of Moon Hill and jostle past the gaggle of water sellers at the gate (stock up), it's a solid half-hour ascent up the steps, through tunnels of bamboo and a crescendo of cicadas, to the top.

Here rises **Moon Arch,** which gives the hill its name. The true summit, a further five-minute climb, offers breathtaking views: Below is a canvas splashed with rivers, emerald-green karst peaks, and little hamlets. The best time of day is early in the morning or approaching twilight. Hawkers will draw your attention to an ancient **Big Banyan Tree,** visible below.

Near Moon Hill, guides pounce to show you **Black Buddha Caves** and the **New Water Caves.** The subterranean caverns contain streams, waterfalls, and pools; expect to get very muddy.

Riverside Excursions

Yangshuo also puts you within range of villages along the Li River. Pretty **Fuli** can be reached by boat, bus, or bike; an alternative is to rent an inner tube (in summer) from one of the cafés or perhaps a raft or kayak. Market day is a tempting occasion to catch the local minorities: It's held twice a week.

The other road much traveled is to **Xingping,** which you will have sailed by if you took the Li River cruise from Guilin (see pp. 282–283). The scenery around Xingping is a condensation of this attractive region, enveloped by peaks. The picturesque village is hewn from stone and has a few places where you can overnight. Farther up the Li River you will come to the village of **Yangdi** (see p. 283), which you can also reach from Yangshuo.

EXPERIENCE: Cycle Around the Southwest

Based in Yangshuo, Bike China ***(42 Guihua Lu, 2nd Floor, tel 0773 882-6521, www.bikeasia.com)*** **provides a whole range of adventure cycling tours ranging from China and Tibet to Southeast Asia. The tours they offer are rated by difficulty level and include everything from ambitious four-week cycling adventures across the Tibetan Plateau to eight-day trips along Tiger Leaping Gorge and the foothills of the Himalaya to ten-day expeditions through the rice terraces of Guangxi Province. Trips are largely designed for those who already enjoy adventure cycling, although trips can be created for cyclists of all levels.**

Bike excursions along the **Yulong River** to the southwest of Yangshuo are delightful. Aim for the lovely **Yulong Bridge,** located near the village of Baisha, an ancient traditional bridge spanning the river around 6 miles (10 km) from Yangshuo. You can spend the rest of the day working your way back to Yangshuo through a gorgeous landscape of fields and dreamy peaks. ■

EXPERIENCE: Getting Physical in Yangshuo

Yangshuo (see pp. 284–285) is an excellent place to get some exercise. You can spend some time learning tai chi, or set out on a once-in-a-lifetime rock-climbing adventure.

Tai Chi

Even though most people study the art for its health-giving properties, tai chi or *taiji quan* (literally "supreme ultimate boxing") is a form of *gongfu* (see pp. 124–125). In its deeper form, tai chi is a powerful system of self-defence, although learning this aspect of the art entails hard work and dedication.

For short-stay practitioners or for those who want to get a feel for the art, the **Yangshuo Taichi Health Center** *(tel 0773 890-0125, www.chinasouth-taichi.com, $$$)* teaches lessons by the hour. Longer-stay students will want to sign up for weekly or monthly courses.

The center teaches two different styles of tai chi, Yang style and Chen style (both taught in English). The **Yang style** is far more common, with its higher and rounded postures. It is excellent for exercising the joints. Punches and steps are interlaced with kicks, some of which are quite high. The tempo of the Yang style is meditatively slow. The full form (with 108 postures) takes around 20 minutes to complete, while the shorter form is much quicker.

More useful as a fighting form, the **Chen style** is clearly more influenced by Shaolin boxing. Postures are much lower, with the occasional fast and snappy punch thrown out to exercise the upper body as well as the legs. When done properly, the Chen form is very tiring but will greatly strengthen your legs.

If you want to take your studies a stage further, the center also teaches push hands *(tuishou).* Push hands is a two-person routine for training the basic precepts of tai chi as a fighting art and teaching the student to relax when under attack. The students link their hands at the wrist, and each student takes turns pushing and then rolling back, absorbing the pressure of the other student. The object is to throw your "opponent" off balance while remaining balanced yourself. Push hands experts can throw an opponent off balance with just a mere touch by quickly manipulating their center of gravity.

The center also offers classes in tai chi weapons forms and *qigong.*

INSIDER TIP:

Rent a mountain bike and ride along the scenic Yulong River from Moon Hill to Dragon Bridge. Ask at your hotel for a map, or just use the river as your guide.

—SUSAN STRAIGHT
National Geographic Books editor

Rock Climbing & More

With its abundance of karst peaks and divine scenery, Yangshuo was one of the first rock-climbing destinations in China to become popular. Whether you're a thorough greenhorn or an unfazed expert, plenty of climbing opportunities are at hand. Hundreds of bolted routes exist, scattered across the idyllic landscape, and more are being added to the list each year.

With experienced Chinese and foreign guides, **ChinaClimb** *(45 Xianqian Jie, tel 0773 881-1033, www.chinaclimb.com, $$$$)* in the Lizard Lounge is the leading outfit in town, offering a whole variety of adventure options, from guided climbs for beginners to two-week trips for seasoned climbers.

ChinaClimb can also arrange trips to other parts of China and offers mountain biking, caving, kayaking, camping, farm visits, and other activities. Autumn is generally considered to be the best season for climbers in Yangshuo.

Beihai

Poking into the sea on a stub of land east of Vietnam, Beihai and its beaches are still a backwater, but the city was once a treaty port, swarming with European traders. It preserves its crumbling concession architecture so typical of port towns along China's coast to the west.

A traditional Chinese wooden fishing boat waits to be taken out on the water.

If you're planning a trip to Hainan Island (see pp. 218–219) from Yangshuo, Guilin, or Nanning, spend a day here before you hop on a ferry to the southern climes. The city is awash with pearls that have been cultivated here for thousands of years, and sea breezes funnel through the boulevard's banyans.

The historic Western quarter of embassy buildings, schools, and churches was shoehorned into an area along Zhongshan Lu in the north of town. Here shaded sidewalks run under arcades created by the overhanging upper stories supported on pillars. The grand old **British Consulate** building, within the No. 1 Middle School, stands not far from **Zhongshan Park. Dijiao,** a nub of land in the northwest of town, is the heart of Beihai's fishing community.

Silver Beach (Yintan), just 6 miles (10 km) to the south of Beihai *(take bus No. 3),* is touted as one of China's best, but remember that beach culture is still in its infancy in China. That said, this is a clean stretch of white sand.

A 22-mile (35 km) boat trip to the south brings you to the small volcanic island of **Weizhou (Weizhoudao).** The island supports a French cathedral attended by a respectful congregation. Chinese Catholics sought sanctuary here, and many locals are still nominally Roman Catholic. ■

Beihai

Map 263 E1

GETTING TO WEIZHOU: Three fast ferries *($$–$$$)* leave from the International Ferry Terminal in Beihai daily at 8:30 a.m., 11:15 a.m., and 4 p.m. It takes 70 minutes to reach the island.

More Places to Visit in the Southwest

Anshun

The pleasant city of Anshun, in Guizhou Province, is close to **Huangguoshu Falls (Huangguoshu Pubu).** Located 28 miles (45 km) to the southwest, the falls are the highlight of a vast scenic area riddled with caves and karst peaks. They cascade through a region populated by the Bouyei minority.

263 D3 **CTS Visitor Information**
Tashan Donglu 0853 323-4662

INSIDER TIP:

If you happen to trek all the way to the town of Tacheng in Yunnan Province, go a little farther up the mountains to see the Yunnan black snub-nosed monkey, unique to this mountainous area.

—CRISTINA MITTERMEIER
National Geographic grantee

Guiyang

Capital of Guizhou Province, Guiyang puts you within reach of Huangguoshu Falls, Kaili (see below), and the southeast. Near the summit of the mount in **Qianling Park (Qianling Gongyuan),** in the northeast section of town, the impressive **Hongfu Temple** boasts excellent views. The **Qianming Temple** is just north of the Nanming River, near a flourishing market selling birds and flowers. The **provincial museum** *(Beijing Lu, closed Mon., $),* in the north of town, focuses on Guizhou's ethnic minorities.

263 D3 **CITS Visitor Information**
20 Yan'an Zhonglu 0851 690-1660

Kaili & Around

Less popular than Yunnan Province, this region is also less commercialized (which means more primitive facilities). Probe the small towns and villages such as Chong'an, Shibing, Zhenyuan, Leishan, and Yongle.

263 D3 **CITS Visitor Information**
Yingpan Hotel, 53 Yingpan Donglu
0855 822-2506

Nanning

Capital of the Guangxi Zhuang Autonomous Region, Nanning is a useful juncture for those bound for Vietnam. **Guangxi Provincial Museum** (Guangxi Bowuguan, $) on Minzu Dadao in the southeast of the city introduces elements of regional minority culture and history. Fifteen miles (24 km) to the northwest are the stalactite-encrusted **Yiling Caves** *($).* The attractive and historical Qing dynasty town of **Yangmei,** 16 miles (26 km) west of Nanning, makes for an interesting and popular day trip.

263 D2 **CTS Visitor Information**
40 Xinmin Lu 0771 280-4960

Sanjiang & Longsheng

These two towns in north Guangxi Province are portals to enticing minority villages and the region's stunning landscape. Sanjiang is an enclave of the Dong minority, while Longsheng is an authentic jumble of Zhuang, Dong, Yao, and Miao minorities.

The undulating region surrounding Longsheng (a three- to four-hour bus ride from Guilin to the northwest) is delightfully sculptured with rice terraces, but the highlights for their sheer scale are **Dragon's Spine Rice Terraces** at Longji, 12 miles (19 km) from Longsheng. Yao farmers are behind the genius of these layered slopes.

Another 30 miles (48 km) to the west of Longsheng lies the **Chengyang Wind and Rain Bridge (Fengyuqiao),** not far from Sanjiang. Set in a fertile valley amid Dong villages, the bridge was built by the villagers in 1916.

263 E3

A region of strong religious persuasion, from the temples of Chengdu to Leshan's colossal Buddha

Sichuan & the Tibetan Plateau

Introduction & Map 290–291

Chengdu & Around 292–295

Experience: Horse Trek Around Songpan 294

Emeishan 296–297

Leshan 298

Dazu 299

Tibet 300–309

Experience: Tibet–Qinghai Railway 303

Feature: Tibetan Buddhism 306–307

More Places to Visit in Sichuan & the Tibetan Plateau 310

Hotels & Restaurants in Sichuan & the Tibetan Plateau 382–383

Tibetan girl wearing a traditional fur hat

Sichuan & the Tibetan Plateau

Despite being distinct entities, Sichuan and Tibet (collectively called *chuanzang diqu* in Chinese) culturally and geographically fuse at their mountainous seam. Many travelers clamber onto Tibet, the Roof of the World, from Sichuan ("four rivers"), sampling some of the land's spiciest food en route.

Settled at an early date by the Han Chinese, the populous province of Sichuan was known as the Kingdom of Shu during the Three Kingdom era (A.D. 220–265). The name Shu still refers to Sichuan today.

Sichuan's encompassing mountainous fringe and remoteness were strategically attractive to the Nationalists, who made it their stronghold during the war with Japan between 1937 and 1945. Its geographic isolation has not stopped it from becoming one of China's wealthier provinces (the fact that Deng Xiaoping hailed from the province probably helped).

The province's capital is pleasant Chengdu, which sidesteps the worst that industrialization can throw at it. It's an attractive portal to the Buddhist shrine of Leshan, where you can size up the world's largest stone Buddha statue and take rigorous hikes up the holy mountain of Emei Shan. Outside Chengdu, Qingcheng Shan tempts with its Taoist mysteries. The reserve of Jiuzhaigou is a bracing slice of scenery in the far north, and the Tibetan influence grows steadily the farther west you go.

Sichuan is famous for its cuisine *(chuancai)*, a smoldering concoction of herbs and spices that frequently puts curry in the shade. It is also now known worldwide for the 7.9-magnitude earthquake that devastated the region just before the summer Olympics in 2008.

To the west, Tibet towers across its eponymous plateau. A remote society for so long preserved by the rarefied atmosphere of Tibetan Buddhism, its idiosyncratic way of life wrestles with the long arm of Beijing, especially

Area of map detail

Beijing

now that the railway to Lhasa has been completed, bringing huge influxes of outsiders. Even so, Tibet remains an enthralling land of mountains, monasteries, and monks with one of the world's most extraordinary cultures. Its remoteness has long seduced Western travelers, but anti-Chinese disturbances in Tibet, and their anniversaries, can seal off Tibet from foreign exploration for weeks, if not months.

The Tibetan capital, Lhasa, is physically dominated by the looming grandeur of the Potala Palace and animated by the spiritual presence of the Jokhang Temple. Explorations beyond the capital will bring you to more monastic societies and the great Buddhist temples at Gyantse and Shigatse.

The vast province of Qinghai, famed for its Ta'er Monastery and raw landscapes, is part of the Tibet-Qinghai Plateau and the historic lands of Tibet that also reach into Gansu Province.

Cleaved from Sichuan Province, Chongqing (see p. 150) is a highly populated municipality serving as the gateway to the Three Gorges (see pp. 146–149). ■

NOT TO BE MISSED:

The sacred Taoist mountains of Qingchengshan 294–295

Tea in a Chengdu teahouse 295

Clambering up, and then back down, the sacred Buddhist mountain of Emeishan 296–297

Sizing up the world's largest Buddha at Leshan 298

The spectacular journey to Lhasa on the Roof of the World 301–302

Exploring the magnificence of the vast Potala Palace in Lhasa 304

Immersing yourself in the awe-inspiring north Sichuan scenery of outstanding Jiuzhaigou 310

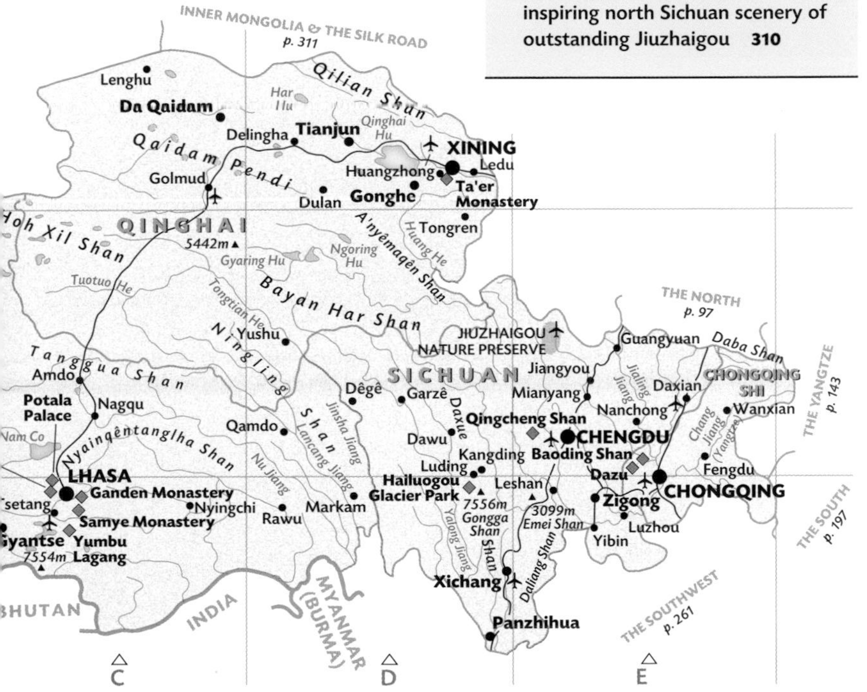

Chengdu & Around

Chengdu, capital of Sichuan Province, manages to preserve a sense of history despite wholesale modernization. Apart from its fine temple architecture, teahouse atmosphere, and giant pandas, it provides an intriguing gateway to Tibet. The city is also the heartland of searing Sichuan cuisine and a springboard for Buddhist pilgrims to Leshan and Emeishan.

Modern, bustling Chengdu also offers traditional pleasures.

Chengdu
291 E2 & 293

Visitor Information
0288 8292-8555

Qingyang Temple
293
Wenhua Gongyuan
$

Founded by the Qin before they completely unified China in 221 B.C., Chengdu prospered as a commercial center during the Tang dynasty. It later introduced paper money in the tenth century. The city also earned a reputation for its brocades and satins, winning it the name Jincheng, or "brocade city."

Chengdu's vast imperial palace was destroyed in the 1960s. The city is blessed, however, with some fine temples, and its layout is redolent of Beijing with its wide streets. Vehicles choke the town center, presided over by a gargantuan statue of Chairman Mao, while charming backstreets of traditional timber houses have somehow survived.

Taoist & Buddhist Temples

Qingyang Palace (Qingyang-gong), "green goat palace," lies in the western part of the city. A typical Taoist motif here is the octagonal eight-diagram pavilion, a design reflecting the eternal principle of the bagua, or the eight trigrams of Taoist philosophy. The eight trigrams represent all natural phenomena, combining to form the 64 hexagrams of the *Book of Changes (Yi Jing* or *I-Ching)* (see p. 54).

In front of the pavilion, a stone tablet depicts the yin/yang symbol (for the female/male, dark/light principle in nature), surrounded by the bagua. Inside, a statue of Laozi, the founding father of Taoism, rides through the Hangu Pass on his green ox. Laozi compiled his mystical musings into a succinct volume and deposited them with the gatekeeper at the pass, before continuing on his journey west (to become the Buddha, some say).

In front of the San Qing Hall is another plaque representing the yin/yang symbol, circled by the 12 animals of the Chinese zodiac. The characters on the right-hand lintel of the hall, which houses two statues of Taoist deities, note, "The sun and moon, the two wheels, are the eyes of heaven and earth."

Wenshu Temple (Wenshuyuan) is a large Buddhist complex in the northern section of the city. The four massive guardians, two on either side as you enter, are vividly painted. Inside the compound lies a cluster of temples and a large teahouse where Chengdu citizens gather to relax and read the paper. The rear of the temple complex has a small network of paths through greenery that makes for a pleasant sojourn. The most fascinating spectacle at the temple is the number of worshippers who congregate here to *baifo* (pray to Buddha); the best time to witness this is on a weekend. The market street outside throngs with stalls selling religious accoutrements.

Zhaojue Temple, a much restored Tang dynasty structure in the northeast section of town, has a main hall with three gilt Buddhas and is more interesting than the adjacent **zoo (Dongwuyuan).** Somnolent pandas reside at the zoo, but if you want to see one of these lovable creatures, it is better to visit the Giant Panda Breeding Research Base (see p. 295).

Wuhou Temple, situated southwest of the Jin River, is a monument to the Three Kingdoms period of Chinese history. Wuhou translates as "minister of war" and refers to Zhuge Liang, a famous military tactician of the period.

INSIDER TIP:

Chengdu is known for its fantastic Sichuan cuisine. Try the stuffed wontons known as *chao shou* or the *zhong shui jiao* (dumplings)

—MARY STEPHANOS
National Geographic contributor

Wenshu Temple
- 293
- Wenshu Yuan Jie
- 0200 674 2375
- $

Wuhou Temple
- 293
- 231 Wuhou Ci Jie
- $$

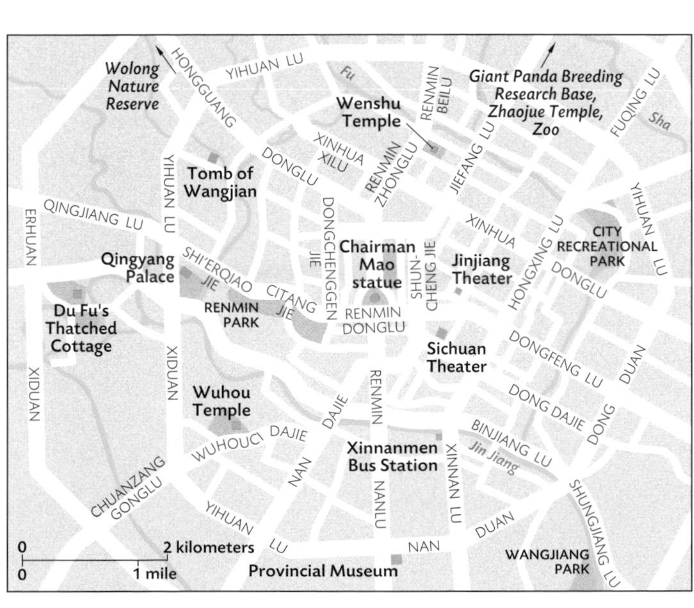

Du Fu's Thatched Cottage
293
38 Qinghua Lu
$

GETTING TO QINGCHENGSHAN: Buses (90 min.) leave regularly from Chengdu's Xinnanmen bus station in the morning for Qingchengshan. The last bus back leaves Qingchengshan at around 6 p.m.

Du Fu's Thatched Cottage

Widely considered to be China's greatest poet, Du Fu was a Confucianist poet of the Tang dynasty, and his cottage is an essential place of homage for Chinese. He is revered for his lyrical rendering of a lifetime of great suffering. Li Bai, his hard-drinking and errant confrère, is often mentioned in the same breath, although the two were very different in character and style (see p. 51).

For the curious, you will find Du Fu's thatched cottage and places described by him in the 200 or more poems he composed here. There are also models of how the estate changed over the centuries, with English captions. An interesting sideshow chronicles visits to the cottage by a number of statesmen and politicians, including Mao Zedong, Zhu De, Liu Shaoqi (the disgraced ex-Communist Party chairman), Deng Xiaoping, Li Ruihuan, and the great playwright Cao Yu.

EXPERIENCE: Horse Trek Around Songpan

If you are heading to Jiuzhaigou from Chengdu by bus outside of the winter months, stop off at the historic town of Songpan for excellent opportunities to ride horses into the splendid woods and up to lakes in the mountains around town. One long-established and dependable operation in town is Shunjiang Horse Treks *(tel 0837 880-9118)*, which can arrange everything from one-day treks to two-week journeys from town.

Qingchengshan

If you haven't the time or energy to climb the holy Buddhist peak of Emeishan (see pp. 296–297), the Taoist mount of Qingchengshan, 40 miles (64 km) west of Chengdu, is a much smaller, more manageable alternative.

Qingchengshan *($$$$)* is a sacred Taoist destination, and the climb is bordered by pines, pools, cool streams, and wayside temples. It isn't as rigorous as Emeishan, but the climb can still be grueling.

A number of Taoist temples dot the mountainside. Just by the main gate at the foot of the mountain you'll find the **Jianfu Temple (Jianfugong),** a sanctuary of peace and seclusion. It evokes all the feeling of a hillside Taoist retreat, with huge pines soaring above and moss and grass carpeting the roof and paving stones. The black statue draped in robes facing away from you as you enter is a depiction of Caishen (god of wealth).

From here, the less energetic can ride a cable car *($$)* up to **Yuecheng Lake,** take a boat over to the other side, and continue by cable car to the summit.

Unfortunately, the usual blitz of hawkers lines the route as well; some of them serve a useful purpose, keeping you going with cucumbers, corn cakes *(yumi gao),* and mineral water. The sedan chair carriers are particularly vocal, pouncing on you as you exit the cable car, wanting to carry you to the summit.

At the top is **Shanqing Hall (Shanqinggong),** a Taoist temple that shelters travelers recovering from their climb, and a community

Chengdu's Teahouses

Chengdu has long been famous for its steamy teahouses *(chadian)*, where customers recline on bamboo armchairs and meet with friends. The lid came down on the teapot during the Cultural Revolution, when many of the teahouses, former stomping grounds of the intelligentsia, were closed. Apart from quaffing *cha*, legitimate activities including playing cards, reading the newspaper, and debating; it's an excellent panorama of Chinese social life.

The Wenshu Temple (see p. 293) has an active teahouse, and a large convention of tea drinkers descends on Renmin Park, west of the center of town. A number of teahouses also line the Jin River, which runs through the city.

of blue-clothed monks. (The temple guardians are sensitive to photography.) There's a Taoist restaurant here, but a cursory look at the menu reveals the standard Chinese fare. As you descend again toward the cable car, you will see four large characters on the wall facing you. They are pronounced *dadao wuwei*, which literally means that "the great Way achieves all through inaction."

Behind Qingchengshan is **Qingcheng Houshan,** a wilder mountain area threaded with hiking trails and traversed by gorges.

Other Attractions

The **Monastery of Divine Light (Baoguangsi)** in Xindu, 11 miles (17 km) north of Chengdu, is a vast and alluring Buddhist complex. The Tang dynasty temple suffered a string of calamities before reemerging in its present, reconstructed incarnation. It hosts an assembly of 500 Luohan (see p. 83), a statue of Buddha made from white jade, and a leaning pagoda.

The **Giant Panda Breeding Research Base,** located about 7 miles (11 km) north of Chengdu, tries to preserve the lineage of the giant panda. The animals are free to wander through a sizable domain of bamboo groves and forest. Probing their kingdom along pathways affords an occasional glimpse of the protected animals. The best time to catch sight of them is during feeding hours in the morning (between 8 and 10 a.m.); at other times, they are likely to be sleeping. The base has largely supplanted the attraction of trying to sight pandas at the **Wolong Nature Reserve,** 87 miles (140 km) north of Chengdu. ■

Giant Panda Breeding Research Base

Map 293

Xiongmao Dadao (Take tourist bus 902 from Traffic Hotel.)

0288 351-6748

$$$

www.panda.org.cn

Enjoy an opera performance at one of Chengdu's teahouses.

Emeishan

Emeishan, one of the four sacred Buddhist mountains of China, originally teemed with Taoist hermits and recluses, but it was appropriated by partisans of Buddha in the sixth century. The philosophical founder of Taoism, Laozi, is said to have lived here in a mythical incarnation.

The spirit of the deity Puxian entices devotees up the grueling heights of Emeishan.

The four Buddhist mountains are protected by the Four Heavenly Kings (seen guarding the entrance to temples) of the four directions. Emeishan, the westernmost mountain, is the highest at 10,170 feet (3,099 m). Jiuhuashan is 4,400 feet (1,342 m), and Wutaishan is 10,036 feet (3058 m). The island of Putuoshan is more of a hill. Emeishan is ruled by the deity Puxian, who is generally depicted riding an elephant or holding a lotus flower.

Climbing Emeishan

The best seasons for climbing are spring to autumn—the winter climb can be treacherous. The mountain is often misty, and a sudden change in the weather is possible in any season. Waterproof clothing is important, as are an umbrella, decent shoes (with a good grip), water, and toilet paper.

Most ascend by way of the Wannian Temple, via Xixiang Pond, and up to the summit at almost 10,168 feet (3,100 m); they descend past the pond, Xianfeng Temple, and the Qingyin Pavilion. You will need a day for your ascent and a day to clamber back down.

Minibuses speed you to Wannian Temple from Baoguo Monastery, and from there it's about a ten-hour climb to the summit. Buses from Qingyin Pavilion return to Baoguo Monastery. Alternatively, you can take a minibus to Jieyin Pavilion and then transfer to a cable car going to the summit. Many temples provide food and spartan shelter.

Temples

Many of Emei's temples have vanished in the swirl of time, but some gems remain. **Baoguo Monastery** was originally built by a Taoist, and some Taoist elements remain. A feature of the **Fuhu Monastery (Crouching Tiger Monastery),** farther on, is its Ming dynasty copper pagoda with a plethora of Buddhist images and a complete text of the Garland Sutra (almost 200,000 characters) of the Hua Yan Buddhist school.

Qingyin ("pure sound") Pavilion echoes the sound of the nearby confluence of the **Black Dragon** and **White Dragon** waters. Higher up the path at 3,345 feet (1,020 m) is the **Wannian Temple** ("temple of ten thousand years"). Founded in A.D. 268, it was embellished during the reign of Wanli (see p. 37) with a huge beamless hall to house an enormous copper and bronze figure of Puxian on his elephant. The original wooden structure burned down, so the present one was made of brick. The hall was apparently modeled on a tower at Kublai Khan's summer lodge in Chengde (see pp. 118–119).

Xianfeng ("immortal peak") Temple is located near a network of formations known as the **Jiulao ("nine immortals") Caves.** Near the intersection of the two major trails, **Xixiang ("washing elephant") Pond** is where Puxian bathed his elephant; bathing the elephant is a Buddhist metaphor for the cleansing of the world from one's mind.

It's an exhausting hike to the **Jinding Temple** on the summit, fronted by a glittering 157-foot-tall (48 m) statue of Puxian. En route, you will pass many temples that have fallen victim to the ravages of time and weather.

INSIDER TIP:

Before climbing Emeishan, buy a bamboo walking stick. It will help you climb and protect you against wild monkeys.

—JINZHONG FU
National Geographic grantee

If you're lucky, you will see **Buddha's Glory** *(foguang),* a light effect in the clouds below. Sunlight shining on water droplets causes rainbows. In ages past, devotees overcome by the ethereal lights would cast themselves into the glow, only to be dashed on the rocks below. A chance of this glimpse of the divine is still the reason many climb Emeishan.

The mountain sees an eclectic mix of pilgrims winding their way to the top. It is a victim of its own popularity, but don't be deterred by the hawkers, for the landscape is spectacular. ■

Emeishan
Map 291 E1
$ $$$$$ (admission)

Visitor Information
✉ Emeishan
☎ 0833 559-2404

Leshan

Presiding over the confluence of the Dadu and Miu Rivers that sweep past the foot of Lingyun Hill at Leshan, not far from Emeishan, is a huge statue of Buddha. Carved from the rock face, it is a staggering 233 feet (71 m) high and is even more impressive for having been created more than 1,200 years ago during the Tang dynasty.

Leshan's carved stone Buddha

Leshan
291 E1
$$

Great Buddha Temple
$$$

The Chinese have a saying: "Buddha is a mountain, mountain is Buddha." This Buddha's head alone is an awesome 50 feet (15 m) high; his ears come in at a lengthy 20 feet (7.5 m), and his sizable feet can hold an audience of 100 sightseers, while he looks down with his 10-foot-wide (3 m) eyes. The Buddha represented is the Maitreya Buddha, the Buddha of the future. The outsize deity *(dafo)* is more of a marvel to behold for its scale rather than for any exquisite carving. Haitong, a devout monk from nearby **Lingyun Temple (Lingyunsi),** made this his labor of love, starting in 713, but he died before its completion 90 years later. He embarked on the project so that Buddha's presence would calm the turbulent waters of the Dadu and Min Rivers below.

Amazingly, the big Buddha—the world's largest stone Buddha statue—has survived civil war and bouts of anti-Buddhist hooliganism. The statue was at one time covered by a protective wooden building, but this was destroyed during the Ming dynasty. An elaborate drainage system prevents the worst effects of weathering.

Steps cut into the rock next to the statue funnel visitors up and down. Above Buddha's crown and at the top of the stairs is the **Great Buddha Temple (Dafosi).**

Climbing up, you pass the impressive Tang dynasty **Wuyou Temple.** Across a bridge you come to the **Oriental Buddha Park (Dongfang Fodu)** *($$$),* with its assembly of Buddhist images, including a reclining Buddha. A museum displays Han dynasty tomb relics. Continuing north brings you to the big Buddha.

Bus 13 runs to the Great Buddha Temple from town, and tour boats *($$)* make the 20- to 30-minute journey along the river from Leshan pier for waterborne perspectives of the statue. ■

Dazu

The Buddhist carvings at Longmen, Dunhuang, and Yungang are loudly trumpeted as the most important monuments to Buddhist art in China, but Dazu County in Sichuan has an equally important, if more scattered, collection.

The most successful carvings in Dazu, 70 miles (112 km) north west of Chongqing (see p. 150), are recognizably human and less preoccupied with divinity. The tribe of figures includes Taoist and Confucian parables among the Buddhist allegories.

Carved between the late Tang and Qing dynasties, principal pieces emerged from the hands of Song dynasty craftspeople. The main figures are clustered in two groups, one on Beishan ("north hill") and the other on Baodingshan ("precious summit").

Beishan

Beishan *($$$)*, located just over a mile (1.6 km) north of Dazu, is home to a large community of weather-beaten effigies in niches carved from the hillside. Some niches shelter exquisite faces—delicate Guanyins amid other tender-looking bodhisattvas.

The pantheon is a varied cast: Samantabhadra, Manjushri, Ksitigarbha (god of the underworld), and others, plus crowds of small effigies of Buddha. In the **Thousand Buddha Cave** (niche No. 155), the Peacock King presides over a dominion of miniature carved Buddhas.

Baodingshan

Baodingshan *($$$)*, situated 10 miles (16 km) northeast of Dazu, boasts 10,000 figures, a massive project initiated in the Southern Song dynasty by Zhao Zhifeng, a monk of the Tantric or esoteric school of Buddhism. The statues are located on a horseshoe-shaped cliff beneath a hill, capped by temples.

The most commanding piece is the reclining Buddha, a 100-foot (30 m) Sakyamuni (see p. 82) issuing his final teachings.

Other stories are charmingly told. The baby Buddha, for instance, bathes in a stream of water issuing from a dragon's mouth (niche No. 12). Some, such as the figures stressing filial piety (niche No. 15), are instructive parables, while others caution with fear. The illustration of hell (niche No. 21) is a ghastly presentiment of what awaits evildoers. ■

Dazu

291 E2

NOTE: Youth hostels in Chongqing are the best source of travel advice for Dazu.

The carvings at Dazu relate stories from Buddhist belief.

Tibet

A vast land of high plateaus and towering mountain peaks, Tibet has long captivated the Western imagination. Its epithets—Roof of the World, Shangri-La, and the Land of Snows—suggest a tempting otherworldliness, but its troubled modern history and ongoing development have sadly diluted much of its mystery. Travel to and within the territory remains tricky, even with the railway, and Tibet is periodically closed to foreigners for political reasons.

Invocations from prayer flags are carried aloft on the wind.

After centuries of isolation and little communication with the outside world, Tibet was unable to resist the Chinese invasion of 1951. A Tibetan revolt in 1959 was mercilessly crushed by the Chinese, and more than 100,000 Tibetans fled the country, including the Dalai Lama. Tibetan culture faced annihilation during the Cultural Revolution (see pp. 44–45), when thousands of monasteries were destroyed.

Today Tibet exists as an autonomous region within China. Periodic splutters of revolt are ruthlessly suppressed, and China wages a constant propaganda war against the "Dalai clique" government in exile.

Travel for foreigners within Tibet can be difficult. Permit requirements are imposed on all foreign travel to Tibet (which must be arranged through a travel agency), and other areas outside Lhasa Prefecture and Shigatse require further permits (see Travelwise p. 354 for details). Tibet can be closed at a moment's notice. Since deadly Lhasa riots in March 2008, the authorities have marked the anniversary by closing Tibet to foreign travelers for weeks on end.

If planning travel to Tibet, avoid this time of year and check with travel agents on accessibility. Transport beyond the main sights around Tibet is basic, and you will need to rent a four-wheel-drive vehicle to just scratch the surface of this huge land.

Nonetheless, with its magnificent scenery and unique culture, the mountain kingdom offers an unforgettable experience. It's worth the extra effort.

Lhasa

Lhasa, holy capital of Tibet, guards the flame of Tibetan heritage that Chinese modernization has failed to extinguish. The Potala Palace gazes down on a city stormed, but not completely ransacked, by Han Chinese culture while the beguiling portals of Lhasa's myriad temples, especially the fabulous Jokhang Temple, access the mysterious realms of Tibetan Buddhism.

Sitting in a valley on the Kyichu River, the historic districts of Lhasa do battle with a final, drab encroachment of Chinese government housing. The old Tibetan town in the west has a footing back in the distant seventh century, and it is here that traditional culture flourishes. This is also where Lhasa keeps her cultural jewels.

Jokhang Temple: One of the oldest buildings in Lhasa, the labyrinthine Jokhang Temple (Dazhaosi) is also the holiest of Tibet's temples. A palpable sense of reverence accompanies a visit here. The temple was consecrated in A.D. 647 on a strict geomantic scheme, and it has undergone considerable embellishment and renovation through the centuries. A major period of restoration followed great damage during the Cultural Revolution. Now literally deluged with Tibetan art, the building is illuminated by a constellation of guttering candles.

The temple is divided into inner and outer sanctums. A prayer-wheel-lined pilgrim route called the **Nangkhor** ("inner pathway") surrounds the quadrangular **inner Jokhang,** itself a sacred repository of chapels, halls, and precious statuary on a number of floors. You can visit the ornamented roofs that cap the Jokhang.

An extension of chapels and halls, the **outer Jokhang** wraps

Lhasa

291 C1

Lhasa Tourism Bureau

33 Jiangsu Lu

0891 634-2884

Jokhang Temple

291 C1

East of Barkhor Square

Inner chapels open a.m.

$$

Altitude Sickness

Many visitors to Tibet experience at least a few symptoms of altitude sickness after arriving in Lhasa. As many new arrivals have reached the high altitude of Tibet at speed (either by plane or train), it is important to rest for a few days before exerting yourself. Common symptoms of altitude sickness include headache, nausea, shortness of breath, tiredness, and a general physical malaise. If you are experiencing any of these symptoms, it is imperative you do not ascend to a higher altitude, otherwise they could develop into something more serious, with potentially fatal complications. Medications such as Diamox can be prescribed for altitude sickness, but you should discuss their use with your doctor.

Ramoche Temple
✉ Xiaozhaosi Lu
$ $$

Norbu Lingka
✉ Mirik Lam
$ $$

TANTRIC BUDDHISM: Tantric Buddhism is a creed that seeks enlightenment through inner experience and growth, and it is symbolized by exotic images of male and female coupling.

around the holy inner core. On the periphery of the outer Jokhang is the **Barkhor,** the middle pilgrim circuit, a holy place of perambulation, around which pilgrims circle in a clockwise direction (don't go against the flow). It has also become a focus for market stalls and a crush of traders from other parts of Tibet. The whole melds into a fusion of color and activity, where you can pick up that prayer wheel you were after, or a double-*dorje* (scepterlike object).

Other Lhasa Monasteries: Near the Barkhor and the Jokhang are other temples worth seeking out. These include the **Meru Nyingba Monastery** and the **Ani Tshamkhung Nunnery. Tengyeling Monastery,** northwest of Barkhor Square, was built in the 17th century after Lhasa was reinstated as capital of Tibet. Lhasa also shelters a Muslim community. The largest mosque is the **Gyel Lhakhang,** towering southeast of Barkhor Square.

Ramoche Temple, half a mile (0.8 km) north of Barkhor Square, is about the same age as the Jokhang. It was burned down early on, rebuilt, damaged by the Mongols, and then served time under the local Communist division in the 1960s.

Norbu Lingka (Luobu Linka), in the western part of Lhasa, has been used as the Summer Palace since the mid-18th century. It's a 98-acre (40 ha) park split into palaces, opera grounds, and government buildings; it also contains a zoo. As with the Potala Palace, the complex has mushroomed over the centuries.

Around Lhasa: Five miles (8 km) north of Lhasa, **Drepung Monastery** (Zhebangsi, $$) was founded in the 15th century. At one time more than 10,000 monks lived here in what was the

Prayer wheels represent the law of Buddha set in motion.

largest monastery in the world. It has managed to survive amid civil war, Mongol incursions, and the Cultural Revolution.

The temple's contingent of monks is sadly much reduced today, with only 700 remaining. Numerous halls and chapels constitute the complex, including the large golden-roofed **Assembly Hall (Tsokchen Lhakhang).** The holiest site is the **Jampa Tongdrol Lhakhang,** adorned with a 50-foot (15 m) image of the Maitreya Buddha.

Less than a mile (1.6 km) southeast of Drepung Monastery is **Nechung Monastery** *($$),* home of the State Oracle and Pehar, defender of the faith (Dharmapala), who resided for 700 years at the Samye Monastery and then relocated to Nechung Monastery. Pehar is most actively worshipped by followers of the Yellow Hat Sect (see sidebar p. 304).

A disciple of Tsongkhapa (creator of the Yellow Hat Sect) founded **Sera Monastery** *($$)* in 1419. On the northern outskirts of Lhasa, it was formerly a major community. The largest building is the Great Assembly Hall, in which hang vast *thangkas* (Buddhist banners). Sera also contains three colleges devoted to esoteric Tantric study.

Pawangka Monastery, 5 miles (8 km) northeast of Lhasa, is possibly older than the Jokhang Temple. The current three-tiered structure was originally a tower built by the pioneering king of ancient Tibet, Songtsen Gampo.

Ganden Monastery *($$),* 28 miles (45 km) east of Lhasa off the Lhasa–Sichuan road, was built by Tsongkhapa in 1409. This flourishing monastery suffered enormous destruction during the Chinese invasion. Many structures are associated with Tsongkhapa, including a stupa that contains his relics.

EXPERIENCE: Tibet–Qinghai Railway

Completed in 2006, the 1,250-mile-long (1,956 km) Lhasa–Qinghai Railway crosses the Tangula Pass through hundreds of miles of breathtaking scenery, including spectacular high-altitude lakes and soaring mountain panoramas. This is the world's highest railway, with a maximum elevation of 16,640 feet (5,072 m). During loftier stretches, oxygen is pumped into the specially designed train carriages. You can get on the train in Beijing, Shanghai, Chengdu, and Guangzhou as long as you have a Tibet Tourism Permit (see Travelwise p. 354).

Lying among magnificent mountain scenery 120 miles (193 km) north of Lhasa is **Namtso Lake (Namucuo),** at more than 15,000 feet (4,570 m) the world's highest lake, with accommodation available near the lakeside **Tashidor Monastery.** Only attempt this trip after long acclimatization in Lhasa.

Probably founded between 775 and 779, **Samye Monastery** *($$)* was Tibet's first monastery. Its founding symbolized the vanquishing of primitive belief in Tibet by Buddhism. The very earliest of the monastery's structures have succumbed to an unfortunate concoction of fire, civil war,

Potala Palace
291 C1
Open 9 a.m.–3 p.m.
$$$ (Note: Tickets for the palace are limited and must be purchased at the ticket office the day before your visit.)

earthquake, and Chinese politics. Difficult to reach (and a permit is officially required), it lies 19 miles (30 km) northwest of Tsetang, north of the Yarlung Zangbo (Brahmaputra) River. The journey there involves a multiple bus-ferry-truck trip.

Yumbu Lagang, 7 miles (11 km) southwest of Tsetang, is a reconstruction of Tibet's oldest building. Rebuilt many times, the palace was constructed on a hilltop for the first king of Tibet in the second century B.C.

Potala Palace

A huge walled castle of a building towering on the slopes of Red Mountain (Mount Marpori), the Potala Palace (Budalagong) is Lhasa's dominating feature. With the Dalai Lama in exile, the Potala has been put on show, but the palace remains a potent symbol of Tibetan nationhood.

This awesome fortresslike palace springs from the hillside above Lhasa, occupying your first impressions of the city. It takes its name from Mount Potalaka, sacred home of the bodhisattva of mercy, Avalokiteshvara, known in China as Guanyin. Two distinct sections make up Potala, the **White Palace** (built between 1645 and 1653) and the **Red Palace** (between 1690 and 1693).

The outer and larger section, the White Palace constituted the winter residential quarters of the Dalai Lama (who is the physical incarnation of Avalokiteshvara) and the governmental headquarters. The Red Palace within is a magnificent realm of temples and spiritual buildings.

The huge walls surrounding the palace of a thousand rooms are fortified, with watchtowers on the southern corners.

The Potala Palace's first stones were laid in the seventh century A.D., but time has taken its toll and only a few structures remain from that period. The building underwent a great period of reconstruction with the fifth Dalai Lama in the 17th century, when Lhasa was restored as the capital of Tibet. The palace's dimensions grew during the 18th century, and it was considerably renovated in the 20th century. Though shelled during the 1959 uprising, the building survived the tumult of the Cultural Revolution. Many rooms remain off-limits.

White Palace: Overlooking the **Eastern Courtyard,** the White Palace was the administrative hub. Visit the Dalai Lama's private quarters on the top floor for a fascinating look at the lineage of some of the men who achieved Buddhahood, and access the well-preserved

Yellow & Red Hat Sects

The Gelukpa (Model of Virtue), or Yellow Hat Sect, was founded by Tsongkhapa in the late 14th century. Tsongkhapa wanted to establish a Tibetan Buddhist order that was strictly disciplined and scholarly. The Red Hat Sect opposed the hegemony of the Yellow Hat Sect, but the Yellow emerged as the leading order in Tibet, with the Dalai Lama at its head, and remained the supreme power until 1959.

apartments of the 13th and 14th Dalai Lamas for a taste of their rarefied world. Portraits of the former occupants hang in the chambers, intriguing murals cover the walls, and small chapels bristle with statuary. Many

The Potala Palace is a sanctuary for the goddess of compassion, Avalokiteshvara.

of the chambers formerly served as government boardrooms. The largest chamber here is the **East Main Hall,** which served as a reception hall and the venue for the observance of religious festivals.

Red Palace: The religious sphere is enclosed within the four-story Red Palace, itself enclosed by the White Palace. This sacred plot is made up of numerous temples and the reliquaries for the remains of former Dalai Lamas. The core structure is the West Main Hall.

For a glimpse into Tibetan Buddhism, investigate the chapels. All four levels of the Red Palace lead to a stunning display of mandalas (mystic diagrams), sacred images, and an encyclopedic display of deities. Stupas containing the relics of past Dalai Lamas contribute to the reverential character.

On the fourth floor, the **Phakpa Lhakhang**—holy nucleus—enshrines a sandalwood effigy of the bodhisattva Avalokiteshvara, discovered miraculously in Nepal in the seventh century. A cohort of other sacred images join the effigy.

The **Chogyel Drupuk,** on the third floor, is a venerable old columned chamber replete with images of Avalokiteshvara, Maitreya, Sakyamuni, and portraits of Tibetan royal personages. The second floor consists of closed

(continued on p. 308)

Tibetan Buddhism

Chinese and Tibetan Buddhism widely diverge in both doctrine and ritual. Chinese Buddhism can seem mundane compared with the more exotic, wondrous images that characterize the Tibetan way. Within Tibetan Buddhism lie elements of the older Bon, a primitive Shaman religion indigenous to Tibet that was steered onto the Buddhist path.

Tibetan Buddhist nuns enjoy a light moment.

Buddhism originally penetrated Tibet in the fifth century A.D. Tibet inherited the cream of Indian Buddhism, partly due to the proximity of the two countries. Buddhism's resulting fusion of Tantric and more esoteric elements with Bon forged Tibetan Buddhism, though Bon still survives as an independent faith. The religion ultimately pervaded the whole of Tibetan society. It is startlingly different in culture and belief from the Buddhism followed outside Tibet and is composed of a number of schools.

Peculiar to Tibetan Buddhism is the doctrine of the reincarnating Lama (see sidebar p. 308) and its idiosyncratic pantheon of deities. A number of the latter have terrifying characteristics not associated with Chinese Buddhism, but it should be remembered that Buddhism is a compassionate religion.

Bon

The primitive Bon religion is governed by a priestly class of mediums, exorcists, and miracle workers. Tibetan Buddhism has preserved much Bon technique, including faith healing and miracle working. The ecstatic dances, belief in human flight, spirit languages, and mythical lore of Bon Shamanism were successfully transplanted into Tibetan Buddhism. The Tibetan *Book of the Dead* (a book to be read by a lama to the recently deceased, without touching the body) is shaman in organization.

This helps explain why Tibetan Buddhism is replete with netherworld images. Human skulls and bones have a symbolic and magical function that reaches out from the Bon psyche. Undoubtedly, what survives of the Bon religion in its Buddhist constitution has come under the influence of Buddhist theology, removing much of its potency. Buddhist elements were also absorbed by Bon.

Accoutrements & Motifs

Tibetan Buddhism has a number of talismans and ornaments that serve sacred purposes.

Wheel of Life: Often found decorating temples in Tibet, the wheel depicts the cycle of suffering and rebirth. It hangs from the mouth of the lord of death, who oversees the drama unfolding within its circuit.

Prayer Wheel: This decorated, hollow metal tube on a rod accommodates a roll of paper upon which is written a mantra or invocation. The turning of the wheel is a substitute for the recitation of the mantra. Photographer James Ricalton noted, while visiting China in the early 20th century, that prayer wheels can be attached to windmills, a strong breeze allowing the lama to "consign himself to the arms of Morpheus, and in the morning find himself the very *ne plus ultra* of holiness."

Prayer Flag: Similar to the prayer wheel, the mantra on the prayer flag is carried aloft by the wind.

Phur-bu: This ritual dagger was formerly used for human sacrifice. It is symbolically employed to exorcise evil spirits. The blade is three-sided, and the handle generally sports the head of a deity or some other fierce design.

Kapala: A cup made from a human skull (*kapala* is Sanskrit for "skull"), the Kapala is often used in ceremonies to offer food and drink resembling flesh and blood to deities.

Dorje: This small scepterlike object (*vajra* in Sanskrit), made from either brass or bronze, represents a thunderbolt. A male symbol, it is balanced by the bell, or *dril bu*, a female symbol. The dorje sometimes appears in double form, in the shape of a cross.

Festivals

Monlam, or Great Prayer Festival, is the most momentous festival of the year, held during Tibetan New Year. The celebration reasserts faith in Buddhism and was initiated by the founder of the Yellow Hat Sect, Tsongkhapa (see sidebar p. 304). The Tibetan New Year is a great event, starting on the first day of the first lunar month (usually February or March in the Gregorian calendar).

Some Buddhists have prayer wheels at home.

chapels but displays murals relating to the Potala Palace.

The largest chamber in the palace is the pillared **West Main Hall** on the first floor, which contains the throne of the sixth Dalai Lama, murals on Buddhist and royal themes, *thangkas* (paintings on cloth), and tapestries.

Gyantse & Shigatse

Gyantse & Shigatse
290 B1 & 291 C1

The old town of Gyantse dwells under an authentic Tibetan spell much sought after by travelers. It can easily be visited going to, or returning from, Tibet's second largest city, Shigatse.

Founded in the 15th century, the **Pelkhor Chode Monastery** *($$)* is the most famous sight in Gyantse (Jiangzi), 162 miles (260 km) southwest of Lhasa. The marvelous octagonal **Kumbum** ("place of 100,000 images") stupa rises up within the walls, with 9 tiers, 75 chapels, and 108 gates. Containing a lengthy pilgrim circuit past magnificent murals, the stupa was completed in 1427. Gyantse's hilltop fort, the **Dzong,** dates back to 1268 and has superb views. A museum records the damage done to the fortress by the British Younghusband expedition in 1904, which forced the Dalai Lama to flee to Mongolia.

INSIDER TIP:

To observe the Tibetan antelope and other unique regional wildlife, take the train or highway that runs between Lhasa and Golmud *(www.chinatibettrain.com).*

—GEORGE B. SCHALLER
National Geographic grantee

The former Tibetan capital of Shigatse, at a slightly higher elevation than Lhasa, is noted for **Tashilhunpo Monastery (Zhashilubusi)** *($$),* founded by the first Dalai Lama in 1447 and seat of the Panchen Lama. Once home to nearly 5,000 monks, it now has many fewer. Displayed here is a massive 85-foot (26 m) beatific effigy of Maitreya, the Future Buddha (see p. 82).

Currently undergoing renovation, Shigatse's hilltop fortress ruin sustained damage in the 18th century and later.

Lamas

The Dalai Lama is the head of the Yellow Hat Sect of Tibetan Buddhism (see sidebar p. 304). The name means "Ocean of Wisdom," and he is the physical manifestation of Avalokiteshvara, the salvationary bodhisattva of mercy (called Guanyin in China). Although he fled Tibet in 1959, the current Dalai Lama remains the temporal ruler of the land.

The Panchen Lama is a physical incarnation of the Amitabha Buddha. The Panchen Lamas enjoy successive reincarnations like the Dalai Lamas. When the tenth Panchen Lama died in 1989, after spending most of his life in Beijing, the Dalai Lama chose the reincarnated Panchen Lama, as was the custom. Beijing ignored this decision and chose a different contender.

Xining & Around

One of China's poorest provinces, huge Qinghai is also where the Yellow, Yangtze, and Mekong Rivers begin as snow water. The capital Xining has little to offer, but it's a gateway to the Ta'er Monastery and Qinghai Lake and a staging post for travelers taking the train to Tibet.

Xining's Hui Muslims worship at the **Great Mosque (Qingzhen Dasi)** on Dongguan Dajie. In the mountains northwest of town lies the **Beishan Temple.**

Located 16 miles (26 km) south of Xining in the town of Huangzhong, **Ta'er Monastery** is one of the six great Yellow Hat Sect lamaseries and birthplace of Tsongkhapa, the founder of the Yellow Hat Sect. Its cluster of buildings includes a fine temple, several stupas, and a hall containing yak-butter statues, a historic Tibetan art form.

Important festivals that attract pilgrims take place in the first, fourth, sixth, and ninth lunar months. Ta'er Monastery is easy to reach by bus from Xining.

The Kumbum stupa rises from a courtyard on the Pelkhor Chode Monastery, Gyantse.

Twelve miles (19 km) south of Ledu, a small town 40 miles (64 km) east on the Xining–Lanzhou railway line, is the Lamaist **Qutan Temple,** with some well-preserved frescoes.

Qinghai's other main attraction is **Qinghai Lake (Qinghaihu),** China's largest saltwater lake. Most travelers explore **Bird Island (Niaodao)** *($$)* in the western part of the lake, where thousands of seabirds descend during breeding season (March to June). Some tours from Xining also pass the Ta'er Monastery. Check the latest bird flu reports before visiting. ■

Xining, Qinghai Province

291 D3

Ta'er Monastery

291 D3

Huangzhong

$$$

More Places to Visit in Sichuan & the Tibetan Plateau

Sichuan

Hailuogou Glacier Park: Part of Mount Gonggashan, this (sadly commercialized) glacier in western Sichuan has breathtaking views over a mountainous backdrop. Autumn offers the best weather, but take warm clothes. A guide is included in the entrance fee, but if trekking take food and water.
291 D1 $$$$$

Jiuzhaigou: This huge nature preserve in northern Sichuan is both remote and blessed with some stunning scenery. With its airport connected to Chengdu (with flights to other major Chinese cities planned), Jiuzhaigou attracts huge numbers of domestic travelers, but the reserve remains a gorgeous panoply of lakes, forest, and alpine scenery. In summer and autumn, tours from Chengdu usually include the **Yellow Dragon Temple (Huanglongsi),** between the town of Songpan and Jiuzhaigou. The reserve lies high up, so take warm clothes.
291 D2 & E2 $$$$$

A stupa on the trail to Everest Base Camp

Everest Base Camp & Rongbuk Monastery

If you are Nepal bound, you can stop at Rongbuk Monastery and the Everest Base Camp *(map 290 B1)* for unforgettable mountain scenery. A guesthouse next to the monastery offers accommodations and a restaurant, and tents are available at Everest Base Camp.

Kangding: One popular, but risky, route into Tibet runs along the Sichuan–Tibet highway, which trundles through Kangding in western Sichuan. If you simply want to reach Tibet, fly or take the train; the land route is officially closed to foreigners, and accidents are commonplace on the bad roads. Kangding is dominated by 24,798-foot (7,556 m) **Mount Gonggashan,** and several Tibetan lamaseries and mountain lakes can be found in the surrounding region.
291 D2

Tibetan Plateau

Sakya: The route from Shigatse to the Nepalese border passes through the town of Sakya. Sakya's huge **monastery** *($$)* is simply sublime, with gargantuan walls thrusting out of the earth. The immense structure is a remarkable sight. Political power crystallized here 700 years ago during the period of Yuan Mongol patronage, a relationship aimed at protecting the country from destruction.

Sakya lies at the outer limits of the public transport system for foreigners within Tibet, and if you wish to go farther, you will have to rent your own vehicle. You will also need to obtain an Alien Travel Permit (see Travelwise p. 354) for visits to Sakya.
290 B1 $$

An epic territory of desert, mountain lakes, and the debris of ancient civilizations

Inner Mongolia & the Silk Road

Introduction & Map 312–313
Ürümqi 314–315
Tianchi 316–317
Turpan 318–320
Kuqa 321
Kashgar (Kashi) 322–323
Karakoram Highway 324
Experience: Cycle the Karakoram Highway 324
Hotan 325
Dunhuang 326–327
Experience: Singing Sand Dunes 327
Jiayuguan Fort & Around 328
Lanzhou & Around 329
Xiahe & Labrang Monastery 330
Yinchuan 331
Baotou & Around 332
Hohhot 333

Hohhot's Dazhao Temple, the region's premier Buddhist monastery

Experience: Horseback Riding on the Mongolian Grasslands 333
More Places to Visit in Inner Mongolia & the Silk Road 334
Hotels & Restaurants in Inner Mongolia & the Silk Road 383–384

Inner Mongolia & the Silk Road

China's first open-door policy nourished the country with the trade, religion, and outside contact that flowed along the historic Silk Road (Sichou Zhi Lu). The merchandise traveled in both directions. Bouncing west out of China were bundles of silk, while ivory, gems, fruit, glass, precious metals, and a variety of religions and creeds crept east.

Departing from Xi'an, the silk-laden trade caravans passed through Lanzhou, nudging through the Jade Gate (Yumen) near Jiayuguan before forking at Dunhuang to skirt the dry menace of the Taklimakan Desert (Takelamagan Shamo). Watered by the oases of Turpan, Kuqa, and Hotan, the trails followed northern and southern arms before reuniting at Kashgar. Caravans that blindly strayed into the desert were quickly swallowed up by sand and heard from no more. One route of this ancient highway slipped out of China over the Pamir Mountains to destinations as far away as the Mediterranean. From the southern arm, another road fed into northern India through the lofty Karakoram Highway.

The Silk Road brought riches to several pre-Islamic Buddhist civilizations that flourished in these regions. Surrendering later to the remorseless desert sands or simply forgotten, many were plundered by intrepid European, Russian, and American archaeologists in the early 20th century. The sacred caves at Dunhuang in Gansu Province were singled out for particular attention.

China's arid northwest is a tamer world today, but it remains a place of hostile desert dappled with green oases. A desert for all seasons, the Taklimakan is a searing griddle in summer and frozen wasteland in winter, forcing life to the oasis towns on its boundaries. East of the desert is the lake of Lop Nur, a body of water that has drifted over the ages. Oasis towns, tranquil lakes, snowcapped mountains, Buddhist caves, and remnants of ancient cities add allure to this wilderness. Bumpy bus rides, long train journeys, and less exciting, but quicker, airplane trips cover the huge distances.

Ürümqi is the capital of the Xinjiang Autonomous

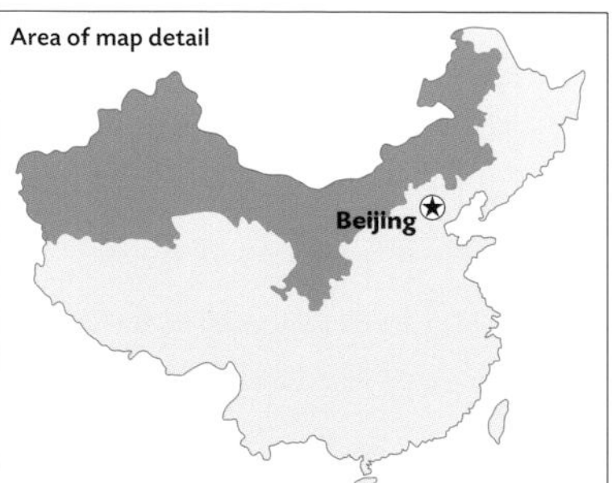

Region (formerly far more grandly called Chinese Turkistan), a region that came under absolute Chinese control only in the Qing dynasty. The city is a communications hub to the rest of Xinjiang, including nearby Heaven's Lake, or Tianchi, the oasis town of Turpan, and Kashgar (Kashi).

The long east–west strip of Inner Mongolia is a very separate cultural and historical entity, an autonomous region bridged to Xinjiang by Gansu Province. Its eastern extremities abut Jilin, Heilongjiang, and Liaoning Provinces.

As in parts of Xinjiang, the huge influx of Han settlers into Inner Mongolia has put a much resented Chinese stamp on the local culture. Mongol pride finds concrete expression in the Mausoleum of Genghis Khan, a memento of those glory days when the Mongol Empire enslaved China. Lamaseries in Hohhot point to the historic allegiance between the Mongols and Tibetan Buddhism.

Pinched between barren Gansu Province and Inner Mongolia, the tiny Ningxia Hui Autonomous Region has a large minority of Hui Chinese, Muslim descendants of Middle Eastern merchants who plied the Silk Road. ■

NOT TO BE MISSED:

A day spent exploring the glorious mountain lake of Tianchi **316–317**

Putting yourself on the edge of Central Asia in Kashgar **322–323**

Touring the fabulous Mogao Caves at Dunhuang **326–327**

The imposing battlements of Jiayuguan Fort, in the deserts of Gansu Province **328**

Labrang Monastery, an 18th-century retreat in the town of Xiahe on the edge of Tibet **330**

Riding a horse on the alluring Mongolian grasslands **333**

Ürümqi

Ürümqi, capital of the vast, dry expanse of the Xinjiang Autonomous Region in China's remote northwest, can be disappointing. The expected thrill of arrival in Xinjiang is dissipated by this very typical Chinese city. No matter, it is an essential staging post to sparkling Tianchi, thirsty Turpan, and exotic Kashgar (Kashi), and there's some excellent Uighur food to be found.

Kazakhs and many other minorities call Ürümqi home.

Xinjiang is best explored with an understanding of the local culture. One excellent step toward this can be found at the newly restored **Xinjiang Autonomous Region Museum,** which has recently benefited from a huge renovation that has banished the stale exhibits and seen the creation of a multi-hall replacement. This is an essential experience for anyone interested in the region: Xinjiang's vanished Buddhist civilizations and cities are all examined, along with Buddhist frescoes, while fascinating pieces of trivia round out the picture.

INSIDER TIP:

Opened in 2010, the Ürümqi zoo on Xinhua Nan Lu showcases a wide range of rare and endangered plains and mountain species.

—JOHN HARE
National Geographic grantee

Some interesting facts can be gleaned. Did you know that more than 8,000 Chinese Russians live in Xinjiang, mainly in the north, and that 18,000 Manchurians also call the region their home?

But the highlight of the museum is its star collection of mummified bodies, which were preserved by the desiccating effects of the arid desert. The body of one woman is about 4,000 years old, unearthed from the region of the Tieban River in 1980. She and several others are of European extraction, revealing a nomadic intrusion into these parts millennia ago by a tribe who spoke a language called Tocharian. The bodies—some of which are children, including a baby—are well preserved and sealed in airtight plastic containers. The main excavation sites are illustrated on a map on the wall.

For those who would like to discover more about the mummies, read *The Mummies of Urumchi* (Macmillan, 1999) by Elizabeth Wayland Barber, who is an expert on ancient textiles. The book is a fascinating and exhaustive piece of forensic detective work, in which the author posits a possible Celtic ancestry for the mummies, after a highly detailed examination of their garments and analysis of the mummified corpses. ■

Ürümqi
312 B2

Xinjiang Autonomous Region Museum
Xibei Lu
Closed 1:30–3:30 p.m.
$

Silk Road Minorities

Xinjiang's largest Turkic group are the **Uighurs,** a Turkic-speaking people of Turkish descent. They are also scattered throughout Kazakhstan and Kirgizstan. The Uighurs are Sunni Muslims who resent the influx of the Han into their province. The more conservative men parade themselves in long coats, knee-high boots, and fur-trimmed hats, while the women swathe themselves in shawls. Far-flung Kashgar (Kashi), on the western rim of the parched Taklimakan Desert, is predominantly Uighur.

A hardy Turkic group, the nomadic **Kazakhs** number more than a million in Xinjiang; many fled to China after the 1917 Russian Revolution. The shores and mountains around Tianchi outside Ürümqi teem with Kazakh families.

Another Turkic-speaking Chinese minority, the **Kirgiz** are also Muslim and nomadic like the Kazakhs. Huge numbers of Kirgiz fled to China from Kirgizstan (Kyrgyzstan) after a 1916 revolt against Russian hegemony; they are concentrated north of Kashgar. Other Turkic-speaking tribes exist in Xinjiang, including the agricultural **Uzbeks** and **Tartars.**

The **Mongol tribes** were united by Genghis Khan, and their descendants are scattered through the provinces of Inner Mongolia, Xinjiang, Qinghai, Tibet, and the northeast. They are typically stocky, shortlimbed, and roundfaced with flat features. Tibetan Buddhism was historically their chosen religion.

The **Hui** (also known as Dungan) are Muslims descended from Chinese converts to Islam. They can be found throughout China but are most concentrated in Gansu, Xinjiang, Qinghai, and Ningxia. Hui men are recognizable for the white caps they wear.

The **Sibo,** a Manchu tribe, live in the northwest with descendants of Manchu troops stationed in Xinjiang during the Qing dynasty.

Originally from Iran, the **Tajiks** today live in far west Xinjiang around the border with Tajikistan, particularly in the town of Taxhorgan (Tashkurgan). They number about 35,000 and speak a form of Persian.

The small community of **Russians** who were living in China was bolstered by refugees from the 1917 Russian Revolution.

Tianchi

From the desert-dry and sand-blown terrain around Ürümqi, capital of Xinjiang Province, rises an unexpected alpine treat—mountains surrounding Tianchi, "heaven's lake," perched at an elevation of 6,560 feet (2,000 m).

Many Kazakh families live along the shores of Tianchi.

Tianchi
312 B2
$$$

Not to be confused with Tianchi in China's northeastern Jilin Province (see pp. 340–341), the lake, located 70 miles (112 km) east of Ürümqi (a 2.5-hour bus ride, $), is spectacularly at odds with the arid terrain below. It is filled with melted snow from the surrounding mountains and ringed by forest. In summer, Tianchi is a breath of fresh air in one of China's oven territories.

How to Visit

You should aim to spend a day here at least, that is unless the weather, which usually obliges with picture-postcard blue skies, is foul (the lake is really accessible only between spring and autumn). The punishing winter clamps the lake in ice and puts it out of reach to travelers.

Some people are so enamored of the lake that they spend months here, shacking up in the delightful Kazakh yurts (see sidebar opposite) that hug the shores. It's easy to understand why: The lake area is a pastoral pleasure with trails winding through deep pine forest, crossing flowery meadows overlooked by mountain goats on precarious perches, skirting streams, and passing Kazakh herders and cattle. If you have time on your hands, this could well be the best way to experience China—one long, unique impression rather than as a series of tourist sights.

You disembark the bus from Ürümqi at a point you will want to leave quickly. This is where the Chinese tour buses grind in, disgorge travelers who clump together for photos and troop off to nearby restaurants for lunch before speeding back to base. (As always, try to avoid weekends and public holidays.) Aim to head off quickly around the paths that ring the lake, climbing and descending the undulating contours of the surrounding pine forest.

Suggested Route

Take the road to the right, and when you encounter the Kazakh horsemen who are generally on hand, turn left onto a concrete path. This soon gives way to a rough path, covered in hoof prints, which guides you into the pine forest carpeting the slopes around the lake. You will probably run into wide-eyed cattle munching vegetation on the slopes.

Threading through the forest, you should find yourself alone, apart from the occasional fellow traveler. After about 20 minutes of walking, follow the path downhill to a small glade beside the water, where cattle graze and yurts form a little community.

Just beyond is an exceptionally tranquil stretch with only the occasional cow for company. If you continue on the trail, you may meet a Kazakh herder or two along the way. A hillside invites you to clamber up, or you can continue on the lower path, as mountain goats scramble over the loose rocks.

The boat cruises are tempting but not essential, for they only take you on a tour of what is far better to tramp through yourself. For a reasonable fee, Kazakh riders will take you up to the snowline, which takes about ten hours.

You'll probably see a number of travelers dragging hiking gear into the region to fully explore what it has to offer, and this is a good option if you have the time.

If you find the 2.5 hour bus ride *($)* back to Ürümqi too daunting a prospect, you should quite easily be able to organize a stay in a yurt for the night; just ask around. These are very cheap, and three daily meals are included in the price. Otherwise, there is a reasonably comfortable guesthouse on the shores of the lake, near the parking lot, where you can stay. ■

Yurts

The shores of Tianchi are dotted with pie-shaped yurts (also called *gher*), nomadic tents used by the Kazakhs who dwell here. They are made from a thick outer skin of hide or thick felt thrown over wooden poles, and they are easily erected and taken down as herders move from pasture to pasture. Felt is the preferred material for nomads because it is quick and easy to produce, not being a woven fabric. Yurts are cozy in the winter and cool in the summer.

Turpan

A sensational journey across a stark landscape from Ürümqi lies the green oasis town of Turpan, thirstily surviving on irrigated snowmelt water from the mountains known as Tianshan. The 30,000-square-mile (77,670 sq km) Turpan depression is China's lowest spot below sea level, blistering in summer (temperatures can soar to 130°F/55°C) and freezing in winter.

Tomb of Xiangfei, a Qing dynasty Uighur concubine

The Drive to Turpan

This is an unforgettable and invigorating experience. The town of Turpan, which lies about 370 miles (595 km) from Ürümqi, was a luxuriant staging post on the northern arm of the Silk Road, imprisoned in the sterile void of the surrounding terrain. The expressway initially passes a long stretch of the **Tianshan range**—a dramatic backdrop that flattens out into a featureless, sweeping plain.

On either side of the road extend huge desiccated swaths of desert. You pass a massive **windmill field** swept by forceful gusts. Some of the scenery here is remarkable—vast plains, snow-capped mountain ranges, and an overwhelming sense of aridity. Step from the air-conditioned chill of your taxi into the summer oven of the Turpan basin, and feel the heat hit you like a frying pan. Farther south at Loulan was the testing range for China's nuclear weapons.

Vineyards

As well as being a well-irrigated oasis, Turpan is also a premier wine-growing region of China. Driving up toward the vineyards, you could almost think that you had accidentally stumbled upon a French wine-growing colony. Vine trellises shade the city, and the prime grape-picking season is from August to September. The viticulture is worth perusing for a taste of the sweet grapes and the comfortable shade that the vines offer.

Wander around the grape markets that cluster about the tourist-designated vineyards, and sit down for a typical Uighur meal: crispy roast lamb skewers (fat clumps of grapes are thrown in for free). If you have developed a taste for kebabs *(yangrouchuan)*, these are some of the best around. The market is a hive of activity, especially at lunchtime: Chefs fan thick clouds of smoke from glowing coals spitting with lamb fat, while hawkers bellow and shout.

The market is presided over by ethnic traders overseeing huge bags that spill over with raisins and grapes. They will also draw your attention to rows of locally fermented wines.

The characteristic buildings with the missing bricks that you see all over Turpan are for drying grapes to make raisins.

Sugongta

Sugongta *($)* is a minaret and mosque, also known as Emin Minaret, on the southeast edge of town. Built in 1778, the simple tower is rather unspectacular.

Kar Wells

The vines in Turpan are watered by an elaborate irrigation project that feeds water in from the melting snows of the Tianshan. The impressive channels were first engineered 2,000 years ago, based on a Persian design. Without them, Turpan would rapidly join the desert. The longest channel is more than 6 miles (10 km) long, and the system in total runs to 3,100 miles (4,990 km). You will probably get an idea of the wells and channels just by visiting the city, but a few wells *(kaner jing)* can be accessed as tourist sights. These unfortunately give little insight into the huge engineering entailed in the project, despite accompanying exhibits, but at least you can climb down the steps and run your fingers through the icy waters.

INSIDER TIP:

The best strategy is to rent a car or take a taxi from Ürümqi to Turpan. Buses also run regularly between the two, departing every 20 minutes or so for the 2.5-hour journey.

—DAMIAN HARPER
National Geographic author

Jiaohe Ruins

The strategically located ruins at Jiaohe *($)*, about 4 miles (6.5 km) west of Turpan, were built on a plateau, originally occupied in the second century B.C. From 108 B.C. to A.D. 450, the city was the capital of the kingdom of Jushi, which was destroyed by fire in a rebellion in the 14th century. There is not much to see here, and the

Turpan
312 B2
Visitor Information
 John's Information Service & Cafe, opposite Turpan Guesthouse, Qingnian Nanlu
0995 852-4237

Kar Wells
 Yaer Village, Turpan

Bezeklik Thousand Buddha Caves
- 6 miles (10 km) north of Gaochang ruins
- $

Gaochang
- 313 C2
- 28 miles (45 km) east of Turpan
- $

Astana Tombs
- 313 C2
- North of the Gaochang ruins
- $

remains of the buildings have taken on the appearance of the eroded landscape. But it is an atmospheric place and pleasant to walk around.

Bezeklik Thousand Buddha Caves

The Bezeklik Thousand Buddha Caves (Baizikelike Shiku), 35 miles (56 km) northeast of Turpan, are a network of grottoes featuring badly damaged Buddhist figures and wall paintings. They are eclipsed by some breathtaking scenery. Take your time to wander around the landscape, sculpted by the wind and redolent of an outtake from an Indiana Jones epic.

The poor condition of the caves can be traced to the energetic and wholesale removal of frescoes by Albert von le Coq (1860–1930), a German Oriental specialist, and Theodore Bartus, his assistant. The grottoes were also defaced by Islamic Uighurs, who had little time for the idolatrous Buddhist art.

Cave No. 27 shelters faintly discernible frescoes, with the best preserved examples clinging to the ceiling. Many of the faces are scratched away, while others appear caked in mud. One of the grottoes pitifully displays the huge figure of a toppled Buddha. Bad lighting in many of the caves doesn't help demystify the divine images. The experience unfortunately speaks more of the destruction of Buddhist art than of its preservation.

The surrounding hills and dunes make for hot and energetic climbs. These are recommended for their stunning views over the arid rock formations (camels will carry you over short distances for a fee). If you are there in summer, don't forget sunscreen and plenty of water.

As you drive to the Bezeklik Thousand Buddha Caves, you will pass the **Flaming Mountains (Huoyanshan),** radiating a fiery hue under the relentless sun. ■

INSIDER TIP:

If you visit Gaochang in the heat of summer, bring plenty of water and hitch a ride on one of the donkey carts at the entrance to get to the site.

—MARY STEPHANOS
National Geographic contributor

Gaochang & the Astana Tombs

To the south of the Bezeklik caves are the ruins of Gaochang, an ancient Uighur capital and later regional capital during the Tang dynasty. The city was destroyed in the 13th century, but outlines of the buildings and other shadows of habitation remain. The Astana Tombs lie to the northwest of the ruins of Gaochang. This is where the dead of Gaochang were buried over a period of 500 years from A.D. 273 to 782. The remains (some corpses, fabrics, and paintings) are remarkably well preserved by the aridity, as are all archaeological sites in the region. They were robbed centuries ago, however, and later turned over by Aurel Stein, a Hungarian-British Orientalist in the early 20th century.

Kuqa

Fed by snow water, the oasis of Kuqa (Kuche) was formerly the seat of a prosperous Silk Road kingdom. The ancient shells of the nearby Kizil Buddhist caves are still decorated with frescoes despite the voracious attentions of European archaeologists.

The sandstone canyon—comparable in scale to the Grand Canyon—lies near Kuqa.

The area was an important juncture on the northern arm of the Silk Road and a center of Buddhist activity. Kumarajiva (A.D. 344–413), one of the most diligent translators of Buddhist sutras, worked here, and the great Chinese traveler Xuanzang—who passed through in the seventh century bringing Buddhist scriptures back to China—described a wealthy kingdom. To the south extends the fierce dryness of the Tarim Basin and to the north, the immense Tianshan range.

As with any Xinjiang town worth its salt, Kuqa hosts a market that draws traders from surrounding desert outposts. Its bazaar is held on Fridays in the old town to the west of the new district. This is a seasoned part of town, decorated with old mosques.

The **Tomb of Molana Eshding Hoja,** in the west part of town, honors this 14th-century Muslim missionary. But Kuqa's showpiece is the **Kizil Thousand Buddha Caves (Kezier Qianfodong)** *($)*, 43 miles (69 km) to the west. There are 236 caves scraped from the rock, many representing the earliest of their type (third century), although only a few are open to the public. Many frescoes were removed and taken to Europe along with other antiquities by Albert von le Coq, but a number of paintings remain.

At **Kizilgaha,** north of Kuqa, is an early **beacon tower** ***(fenghuotai)*** that was a link in a chain of signal posts across the region. ■

Kuqa

312 B2

GETTING THERE:
It's quite a journey to the caves, which generally involves renting a vehicle (CITS can arrange this) or taking a taxi. Take plenty of food and water in case of a breakdown. You can also catch a bus to Baicheng and sort out transport there for the remaining 7 miles (11 km).

Kashgar (Kashi)

Despite the growing Han Chinese stamp, Kashgar is a Central Asian town that has somehow drifted with the sand over the Chinese border from Central Asia. It is the focal point of this western region of what was called Chinese Turkistan, a city of silk markets, exotic bazaars, camel traders, and Islamic aromas. The farthest west of China's towns, Kashgar is pressed up toward bordering Kirgizstan and Tajikistan by the arid sands of the Taklimakan Desert.

Few other markets in the world have as long a history as Kashgar's busy Sunday market.

Kashgar
312 A2
Visitor Information
John's Information Service & Cafe, Seman Hotel, 337 Seman Lu
0998 258-1186
www.johncafe.net

Unlike Ürümqi to the east, Kashgar's persona is overtly Islamic, as 90 percent of the population are Uighur Muslims. Kashgar somehow musters together a Mao statue and a People's Square, but the socialist-housing style that defines the rest of China is delightfully absent.

A few miles east of Kashgar is the sacred resting place of the descendants of Abakh Hoja, a 17th-century Muslim holy man and ruler of this region. The 17th-century hall is capped with a green-tiled dome. It is also believed that Xiangfei, the Fragrant Concubine, is buried here. This Muslim princess was captured by Qing forces and taken to Beijing to serve as the emperor's concubine. The Qianlong emperor (*r.* 1736–1795) built her a tower facing her homeland because she pined for her country, but she committed suicide, coerced by the empress dowager.

Kashgar's famous **Sunday market,** a busy confluence of trade traversing the old Silk Road, has been held here for the past 1,500 years. It rolls dustily into town every Sunday from the desert and throws up an enormous bazaar. This is the trading event of the week, a bustle of farmers and merchants bargaining over camels, sheep, goats, and fabrics; it fans out along Aizilaiti Lu in the east part of town.

Cattle are herded into crowded pens as farmers swarm amid an enthusiastic and boisterous swell. The market offers a wide variety of goods: kitchenware, multicolor fabrics, knives, embroidered rugs and carpets, handicrafts, and food; street-side vendors, serving up flat breads and yogurts, feed the throng.

INSIDER TIP:

The spectacular Karakoram Highway runs south from Kashgar to the Pakistan border, passing by the massifs of Kongur and Mustagh Ata.

—GEORGE B. SCHALLER
National Geographic grantee

During the week, the city's permanent bazaar peddles its wares on lanes that sprout east and west from **Id Kah Square.** The side streets glitter with jeweled knives and ornate boxes, while piles of rugs and carpets, hats, and embroidered caps attract souvenir hunters. Metal is hammered out and shaped on the spot, alongside jewelry shops that twinkle with precious metal, necklaces, and rings.

Id Kah Mosque (Aitigaer Qingzhensi) magnanimously overlooks its eponymous square and is probably the most illustrious example of Islamic architecture in China. A glance at its dome and minarets, tiled in blue and red, reveals an aesthetic that would look at home in Islamabad.

Taklimakan Desert

The Taklimakan desert, or Takelamagan Shamo, was historically a hostile wilderness and graveyard for foolhardy explorers and disoriented caravans. The desert dryly consumes the rivers that penetrate it from the Kunlunshan to the south and the Tianshan range to the north. The ancient Chinese called it the *liu sha,* or "moving sands," for the dunes that crawl across its face. Caravans skirted it along the oasis-stringed perimeter, lest they be led to a dusty death or lashed by one of the epic sandstorms. Winters are freezing and summers searing, with negligible precipitation.

Outside Kashgar

The entry of the Buddhist faith into China along the Silk Road left its traces in the **Three Immortals Cave (Sanxiandong),** 8 miles (13 km) to the north. The frescoes have virtually vanished, and all that remain of the figures are a few minute statues of Buddha.

Twenty-five miles (40 km) west of Kashgar is the simple **Tomb of Mahmud Kashgari,** an 11th-century Uighur academic. ■

Karakoram Highway

The Karakoram Highway feeds dramatically through the mountains over the Khunjerab Pass and across the border into Pakistan. If you plan to visit Pakistan, this can make for an unforgettable entrance, but if you're just plain adventurous, the region offers a spellbinding display of awesome mountain scenery filled with lakes, canyons, and cliffs.

EXPERIENCE: Cycle the Karakoram Highway

Xinjiang & Tibet Expeditions *(83 Aletal Lu, Ürümqi, $$$$$, www.xinjiangtibetexpeditions.com)* **offers three-day bicycle tours of the Karakoram Highway. On the first day, you will be picked up in Kashgar and transported to Tashkurgan. From there, you will make the magnificent two-day return journey to Kashgar, passing Karakul Lake and some simply breathtaking mountain scenery.**

Karakoram Highway
312 A2

NOTE: The border at Khunjerab Pass is officially open April 15–Oct. 31.

Surging through Afghanistan, Pakistan, Kashmir, and China, the Karakoram mountain range boasts **K2 (Qoghir),** the world's second highest peak (28,250 feet/ 8,611 m). The **Khunjerab Pass** (named after the river) is the historic channel that funneled caravans and treasures into and out of China from present-day Pakistan. Today, if you are Pakistan bound, a more modern road will take you there.

From Kashgar (see pp. 322–323), the road as far as the town of Tashkurgan is wild, feeding between the staggering mountain heights of Kongurshan (25,280 feet/7,719 m) and Mustagh Ata (24,600 feet/7,500 m).

Between the two lies the icy beauty of **Karakul Lake (Kalakuli Hu)** *($$),* about a hundred miles (160 km) southwest of Kashgar. The lake, at 12,464 feet (3,800 m), is dwarfed by towering peaks on either side. The waters are breathtakingly serene and a sight to be witnessed. You can overnight here in one of the lakeside yurts for a proper assessment.

You could spend weeks here, and five-day hikes can be arranged from Kashgar. Otherwise, locals will gather with horses for ventures around the lake. Beyond the lake, the road to Tashkurgan passes gorgeous pastures.

Tashkurgan is an eight-hour bus ride from Kashgar. The town is the capital of an autonomous Tajik County, a fascinating border land of cultures and moods. Though diminutive, Tashkurgan's importance was once greater than its size suggests; it often acted as a cornerstone of Great Game politics. Its most famous attraction is the **ruined fort.** Beyond lies the Khunjerab Pass and Pakistan. On the Pakistani side, things get rougher, and there's greater danger from falling rocks (and stones thrown by children). The best season to visit is summer; Tashkurgan lies at an elevation of more than 11,000 feet (3,350 m).

Vehicles can be hired in Kashgar to take you to both the lake and Tashkurgan. Remember to schedule a return for the next day (ask at John's Information Service & Café in Kashgar, see p. 322). ■

Hotan

Also known as Khotan, the oasis city of Hotan (Hetian) lies at the southern extremity of the Taklimakan Desert, washed by a number of jade-bearing rivers. To the south are the ragged Kunlunshan, and the surrounding land is scarred with the withered remains of ancient cities. Hotan is celebrated in China for its indigenous jade, silk, and carpet production.

Like many Silk Road cities in Xinjiang, Hotan was a thriving center of Buddhism before the arrival of Islam in the eighth century. The **Hotan Museum (Hetian Wenbowuguan),** just south of the remains of the old city walls, contains relics that eluded the antique collectors. Among the clutter lie two fascinating mummified bodies like the ones that can be seen in Ürümqi (see pp. 314–315).

Drop in on the **Sunday market** in the eastern part of town for its textures of local life. Hotan, one of the principal suppliers of nephrite jade in China, is renowned for the quality of its green silicate. You may see jade being carved and polished around town, and the main street has a large number of jade shops and stalls.

A statue of Mao overlooks People's Square in Hotan.

At the beginning of the 20th century, European adventurers explored the ruined cities around Hotan, unearthing Roman coins. Hotan's rich pre-Islamic kingdom was formerly embellished with fabulously ornamented Buddhist temples and monasteries. The nearest remains of this prosperous epoch are the ruins at **Yurturgan (Yuetegan),** 6 miles (10 km) to the west, and **Malikurwatur (Malikewate),** 16 miles (25 km) to the south. Despite their former importance, both cities have collapsed under the weight of time, leaving little to posterity. ■

Hotan

312 B1

CITS Visitor Information

23 Tamubake Xilu

0903 202-6090

Chinese Jade

Nephritic jade was first discovered in river deposits in Xinjiang. Its color (generally green) depends on the concentration of metallic oxides present. Its oily feel differentiates it from jadeite, which has a glassy smoothness and impurities that make it white, emerald green, and blue. The jade often seen in Hong Kong is generally the much cheaper and more abundant fluorite (calcium fluoride).

Dunhuang

Dunhuang is an ancient oasis town in the parched deserts of western Gansu Province, sheltering one of the most significant treasure troves of early Buddhist art in China. The caves are only equaled in renown by the grottoes at Longmen and Yungang.

Trekking through the Singing Sand Dunes

VISITING THE CAVES: Getting there and back is easy by minibus from Mingshan Lu in Dunhuang. Bear in mind that you will probably need at least a whole day here as there is a vast amount of detail to explore. Winter trips are not advisable because of the extreme cold.

When Buddhism first entered China, Dunhuang lay on a principal trade route along which flowed emissaries from myriad cultures: Turkish, Mongolian, Christian, Manichean, and Buddhist from Central Asia. The town marked a confluence of artistic styles and philosophies, becoming an important center of Buddhism and a place of devout pilgrimage. Even Hellenistic elements made their way into the art of Dunhuang, via Gandhara in North India.

The most famous grottoes are the **Mogao Caves (Mogao Shiku)** that pierce the desert cliff faces 15 miles (24 km) southeast of Dunhuang. Begun in the fourth century A.D., the caves were gradually adorned over a period of six centuries with paintings and effigies of Buddha, filled with religious manuscripts, and then mysteriously sealed in the 11th century.

It was not until 1900 that the caves were rediscovered, revealing a collection of 50,000 drawings and scrolls. Among these were not only Buddhist sutras but Taoist, Nestorian, and Zoroastrian documents. Collectors acting for large museums in the West were among the first to get wind of their discovery. Further damage was done by refugee White Russians who were forced by the Chinese to hole up in the caves. Subsequent efforts have been made to preserve the color and condition of the frescoes in the 492 caves. Some 45,000 frescoes remain, together with more than 2,000 statues.

The Grottoes

The Mogao Caves are kept behind locked doors, which makes access troublesome. An English-speaking guide opens a selection of caves, a service included in the ticket price. Each cave contains statues of Buddha or bodhisattvas. Representations of Sakyamuni were popular in earlier ages, evolving into a later preference for the salvationary Buddhas, such as Guanyin.

The caves of the Northern Wei are replete with the otherworldly and delicately featured Buddhas characteristic of this era. The earlier figures reveal foreign influence, giving way to the more noticeable Chinese effects of the Sui caves.

Unlike their earlier Northern Wei counterparts, the caves of the Tang dynasty emphasized the art of bodhisattva statues. Tang craftsmen were responsible for almost half of the caves. Other caves, such as **Cave 465,** show scenes of Tantric sexual union and are off-limits, unless you pay a hefty fee.

Highlights: Cave 96 contains a statue of Buddha, 113 feet (34 m) high seated behind the frame of a huge wooden pagoda. This is the Buddha of the future, the Maitreya Buddha. Figures stand on a platform inside the huge **Cave 16,** reached by a passageway adorned with Song bodhisattvas. The adjoining **Cave 17** contained many of the manuscripts that were plundered when the grottoes were rediscovered. **Cave 257** displays typical work from the Northern Wei, telling stories of Buddha's life (in this case the Deer King fable). In **Cave 259,** effigies of Buddha have that distant look sought by Wei craftsmen, and a definite Indian influence in the contours and styling. **Cave 148** has a 55-foot (16.5 m) Buddha, dispensing a final piece of wisdom before entering nirvana.

The entry fee includes an English-speaking guide, who can cast light on these parables in stone. Photography is not allowed. Take a flashlight. Before you tour the caves, it might be worth visiting the Dunhuang Research Centre, where exhibits explain how the caves were discovered and what remains in them.

Crescent Moon Spring & Singing Sand Dunes

About 4 miles (6.5 km) south of Dunhuang is the **Crescent Moon Spring (Yueyaquan),** a lake fed by a spring, set among colossal sand dunes that swirl around the oasis town. You can climb the **Singing Sand Dunes (Mingshashan)** (see sidebar below) for breathtaking views, wander through the setting on a camel, paraglide, or sand surf, all for a fee. ■

EXPERIENCE: Singing Sand Dunes

Several of the cafés in Dunhuang can arrange excursions into the magnificent Singing Sand Dunes, including camel rides and overnight tent camping. Rent a bike from John's Information Service & Café *(22 Mingshan Lu, tel 0937 882-7000)*. Make the trip late in the afternoon when the dunes are cooler. Charley Johng's Café *(21 Mingshan Lu, tel 0937 388-2411)* also arranges longer expeditions across northwest Gansu Province and into Xinjiang.

Dunhuang
Map 313 C2
CITS Visitor Information
Address: 32 Mingshan Lu
Tel: 0937 882-3312

Mogao Caves
Map 313 C2
Address: 15 miles (24 km) southeast of Dunhuang
Price: $$$$

International Dunhuang Project
For information on cave treasures at Dunhuang
www.idp.bl.uk

Singing Sand Dunes
Map 313 C2
Price: $$$

Jiayuguan Fort & Around

While the industrial town of Jiayuguan holds few surprises itself, its fort, 4 miles (6.5 km) to the east, is a monumental culmination to the story of the Great Wall. This spectacular structure traditionally marks the barrier's westernmost extremity.

Jiayuguan Fort
- 313 C2
- Closed 12:30 p.m.–2:30 p.m.
- $$

Overhanging Great Wall
- 313 C2
- $

July 1st Glacier
- 313 C2
- $$

Despite the fort's fame as the terminus of the Great Wall (see pp. 89–94), older Han dynasty sections stretched farther west into the Gobi desert. The vast structure was not built until 1372, soon after the establishment of the Ming dynasty.

The fort controlled the route through the Jade Pass that threaded the Silk Road between the Qilianshan and Black Mountains into this part of Gansu. The Taoist sage Laozi (see p. 54), apocryphally journeyed on his ox through this pass en route to the west. Some say he reached India and became Buddha.

The fort's illustrious **gate towers** rise 35 feet (10.5 m) from the desert. Inside is an assortment of buildings, including a temple and a theater where Qing troops were entertained. You can climb the walls and stroll along the **battlements.** Also included in the price is admission to the informative **Great Wall Museum.**

INSIDER TIP:

The fragile Buddhist frescoes and sculptures at Dunhuang are just a train ride away from Jiayuguan Fort.

—ZHANG YONGJUN
Former researcher, Dunhuang Academy

A reconstructed section of wall, the **Overhanging Great Wall (Xuanbi Changcheng),** lies a few miles north of the fort.

Twelve miles (19 km) east of Jiayuguan is a group of **tombs.** The area is studded with burial mounds, but only some are open, 20 miles (32 km) northwest of Jiayuguan. Most were built during the Wei and Western Jin dynasties.

To escape the summer heat, take a taxi or minibus 80 miles (129 km) south to the **July 1st Glacier** in the chilly heights of the snowcapped Qilianshan. ■

Mao's Words Meet the Gobi Winds

Chinese visitors to Jiayuguan Fort will notice, but probably ignore, the Maoist slogans decorating some of its buildings and walls. Unable to read Chinese, most foreign visitors will not even notice them. And, in fact, some of the slogans have disappeared almost completely. Bleached of their color over the passing decades and scrubbed by the relentless Gobi winds, they survive only as shadows on the brick work and discernible only to a very keen eye.

Slogans painted on walls away from the winds will last longer, but without retouching, they too will eventually vanish. In the meantime, they survive as fascinating examples of China's recent political heritage.

Lanzhou & Around

Lanzhou, capital of impoverished and rugged Gansu Province, was an important staging post on the Silk Road. The corridor of commerce led through the province, leaving a strong regional culture of Buddhist cave art in its wake.

Liuijiaxia Reservoir Canyon, Lanzhou

There's not much to see in Lanzhou itself, but the **Gansu Provincial Museum (Gansusheng Bowuguan)** displays an intriguing collection. The world-famous Han horse of Wuwei, a statue of a flying steed, is the showpiece item. The museum also has an exhibition charting the history of the Silk Road, marked by compelling pieces that made their way into China from Byzantium.

White Pagoda Hill (Baitashan) is an attractive climb capped by a temple of the same name. It lies on the northern bank of the Yellow River, on which Lanzhou sits. **Five Spring Hills Park** to the south is linked to the heights of **Lanshan Park** above by a cable car *($)*.

Forty-six miles (74 km) to the southwest of Lanzhou, at Yongjing, are the carved Buddhist caves of **Binglingsi** *($$)*. The works are chiseled from the walls of a gorge above the Yellow River. The artistic feat was begun in the Northern Wei dynasty, with additions by succeeding dynasties, especially the industrious Tang, Song, and Ming. On display are large effigies of Buddha with attendant wall paintings.

The caves can be visited as a day trip from Lanzhou by taking a three-hour bus ride from Lanzhou followed by a one-hour speedboat ride to the grottoes; ferries also ply the route but are much slower (3.5 hours each way). Winter puts an icy clamp on all ferry tours to the caves because the water is too low.

Xiahe and the **Labrang Monastery** (see p. 330) can also be reached from Lanzhou. ■

Lanzhou
- 313 D1

CITS Visitor Information
- 10 Nongmin Xiang
- 0931 883-5566

Gansu Provincial Museum
- Xijin Xilu
- Closed Mon.
- $

THE AIR: The air quality in Lanzhou (which has a large petrochemical industry) is poor. A report by the Washington-based World Resources Institute lists Lanzhou as having the world's most polluted atmosphere. Bear this in mind if you are asthmatic or have other breathing difficulties.

Xiahe & Labrang Monastery

The prayer flag–garlanded town of Xiahe nestles deep in southwestern Gansu Province, a spiritual beacon turned toward Lhasa. For many, arrival at the Lamaist Labrang Monastery is akin to setting foot in Tibet. Most wayfarers depart Xiahe with fertile memories of a divine enclave and an enchanting sanctuary.

Xiahe
313 D1

Labrang Monastery
313 D1
Xiahe
$

Almost 10,000 feet (3,045 m) above sea level, Xiahe is a long strip of a town abutting the Daxia River. The community wraps itself around the **Labrang Monastery (Labulengsi),** huddled in the center of the town, ringed by a pilgrim's way.

The Labrang Monastery, a flourishing retreat of Tibetan sacred culture far removed from the Chinese knot surrounding it, managed to escape the worst excesses of the Cultural Revolution. It dates back to 1709 and the time of the first Jamyang (the reincarnating Buddha of the monastery). Approximately one thousand monks live here, and six institutes delve into the arts of Buddhism, religious philosophy, astrology, and other esoteric disciplines. There are devotional temple buildings, the monks' living quarters, and a museum, in addition to the institute buildings.

INSIDER TIP:

When visiting towns and cities throughout China, head to a park in the early morning for a glimpse of locals practicing tai chi.

—ALISON WRIGHT
National Geographic photographer

The interiors of the Tibetan monastery buildings are lit with the soft glow of candles, which pick out Buddhist effigies and sacred volumes, monks at prayer, and frescoes. A disastrous electrical fire in 1985 gutted the **Assembly Hall,** but it has since been rebuilt.

Many Western travelers report being warmly received by monks at Labrang and welcomed into their living quarters; you can enter the monastery, however, only as part of a tour with a guide.

At festival time, nomads and pilgrims swarm to the monastery and pitch tents in the surrounding grasslands. The most significant event is the Monlam Festival (4th to 16th day of the first lunar month, just after the Tibetan New Year). It includes the custom of displaying a huge cloth painting or *thangka* of the Buddha, dancing, and an exhibition of Tibetan butter sculpture.

Other noteworthy festivals are held in the second, sixth, seventh, and ninth lunar months (like the Chinese, Tibetans use the lunar calendar).

Opportunities also exist for bicycle and bus trips to the valley, lakes, and yak-grazing grasslands around Xiahe. Most hotels offer bicycle rental. ■

Yinchuan

Yinchuan ("silver river") is an attractive, clean, and easygoing city, capital of the poor and parched Ningxia Hui Autonomous Region. Summers are ferociously hot and winters savage; the unrelenting aridity of the region drives communities to cluster along the life-giving artery of the Yellow River.

Situated on the Lanzhou-Beijing railroad line, Yinchuan is divided into a new town (Xin Cheng) and an old town (Lao Cheng) with most of the city's features and areas of interest in the old town. The two towns are about 5 miles (8 km) apart.

Old Town

A number of monuments in the old town recall Yinchuan's glory as capital of the nomadic Tangut Xi Xia dynasty, which was wiped out by Ghenghis Khan. The predominant ethnic group here are the Hui, Muslim descendants of Silk Road merchants.

Many sights can be seen on foot. Part of the old **Chengtian Monastery,** the **Ningxia Museum (Ningxia Bowuguan)** assembles fragments from the Xi Xia dynasty and items from Hui culture. You can climb up the monastery's brick pagoda.

The old **Drum Tower (Gulou),** on Jiefang Dongjie (the main road running east–west), is just to the west of the **Yuhuang Pavilion (Yuhuangge),** a tower dedicated to the Jade Emperor (see p. 83).

Haibao Pagoda (Haibaota), also called the **North Pagoda (Beita),** lies in the north of the city. It is housed among temple buildings, inside one of which reclines a 23-foot (7 m) Buddha.

The Xi Xia dynasty erected tombs near Yinchuan.

Around Yinchuan

Historical remains scatter throughout the countryside. The Xi Xia emperors are entombed about 30 miles (48 km) to the west. These **tombs (Xixiawangling)** can be visited by trips arranged by CITS (*$*) or by hiring a taxi. These dusty and solemn crypts lack the majesty of other imperial tombs, but they evoke the passing of the dynasty.

Buses run the 12 miles (19 km) to **Yongning** to the south of Yinchuan. Outside town stands the imposing Ming dynasty **Najiahu Mosque (Najiahu Qingzhensi),** busy on Fridays but quiet at other times of the week.

The **Yuhuang Pavilion** in **Pingluo,** 37 miles (60 km) to the north, is another temple structure dedicated to the Jade Emperor. ■

Yinchuan
Map 313 D1
CITS Visitor Information
116 Jiefang Xijie
0951 504-8006 or 0951 504-5555

Ningxia Museum
32 Jinning Nanjie
$ $

Baotou & Around

The city of Baotou, on the northern loop of the Yellow River, may seem little more than an industrial smudge across the map of Inner Mongolia, where few travelers linger, but there is a satisfying assortment of temples. More significant, the symbol of Mongolian national identity, Genghis Khan's Mausoleum near the city of Dongsheng to the south, urges exploration.

More than one thousand monks once lived at Wudangzhao Monastery.

Baotou
313 D2

Mausoleum of Genghis Khan
313 D1
$$$
1.5 hours to Dongsheng by bus, then 2 hours by minibus to mausoleum

Temple hunters should head out of town for the Qing dynasty **Wudangzhao Monastery (Wudangzhao)** *($)* in the mountain foothills 40 miles (64 km) northeast of town. The Tibetan-style Yellow Hat Sect lamasery is wonderfully laid out along passages dividing buildings, with gloomy halls and dark interiors. Staring into the darkness slowly brings the occasional ogrelike statue and diabolical painting to life, along with a host of Buddhist effigies.

For those with an interest in the bloodthirsty chieftain, homage can be paid at the **Mausoleum of Genghis Khan (Chengjisihanling)** outside the city of **Dongsheng,** 68 miles (110 km) to the south. This is the place to get the core of the Mongolian identity in focus. Mongolians travel from all over the far-flung and disparate lands of Inner and Outer Mongolia to pay their respects to the man who set the world ablaze and placed China under the yoke of the Yuan dynasty. The mausoleum has naturally taken its place as an icon of Mongolian nationalism and cultural identity.

The domed buildings, dating from the 1950s, were restored after Cultural Revolution damage. Inside, offerings from visitors are laid in front of a statue of Genghis Khan. Adjacent halls accommodate the remains of his wife and one of his sons. Periodic ceremonies at the mausoleum further indulge the legacy of the man. ■

Hohhot

Hohhot is the capital of steppe-covered Inner Mongolia, lashed by merciless and forbidding winters. A thriving corner of temple architecture survives here, demonstrating the Mongolians' energetic liaison with Tibetan Buddhism.

The name Hohhot originates from its Mongolian name, meaning "blue city." The prospering modern city is today largely Han in character, but evidence of its Mongolian identity can be discerned in the occasional Mongolian script on street signs.

Temples lie in the old part of town to the southwest. **Dazhao Temple** *($)*, off Danan Jie, is the region's premier lamasery, albeit tainted by commercialization. The hall at the rear is a compelling, authentic feature.

The active **Xiletuzhao Temple** nearby, a rather dusty relic with mild Tibetan features, includes a large white **dagoba (stupa).**

The group of brick pagodas at the **Five Pagoda Temple (Wutasi)** rise together from a stone base, carved with Tibetan, Mongolian, and Chinese script.

The Chinese-style **Great Mosque (Qingzhen Dasi),** on Tongdao Jie to the north, marks the confluence of Hohhot's Muslim community. Opposite, on Binhe Lu to the west of Tongdao Jie, the brisk **Bird Market (Binhe Lu Niaoshichang)** sets up its stall on the weekends.

For an understanding of the local culture, visit the intriguing **Inner Mongolia Museum (Neimenggu Bowuguan),** where you'll find yurts (see sidebar p. 317), clothing, and even a mammoth skeleton dug up in the northern part of the province. The **Zhaojun Tomb (Zhaojunmu),** 6 miles (10 km) south of the city, is the crypt of a Han dynasty imperial concubine. There are fine views of the surrounding countryside.

The **grasslands** beyond town lure tour groups. Most of these tours offer contrived evenings in yurts. The nearest grasslands are at **Xilamuren,** 50 miles (80 km) away; taxis can take you there. Shop around for the best price.

The lively summer festival of Naadam, usually held in mid-August, is marked by traditional Mongolian sports such as wrestling and horse racing. ■

Hohhot
Map 313 E2

CITS Visitor Information
✉ 95 Yishuting Nanjie
☎ 0471 680-1710

Five Pagoda Temple
✉ Wutasi Houjie
$ $

Inner Mongolia Museum
✉ Hulunbei'er Lu (at intersection with Zhongshan Donglu)
$ $

EXPERIENCE: Horseback Riding on the Mongolian Grasslands

The nearest grasslands to Hohhot are at **Xilamuren,** around two hours by bus from town. Although the area is quite developed for tourists, there is ample opportunity to hop on a horse (for an hourly fee) and ride off into the grasslands; it's worth paying more for longer on horseback so you can put distance between yourself and the overdeveloped reception area. Round off the day with an evening meal of roast lamb around a campfire and spend the night in a yurt *(ger)*. Buses run to Xilamuren from Hohhot throughout the day; alternatively, tours can be booked through CITS (see above) in Hohhot.

More Places to Visit in Inner Mongolia & the Silk Road

Grasslands

For those who want a glimpse of yurts and a more authentic way of life, CITS, CTS, and hotels in Hohhot can arrange tours to the grasslands. Although you'll need to visit Outer Mongolia to see the real thing, this is the closest you'll get in China itself.

CTS Visitor Information ✉ Inner Mongolia Hotel, Wulanchabu Lu, Hohhot ☎ 0471 230-8056

Hami (Kumul)

The predominantly Han city of Hami in the east of Xinjiang has an attractive Uighur quarter that resists creeping industrialization. If traveling on the Lanzhou/Ürümqi railway, you could jump off here and seek out the **Muslim King Tombs (Huiwangmu)** in the southwest part of town.

Map 313 C2 **CITS Visitor Information** ✉ Building No. 1, Hami Binguan

INSIDER TIP:

The Gansu village of Langmusi *(map 313 D1)* has two Tibetan monasteries and strong Tibetan traditions. You can reach it from the nearby town of Hezuo.

—DAMIAN HARPER
National Geographic author

Linxia

Formerly an important Silk Road staging post, the minaret-studded town of Linxia, southwest of Lanzhou (see p. 329) is noted mainly for its markets and Muslim Hui character. The busy streets throng with people of the Dongxiang and Bao'an minorities. The Taoist **Wanshou Temple** in **Beishan Park (Beishan Gongyuan)** offers views over town.

Map 313 D1

Maijishan

The Maijishan **Buddhist cave carvings** are not far from the town of Tianshui in the southeast corner of Gansu Province. Two cliffs are pockmarked with 194 caves ornamented with figures of Buddha and religious frescoes, ranging from Northern Wei work to the Qing dynasty. The effigies in cave No. 133 of the Western Cliff are the most renowned. Bring a flashlight.

Map 313 D1 $ $$

Zhangye

Midway between Wuwei and Jiayuguan in Gansu is the old garrison town of Zhangye. The spectacular 111-foot (34 m) reclining Buddha in the **Giant Buddha Temple (Dafosi)** is the largest of its type in China.

Forty miles (64 km) south of Zhangye, in the village of **Mati** ("horse's hoof"), activity centers on the cliffside **Mati Temple** *($$)*, a regional focus of the Yellow Hat Sect of Tibetan Buddhism (see sidebar p. 304).

Map 313 D1 **CITS Visitor Information** ✉ 60 Xianfu Nanjie ☎ 0936 824-3445

Zhongwei

The impressive **Gao Temple** is the main reason to come to Zhongwei in Ningxia Province. Comprehensive tours also include the **Shapotou Desert Research Institute,** trips along the Yellow River on leather rafts, and fragments of the **Great Wall** in the Tenger Desert. **Shikong,** not far east of Zhongwei, contains some rather neglected ancient **Buddhist cave art.**

Map 313 D1 **Ningxia Zhongwei Travel Service** ✉ 7 Xi Dajie ☎ 0953 701-2620

The three provinces formerly known as Manchuria—home of Manchu artifacts, Russian heritage, and a glittering winter festival

The Northeast

Introduction & Map 336–337

Dalian 338

Shenyang 339

Tianchi 340–341

Feature: Tigers in China 342–343

Experience: Seeing Manchurian Tigers Up Close 343

Harbin & Around 344-346

More Places to Visit in the Northeast 347–348

Experience: Skiing in the Northeast 347

Hotels & Restaurants in the Northeast 384–385

Statue of Abahai, founder of the Qing dynasty

The Northeast

Cast as an industrial hinterland, the hardy northeast has a reputation for being rather pedestrian. The toughness of the people, however, finds dramatic reflection in an often savage landscape of frozen rivers, volcanic lakes, and jagged mountains. The northeast is also the cradle of the magnificent Manchurian civilization, with a piecemeal history of Russian control that has left a grand inheritance of dashing architecture.

While perhaps this should not be your first port of call in China, the northeast is often unjustly sidelined by travelers. The temple-watcher and sunseeker may leave the northeast feeling cheated, but if you're in search of wilder climes and textures, you will be fully rewarded.

Tourists enjoy dressing in period costumes at the Imperial Palace in Shenyang.

The dynamic port city of Dalian drags the whole of the southernmost Manchurian province of Liaoning behind it. The city has preserved museum-piece Russian architecture while also acting as a blueprint for a new and adept China. This southern upstart eclipses its landlocked provincial capital, but heavily industrialized Shenyang discloses a precious vein of imperial splendor in its Manchurian palace and tombs.

Border fanatics can traipse over to Dandong to gaze North Korea in the face and possibly even penetrate the idiosyncratic state.

The large cities of Jilin Province, sandwiched between Russia, Inner Mongolia, and North Korea, are of the heavyset industrial cast, but the volcanic lake of Tianchi fires the province with mystery. High up in a beautiful alpine landscape of firs and flowers, the lake is within a sublime range of ragged rocks, with crystal waters and melting snow, straddling the border with North Korea.

The exciting and mysteriously named Black Dragon River hints at the shaman origins of these parts of China. The borderlands of Heilongjiang ("black dragon river") Province still support shaman-believing minorities.

Winter's big chill puts many transportation options literally on ice. The icy season, however, yanks the curtain off the glittering Ice Lantern Festival in the province's attractive capital, Harbin. This unlikely but very popular tourist season drags Chinese from all over the land to watch the locals swimming in thick holes cut into the ice-bound river. You will need a strong constitution, but some people say it's very good for the heart. ■

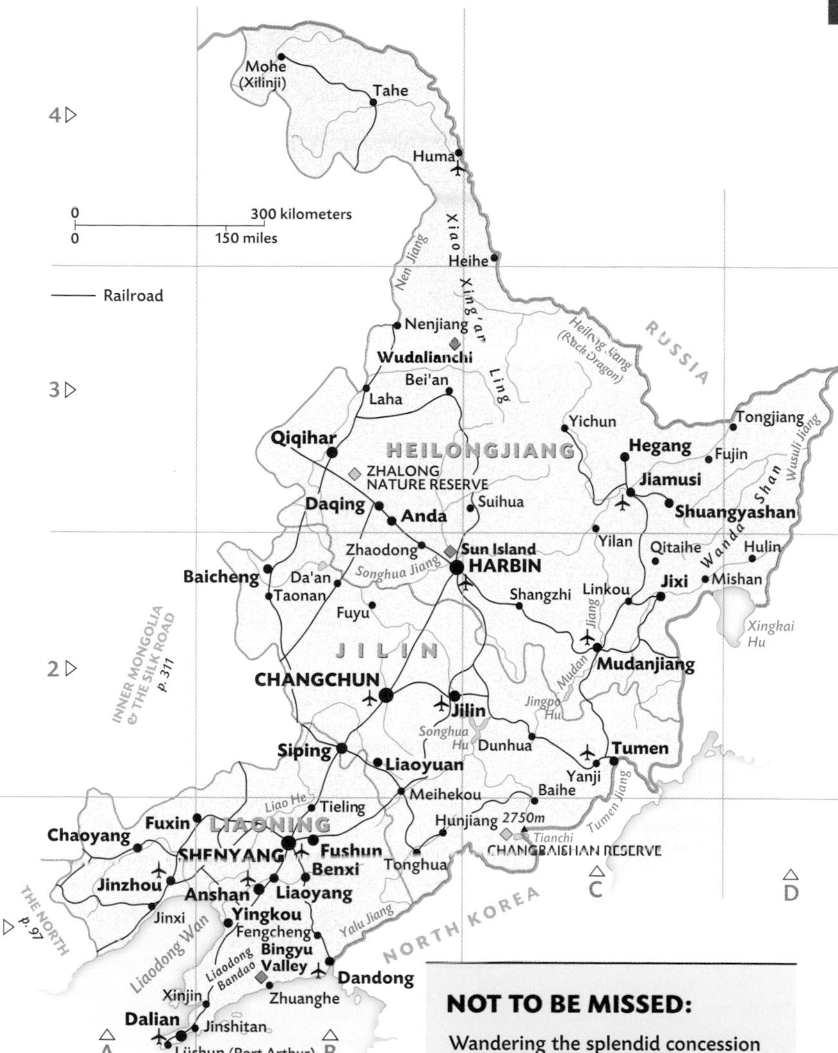

Area of map detail

Beijing

NOT TO BE MISSED:

Wandering the splendid concession districts of Dalian **338**

The Manchu splendor of the Imperial Palace in Shenyang **339**

Views over Tianchi, China's sparkling volcanic lake **340–341**

Visiting Harbin in midwinter for its glittering Ice Lantern Festival **346**

Exploring the northernmost tip of the region at remote Mohe in Heilongjiang Province **347**

A journey to the North Korean border at Dandong **347**

Dalian

The port city of Dalian fosters an upbeat spirit forged from the zeitgeist of reform. This oasis of enviable prosperity, clean buses, lawns, and streets is loved by its citizens. With some grand examples of Russian and Japanese architecture, Dalian is also famed for having China's sole unit of policewomen patrolling on horseback.

Dalian
337 A1
CITS Visitor Information
145 Zhongshan Lu
0411 8367-8019

The ice-free port of Dalian was granted to Russia as a concession in 1898, only to slide into the jaws of the Russo-Japanese War (1904–1905). **Port Arthur** (now known as Lüshan), just to the south, was the scene of Russia's humiliating naval defeat in 1904. Dalian remained under Japanese control until the end of World War II, when it again passed into Russian hands, returning to China in the 1950s.

INSIDER TIP:

For some of Dalian's best seafood, head for the restaurants around Xinghai Square near the beach.

—BO WANG
President, Chinatour.com International

Much of Dalian's charm is a result of its architecture, and building enthusiasts will enjoy the spectacle of **Zhongshan Square** (actually a circle). The city converges on this point, with major streets radiating from here. The wonderful **Dalian Hotel** is a picture. Across the way is the domed Bank of China Building, and the classical pile next to it is the **People's Cultural Hall.**

Decorated with beautiful lawns, **People's Square (Renmin Guangchang)** to the southeast of Zhongshan Square is a popular congregation point for Dalian's citizens. Much of the architecture in what was formerly called Stalin Square is of the monumental, Soviet-style variety. **Tianjin Jie,** east of Shengli Square, is a popular shopping drag.

Around Dalian

Dalian is surrounded by a wealth of beaches, and there's also some dramatic scenery down by the coast. About 3 miles (5 km) southeast is the pebbled beach of **Bangchuidao.** In the vicinity are some splendid vistas, including a stirring stretch west along the coastal road to Laohutan Park, overlooking the sea from the clifftops. Farther along the coastline to the west is a string of sandy beaches—**Fujiazhuang, Silver,** and **Gold.** Farther westward again lies the attractive beach of **Xinghai Park.**

Thirty-seven miles (60 km) north of Dalian is **Jinshitan** ("golden stone beach"), a popular weekend getaway noted for its rocky landscape formations, caves, and beach area. ■

Shenyang

Shenyang is the capital of Liaoning Province and is the most southerly of the three provinces that made up Manchuria. Historically, the city was fought over by the Russians and Japanese and was left a ragged mess after World War II. Today it is principally driven by heavy industry.

Strong echoes of the Forbidden City (see pp. 60–66) exist in the design of the walled **Imperial Palace,** dating from 1625, although it is mainly Manchu in concept. The palace is smaller than its counterpart in Beijing, but it was here that the Qing dynasty was inaugurated in 1636 (before going on to consume the rest of China).

The buildings are laid out on a north–south axis, with halls on either side displaying weapons and exhibitions of ceramics and jade. Notable halls are the **Dazheng Hall, Chongzheng Hall,** and **Wensu Hall.** Some were used for the shamanistic rites that formed the belief system of the Manchu (see pp. 37–38).

Historically bedeviled by a lumbering state enterprise sector, Northeast China has, in recent years, been confronting the harsh truths of economic reform by heavily shedding industrial jobs. Shenyang has its own potent symbol of political backwardness, a **Mao statue** in Zhongshan Square in the center of town—evocative of all that was wrong with China, when the proletariat gaily reached for a future that never quite dawned. Inspect it closely, for there are numerous stories etched into the stone, but the overall message is the unmistakable folly of megalomania.

The North Tomb stands at the heart of Beiling Park.

In the northern suburbs is the magnificent **North Tomb (Beiling).** Entombed here is Abahai (1592–1643), founder of the Qing dynasty, and his wife. Built in the mid-17th century, with later additions, the tomb rests at the end of a statue-lined avenue inside a vast park. Southeast of North Tomb, off Chongshan Lu, is the restored **North Pagoda,** with halls that are decorated with a series of celestial images and statues.

Five miles (8 km) east of Shenyang is **East Tomb** *($),* the final resting place of Abahai's father, Nurhachi (1559–1626). The Manchurian chieftain (also known as Kundulun Khan) brought together the scattered northeastern Jurchen tribes into the capable fighting force that invaded China. ■

Shenyang

337 B1

Liaoning Tourism Bureau

113 Huanghe Dajie

0428 8680-7316

Imperial Palace

Shenyang Lu

$$

North Tomb

Taishan Lu

$

Tianchi

Tianchi ("heaven's lake") in Jilin Province—one of the prime sights of China's northeast—is a volcanic lake on the North Korean border in the Changbaishan ("ever white mountains") Reserve. The perfect antidote to congested cities, it is a blessed retreat for volcanologists, geologists, and adventure seekers. Its photogenic panorama includes snarling rock formations, a mirror-smooth lake, emerald green pines, and all the drama of a volcanic presence.

Accessible only in summer, the volcanic lake of Tianchi is a dramatic destination.

Tianchi
337 C1

China's largest nature reserve is a treasure chest for the natural scientist. The region is thickly covered in deciduous and coniferous forests, with alpine meadows on the higher reaches. There is also a wealth of medicinal plants and animal species, along with rare sightings of the Manchurian tiger (see pp. 342–343).

The peaks of the **Changbai Mountains (Changbaishan)** (*$$$$*) cluster around a number of dormant volcanoes and crater lakes in a belt that has heavy precipitation. The highest peaks (8,000 feet/2,438 m) of this beautiful range are covered by snow for half the year. Rivers plunge from Tianchi, cascading into spectacular waterfalls.

The lake is the goal for most travelers, but many do not take the time to fully appreciate the spectacle. At 7,200 feet (2,195 m), the air is getting thin, but not dangerously so. Three miles (5 km) from north to south and just over 2 miles (3 km) from east to west, the lake is 8 miles (13 km) in circumference. Clear weather adds sharp definition to the jagged rocks and peaks and makes for dramatic images.

Before You Go

The Changbai Mountains cleave Liaoning and Jilin Province from North Korea. Tianchi straddles the North Korean border, and the lake cannot be circumnavigated, so stick to the northern perimeter. The whole region on the Chinese side in Jilin is called the Korean Autonomous District, populated by Chinese of Korean ancestry.

Chinese tour buses descend on Tianchi for swift assaults on the area. Chinese visitors habitually discard Styrofoam lunch boxes, chopsticks, and plastic water bottles, festooning the crags with detritus. To escape the main concentration of tourists, chart your own route around the immediate reaches of the lake. It's relatively simple to get away from tourists; they tend to herd together at the main assembly point.

If you set off around the lake on your own, watch out for sharp rocks, as well as dense cloud cover that can suddenly appear. Weather at such high elevations can change quickly. You can rent People's Liberation Army (PLA) overcoats and waterproof jackets from the gaggle of women who wait at the Tianchi bus stop.

Guides are at hand for those who want to access the highest reaches of the lake for sublime views down to the water. Take a wide-angle lens to encompass the whole circle of the volcano's rim (but don't bother to hike up if the weather is not good).

Getting to the Reserve

Getting to Changbaishan, formerly called Puxianshan after the bodhisattva, is quite a journey. The lake is realistically accessible only from late June to September, when the ice and snow that grip the volcano for the rest of the year melts. The occasional snowmobile makes the trek out from Baihe (a very small town closest to the mountains) during the frozen months, but this can be extremely hazardous. For the intrepid, guesthouses are plentiful in the Changbaishan region.

You can get to Baihe either from Shenyang (see p. 339) via Tonghua, or from Dunhua (see map p. 337). Alternatively you can fly to Yanji, head back to Antu, and then get a bus to Baihe. From Baihe, buses leave from the square in front of the train station (from 6 a.m. to noon). Or you can rent a car with a driver. ■

The Tianchi Monster

Some people say that beneath the surface of Tianchi lurks a Loch Ness–style monster—or monsters. For more than a century, visitors to the lake have claimed to have sighted the monster, and argument has raged along the lake shore about just what kind of creature it might be: seal, buffalo, or something else?

Recent sightings at Tianchi describe a creature with a human-like head, long neck, and gray body. A researcher at the National Academy of Science in North Korea has a theory: The creatures are the mutant offspring of trout released into the lake by North Koreans more than 50 years ago.

Tigers in China

China offers a precarious abode to the tiger, one of the world's most fascinating and majestic species. As in other countries, the tiger in China is on the verge of extinction in the wild. The 20th century saw three subspecies wiped out completely in other countries, largely because of hunting, forest degradation, and encroachment on habitat.

The huge Siberian tiger is a protected species struggling for survival in China's northeast.

The tiger casts a spell over the Chinese imagination. It belongs to one of the 12 animals of the Chinese astrological calendar and is represented by wood in the cycle of the five elements (see p. 256). The white tiger denotes the guardian of the eastern direction in *fengshui* (see p. 256). The markings above and between a tiger's eyes resemble the Chinese character for "king" *(wang)*, three horizontal lines joined by a vertical line. The tiger lends its movements to one of the more vigorous of Shaolin *gongfu* (see pp. 124–125) styles, where the tendons of the forearm and hands are conditioned like steel and the legs strengthened for leaping.

Tiger parts are prized in the Far East for their alleged medicinal properties, and consequently Chinese tigers have been trapped to feed the traditional medicine market in China, Taiwan, Japan, Korea, and Chinese communities the world over. China is a signatory to the Convention on International Trade in Endangered Species of Wild Fauna and Flora (CITES). The market within China has been banned, but illegal hunting continues.

Because they are so elusive, it's hard to determine exactly how many tigers still exist in the wild. Today Chinese tigers are being enticed to return to sanctuaries, reserves, and zoological parks. The Siberian Tiger Park (see sidebar below) is part of a large program to breed animals in captivity and release them back into the wild. There are problems of inbreeding with captive animals, especially where there is a very small natural population in the wild.

INSIDER TIP:

The Siberian Tiger Park near the city of Harbin is home to the largest contiguous population of tigers in the world. The park is affiliated with China's Northeastern Forestry Institute.

—KIRSTEN CONRAD
Conservationist

Siberian Tiger

The world's largest tiger, the Siberian (Manchurian or Amur) tiger *(Panthera tigris altaica)*, is a fascinating specimen. Sadly, it dwindles on the cusp of extinction in its homeland of Manchuria, Russia, and North Korea, but it has been seen in the Changbaishan region of China's northeast, which adjoins North Korea.

A far larger and heavier cat than other tiger subspecies found in China, with males weighing up to 800 pounds (360 kg) and reaching 9 feet (2.8 m) in length, it has a yellowish-orange fur ribbed with black stripes. Its eyes are yellow, and its night vision is excellent (for hunting).

Siberian tigers are on the Endangered Species List, and considerable conservation efforts are being made to rescue them from certain oblivion. These animals are not very sociable, tending to lead solitary lives. They mate in winter and spring, and the litter typically consists of two to four cubs.

Only 200 to 300 tigers survive in the wild (mostly in Russia), with another thousand or so in zoological parks and reserves such as the Siberian Tiger Park in Harbin. In captivity, they can expect to live much longer than in the wild and yield offspring.

Indochina Tiger

The Indochina tiger *(Panthera tigris corbetti)* is possibly vanishing more rapidly than any other subspecies. About 1,200 to 1,800 of these animals survive in China, Vietnam, Laos, Myanmar (Burma), and Thailand. The only specimens that now exist in China are a handful of animals that live in reserves in Xishuangbanna in southern Yunnan Province (see pp. 276–279).

South China Tiger

About 30 South China, or Amoy, tigers *(Panthera tigris amoyensis)* survive in the wild, with about 50 in captivity. This is the only tiger indigenous to China. It numbered 4,000 in the early 1950s but was almost bludgeoned into extinction when it was hunted as a pest. Evidence of its existence has been found in the provinces of Hunan, Fujian, Guangdong, and central Jiangxi.

EXPERIENCE: Seeing Manchurian Tigers Up Close

The Siberian Tiger Park ***(88 Songbei Jie, Songbei District, Harbin, tel 0451 8808-0098, $$)*****—China's largest reserve for the breeding of the Siberian tiger—allows visitors to observe these impressive animals from walkways or from within the confines of minibuses driven through the grounds. More than a hundred cubs are born here every year. Built in 1996, the park is located 10 miles (15 km) north of Harbin** **(see pp. 344–346).**

Harbin & Around

A stately memento of Russia's former influence here, Harbin is capital of Heilongjiang ("black dragon river") Province. The city's visual appeal is great: Russian Orthodox churches, onion domes, and fancy pockets of cobbled streets. Take a deep breath of the glacial Harbin winter and feel it punch you in the chest. This is the season when Harbin's picturesque streets swarm with out-of-towners, lured by the twinkling of the city's renowned Ice Lantern Festival.

The Church of St. Sophia glows beautifully at night.

The attractive historic quarter lies north of the train station. The China Eastern Railway put Harbin on the map, linking it to Vladivostok (250 miles/402 km southeast) and to Russian-controlled Dalian (see p. 338). Russian influence periodically waned (such as after the disastrous Russo-Japanese War), but there was a continual presence here (with Russians outnumbering the Chinese for a while). Today, the hotels that flank the train station overflow with Russian visitors, who flock to Harbin to shop.

The **Church of St. Sophia (Dongzheng Jiaotang)** is the premier example of Russian Orthodox church architecture in China. Some churches, most notably the small, wooden **St. Nicholas,** failed to survive the battering of wars and the Cultural Revolution. Fortunately, this proud and charismatic church in Harbin remains despite the foliage that indiscreetly pokes from rooftop niches.

Built in 1899, the church is a gorgeous pile of round arches and red brick capped by a turquoise dome and adjacent towers, where Byzantine curls and flourishes confidently assert themselves. Within the church is the **Harbin**

Unit 731

During World War II, Japan wanted to beat the West in the race to develop unconventional means of warfare. The Unit 731 Japanese Germ Warfare Division aimed to develop a host of pathogenic weapons—including anthrax, plague, typhoid, and cholera—using British, Chinese, and Korean prisoners of war as test subjects.

At the end of the war, fleeing Japanese troops left the remains of the infamous Unit 731 experimental germ-warfare laboratory behind. Today, this horrible scar of the war with Japan operates as a museum. Located around 10 miles (16 km) to the south of Harbin, the **Unit 731 Museum** *(closed 11:30 a.m.–1 p.m., English or Mandarin audio guide: $)* tells the story of Unit 731 through the few buildings that remain and a film presentation.

The display is not as engrossing as its equivalent in Nanjing (see pp. 160–163), as it consists only of a few rooms and remnants of the base, but for historians of the war with Japan, and for those keen to better understand why many Chinese still harbor suspicions about the Japanese, it is essential viewing.

Architecture & Arts Centre, with photographs on local history.

Zhongyang Dajie, in the heart of **Daoliqu,** Harbin's most graceful neighborhood, is the main boutique-lined street that conveys shoppers to the Songhua River. Wander past Russian spires and turrets and around the side streets that lazily meander off Zhongyang Dajie. The street is currently undergoing a defiant modernization of boutiques and fast-food restaurants, yet the local mood has not been completely trampled.

The misnomer of the **Modern Hotel** disguises its 1906 origins. This civilized Russian hotel is a stylish place brimming with character. Pop inside for a feel of the place and a glance at the lobby, or reserve a room.

Standing at the northern end of Zhongyang Dajie by the Songhua River, the modern **Flood Control Monument** is a reminder that Harbin often suffered serious flooding. The embankment that runs along the river has a ponderous Russian ring to it: **Stalin Park** (much of the northeast still has one foot in the era of Sino-Soviet camaraderie). This is the main area of Harbin's summer tourist industry, jammed with vendors selling hot sweet potatoes and cooked river snails. Boats of all kinds chug to and fro across the river to Sun Island.

In winter, arctic temperatures transform the river into a glacier. The locals show their contempt for the cold by carving holes in the ice and swimming in the slush that lies beneath.

INSIDER TIP:

Harbin's flourishing Nangang District *(near the Dragon Tower on Changjiang Lu)* boasts stellar local cuisine.

—BO WANG
President, Chinatour.com International

Harbin
Map 337 B2
CITS Visitor Information
✉ 68 Hongjun Jie
☎ 0451 5366-1191

Church of St. Sophia
✉ Toulong Jie (near Diduan Jie)

Modern Hotel
✉ 89 Zhongyang Dajie
☎ 0451 461-5846

Zhaolin Park

To the east is Zhaolin Park (Zhaolin Gongyuan), the annual venue for the **Ice Lantern Festival (Bingdengjie)** *($$)*. This very popular fairyland extravaganza sees carvers shaping ice to look like animals, fantastic creatures, and historic buildings. The sculptures are colorfully illuminated from within.

The festival is held from January to March, but it's worth phoning a hotel in Harbin to check before you sled over. If you do visit Harbin in winter, prepare yourself for the extreme temperatures; buy a good padded down jacket, thick gloves, lip balm, long johns, and warm boots.

Sun Island

Sun Island (Taiyangdao), on the opposite side of the Songhua River, sounds welcoming, unless you happen to arrive in midwinter. Spring and especially summer promise long walks and camping opportunities. The island is a huge expanse of parks, paths, and the excellent **Siberian Tiger Park (Dongbeihu Linyuan),** a noble attempt to stave off extinction for the massive Siberian tiger (see sidebar p. 343).The park's objective is to rear tigers for their eventual release into the wild, where numbers have fallen precipitously.

The park is an excellent opportunity to see the animals outside of a typical zoo setting, but be prepared before you go. The tigers may appear institutionalized and quite ill prepared for reintroduction into the wild. More disturbing for some visitors is the live feeding show: Even cattle are fed to the tigers, which asphyxiate the cattle first with their powerful jaws before feeding. ■

Locals exercise in Stalin Park on the bank of the Songhua River.

More Places to Visit in the Northeast

Bingyu Valley

Located about 150 miles (240 km) north of Dalian (see p. 338), Bingyu Valley (Bingyu Gou) is a gully of precipitous rock formations pinched by forested mountains. It's an impressive natural wonder but only worth considering if you have a lot of time, because traveling there is a lengthy operation. The best way to reach Bingyu Valley is by bus from Dalian to Zhuanghe, and then by minibus.

337 B1 $$$$

Black Dragon River

Snaking along the border between China and Russia, this river lends its dark name to Heilongjiang Province. The Black Dragon River penetrates areas of Siberian forest, and summer boat trips can be made between **Tongjiang, Heihe,** and **Huma.** This is the shrinking homeland of minorities such as the Shaman Oroqen and the Daur. You can't go farther north than **Mohe,** also on the river, from where you can witness the aurora borealis (northern lights). Winter trips along the Black Dragon River are out of the question as the temperature can fall as low as minus 60°F (-50°C).

337 C3

Changchun

Changchun is the rather dull capital of Jilin Province. Its **Puppet Emperor's Palace & Exhibition Hall** is where you can unearth vestiges of the life of Henry Puyi, the last emperor. His lamentable life was retold by Italian film director Bernardo Bertolucci in his epic film *The Last Emperor* (1987). The puppet king was manipulated by the Japanese and stage-managed as emperor of Manchukuo (Japan's policy of taking over China began with Manchuria) in 1934, with Changchun as its capital. The palace was his residence and is a spiritless reminder of the tragicomedy of Puyi's life. You can walk through his domain of small rooms and trace his unfortunate story through the photos on the walls. An exhibition at the rear deals frankly with the Japanese occupation of Manchuria.

337 B2 **CITS Visitor Information**
Changbai Shan Hotel, 1448 Xinmin Dajie
0431 566-6541

EXPERIENCE: Skiing in the Northeast

While few people come to China specifically to ski, if you find yourself in China during the winter months, consider a trip to one of the nation's increasingly popular ski slopes. China's largest and best equipped ski resort is the Sun Mountain Resort *(tel 0451 5345-8888, www.yabuliski.com)* at Yabuli. A former hunting ground, the resort is located about 112 miles (180 km) southeast of Harbin (see pp. 344–346) in Heilongjiang Province. Trains and buses run to Yabuli from Harbin, or you can book passage online. Sun Mountain Resort, which is suitable for both novices and experts, has hosted a variety of national and international skiing competitions. It was largely revamped in 2009, which resulted in upgraded facilities but also increased prices. The skiing season here runs from November to late March, but note that the weather can get pretty bitter here, and temperatures have dipped far below zero.

Dandong

The city of Dandong borders North Korea on the Yalu River, and its main attraction is the opportunity to get close to the Democratic People's Republic of Korea. This can be done by taking a speedboat along the river to peer at a sad panorama of idling soldiers and barking dogs. The half-destroyed bridge that crosses the rivers between the two countries is known as the Sino-Korea Friendship Bridge and was the work of the U.S. Air Force during the Korean War, during which 200,000 Chinese died.

Magnificent **Fenghuangshan** is a mountain decorated with charming temples. It lies 32 miles (51 km) to the northwest of Dandong. **Hushan Great Wall** marks the eastern beginning of the portion of the Great Wall built during the Ming dynasty.

337 B1 **CITS Visitor Information**
20 Shiwei Lu 0415 213-5854

Jilin

The city of Jilin (known in the West as Kirin) is most famous for its winter phenomenon of ice-rimmed trees. Water from the nearby hydroelectric plant flows into the river and keeps it from freezing; the evaporating water condenses on the frozen branches of riverside trees, encrusting them with ice.

Locals are proud of the **Catholic church,** on the north shore of the Songhua River by Jilin Bridge, which suffered a dressing-down during the Cultural Revolution. Not far east

INSIDER TIP:

Hunchun, 251 miles (404 km) from Jilin, is only a half-hour drive from the borders of North Korea and Russia.

—KIRSTEN CONRAD
Conservationist

of the church, the magnificent **Confucius Temple (Wenmiao)** displays an interesting exhibition featuring the archaic methods of the imperial examinations. The main temple presents a statue of Confucius surrounded by sacred objects.

337 B2 **CITS Visitor Information**
1 Chongqing Jie 0432 244-1304

Jingpo Lake

As with many natural marvels in China, Jingpo Lake (Jingpo Hu) is a victim of its own popularity. Legions of Russians and Chinese descend here to navigate boats around this island-studded lake on the Heilongjiang–Jilin border, and a resortlike character results. To capture a more meditative mood, rent a fishing rod (in summer), and find yourself a quiet perch on the shore.

337 C2

Xingcheng

The walled town of Xingcheng (see map p. 337), near the Liaoning coastline, is well worth exploration, especially if you are interested in historic towns. Most of Xingcheng is modern and unattractive, but the old city walls—with a gate at each of the cardinal points—preserves the architectural logic of this Ming dynasty defensive settlement built on the wrong side of the Great Wall.

Xingcheng's city walls were built in 1428 and remain intact, which is quite unusual for old towns across China. The best thing to do is climb the walls and hike around them, which takes a couple of hours but gives the best views. The town's drum tower is naturally positioned at the heart of the old town, while Xingcheng's venerable Confucius Temple dates to the 15th century. In the stifling summer months, cool off by wandering along the sandy beaches on the Bohai coastline beyond town, reachable by bus.

Xincheng can be reached by bus or train from Beijing, Shenyang, or Shanhaiguan. If you want to spend the night, finding a hotel in town is a fairly straightforward endeavor.

Travelwise

Planning Your Trip 350
How to Get to China 351–352
Getting Around 352–354
Practical Advice 354–360
Emergencies 360
Hotels & Restaurants 361–385
Shopping 386
Entertainment 387
Museums 388
Language Guide 389
Menu Reader 390

A young family enjoys an outing at the North Tomb in Shenyang.

TRAVELWISE

PLANNING YOUR TRIP

Climate & When to Go

China is a vast land with large disparities in climate, so you have to decide where you are going before deciding when. Summer is hot the land over, humid along the southern coastline and in the Yangtze region, and arid in the northwest. Rains are generally heavy in July and August, especially in the south. The southern reaches of Guangdong, Guangxi, and Yunnan Provinces, Hong Kong, Macau, and Hainan Island all lie in a tropical zone, with sweltering summer humidity. Late autumn, winter, and early spring are comfortable seasons to visit Hong Kong and Macau.

Typhoons can scuttle travel plans, blowing in along the southern coastline (and Hainan Island) during the summer.

Winters north of the Yangtze River are bitterly cold, especially in Tibet, the northwest, Inner Mongolia, and the northeast. High-elevation destinations will be very cold in winter, and many places such as Jiuzhaigou and Tianchi are inaccessible during winter months. You would not want to visit Jiayuguan or Dunhuang in Gansu Province during winter, and the Turkic northwest is just as inhospitable. On the other hand, Harbin in the northeast makes a tourist season out of its harsh winter.

Beijing endures hot summers and bitterly cold winters, but it can realistically be visited in any season, although autumn—a very short season in the capital—is definitely the best.

Shanghai is miserable in winter and extremely hot and muggy in summer, with spring and autumn the best seasons to visit.

Central and southern Yunnan Province experience a relatively mild winter. Hainan Island is very comfortable in winter.

Festivals & Holidays in the People's Republic

Traveling in China during festival season can be a spectacular way to see the nation in full celebration. Note, however, that hotel prices rise during festival season, and bus tickets can be in short supply, especially during Chinese New Year. Moreover, domestic travelers flood tourist sights around China during these holiday periods, making it a very busy time to travel for leisure.

Yuandan (Western New Year) January 1
Chun Jie (Chinese New Year, Spring Festival) Falls anywhere from late January to early March, but usually February (most significant festival of the year; five-day holiday)
Yuanxiao Jie (Lantern Festival) Fifteenth day of first lunar month (usually mid- to end of February)
Qingming Jie (Tomb-Sweeping Festival) One-day holiday in first week of April
Wuyi Laodong Jie (Labor Day, May Day) May 1, three-day national holiday
Wusi Qingnian Jie (International Youth Day) May 4
Duanwu (Dragon Boat Festival) Fifth day of fifth lunar month (normally held in June)
Liuyi Ertong Jie (Children's Day) June 1, holiday for schoolchildren
Communist Party Founding Anniversary July 1
Zhongqiu Jie (Mid-Autumn Festival) Fifteenth day of the eighth lunar month
Guoqing Jie (National Day) October 1, state holiday, one-week holiday

Both Hong Kong and Macau celebrate other festivals; for details check with the Hong Kong Tourism Board *(tel 0852 2508-1234, www.discoverhongkong.com)* or the Macau Government Tourist Office *(tel 0853 2831-5566, www.macautourism.gov.mo)*.

Further Reading

Before traveling to China, it's worth reading a few titles to arm yourself with a vision of your destination. Suggestions include the following:

The Hermit of Peking, by Hugh Trevor-Roper. Classic investigative scholarship into the colorful life of Edmund Backhouse, the eponymous hermit and Sinologist.
The Classic of the Way and Its Power (Daode Jing), by Laozi. Taoist classic.
Tao: the Watercourse Way, by Alan Watts. An insightful introduction to the Way and its mysteries.
When a Billion Chinese Jump, by Jonathan Watts. A sober study of China's environmental travails by the excellent journalist from the *Guardian.*
Foreign Devils and the Silk Road, by Peter Hopkirk. Thrilling history of antiques hunters in Chinese Turkistan in the early 20th century.
Red Dust, by Ma Jian. Off-beat China travelogue.
The Writing on the Wall: China and the West in the 21st Century, by Will Hutton. An incisive analysis of China's economic model of development.
The Search for Modern China, by Jonathan Spence. Huge post-Ming history lovingly executed by well-known Sinologist.
The Tyranny of History: The Roots of China's Crisis, by W. J. F. Jenner. Critical look at the oppressive nature of China's traditions and the nation's conservatism.
Wild Swans, by Jung Chang. Popular biography charting the trauma of recent Chinese history.

Concise English-Chinese, Chinese-English Dictionary, Oxford University Press. Excellent, exhaustive, concise dictionary.

What to Take

Travel as lightly as possible. A collapsible umbrella is useful. Take jeans, or a light pair of quick-dry trousers, a waterproof jacket, and waterproof or durable shoes. A sun hat, sunscreen, first-aid kit, bug repellent, and lip balm are also necessary.

A thick, padded jacket, long underwear, warm socks, and gloves are essential if you plan to travel in North China, Tibet, the northeast, Inner Mongolia, or the northwest in winter. A durable backpack is recommended for more independent travel.

You will find a phrase book, money belt (essential), Swiss army knife (important), alarm clock, small flashlight, and camera helpful. Diarrhea tablets can be lifesavers on a long-haul bus trip. Also pack antiperspirant/deodorant (hard to find).

Most hotels provide disposable toothbrushes and toothpaste, but it's best to bring your own. Name or business cards are a good idea as the Chinese take giving and receiving cards very seriously.

Reading material is essential: Much of the fiction available in China is hard-going. Hong Kong is a good place to stock up on literature. An MP3 player or iPod is crucial for long bus and train journeys.

If you enjoy photography, stock up on batteries (go for well-known brands such as Duracell) in the cities and towns as prices can be extortionate at tourist sights.

HOW TO GET TO CHINA

Passports & Visas

A valid passport and visa are required for entry into China. Your passport must be valid for at least six months after the visa expiration date. Thirty-day tourist visas (type L) are usually issued, visa prices are rising steadily, and there may be handling charges. Contact your nearest Chinese Embassy for more information.

If you are planning to stay for a long period, register your passport with your nearest embassy or consulate (see p. 360).

Make a photocopy of your passport (the page with your photo, passport number, and other details) in case of loss or theft while in China; contact the Public Security Bureau (see p. 355) and your nearest consulate or embassy immediately if you discover that your passport has been lost or stolen. Your passport will also serve as an invaluable proof of identity while in China, but don't hand it over as a deposit if you can avoid it.

If you want to extend your stay in China, take your visa to the Public Security Bureau (PSB; see p. 355) for consideration (it will charge a small fee). You will need a letter of invitation from a host company if you wish to work in China.

Hong Kong

A valid passport is needed to visit Hong Kong. British citizens can stay visa-free for six months. Australian, Canadian, United States, New Zealand, Western European, and European Union citizens can stay for three months. Citizens of a number of Middle Eastern, Southeast Asian, and former Soviet-bloc countries require a visa. If you are entering Hong Kong from China, you will need a reentry visa to return to China. Contact the Hong Kong Immigration Department *(2nd Floor, Immigration Tower, 7 Gloucester Rd., Wan Chai, tel 0852 2852-3047, www.immd.gov.hk).*

Macau

A valid passport is needed to visit Macau. Visitors from the European Union can stay for 90 days; citizens of the United States, Canada, Australia, New Zealand, Israel, and South Africa can stay for 30 days. Hong Kong residents and Portuguese passport holders can stay for one year without a visa. Nationals of other countries need a visa, which can be obtained on arrival in Macau. Entering Macau from China, you will need a reentry visa to return to China.

Chinese Embassies & Consulates Abroad

Australia

Chinese Embassy 15 Coronation Dr., Yarralumla, ACT 2600, tel 02 6273-5848, fax 02 6273-4878, www.au.chineseembassy.org

Canada

Chinese Embassy 515 St. Patrick St., Ottawa, Ontario K1N 5H3, tel 613/789-3434, fax 613/789-1911, www.chinaembassycanada.org

Chinese Consulate 240 St. George St., Toronto, Ontario M5R 2N5, tel 416/964-7260, fax 416/324-6468, http://toronto.china-consulate.org; other consulates in Vancouver and Calgary

France

Chinese Embassy 11 Av. George V, 75008 Paris, tel 1 4952 1950, www.fr.chineseembassy.org

Consular Department 20 Rue de Washington, 75008 Paris, tel 1 5375 8805

Hong Kong

Visa Office Ministry of Foreign Affairs of the PRC, 5th Floor, Low Block, China Resources Building, 26 Harbour Rd., Wan Chai, Hong Kong Island, tel 0852 3413-2300

Italy

56 Via Bruxelles, 56-00198, Rome, tel 06 8413-458 or 06 8413-467

Japan
3-4-33 Moto-Azabu, Minato-ku, Tokyo, tel 03 3403-3388, www.china-embassy.or.jp

Netherlands
Willem Lodewijklaan 10, 2517 The Hague, tel 070 306-5061, fax 070 355-1651, www.china embassy.nl

New Zealand
2–6 Glenmore St., Wellington, tel 04 4721-3821, www.china embassy.org.nz (consulate in Auckland)

United Kingdom
49-51 Portland Pl., London, tel 020 7299-4049, fax 020 7636-2981, www.chinese-embassy.org .uk; 43 Station Rd., Edinburgh EH12 7AF, tel 0131 337-3220

United States
Chinese Embassy 3505 International Pl., NW, Washington, DC 20008,tel 202/495-2266, www.china-embassy.org

Chinese Consulate 100 West Erie St., Chicago, IL 60654, tel 312/803-0095, fax 312/803-0110, www.chinaconsulate chicago.org

Chinese Consulate 443 Shatto Pl., Los Angeles, CA 90020, tel 213/807-8088, fax 213/ 380-8091, http://losangeles .china-consulate.org

Chinese Consulate 520 12th Ave., New York, NY 10036, tel 212/244-9456, fax 212/ 502-0245, www.nyconsulate .prchina.org

Chinese Consulate 1450 Laguna St., San Francisco, CA 94115, tel 415/852-5941, fax 415/563-0494, www.chinaconsulatesf.org

Airports
Most international flights arrive at Beijing's **Capital International Airport** *(tel 962-580, within Beijing only; flight info tel 010 6454-1100; http://en.bcia.com.cn)* or in Shanghai, Guangzhou, Hong Kong, or Macau.

In Beijing, you can take the Airport Express, a bus, or a taxi from the airport to the city *(45 min.)*.

Shanghai's **Pudong Airport** *(tel 021 96990, www.shairport.com)* is linked to the city by bus, taxi, Maglev (see sidebar p. 189), and subway (the latter connects with Hongqiao Airport in the west of town).

Hong Kong International Airport *(tel 0852 2181-8888, www.hkairport.com)* at Chek Lap Kok is connected to the city by airport train, airbus, or taxi.

Rail
China can be reached by rail from Europe aboard the **Trans-Mongolian Express** or the **Trans-Manchurian Express,** which terminates in Beijing. Both routes connect Beijing to Moscow, from where you can continue to Western Europe. This is a fascinating, but time-consuming, means of reaching China (five or more days). Returning to Europe this way is popular.

Contact **CITS** (China International Travel Service) in Beijing *(Beijing International Hotel, 9 Jianguomennei Dajie, tel 010 6512-0507)*. Tourist or transit visas must be arranged. A number of travel agents outside of China can arrange tickets; White Nights *(www.wnights.com)* is an example.

GETTING AROUND
Traveling Around China
By Air
This is the most sensible option for those who have little time, but tickets are expensive. China's airline, CAAC, has been split into regional airlines (such as China Southern Airlines, China Southwest Airlines), with a much improved safety record over the past decade.

Air tickets can generally be bought quickly through CITS, your hotel travel desk, or airport ticketing offices. Discounting is common on domestic tickets, although you may have to pay full price to large cities on the weekend. Tickets are one-way, and delays are common.

All provincial capitals have their own airports, as do numerous large cities and popular tourist destinations. Airports vary in distance from the city center, but most have buses that convey passengers to air ticketing offices in town; taxis are abundant. The better hotels have shuttle buses that wait for passengers at the airport. Departure tax (Y50) is generally included in the ticket price. Insurance is offered as an optional extra. Airline meals on domestic flights are generally of very poor quality.

By Bicycle
Bicycle *(zixingche)* travel is one of the best ways around town, unless you are in Chongqing (the only city without bikes due to its steep inclines). Ask if your hotel has bike rental—check the brakes and the tires before setting out.

Many large cities and tourist destinations, such as Beijing, Hangzhou, Suzhou, Nanjing, and Yangshuo, have cheap bike rental. If you plan to stay in China for a while, buy a bike and join the throng. Cheap and efficient bicycle repairmen line the road throughout Chinese cities. Theft is very common, however, so lock your bike.

By Boat
Maritime and river boat routes are dwindling due to alternative forms of transportation. Hydrofoils ply the waters between Hong Kong and Macau, and boats still journey to Hainan Island, from Yantai to Dalian, and from Shanghai to Putuoshan, but many other routes have ground to a halt. The

most popular river route is along the Yangtze River; boats can be taken along the Li River and the Grand Canal, but elsewhere routes are limited.

By Bus

Large government-run buses *(gonggong qiche),* private buses, and minibuses travel all over China. You will find that bus tickets are easier to procure than rail tickets, but as with rail tickets, you can only travel single and not round-trip. State-owned buses leave on schedule and are the cheapest option, but they are also the most uncomfortable.

Private buses offer travelers more comfort and often have such luxuries as onboard toilets. Sleeper buses navigate the night roads through the land. Private minibuses *(xiaoba)* are faster but run mainly on local routes, often departing only when they are completely full with passengers. Private minibuses can become very crowded, making travel both uncomfortable and dangerous.

Buses can be dangerous in the more peripheral regions of China—such as Tibet, Yunnan Province, Hainan Island, and parts of Sichuan Province—and should be taken only if there is no other alternative. Driving standards are appalling, and accidents are common. Keep a close eye on your bag and belongings, especially on sleeper buses.

Urban bus fleets in the larger cities are being slowly modernized, but aged beasts survive. Cities such as Beijing, Shanghai, and Dalian sport modern fleets. Pay the driver as you board, or pay the ticket seller on the bus. Trips within cities are cheap, and most trips should cost around Y1–Y2 (about 12 cents). Some cities also have electric trams (e.g., Hong Kong).

Outside Hong Kong and Macau, bus stops have signs only in Chinese, making navigation difficult. Keep a close eye on your belongings, as the crowded environment is perfect for pickpockets.

By Car

Until recently, it was impossible for tourists to rent cars while traveling in China, but this is now possible as long as you undertake a short test and fill out the necessary paperwork upon arrival at either Beijing Capital International Airport or Shanghai Pudong International Airport. Once you have done so, you will be issued a three-month temporary driving license.

Cars can be rented at a number of places in Hong Kong, but the excellent public transportation system obviates the need. If you want to drive, contact Avis *(Shop 46, Peninsula Centre, 67 Mody Rd., Tsim Sha Tsui, tel 0852 2890-6988)* or the Hong Kong Tourist Board for further information.

In Macau, vehicles can be rented from Avis Rent-A-Car *(tel 0853 2833-6789, www.avis.com.mo)* at the Macau Ferry Terminal.

If you can't face the anarchic chaos on the roads, hire a car with a driver from your hotel. Alternatively, negotiate a fee with a taxi driver (see By Taxi section below). In Beijing, try Hertz at Jianguo Hotel *(5 Jianguomenwai Dajie, tel 0800 810-8833),* or ask for help at your hotel.

By Pedicab

Pedicabs, or three-wheeled bicycles *(sanlunche),* offer a relatively cheap but slow amble around town. Because they are often operated by old men, it's usually cheaper, and far quicker, to take a taxi. Rip-offs are frequent, so if you do decide to take a pedicab, make sure you agree on an unambiguous price before setting off.

By Subway

China's metropolitan subway system *(ditie)* is growing quickly. The cities of Beijing, Shanghai, Hong Kong, Shenzhen, Guangzhou, Tianjin, and Nanjing all have systems; Xi'an and Hangzhou are soon to follow with subways of their own. Of them all, Hong Kong has the best system; Shanghai's is the world's largest. Light rail systems are also becoming increasingly widespread (e.g., Beijing, Wuhan, Shanghai). Trains are punctual, reliable, and cheap.

By Taxi

This is by far the fastest and most hassle-free way around town. Taxi rates vary but typically are Y5–Y12 ($1US–$2US for the first 3–4 km (1.8–2.5 miles) and from then on Y1.4–2 (20–30 cents) per kilometer (0.6 mile). Prices vary depending on the city and the size of the taxi, but it costs very little to travel around town by cab.

Taxis are ubiquitous and display a light when unoccupied. Insist that the driver use the meter *(dabiao).* Ask for a receipt, as the number of the cab will be upon it, which is important to have in case you leave anything in the vehicle or have cause for complaint. Tipping is unnecessary and sometimes refused. Do not expect the driver to understand any English except the names of the larger hotels.

Taxis can often be used to take you to places out of town cheaper than joining a tour. Drivers will charge a flat fee and may well expect you to pay for lunch.

By Train

Traveling around China by train *(huoche)* is a fun and exciting way to chart the land. The rapid development of the high-speed rail system throughout China means that major cities and large towns are far closer together time-wise; look out for C-, D-, G-, and Z-class trains, which are the fastest, most comfortable, and most convenient. Traveling by train is also a great way to practice your Chinese.

Try to buy your tickets early through your hotel travel desk—otherwise you can try your luck at the station, but expect a long line. Don't expect to obtain a ticket on the day of departure unless it's for a local train, and plan a few days ahead at all times (buying your outbound ticket as soon as you arrive at a destination is very good planning). Tickets are typically single trip, rather than return.

Standards of comfort are excellent on the high-speed express trains, but expect very basic conditions on older rolling stock.

Tickets come in various classes: hard seat *(yingzuo)*, soft seat *(ruanzuo)* on certain routes, hard sleeper *(yingwo)*, and soft sleeper *(ruanwo)*. Hard seat is fine for short journeys, but you will find yourself among watermelon seed shells, litter, and standing passengers waiting to pounce on your seat if you vacate it for an instant.

For journeys of more than five hours, a sleeper ticket is important. A hard sleeper ticket puts you on a reasonably comfortable bunk bed in a crowded, doorless, six-bed compartment in a carriage. You have a choice of upper *(shang)*, middle *(zhong)*, or lower *(xia)* berth. The middle berth is generally the best option as the lower bunk is used as a bench by all and sundry, while the top bunk is quite a climb and space is more limited.

Soft sleeper (much more expensive) puts you in your own four-berth compartment (with door). If you are traveling by sleeper, the ticket collector will come and exchange your ticket for a metal or plastic version, which will be swapped before you arrive at your final destination. You can often upgrade *(bupiao)* your ticket once aboard the train.

Traveling Around Tibet

Just reaching Tibet may be hard since it is periodically closed to foreign travelers (often in March), and travel within the region is restricted to certain areas.

The first thing you will need to obtain for travel to Tibet is a valid Chinese visa. When you apply for a visa in the Chinese Embassy in your country, the form will ask you to list which provinces and cities you plan to visit. If you plan to visit Tibet, putting this on your application may raise eyebrows among the officials at the embassy. Suffice it to say, you can always modify your itinerary as you see fit once you have arrived in China.

Because of Tibet's aim for autonomy from Beijing, China is highly sensitive to individual Western travelers roaming at will around the land. To control movement within the region, individuals are forced into tour groups (which charge high rates) on permits issued by the Tibet Tourism Bureau. Such permits can be purchased through travel agencies in China. This will get you to the Tibetan Autonomous Region (TAR).

If you want to travel outside the city of Lhasa, you will need a further Alien Travel Permit (ATP), issued by the PSB (see p. 355). The best way to obtain the permit is through a travel agency in Lhasa (see p. 301) so that you are officially part of a tour group. Destinations that do not require an Alien Travel Permit (at the time of writing) include Lhasa and Shigatse; travelers to the Everest Base Camp, Gyantse, and Samye Monastery will need a permit.

With the new railway, Lhasa is now linked by train to numerous stations in China, including Shanghai and Beijing. Flights to Lhasa depart from numerous domestic airports, including Beijing, Shanghai, Guangzhou, Chengdu, and Zhongdian. Travel agencies sell package deals including travel permits charged to your air ticket; the tour is nominal, and members later go their own way. The best time to visit Tibet is from April to June and September to November.

PRACTICAL ADVICE

Bargaining

Foreigners are often massively overcharged (especially in tourist areas), and bargaining is expected unless prices are clearly marked. Top-end hotels sometimes sell local wares (such as oil paintings) that you can find for a tenth of the price if you investigate local markets. If the item is unmarked, the seller may quote a price from out of the air. Feel free to haggle, but don't be pushy.

Communications

E-Mail, Internet, & Wi-Fi

Internet cafés *(wangba)* are plentiful in large cities and towns. Internet services in pricier hotels are overpriced. Very cheap Internet cafés are usually open 24 hours. Wi-Fi is also increasingly commonplace, especially in cafés, bars, restaurants, and hotels.

The Internet in China is obsessively monitored by a huge army of censors, but it is usually possible to get online to read Western newspapers. In Beijing and some other cities, you will be asked for your passport before going online at Internet cafés. Most hotels can provide fax service.

Language

Don't expect the people in China to understand English, but treat it as an enjoyable surprise when they do. Luxury hotels generally offer passable, but limited, standards of English. Youth hostels always have good English speakers, but cheaper hotels do not. Patience is an essential ingredient to communication success. Don't expect restaurant staff to understand you, and expect to do a lot of pointing.

You will quickly find yourself in a forest of Chinese signs with very few recognizable English words. A comprehensive phrase book is an essential companion. See the Chinese language sections (pp. 358, 389–390).

Post Offices

From China, airmail letters sent to the United States, Britain, and

Australia should take between four days and a week to reach their overseas destinations. Be sure to mark the envelope "airmail/par avion." Stamps are sold at the counter; there are no machines. Envelopes are often gumless; glue is available at the post office. Don't expect anyone to speak English.

As well as regular post offices, large top-end hotels have their own post offices; other hotels should have a mail service. Most cities and large towns have *poste restante* services, and larger hotels should hold mail until you arrive.

Telephone

If you are going to use a public telephone, it's best to buy a phone card *(dianhuaka)*. Prepaid cards come in various denominations and can be used for international calls; card phones are increasingly plentiful. If you can't find one, try the nearest large hotel.

For cell phone users, SIM cards can be bought from shops such as China Mobile or even at newspaper stands; you will get a phone number and around Y50 ($8US) worth of credit. Cards can be topped up with a credit charging card bought from the same kind of outlet. China's country code is 86.

Useful Numbers in China

International assistance	115
Local directory enquiries	114

Crime

Most travelers feel very safe while they are journeying through China. Most serious crime occurs between Chinese without the involvement of foreigners. Pickpocketing is a problem, however, so spread your money among a number of pockets and wear a money belt. If changing money on the streets, caution is strongly advised. When traveling on buses between cities, keep a close eye on your bag.

Not a crime as such, but be on the alert for English language learners who befriend foreigners (especially in Guangzhou and Shanghai) and lead them to expensive restaurants, where they are left to foot the bill for pricey meals and drinks. Also watch out for the fake art students who prey on tourists around sights such as Tiananmen Square in Beijing, shepherding them to overpriced art galleries.

The **Public Security Bureau** *(gonganju)*, more often called the PSB, is China's police force and an austere and bureaucratic organization par excellence. You can find PSB stations in Beijing *(2 Andingmen Dongdajie, tel 010 8402-0101)*, Shanghai *(1500 Minsheng Lu, Pudong, tel 021 6854-1199)*, and Guangzhou *(Jiefang Beilu, tel 0208 311-6688)*, though every city has a main PSB office, where you can report crime or extend your visa. You are unlikely to have a run-in with the PSB, unless you have overstayed your visa.

Culture

Banquets

If you are called upon to attend a Chinese banquet—enjoy it! In the middle of the dinner table is a small, circular table that is laden with all the dishes and rotated. If you are the guest of honor, the important dishes will be passed to you to sample. This can be a bit of a challenge, especially when specialties such as huge sea snails and snake sail into view, with all eyes upon your reaction.

Before the banquet begins, the host will have made sure that there is plenty to drink on hand. The preferred tipple is *baijiu,* a clear and ferocious spirit that hits like a sledgehammer. Too much of this drink at dinner will have you rapidly talking nonsense.

If you smoke, it is essential that you offer your pack to everyone around the table. It's bad form to guard your cigarettes, and generosity is essential. If your host smokes, a carton (never just a pack) of Marlboro or Dunhill will make you friends for life.

Beggars

Chinese economic reforms have removed many safety nets for society's more impoverished. Rural hopefuls travel to the large cities in search of work; some end up penniless and hungry. Foreigners are natural targets for beggars. They will gravitate toward you if you give money to other vagrants, and they collect outside temples.

Karaoke

The Chinese take karaoke *(kala OK)* very seriously. If you are entertained by Chinese at a banquet (see the Banquets section above), at some stage of the evening the karaoke equipment will be wheeled out and you will be exhorted to sing the one Western song on the menu (just pray it's not "Bohemian Rhapsody").

If you are checking into one of the cheaper hotels, inquire where the karaoke lounge is and ask for the room farthest from that point if you want any sleep.

Lining Up

Standing in line is an alien concept that is only slowly gaining ground in China. Be prepared to join a jostling mass with no beginning or end, all elbows and bellowing voices, and no referee. Polite attempts at lining up are generally trampled.

Settling the Bill

In China, meal bills are rarely divided up in the Western fashion, and the honor of paying typically falls on one person (it is not uncommon to see a polite scramble for the bill at the conclusion of a meal). Don't attempt to pay for your share, but make an attempt to pay for the entire meal yourself (which will probably be politely refused, unless you are the host).

Smoking
China is a tobacco company's paradise, and the country is largely addicted to nicotine. The authorities have tried to limit smoking in certain places, and the situation has much improved. Smokers on trains are now largely consigned to the carriage ends, but you will still see travelers light up on rural buses. If you dislike smoking, you may find China hard to stomach. If you smoke, most Chinese cigarettes are cheap and have a strong, dry flavor.

Spitting
Posters exhort against spitting and fines are sporadically levied on offenders, but spitting carries on wholesale, even in crowded buses and trains. Apart from being very unpleasant, this is a main transmission route for airborne diseases.

Taboos
Frank political discussions with Westerners are shunned by most Chinese people. The Chinese are not given to speaking openly about their concerns, and they may be sensitive to the implications of discussing such issues with you. It is tempting to proselytize when in China, but it leads nowhere.

Customs
If you are visiting China for six months or less, you may bring into the country two bottles of alcohol and 400 cigarettes or the equivalent in tobacco. If you plan to stay longer than six months, you may import four bottles of alcohol and 600 cigarettes or the tobacco equivalent.

Generally you may enter China with one of each of the following: camera, portable tape recorder, portable movie camera, portable video camera, and portable computer. A reasonable quantity of perfume is allowed for personal use.

Travelers to China should be aware that "articles which are detrimental to the political, economic, cultural, and moral interest of China" (apart from the obvious arms, explosives, poisons, etc.) are subject to wide interpretation, but most things that are not inflammatory should be admitted. The death sentence can be administered to drug traffickers.

If you are leaving China with any items that are of antique value, you should take them to the cultural administration department first for verification and issuing of an export license.

Electricity
China's electrical current is 220V, 50-cycle A/C. Plugs come in a variety of shapes (usually two or three flat or round pins), so a conversion plug is useful.

Entrance Tickets
Virtually all sights in China (museums, parks, temples, etc.) require that you buy a ticket. Prices are very reasonable, but for many sights these are going up way ahead of inflation and sometimes by as much as a hundred percent per year. Entrance to small temples should cost around Y5–Y10 ($1US–$1.50US), but drawcard temples can cost up to Y100 ($15US). Large outdoor destinations such as Huangshan and Wutaishan can be very expensive.

Female Travelers
China is generally a very safe travel destination for women, but, as with any other destination in the world, individual travel has its own set of risks. Sexual harassment exists in China, but cases are rare.

Health
In China's large cities, you can generally find decent medical assistance in time of need. Medical services in rural or far-flung regions, however, are usually far more basic.

Contact Organization
If you live in the United States and would like more information about health issues in China, contact the Centers for Disease Control and Prevention *(tel 800 311-3435, www.cdc.gov).*

Dental Care
It's a good idea to have your teeth checked and any work done before visiting China. Standards of dental care vary; expect only the most basic in remoter regions.

Diseases
Bilharzia/Schistosomiasis: This parasitic disease is caused by a worm living in contaminated water, found in South China and the Yangtze River basin. Worm larvae enter the skin, initially causing a rash and later fever, abdominal pain, diarrhea, and fatigue. When in China, stick to the hotel swimming pool.

Cholera: This intestinal infection caused by contaminated food is contracted mainly in areas of poor sanitation and is generally avoided if you follow the procedures described in the Food & Water section (see p. 357). The available vaccine offers little protection against cholera.

Diarrhea: Diarrhea *(la duzi)* is reaction to unfamiliar bacteria. It can be persistent and ruin a vacation. Avoid eating meat, and drink a lot of water to prevent dehydration. If problems persist for more than five days, or worsen, you may have dysentery.

Giardia: This parasite lurks in contaminated water. Symptoms are fever, nausea, rashes, and severe diarrhea. The condition is treatable with drugs.

Hepatitis C: There is no vaccine for Hepatitis C *(bing ganyan)*. Transmission routes are the same as for Hepatitis B (see Immunizations below), so avoid associated high-risk activities.

HIV: Precautions against HIV *(aisibing)* infection are the same as elsewhere in the world. Taking your own medical pack that includes needle/syringe is a good idea if traveling beyond the large cities. Take extra condoms if voyaging to rural regions of China as they can be difficult to buy. If you are HIV-positive, entry to China may prove difficult, and if you are planning to live or work in China for more than six months, you will require an HIV test.

Malaria: A parasitic disease spread by the bite of the female mosquito, malaria *(nueji)* is potentially fatal, causing fever and possible organ damage. The disease is not a large threat in China, but travelers to the tropical regions of Hainan Island and south Yunnan Province face a possible risk of contracting it. Visitors to the rural regions of the south and southwest during summer might face exposure, but malaria mosquitoes are virtually absent from China's cities.

If you are traveling to high-risk areas, discuss medications with your doctor. Otherwise, prevention is the best strategy. Using mosquito repellent (containing DEET), wearing long sleeves and pants, and using a mosquito net (preferably impregnated with insecticide), are all effective safeguards against malaria. Consult a doctor as quickly as possible if you suspect you have contracted the disease.

Environmental Health

Air pollution is a serious problem in China, largely because of increasing industrial and vehicle emissions in the rapidly expanding economy. Large cities such as Beijing, Lanzhou, and Jilin suffer from dangerous levels, especially in winter (on bad days equivalent to smoking two packs of cigarettes a day). Those with respiratory problems such as asthma should speak to their doctors before traveling and make sure they take sufficient medication with them.

Food & Water

Thoroughly wash fruit and vegetables bought at markets (human manure is used in agriculture). Avoid eating shellfish and seafood unless you are by the sea. Very spicy food is safer than mild foods. Eat more vegetable than meat dishes if possible. Chew your rice softly—occasional stones can lead to costly dental repairs.

Avoid drinking water straight from the tap, even in Shanghai. All hotels provide either mineral water *(kuangquanshui)* or boiled water *(kaishui)* in thermos flasks. Always buy bottled mineral water, available all over China, and take water purification tablets for emergencies.

Heatstroke & Sunburn

China's tropical south, southwest, and arid northwest can be extremely hot in summer; the rest of the country can also roast uncomfortably. Take sunscreen, sunglasses, and a wide-brimmed sun hat, and drink plenty of water. Prickly heat is caused by a blockage of the sweat pores. Heatstroke is caused by overheating, marked by headaches and a feeling of malaise, potentially leading to delirium and death.

High Elevation

High-elevation travel in China can be extremely cold, so take warm, waterproof clothing and shoes. Altitude sickness is also a risk, especially for travel in Tibet. Decreased oxygen levels and air pressure at elevations over 10,000 feet (3,000 m) can result in altitude sickness. Symptoms vary according to speed of ascent, age, fitness, and other factors and can include headache, nausea, breathlessness, and mental impairment. If suffering from altitude sickness, it is imperative to reach a safer elevation quickly. When traveling to Lhasa and beyond, spend two days gently acclimatizing. The risk of sunburn is also greater at high elevation.

Hypothermia & Frostbite

Parts of China can be dangerously cold in winter, especially the far north and at high elevations. Wind chill or wet clothing can make the situation rapidly worse. Hypothermia sets in when the body's core temperature drops. Symptoms include numbness, slurred speech, lethargy, and poor coordination; death may follow.

Frostbite may occur in temperatures below freezing. If visiting Tibet and other cold regions in winter, it is imperative to take adequate warm, waterproof clothing, gloves, and shoes. Long bus rides can prove fatal if a breakdown coincides with a deterioration in the weather, so take extra clothing and gloves.

Immunizations

First discuss what you may need in terms of immunizations with your doctor or nurse. Check that your immunizations for diphtheria, polio, and tetanus are up-to-date. Consult your doctor well in advance of when you plan to travel. The following immunizations are recommended:

Hepatitis A: In China, Hepatitis A *(jia ganyan)* is often spread through the consumption of contaminated food and water and in areas of poor sanitation.

Hepatitis B: China is a high-risk country for the contraction of Hepatitis B *(yi ganyan)*. The disease is spread through the same channels as HIV/AIDS (contaminated blood, sharing contaminated needles or syringes, and sexual activity). Avoid high-risk activities and take your own first-aid kit that has sterile syringe needles.

Typhoid: Immunization against typhoid (which is transmitted in areas with poor sanitation and contaminated food and water) is probably not necessary if you are staying in clean conditions while traveling in China. If you are unsure of your itinerary, however, err on the side of caution and get immunized.

Yellow Fever: Immunization against yellow fever is essential if you are traveling from an infected country.

Insurance

If you fall ill in China and expect to receive a high standard of care in a Chinese medical facility, health insurance is essential. Make sure that medical coverage in your travel insurance is adequate. If your stay in China is extended, take out international medical insurance before going.

Medical Care

Chinese state hospitals are basic, and they will treat you for a fee. The larger cities (Hong Kong, Macau, Shanghai, Guangzhou, Beijing, etc.) have private foreign clinics, where you can receive high levels of medical assistance (albeit costly). Taking out medical insurance before you travel to China is highly advisable.

Pharmacies are plentiful and can be identified by a green cross. Many Chinese pharmacies, like Watson's in Hong Kong and other large cities, sell prescription drugs over the counter.

Medical Conditions

Carry a record of any medical conditions you may have and the proper names (not just the trade names) of any prescribed medication you may be taking.

Language

Chinese is a tonal language, spoken as a mother tongue by approximately 1.2 billion people. The majority speak Mandarin, a dialect spread over much of North China and used nationwide as a lingua franca.

The most versatile Chinese dialect is Mandarin (*putonghua* or "common tongue"). You can use it in all parts of China (including Hong Kong and Macau), but as a very rough guide, you will find that the farther away you are from Beijing, the more widespread the use of other dialects. It is not worth trying to learn other tongues for other dialect *(fangyan)* regions, for even in other dialect areas such as Cantonese and Shanghainese, Mandarin is readily understood.

Cantonese is a dialect spoken in south China, specifically in Hong Kong, Macau, Guangdong Province, and parts of Guangxi Province. Mandarin is not easy to learn, but it's worth trying to pick up as much as you can during your trip.

Written Chinese

Alphabets use letters to make up the sounds of words. Written Mandarin is the only major language in the world without an alphabet. Instead it uses "pictures" or "characters" to describe the written word. Like Mandarin, other dialects of Chinese, such as Cantonese, also essentially use pictures.

Pronunciation

This guide has used Chinese names in pinyin to name places of note. Below are some of the pinyin pronunciations you should pay attention to:

Vowel sounds

a	as in father
ai	as in fight
ao	as in cow
ang	as in sung
e	as in duh
ei	as in weigh
eng	as in lung
i	"ee"; "er" sound after r, c, ch, s, sh, zh, and z
ian	as in yen
ie	as in yellow
ou	as in oak
o	as in more
u	as in noodle
ui	as in way
uo	as in wart

Consonant sounds

c	as in cats
ch	as in catch
q	in between "ts" and "ch"
r	as in run
s	as in shine
x	"s" as in sing
z	"ds" as in duds
zh	"dge" as in dredge

For useful words and phrases see pp. 389–390.

Media

Chinese-language Newspapers

The main Chinese newspaper is the *People's Daily (Renmin Ribao)*; it faces tough censorship, so reporting is one-sided. A clutch of similar papers exists, including the *People's Liberation Army Paper (Jiefangjun Bao)* and *Worker's Paper (Gongren Bao)*.

English-language Newspapers

The *China Daily* is China's English-language paper, and like the Chinese-language papers, it strongly reflects the Communist Party line.

The large five-star hotels generally have bookstores that sell the *International Herald Tribune, Newsweek, Time, Far East Asian*

Economic Review, and *Wall Street Journal* (sometimes trimmed of unappetizing opinion).

Some cities (Guangzhou, Kunming, Hong Kong, Shanghai, and Beijing) have enterprising local-events magazines that are worth picking up at expat bars.

The two leading Hong Kong newspapers—the *Hong Kong Standard* and *South China Morning Post*—are available in decent hotels throughout China.

Television

You will generally encounter Chinese television in your hotel room. Superior hotels will also provide CNN, MTV, and HBO (it is almost impossible to access CNN or BBC World outside of four- and five-star hotels).

CCTV, the Chinese broadcaster, feeds the nation a diet of historical costume epics, glitzy game shows, and patriotic extravaganzas. CCTV 9 is the domestic English-language channel, with censored news and flat content.

Money Matters

People's Republic of China

The currency of the People's Republic of China is the RMB (renminbi), also called the yuan (Y), or *kuai* in spoken Chinese. One yuan is divided into ten jiao *(mao)*. One jiao is divided into ten fen (rarely used). Paper bills come in denominations of 1, 2, and 5 jiao, and 1, 2, 5, 10, 20, 50, and 100 yuan, but nickel and bronze equivalents exist for the smaller units.

Be on your guard against the large number of forged bills in circulation and black-market money-changers on the streets.

Credit cards can be used at most hotels above a three-star ranking; four- and five-star hotels should accept all major credit cards (Visa, MasterCard, Amex, Diners Club). Most cheap restaurants do not accept international credit cards and may take only cash.

Hong Kong & Macau

In Hong Kong, the Hong Kong dollar is used (pegged to the US$), and in Macau the currency is the pataca.

Opening Hours

Banks, businesses, and government offices are officially open weekdays, roughly from 8:30 a.m. to 6 p.m., some with an hour or two lunch break; some bank branches also open on weekends.

Temples, museums, zoos, and other tourist sites are generally open daily, from 8 or 9 a.m. to 5 p.m. Opening hours for tourist sights are generally longer in summer than in winter months.

Places of Worship

A number of active Christian churches are mentioned in the text, some holding regular services. If visiting Chinese temples, there is no strict dress code, but be quiet and respectful as you would when visiting any other place of worship.

Racism

Despite being a multiethnic society, China's ethnic minorities are close to Han Chinese in appearance. This leaves the Chinese with little experience of other races and very conservative ideas about how to deal with them. Although white travelers from wealthy Western countries will be treated reasonably (sometimes surprisingly) well, Chinese prejudice often increases the darker the skin color.

Restrooms

Most hotels apart from those on the lowest rung will equip you with a Western toilet; beyond that, however, expect to acquaint yourself with the Chinese squat toilet. These vary, but as a rough guide, the farther you stray from the large towns, the more gruesome they become. Often there is little privacy. Toilets in rural backwaters can be sordid. Always carry toilet paper.

Time Differences

China is eight hours ahead of Greenwich mean time (GMT). Despite China's size, Beijing time is followed by the whole land. Noon in Beijing is 11 p.m. of the day before in New York, 8 p.m. in Los Angeles, 5 a.m. in Paris, 4 a.m. in London, 2 p.m. in Melbourne, and 4 p.m. in Wellington. Time zone clocks in hotel foyers are often haywire, so don't rely on them.

Tipping

Tipping is generally not done in China. Some smarter restaurants may add a service charge to the bill, so don't leave a tip. Cheaper restaurants never expect tips, nor do taxi drivers. The only exception is hotel porters, who may expect a small something.

Travelers With Disabilities

Disabled travelers will find China inadequately equipped. Public transportation remains largely inaccessible to travelers with disabilities, and only the best hotels and restaurants are prepared.

Vegetarians

Those travelers on a vegetarian diet will find it hard-going in China. The Chinese are eating greater amounts of meat, and the philosophy of vegetarianism for secular reasons is virtually unknown. Vegetarianism does exist for religious reasons, however, and Buddhist temples and restaurants are your best bet for meat-free meals. Otherwise, most restaurants offer a large, if unimaginative, range of vegetable dishes *(sucai),* many of which are prepared with meat-based cooking oils. Some vegetarian restaurant options are noted in the restaurant index.

Weights & Measures

The metric system is used in China, alongside its own system. The only Chinese measurement you are likely to see is the unit of weight: 1 *jin* (Cantonese: *gan*) weighs 1.1 pounds (0.5 kg). The Chinese use both kilometers *(gongli)* and miles *(yingli)*, as well as meters *(mi)*.

EMERGENCIES

Accidents

Vehicle accidents are common in China. Minibus drivers pack passengers in until you can't move, and the law pays no attention. This, coupled with low driving standards and high-speed racing on terrible roads, frequently leads to disaster. There's not much you can do to avoid this, but be aware of the perils of traveling on China's roads and try to remain alert. Gaping holes in city sidewalks are common; look where you are going (especially at night).

Emergency Phone Numbers

The following telephone numbers apply to the larger cities (Beijing, Shanghai, and Guangzhou):

Police 110
Fire 119
Ambulance 120

Foreign Embassies & Consulates in China

Australia

Embassy 21 Dongzhimenwai Dajie, Sanlitun, Beijing, tel 010 5140-4111, www.china.embassy.gov.au

Consulate CITIC Square, 1168 Nanjing Xilu, 22nd Floor, Shanghai, tel 021 2215-5200, www.aus-in-shanghai.com.cn

Consulate Development Center, 12th Floor, 3 Liujiang Dadao, Guangzhou, tel 020 3814-0111, fax 020 3814-0112

Canada

Embassy 19 Dongzhimenwai Dajie, Sanlitun, Beijing, tel 010 5139-4000, fax 010 6532-4072, www.canada.org.cn

Consulate Shanghai Center, Room 604, 1376 Nanjing Xilu, Shanghai, tel 021 3279-2800, www.shanghai.gc.ca

Consulate China Hotel Office Tower, Room 801, Liuhua Lu, Guangzhou, tel 020 8611-6100

France

Embassy 3 Dongsan Jie, Sanlitun, Beijing, tel 010 8532-8080, fax 010 6532-4757, www.ambafrance-cn.org

Consulate United Plaza, Room 1204, 1468 Nanjing Xilu, Shanghai, tel 010 8532-8080, fax 010 6532-4757, www.ambafrance-cn.org

Consulate Guangdong International Hotel, Main Tower, Room 810, 8th Floor, 339 Huanshi Donglu, Guangzhou, tel 020 2829-2000, fax 020 2829-2001, www.ambafrance-cn.org

Germany

Embassy 17 Dongzhimenwai Dajie, Sanlitun, Beijing, tel 010 8532-9000, fax 010 6532-5336, www.peking.diplo.de

Consulate 181 Yongfu Lu, Shanghai, tel 021 3401-0106

Consulate Yuehai Tianhe Bldg., Main Tower, 14th Floor, 208 Tianhe Lu, Guangzhou, tel 020 8313-0000, fax 020 8516-8133

Japan

Embassy 7 Ritan Lu, Beijing, tel 010 6532-2361, www.cn.emb-japan.go.jp

Consulate 8 Wanshan Lu, Hong-qiao, Shanghai, tel 021 5257-4766

New Zealand

Embassy 1 Dong Erjie, Ritan Lu, Beijing, tel 010 8532-7000, fax 010 6532-4317, www.nzembassy.com/china

Consulate The Centre, 16th Floor, 989 Changle Lu, Shanghai, tel 021 5407-5858

South Korea

Embassy China World Trade Center, 3rd & 4th Floors, 1 Jianguomenwai Dajie, Beijing, tel 010 6505-2608, fax 010 6505-3067

United Kingdom

Embassy 11 Guanghua Lu, Beijing, tel 010 5192-4000, www.ukinchina.fco.gov.uk

Consulate Shanghai Centre, 3rd Floor, Suite 319, 1376 Nanjing Xilu, Shanghai, tel 021 3279-2000, fax 021 6279-7651

Consulate Guangdong International Hotel, Main Tower, 2nd Floor, 339 Huanshi Donglu, Guangzhou, tel 020 8314-3000, fax 020 8332-7509

United States

Embassy 3 Xiushui Beijie, Beijing, tel 010 8531-3000/4000, fax 010 8531-4200, http://beijing.usembassy-china.org.cn

Consulate 1469 Huaihai Zhonglu, Shanghai, tel 021 6279-7662; Westgate Tower, 8th Floor, 1038 Nanjing Xilu, Shanghai, tel 021 3217-4650, emergency 021 6433-3936, http://shanghai.usembassy-china.org.cn

Consulate Tian Yu Garden, 5th Floor, 136–142 Linhe Zhonglu Guangzhou, tel 020 8121-8000, fax 020 8121-8428, http://guangzhou.usembassy-china.org.cn

Vietnam

Embassy 32 Guanghua Lu, Beijing, tel 010 6532-1155

Hotels & Restaurants

Accommodations in China, albeit quite uniform in appearance, come in a variety to suit all budgets. Facilities and standards, reflected in the price, have come a long way over the past two decades. A major part of the China experience is the nation's cuisine, and you will find a vast number of restaurants with a blinding array of flavors and regional dishes.

Accommodations

Accommodations in China range from cheap, low budget to five-star hotels of international quality. The country's cheaper hotels are called *binguan* (guesthouse); more expensive hotels are called *jiudian* (wine shop), *da jiudian* (large wine shop), or *fandian* (literally "restaurant").

China rates its hotels from one to five stars. Very cheap accommodations *(zhaodaisuo)* are generally off-limits to foreigners *(waiguoren)*, but a growing band of youth hostels operating throughout the country has rushed to fill the gap. See *www.yhachina.com* for a growing list of Hosteling International–affiliated hostels. Otherwise, hotels of two stars and above should accept foreigners.

The vast majority of hotels in China are of recent and unimaginative construction, which results in an aesthetically bland choice for travelers. Outside of Hong Kong, Macau, Beijing, Shanghai, and Guangzhou, luxury hotels may struggle to make the grade. You will encounter many hotels whose five-star ranking is undeserved and four-star hotels that should be ranked lower. Into the mix are thrown charming courtyard hotels (Beijing), Hakka roundhouse hotels (Yongding), and concession-era villa hotels (Shanghai).

Some more remote parts of China are without four- or five-star hotels; in this case, the best alternatives have been listed. Youth hostels are often an excellent choice as they frequently have decent and affordable double or twin rooms, and staff are always English-speaking and generally knowledgeable about the surrounding area.

Single rooms are rare, and you will usually find yourself in a double or twin. When registering at a hotel, you will have to complete a form and hand over your passport for inspection; you generally have to pay a deposit. Breakfast is sometimes complimentary, but rarely in cheaper establishments. International credit cards are not widely accepted at cheaper hotels (below three stars), so be prepared to pay cash. If a hotel takes credit cards in the list of recommended hotels following, this is indicated. Checkout *(tuifang)* is generally noon.

Most four-star hotels and above should have foreign-exchange counters. Apart from the major holiday periods (Chinese New Year, first week of May, and first week of October), hotels never charge the rack rate, so ask for the discounted rate. Smarter hotels assess a 10 to 15 percent service charge not levied at cheaper establishments.

The following list is a recommended selection of the most appealing hotels and restaurants within their class.

Grading System

✪✪✪✪✪ This category affords an internationally recognized level of luxury and a very high degree of service. Expect to receive decent English-language skills, newspaper delivery, nightly turndown, free airport shuttle, limousine service, room safe, in-room movies, 24-hour business center, in-room tea- and coffee-making facilities, minibar, excellent restaurants and shopping facilities, a swimming pool, Wi-Fi zones, and more. Full Western breakfast will include bacon, eggs, sausage, toast, and so on.

✪✪✪✪ Four-star hotels may offer some, if not all, of the above including business and travel desks, stores, health clubs, and efficient amenities—but they may lack the professionalism and excellence reserved for five-star status. They often appear much more tarnished than five-star hotels. Double rooms will be clean and spacious. Your stay will be comfortable, yet affordable. Virtually all hotels in China have restaurants; four- and five-star hotels should have a Western as well as a Chinese restaurant.

✪✪✪ At three-star hotels, you can expect a decent level of service and restaurant food. They are, however, only modestly equipped to deal with foreigners, and English skills will be moderate at best. Three-star hotels offer large, clean double rooms, and suites should also be available. Rooms should have a minibar and perhaps tea- and coffee-making facilities. Most three-star hotels have in-room broadband Internet access, a travel desk for procuring air and train tickets, and a basic business center *(shangye zhongxin)*.

✪✪ Two-star hotels are simple and often unprofessional, so don't expect much more than a roof over your head. This standard is usually the cheapest type of hotel that takes foreign guests, although you may be accepted by those with no star ranking. Standard double rooms *(putong shuangren fang)* include separate bathroom *(weishengjian)*, television *(dianshi)*, and telephone *(dianhua)*. Air-conditioning *(kongtiao)* is available at all hotels in China except the very cheapest. A common Internet area may be available. English skills could be basic. Some two-star hotels do offer excellent quality within their league, and these have been listed below.

Red stars (✪), ranging from two to five, are awarded to hotels recognized for excellence within their own star rating for consistent, superior levels of hospitality, service, food, and comfort.

Please note: Unless otherwise stated, all rooms have telephone, television, and bathroom. Room prices are given only for guidance and do not take into account seasonal variations. Prices given are per double room.

Restaurants

Better Chinese restaurants *(fandian/canguan)* generally have a large number of tables, with separate banquet/dining rooms at the wings (for private groups). Nonsmoking sections are rare except in expensive, or hotel, restaurants, but the pricier banquet rooms *(danjian)* can be used for this purpose.

English menus can be a rarity except in more expensive hotels or those located along routes much traveled by Westerners. Food is not necessarily served in a particular order, and you will probably have to remind the waitress to bring your rice *(baifan).* The Chinese eat many dishes at the same time, rather than courses.

Many restaurants in China do not take credit cards, so check first or carry enough cash at all times. There is no need to tip at most restaurants (see p. 359), but smarter establishments may preempt you by adding a gratuity.

Not included in the following list of restaurants are fast-food outlets that are plentiful. McDonald's and KFC (often the only English words taxi drivers recognize) can be found in large towns and cities throughout China. Other familiar names are T.G.I. Friday's, Häagen Dazs, and Starbucks.

Chopsticks

If you don't know how to use chopsticks, you might as well use your time in China learning the skill (once learned, you won't forget). They come in disposable bamboo, lacquer, or imitation ivory; occasionally you will see a silver pair. Practice with a pair of pencils, if you like. Hold them so that your middle finger acts as the fulcrum, with pressure from the thumb and second finger. The other two fingers are not used.

When you are not using your chopsticks, do not thrust them upright into your bowl of rice, but place them across your plate or on the chopstick rest (provided in smarter restaurants).

Sichuan Hotpot

The huge Yangtze city of Chongqing (see p. 150) is one of the best places to sample a flaming Sichuan hotpot *(huoguo).* The hotpot is divided into two compartments, one hot and the other milder, or is just plain hot. Into the boiling furnace of each are liberally thrown skewers of sliced meat and vegetables. The experience guarantees a warm afterglow in winter. Chongqing is China's hotpot capital, and suitable restaurants can be found throughout the city.

Organization

The hotels and restaurants listed here have been grouped first according to their region, then listed alphabetically by price in descending order.

Credit Cards

Abbreviations used are: AE (American Express), DC (Diners Club) MC (Mastercard), V (Visa)

PRICES

HOTELS

An indication of the cost of a double room in the high season is given by **$** signs.

$$$$$	Over $350
$$$$	$180–$350
$$$	$100–$180
$$	$40–$100
$	Under $40

RESTAURANTS

An indication of the cost of a three-course meal without drinks is given by **$** signs.

$$$$$	Over $100
$$$$	$75–$100
$$$	$50–$75
$$	$30–$50
$	Under $30

BEIJING

PARK HYATT BEIJING
$$$$$ ✪✪✪✪✪

2 JIANGUOMENWAI DAJIE, CHAOYANG DISTRICT
TEL 010 8567-1234
FAX 010 8567-1000
www.beijing.park.hyatt.com

Enjoy a stratospheric meal in China Grill, with magnificent views over the city, or go for a dip in the pool, also with breathtaking panoramas standard. Service is attentive and top notch, rooms are spacious and highly comfortable, while the hotel design and facilities are excellent. Well located for subway access. Five restaurants and a bar; Wi-Fi.

237, 18 suites
All major cards

KERRY CENTRE HOTEL (JIALI ZHONGXIN FANDIAN)

$$$$ ✪✪✪✪
KERRY CENTRE,
1 GUANGHUA LU
TEL 010 6561-8833
www.shangrila.com/beijing/kerrycentre
Owned by the premier Shangri-La group, this modern hotel is a sophisticated and impressive business choice. Situated in east Beijing within reach of the embassy and commercial districts. Chinese restaurant and a hip 24-hour bar, Centro.
487 All major cards

PENINSULA BEIJING (WANGFU FANDIAN)

$$$$ ✪✪✪✪✪
8 GOLDFISH LANE
(JINYU HUTONG)
TEL 010 8516-2888
FAX 010 6510-6311
www.peninsula.com
Owned by the Peninsula group, the Peninsula Beijing is a sumptuous and well-polished hotel situated near the fashionable shopping experience of Wangfujing. Traditional Chinese motifs on the exterior, shopping arcade, and a range of restaurants, from the *siheyuan*-style Huang Ting to the celebrated Jing, and lobby lounge and bar. The Forbidden City is not far away. Mercedes/Rolls Royce limousine service.
530 All major cards

SOMETHING SPECIAL

ST. REGIS

$$$$ ✪✪✪✪✪
12 JIANGUOMENWAI DAJIE
TEL 010 6460-6688
FAX 010 6460-3299
www.stregis.com
Centrally located, the St. Regis is Beijing's most prestigious and elegant hotel and first choice for visiting dignitaries. The sumptuous foyer is a taster for the unbridled luxury throughout, which extends to a gamut of top-notch restaurants and bars, a profusion of five-star facilities, and 24-hour butler service.
273 All major cards

PARK PLAZA HOTEL

$$$ ✪✪✪✪
97 JINBAO JIE
TEL 010 8522-1999
www.parkplaza.com
This excellently located hotel is a great value, tucked away behind the Regent Beijing near Wangfujing Dajie. Crisp and modern, the hotel is understated and relaxed. Rooms are stylish, and Wi-Fi is available.
262 All major cards

LÜSONGYUAN HOTEL (LÜSONGYUAN BINGUAN)

$$ ✪✪
22 BANCHANG HUTONG
TEL 010 6404-0436
FAX 010 6403-0418
www.lusongyuanhotel beijing.cn
An enterprising and historic *siheyuan* (walled courtyard) hotel lost down a charming alley in a *hutong*-riddled area of Beijing. The hotel boasts traditional Qing dynasty courtyard architecture, and a garden and offers bike rental and *hutong* tours. Its central location just off the alley of Nanluogu Xiang makes it very popular, so reservations are recommended.
60 All major cards

PEKING INTERNATIONAL YOUTH HOSTEL

$$ ✪✪
5 BEICHIZI ERTIAO
TEL 010 6526-8855
www.peking.hostel.com
There's little to fault this excellent and well-managed hostel, least of all the superb location in a *hutong* just east of the Forbidden City. Rooms are small but pleasant; common areas are charming and homey, with a tranquil Beijing courtyard ambience. Wi-Fi available.
80 No credit cards accepted

HAOYUAN HOTEL (HAOYUAN BINGUAN)

$
53 SHIJIA HUTONG
TEL 010 6512-5557
www.haoyuanhotel.com
Pleasant and quiet courtyard (*siheyuan*) hotel, enjoying an excellent location in a *hutong* not far east of Wangfujing, Beijing's main shopping street. Very popular with foreigners. Clean rooms. Lovely VIP room.
20 No credit cards accepted

CAPITAL M

$$$$
2 QIANMEN DAJIE, 3RD FLOOR
TEL 010 6702-2727
www.capital-m-beijing.com
Bringing the success of Shanghai's M on the Bund to Beijing, Michelle Garnaut has found herself a perfect perch overlooking Qianmen, just south of Tiananmen Square. The modern European menu is excellent, as are the views from the terrace.
50+ Subway: Qianmen All major cards

FACE

$$$
26 DONGCAOYUAN (S OF GONGRENTIYUCHANG NANLU)
TEL 010 6551-6788
www.facebars.com
Taking its cue from its vastly popular Shanghai namesake, Face is a stylish and elegantly decorated cocktail bar tucked away off the road to the south of the Workers' Stadium.
50+ All major cards

VINEYARD CAFÉ
$$
31 WUDAOYING HUTONG
TEL 010 6402-7961
http://vineyardcafe.cn

Come here for the legendary full-size English breakfast, which will fuel you enough for an expedition to the Great Wall or a day at the Forbidden City. The lunch and dinner menus are also excellent.

Closed Mon. Subway: Yonghegong All major cards

XIAO WANG'S HOME RESTAURANT
$$
2 GUANGHUA DONGLI
TEL 010 6594-3602

This excellent multifloor restaurant has been in business for more than a decade. The Chinese homestyle food is very tasty, the service swift and friendly (if rather harassed), and the engaging, fun ambience a million miles from huge banquet-style Chinese restaurants. Another branch operates in Ritan Park.

30+ Subway: Yonganli All major cards

QIANMEN QUANJUDE ROAST DUCK (QIANMEN QUANJUDE KAOYADIAN)
$–$$
30 QIANMEN DAJIE
TEL 010 6511-2418
www.qmquanjude.com.cn

This is one of the ancestral homes of roast duck *(kaoya)*, dating back to the 19th century and divided into sections for differing budgets. This vast place may be a major stopping-off point for tour groups, but you can't argue with the excellent duck value. Order your bird and the pancakes; onion and plum sauce will automatically arrive. There are other branches at 143 Qianmen Xidajie *(tel 010 6301-8833)* and 9 Shuaifuyuan Hutong *(off Wangfujing Dajie, tel 010 6525-3310).*

1,000+ Subway: Qianmen Closed 1:30 p.m.–4:30 p.m. AE

AJISEN (WEIQIAN LAMIAN)
$
FF08, BASEMENT
ORIENTAL PLAZA
TEL 010 8518-6001
www.ajisen.com.cn

Conveniently located right at the foot of Wangfujing Dajie, this branch of the nationwide noodle chain is typically packed with diners unanimous in their adoration of their filling and tasty Japanese noodle and rice dishes (pay at the start of the meal).

60 All major cards

BAGUOBUYI
$
89-3 DIANMEN DONGDAJIE
TEL 010 6400-8888
www.baguobuyi.com

It's a feat finding an authentic Sichuan meal outside its heartland in the west of China, but the dishes of Baguobuyi—with a branch in Chengdu—are a close second best, delivered up in a fun, garrulous, and centrally located restaurant to the east of the north gate of Beihai Park.

300+ Closed 2:15 p.m.–5:15 p.m. No credit cards accepted

BOOKWORM CAFÉ
$
BLDG. 4, NAN SANLITUN LU
TEL 010 6586-9507
www.beijingbookworm.com

A haven for bibliophiles citywide, Bookworm has wormed its way into the expat consciousness as the heartiest place for a good cup of coffee, a bite to eat, and a book to read. Join the sedate hordes thumbing through hard-to-find fiction/nonfiction, and take time out from Beijing's usual café scene.

100 No credit cards accepted

HUTONG PIZZA
$
9 YINDINGQIAO HUTONG
TEL 010 8832-8916

Apart from the charming *hutong* setting (hidden away just off Qianhai and Houhai lakes), a delightful upstairs hideaway, and a tasty menu, this pizzas here are large enough to feed a horse—and a famished one at that. The restaurant can take some finding, but persevere: It's well worth it.

All major cards

LIQUN ROAST DUCK RESTAURANT (LIQUN KAOYADIAN)
$
11 BEIXIANGFENG HUTONG
(S OF XIDAMOCHANG JIE, SE OF QIANMEN)
TEL 010 66705-5578

Small and quiet, the unsophisticated Liqun is tricky to find (follow the signs in the surrounding tangle of *hutongs*), but the duck has long won praise from Beijing's picky duck diners. Phoning ahead for a reservation is advised; otherwise you may have a long wait (but it's worth it).

80 No credit cards accepted

MAKYE AME (MAJI AMI)
$
A11 XIUSHUI NANJIE
JIANGUOMENWAI
TEL 010 6506-9616
http://en.makyeame.cn

Dishes from the Land of Snows in a marvelous Tibetan setting at this upstairs restaurant behind the Friendship Store. English menu.

60 No credit cards accepted

PASSBY BAR (GUOKE)
$
108 NANLUOGU XIANG
TEL 010 8403-8004
Nanluogu Xiang is a lovely old north–south *hutong* east of the lake of Qian Hai with traveler-friendly watering holes and restaurants. Age has hardly dented the popularity of this charming courtyard bar.
60 Subway: Gulou
No credit cards accepted

THE NORTH

CHENGDE

MOUNTAIN VILLA HOTEL (SHANZ-HUANG BINGUAN)
$ ✪✪✪
127 LIZHENGMEN LU
TEL 0314 209-1188
www.hemvhotel.com
Excellent location south of the main entrance to the Bishu Shanzhuang resort in the north of town, this long-serving mid-range hotel has a decent variety of large and clean rooms, suiting a range of budgets.
340 All major cards

DATONG

GARDEN HOTEL (HUAYUAN DAFAN-DIAN)
$$$ ✪✪✪✪
59 DA NANJIE
TEL 0352 586-5825
FAX 0352 586-5894
www.huayuanhotel.com.cn
Datong's most pleasant hotel offers a great blend of comfort and elegance in a central location just south of the old town and a short walk from the sights. Rooms come with attractive furniture and broadband Internet. Chinese and Western restaurants.
108 All major cards

HUASHAN

There are a number of hotels in Huashan Village (at the foot of the mountain) and along Yuquan Lu leading up to the Yuquan Temple. Hotels also dot the slopes and peaks of Huashan, but facilities and services are more basic. Food and water can be bought along the path up the mount.

JINAN

CROWNE PLAZA JINAN (JINAN GUIHE HUANG-GUAN JIARI JIUDIAN)
$$$$ ✪✪✪✪✪
3 TIANDITAN JIE
TEL 0531 8602-9999
FAX 0531 8602-3333
www.crowneplaza.com
An elegant hotel bursting with restaurants and facilities, the Crowne Plaza is perfectly geared to travelers, combining elegance and excellence.
306 All major cards

KAIFENG

DAJINTAI HOTEL (DAJINTAI BINGUAN)
$ ✪✪
23 GULOU JIE
TEL 0378 255-2888
FAX 0378 255-5189
Just around the corner from Kaifeng's lively night market, the Dajintai has a central location and perfectly adequate rooms. Breakfast is included.
120 No credit cards accepted

DONGJING HOTEL
$ ✪✪✪
14 YINGBIN LU
TEL 0378 398-9388
FAX 0378 595-6661
Kaifeng is sadly not blessed with great hotels, but the Dongjing at least offers a reasonably pleasant location (in the southwest within the city walls), a business center, and a complimentary breakfast. CITS north of the hotel. Chinese and Western cuisine. Also, there's a shopping center, post office, ticketing office.
300+ V

LUOYANG

PEONY HOTEL (MUDAN DAJIUDIAN)
$$ ✪✪✪
15 ZHONGZHOU XILU
TEL 0379 6468-0000
FAX 0379 6468-0000
The Peony is a centrally located, inexpensive, mid-ranking hotel. All rooms are furnished with satellite TV.
196 All major cards

QINGDAO

CROWNE PLAZA (YIZHONG HUANGUAN JIARI JIUDIAN)
$$$$ ✪✪✪✪✪
76 XIANGGANG ZHONGLU
TEL 0532 8571-8888
FAX 0532 8571-6666
www.ichotelsgroup.com
The sparkling tower of the Crowne Plaza is a modern, hallmark hotel in Qingdao's busy commercial district. Rooms are perfectly equipped for business travelers, and there's a huge selection of fine restaurants. Breakfast included, and Wi-Fi available.
388 All major cards

SHANGRI-LA HOTEL QINGDAO (XIANG-GELILA JIUDIAN)
$$$ ✪✪✪✪✪
9 XIANGGANG ZHONGLU
TEL 0532 8388-3838
FAX 0532 8388-6868
www.shangri-la.com
The Shangri-La is a high-quality fixture among the charms of

Qingdao. Excellent amenities, facilities, and standards of service. Executive floors offer an even higher level of service. Chinese restaurant, café, and pub. Tennis courts.

502 All major cards

AJISEN (WEIQIAN LAMIAN)

$

1ST FLOOR, CARREFOUR,
21 XIANGGANG ZHONGLU
TEL 0532 8580-6375
www.ajisen.com.cn

Bowls of spicy, searing noodles are the specialty at this ever busy Japanese hot spot. Excellent, filling food, served up at speed by attentive waitstaff.

150 No credit cards accepted

CHUNHE LOU

$

146 ZHONGSHAN LU
TEL 0532 8282-4346

The best way to sample Qingdao dishes is to visit one of the city's many seafood restaurants, but this old-timer in the historic part of Qingdao remains one of the town's most famous eateries.

400 No credit cards accepted

QUFU

QUELI HOTEL (QUELI BINSHE)

$ ✪✪✪

1 QUELI STREET
TEL 0537 486-6818
FAX 0537 441-2022
www.quelihotel.com

Facing both the Confucius Temple and the Confucius Mansions, the Queli is admirably presented in architecture of traditional Chinese style. Nothing special, but reasonably pleasant and well situated.

160+ MC, V

SHAOLIN TEMPLE

It is possible to stay in accommodations near the temple, but the best strategy is to stay in Luoyang or Zhengzhou. If you are stuck here, try the **Shaolin International Hotel** *(20 Shaolin Dadao, tel 0371 6285-6868, www.shaolinhotel.com)* in neighboring Dengfeng the principal tourist hotel in the area with adequate facilities. Other hotels and restaurants can be found in Dengfeng.

TAISHAN

SHENQI GUESTHOUSE (SHENQI BINGUAN)

$$ ✪✪✪

10 TIAN JIE
TEL 0538 822-3866
FAX 0538 821-5399

Sun worshippers can snuggle up away from Taishan's chill in this two-story hotel, the best in the summit area. You will be awakened well before sunrise. Suites available.

50+ No credit cards accepted

TAISHAN HOTEL (TAISHAN BINGUAN)

$$ ✪✪✪

26 HONGMEN LU
TEL 0538 822-4678
FAX 0538 822-1432

The most popular choice for climbers, this hotel puts you at the start of the road up Taishan, just north of the most interesting part of town. Rooms are divided between newer, more expensive rooms and older, cheaper ones. Breakfast, shop, and ticketing service.

100+ All major cards

TIANJIN

RAFFLES TIANJIN

$$$$

219 NANJING LU
TEL 022 2321-5888
www.raffles.com

The old days when Tianjin was limited to just a handful of five-star hotels and a band of fuddy-duddy concession-era hotels are thankfully over. High up in the Tianjin Centre West Tower, the Raffles Tianjin is a breathtaking new hotel boasting gorgeous and ample rooms, along with butler service around the clock. Although the Raffles was unable to obtain a period property like its sister hotels in Beijing, the hotel is still the best in town, and the cental location is excellent. Wi-Fi is also available.

116 All major cards

HYATT REGENCY (KAIYUE FANDIAN)

$$$ ✪✪✪✪

219 JIEFANG BEILU
TEL 022 2330-1234
FAX 022 2331-1234
www.hyatt.com

PRICES

HOTELS

An indication of the cost of a double room in the high season is given by **$** signs.

$$$$$	Over $350
$$$$	$180–$350
$$$	$100–$180
$$	$40–$100
$	Under $40

RESTAURANTS

An indication of the cost of a three-course meal without drinks is given by **$** signs.

$$$$$	Over $100
$$$$	$75–$100
$$$	$50–$75
$$	$30–$50
$	Under $30

The four-star Hyatt is an elegantly styled hotel benefiting from an excellent position on Tianjin's historic Jiefang Lu near the Hai River. This may not be Tianjin's most lavish hotel, but complete top-to-bottom renovations in 2012 have restored sparkle and competitive panache.

450 All major cards

XIANG WEI ZHAI

$–$$ ○○○○

HYATT REGENCY
219 JIEFANG BEILU
TEL 0222 2331-8888

This pleasantly designed dumpling restaurant is a joy. The name means "countryside flavor," pointing to its emphasis on traditional simplicity. Try the crab and chive dumpling or the seafood and noodle soup, and wash it down with Chinese tea. Inexpensive and all very worthwhile. Service charge included. English menu.

44 All major cards

GOUBULI

$

77 SHANDONG LU
TEL022 2730-2540
www.chinagoubuli.com

The famous Goubuli, located just off the shopping drag of Binjiang Dadao, has been serving up its trademark specialty steamed buns *(baozi)* for more than a hundred years. The buns come in almost a hundred varieties (pork, chicken, shrimp, vegetable, and more), and a selection of tasty and good-value set meals is also available. There are other branches dotted around China.

300+ No credit cards accepted

YY BEER HOUSE

$

3 AOMEN LU
TEL 022 2339-9634

This fantastic Thai restaurant just south off Nanjing Lu has a magnificent selection of beers, bubbly staff, great food, and frequent lines.

80 All major cards

WUTAISHAN/TAIHUAI

FOYUAN LOU

$$

BEHIND SHUXIANG TEMPLE, S OF TAIHUAI VILLAGE
TEL 0350 654-2659

Just beyond the top of the mighty steps leading to Shuxiang Temple is this lovely hotel, right next to the temple and accessed through heavy traditional-style doors. Rooms are comfortable and presentable and service rather hesitant, but the unbeatable location steals the show.

No credit cards accepted

XI'AN

SOFITEL ON RENMIN SQUARE (SUOFEITE RENMIN DASHA)

$$$$$ ○○○○○

319 DONG XIJIE
TEL 029 8792-8888
FAX 029 8792-8999
www.sofitel.com

Undoubtedly Xi'an's top choice, the Sofitel on Renmin Square is a stunning top-league addition to Xi'an's growing galaxy of hotels, with eye-catching flair, exemplary service throughout, and elegant, modern rooms. Wi-Fi zone, two bars, and four restaurants.

432 All major cards

HYATT REGENCY XI'AN (XIAN KAIYUE FANDIAN)

$$$ ○○○○○

158 DONG DAJIE
TEL 029 8769-1234
www.xian.regency.hyatt.com

The uninspiring exterior conceals a grand and sophisticated center. Situated well within the city walls, this is the only five-star hotel in the thick of it. Bill Clinton made this his port of call when last in town. Service is crisp and efficient. Tennis court.

404 All major cards

CITY HOTEL X'IAN (XIAN CHENGSHI JIUDIAN)

$ ○○○

70 NAN DAJIE
TEL 029 8721-9988
FAX 029 8721-6688
www.cityhotelxian.com

A centrally located hotel very close to the Bell Tower, the City Hotel is popular and inexpensive, with comfortable rooms and staff who are used to dealing with foreign guests. Business centers, Chinese and Western restaurant.

133 All major cards

LAO SUNJIA

$

DONG DAJIE
TEL 029 8742-1858
www.xa-lsj.com

Serving diners for more than a century, this *laozihao* (established restaurant) is clearly doing something right. Its consistently excellent signature item is *yangrou paomo,* a tasty soup of noodles, bread, and lamb—perhaps Xi'an's best known dish. There are several branches in town.

20+ No credit cards accepted

ZHENGZHOU

HOLIDAY INN CROWNE PLAZA (HUANGGUAN JIARI FANDIAN)

$$$ ○○○○○

115 JINSHUI LU
TEL 0371 6595-0055
www.crowneplaza.com

A finely serviced hotel, with facilities of international standards and decent restaurants.

Nightclub, barber, and beauty salons also on site.
222 All major cards

YANGTZE REGION

CHONGQING

MARRIOTT HOTEL
$$$–$$$$ ✪✪✪✪✪
77 QINGNIAN LU
TEL 023 6388-8888
FAX 023 6388-8777
www.marriott.com
The glittering tower of the Marriott supplies five-star comfort and facilities in the heart of Chongqing. Adventurous travelers may be tempted away to visit one of the city's many hotpot *(huoguo)* restaurants, but the Marriott is equipped with splendid restaurants, including Chinese and Japanese.
498 All major cards

HANGZHOU

GRAND HYATT REGENCY (HANGZHOU KAIYUE JIUDIAN)
$$$$ ✪✪✪✪✪
28 HUBIN LU
TEL 0571 8779-1234
FAX 0571 8779-1818
www.hangzhou.regency .hyatt.com
The huge Hyatt comes replete with international standard five-star facilities and amenities, with fully equipped rooms and a fine location on the east side of West Lake.
390 All major cards

SHANGRI-LA HOTEL HANGZHOU (HANGZHOU XIANGGELILA FANDIAN)
$$$–$$$$ ✪✪✪✪✪
78 BEISHAN LU
TEL 0571 8797-7951
FAX 0571 8707-3545
www.shangri-la.com
Located in 30 acres (12 ha) of landscaped gardens on the shore of West Lake, the Shangri-La is one of the best hotels in town, bursting with fine dining opportunities and eager to please. Chinese and Italian restaurant, American bar and café. Billiards, bike rental.
387 All major cards

MINGTOWN YOUTH HOSTEL
$
101–11 NANSHAN LU
TEL 0571 8791-8948
Don't be put off by the youth hostel designation; this place right by West Lake on the east shore has popular single and double rooms, plus a great bar.
No credit cards accepted

LOUWAILOU (LOUWAILOU CAIGUAN)
$$ ✪✪✪
30 GUSHAN LU
TEL 0571 8796-9023
FAX 0571 8799-7264
www.louwailou.com
Hangzhou's most famous eatery feeds everyone on immortal local recipes (Sudong po pork and beggar's chicken) and offers long views over West Lake from Solitary Hill Island. Specialties: West Lake vinegar fish *(xihu cuyu)* and Longjing shrimps *(longjing xiaren)*. English menu.
1,400 All major cards

HUANGSHAN/TUNXI

BEIHAI HOTEL (BEIHAI BINGUAN)
$$–$$$ ✪✪✪✪
TEL 0559 558-2555
FAX 0559 558-1996
www.hsbeihaihotel.com
This utilitarian hotel is poised within reach of Huangshan sunrise viewing area. Four-bed rooms available.
100+ No credit cards accepted

XIHAI HOTEL (XIHAI FANDIAN)
$$–$$$ ✪✪✪
SUMMIT AREA
TEL 0559 558-8987/8888
FAX 0559 558-8988
www.hsxihaihotel.cn
The modern Xihai is not cheap, but it is one of the more comfortable entrées to watching the sunrise the next day. Nightclub, snooker.
150 All major cards

OLD STREET HOTEL (LAOJIEKOU KEZHAN)
$$ ✪✪✪✪
1 LAOJIEKOU, TUNXI
TEL 0559 233-9188
FAX 0559 253-1313
www.oldstreet-hotel.com
For those using Tunxi as a hopping-off point to Yixian and Shexian, and even nearby Huangshan, this pleasant hotel at the western tip of Old Street (Lao Jie) has traditional-style rooms with wooden floors. Breakfast included.
33 MC, V

JIUHUASHAN

As with all sacred mountain destinations in China, Jiuhuashan offers poor quality hotels. There are a number of hotels in Jiuhua village, including the **Julong Hotel** *(Julong Dajiudian, tel 0566 501-1368, fax 0566 501-1022, no credit cards accepted)*, an unsurprising establishment. Pleasant accommodations can also be found at the homey **Nanyuan Hotel** *(26 Furong Lu, tel 0566 501-1122)*, near the Tonghui Nunnery. Restaurants muster along the main street, Jiuhua Jie. Food and drink can also be found on the way up the mountain.

MOGANSHAN

MOGANSHAN 23

$$$

23 MOGANSHAN
(NEAR DEQING, ZHEJIANG)
TEL 0572 803-3822
www.moganshanhouse23.com

This lovely stone villa, with a garden restored to its period charms, is the best place to stay on Monganshan. Book well ahead, however, since it's very popular. If it's booked, ask about House 25, with an additional two rooms. Breakfast included.

6 No credit cards accepted

NANJING

JINLING HOTEL (JINLING FANDIAN)

$$$$ ✪✪✪✪✪

XINJIEKOU SQUARE
TEL 025 8471-1888
FAX 025 8471-1666
www.jinlinghotel.com

Centrally located, first-class hotel with excellent rooms. The executive suites are intelligently and thoughtfully designed. Standard rooms also of distinctive high quality. Boasts a legion of restaurants, both Eastern and Western (including revolving restaurant). Despite mainly catering to Chinese guests, the hotel is welcoming to Westerners.

600 All major cards

JINGLI HOTEL (JINGLI JIUDIAN)

$$ ✪✪✪

7 BEIJING XILU
(W OF THE DRUM TOWER)
TEL 025 8331-0818
FAX 025 8663-6636
www.jinglihotel.com

This clean three-star hotel offers good value and strives to be a cut above the rest. Put yourself in an executive suite for $130. Its central location puts you within striking distance of Nanjing's sights. Chinese restaurant, Internet access, and business center.

131 All major cards

NANSHAN EXPERT'S BUILDING HOTEL (NANJING ZHUANJIA LOU)

$ ✪✪✪

NANJING NORMAL UNIVERSITY,
122 NINGHAI LU
TEL 025 8329-2888

With comfortably redecorated rooms, this hotel has been elevated from its former backpacker incarnation into a more tasteful mid-range option. Yet the wonderful setting remains the same, located in the quiet heart of Nanjing Normal University, the grounds of which have a rare beauty. Amid the gorgeous traditional rooftops and the dry chorus of cicadas, the hotel today welcomes a wide variety of travelers.

200+ No credit cards accepted

PUTUOSHAN

PUTUOSHAN HOTEL (PUTUOSHAN DAJIUDIAN)

$$ ✪✪✪✪

93 MEICEN LU
TEL 0580 609-2828
FAX 0580 609-1818
www.putuoshanhotel.com

One of the most superior hotels to have arrived on the island, this four-star hotel offers comfort and a decent range of amenities.

160 MC, V

SANSHENGTANG (SANSHENGTANG FANDIAN)

$

121 MIAO ZHUANGYAN LU
TEL 0580 609-3688
FAX 0580 609-1140

This budget hotel was formerly a Buddhist nunnery in keeping with the sacred character of the island. Diverse range of rooms, just a ten-minute walk from the ferry terminal, not far from Puji Temple. Ticketing service available.

100+ No credit cards accepted

RESTAURANTS IN PUTUOSHAN

Recommending a decent restaurant in Putuoshan is difficult because they are in short supply. Outside of hotel restaurants, decent small seafood eateries can be found not far from the ferry terminal and around the Puji Temple.

SHANGHAI

PORTMAN RITZ-CARLTON (BOTEMAN DAJIUDIAN)

$$$$$ ✪✪✪✪✪

SHANGHAI CENTER,
1376 NANJING XILU
TEL 021 6279-8888
FAX 021 6279-8800
www.ritzcarlton.com

The Ritz-Carlton remains one of Shanghai's leading hotels, with recent renovations keeping it well within the front-runners in this highly competitive market. The first-class standards that make this one of the very best busness hotels in Shanghai are still at the forefront. Spacious guest rooms; Chinese, Japanese, and Western restaurants. Squash, racketball, and tennis courts. Restaurant and service-equipped Shanghai Center on your doorstep.

564 Subway: Jing'an Temple All major cards

ASTOR HOUSE HOTEL
$$$$ ✪✪✪
15 HUANGPU LU
TEL 021 6324-6388
www.astorhousehotel.com
Until recently called the Pujiang Hotel, this noble and well-renovated relic sits north of Suzhou Creek, overseen by staff putting a shine to its sense of history. This is one of the most rewarding addresses in the city for those who want decent mid-range comfort near the Bund. Restaurants and bar.
146 All major cards

FAIRMONT PEACE HOTEL (HEPING FANDIAN)
$$$$ ✪✪✪✪
20 NANJING DONGLU
TEL 021 6321-6888
www.fairmont.com
Closed for renovation in 2007, the landmark Peace Hotel reopened at the tail end of 2010. The art deco features have all been preserved, hunting down the stained glass is a worthwhile recreation, and the old jazz band is still strumming away. Wi-Fi available.
270 Subway: East Nanjing Lu All major cards

PARK HYATT SHANGHAI
$$$$ ✪✪✪✪✪
100 CENTURY AVENUE
TEL 021 6888-1234
FAX 021 6888-3400
www.parkhyattshanghai.com
Deftly knocking the neighboring Grand Hyatt off its perch as the city's highest hotel above ground level, the Park Hyatt rests at the pinnacle of luxury in Shanghai. Filling the 79th to the 93rd floors of the towering Shanghai World Financial Center, the hotel has spared no expense in wowing guests with a combination of cool styling and fashionable rooms bursting with gadgets and wrap-around views that extend forever.
174 All major cards

URBN
$$$$ ✪✪✪✪
183 JIAOZHOU LU
TEL 021 5153-4600
FAX 021 5153-4610
www.urbnhotels.com
Shanghai's first carbon-neutral hotel, URBN is a very cool boutique hotel with a lovely location out of the action. Aimed squarely at the green and environmentally aware traveler, the emphasis on recycling and carbon neutrality extends to carefully considered and designed rooms.
26 Subway: Jing'an Temple All major cards

PUDONG SHANGRI-LA SHANGHAI (XIANGELI-LA JIUDIAN)
$$$ ✪✪✪✪✪
33 FUCHENG LU, LUJIAZUI, PUDONG
TEL 021 6882-8888
FAX 021 6882-6688
www.shangri-la.com
Facing the Bund from the riverside borders of Pudong, the Shangri-La enjoys a prestigious view over old Shanghai and provides excellent service. The premier rooms in the stunning Tower Two annex are Shanghai's roomiest at 581 square feet (54 sq m). Chinese and Japanese restaurants and coffee shop. Limousine service.
981 Subway: Lujiazui All major cards

OLD HOUSE INN
$$ ✪✪✪
NO. 16 LANE 351
OFF HUASHAN LU
TEL 021 6248-6118
FAX 021 6249-6869
www.oldhouse.cn
A stylish boutique hotel in a building dating from the 1930s, with a handful of traditionally styled rooms. There's a genuine antique charm about this place on the edge of the French Concession. Breakfast included.
12 MC, V

PARK HOTEL (GUOJI FANDIAN)
$$ ✪✪✪✪
170 NANJING XILU
TEL 021 6327-5225
FAX 021 6327-6958
www.parkhotel-shanghai.com
Excellently located hotel overlooking Renmin Square and encasing a splendid art deco interior. Built in 1934, the Park is one of the old guard—not the most sophisticated but distinguished nonetheless. Chinese and Western restaurants, nightclub, shopping arcade.
180 Subway: People's Square All major cards

PRICES

HOTELS
An indication of the cost of a double room in the high season is given by **$** signs.

$$$$$	Over $350
$$$$	$180–$350
$$$	$100–$180
$$	$40–$100
$	Under $40

RESTAURANTS
An indication of the cost of a three-course meal without drinks is given by **$** signs.

$$$$$	Over $100
$$$$	$75–$100
$$$	$50–$75
$$	$30–$50
$	Under $30

CAPTAIN HOSTEL (CHUANZHANG QINGNIAN JIUDIAN)
$
37 FUZHOU LU
TEL 021 6323-5053
FAX 021 6321-9331
www.captainhostel.com.cn

Located just a chopstick's throw away from the Bund, the Captain Hostel comes up trumps with good-value dorm accommodations (but less value on double rooms) and a handy bar on the top floor with killer views.

105 Subway: Middle Henan Road MC, V

T8
$$$
8 NORTH BLOCK
181 TAICANG LU
TEL 021 6355-8999
www.t8shanghai.com

Serving up its signature international dishes from the stylish restaurant/shopping hub of Xintiandi, T8 easily ranks itself among the best of Shanghai's dining experiences in an increasingly competitive market of top chefs and hard-to-please diners. Lunchtime set menus.

150 All major cards

M ON THE BUND (MISHI XICANTING)
$$
20 GUANGDONG LU, 7TH FL.
TEL 021 6350 9988
www.m-onthebund.com

If you are in the area of the Bund, you could do far worse than visit this international eatery. It boasts a fine view of the waterfront and fantastic, acclaimed dining.

130 All major cards

QUANJUDE (QUANJUDE KAOYADIAN)
$$
786 HUAIHAI ZHONGLU
TEL 0216 433-7286 OR 0216 6433-5799
www.quanjude.com.cn

Feverishly busy on weekends, Shanghai's Quanjude can't match its parent in Beijing but is still essential feasting for *kaoya* (Peking duck) enthusiasts. The waitresses are hectically efficient, and banquet rooms (one called the Forbidden City) wait on the wings. Wash it all down with sweet *babao cha* (eight treasures tea). English menu.

60 All major cards

1221
$
1221 YAN'AN XILU
TEL 021 6213-2441

Despite a far-flung location in the city's west, this restaurant is much loved by both local and expat diners. The chefs have hit the nail on the head with some first-rate and inventive Shanghai dishes. Try the onion cakes, and wash them down with some sweet and refreshing *babao cha* (eight treasures tea).

100+ All major cards

GONGDELIN VEGETARIAN RESTAURANT (GONGDELIN SUSHI CHU)
$
445 NANJING XILU
TEL 021 6327-0218

Recently renovated, the stylish Gongdelin (look for the sign that says "Godly Restaurant") serves tasty dishes resembling meat, but without a fiber of flesh. Examples include vegetable chicken *(suji)* and vegetable duck *(suya)*. 50 tables. English menu.

50 No credit cards accepted

HUXINTING TEAHOUSE (HUXINTING CHALOU)
$
257 YUYUAN LU
TEL 021 6373-6950

Emerging from the pond in the heart of the Yuyan Bazaar, the old teahouse is a charming fragment of yesteryear and an excellent place to sample Chinese brews. Two floors. English menu.

180 No credit cards accepted

NANXIANG STEAMED BREAD SHOP (NANXIANG MANTOUDIAN)
$
85 YUYUAN LU
TEL 021 6355-4206

Packed on weekends, Nanxiang offers gorgeous prix fixe meals of steamed buns *(xiaolongbao)*, Shanghai's favorite dumpling. Try the delicious crabmeat variety *(xiefen xiaolong)*, accompanied by a thin soup textured with strips of egg. Takeout.

33 All major cards

NEW HEIGHTS
$
THREE ON THE BUND, 7TH FL.
TEL 021 6321-0909

For some of the best nocturnal views in town, grab a drink and head out to the terrace for a wide-angle Pudong panorama.

30+ Subway: East Nanjing Road All major cards

WUYUE RENJIA MIANGUAN
$
10, ALLEY 706, HUAIHAI ZHONGLU
TEL 021 5306-5410

Perfect for a full-blown meal or a swift snack, this popular and traditionally styled noodle house delivers bowl after bowl of delicious soup noodles and wontons. No English menu.

40 No credit cards accepted

SHAOXING

XIANHENG HOTEL (XIANHENG DAJIUDIAN)
$$$ ✪✪✪✪

680 JIEFANG NANJIE
TEL 0575 806-8688
FAX 0575 805-1028
www.xianhengchina.com

Smart and not overly expensive choice located in the south of Shaoxing. Tennis courts.

200+ All major cards

SUZHOU

SHERATON SUZHOU & TOWERS
$$$$ ✪✪✪✪✪

388 XINSHI LU
TEL 0512 6510-3388
FAX 0512 6510-0888
www.sheraton-suzhou.com

Located north of the Panmen scenic area, the Sheraton Suzhou is the best in town, deftly embracing the local architectural vernacular with its upturned eaves, waterways, bridges, and gorgeous gardens. Tennis courts.

484 All major cards

BAMBOO GROVE
$$$ ✪✪✪✪

168 ZHUHUI LU
TEL 0512 6520-5601
FAX 0512 6520-8778
www.bg-hotel.com

One of Suzhou's few top-end hotels, the well-positioned Bamboo Grove, picturesquely surrounding a rock pool with ducks, deals with large numbers of Western travelers. The decor is beginning to look a bit threadbare, but the huge servings of bacon at breakfast are highly recommended. Evening live music in foyer bar.

405 All major cards

SONGHELOU (SONGHELOU)
$

18 TAIJIAN NONG,
141 GUANQIAN JIE
TEL 0512 6523-3270

The long-standing Songhelou dishes up standard Eastern Chinese seaboard fare, such as squirrel-shaped mandarin fish and *gu su* marinated duck, at tourist prices. The restaurant is near the Xuanmiao Temple. English menu.

220 AE

IA YOU FANG

This street lined with restaurants just north of the Garden of Happiness is popular with the locals (and that's where it counts), there is little to distinguish one eatery from another, so take your pick.

WUHAN

SHANGRI-LA HOTEL (XIANGGELILA DAFANDIAN)
$$$$ ✪✪✪✪

700 JIANSHE DADAO, HANKOU
TEL 027 8580-6868
FAX 027 8577-6868
www.shangri-la.com

This notable luxury hotel, Wuhan's first of an international standard, prides itself on a philosophy of cultured Oriental hospitality. The service is friendly and assured, unobtrusive yet caring, and the amenities are all first class. Chinese restaurant, Western café, and restaurant. Horizon Club (executive) floors. Excellent business facilities. Outdoor tennis court.

520 All major cards

JIANGHAN HOTEL (JIANGHAN FANDIAN)
$$ ✪✪✪✪

245 SHENGLI JIE
TEL 027 8281-1600
FAX 027 8281-4342
www.jjhotel.com

A colonial edifice in the heart of Hankou not far from the old Hankou train station. Built by the French early in the 19th century, the hotel is knee-deep in history. It's an excellent place from which to patrol the old concession architecture in riverside Hankou. Shops, restaurants (Cantonese/Chiu Chow, Northern Chinese).

110 All major cards

WUXI

NEW WORLD COURTYARD WUXI
$$$ ✪✪✪✪

335 ZHONGSHAN LU
TEL 0510 8276-3388
FAX 0510 8276-3388
www.marriott.com

Located in the center of town, the Marriott-run, 36-story New World Courtyard is the tallest tower in Wuxi. Guest rooms are supplied with daily newspapers, satellite TV, coffee, in-room safe, and Internet access. Chinese and Japanese restaurants.

277 All major cards

MILIDO HOTEL
$$ ✪✪✪

2 LIANGXI LU
TEL 0510 586-5665
FAX 0510 580-1668

Situated near the Grand Canal, the Milido Hotel is one of the most upmarket places in town, with good service and inexpensive rooms making for an enjoyable stay. Business center. Bike rental.

188 All major cards

YANGZHOU

XIYUAN HOTEL
$$$$ ✪✪✪✪

1 FENGLE SHANGJIE
TEL 0514 8780-7888

FAX 0514 8723-3870
Excellently located hotel attractively set in greenery and near the canal, with pleasant rooms.
250 All major cards

YICHANG

TAOHUALING HOTEL (TAOHUALING BINGUAN)

$ ✪✪✪✪

29 YUNJI LU
TEL 0717 623-6666
FAX0717 623-8888

Built in 1957, the Taohualing is a renovated hotel in the center of town. Postal service, ticketing office, bowling, business center. Breakfast is included.
282 All major cards

ZHENJIANG

INTERNATIONAL HOTEL (ZHENJIANG GUOJI FANDIAN)

$$ ✪✪✪✪

218 JIEFANG LU
TEL 0511 502-1888
FAX 0511 502-1777

Zhenjiang's best hotel, the four-star International is centrally located and has a revolving restaurant on the 29th floor.
430 All major cards

YANCHUN HOUSE (YANCHUN JIULOU)

$ ✪✪✪

17 RENMIN LU, OFF DAXI LU
TEL 0511 501-0478

This is Zhenjiang's most famous eatery, serving up dim sum and local specialties, not far from the museum in the north of town. Water is poured into your teacup—containing sugar, dried chamomile flowers, and berries—from an impressive distance by sharpshooter waiters. No English menu.
230 No credit cards accepted

THE SOUTH

DINGHUSHAN

DINGHU SUMMER RESORT (DINGHU BISHU SHANZHUANG)

$ ✪✪

TEL 0758 262-1668
FAX 0758 262-1665

You may want to stay at Dinghushan for a while before the grind back to Guangzhou. The resort, not far from the bus stop, has a good range of amenities. Travel center, currency exchange.
47 No credit cards accepted

GUANGZHOU

GRAND HYATT GUANGZHOU

$$$$$ ✪✪✪✪✪

12 ZHUJIANG XILU
TEL 020 8396-1234
FAX 020 8550-8234
www.guangzhou.grand.hyatt.com

Spacious standard rooms come with granite bath, iPod docking stations, and huge windows at this excellent hotel in the Tianhe business district. Smart dining options include the natty **G** on the 22nd floor, serving fantastic seafood and grills. Wi-Fi available.
350 All major cards

WHITE SWAN HOTEL (BAITIAN'E BINGUAN)

$$$ ✪✪✪✪✪

1 SHAMIAN NANJIE, SHAMIAN ISLAND
TEL 020 8188-6968
www.whiteswanhotel.com

The White Swan is not a new hotel and it's lost some of its shine, but it sits commandingly on picturesque Shamian Island, replete with five-star amenities and service. The hotel is very popular with couples coming to China to adopt Chinese children. Impressive fountain in foyer and well-stocked shopping arcade. Pearl River night cruise. Nine restaurants. Limousine service. Tennis and squash courts.
843 All major cards

SHAMIAN HOTEL (SHAMIAN BINGUAN)

$ ✪✪

52 SHAMIAN NANJIE
TEL 020 8121-8288
FAX 020 8121-8628
www.gdshamianhotel.com

A budget hotel offering an affordable and pleasant stay and a view over the Pearl River. The standards are rudimentary but serviceable, and with the rest of the island as your back garden, does it matter?
50 No credit cards accepted

BANXI (BANXI JIUJIA)

$$

151 LONGJIN XILU
TEL 0208 181-5718 OR 0208 8181-5955

This famous restaurant in west Guangzhou is the place to come for the full social event around the eating of Cantonese dim sum (especially on weekends). The rest of the menu is a cavalcade of tasty regional Cantonese cuisine *(yuecai)*.
1,500–2,000 No credit cards accepted

DONGBEIREN

$

1 TAOJIN BEILU, 2ND FL.
TEL 020 8357-5276
www.dongbeiren.com.cn

This funky little chain of restaurants serves up fantastic dumplings *(jiaozi)* from China's Manchurian region. Nineteen different types of handmade dumplings. Professional service, gregarious, and fun. English

menu. Also at 36 Garden Building, **Tianhe Nanlu** *(tel 8750-1711)*, and **668 Renmin Beilu** *(tel 020 8136-1466)*.
40–50 No credit cards accepted

GUANGZHOU (GUANGZHOU JIUJIA)
$
2 WENCHANG LU
TEL 020 8138-0388
www.gzr.com.cn
The Guangzhou has been serving up Cantonese cuisine since 1936 and has spawned several branches. The restaurant is busy (perhaps phone for a reservation), the food authentic and well presented, the menu extensive, and the dim sum very popular. English menu.
500+ Closed 3 p.m.–5:30 p.m. All major cards

HAINAN ISLAND

Winter season is the high season on Hainan Island. If you travel after March, hotel rooms will be up to 40 percent cheaper.

SOMETHING SPECIAL

HILTON SANYA RESORT & SPA (XIERDUN WENQUAN DUJIA JIUDIAN)
$$$$ ✪✪✪✪✪
WENLING LU NANDUAN
TEL 0898 8858-8888
FAX 0898 8858-8588
www.sanya.hilton.com
Bringing its brand of excellence to the beachfront of Yalong Bay, this new resort from Hilton has all you need for intensive comfort and relaxation. The private beach is lovely, the views from the rooms are all you could want, and hotel staff are highly attentive without being intrusive.
501 All major cards

GLORIA RESORT SANYA (KALAI DUJIA JIUDIAN)
$$$–$$$$ ✪✪✪✪✪
YALONG BAY
TEL 0898 8856-8855
FAX 0898 8856-8533
www.gloriaresort.com
Enjoying an enviable location on Hainan's most pristine beach, the Gloria Resort is the perfect place to unwind. Rooms come with in-house movies, minibar, and fabulous views. Restaurants and full range of resort facilities.
403 All major cards

MERITUS MANDARIN HAIKOU
$$$ ✪✪✪✪✪
18 WENHUA LU
TEL 0898 6854-8888
FAX 0898 6851-1228
www.meritushotels.com
Located in the financial district of the provincial capital, Haikou's best hotel, the 23-story Meritus Mandarin supplies the full range of international standard facilities and services. Chinese and Italian restaurants. Tennis courts.
318 All major cards

LUSHAN

LUSHAN VILLA HOTEL (LUSHAN BIESHU CUN BINGUAN)
$$$
182 ZHIHONG LU
TEL 0792 828-2927
FAX 0792 828-2927
The hotel has a number of villas and cottages tucked away in the forest and is one of the best ways to appreciate Lushan's charming character. Wide range of prices.
100+ No credit cards accepted

PRICES

HOTELS

An indication of the cost of a double room in the high season is given by **$** signs.

$$$$$	Over $350
$$$$	$180–$350
$$$	$100–$180
$$	$40–$100
$	Under $40

RESTAURANTS

An indication of the cost of a three-course meal without drinks is given by **$** signs.

$$$$$	Over $100
$$$$	$75–$100
$$$	$50–$75
$$	$30–$50
$	Under $30

LUSHAN YUNTIAN VILLA (LUSHAN YUNTIAN BIESHU)
$$ ✪✪✪
GULING ZHENGJIE
TEL 0792 829-3555
Too many of Lushan's hotels are slowly going to seed. This alternative—centrally located in Guling—brings a fresh approach to its original villa architecture.
30 No credit cards accepted

WULINGYUAN

DRAGON INTERNATIONAL HOTEL (XIANGLONG GUOJI DAJIUDIAN)
$$ ✪✪✪✪
46 JIEFANG DONGLU, ZHANGJIAJIE CITY
TEL 0744 822-6888
FAX 0744 822-2935
This is the best choice if you want to stay in Zhangjiajie City

rather than the village. The hotel is decidedly a tour-group hotel but plusher than the more basic accommodations in Zhangjiajie Village. Tours of Wulingyuan, rafting, and cave trips can easily be arranged by the tourist center here.

200+ All major cards

PIPAXI HOTEL (PIPAXI BINGUAN)
$$

TEL 0744 571-8888
www.pipaxi-hotel.com

Quietly hidden away, yet still only a short walk to the gates of Wulingyuan, the popular Pipaxi Hotel offers pleasant and comfortable rooms and a measure of tranquillity.

180 No credit cards accepted

XIAMEN

MILLENNIUM HARBOUR VIEW HOTEL (JIARI HUANGGUAN HAIJING DAJIUDIAN)
$$$$ ✪✪✪✪

12-8 ZHENHAI LU
TEL 0592 202-3333
FAX 0592 203-6666
www.millenniumxiamen.com

Once managed by Holiday Inn, this is a hospitable and affordable hotel in the heart of town, with towering views over Gulangyu. Rooms are routinely heavily discounted.

367 All major cards

GULANGYU INTERNATIONAL YOUTH HOSTEL (GULANGYU GUOJI QINGNIAN LUGUAN)
$

18 LUJIAO LU
TEL 0592 206-6066

It is infinitely preferable to stay on Gulangyu rather than in Xiamen, so hop on a ferry. Conveniently located just a short walk up from the ferry pier, this charming hostel operates from an old Gulangyu villa. Rooms are spacious and inviting. Book ahead as it can be busy. Internet available.

6 No credit cards accepted

HONG KONG & MACAU

HONG KONG

MANDARIN ORIENTAL
$$$$$ ✪✪✪✪✪

5 CONNAUGHT RD., CENTRAL, HONG KONG ISLAND
TEL 0852 2522-0111
www.mandarinoriental .com

Thoroughly renovated in 2006, the Mandarin Oriental is a landmark in Hong Kong's dazzling hotel firmament. First-class service and facilities.

542 Subway: Central All major cards

SOMETHING SPECIAL

THE PENINSULA
$$$$$ ✪✪✪✪✪

SALISBURY RD., KOWLOON
TEL 0852 2920-2888
FAX 0852 2722-4170
www.peninsula.com

Highly sophisticated, grand, and elegant, this hotel makes your stay an event, with some of the territory's most distinguished experiences (see Felix, p. 376) and *the* place to come for afternoon tea. The corner suites are equipped with magnificent wide vistas, and the harborside view is out of this world. Even if you feel you can't quite afford the cost, it's well worth throwing caution to the wind for gilt-edged memories. First-class shopping arcade. Rolls Royce fleet. Helicopter service.

300 Subway: Tsim Sha Tsui All major cards

RITZ-CARLTON HONG KONG
$$$$$

INTERNATIONAL COMMERCE CENTRE, 1 AUSTIN ROAD, KOWLOON
TEL 0852 2263-2263
FAX 0852 2263-2260
www.ritzcarlton.com

One of the world's highest hotels above ground level, the brand-new Ritz-Carlton occupies floors 102 to 118 of the dazzling International Commerce Centre, with rooms looking out onto a breathtaking panorama. Rooms are state-of-the-art, providing a high degree of comfort and convenience. A dip in the hotel's pool is a most for quite stunning views, rounded off with a drink on the rooftop bar. Wi-Fi available.

312 All major cards

ISLAND SHANGRI-LA
$$$$ ✪✪✪✪✪

PACIFIC PLACE, SUPREME COURT RD., CENTRAL, HONG KONG ISLAND
TEL 0852 2877-3838
FAX 0852 2521-8742
www.shangri-la.com

Encased by one of the most attractive buildings on Hong Kong Island, the interior of the Shangri-La is equally breathtaking. One of the jewels in the Shangri-La crown with panoramic views over to Kowloon. Chinese, Japanese, French, and seafood restaurants.

565 Subway: Admiralty All major cards

SOMETHING SPECIAL

THE UPPER HOUSE
$$$$

88 QUEENSWAY, PACIFIC PLACE, ADMIRALTY
TEL 0852 2918-1838
www.upperhouse.com

This fastidiously neat boutique Hong Kong Island-side hotel is

a master class in style, from the gorgeous rooms to the lovely lawn. Wi-Fi available.
117 All major cards

JIA

$$$

1–5 IRVING ST., CAUSEWAY BAY
TEL 00852 3196-9000
FAX 00852 3196-9001
www.jiahongkong.com

!t's never going to be everyone's cup of tea, but the Philippe Starck-designed Jia will be an instant hit with trendy young travelers in search of a super-chic boutique space to hang their hat in Honkers. While not spacious, the open-plan studios (with kitchen) are fine for short stays, and the snappily attired staff nudges the hotel into seriously cool territory. Guests enjoy free access to a nearby health club.
57 Subway: Causeway Bay All major cards

KOWLOON HOTEL

$$$ ✪✪✪✪

19–21 NATHAN RD., KOWLOON
TEL 00852 2929-2888
FAX 00852 2739-9811
www.thekowloonhotel.com

The Kowloon Hotel enjoys an excellent location on Kowloon's "Golden Mile," within range of most sights of note and a short walk from the Star Ferry Pier. Convenient and inexpensive, standard rooms may not be spacious but are fine for short-stay travelers, coming computer-equipped (aim for rooms on upper floors if you want good views). Good choice of restaurants, shopping arcade.
736 Subway: Tsim Sha Tsui All major cards

SALISBURY YMCA

$$$

41 SALISBURY RD.
TEL 832 2268-7888
www.ymcahk.org.hk

The dorms here are good value, and the location just down from the Peninsula is excellent, but double rooms are simple. It's not upscale, but this is one of the best mid-range options in town; maximum stay is seven nights.
380 Subway: Tsim Sha Tsui All major cards

DYNASTY

$$$$

4TH FLOOR., NEW WORLD HOTEL, 22 SALISBURY RD., TSIM SHA TSUI
TEL 0852 2369-4111 EXT 6361

Cantonese dining in a traditional Chinese teahouse ambience. One of Hong Kong's finest Cantonese restaurants; specialties include baked silver cod and steamed sliced pork with preserved shrimp paste. Excellent wine list. No prix fixe meals.
88 Subway: Tsim Sha Tsui All major cards

FELIX

$$$$

PENINSULA
TEL 852 2315-3188
www.peninsula.com

Felix takes dining to new heights on the 28th floor of the Peninsula. The work of French designer Philippe Starck, the restaurant is imaginatively theatrical, and the views are as inspiring as the dishes. Felix has its own mood-lighting-equipped elevator. International/Pan-Asian cuisine. Three bars (the Wine Bar, the Balcony, and the American Bar) and dance floor. Smart/casual dress code.
110 Subway: Tsim Sha Tsui All major cards

MAN WAH

$$$$

25TH FLOOR, MANDARIN ORIENTAL , 5 CONNAUGHT RD., CENTRAL
TEL 0852 2522-0111 EXT 4025
www.mandarinoriental.com

With views over Victoria Harbour, the hallmark hotel's elegant Chinese restaurant offers a feast of Cantonese flavors in a refined, traditional Chinese setting. Signature dishes include fillet of sole in black bean sauce, beggar's chicken, and stuffed prawns, with dim sum served on weekends and public holidays.
130 Subway: Central All major cards

BAR

$$$ ✪✪✪✪✪

THE PENINSULA, 1ST FL. SALISBURY RD., TSIM SHA TSUI
TEL 0852 2920-2888 EXT 3163
www.peninsula.com

The Bar is expensive, but the highly civilized ambience and sterling service are almost peerless. A hushed, seductive, and superlative tavern, but no formal restaurant. Smart/casual dress code.
46 Subway: Tsim Sha Tsui All major cards

HUNAN GARDEN

$$$

3RD FLOOR, THE FORUM, EXCHANGE SQUARE, CENTRAL
TEL 0852 2868-2880

This restaurant expertly re-creates the fiery aromas of Hunan cuisine. Elegantly decorated ambience and fine presentation. The chicken in spicy sauce will set you in the right direction. Good wine list. Prix fixe meals.
300+ Subway: Central Closed 3 p.m.–6 p.m. All major cards

HUTONG

$$$

1 PEKING RD., 28TH FLOOR, TSIM SHA TSUI, KOWLOON
TEL 0852 3428-8342
www.aqua.com.hk

The faux Beijing *hutong* styling is simply seductive—if highly contrived—and the jaw-dropping views better still at this outstanding Kowloon restaurant. The cuisine is north Chinese with some spicy Sichuan dishes thrown in for added piquancy. Reserve ahead; minimum charge per person.
30+ Subway: Tsim Sha Tsui Closed 2:30 p.m.–6 p.m. All major cards

JIMMY'S KITCHEN
$$$
BASEMENT, SOUTH CHINA BUILDING, 1 WYNDHAM ST., CENTRAL
TEL 0852 2526-5293
www.jimmys.com
An old-timer that has seen a lot of restaurants close around it. Jimmy's plentiful European menu has a loyal fan base. Try the escargots in garlic butter or char-grilled king prawns, and round it all off with hot apple crumble. English menu.
120 Subway: Central Closed 3 p.m.–6 p.m. All major cards

KUNG TAK LAM
$$$
1 PEKING RD., 7TH FL., TSIM SHA TSUI, KOWLOON
TEL 0852 2312-7800
The famous vegetarian name Gongdelin (Kung Tak Lam in Cantonese) brings its appetizing Shanghai Buddhist menu to Hong Kong with this meat- and MSG-free restaurant. The emphasis is on dishes that resemble meat but are made without a shred of flesh.
30 AE, MC, V

PEAK LOOKOUT
$$$
121 PEAK RD., THE PEAK, HONG KONG ISLAND
TEL 0852 2849-1000
www.peaklookout.com.hk
Formerly the Peak Café, the relaxing colonial setting of the Lookout on Victoria Peak is splendid, with a respected menu celebrating Asian and International cuisine. The restaurant is notable for its seafood dishes, and there's a much celebrated alfresco dining area on the terrace. Breakfast is served Saturday, Sunday, and public holidays (8:30 a.m.–11:30 a.m.).
250 Peak Tram Station MC, V

YUNG KEE
$$$
32–40 WELLINGTON ST., CENTRAL
TEL 0852 2522-1624
www.yungkee.com.hk
Dating back to 1942 and one of Hong Kong's most famous Cantonese diners, four-floor Yung Kee's specialty dish is its splendid roast goose. There's much more to the menu than fowl, including dim sum and a host of other Cantonese dishes.
60+ Subway: Central All major cards

CLUB 71
$$
BASEMENT, 67 HOLLYWOOD RD., CENTRAL
TEL 0852 2858-7071
You trip over chic bars by the bundle in Hong Kong, but for the more no-frills crowd, Club 71 is one of NoHo's (North of Hollywood Road) choice spots for intelligent discussions over drinks.
50 Subway: Central or Sheungwan MC, V

TUTTO BENE
$$
7 KNUTSFORD TERRACE TSIM SHA TSUI
TEL 0852 2316 2116
www.mhihk.com
Quietly tucked away in an alley of restaurants and bars east off Nathan Road, Tutto Bene delivers quality, inexpensive Italian food and good service in an agreeable setting. There's an alfresco dining option at one of the tables parked outside. Wi-Fi.
100 Subway: Tsim Sha Tsui Closed for lunch All major cards

BOOKWORM CAFÉ
$
79 MAIN ST., YUNG SHUE WAN, LAMMA ISLAND
TEL 00852 2982-4838
http://bookwormcafe.com.hk
The Wi-Fi–equipped Bookworm long ago won acclaim as a much loved used bookshop and veggie café rolled into one.
12 MC, V

ORGANIC
$
10 SHELLY ST., CENTRAL
TEL 00852 2810-9777
www.lifecafe.com.hk
First stop for vegetarians and vegans alike or simply those aiming at a first-rate detox.
50 Subway: Central All major cards

LUK YU TEAHOUSE & RESTAURANT
$
24–26 STANLEY ST., CENTRAL
TEL 0852 2523-5464
One of Hong Kong's most famous Cantonese teahouses, Luk Yu is a very popular place to *yum cha* (drink tea, relax) and eat excellent dim sum. The service (cantankerous aged waiters) flags way behind, but everyone's used to it. Reservations recommended. Dim sum daily.
300 Subway: Central All major cards

STEAM & STEW INN
$
21–23 TAI WONG ST. EAST, WAN CHAI, HONG KONG ISLAND
TEL 0852 2529-3913
The air heavy with steamy aromas and the boiled infusion of Cantonese herbs and

spices, the emphasis here is not so much on elegance as on authentic, healthy dinner preparations. Highly popular. MSG-free dining. Prix fixe meals. No wine. English menu.
100+ Subway: Wan Chai Closed 2:30 p.m.–5:30 p.m. MC, V

MACAU

Before heading to Macau, be aware that you can get a much cheaper room (up to 50 percent off) if you book your ticket and hotel room through one of the numerous outlets in the Shun Tak Centre at the Macau Ferry Terminal, Sheung Wan, Hong Kong Island.

If you arrive in Macau without a room, a number of mid-range and upscale hotels have counters at the hydrofoil pier where you can negotiate a price much lower than the walk-in price. Hotel rooms are far cheaper during the slack weekday period, with large price hikes on weekends (when large numbers of Hong Kong Chinese come to Macau). A number of shuttle buses run to hotels from the pier.

POUSADA DE SAO TIAGO
$$$$$ ✪✪✪✪✪
AVENIDA DE REPUBLICA
TEL 0853 2837-8111
FAX 0853 2855-2170
www.saotiago.com.mo

Perched on the southern tip of the peninsula overlooking the harbor, this hotel is delightfully incorporated into the 17th-century Barra Fort (Fortaleza da Barra), which also contains the Chapel of St James. Indulge in a drink or meal on the terrace. The elegant hotel has a limited number of rooms, each equipped with its own balcony affording splendid views, so reservations are much recommended. Complementary pier transfer and shuttle service.
12 All major cards

WESTIN RESORT MACAU
$$$$ ✪✪✪✪✪
1918 ESTRADA DE HAC SA, COLOANE
TEL 0853 2887-1111
FAX 0853 2887-1122
www.westin.com/macau

Located on Hac Sa Beach on Coloane, the Westin is a popular resort with a plethora of five-star facilities, including a championship golf course, both indoor and outdoor pools, and tennis courts, while the Kids Club can lend a hand with children. Rooms all have terraces and sea views, and come with the trademark Westin Heavenly Bed.
208 All major cards

ROCKS HOTEL
$$$ ✪✪✪✪
FISHERMAN'S WHARF
TEL 0853 2878-2782
FAX 0853 2872-8800
www.rockshotel.com.mo

Lovely Victorian-esque boutique hotel down along Fisherman's Wharf on the eastern side of the Macau peninsular, with tasty harbor views and period charms. Shuttle bus from ferry terminal.
72 All major cards

HOLIDAY INN
$$–$$$
82–86 RUA DE PEQUIM
TEL 0853 2878-3333
www.macau.holiday-inn.com

A reliably decent hotel, equipped with an efficient range of amenities and services. Nightclub, cable TV, gym. Situated within easy reach of the hydrofoil pier. Shuttle bus.
410 All major cards

MEZZALUNA
$$$ ✪✪✪✪
MANDARIN ORIENTAL HOTEL, 956 AVENIDA DE AMIZADE
TEL 0853 8793-3861
www.mandarinoriental.com

Fine, upscale Italian restaurant in one of the territory's premier hotels. Nice setting, fresh pasta, very successful pizza. Dress code. Reservations recommended. English menu.
58 All major cards

FAT SIU LAU
$$
64 RUA DE FELICIDADE
TEL 0853 2857-3580

Dating to the early 20th century and located at the center of Macau, this celebrated old Macanese restaurant has a name that means "Buddha Laughing Building." The standout dish is the "Shek Ki Superb Roasted Pigeon," prepared using a technique that has remained confidential for more than a century. Additional branches can be found on Avenida Dr. Sun Yat-Sen (*tel 0853 2872-29222*) and on the island of

PRICES

HOTELS

An indication of the cost of a double room in the high season is given by **$** signs.

$$$$$	Over $350
$$$$	$180–$350
$$$	$100–$180
$$	$40–$100
$	Under $40

RESTAURANTS

An indication of the cost of a three-course meal without drinks is given by **$** signs.

$$$$$	Over $100
$$$$	$75–$100
$$$	$50–$75
$$	$30–$50
$	Under $30

Taipa *(181–185 Rua do Regedor, tel 0853 2882-5257)*
30+ AE, MC, V

PINOCCHIO
$$
4 RUA DO SOL, TAIPA VILLAGE
TEL 0853 2882-7128
Huge Portuguese restaurant in picturesque Taipa Village, waylaying tourists with a mammoth menu including roast lamb, deep-fried sardines, curried crab, and grilled squid. Weekend reservations recommended. English menu. A choice of other restaurants peppers Rua da Cunha around the corner.
300+ All major cards

SOMETHING SPECIAL

RESTAURANTE FERNANDO
$$ ○○○○
9 HAC SA BEACH, COLOANE
TEL 0853 2888-2264
www.fernando-restaurant.com
An excellent wine list accompanies superb Portuguese dining at this noteworthy eatery on Coloane's eastern shore. Fernando conjures up some fine magic with lamb, clams, shrimps, prawns, and Portuguese recipes in a simple setting. The restaurant has a stunning reputation, so weekend reservations are necessary if not mandatory.
100+ No credit cards accepted

RESTAURANTE LITORAL
$$
261A RUA DO ALMIRANTE SERGIO
TEL 0853 2896-7878
www.restaurante-litoral.com
One of Macau's best restaurants for Macanese and Portuguese cuisine, with a charming interior.
30+ AE, MC, V

A LORCHA
$
289A RUA DO ALMIRANTE SERGIO
TEL 0853 2831-3193
If you've done the walk south to the Maritime Museum/ A-Ma Temple, treat yourself at A Lorcha. A feast of Portuguese flavors is conjured up by fine chefmanship; raw codfish salad, African chicken, pork knuckles, and other temptations. English menu. Weekend reservations recommended.
60 Closed Tues.
AE, MC, V

MARGARET'S CAFÉ E NATA
$
GUM LOI BUILDING, 17 RUA COMMANDANTE
TEL 0853 710-032
Sit in the square outside and work your way through one of the breakfasts: egg tarts, sandwiches, cheesecake, and coffee. English menu. Also at Rua Almirante Costa Cabral not far from the Lou Lim Ieoc Gardens *(tel 0853 527 791)*.
50 No credit cards accepted

NGA TIM CAFÉ
$
8 RUA CAETANO, COLOANE VILLAGE
TEL 0853 2888-2086
Picturesquely situated opposite St. Francis Xavier's, this café is a feast of good-value Macau and Portuguese food, with a fine reputation for seafood.
64 MC, V

THE SOUTHWEST

BEIHAI

SHANGRI-LA HOTEL (XIANGGELILA FANDIAN)
$$ ○○○○
33 CHATING LU
TEL 0779 206-2288
FAX 0779 205-0085
www.shangri-la.com
By far Beihai's best hotel, facing the sea with spacious but affordable rooms. As with all Shangri-La hotels, executive floors provide a superior degree of comfort and service. Chinese and Western restaurants. Half an hour from the international airport. Horizon Club (executive) floors. Bike rental.
364 All major cards

DALI

JADE EMU
$
XIMEN CUN
TEL 0872 267-7311
www.jade-emu.com
Located just outside Dali's West Gate, this excellent and homey hostel has clean dorms and doubles, offering great value and a chance to escape the hubbub in town. The Australian-Chinese management means staff is very switched on to travelers' needs, with all kinds of helpful advice.
25 All major cards

JIM'S TIBETAN GUEST HOUSE
$
13 YUXIU LU
TEL 0872 267-17824
www.china-travel.nl
Half-Hui, half-Tibetan, English-speaking Jim has been wooing guests for many years in Dai, with a combination of charming rooms and fine dining, and if that doesn't get you going, he'll lay his 40 percent proof No. 1 special on you: a stunning pink-elephant-inducing spirit seasoned with an exotic spray of herbs. Jim can also arrange a multitude of area tours. Wi-Fi.
7 No credit cards accepted

MCA HOTEL (HUALANG JIUDIAN)
$ ✪✪
WENXIAN LU
TEL 0872 267-3666 OR 0872 267-1999
www.mcahotel.com
The hotel has a large and popular range of rooms, from doubles to family rooms. There's bike rental, ticketing, and Internet access.
48 No credit cards accepted

CAFÉ DE JACK
$
82 BO'AI LU
TEL 0872 267-1572
A veritable old-timer and much respected standby in Dali's ever shifting galaxy of bars and restaurants, Café de Jack is a snug spot with a mixed menu of good-value local Bai and Western dishes, vegetarian options, and cups of steaming Yunnan coffee.
No credit cards accepted

CLOCK TOWER CAFÉ
$
YANGREN JIE
TEL 0872 267-1883
With a great roof-terrace bar, this recommended three-floor outfit is very popular with travelers for its winning Western menu and breakfasts.
No credit cards accepted

DRAGON'S BACKBONE

LONGYING HOTEL (LONGYING FANDIAN)
$
PING'AN
TEL 0773 758-3059
With excellent views from its terrace, this handy hotel with good rooms and a pleasant atmosphere is situated at the top of Ping'an village, making a great base for treks around the rice terraces.
40 MC, V

GUILIN

BRAVO HOTEL
$$$ ✪✪✪✪
14 RONGHUA NANLU
TEL 0773 289-8888
FAX 0773 289-3999
www.glbravohotel.com
Among the best hotels in town, this former Holiday Inn offers good value and a decent range of four-star amenities. Service is efficient, restaurants good, and some rooms overlook the river.
259 All major cards

GUILIN FUBO HOTEL (GUILIN FUBOSHAN ZHUANG)
$$ ✪✪✪
121 BINJIANG LU
TEL 0773 282-9988
FAX 0773 282-2328
This clean three-star hotel is popular with Westerners. Spread over only a few floors like all hotels in Guilin (height restrictions protect the view), the Fubo is in a splendid location next to Fuboshan (Wave-subduing Hill) and the Li River. Chilled water delivered to your room.
150 All major cards

SHERATON GUILIN (GUILIN DAYU DAFANDIAN)
$$ ✪✪✪✪✪
15 BINJIANG NANLU
TEL 0773 282-5588
FAX 0773 282-5598
www.sheraton.com
Overlooking the Li River, the Sheraton has a majestic location and offers excellent facilities with very comfortable rooms. Restaurants include Chinese and Western fine dining options and a popular bar.
430 All major cards

JINGHONG

NEW TAI GARDEN HOTEL (DAIYUAN JIUDIAN)
$ ✪✪✪✪
61 MINHANG LU
TEL 0691 212-3888
www.newtgh.com
Jinghong's luxury option sports clean and attractive rooms and a bright, marbled interior. The hotel's restaurant and entertainment options are mainly Chinese (heavy on the karaoke), but the service is efficient, and Jinghong's remorseless tacky character is kept at bay—a different world from the rest of Jinghong. The breakfast—coffee, pancakes, sausage, egg, and toast—is excellent.
172 All major cards

MEI MEI CAFÉ (MEI MEI KAFEIDIAN)
$
MENGLONG LU
TEL 0691 216-1221
The Mei Mei ("pretty pretty") Café serves up pineapple shakes, burgers, and BLT sandwiches to enthusiastic backpackers. Settle into a rattan chair and reach for the gripping travelers' tales notebooks (with recommended sorties into the undergrowth around town). Book exchange and Internet.
20 No credit cards accepted

KUNMING

KUNMING HOTEL
$$ ✪✪✪✪
52 DONGFENG DONGLU
TEL 0871 316-2063 OR 0871 316-2172
www.kunminghotel.com.cn
For a four-star hotel, the lobby is a tad overblown, but the glitter, shine, and sparkling chandeliers are a presage of clean rooms along elegant corridors, especially on the

executive floors. The exterior is certainly more stylish than the Holiday Inn opposite. Staying here puts you in the heart of the city, within striking distance of decent bars and restaurants. Tennis court.

236 All major cards

CAMELLIA HOTEL (CHAHUA BINGUAN)
$
96 DONGFENG DONGLU
TEL 0871 316-3000
FAX 0871 314-7033
www.kmcamelliahotel.com

Kunming's budget option, the Camellia dorms play host to most of the backpackers that drift into town. Very cheap and with no frills, this is the place to trade tales from the road with like-minded veterans on the Yunnan circuit. Bicycle rental.

279 All major cards

YUQUANZHAI VEGETARIAN RESTAURANT
$$
22 YUANTONG JIE
TEL 0871 511-1809

With a handy English menu proferred to its numerous foreign diners, this veggie eatery has done excellent business. Following the Buddhist tradition of preparing vegetables to resemble meat but without an ounce of flesh, Yuquanzhai is a reliably good, indeed fascinating, dining option.

No credit cards accepted

HALFWAY HOUSE
$
OFF DONGFENG XILU
TEL 0871 535-2702

Dependable and long-standing lbar west of Greenlake Park in the northwest of town. Live music picks things up; otherwise it's a decent and welcoming place.

No credit cards accepted

LIJIANG

BANYAN TREE LIJIANG
$$$$ ✪✪✪✪
YUERONG LU, SHUHE (NEAR LIJIANG)
TEL 0888 533-1111
FAX 0888 533-2222
www.banyantree.com

Located near the ancient village of Shuhe, the hotel gets you away from the crowds that increasingly fill Lijiang. With a splendid variety of delightfully dressed rooms and villas (some with pool), the top-notch views to Jade Dragon Snow Mountain are simply gorgeous. The spa also gets rave reviews, and service is virtually faultless.

55 villas All major cards

ZEN GARDEN HOTEL
$$$
36 XINGREN XIADUAN
TEL 0888 518-9799
www.zengardenhotel.com

The Lijiang old town can be a busy place, despite—or, in fact, because of—its picturesque charm. With its lovely design, tranquilizing mood, and stress-busting ambience, the Zen Garden Hotel is an appealing old-town choice, with attractive suites and double rooms.

14, 2 suites All major cards

DONGBA HOTEL
$
109 WENZHI XIANG
TEL 0888 512-1975
www.dongbahotel.com

Ever popular old-town hotel—named after the ancient Dongba culture—and ever inexpensive, with loads of character and charm, some fantastic single and double rooms, and a welcoming atmosphere.

10 No credit cards accepted

BLUE PAGE VEGETARIAN (LANYE SUSHI CANGUAN)
$
69 MISHI ALLEY, XINYI JIE, OLD TOWN
TEL 0888 518-5206

This rather frugal and snug restaurant is a lovely place to enjoy meat-free dishes. The Dali toasted cheese sandwich is scrumptious. Candles create a soothing mood.

20 No credit cards accepted

SAKURA CAFÉ (YINGHUA WU)
$
123 CUIWENDUAN, XINHUA ST., OLD TOWN
TEL 0888 518-7619 OR 0888 312-6766
www.sakura.yn.cn

An engaging and comfortable mishmash of Italian, Korean, Japanese, and Naxi cuisine with travel advice thrown in, Sakura Café is picturesquely sited next to the canal in Lijiang's old town. Internet.

50 No credit cards accepted

SANJIANG

CHENGYANG BRIDGE HOSTEL (CHENGYANG QIAO ZHAODAISUO)
$ ✪✪
TEL 0772 861-2444

Dong-style hotel with riverside balconied restaurant near the bridge. Simple provisions and basic accommodations.

No credit cards accepted

YANGSHUO

Xi Jie is a street full of restaurants and cafés serving up drinks, dishing up Western and local snacks, and dispensing travel advice. Among the best choices are the **Red Star Express** at No. 66, **Minnie Mao's** at No. 83, the **Under the Moon Café,** and **Lisa's** café, bar, and guesthouse.

YANGSHUO MOUNTAIN RETREAT
$$$$
WANGGONGSHANJIAO, GAOTIAN VILLAGE
TEL 0773 877-7091
www.yangshuomountainretreat.com
Well away from the hubbub and idyllically located near the Yulong River, this gorgeous retreat has excellent rooms looking onto stunning views.
29 MC, V

MING YUAN
$
50 XI JIE
TEL 134 5736-9680
A more civilized alternative to some of Yangshuo's hyped-up restaurants and bars, petit and enjoyable Ming Yuan offers an impressive range of coffees.
5 No credit cards accepted

SICHUAN & THE TIBETAN PLATEAU

CHENGDU

HOLIDAY INN CROWNE PLAZA CHENGDU (ZONGFU HUANGGUAN JIARI JIUDIAN)
$$$ ✪✪✪✪✪
31 ZONGFU LU
TEL 028 8678-6666
FAX 028 8678-9789
www.holidayinn.com
One of Chengdu's best. It is in need of a renovation to reintroduce zest, sparkle, and shine, but the location is excellent.
433 All major cards

JINJIANG HOTEL (JINJIANG BINGUAN)
$$$ ✪✪✪✪✪
80 RENMIN NANLU
TEL 028 8550-6666
FAX 028 8550-6550
www.jjhotel.com
By the banks of the Jinjiang River, this is one of Chengdu's smartest hotels, despite its age and the more recent competition in town. Facilities are extensive and rooms decent. Bowling alley, medical clinic, airport shuttle bus. Tennis courts.
523 All major cards

TRAFFIC HOTEL (JIAOTONG FANDIAN)
$ ✪✪
77 LINJIANG LU
TEL 028 8545-1017
FAX 028 8544-0977
www.traffichotelchengdu.cn
Well above average for the budget category, but the service can be perfunctory. The double rooms are spacious, dry, and reasonably clean, and a useful bulletin board puts you in touch with fellow travelers. The hotel's Travel Bureau speaks good English and can set you on your way to Tibet. Double rooms come with complimentary breakfast. Business center. Bike rental.
150 AE, MC, V

SOMETHING SPECIAL

BAGUOBUYI (BAGUOBUYI FENGWEI JIULOU)
$$
20 RENMIN NANLU SIDUAN
TEL 028 8553-1688
www.baguobuyi.com
The waitresses here deliver the finest Sichuan food money can buy. The atmosphere is relaxed but mildly exuberant. There's no English menu. Stick to the cheap plates; the pricier ones are more exotic (like tortoise). The delectably simple *suancai shaoniurou*, chunks of beef with crumbling potatoes settled in a wash of hot sauce, is pure heaven. The *dandan mian* (spicy noodles) are a sharp and fiery accompaniment.
400+ AE, MC, V

PRICES

HOTELS
An indication of the cost of a double room in the high season is given by **$** signs.

$$$$$	Over $350
$$$$	$180–$350
$$$	$100–$180
$$	$40–$100
$	Under $40

RESTAURANTS
An indication of the cost of a three-course meal without drinks is given by **$** signs.

$$$$$	Over $100
$$$$	$75–$100
$$$	$50–$75
$$	$30–$50
$	Under $30

CHEN MAPO DOUFU (CHEN MAPO DOUFU DIAN)
$
197 XIYULONG JIE
TEL 028 8675-4512
www.chenmapo.com
The classic Sichuan dish, *mapo doufu,* must be sampled while in Chengdu. A number of restaurants claim a lineage to the original Chen Mapo Doufu restaurant, as does this one in the city center.
300+ No credit cards accepted

DAZU

It's better to visit Dazu as a day trip from Chongqing, because accommodations are limited and poor in quality.

EMEISHAN

The temples and monasteries on Emeishan all provide very basic accommodations. At the base of the mountain near the bus station is the popular **Teddy Bear Hotel** *(tel 0833 559-0135)*. The **Hongzhushan Hotel** (**$ ✪✪✪**; *tel 0833 552-5888, fax 0833 333-788)* is a three-star option south of Baoguo Monastery that takes major credit cards and has reasonable villa accommodations. Use the hotel's travel agency to procure bus tickets.

TEDDY BEAR CAFÉ

$

On the main road leading to the Baoguo Monastery, the Teddy Bear Café is a magnet for Western travelers heading to Emeishan. Try the spicy Sichuan dishes, such as *suancai yu*, or sample the Western food. Very useful travel advice.

100+ No credit cards accepted

LHASA

LHASA HOTEL (LASA FANDIAN)

$$ ✪✪✪

1 MINZU LU

TEL 0891 683-2221

FAX 0891 683-5796

This three-star hotel north of the Norbu Lingka is about as good as it gets in Lhasa. Five restaurants (Western, Tibetan and Nepalese, Chinese); business center; ticketing office.

450 All major cards

SNOWLANDS RESTAURANT (XUEYU CANTING)

$

4 ZANGYIYUAN LU, NEXT TO SNOWLANDS HOTEL

TEL 0891 633-7323

Popular with travelers, this restaurant serves decent Chinese, Western, Indian, and Tibetan dishes; English menu available.

40 No credit cards accepted

INNER MONGOLIA & THE SILK ROAD

DUNHUANG

SILK ROAD DUNHUANG (DUNHUANG SHANZHUANG)

$$$ ✪✪✪

DUNYUE LU

TEL 0937 888-2088

FAX 0937 888-2086

www.the-silk-road.com

Settled near the Mingsha Hills south of Dunhuang City, this modern but traditionally designed hotel artfully blends into the topography of the region and is ideally located for trips to Crescent Moon Lake. Chinese and international restaurants and popular rooftop bar for views of the dunes. Live entertainment and shuttle bus provided.

300 All major cards

DUNE GUESTHOUSE

$–$$ ✪✪

N OF MINGSHA HILLS

TEL 0937 388-2411

www.the-silk-road.com

This excellent place enjoys a splendid location just a few minutes' walk north of the Mingsha Hills. There's a wide range of accommodations, from dorms to double rooms and huts in the garden.

No credit cards accepted

JOHN'S INFORMATION SERVICE & CAFÉ

$

22 MINGSHAN LU, NEXT TO FEI TIAN HOTEL

TEL 0937 882-7000

www.johncafe.com

Travelers come here for clues on exploring the area. Outdoor terrace; train and air tickets arranged. Chinese and Western food. Tours and bike rentals. Internet access.

50+ No credit cards accepted

HOHHOT

SHANGRI-LA

$$$$ ✪✪✪✪✪

5 XILINGUOLE NANLU

TEL 0471 336-6888

FAX 0471 336-6666

www.shangri-la.com

Excellently located, Hohhot's finest hotel offers comfortable rooms, fine restaurants, and tip-top service. Wi-Fi available.

375 All major cards

JIAYUGUAN

GREAT WALL HOTEL (CHANGCHENG BINGUAN)

$ ✪✪✪

6 JIANSHE XILU

TEL 0947 622-5213 OR 0947 622-5288

FAX 0947 622-6016

This fortress-like hotel in the south of town is good value and reasonably well equipped. Bike rental, travel agency.

160 All major cards

KASHGAR (KASHI)

QINIBAGH HOTEL (QINIWAKE BINGUAN)

$ ✪✪

93 SEMAN LU

TEL 0998 298-2103

FAX 0998 298-2299

Occupies the same site as the former British Consulate building, not far from Id Kah Square. Breakfast included. Business center. Internet access.

140 No credit cards accepted

JOHN'S INFORMATION SERVICE & CAFÉ (YUEHAN ZHONGXI CANTING)

$

SEMAN HOTEL, 170 SEMAN LU

TEL 0998 258-1186

www.johncafe.com
This reliable outpost in the Seman Hotel is a favorite backpacker meeting ground and a source of useful advice for traveling around the region. Coffee, pancakes, Chinese dishes. It can organize trips around Kashgar's sights and into the Taklimakan Desert. Internet access, bike rental, English menu.
100+ No credit cards accepted

LANZHOU

JJ SUN HOTEL
$$$ ✪✪✪✪
589 DONGGANG XILU
TEL 0931 880-5511
www.jinjiangsunhotel-lanzhou.com
It's not the nearest hotel to the train station, but the JJ Sun is affordably comfortable with large rooms and decent comfort all around.
235 All major cards

TURPAN

OASIS HOTEL (LÜZHOU BINGUAN)
$ ✪✪✪
41 QINGNIAN LU
TEL 0995 852-2491
FAX 0995 852-3348
One of Turpan's better hotels, the recently renovated Oasis has decent double rooms, a good choice of restaurants, and bicycles to rent.
191 All major cards

JOHN'S INFORMATION SERVICE & CAFÉ
$
OPPOSITE TURPAN HOTEL (TULUFAN BINGUAN), QINGNIAN NANLU
TEL 0995 852-4237
www.johncafe.com
Chinese and Western food, chilled drinks, plus all the information you need for exploring the dry locality of Turpan. John Hu, the owner, is an intrepid entrepreneur who has other café outposts in Kashgar, Ürümqi, and Dunhuang. Internet access. English menu.
50+ No credit cards accepted

ÜRÜMQI

HOI TAK HOTEL (HAIDE JIUDIAN)
$$$$ ✪✪✪✪✪
HOLIDAY INN
1 DONGFENG LU
TEL 0991 232-2828
FAX 0991 232-1818
www.hoitakhotel.com
The 33-story tower in the center of town offers reasonably equipped and acceptable rooms and facilities, including a bowling alley and a large range of international dining options, including Muslim and Chinese.
318 MC, V

SHERATON ÜRÜMQI HOTEL
$$$$ ✪✪✪✪✪
9 YOUHAO BEILU
TEL 0991 699-9999
FAX 0991 699-9888
www.starwoodhotels.com
Slightly hobbled by a non-central location, in terms of service, rooms, and restaurants the Sheraton is the most luxurious choice in town, bringing international standards of hospitality to the Xinjiang capital. With a fine choice of restaurants and cafés, the hotel also boasts the full range of facilities, including a nightclub and executive floors for extra pampering.
398 All major cards

FUBAR
$
40 GONGYUAN BEIJIE
TEL 0991 584-4498
This is an excellent place to enjoy a pint, knock back an imported beer., and munch on some tasty pub food. Frequented by locals and Western travelers in Xinjiang, Fubar is a great place to stock up on travel advice. There'a another outlet in Kashgar.
All major cards

XIAHE

OVERSEAS TIBETAN HOTEL
$$ ✪✪
77 RENMIN XIJIE
TEL 0941 712-2642
www.overseastibetanhotel.com
Run by the indefatigable Lohsang, this hotel is near Labrang Monastery and comes with the Everest Café attached. Double rooms are good.
40 No credit cards accepted

THE NORTHEAST

CHANGCHUN

SHANGRI-LA CHANGCHUN (XIANGGELILA JIUDIAN)
$$$ ✪✪✪✪
569 XIAN DALU
TEL 0431 8898-1818
FAX 0431 8898-1919
www.shangri-la.com
The finest rooms in the city and superlative service. The Shangri-La chain offers the very best, from the impressive lobby to the clean-cut rooms. Two Chinese restaurants, coffee shop, nightclub, delicatessen. Horizon Club. Tennis courts. Limousine service.
458 All major cards

DALIAN

SHANGRI-LA HOTEL (XIANGGELILA

DAJIUDIAN)
$$$$ ✪✪✪✪✪
66 RENMIN LU
TEL 0411 8252-5000
FAX 0411 8252-5050
www.shangri-la.com
Just down Renmin Lu from Zhongshan Square, the superb Shangri-La (one of Dalian's various five-star hotels) puts you in the lap of luxury right in the heart of town. Chinese and Japanese restaurants. Horizon Club executive floor. American bar and café, delicatessen. Limousine service. Tennis courts.
562, 191 apartments All major cards

DALIAN HOTEL (DALIAN BINGUAN)
$$ ✪✪✪
4 ZHONGSHAN SQUARE
TEL 0411 8263-3111
FAX 0411 8263-4363
www.dl-hotel.com
Adorning Dalian's elegant hub on Zhongshan Square, the Dalian Hotel is a fine historic building and inexpensive. Centrally located and stylish. Breakfast included.
220 All major cards

NOAH'S ARK
$
32 WUSI LU
TEL 0411 8369-2798
Dependable bar for live music, beer, Western food, and a local Chinese crowd. Wi-Fi.
No credit cards accepted

1–55 COFFEE STOP & BAKERY
$
67 GAOERJI LU
TEL 0411 8369-5755
Very comfortable spot serving up fine brews and some great Western food including breakfasts. Relaxing patio and Wi-Fi access.
No credit cards accepted

DANDONG

CROWNE PLAZA DANDONG
$$$$
158 BINJIANG DONGLU
TEL 0415 318-9999
FAX 0415 319-8888
www.crowneplaza.com
Dandong's most luxurious hotel is not the most central option, but rooms are lovely and dining options superb.
356 All major cards

HARBIN

SHANGRI-LA HOTEL (XIANGGELILA DAJIUDIAN)
$$$ ✪✪✪✪
555 YOUYI LU, DAOLI DISTRICT
TEL 0451 8485-8888
FAX 0451 8462-1666
www.shangri-la.com
An 18-story, first-class hotel near the Songhua River in the Daoli District. Horizon Club (executive) floors feature free suit pressing, newspaper delivery, lounge facilities, breakfast buffet, drinks, and excellent business facilities. Limousine service. Chinese and Western restaurants. Tennis courts.
346 All major cards

HOLIDAY INN (WANDA JIARI JIUDIAN)
$$ ✪✪✪✪
90 JINGWEI JIE
TEL 0451 8422-6666
FAX 0451 8422-1663
www.holidayinn.com
Perched at the end of fashionable Zhongyang Dajie, the Holiday Inn is a reliable, if rather predictable and unexciting, welcoming sign. Clinic, snooker. Airport transportation.
157 All major cards

HUAMEI WESTERN RESTAURANT (HUAMEI XICANTING)
$
112 ZHONGYANG DAJIE, ACROSS FROM THE MODERN HOTEL
TEL 0451 8467-5574
There are plenty of places around town steaming with Northeast Chinese *jiaozi* (dumplings), but this is the place to further capitalize on Harbin's Russian ingredients. English menu.
400–500 All major cards

JILIN

JIANGCHENG (JIANGCHENG BINGUAN)
$ ✪✪✪
4 JIANGWAN LU
TEL 0432 245-7721
FAX 0431 245-8973
One of the city's better hotels, but that's not saying much. The Jiangcheng is at least cheap and well situated for trips to the Catholic church, the Confucius Temple, and the icicle shows along the Songhua River in winter. CITS can be found in the hotel. Free breakfast.
100 All major cards

SHENYANG

TRADERS (SHANGMAO FANDIAN)
$$$ ✪✪✪✪
68 ZHONGHUA LU
TEL 024 2341-2288
www.shangri-la.com
An elegant link in the Shangri-La chain of hotels, Traders is a fastidious, stylish port of call in downtown Shenyang. Chinese restaurant, bar, and coffee shop. Traders club. Shopping center next door. Limousine service.
592 All major cards

Shopping

Tourist shops such as the Friendship Stores, present in most large cities, are mediocre but useful for souvenirs and presents (silk, cloisonné, ceramics, etc.). Objects of interest often surface in street markets, surrounded by fake antiques and litter from the Cultural Revolution. The most interesting items lie off the beaten track, away from the tourist routes, so dig far and deep. See Customs (p. 356) for export restrictions.

BEIJING

Also see p. 96.

Shopping Malls

Oriental Plaza
1 Dongchang'an Jie
Vast, glittering shopping complex at the foot of Wangfujing Dajie boasts top-of-the-line goods.

Village
19 Sanlitun Lu
Tel 010 6417-6110
www.sanlitunvillage.com
Boasts the world's largest branch of Adidas, a large selection of other brands, and a stellar choice of restaurants and bars.

SHANGHAI

Bookshop

Shanghai Museum Shop
Shanghai Museum
201 Renmin Dadao
Tel 021 6372-3500
Subway: Renmin Square
First-class range of books on Chinese arts and history, plus a fine array of gifts and postcards.

Department Stores

Nanjing Donglu
Partly pedestrianized street running west from the Peace Hotel and the Bund.

Nextage (Xinshiji Shangsha)
1111 Pudong Nanlu
Asia's largest department store.

Plaza 66
1266 Nanjing Xilu
One of the smartest and slickest malls in the city, with a fleet of top designers.

HONG KONG

North Hong Kong Island is carpeted with top names, including **Marks & Spencer** *(Central Tower, 28 Queen's Rd. Central, Central, tel 2921-8059; Times Square, 1 Matheson St., Causeway Bay, tel 2923-7970; Cityplaza 1, 111 Kings Rd., Taikoo Shing, Quarry Bay, tel 2922-7234)* and **Sogo** *(East Point Centre, 555 Hennessy Rd., Causeway Bay, tel 2833-8338).*

Shopping Malls

IFC Mall
1 Harbour View St., Central
www.ifc.com.hk
Highly slick mall in Central for top-brand shopping.

Pacific Place
88 Queensway
Home to a movie theater, restaurants, and shops, and backed up by two five-star hotels, Pacific Place is an excellent shopping experience. Easily reached by tram from Central (five minutes) or subway (Admiralty MTR).

Prince's Building
5 Ice House St., Central
Very elegant retail environment across from the Mandarin Oriental Hotel. Top names, top prices, and sophisticated design.

Chinese Medicine

Eu Yan Sang Ltd.
Eu Yan Sang Tower,
11–15 Chatham Rd. South, Kowloon
Tel 0852 2366-8321
Take a fantastic tour through the exotic world of Chinese medicine at this premier outlet.

Bookshops

Swindon Book Co. Ltd
Anson House, 13–15 Lock Rd., Tsim Sha Tsui, Kowloon
Tel 0852 2366-8001
Varied collection and knowledgeable staff. English-language books.

Souvenirs/Arts & Crafts/Chinese Emporiums

Yue Hwa Chinese Products Emporium Ltd.
301-309 Nathan Rd., Tsim Sha Tsui, Kowloon
Tel 0852 2384 0084
Chinese ceramics, cloisonné, clothes, and furniture in a large store. Also at 39 Queen's Road, Central, tel 0852 2522 2333.

Music/CDs

HMV
Shop UG06, UG Level, iSquare
63 Nathan Rd., Tsim Sha Tsui, Kowloon
Tel 0852 2302-0122
Subway: Tsim Sha Tsui
Magnificent range of CDs to stock up with before setting out. Low prices. Also located at 1/F, Style House, Park Ln., Causeway Bay, tel 0852 2504-3669, subway: Causeway Bay.

MACAU

Wandering the streets is the best way to shop in Macau. The region around Rua de Caldeira, near the Inner Harbour in the west of the peninsula, is an excellent place to find the dried, sugared meats popular in Macau.

Entertainment

The growing number of expatriates and travelers to China has guaranteed an increasingly adventurous drinking and dancing scene that didn't really exist 15 years ago. Excluding Hong Kong, cinemas are for Chinese audiences unless you speak Chinese. Beijing, Shanghai, Guangzhou, Hong Kong, Kunming, and a few other more entrepreneurial cities have entertainment magazines for expatriates, available at Western bars. Below is a selection of theaters, shows, and venues in China.

BEIJING

Acrobats

Beijing Chaoyang Theatre (Beijing Chaoyang Juchang)
36 Dongsanhuan Beilu
Tel 010 6507-2421
www.bjcyjc.com
The Beijing Chaoyang Theatre offers daily performances of rubber-jointed contortionists and other fearless artists.

Beijing Opera

Liyuan Theatre (Liyuan Juchang)
Qianmen Jianguo Hotel,
175 Yongan Lu
Tel 010 6301-6688 ext. 8860
www.liyuantheatre.cn
The Liyuan Theatre stages nightly performances of classic opera tales. The tales may be incomprehensible to a Western audience, but they are always fun.

SUZHOU

Every evening a cultural performance is held at the **Master of the Nets Garden,** featuring musical compositions and Chinese opera. Performances take place between 7:30 p.m. and 10 p.m.; tickets cost Y100 and can be bought at the garden.

SHANGHAI

Acrobats

Shanghai Acrobatics Theatre
Shanghai Centre Theatre,
Shanghai Centre,
1376 Nanjing Xilu
Tel 021 6279-8663
www.shanghaicentre.com/theatre
One of the best venues in China for the legendary performances of Chinese acrobats.

Jazz

Peace Bar Jazz Band
Peace Hotel, 20 Nanjing Donglu
Tel 021 6321-6888 ext 6210
Vintage strummers, some members of the Peace Bar Jazz Band have amazingly struggled on longer than the Rolling Stones. The old-timers go through a succession of pre-Revolution jazz numbers that have been their staple since days long gone. Nightly, 8 p.m.–2 a.m.

HONG KONG

Hong Kong Dolphinwatch
1528a Star House
3 Salisbury Rd.,
Tsim Sha Tsui, Kowloon
Tel 0852 2984-1414
www.hkdolphinwatch.com
Hong Kong Dolphinwatch puts on an ecological sideshow with waterborne tours to see Hong Kong's dwindling population of pink dolphins *(Sousa chinensis).*

Movie Theaters

UA Queensway
Ground Floor, Pacific Place
88 Queensway, Admiralty
Tel 0852 2869-0394
Subway: Admiralty

UA Times Square
Ground and 2nd floor,
Times Square
1 Matheson St., Causeway Bay
Tel 0852 3516-8811
Subway: Causeway Bay

MACAU

Macau Cultural Centre (Omoon Manfa Zhongsam/ Centro Cultural de Macau)
Avenida Xian Xing Hai
Tel 0853 2870-0699
Fax 0853 2875-1395
E-mail: mccpm@macau.ctm.net
www.ccm.gov.mo
Cinema, theater, concerts of classical music, performances of Chinese opera, musicals, and more. The Cultural Centre consists of auditoriums, conference halls, museum space (including the Macau Museum of Art), and a multimedia center. The building itself is a dynamic addition to the Macau skyline.

Macau Bars

Macau has a reputation as a gambling destination, but there are several bars where you don't have to listen to the constant clatter of slot machines. Near the ruins of St. Paul on the Macau Peninsula, **Macau Soul** *(31a Rua de Sao Paulo, near Travessa de Paixao, tel 0853 2836-5182, closed Wed., http://macausoul.com)* has live jazz, blues, swing, country, folk, and a good atmosphere. On Taipa, the **Old Taipa Tavern** *(21 Rua dos Negociantes, tel 0853 2882-5221)* also has weekly live music.

Gambling

Gambling is illegal in Hong Kong and mainland China, so most Chinese gamblers storm Macau on weekends.

Macau's casinos include the **Casino Lisboa,** the **Altira Macau,** the **Sands Macau,** and the vast **Venetian Macau.**

Shows

The **Crazy Paris Show** is a revue-style show performed nightly in the Grand Lisboa Hotel *(tel 0083 2828-3838).*

Museums

Particularly notable museums are mentioned in the main text; this list is a further selection of museums of general interest throughout China. Telephone numbers are given, but we cannot guarantee and English reply.

BEIJING

Natural History Museum (Ziran Bowuguan)
$
126 Tianqiao Nandajie
Tel 010 6702-4431
Huge and absorbing trawl through evolution and the natural world. Just west of the Temple of Heaven. Sporadic English translations. No tickets sold after 4 p.m.

China Art Gallery (Zhongguo Meishuguan)
$
1 Wusi Dajie
Tel 010 6400-6326
East of Jingshan Park with exhibitions of contemporary Chinese art. No English captions. No tickets sold after 4 p.m.

Lu Xun Museum (Lu Xun Bowuguan)
$
19 Gongmenkou Ertiao
Tel 010 6616-4168
Subway: Fuchengmen
Dedicated to China's famous novelist. No English captions. No tickets sold after 3:30 p.m.

TIANJIN

Tianjin Opera Museum (Tianjin Xiju Bowuguan)
$
31 Nanmennei Dajie
Tel 022 2727-3443
Offers an historical look at local opera with performances.

SUZHOU

Suzhou Museum (Suzhou Bowuguan)
204 Dongbei Jie
Tel 0512 6757-5666
www.szmuseum.com
This I. M. Pei–designed museum balances splendid modern architecture with a fascinating collection of cultural displays.

Suzhou Silk Museum (Suzhou Sichou Bowuguan)
$
2001 Renmin Lu
Close to the North Pagoda, this excellent museum charts the history of silk production (sericulture), a process intimately tied to the prosperity of Suzhou.

SHANGHAI

First National Congress of the Chinese Communist Party (Zhonggong Yidahuizhi Jinianguan)
$
76 Xingye Lu (corner of Huangpi Nanlu)
Tel 021 6328-5266
Subway: South Huangpi Road
The CCP was founded here in July 1921. English captions.

Former Residence of Sun Yat-sen (Sun Zhongshan Guju)
$
7 Xiangshan Lu
Tel 021 6437-2954
Sun Yat-sen, lived in this two-story Western-style house.

LUSHAN

Lushan Museum (Lushan Bowuguan)
Traces the urban and natural history of Lushan.

People's Hall Renmin Juchang)
$
504 Hexi Lu
Tel 0792 828-2584
Venue of a Communist conference in 1959 that shaped turbulent Chinese politics in the 1960s.

CHANGSHA

Hunan Provincial Museum (Hunansheng Bowuguan)
3 Dongfeng Lu
Tel 0731 451-4629
The museum contains fascinating Western Han artifacts from Mawangdui, including the mummified remains of a Han woman.

HONG KONG

University Museum & Art Gallery
Hong Kong University, 94 Bonham Rd., Kennedy Town, Hong Kong Island
Tel 0852 2975-5600
Antique bronzes and ceramics displayed among the magnificent old Edwardian architecture of the university. Closed Sun. mornings.

Lei Cheng Uk Han Tomb Museum
41 Tonkin St., Sham Shui Po, Kowloon
Tel 0852 2386-2863
Subway: Cheung Sha Wan
The museum houses the earliest historical relic in Hong Kong, a 2,000-year-old Han dynasty tomb. Closed Thurs., some public holidays., & Sun. a.m.

KUNMING

Yunnan Provincial Museum (Yunnansheng Bowuguan)
118 Wuyi Lu
Tel 0871 316-3694
Concentrates on the province's ethnic customs.

CHENGDU

Sichuan Provincial Museum (Sichuansheng Bowuguan)
3 Renmin Nanlu
Tel 028 8522-8796
Extensive collection of artifacts from Sichuan.

Language Guide

Useful Words & Phrases

Hello *nihao*
Goodbye *zaijian*
Thank you *xiexie*
Pardon me *dui bu qi*
I *wo*
We, us *women*
You (sing.) *ni*
You (plur.) *nimen*
He, she *ta*
Them, they *tamen*
My name is... *wo jiao...*
What is your name? *ni gui xing?*
I want... *wo yao...*
Do you have...? *ni you mei you...?*
I do not have... *wo mei you...*
I understand *wo mingbai*
I don't understand *wo bu mingbai*
No problem *mei wenti*
I am American *wo shi meiguoren*
I am English *wo shi yingguoren*
I am Australian *wo shi aodaliyaren*
America *meiguo*
England *yingguo*
Australia *aodaliya*
Canada *jianada*
New Zealand *xinxilan*
China *zhongguo*
France *faguo*
Germany *deguo*
Toilet *cesuo*
Where is...? *zai nar...?*
Where is the toilet? *cesuo zai nar?*
How much is...? *duoshao qian...?*
Water *shui*
How much is the beer? *pijiu duoshao qian?*
Too expensive *tai gui le*
Vegetables *cai*
Fruit *shuiguo*
Money *qian*
I don't like... *wo bu xihuan...*

Numbers

one *yi*
two *er*
two (when followed by a noun) *liang*
three *san*
four *si*
five *wu*
six *liu*
seven *qi*
eight *ba*
nine *jiu*
ten *shi*
11 *shiyi*
20 *ershi*
21 *ershiyi*
30 *sanshi*
100 *yi bai*
200 *liang bai*
1,000 *yi qian*
10,000 *yi wan*
1,000,000 *yi bai wan*
0 *ling*

Restaurant

Beef *niurou*
Beer *pijiu*
Chicken *jirou*
Chopsticks *kuaizi*
Coffee *kafei*
Dumplings *jiaozi*
Fork *chazi*
Knife *daozi*
Lamb *yangrou*
Menu *caipu/caidan*
Plate *panzi*
Pork *zhurou*
Tea *cha*
Tofu *doufu*
Waitress *xiaojie*
Water *shui*
Wine *putaojiu*
I am vegetarian *wo chisu*
Warm/hot *re*
Cold *leng*
The bill, please *qing jiezhang/mai dan*

Hotel

Do you have any rooms? *you mei you kong fangjian?*
Bed *chuangwei*
Check out *tuifang*
Deluxe room *haohuafang*
Double room *shuangrenfang*
Passport *huzhao*
Reception *zongfuwutai*
Standard room *biaozhunfang*
Toilet paper *weishengzhi*

Time

Today *jintian*
Tomorrow *mingtian*
Yesterday *zuotian*
What time is it? *ji dian zhong?*

Getting Around

Airplane *feiji*
Airport *jichang*
Bicycle *zixingche*
Boarding pass *dengjika*
Bus *gonggong qiche/bashi*
Car *qiche*
Map *ditu*
Medium-size bus *zhongba*
Small bus *xiaoba*
Subway *ditie*
Taxi *chuzu qiche*
Ticket *piao*
Train *huoche*
I want to go to... *wo xiang qu...*
How far is it? *duo yuan?*
Give me a receipt, OK? *gei wo yi ge shoutiao, hao bu hao?*

Emergency

Ambulance *jiuhuche*
Antibiotics *kangjunsu*
Doctor *yisheng*
Fire! *zhao huo le!*
Help! *jiuming a!*
Hospital *yiyuan*
Police *jingcha*
Public Security Bureau (PSB) *gonganju*
I feel ill *wo bu shufu*

Directions

North *bei*
South *nan*
East *dong*
West *xi*
Left *zuo*
Right *you*
Inside *limian*
Outside *waimian*

Post Office

Envelope *xinfeng*
Letter *xin*
Post office *youju*
Telephone *dianhua*

Sightseeing

Avenue *dadao*
Lake *hu*
Main street *dajie*
Mountain *shan*
River *he, jiang*
Road *lu*
Street *jie*
Temple *simiao/si/guan*

Menu Reader

Beijing (Peking), north, & northeastern dishes in Beijing & the north

Beijing duck	*Beijing kaoya*
Braised fish in soy sauce	*hongshao yu*
Braised spare ribs in soy sauce	*hongshao paigu*
Drunken crab	*zuixie*
Drunken shrimps	*zuixia*
Dumplings	*shuijiao*
Egg and tomato soup	*xihongshi jidan tang*
Hotpot	*huoguo*
Steamed crab	*qingzheng pangxie*
Stewed pork with rice noodles	*zhurou dun fentiao*
Stewed ribs with potatoes	*paigu dun tudou*

Shanghai/Eastern Chinese dishes in Shanghai, Jiangsu, & Zhejiang Province

Beggar's chicken	*fugui ji*
Cold spiced beef	*xuxiang niurou*
Drunken pigeon with wine sauce	*zuixiang ruge*
Fried crab with salty egg	*xiandan chaoxie*
Quick-fried freshwater shrimps	*qingchao xiaren*
Shanghai crab in wine	*zuixie*
Shanghai dumplings	*xiaolongbao*
Smoked fresh yellow fish	*xun xinxian huangyu*

Cantonese/Chaozhou dishes in Hong Kong, Macau, & the South (Cantonese in parentheses)

Barbecued pork buns	*cha shao bao (cha siu bao)*
Deep-fried shrimp	*suzha fengwei xia*
Fried dumplings	*guo tie (wok tit)*
Pork and shrimp dumplings	*shao mai (siu mai)*
Rice-flour rolls w/shrimp or pork	*chang fen (cheung fan)*
Shrimp dumplings	*xia jiao (ha gau)*
Spare ribs	*paigu (paigwat)*
Spring rolls	*chun juan (chun guen)*
Barbecued pork	*chashao (chasiu)*
Deep-fried stuffed chicken wings	*cuipi niang jiyi*
Roast crispy pigeon with soya sauce	*shengchou huang cuipi ruge*
Shark's fin soup	*dayuchi tang (daiyuchee tong)*
Steamed crab	*zhengxie (jinghai)*

Sichuan dishes in Chengdu & Chongqing

Chicken with chili	*lazi jiding*
Eggplant in hot fish sauce	*yuxiang qiezi*
Fish and cabbage in spicy soup	*suancai yu*
Hot-and-sour soup	*suanla tang*
Mapo tofu (tofu with pork in spicy sauce)	*mapo doufu*
Meat strips in hot fish sauce	*yuxiang rousi*
Pork slices in chili	*shuizhu roupian*
Spicy noodles	*dandan mian*

INDEX

Bold page numbers indicate illustrations.
CAPS indicates thematic categories.

A
A-Ma Temple, Macau 255
Aberdeen, Hong Kong 237
Accidents 360
Air pollution 329, 357
Air travel 8, 352
Alcohol regulations 356
Altitude sickness 301, 357
Ancient Observatory, Beijing 76
Anshun 288
Anyang 142
Appliances, electronic 356
Architecture 44, 117, 152, 193, **194,** 194–195
Art galleries *see* MUSEUMS
Arts & culture 48–56
- Buddhist **12,** 13, 33
- ceramics **52,** 52–53, **53,** 215
- Chinese opera **4,** 56
- film 56
- literature 51, 54–55
- music **54,** 55–56, 273
- painting 48–50, 51

Astana Tombs 320
Astor House Hotel, Shanghai 184
Astrology 246
ATMs 10
Automobile rentals 353, 360

B
Badachu, near Beijing 89
Badaling 92–93
Baisha 273–274
Bamboo Temple, Kunming 265
Bank of China Building, Shanghai 185
Bank of China Tower, Hong Kong 227–228
Banpo Museum, Xi'an 104
Banquets 355
Baodingshan 299
Baotou 332, **332**
Bargaining 354
Beggars 355
Beihai 287, **287,** 379
Beihai Park, Beijing 67, **67,** 68
Beijing 57–96
- bike ride 68–69
- churches 81
- cooking lessons 25
- entertainment 387
- expat magazine 187
- hiking 96
- hotels 73, 362–363
- *hutongs* **57, 72,** 72–73
- maps 58–59, 69, 91
- name 35
- notable museums 388
- restaurants 363–365, 390
- shopping 386
- suggested itinerary 9
- surrounding area 88–96
- transportation 61
- 798 Art District 96
- Ancient Observatory 76
- Beihai Park 67, **67,** 68
- Capital Museum 96
- Confucius Temple 79, **79**
- Cow Street Mosque 80
- Dongyue Temple 81
- Fayuan Temple 80, **80**
- Forbidden City **60,** 60–66, **62–63, 64, 66**
- Great Bell Temple 96
- Great Wall 89–94
- Jingshan Park 67
- Lama Temple **11,** 78
- Liulichang 96
- Marco Polo Bridge 96
- Old Summer Palace 87, **87**
- South Cathedral 81
- Summer Palace **84,** 84–86
- Temple of Heaven **74,** 74–75
- Tiananmen Square 45, **46–47,** 47, **70,** 70–71
- Western Hills 88–89
- White Clouds Temple 81
- White Dagoba Temple 96
- Zhihua Temple 81

Beishan 299
Bell Tower, Beijing 69
Bezeklik Thousand Buddha Caves, Turpan 320
Big Wild Goose Pagoda, Xi'an 103
BIKE RIDES
- Beijing 68–69
- Suzhou 170–171

Biking 259, 285, 324, 352
Bilharzia/schistosomiasis 356
Binglingsi 329
Bingyu Valley 347
Bird flu 243
Birding 242–243
Black Dragon River 347
Blind massage 76
Blue Wave Pavilion, Suzhou 169
Boat trips
- overview 352
- Grand Canal 177
- Hong Kong ferries 230, 231–232, 248
- Huangpu River Cruise 196
- Li River 282–283
- Macau ferry 251
- Pearl River, Guangzhou 215
- Three Gorges cruise 146–149

Bon (religion) 306–307
Botanical gardens *see* GARDENS
Bright Filial Piety Temple, Guangzhou 213
Buddha's Glory (light effect) 297
Buddha's Summit Peak 180–181
Buddhism 32–33
- art **12,** 13, 33
- beginnings 31
- cave-temples **112,** 114–115, **122,** 122–123
- festivals 307
- giant stone Buddha 298, **298**
- gods & goddesses 82–83
- lamas 308
- nuns **306**
- prayer flags **300,** 307
- prayer wheels **32, 302,** 307, **307**
- stone carvings 298, **298,** 299, **299**
- Tantric 302
- temples 157–158, 293
- Tibetan 304, 306–307, 308
- Yellow & Red Hat Sects 304

Bund, Shanghai **18–19, 184,** 184–187, **187**
Bus travel 117, 352–353

C
Calligraphy 55
Camoes Gardens, Macau 253
Cangshan Mountains 270
Cantonese language 230
Capital Museum, Beijing 96
Car rentals 353, 360
Casinos 255, **255,** 260
Cathedrals *see* CHURCHES
Causeway Bay, Hong Kong 232
Caves
- Inner Mongolia & the Silk Road 320, 321, 323, 326–327, 329, 331
- The North **114,** 114–115, **122,** 122–123
- The South 202
- The Southwest 281
- Yangtze region 172, 181

Central District, Hong Kong 226–230
Central-Midlevels Escalator, Hong Kong 231
Ceramics **52,** 52–53, **53,** 215
Changbai Mountains 340–341
Changchun 347, 384
Changzhou 196
Chapel of St. Francis Xavier, Coloane 259
Chen Family Temple, Guangzhou 214
Chengde **118,** 118–120, **120,** 365
Chengdu **292,** 292–295, **295,** 382, 388, 390
Cheung Chau 248–249
Chiang Kai-shek 41–42, 204
China National Museum, Beijing 71
Chinese language *see* Language
Chinese opera **4,** 56
Ching Chung Koon Temple, Tuen Mun 241

Cholera 356
Chongqing 150, **150,** 368, 390
Chopsticks 362
Christ Church, Qingdao 138
Christianity 33
  see also CHURCHES; Taiping Rebellion
Chuandixia 89
CHURCHES
  worship services 359
  Beijing 81
  Chapel of St. Francis Xavier, Coloane 259
  Christ Church, Qingdao 138
  Church of St. Sophia, Harbin **344,** 344–345
  Guangzhou 212–214
  St. John's Cathedral, Hong Kong 228
  St. Michael's Catholic Church, Qingdao 138
  São Paulo, Macau 252
  Shanghai 195
  South Cathedral, Beijing 81
  Wanghailou Cathedral, Tianjin 116
  Xi Kai Cathedral, Tianjin 117
Cigarettes 356
Cinema 56
Cixi, Qing Empress 39–41, 85, 95
Climate 21–22, 248, 350
Clothing, suggested 351
Coloane (island), Macau 259
Communications 354–355, 358–359
Concession architecture 117
Confucianism 33, 130–131, 156–157
Confucius 28, 130, **130**
Confucius Temple, Beijing 79, **79**
Confucius Temple, Nanjing 162
Confucius Temple, Qufu 132
Confucius Temple, Tianjin 117
Consulates 351–352, 360
Cormorant fishing **2–3,** 269
Couples Garden, Suzhou 169
Courtyard hotels 73
Cow Street Mosque, Beijing 80
Credit cards 10, 359
Crime 281, 355
Culture 14–15, 355–356
  see also Arts & culture
Currency 10, 16, 359
Customs (border control) 356
Customs (etiquette) *see* Etiquette
Customs House, Shanghai 186, **187**

D

Da Xiangguo Temple, Kaifeng 126
Dai Temple, Tai'an 134
Dalai Lama 308
Dali **268,** 268–271, **271,** 379–380
Dali Museum, Dali 268–269
Dalian 338, 384–385
Damenglong 279
Daming Temple, Yangzhou 166
Dandong 347–348, 385
Datong 10, **112,** 112–113, 365
Dazu 299, **299,** 382
Dehang 202
Dental care 356
Dian, Lake 265–266
Diarrhea 356
Dingshan 172
Disabilities, travelers with 359
Diseases 356–357
Dongyue Temple, Beijing 81
Dragon Well 175
Dragons **50,** 65
Drepung Monastery, Tibet 302–303
Du Fu 51, 294
Dunhuang 11, **326,** 326–327, 383
Dynasties 28

E

E-mail 354
Economy 16–17
Eight Immortals Temple, Xi'an 102–103
Electricity 356
Electronic appliances 356
Elephants 279
Elevation 301, 357
Email 354
Embassies 351–352, 360
Emeishan **296,** 296–297, 382–383
Emergencies 360, 389
English-language newspapers 358–359
Entertainment **4,** 387–388
Erhai Lake 269, 270
Escalator, longest outdoor 231
Etiquette 10, 355–356, 359
Everest Base Camp 310, **310**
Ex-Government House, Hong Kong 228
Expat magazines 187
EXPERIENCES
  Beijing blind massage 76
  Beijing classes 77, **77**
  Beijing cooking lessons 25
  Beijing courtyard hotels 73
  Beijing hiking 96
  Chaundixia village life 89
  Great Wall hotels 92
  Hakka lodging 210, **210**
  Hong Kong tai chi classes 237
  Jiankou Great Wall 90, **90**
  Karakoram Highway cycling 324
  Luoyang Peony Festival 121
  Macau biking & hiking 259
  MacLehose Trail 240
  Moganshan trek 167
  Naxi music 273
  Northeast skiing 347
  Pingyao's town walls walk 109
  Qingdao brewery 141
  Shanghai cooking lessons 25
  Shanghai M50 art 190
  Shanghai Zhujiajiao 192
  Siberian Tiger Park 343
  Singing Sand Dunes 327
  Songpan horse trek 294
  Southwest biking 285
  Tibet-Qinghai Railway 303
  wing chun gongfu 231
  Xian Muslim Quarter cuisine 102
  Yangshuo activities 286

F

Face *(mianzi)* 10
Famen Temple, Xi'an 104
Fayuan Temple, Beijing 80, **80**
Female travelers 356
Fengdu 147
Fenghuang **200,** 200–201
fengshui 156, 238, 256–257
Festivals
  calendar 350
  Cheung Chau Bun Festival 248
  Ice Lantern Festival 346
  Labrang Monastery 330
  Peony Festival, Luoyang 121
  Third Moon Fair, Dali 270
  Tibetan Buddhism 307
  Water-splashing Festival 277
Film 56
Fishing, cormorant **2–3,** 269
Five Genies Temple, Guangzhou 214
Flower Pagoda, Guangzhou **157**
Flu, avian 243
Food & drink **24,** 24–25
  banquets 355
  cooking lessons 25
  health concerns 357
  Kunming 266
  vegetarians 359
  Xian's Muslim Quarter 102
  see also Restaurants
Forbidden City, Beijing **60,** 60–66, **62–63, 64, 66**
Foreigner's Street, Dali 269
Fortune-telling 238, 246
Foshan 220
French Concession, Shanghai 192–193, **194,** 195
Frostbite 357

G

Gambling 255, **255,** 260
Ganden Monastery, Tibet 303
Ganlanba 278–279
Gansu Provincial Museum 329
Gantong Temple, Dali 271
Gaochang 320
GARDENS
  Jinghong 276–277
  Macau 253, 260
  Shanghai 191, **191**
  Suzhou **168,** 168–169
  Yangzhou 166
Geography 20–21
Giant pandas **8,** 295
Giardia 357
Gods & goddesses 82–83, 181
Golden Temple, Kunming 265
gongfu (kung fu) **124,** 124–125, **125,** 128–129, 231

Grand Canal **176,** 176–177, **177**
Grasslands 334
Great Bell Temple, Beijing 96
Great Mosque, Tianjin 116
Great Mosque, Xi'an 101–102
Great Wall **26–27,** 89–94, **93**
Guangzhou **157, 211,** 211–217, **213, 214, 216,** 373–374
guanxi (contacts) 10
Guanyin (goddess) 181, 254
Guanyin Temple, Dali 270–271
Guia Fort, Macau 260
Guilin **280,** 280–281, 380
Guiyang 288
Guiyuan Temple, Wuhan 151
Gulangyu Island **206,** 206–208
Guling 203–204
Gyantse, Tibet 308

H

Hac Sa Beach, Coloane 259
Haikou 218–219
Hailuogou Glacier Park 310
Hainan Island **17, 218,** 218–219, 374
Hakka people 209, **209,** 210, **210,** 233, 241, 242
Hall of Prayer for Good Harvests, Beijing 74–75
Hami (Kumul) 334
Hanging Monastery, Datong **112,** 113
Hangzhou 173–175, **174, 176,** 368
Happy Valley, Hong Kong 232
Harbin **344,** 344–346, 385
Health 243, 301, 329, 356–358
Heatstroke 357
Hengshan 220
Hepatitis 357, 358
High elevation 301, 357
High-speed trains 151, 189
Hiking
  Beijing 96
  Hong Kong 237, 240, 250
  Inner Mongolia 317
  Macau 259
  The North 108, **108,** 133–135
  Sichuan & Tibetan Plateau 296–297
  The Southwest 270, 273, 274–275, 281
  Yangtze region 154–155, 167
History 26–47
HIV 357
Hohhot **311,** 333, 383
Holidays *see* Festivals
Hong Kong 221–250
  bird flu 243
  entertainment 387
  expat magazine 187
  fengshui 256, **257**
  ferries 230, 231–232, 248
  hotels 235, 375–376
  maps 222–223, 224–225, 227, 235
  maps for sale 237, 240
  markets 231, 260
  money matters 359
  museum pass 236
  notable museums 388
  passports & visas 351
  restaurants 376–378, 390
  shopping 386
  tai chi classes 237
  transportation 230, 231–232, 354
  typhoons 248
  Central District walk 226–228
  Hong Kong Island 229–233, 237
  Mong Kok 260
  New Territories 239–245
  Outlying Islands 247–250
  Peng Chau 260
  Ping Chau 260
  Plover Cove Reservoir 260
  Tap Mun Chau 260
  Tsim Sha Tsui walk 234–236
  Tung Lung Chau 260
  Wong Tai Sin Temple 238
  Yau Ma Tei 260
Hong Kong and Shanghai Bank, Hong Kong 227
Hong Kong and Shanghai Bank, Shanghai 186
Hong Kong Cultural Centre 234–235
Hong Kong Island 229–233, 237
Hong Kong Park, Hong Kong 228
Hong Kong Trail 237
Hong Kong Wetland Park 244
Hong Xiuquan 164, 165
Hongcun 153, **153**
Horse racing 232, **233**
Horseback riding **275,** 294, 333
Hotan 325, **325**
Hotels 361–385
  accommodations 361–362
  grading system 361–362
  Beijing 73, 362–363
  Great Wall 92
  Hakka earth buildings 210, **210**
  Hong Kong 235, 375–376
  Inner Mongolia & the Silk Road 383–384
  language guide 389
  Macau 378
  The North 365–368
  The Northeast 345, 384–385
  Sichuan & Tibetan Plateau 382–383
  The South 210, **210,** 373–375
  The Southwest 267, 275, 379–382
  Yangtze region 184, 185–186, 368–373
Huaisheng Mosque, Guangzhou 213–214
Huangguoshu Falls 288
Huangpu River cruise **14–15,** 196
Huangshan **154,** 154–155, 368
Huaqing Pool, Xi'an 104
Huashan 108, **108,** 365
Huashilou, Qingdao 139
Huayan Monastery, Datong 112–113
Hubei Provincial Museum, Wuhan 151–152
Humble Administrator's Garden, Suzhou **168,** 169
hutongs **57, 72,** 72–73
Hypothermia 357

I

Ice Lantern Festival 346
Id Kah Mosque, Kashgar 323
Immunizations 357–358
Imperial Palace, Shenyang **336,** 339
Influenza 243
Inner Mongolia & the Silk Road 311–334
  grasslands 334
  horseback riding 333
  hotels & restaurants 383–384
  map 312–313
  the Silk Road minorities 315
  yurts 317
  Baotou 332, **332**
  Dunhuang 11, **326,** 326–327, 383
  Gaochang & Astana Tombs 320
  Hami (Kumul) 334
  Hohhot **311,** 333, 383
  Hotan 325, **325**
  Jiayuguan Fort 328, 383
  Karakoram Highway 324
  Kashgar **322,** 322–323, 383–384
  Kuqa 321, **321**
  Lanzhou 329, **329,** 384
  Linxia 334
  Maijishan 334
  Taklimakan Desert 323
  Tianchi **316,** 316–317
  Turpan **318,** 318–320, 384
  Ürümqi **314,** 314–315, 384
  Xiahe & Labrang Monastery 330, 384
  Yinchuan 331, **331**
  Zhangye 334
  Zhongwei 334
Insurance 358
Internet 354
Iron Pagoda, Kaifeng 126
Islam 33
  see also MOSQUES
Itineraries, suggested 9–11

J

Jade 325
Jade Buddha Temple, Shanghai 192
Jade Dragon Snow Mountain **20–21,** 273
Jewish communities 33, 126, 186
Jianfu Temple, Qingchengshan 294
Jiankou 90, **90**
Jiaohe Ruins, Turpan 319–320
Jiaozhou Bay Bridge 141
Jiayuguan Fort 328, 383

Jietai Temple, Beijing 89
Jilin 348, 385
Jinghong 276–277, **278,** 380
Jingpo Lake 348
Jingshan Park, Beijing 67
Jinmen (island) 208
Jinshan Temple, Zhenjiang 167
Jiuhuashan 159, 368
Jiuzhaigou 310
Jokhang Temple, Lhasa 301–302
Judaism 33, 126, 186

K

Kaifeng 126, 365
Kangding 310
Kar Wells, Turpan 319
Karakoram Highway 324
Karakul Lake 324
Karaoke 355
Kashgar **322,** 322–323, 383–384
Kat Hing Wai 242
Kilns 215
Kowloon, Hong Kong 234–236
Koxinga 207
Kun Iam Temple, Macau 254
Kung fu *see gongfu*
Kunming **264,** 264–266, **266,** 380–381, 388
Kunming Lake, Beijing 86
Kuqa 321, **321**
Kwun Yam (Goddess of Mercy) 83

L

Labrang Monastery 330
Lama Temple, Beijing **11,** 78
Lamma Island 247–248
Lan Kwai Fong, Hong Kong 228
Land & landscape **20–21,** 20–23
Language
  Cantonese 230
  classes 77
  Mandarin 230
  menu reader 390
  overview 358
  pronunciation 358
  travel tips 354
  useful words & phrases 389
  written Chinese 358
Lantau Island **247, 249,** 249–250
Lanzhou 329, **329,** 384
Laoshan 140–141
Leshan 298, **298**
Lhasa, Tibet 301–304, 383
Li Bai 51, 148
Li River **280, 282,** 282–283
Lijiang **20–21, 54, 272,** 272–275, **275,** 381
lilong (lanes) 193
Linggu Temple, Zijinshan 163
Lingyin Temple, Hangzhou 175
Linxia 334
Lion Grove, Suzhou 169
Lions, symbolism 65
Literature 51, 54–55
Little Three Gorges 149
Liulichang, Beijing 96
Long March 42
Longmen Caves **122,** 122–123
Longsheng 288
Lou Lim Ieoc Gardens, Macau 260
Lu Xun 55, 178, 179, 388
Luohan Temple, Chongqing 150
Luoyang 121, 365
Lushan **203,** 203–204, 374, 388

M

M50 complex, Shanghai 190
Macartney, Lord George 119
Macau 251–260
  casinos 255, **255,** 260
  entertainment 387
  hotels 378
  islands 258–259
  maps 222–223, 253
  money matters 359
  passports & visas 351
  restaurants 378–379, 390
  shopping 386
  transportation 251, 354
  Grand Prix 254
  Guia Fort 260
  Lou Lim Ieoc Gardens 260
  Macau Peninsula **252,** 252–255
MacLehose Trail 240
MagLev train, Shanghai 189
Mai Po marshes **242,** 242–244, **244–245**
Maijishan 334
Main Palace, Chengde 119
Malaria 357
Man Mo Temple, Hong Kong 231
Mandarin language 77, 230
Manners *see* Etiquette
Mansion of Prince Gong, Beijing 68
Manting Park, Jinghong 277, **278**
Mao Zedong 17–18, 41–44, **43,** 45, 63, 70, 328, 339
Maps
  purchasing 237, 240
  Beijing 58–59, 69
  Beijing area 91
  Central District, Hong Kong 227
  Chengdu 293
  Guangzhou 212
  Guilin 281
  Gulangyu Island 207
  Hangzhou 173
  Hong Kong 222–223, 224–225, 227, 235
  Inner Mongolia & the Silk Road 312–313
  Li River 283
  Macau 222–223, 253
  Macau Peninsula 253
  Nanjing 161
  The North 98–99
  The Northeast 337
  Qingdao 137
  Shamian Island 217
  Shanghai 183, 185
  Sichuan 290–291
  The South 199
  The Southwest 262–263
  Suzhou 171
  Three Gorges 146–147
  Tibetan Plateau 290–291
  Tsim Sha Tsui, Hong Kong 235
  Xi'an 101
  Yangtze region 144–145
Marco Polo Bridge, Beijing 96
Maritime Museum, Macau 255
Martial arts *see gongfu;* Tai chi classes
Massages 76
Master of the Nets Garden, Suzhou 168–169
Mausoleum of Sun Yat-sen, Zijinshan 162–163, **163**
Measurements 360
Media 358–359
Medicine & health *see* Health
Meilu Villa, Guling 204
Meizhou 220
Memorial of the Nanjing Massacre, Nanjing 162
Mengla 279
mianzi (face) 10
Ming City Wall, Nanjing 160–161
Ming dynasty 37
  tombs **94,** 94–95, 163
Minorities 219, 315
Miu Fat Monastery 241
Modern Hotel, Harbin 345
Moganshan 167, 369
Mogao Caves 326–327
MONASTERIES **44–45**
  Hanging Monastery, Datong **112,** 113
  Huayan Monastery, Datong 112–113
  Labrang Monastery 330
  Miu Fat Monastery 241
  Puji Monastery 180
  Ta'er Monastery, Xining 309
  Taiqing Palace, Laoshan 140–141
  Tibet 302–304, 308, **309**
  Tibetan 274
  Wudangzhao Monastery 332
  see also TEMPLES
Monastery of Divine Light, Xindu 295
Money matters 10, 16, 359
Mong Kok, Hong Kong 260
Monkey Island 219
Monte Fort, Macau 252
Moon Hill, Yangshuo 284–285
MOSQUES
  Cow Street Mosque, Beijing 80
  Great Mosque, Tianjin 116
  Great Mosque, Xi'an 101–102
  Guangzhou 212–214
  Id Kah Mosque, Kashgar 323
  Kunming 264–265
Movies 56
Mudu 196
MUSEUMS
  notable 387–388

opening hours 359
798 Art District, Beijing 96
Banpo Museum, Xi'an 104
Capital Museum, Beijing 96
China National Museum, Beijing 71
Dali Museum, Dali 268–269
Gansu Provincial Museum 329
Hong Kong Cultural Centre 234–235
Hong Kong museum pass 236
Hotan Museum 325
Hubei Provincial Museum, Wuhan 151–152
M50 complex, Shanghai 190
Maritime Museum, Macau 255
Memorial of the Nanjing Massacre, Nanjing 162
Qin Warrior Museum 106
Sam Tung Uk Museum, Tsuen Wan 241
Shaanxi Museum of History, Xi'an 103–104
Shanghai Museum 189–191
Suzhou Museum 170, 388
Taiping Museum, Nanjing 161–162
Unit 731 Museum, Harbin 345
Xi'an Forest of Stone Tablets Museum, Xi'an 102
Xinjiang Autonomous Region Museum, Ürümqi 314–315
Music **54,** 55–56, 273
Mutianyu 93

N

Nanchan Temple, Taihuai 111
Nanjing **160,** 160–163, **163,** 165, 369
Nanjing Massacre 162
Nanluogu Xiang, Beijing 69
Nanning 288
Nanputuo Temple, Xiamen 205, **205**
Nathan Road, Hong Kong 235–236
Naxi people **54,** 273
Nechung Monastery, Tibet 303
New Territories, Hong Kong 239–245
Newspapers 358–359
Nine Dragon Screen, Datong 113
Ningbo 196
Norbu Lingka, Lhasa 302
The North 97–142
hotels & restaurants 365–368
map 98–99
terra-cotta warriors **30, 97,** 103, 105–106, **106, 107**
Anyang 142
Chengde 118–120, 365
Datong 10, **112,** 112–113, 365
Huashan 108, **108,** 365
Jiaozhou Bay Bridge 141
Kaifeng 126, 365
Longmen Caves **122,** 122–123
Luoyang 121, 365
Penglai 142
Pingyao 109–110, **110**
Qingdao 136–141, 365–366
Qufu **131,** 132, **132,** 366
Shanhaiguan 142
Songshan **127,** 127–129, **128**
Taihuai 111, 367
Taishan **133,** 133–135, **135,** 366
Taiyuan 142
Tianjin 116–117, 366–367, 388
Wutaishan 111
Xi'an 10, **100,** 100–104, 367
Yungang Caves **114,** 114–115
Zhengding 142
Zoucheng 142
North Cathedral, Beijing 68
North Macau 254
The Northeast 335–348
hotels 345, 384–385
map 337
restaurants 384–385
skiing 347
tigers **342,** 342–343
Bingyu Valley 347
Black Dragon River 347
Changchun 347, 384
Dalian 338, 384–385
Dandong 347–348, 385
Harbin **344,** 344–346, 385
Jilin 348, 385
Jingpo Lake 348
Shenyang **336,** 339, 385
Tianchi **340,** 340–341
Xingcheng 348

O

Old city, Shanghai **191,** 191–192
Old Summer Palace, Beijing 87, **87**
Opera **4,** 56
Orchid Pavilion, Shaoxing 179
Outlying Islands, Hong Kong 247–250

P

Packing tips 351
Painting 48–50, 51
PALACES
Forbidden City, Beijing 60–66
Imperial Palace, Shenyang **336,** 339
Main Palace, Chengde 119
Norbu Lingka, Lhasa 302
Old Summer Palace, Beijing 87, **87**
Potala Palace, Lhasa 304–305, **305,** 308
Summer Palace, Beijing **84,** 84–86
Panchen Lamas 308
Pandas **8,** 295
PARKS
Beihai Park, Beijing 67, **67,** 68
Hailuogou Glacier Park 310
Hong Kong Park 228
Hong Kong Wetland Park 244
Jingshan Park, Beijing 67
Kowloon Park, Hong Kong 235, **236**
Mai Po marshes **242,** 242–244, **244–245**
Manting Park, Jinghong 277, **278**
Seven Star Park, Guilin 280–281
Shouxi Lake Park, Yangzhou 166
Siberian Tiger Park 343, 346
Wulingyuan 202, 374–375
Xiaoyushan, Qingdao 139
Zhaolin Park, Harbin 346
Passports & visas 351, 354
Pawangka Monastery, Tibet 303
Peace Hotel, Shanghai 185–186
Peak Tram, Hong Kong 230
Pearl River cruises 215
Pedicabs 353
Peking Man Site 27
Pelkhor Chode Monastery, Gyantse 308, **309**
Peng Chau, Hong Kong 260
Penglai 142
Peninsula Hong Kong 235
Peony Festival, Luoyang 121
Perfume 356
Ping Chau, Hong Kong 260
Pingyao 109–110, **110**
Plover Cove Reservoir, Hong Kong 260
Poetic painting 51
Poetry 51
Politics & economy 16–18
Pollution 22–23, 329, 357
Porcelain *see* Ceramics
Post offices 354–355, 389
Potala Palace, Lhasa 304–305, **305,** 308
Pottery *see* Ceramics
Propaganda Poster Art Centre, Shanghai 193
Pudong, Shanghai 187, **188,** 188–189
Puji Monastery 180
Putuoshan 180–181, 369
Putuozongcheng Temple, Chengde **118,** 120, **120**
Puyi, Emperor 41, 42, 347

Q

qigong 77, **77**
Qin Warrior Museum 106
Qing dynasty 37–41, 95, **335,** 339
Qingchengshan 294–295
Qingdao 136–141, 365–366
Qinghai Lake 309
Qinghefang Old Street, Hangzhou 175
Qingping Market, Guangzhou **214,** 214–215
Qingyang Temple, Chengdu 292
Qingyuanshan 220
Qinshi Huangdi, Emperor 29,

104, 105
Quanzhou 220
Qufu **131,** 132, **132,** 366
Qutang Gorge 148

R

Racism 359
Ramoche Temple, Tibet 302
Reading, recommended 350–351
Reed Flute Cave, Guilin 281
Religion 16, 17–18, 32–33, 82–83
see also specific religions
Restaurants 361–385
language guide 389, 390
settling the bill 355–356
tipping 359
vegetarians 359
Beijing 363–365, 390
Hong Kong 376–378, 390
Inner Mongolia & the Silk Road 383–384
Macau 378–379, 390
The North 365–368
The Northeast 384–385
Sichuan & Tibetan Plateau 382–383
The South 373–375, 390
The Southwest 379–382
Yangtze region 368–373
see also Food & drink
Restrictions on travel 11
Restrooms 359
Rock climbing 286
Rongbuk Monastery 310

S

Sai Kung Peninsula 239
St. John's Cathedral, Hong Kong 228
St. Michael's Catholic Church, Qingdao 138
Sakya 310
Sam Tung Uk Museum, Tsuen Wan 241
Samye Monastery, Tibet 303–304
Sanjiang 288, 381
Sanya **17,** 219
São Paulo (St. Paul's), Macau 252
Sedan chairs 66
Sera Monastery, Tibet 303
798 Art District, Beijing 96
Seven Star Park, Guilin 280–281
Sha Tin 240
Shaanxi Museum of History, Xi'an 103–104
Shamian Island **216,** 216–217
Shanghai **14–15,** 182–195
architecture 193, **194,** 194–195
cooking lessons 25
entertainment 387
expat magazine 187
hotels & restaurants **24,** 184, 185–186, 369–371, 390
Jewish history 186
maps 183, 185
notable museums 388
shopping 386
suggested itinerary 10
temples 192
transport card 183
Bund **18–19, 184,** 184–187, **187**
French Concession 192–193, **194,** 195
M50 complex 190
MagLev 189
old city **191,** 191–192
Pudong 187, **188,** 188–189
Shanghai Museum 189–191
Zhujiajiao 192
Shanhaiguan 142
Shantou 220
Shaolin Temple **124, 128,** 128–129, 366
Shaoxing **178,** 178–179, 372
Shaping 271
Shenyang **336,** 339, 385
Shenzhen **198**
Sheung Wan, Hong Kong 231–232
Shexian 153
Shigatse, Tibet 308
shikumen (housing) 193
Shopping 354, 386
Shouxi Lake Park, Yangzhou 166
Siberian Tiger Park 343, 346
Sichuan 289–299, 310
hotels & restaurants 382–383
hotpot 362
map 290–291
Chengdu **292,** 292–295, **295,** 382, 388, 390
Dazu 299, **299,** 382
Emeishan **296,** 296–297, 382–383
Hailuogou Glacier Park 310
Jiuzhaigou 310
Kangding 310
Leshan 298, **298**
Silk Road *see* Inner Mongolia & the Silk Road
Silver Beach, Beihai 287
Simatai 93–94
Singing Sand Dunes **326,** 327
Six Harmonies Pagoda, Hangzhou 175
Skiing 347
Small Wild Goose Pagoda, Xi'an 103
Smoking 356
Songpan horse trek 294
Songshan **127,** 127–129, **128**
Songyang Academy 127
The South 197–220
hotels 210, **210,** 373–375
map 199
restaurants 373–375, 390
Fenghuang **200,** 200–201
Foshan 220
Guangzhou **157, 211,** 211–217, **213, 214, 216,** 373–374
Gulangyu Island walk 206–208
Hainan Island **17, 218,** 218–219, 374
Hakka *tulou* 210, **210**
Hengshan 220
Lushan **203,** 203–204, 374, 388
Meizhou 220
Qingyuanshan 220
Quanzhou 220
Shamian Island walk 216–217
Shantou 220
Wulingyuan 202, 374–375
Xiamen **13,** 205, **205,** 375
Xiqiao Hills 220
Yongding County 209, **209**
Zhuhai 220
South Cathedral, Beijing 81
South Macau 254–255
The Southwest 261–288
hotels & restaurants 267, 275, 379–382
map 262–263
Anshun 288
Beihai 287, **287,** 379
Dali 268–271, 379–380
Guilin **280,** 280–281, 380
Guiyang 288
Kunming **264,** 264–266, **266,** 380–381, 388
Li River **280, 282,** 282–283
Lijiang **20–21, 54, 272,** 272–275, **275,** 381
Longsheng 288
Nanning 288
Sanjiang 288, 381
Stone Forest 267
Xishuangbanna 276–279
Yangshuo 282, 284–286, 381–382
Spitting 356
Statue Square, Hong Kong 226–227
Stone Forest 267
Subways 353
Summer Palace, Beijing **84,** 84–86
Sun Island 346
Sun Yat-sen 41, 162–163, 388
Sunburn 357
Suzhou **168,** 168–171, **170,** 372, 387, 388
Symbolism 52–53, 65
Synagogues 186

T

Taboos 356
Ta'er Monastery, Xining 309
Tai chi classes 237, 286
Tai Mo Shan 241
Tai Po 240
Taihu, Lake 172, **172**
Taihuai 111, 367
Taipa (island), Macau 258–259
Taiping Museum, Nanjing 161–162
Taiping Rebellion 164–165, **165**
Taiqing Palace, Laoshan 140–141
Taishan **133,** 133–135, **135,** 366
Taiyuan 142
Taklimakan Desert 323
Tantric Buddhism 302
Taoism 32, 83, 133, **135,** 158, 292, 294–295

Tap Mun Chau, Hong Kong 260
Tashilhunpo Monastery, Shigatse 308
Tashkurgan 324
Taxis 353
Tea & teahouses 175, 295, **295**
Telephones 16, 355, 360
Television 359
TEMPLES 156–158
  etiquette 359
  fengshui 156, 238
  A-Ma Temple, Macau 255
  Beijing area 89
  Big Wild Goose Pagoda, Xi'an 103
  Chengde **118,** 119–120, **120**
  Chengdu 292–293
  Ching Chung Koon Temple, Tuen Mun 241
  Confucius Temple, Beijing 79, **79**
  Confucius Temple, Nanjing 162
  Confucius Temple, Qufu 132
  Confucius Temple, Tianjin 117
  Da Xiangguo Temple, Kaifeng 126
  Dai Temple, Tai'an 134
  Daming Temple, Yangzhou 166
  Dongyue Temple, Beijing 81
  Eight Immortals Temple, Xi'an 102–103
  Emeishan 297
  Famen Temple, Xi'an 104
  Fayuan Temple, Beijing 80, **80**
  Ganlanba Temple 278
  Gantong Temple, Dali 271
  Great Bell Temple, Beijing 96
  Guangzhou **157,** 212–214
  Guanyin Temple, Dali 270–271
  Guiyuan Temple, Wuhan 151
  Jinshan Temple, Zhenjiang 167
  Jiuhuashan 159, **159**
  Jokhang Temple, Lhasa 301–302
  Kun Iam Temple, Macau 254
  Kunming 264–265
  Lama Temple, Beijing **11,** 78
  Lingyin Temple, Hangzhou 175
  Longmen Caves **122,** 122–123
  Luohan Temple, Chongqing 150
  Man Mo Temple, Hong Kong 231
  Monastery of Divine Light, Xindu 295
  Nanchan Temple, Taihuai 111
  Nanputuo Temple, Xiamen 205, **205**
  Qingchengshan 294–295
  Shanghai 192
  Taihuai 111
  Temple of Heaven, Beijing **74,** 74–75
  Temple of Yue Fei, Hangzhou 174
  Ten Thousand Buddhas Monastery, New Territories **239,** 240, **241**
  Tianhou Temple, Tianjin 116–117
  West Garden Temple, Suzhou 170–171
  White Clouds Temple, Beijing 81
  White Dagoba Temple, Beijing 96
  White Horse Temple, Luoyang 121
  Wong Tai Sin Temple, Hong Kong 238
  Xuanmiao Temple, Suzhou 170
  Yungang Caves **114,** 114–115
  Zhihua Temple, Beijing 81
  Zhonghe Temple, Dali 269–270
  see also MONASTERIES
Ten Thousand Buddhas Monastery, New Territories **239,** 240, **241**
Terra-cotta warriors **30, 97,** 103, 105–106, **106, 107**
Third Moon Fair, Dali 270
Three Gorges cruise 146–149
Three Pagodas, Dali 270
Tiananmen Square, Beijing 45, **46–47,** 47, **70,** 70–71
Tianchi, Jilin **340,** 340–341
Tianchi, Xinjiang **316,** 316–317
Tianhou Temple, Tianjin 116–117
Tianjin **116,** 116–117, 366–367, 388
Tibet-Qinghai Railway 303
Tibetan Buddhism **300,** 304, **305, 306,** 306–307, **307,** 308
Tibetan Plateau 300–310
  altitude sickness 301
  hotels & restaurants 382–383
  map 290–291
  transportation 303, 354
  Everest Base Camp 310, **310**
  Gyantse 308
  Lhasa 301–304, 383
  Potala Palace 304–305, **305,** 308
  Rongbuk Monastery 310
  Sakya 310
  Shigatse 308
  Tibet–Qinghai Railway 303
  Xining 309
Ticket prices 356
Tiger Leaping Gorge 274–275
Tigers **342,** 342–343, 346
Time differences 359
Tipping 359
Toilets 359
Tongli 196
Tourist information 9
Trains 8–9, 151, 189, 303, 352, 353–354
Transportation
  Beijing 61
  in China 8–9, 352–354
  to China 352
  high-speed trains 151, 189
  Hong Kong 230, 231–232, 354
  Macau 251, 354
  Shanghai 183
  Tibet 303, 354
Travel restrictions 11
Traveler's checks 10
Tropical Flowers & Plants Garden, Jinghong 276–277
Tsim Sha Tsui, Hong Kong 234–236
Tsingtao beer 140, **140,** 141
Tsuen Wan 240–241
Tuen Mun 241
tulou (earth building) 209, **209,** 210, **210**
Tung Lung Chau, Hong Kong 260
Turpan **318,** 318–320, 384
Typhoid 358
Typhoons 248

U

Unit 731 Museum, Harbin 345
Ürümqi **314,** 314–315, 384

V

Vegetarians 359
Victoria Peak, Hong Kong 229–230
Vineyards 318–319
Visas & passports 351, 354
Visitor information 9

W

WALKS
  Gulangyu Island **206,** 206–208
  Hong Kong's Central District 226–228
  Hong Kong's Tsim Sha Tsui 234–236
  Qingdao 137–139
  Shamian Island **216,** 216–217
  Shanghai **184,** 184–187, **187**
Wan Chai, Hong Kong 232–233
Wanghailou Cathedral, Tianjin 116
Wannian Temple, Emeishan 297
Wanxian 148
Water, drinking 357
Water-splashing Festival 277
Weather 21–22, 248, 350
Weights & measures 360
Weizhou (island) 287
Wenshu Temple, Chengdu 293, 295
West Garden Temple, Suzhou 170–171
West Lake, Hangzhou 173–175
Western Hills, Beijing area 88–89
White Clouds Temple, Beijing 81
White Dagoba Temple, Beijing 96
White Horse Temple, Luoyang 121
Wi-Fi 354
Wilson Trail, Hong Kong 237
wing chun gongfu 231

Women, as travelers 356
Wong Tai Sin Temple, Hong Kong 238
Wooden Pagoda, Yingxian 113
World War II 345
Wuchaomen Park, Nanjing 161
Wudangshan 196
Wudangzhao Monastery 332
Wuhan 151–152, 372
Wuhou Temple, Chengdu 293
Wulingyuan 202, 374–375
Wutaishan 111
Wuxi 172, 372
Wuyuan 204

X

Xi Jie 284
Xi Kai Cathedral, Tianjin 117
Xiahe 330, 384
Xiamen **13,** 205, **205,** 375
Xi'an 10, **100,** 100–104, 367
Xi'an Forest of Stone Tablets Museum, Xi'an 102
Xiaoyushan, Qingdao 139
Xidi 153
Xingcheng 348
Xingping 285
Xining 309
Xinjiang Autonomous Region Museum, Ürümqi 314–315
Xintiandi, Shanghai 193
Xiqiao Hills 220
Xishuangbanna **276,** 276–279, **278**
Xizhou 271
Xuanmiao Temple, Suzhou 170

Y

Yangshuo 282, **284,** 284–286, 381–382
Yangtze region 143–196
 hotels & restaurants 184, 185–186, 368–373
 map 144–145
 Changzhou 196
 Chongqing 150, 368, 390
 Grand Canal 176–177
 Hangzhou 173–175, **176,** 368
 Huangpu River cruise **14–15,** 196
 Huangshan 154–155, 368
 Jiuhuashan 159, 368
 Lake Taihu 172, **172**
 Mudu 196
 Nanjing 160–163, 165, 369
 Ningbo 196
 Putuoshan 180–181, 369
 Shanghai 10, **14–15, 18–19, 24,** 25, 182–195, 369–371, 386, 387, 388, 390
 Shaoxing 178–179, 372
 Shexian 153
 Suzhou 168–171, 372, 387, 388
 Three Gorges cruise 146–149
 Tongli 196
 Wudangshan 196
 Wuhan 151–152, 372
 Yangzhou 166, 372–373
 Yixian 153
 Zhenjiang 167, 373
 Zhouzhuang 196
Yangtze River Bridge 163
Yangzhou 166, **166,** 372–373
Yau Ma Tei, Hong Kong 260
Yellow fever 358
Yinchuan 331, **331**
Yixian 153
Yongding County 209, **209**
Yuantong Temple, Kunming 264
Yue Fei 174
Yuexiu Park, Guangzhou 215
Yungang Caves **114,** 114–115
Yurts 317
Yuyuan Gardens, Shanghai 191, **191**

Z

Zhang Ji 171
Zhangye 334
Zhaojue Temple, Chengdu 293
Zhaolin Park, Harbin 346
Zhengding 142
Zhenjiang 167, 373
Zhihua Temple, Beijing 81
Zhonghe Temple, Dali 269–270
Zhongwei 334
Zhongyue Temple 128
Zhouzhuang 196
Zhuhai 220
Zhujiajian 181
Zhujiajiao, Shanghai 192
Zijinshan 162–163
Zodiac 246
Zoucheng 142

ILLUSTRATIONS CREDITS

All photographs by Alison Wright unless otherwise noted.

Cover, Justin Guariglia/Eightfish/Getty Images; Spine, Wilfried Krecichwost/Getty Images; 4, bendao/Shutterstock; 8, Eric Issel/Shutterstock; 18-19, Xiaoyang Liu/CORBIS; 23, Lian Deng/National Geographic My Shot; 29, O. Louis Mazzatenta; 32, David Evans/NationalGeographicStock.com; 36, Dean Conger/NationalGeographicStock.com; 40, Antonio Abrignani/Shutterstock; 43, Giraudon/The Bridgeman Art Library International ; 50, O. Louis Mazzatenta/NationalGeographicStock.com; 53, Tony Law/NationalGeographicStock.com; 64, Shutterstock; 66, Wei Xia/National Geographic My Shot; 70, Paul Chesley/NationalGeographicStock.com; 77, Qiao Qiming/CORBIS; 79, Roman Sigaev; 80, claudio zaccherini/Shutterstock; 88, loong/Shutterstock; 90, Pius Lee/Shutterstock; 100, Greg Girard/NationalGeographicStock.com; 110, Stringer/Getty Images; 118, Raymond Gehman/NationalGeographicStock.com; 120, Mikhail Nekrasov/Shutterstock; 133, Gregs/Shutterstock; 135, Daryl H/Shutterstock; 147, David Evans/NationalGeographicStock.com; 148, Tim Graham/Getty Images; 154, Jun Mu/Shutterstock; 172, Don Klumpp/Getty Images; 174, Tim Robberts/Getty Images; 176, James L. Stanfield/NationalGeographicStock.com; 177, Dean Conger/NationalGeographicStock.com; 180, Martin Gray/NationalGeographicStock.com; 200, Hung Chung Chih/Shutterstock; 203, zhu difeng/Shutterstock; 209, Chen Z./Shutterstock; 210, Jun Mu/Shutterstock; 233, Pete Ryan/NationalGeographicStock.com; 234, Pete Ryan/NationalGeographicStock.com; 236, Ian D Walker/Shutterstock; 272, loong/Shutterstock; 276, JingAiping/Shutterstock; 278, JingAiping/Shutterstock; 287, StockHouse/Shutterstock; 292, Fenghui/Shutterstock; 295, Paul Madland 296, Stringer/Getty Images; 299, steve estvanik/Shutterstock; 305, Hung Chung Chih/Shutterstock; 310, Doug Pierson; 316, Tatiana Grozetskaya/Shutterstock; 318, Wikipedia; 321, George Steinmetz/NationalGeographicStock.com; 325, Carolyn Drake; 329, Bill Perry/Shutterstock; 331, dengmh3602/Shutterstock; 340, cheng-hsien/Shutterstock.

National Geographic
TRAVELER
China

Published by the National Geographic Society
John M. Fahey, Jr., *Chairman of the Board and Chief Executive Officer*
Timothy T. Kelly, *President*
Declan Moore, *Executive Vice President; President, Publishing*
Melina Gerosa Bellows, *Executive Vice President, Chief Creative Officer, Books, Kids, and Family*

Prepared by the Book Division
Barbara Brownell Grogan, *Vice President and Editor in Chief*
Jonathan Halling, *Design Director, Books and Children's Publishing*
Marianne R. Koszorus, *Design Director, Books*
Barbara Noe, *Senior Editor*
Carl Mehler, *Director of Maps*
R. Gary Colbert, *Production Director*
Jennifer A. Thornton, *Managing Editor*
Meredith C. Wilcox, *Administrative Director, Illustrations*

Staff for This Book
Mary Stephanos, *Project Editor*
Kay Kobor Hankins, *Art Director*
Linda Makarov, *Designer*
Adrian Coakley, *Illustrations Editor*
Michael McNey and Mapping Specialists, *Map Production*
Rob Waymouth, *Illustrations Specialist*
Connie Binder, Judy Burke, Seferina Liriano, and Jane Sunderland, *Contributors*

Travel Publications
Keith Bellows, *Vice President, Editor in Chief*

Manufacturing and Quality Management
Christopher A. Liedel, *Chief Financial Officer*
Phillip L. Schlosser, *Senior Vice President*
Chris Brown, *Technical Director*
Nicole Elliott, *Manager*
Rachel Faulise, *Manager*
Robert L. Barr, *Manager*

National Geographic Traveler: China (Third Edition)
ISBN: 978-1-4262-0858-4

First edition: Edited and designed by AA Publishing (a trading name of Automobile Association Developments Limited, whose registered office is Norfolk House, Priestley Road, Basingstoke, Hampshire, England RG24 9NY. Registered number: 1878835).

Area map illustrations drawn by Chris Orr Associates, Southampton, England
Cutaway illustrations drawn by Maltings Partnership, Derby, England

The information in this book has been carefully checked and to the best of our knowledge is accurate. However, details are subject to change, and the National Geographic Society cannot be responsible for such changes, or for errors or omissions. Assessments of sites, hotels, and restaurants are based on the author's subjective opinions, which do not necessarily reflect the publisher's opinion.

The National Geographic Society is one of the world's largest nonprofit scientific and educational organizations. Founded in 1888 to "increase and diffuse geographic knowledge," the Society works to inspire people to care about the planet. National Geographic reflects the world through its magazines, television programs, films, music and radio, books, DVDs, maps, exhibitions, live events, school publishing programs, interactive media and merchandise. *National Geographic* magazine, the Society's official journal, published in English and 33 local-language editions, is read by more than 40 million people each month. The National Geographic Channel reaches 370 million households in 34 languages in 168 countries. National Geographic Digital Media receives more than 15 million visitors a month. National Geographic has funded more than 9,600 scientific research, conservation and exploration projects and supports an education program promoting geography literacy. For more information, visit www.nationalgeographic.com.

For more information, please call 1-800-NGS LINE (647-5463) or write to the following address:

National Geographic Society
1145 17th Street N.W.
Washington, D.C. 20036-4688 U.S.A.

For information about special discounts for bulk purchases, please contact National Geographic Books Special Sales: ngspecsales@ngs.org

For rights or permissions inquiries, please contact National Geographic Books Subsidiary Rights: ngbookrights@ngs.org

The Library of Congress cataloged the first edition as follows:
Harper, Damian.
The National Geographic traveler : China / Damian Harper.
p. cm.
Includes index.
ISBN 0-7922-7921-2
1. China--Description and travel. I. Title: China. II. Title.

DS712 .H365 2001
915.104'6--dc21

00-052682

Printed in Hong Kong
14/THK/2